# THE CREATION AND AMENDMENT
OF CONSTITUTIONAL NORMS

*Edited by Mads Andenas*

# CENTENARY SERIES

## COMPARATIVE LAW

*Comparative Criminal Procedure*
Eds. J. Hatchard, B. Huber and R. Vogler
*National and International Perspectives on Law and Privatisation*
Ed. John F. McEldowney
*The Creation and Amendment of Constitutional Norms*
Ed. Mads Andenas

## EUROPEAN LAW

*The Role and Future of the European Court of Justice*
A Report of the EC Advisory Board of
the British Institute chaired by
The Rt. Hon. The Lord Slynn of Hadley
*Enhancing the Legal Position of the European Consumer*
Ed. Julian Lonbay

## HUMAN RIGHTS

*Human Rights as General Norms and a State's Right to Opt Out:
Reservations and Objections to Human Rights Conventions*
Chinkin and Others. Ed. J.P. Gardner

## PRIVATE INTERNATIONAL LAW

*Topics in Choice of Law*
A.J.E. Jaffey

## PUBLIC INTERNATIONAL LAW

*The International Court of Justice: Process, Practice and Procedure*
Bowett and Others
*The Changing Constitution of the United Nations*
Ed. Hazel Fox
*The International Law Commission and the Future of International Law*
Eds. M.R. Anderson, A.E. Boyle, A.V. Lowe
and C. Wickremasinghe
*The International Lawyer as Practitioner*
Ed. Chanaka Wickremasinghe

# THE CREATION AND AMENDMENT

# OF CONSTITUTIONAL NORMS

*Edited by Mads Andenas*

B.I.I.C.L.
2000

Published by
The British Institute of International and Comparative Law
17 Russell Square, London WC1B 5JP

©The British Institute of International
and Comparative Law, 2000

**British Library Cataloguing-in-Publication Data**

ISBN 0 903067 90 0

All rights reserved. No part of this publication
may be reproduced or transmitted in any form or by any means,
electronic, mechanical, photocopying, recording or
otherwise, or stored in any restricted system of
any nature without the written permission of the publisher.

Printed by Page Bros., Norwich

# THE CENTENARY SERIES

The Centenary Series has established itself as an authoritative series of books reflecting the broad range of scholarly activities undertaken by the British Institute of International and Comparative Law.

The background for the series was the following:

The British Institute was created in 1958 from the merger of the Society of Comparative Legislation, itself created in 1895, and the Grotius Society which was established in 1915. As a result of the ceremonies to mark the Centenary of the first of these constituent Societies, the idea was born to establish a Centenary Series grouping the Institute's publications.

This series epitomises the role and purpose of the Institute as an independent, self-governing body, dedicated to the analysis and development of public and private international law, comparative law, the law of the European Union and Commonwealth law. The Institute undertakes this work through discussion, analysis, research and publication, and seeks to act as a bridge between academic and practising lawyers. Its commitment is to the accurate analysis and development of law as it is practised.

In keeping with this role, the Institute's Centenary Series has been divided into separate series for each of the principal disciplines of the Institute. The continued expansion of the Institute's work under the guidance of the Sections of its Advisory Board have resulted in a significant number of publications which can conveniently each be grouped in their separate series. As a result, a subject series has been established for each of public and private international law, human rights law, comparative law, and European law. Nevertheless, the common theme of the Institute's commitment to the analysis of law in practice ensures that the whole Centenary Series has a coherence and a common connection.

The Centenary series has, therefore, a two-fold object: first, it provides the mechanism for ensuring that the work of the Institute's members and supporters is more widely known and readily accessible to lawyers, whether academic or practising, throughout the world. In this respect, the series reflects the worldwide distribution of the Institute's principal periodical publication, the *International and Comparative Law Quarterly*

The second aim is to contribute to the development of transnational law through comparison and so to reinforce the development of regional and international legal structures based upon the accurate analysis of the operation of law in practice.

Mads Andenas.
Director
The British Institute of International and Comparative Law

London, December 2000

# TABLE OF CONTENTS

    Page

Introduction
    *Mads Andenas*    ix

Establishing Popular and Durable National Constitutions in Commonwealth Africa
    *John Hatchard*    1

The Judicial Enforcement of Constitutional Human Rights in Commonwealth Countries: The Right to Participation in Parliamentary Processes
    *Peter Slinn*    25

The Constitution of the Commonwealth of Australia
    *Leslie Zines*    41

The Creation and Amending Process in the Brazilian Constitution
    *Luciano Maia*    54

The Ongoing Search for an Acceptable Amending Formula in Canada
    *Christopher Ram*    87

From Abolition to Amendment: Life and Death of Constitutions in France
    *Sophie Boyron*    133

Constitutional Change in the Federal Republic of Germany and the Effects of Germany's EU membership on the German Basic Law
    *Sven Reckewerth*    157

The Politics of Constitutional Amendment: Hungary's Lasting Transitory Constitution
    *György Szoboszlai*    174

The Judicial Role in Constitutional Amendment in India:
   The Basic Structure Doctrine
      *Mathew Abraham*                                             195

Creation and Amendment of Constitutional Norms
   in Ireland
      *Padraic Taylor*                                             205

Constitutional Revisions and Reforms: The Italian
   Experience
      *Paolo Galizzi*                                              235

The Constitutional Amendment Process in Malaysia
      *Andrew Harding*                                             250

Why the Judicial Annulment of the Constitution of 1999
   is Imperative for the Survival of Nigeria's Democracy
      *Tunde I. Ogowewo*                                           265

Ethnicity, Conflict and Constitutional Change in Rwanda
   and Burundi
      *Guglielmo Verdirame*                                        302

Constitutional Change in the United Kingdom
      *Peter Oliver* and *Adam Tomkins*                            319

The Changing Constitution: American Constitutional
   Amendment and the Limits of Article V
      *Stephen Tierney*                                            358

The Creation and Amendment of Constitutional Norms:
   A Comparison
      *Andrew Harding*                                             390

# INTRODUCTION

Mads Andenas[*]

## I.

"The Creation and Amendment of Constitutional Norms" is an ambitious topic. In any jurisdiction it goes straight to the very foundations of the legal system. It will invariably bring up unresolved issues on a black letter law level. There are reform issues: amending the amendment provisions is discussed in the lifetime of most constitutions. On a more theoretical level one seeks answers to questions such as what constitutes a legal system, or what constitutes a legal system at any given time or over a period of time.

The creation and amendment of constitutional norms is an important topic for on-going political discussions of theories of constitutionalism, for instance at present in the European Union, or in many new or old federal State systems. It is an important topic for the status of human rights and their legal recognition. And it is of particular significance in countries where a new political regime requires a new constitutional order.

From all of these different perspectives, much could be gained by comparative research. It may assist in finding models for resolving domestic problems. Seeing other solutions may provide useful insights about the domestic system. All the traditional benefits of comparative research should obtain here.

Rigorous and sustained research could also provide a fertile field for trying out general and fundamental theories of law and legal constitutions. Is there, for instance, support for a Habermasian communications theory or a Rawlsian liberal theory?

Comparative public law is, in spite of some notable contributions, in a rather sorry state. There is too little of it, and what there is remains too descriptive. There is too little of it, not the least if one considers the many issues which public law covers. Constitutional law has traditionally lent itself more to comparative study than most other areas of public law but even here one is far from the critical mass

---

[*] The Director, The British Institute of International and Comparative Law, London, and Fellow, Harris Manchester College, University of Oxford.

of research that could create the level of interchange that is necessary for an academic discipline to be brought into existence. The lack of comparative research in public law is not the case in the UK alone; it is a general problem. In the proud comparative law traditions of France and Germany it is private law that has occupied the dominant position. In a somewhat flawed historical perspective, public law is perceived as the younger discipline. The lack of comparative scholarship, then, partly follows from that, and also from the particularly "national" nature of public law (another assumption equally flawed).[1]

Recent experiences from the UK, in spite of its traditionally open and international orientation, demonstrate some unfortunate consequences of this situation. The UK has over a period of very few years undergone rather fundamental constitutional change with the introduction of a new federal structure (devolution for Scotland and Wales and new arrangements in Northern Ireland), a new bill of rights (the introduction into domestic UK law of the European Human Rights Convention) and new access to information legislation. When the UK government recently proposed new legislation on freedom of access to information it did look to other countries. It made reference to Australia, Canada, New Zealand and the US. There was also a very short reference to Sweden (having the oldest freedom of information legislation). I suspect that the text was taken verbatim from the papers previously published by the New Zealand and Australian governments.[2]

---

[1]   I never understood Kahn-Freund's rejection in particular of comparative public law scholarship which he largely wrote off as a misuse of comparative law in his entertaining but misconceived article "On Uses and Misuses of Comparative Law" (1974) 37 MLR 1. Reading it as an undergraduate it seemed so obviously wrong. (More critical reading at a later stage in life shows that Kahn-Freund of course qualifies his statements much more than the undergraduate or some other writers claiming his support acknowledged.) The amount of borrowing, and to good use, in constitutional law is overwhelming. All the great written constitutions of the world, all of them, were based on importation of institutions, concepts and rules. This usually applies also to constitutional amendments. Kahn-Freund's assumptions about the nature of national legal traditions, and his examples, on closer examination, are fundamentally flawed. Other areas of public law, not the least recent reforms and developments in the administrative law of the years just before and since his article support this rejection. And the development of European Union public law and the European Human Rights Convention provide further support. As does the emergence of international criminal law with the War Crimes Tribunal etc etc.

[2]   The study of Commonwealth law is of course of great importance. Its value is recognised by the UK courts in that Commonwealth authorities are accepted as persuasive authorities - none more so than those from the highest Australian and New Zealand courts. In this field there are also valuable contributions made in academic legal scholarship, also by the many UK academics whose backgrounds are from those jurisdictions. But much comparative work is undertaken in the very judgments of UK courts, generally no doubt well assisted by counsel. These influences can eventually assist in how to deal with European law, as in the instance mentioned in the main text of the UK borrowing from New Zealand a model for implementing the European Human Rights Convention as a Bill of Rights which allows courts to review the constitutionality of parliamentary legislation. The inspirational and authoritative book by Leslie Zines (also a contributor to this book) *The High Court and the Constitution* (4th ed., 1997) shows how the Australian High Court has approached the legal concepts of legitimate expectations and proportionality, and is using European authorities, within a common law framework.

There was no reference to the extensive legislation and practice of France or Germany, or to the European Union or the European Human Rights Convention. The European Human Rights Convention was introduced into domestic UK law without any look at other countries recently having gone through a parallel process. It borrowed from New Zealand instead. Devolution took place in the UK without any of the official documents making use of the experiences of the older federal states of Europe or newer models. At least open references were made to foreign systems and some use clearly made of them. The flaws can to some extent be explained by the limited scholarship that could have made the relevant sources more readily available to the government. No doubt the study of foreign law should be developed and also provide comparison which could enlighten the policy maker. The UK experience shows the need for public law scholarship.

And not only the UK experience. The overviews of foreign laws that one finds in the public documents of law reform commissions of many countries are usually of little help. They are often brief, superficial and descriptive, added after the real work is done and by research assistants. Even in the European Court of Justice, with all its comparative law expertise on the Court itself and submissions from the governments of the many Member States, important developments have taken place without any study of the systems of the Member States. For instance, when the Court of Justice established the principle of tort liability for breach of EC law for Member States, it seems it did so without even calling upon its internal research resources to provide a study of the laws of the Member States. This was omitted even though the Treaty provision[3] called for a liability "in accordance with the general principles common to the laws of the Member States". At this stage there was no independent academic research which could be of much assistance to the Court in this respect. Just calling for a comparative table could perhaps have caused more confusion than useful input. So the omission was perhaps not a mere oversight.

In his concluding contribution to this book,[4] Andrew Harding is critical of the limited comparative public law scholarship, and rightly so. But his contribution shows that it is possible to make much out of a project such as this book. Many colleagues are interested and will contribute. They will produce material which can provide the basis for ambitious comparative analysis. Further dialogue and research can actually produce that much needed comparative analysis.

Comparative public law is certainly an area of priority for the British Institute of International and Comparative Law. This book will be a most helpful contribution in the development of the Institute's programme. The aims of the

---

This may sound too much of a paradox, but also in terms of dealing with European law there is much to learn from the Australian High Court!

[3] Now Article 288 EC.
[4] Chapter 17, "The Creation and Amendment of Constitutional Norms: A Comparison", *infra*, p. 390.

Institute's programme are both to contribute to the emergence of the discipline of comparative public law and to make use of the discipline in the discussion of law reform in the UK, and at a European, Commonwealth and international level.

II.

So "The Creation and Amendment of Constitutional Norms" is an ambitious topic. How relevant is it? From an historical perspective it may seem as though it is people and armies who change constitutions. Great events spring to mind, such as the American War of Independence, the French Revolution and the Russian Revolution. However, such rare extremes aside, constitutional change within the rule of law requires that certain procedures be followed. Even the people's voice cannot govern constitutional change unless a procedure indicates how that voice is to be understood.

The contributions in this book demonstrate the extent to which constitutional amendment procedures allow for a massive amount of variation. Each country's amending formula (and they may be more than one) provides an insight into the intricacies and peculiarities of that country's social and political culture. This can of course pose a problem in the context of comparative research. It may be difficult to arrive at any meaningful comparison.

To take the example of the post-war German constitution's provisions protecting human rights: they make the core rights apparently unamendable.[5] The Australian constitution shows its American influence in including the Australian people in its amending formula.[6] Neighbouring New Zealand sticks much closer to the "unwritten" or uncodified UK model.[7]

But recently drafted amending formulae show that much has been learned from other countries' experience. One example here is the detailed Canadian constitutional amending provisions.[8] They must be an especially good outcome of the processes that could be studied in other countries' constitutional law.

A different perspective on the creation and amendment of constitutional norms is presented in jurisdictions where a new constitution has been adopted. One dimension of this perspective is what happens if it is abolished, say after 50 years. In Estonia the post-Communist State reverted to the constitution of the new national State that emerged after the First World War.[9] They have had to review the rights of individuals, for instance of foreign language speaking residents, but otherwise have kept the pre-war constitution. What if you cannot abolish the constitution but

---

[5] See S. Reckewerth "Constitutional Change in the Federal Republic of Germany", *infra*, p. 157.
[6] See L. Zines's chapter on "The Constitution of the Commonwealth of Australia", *infra*, p. 41.
[7] See P. Oliver and A. Tomkins, "Constitutional Change in the United Kingdom", *infra*, p. 319.
[8] See C. Ram, "The Ongoing Search for an Acceptable Amending Formula in Canada", *infra*, p. 87.
[9] See *infra*, p. 285.

you wish to set aside certain provisions? There could be very legitimate reasons for this. For instance provisions giving broad immunities to people who committed crimes during and after a coup. Then the same people had the constitution adopted with the immunities as their terms for giving way to a new political order. This is a pressing issue in several countries such as Chile. In other countries setting aside the constitution adopted under such circumstances can be imperative for the continuation of a democratic constitutional order.[10] Answers to these questions could be developed in a more extensive doctrine of creation and amendments of constitutional norms, and comparative scholarship could provide a basis for such a doctrine.

As already suggested, the creation and amendment of constitutional norms could provide a fertile field for trying out fundamental theories of law and legal systems. In addition to being of interest for practical reasons, the study of constitutional amendment brings us close to some of the most fundamental theoretical questions in law. This should not be surprising, given that at the level of the amending formula we are looking at the space in which law, politics, history and philosophy meet. This is, after all, where the *Grundnorm* or ultimate rule of recognition is located.

Theoretical questions include the following. Does the attribution of supreme constitution making power necessarily mean that such power is also unlimited? And, second, if an amending formula is put in place by the vote of a constituent assembly, does the amending formula then govern conclusively? Or is it still possible to resort to this or another constituent body in order to amend the constitution, or amend the amending formula?

A third, and related, question is this. Does the amendment of the amending formula represent a "disguised revolution" or "magical act" as some writers have suggested (including Sir William Wade and Alf Ross)? Or does it instead amount to legally valid change?

A fourth question. How does one analyse a breach of constitutional rules which is nonetheless intended to have legal consequences and preserve overall legal continuity (as in the case of constitutional necessity, e.g. Cyprus) and respect for constitutional rules which is nonetheless intended to create a discontinuity (as in the case of Commonwealth devolution)?

And a final question. How does the theory of legal systems tie in to the process of constitutional amendment (thinking for example of Commonwealth devolution, ever-closer European union or State secession)?

---

[10] See T. I. Ogowewo, "Why the Judicial Annulment of the Constitution of 1999 is Imperative for the Survival of Nigeria's Democracy", *infra*, p. 265.

### III.

In this collection, these sorts of questions are very much present, whether in the foreground or in the background of the different contributions.

There is one great advantage of the wide range of amendment experience covered in this book. Despite each country's relatively limited experience of constitutional amendment (typically it occurs only infrequently[11]), each can learn lessons from the experiences of others. Such lessons may just as often lead to the conclusion that a certain procedure should not be borrowed as to the conclusion that it should be.

One example is the amending formula which protects the constitution from change except where the usual two-thirds parliamentary majority has been obtained. It may be perfect for most countries. It is inappropriate for a country in which the ruling party regularly obtains more than two-thirds of the seats in general elections.

A famous example of helpful borrowing is the now-familiar concept of double-entrenchment. Double-entrenchment remedies the fault line created where the amending formula itself is only protected from amendment by, say, majority vote. That would allow a rigid amending formula to be by-passed. The double-entrenchment makes clear that the amending formula itself is protected.

Even though it might seem that amending formula issues have no place in United Kingdom constitutional law, most of the discussion can be reformulated in terms of the traditional debates on parliamentary sovereignty. And, furthermore, the wider definition of "constitutional" that one finds in the UK serves as a useful reminder that all constitutions change and evolve according to the development of non-formal rules.

Andrew Harding suggests that the different contributions to this book and the discussion that took place at a seminar where most of them were presented could lead to the following prescription. Constitutional amendments should be made difficult, once the constitution has settled into its foundations.[12] This is an interesting conclusion, with consequences, perhaps further prescriptions, for a hierarchy of norms and constitutional review by courts.

It is clear to me that this book is a contribution to the theoretical comparative public law scholarship. It also contributes to the applied comparative public law

---

[11] New constitutions or constitutional amendments may not be expected to be a regular occurrence in stable political systems. The two oldest constitutions still in force, those of the United States and Norway, are not that much amended but proposals for amendment are a more permanent presence. The oldest constitutions can in some respects have the most modernised rights catalogues: the Norwegian 1814 Constitution has provisions about the right to work, workers' co-determination and an unpolluted environment, and the protection of the rights of the *Sami* minority.

[12] Chapter 17, "The Creation and Amendment of Constitutional Norms: A Comparison", *infra*, p. 390 at 406.

scholarship that Kahn-Freund attacked.[13] I am convinced that the reader will agree with me in how wrong Kahn-Freund was.[14]

---

[13] See the realistic appreciation of the role of applied comparative public law scholarship in J. Bell, "Mechanisms for Cross-Fertilisation of Administrative Law in Europe" in J. Beatson and P. Tridimas (eds.) *New Directions in European Public Law* (1998) p. 147, who points out both the national character of the public law traditions and that "international interaction and collaboration ... will continue to shape [their] development".

[14] A modern programme for comparative scholarship is set out in B.S. Markesinis "Comparative Law, A Subject in Search of an Audience" (1990) 53 MLR 1 and in B.S. Markesinis *Foreign Law and Comparative Methodology* (1997). See also the powerful summing up of these constructive views on the application of comparative public law in B.S. Markesinis, J.-B. Auby, D. Coester-Waltjen, S.F. Deakin (eds.) *Tortious Liability of Statutory Bodies: A Comparative and Economic Analysis of Five English Cases* (1999), for instance at pp. 3-4 and 107-8.

## Chapter One

## ESTABLISHING POPULAR AND DURABLE NATIONAL CONSTITUTIONS IN COMMONWEALTH AFRICA[1]

### John Hatchard

*The People themselves must be involved in the formulation and adoption of their Constitution because ... a Constitution imposed on the people by force cannot be the basis of a stable and peaceful Government of the people*[2]

A constitution enjoys a special place in the life of any nation, for it deals not only with the exercise of political power but also the relationship between political entities and between the State and persons. Being the supreme law, it shapes the organisation and development of a society both for the present and for future generations. As the Preamble to the Constitution of Uganda declares:

WE THE PEOPLE OF UGANDA COMMITTED to building a better future by establishing a socio-economic and political order through a popular and durable national Constitution ... DO HEREBY ... solemnly adopt, enact and give to ourselves and our posterity, this Constitution of Uganda.

Thus the making of a national constitution is a serious business and the drafters of the document have got to 'get it right'. In the African context, however, examples of constitutions that got it wrong abound. Indeed, prior to 1990 the constitutional picture was bleak with the majority of Commonwealth African States experiencing the suspension or abrogation of their constitutions by the military and/or the rigidity of a one-party state. The 1990s have brought about a dramatic change with most sub-Saharan African States adopting new constitutions providing for, amongst other things, a multi-party system, a wide-ranging Bill of Rights and mechanisms for promoting good governance and accountability. Central to the task of constitution-making is the development of an effective and acceptable procedure

---

[1] There are Botswana, Cameroon, The Gambia, Ghana, Kenya, Lesotho, Malawi, Mauritius, Mozambique, Namibia, Nigeria, Seychelles, Sierra Leone, South Africa, Swaziland, Tanzania, Uganda, Zambia and Zimbabwe.
[2] Guidelines on Constitutional Issues Uganda Constitutional Commission, 1991, 1.

leading to the creation of an autochthonous document that reflects the needs and aspirations of the people as a whole. This is crucial if an *ethos of constitutionalism* is to be established: i.e. a recognition by the people that the document is 'their constitution' upon which they were consulted and which they endorsed, which contains provisions that are meaningful to them and from which they can derive demonstrable benefits. Further, that it is a document that will stand the test of time and enjoy public support to enable it to withstand better any attempt to undermine it.

This chapter first provides an overview of the process of making the independence constitutions in much of Commonwealth Africa, examines their fate and then argues that the procedure for making them contributed to their failure. The discussion then focuses on the procedure for making the new constitutions of the 1990s and the mechanisms for their amendment and considers whether these have produced truly autochthonous documents that are capable of helping to establish an ethos of constitutionalism.

## I. THE PROCESS OF MAKING THE INDEPENDENCE CONSTITUTIONS AND ITS AFTERMATH: AN OVERVIEW

A The Making of the Independence Constitutions

The newly independent States in Commonwealth Africa[3] started life with a Constitution bestowed upon them by Britain. Not surprisingly, the Westminster model was chosen for, as Dale suggests, it was the one Whitehall knew and thought the best.[4] A similar procedure was used for the making of most of the new constitutions: i.e. a constitutional conference was held at Lancaster House in London at which the nationalist leaders met with British government officials and the new Constitution duly agreed to. In most cases it actually came into existence through the somewhat obscure means of being placed in a schedule to an Order in Council made by Her Majesty in exercise of the powers by which, under Act of Parliament and the Prerogative, she legislated for dependent territories.[5] This method was defended by De Smith[6] on the ground that the possible upsetting by Parliament of delicately balanced compromises arrived at after strenuous negotiations might have had 'unfortunate repercussions' in the new State. He also emphasised the need for speed and the fact that it was impracticable to expect

---

[3] The discussion in this section excludes Namibia, Mozambique and Cameroon which did not join the Commonwealth until the 1990s and South Africa which also had a very different constitutional history.

[4] Sir William Dale 'The Making and Re-Making of Commonwealth Constitutions' (1993) 42 *ICLQ* 67 at 68. The main features of the model are the diffusion of executive power (a separate Head of State and Head of Government); the partial fusion of the organs of government; a parliamentary opposition party; and the responsibility of the executive to the legislature.

[5] For details see K. Roberts-Wray *Commonwealth and Colonial Law* London, 1966 esp at 264.

[6] S A De Smith 'The Independence of Ghana' (1957) 20 MLR 347 at 356.

Parliament to dispose of a Bill containing the entire Constitution and adhere to the set timetable.[7]

This view entirely overlooks the fact that there was little or no opportunity for public debate on the Independence Constitution in the new State itself and that the process ensured that the nationalist leaders themselves had no genuine choice as to the structure and content of the document. Certainly Kanyeihamba asserts that the reasons for a constitutional conference in London were political and expedient. He argues that delegates who are in a strange country far from their families and not able to consult readily with colleagues back home are likely to be 'less difficult' during negotiations than if they are operating on home ground. Thus pressure can be brought to bear on delegates 'to conclude that the Westminster model of Government is the best for their own country'.[8] He adds that British hospitality was also used to disarm delegates: 'At the beginning of the conference, you might have been suspicious of the motives [of your host]. At the end you are likely to accept his suggestions, not that they are any better than before, but because you remember the trouble he took to make you comfortable at the London Hilton'.[9] Certainly the procedure suited British interests and, even as late as 1979, the 'Lancaster House experience' was used to bring Zimbabwe to independence.

The process ensured that the Independence Constitutions often paid insufficient attention to the specific needs, circumstances and realities of the new State. One particular area of difficulty concerned the diffusion of executive power. As Nwabueze rightly notes, conflict is necessarily to be expected in an arrangement whereby the executive authority is vested in one person and exercised by another. In Britain, the division between the Queen as Head of State and the Prime Minister as Head of Government is a product of history but such conditions were entirely lacking in the new States and rapidly led to conflict and frustration and consequent disenchantment with the Westminster system.[10]

B. The Aftermath

The futility of forcing the Westminster model on the newly independent States, in the words of Karugire 'a triumph of hope over experience', inevitably led to constitutional instability and a round of constitution-making and amendment. For example, in Tanganyika a presidential system was installed within just ten months of independence whilst in Nigeria conflict between the President and the Prime Minister occurred on several occasions which did great harm to the federation and

---

[7] Roberts-Wray (above at 264-5) criticises this view pointing out that those with the task of preparing Orders in Council 'find that the time allowed for terminating a hundred years or more of dependent status is cut very close to the verge of impossible'.

[8] G W Kanyeihamba *Constitutional Law and Government in Uganda* East African Literature Bureau, Nairobi, 1975, 56.

[9] Above at 56.

[10] B O Nwabueze *Constitutionalism in the Emergent States* Hurst, London, 1973, 56.

contributed to its later constitutional instability.[11]

The experience of Uganda perhaps epitomises the problem. A detailed examination is beyond the scope of this chapter; suffice to note that the Constitution of Uganda 1962 contained the seeds for many years of constitutional instability for, in particular, it gave Buganda a special and privileged constitutional position. Friction between the Baganda and the central government led, in 1966, to Prime Minister Milton Obote, with the support of the military, suspending the Independence Constitution, declaring himself Executive President vested with wide-ranging powers and sweeping away the special position and privileges of the Baganda people. To legalise his actions, Obote summoned parliament to rubber stamp a new interim Constitution. With a heavy military presence outside the parliament building, Obote informed MPs that there was now a provisional Uganda Constitution and added 'If you go down to your pigeon-holes you will find copies of the new Constitution'. Thoroughly intimidated, the parliamentarians endorsed the 'Pigeon-hole' Constitution. The following year, the government drafted a new Constitution which was duly endorsed by the National Assembly (acting as a Constituent Assembly).[12] This vested still further extensive powers in the President which were further enhanced following the 1969 declaration of a nationwide state of emergency. Constitutionalism was dead and a reign of terror substituted that lasted for nearly two decades.[13]

The Uganda experience is one of many where the Independence Constitution was replaced (or, in some States, radically amended) so as to entrench and enhance the political power of the ruling elite and to eliminate political opposition. In many cases the creation of an all-powerful executive president was coupled with the introduction of a one-party state, a situation epitomised by the experience of Malawi: here parliament duly approved constitutional amendments providing that 'The ... President shall be Ngwazi Dr. H Kamuzu Banda, who shall hold the office of President for his lifetime'[14] and outlawing all political parties other than the President's Malawi Congress Party. As a result, parliament became a purely rubber-stamp body and national and local elections became meaningless. Constitutional changes also led to the establishment of one-party states in many other Commonwealth African countries, including Ghana, Kenya, Tanzania, Uganda and Zambia.

Constitutional stability was not assisted by the weak amendment mechanism provided for in the Westminster model. The requirement for the support of two-

---

[11] See, in particular, Nwabueze, above, 58 *et seq*. By 1964 the lesson seems to have been learned with Zambia attaining her independence based on the presidential system. Even so, the Constitution of Zimbabwe 1979 provided for a non-executive President who was replaced by an Executive President within a few years.
[12] Although many amendments were proposed by individuals, political parties and associations, some of which led the government to drop some of its own proposals.
[13] For a brief but useful account see D Mukholi *Uganda's Fourth Constitution: History, Politics and the Law* Fountain Publishers, Kampala, 1995, 11-24.
[14] See s. 9 Constitution of Malawi 1966 (as amended).

thirds of all the members of the legislature for any constitutional amendment proved ineffective even in the ostensibly 'multi-party' States, particularly because of the weakness of parliamentary opposition (a situation often engineered by the actions of the ruling party itself).[15] Further, there was little public consultation over the proposed changes, a point epitomised by the 'Pigeon-hole' Constitution in Uganda. Thus governments were able to make new Constitutions or amend existing ones with the minimum of effort.

Up to 1990, therefore, the main characteristic of the constitution-making and amendment process in Commonwealth Africa was the effort made by the ruling elite to 're-design' the Constitutions so as to enhance executive power, to remove or reduce checks and balances and to restrict or eliminate the enjoyment of fundamental rights. Significantly, there was little or no consultation with the people about constitutional reform and as a result, the concept of a 'popular' Constitution was non-existent. In short, constitutions were largely instruments of oppression.

## II. THE NEW CONSTITUTIONS OF THE 1990s

The 1990s have seen an almost complete transformation of the constitutional picture in Commonwealth Africa with new constitutions in Cameroon (1995); Ghana (1992); Lesotho (1994); Malawi (1994); Mozambique (1990); Namibia (1990); Seychelles (1992); Sierra Leone (1991); South Africa (1994 and 1996); Uganda (1995); and Zambia (1991 and 1996).[16] All provide for a multi-party state,[17] free and fair elections; a wide-ranging Bill of Rights and an Office of the Ombudsman and/or a Human Rights Commission. Elsewhere, both Kenya and Tanzania have amended their Constitutions and returned to a multi-party state.[18] Thus in the space of a few short years, the *de jure* one-party state has changed from

---

[15]  There were also special provisions relating to federal states.

[16]  The Constitution in The Gambia 1996 contains similar provisions: however, given the transformation of the former military dictator into the new civilian president, concern remains about the democratic nature of the country. The 1999 Constitution of Nigeria that was used to return the country to civilian rule is also subject to considerable criticism. As Justice Akinola has noted: '... the Constitution was simply imposed upon this country [by the military] without our consent, and what is worse, it has been made to tell an obvious lie against all of use, one hundred and ten million of us less, of course, a few number of men who you can almost count on your finger tips, by alleging that 'WE the People of the Federal Republic of Nigeria - make, enact and give ourselves' this Constitution. See unpublished paper 'The Functions of the Judiciary and the Separation of Powers under the Constitution of the Federal Republic of Nigeria'.

[17]  At present, Uganda retains the 'movement political system' which has individual merit as the basis for election to political office: see Art 70 Constitution of Uganda. However, provision is made for a return to a multi-party system at a later date following free and fair elections or a referendum: see Art 69 Constitution of Uganda.

[18]  Botswana and Zimbabwe have retained their independence constitutions and remain multi-party states. Swaziland is the exception with the constitution remaining suspended although a Constitutional Review Commission is currently at work on a new document.

a frightening reality to an historical anachronism.[19] The overt influence of the armed forces has also waned although the years of military government in Nigeria that ended in 1999 provide a stark reminder of the vulnerability of a Constitution.

So much euphoria; so much hope: but the question remains as to whether these new Constitutions are a break with the past, are really capable of meeting the needs of the people and are truly autochthonous documents. Is the hope of the Ugandan people of establishing a 'socio-economic and political order through a popular and durable Constitution' possible to fulfil in practice? This is dependent upon many factors, not the least of which being the political will to make them succeed. However, the first step is to produce an autochthonous Constitution and to do this requires the development of an effective and acceptable procedure for doing so. This issue is explored in the next section.

### III. MAKING THE NEW CONSTITUTIONS OF COMMONWEALTH AFRICA

Unlike the independence documents, most of the new Constitutions of Commonwealth Africa contain a Preamble to the effect that 'We the People give Ourselves this Constitution'. To have any real meaning the document must be the product of a process in which the people themselves actually played an active and effective role. This involves (a) obtaining the views of the people on the contents of the new Constitution; (b) having the Constitution itself adopted by a fully representative body; and (c) having the document approved by the people in a referendum.

A. Obtaining the Views of the People on the Contents of the New Constitution

Many countries have used a constitutional commission to obtain the views of the people on the contents of their new Constitution. This has several advantages: it is an inclusive process; it raises public awareness of the constitution-making process itself; and it enhances the chances of including issues of importance to the people in the new Constitution. Such an approach is time-consuming and expensive[20] but it is undoubtedly worthwhile if the ensuing document genuinely reflects the views of the people. The experience of Lesotho, Nigeria, Uganda and Zambia neatly illustrate the strengths and weaknesses of this approach.

As noted earlier, after independence in 1962 Uganda experienced untold

---

[19] The underlying reasons for such a change are well-known. These include, firstly, the dramatic alteration in the international political climate resulting from the ending of the Cold War and the collapse of the Soviet Union; secondly the linking of aid with good governance by Western countries; and thirdly, so far as Commonwealth countries are concerned, the impact of the 1991 Harare Commonwealth Declaration with its emphasis on good governance, accountability and the rule of law.
[20] Although it is an exercise that is likely to attract foreign aid. For example, the Mwanakatwe Commission in Zambia (discussed below) was funded by USAID.

political instability and the later Constitutions were made with little or no public consultation. Upon assuming power in 1986, the National Resistance Movement government decided to 'give the people of Uganda an opportunity to make their new Constitution', declaring that the people themselves

must be involved in the formulation and adoption of their Constitution because ... a Constitution imposed on the people by force cannot be the basis of a stable and peaceful Government of the people.[21]

As a result, a twenty-one member Constitutional Commission was established. It toured the country obtaining the views of the populace through a series of seminars, workshops, debates and discussions and also had an opportunity to gather views from the many Ugandans living abroad. It also published a document entitled *Guidelines on Constitutional Issues*[22] which was written in a clear and simple manner and which sought to assist Ugandans to understand the relevant constitutional issues and to enable them to contribute actively to the making of the new Constitution. The Commission received 25,542 submissions and, based on these, it proceeded to produce a draft Constitution. A representative Constituent Assembly (see below) then debated the draft and adopted and enacted the new Constitution of Uganda 1995. Indeed, the Preamble proudly proclaims that, 'We the People of Uganda ... fully participated in the Constitution-making process'.

A slightly different consultative procedure was adopted in Lesotho. During 1990 and 1991 a National Constituent Assembly made up of 108 appointed members was set up to draft a new Constitution. The Assembly, which included members of the ruling Military Council, Council of Ministers, all Principal Chiefs and politicians, held consultations using the 1966 Independence Constitution as its starting point. In September 1991 a preliminary draft was published and the Assembly then appointed a constitutional commission, known as the National Constitutional Commission, to carry out a widespread consultation exercise to assess public reaction to the document before it was adopted. This was preceded by a high profile information programme: proceedings of the National Constituent Assembly were broadcast on the radio; ninety-three public meetings were convened at which the proposals of the Assembly were explained and discussed; and a booklet entitled *Report on Changes to the 1966 Independence Constitution* and written in simple language was made available at a low price. The Commission then held sixty-six meetings nationwide, heard evidence from 1272 people and received twenty-two written submissions. Finally the report was presented to the National Constituent Assembly which adopted it virtually intact[23] and the

---

[21] Guidelines on Constitutional Issues Uganda Constitutional Commission, 1991, 1.
[22] Uganda Constitutional Commission, 1991, Kampala.
[23] The Assembly recommended that the draft Constitution be revised to take into account the recommendations of the Commission.

Constitution came into force following the election of a National Assembly.[24]

Another useful illustration concerns the making of the 1989 Constitution of Nigeria which was characterised by a protracted government debate and a series of formal consultations. The decision by the then military government to return the country to civilian rule led to the establishment of a sixteen-member Political Bureau in January 1987 charged with identifying Nigeria's past political problems and collecting views about its political future. Its report highlighted a sharp division of opinion on many points but led to the preparation of a White Paper in which the government set out its views on the report of the Bureau. The next stage was the preparation of a draft Constitution by a Constitution Review Committee chaired by a judge. The public was invited to submit comments and over 400 memoranda were received. The draft was then put to a Constituent Assembly (see below).

The situation in Zambia was more complex. Whilst the country probably heads the world league table for establishing constitutional commissions, these demonstrate considerable flaws in their operation. Prior to the establishment of the Second Republic, the Chona Commission was set up in 1972 and travelled extensively around the country seeking views on the type of government the people wanted. However, its work was undermined by two factors. Firstly, the government had already announced that Zambia would change from a multi-party state to a one-party state. Secondly, the Commission reported directly to the Government which was therefore able to discard any recommendations it did not like. This led to the swift rejection of the main recommendations of the Commission that were aimed at placing safeguards on the exercise of presidential power and meant that the 1973 Constitution was essentially a creation of the ruling elite who transformed the country into an effective one-party dictatorship. When political change became inevitable in 1991, the Government of President Kaunda again adopted the 'pick and choose' approach to the recommendations of a second constitutional commission. However, this action provoked such a political storm that eventually the churches organised a national conference and mediated the dispute between the main political parties. It was still recognised that the new 1991 Constitution was unsatisfactory and the Movement for Multi-Party Democracy (MMD) (which won the subsequent 1991 general election) pledged that it would replace the document with one that would be above partisan politics. Perhaps wary of yet another constitutional commission, initially the Ministry of Legal Affairs set up a seven-person task force chaired by the Attorney-General to review the Constitution. As Ndulo and Kent point out, 'the government was persuaded that it was unwise to leave a task of this magnitude in the hands of a few under the chairmanship of the principal legal advisor to the government'.[25] This led the government to appoint the Mwanakatwe Commission. Its report made many important recommendations for strengthening fundamental rights and freedoms but, regrettably, the government of

---

[24] See Lesotho Constitution (Commencement) Order 1993.
[25] M. Ndulo and R. Kent, 'Constitutionalism in Zambia: Past, Present and Future' (1996) 40 *Journal of African Law* 256 at 271.

President Chiluba employed the same 'pick and choose' tactics as his predecessor. The result was yet another flawed Constitution.[26]

The work of the three constitutional commissions in Zambia was essentially an exercise in futility because they reported directly to government which had the final say on the fate of their recommendations and was free to reject any which it did not like. This action was defended by the MMD Government in a pamphlet published in response to widespread public criticism of its 'pick and choose' tactics.[27] It argued that according to 'constitutional practice in the Commonwealth, an independent commission such as Mwanakatwe was required to submit its proposals to the government which has the power and freedom to reject, accept, amend or note the proposals'. This is questionable. Certainly some Commonwealth States have employed the pick and choose method but given the experience of Uganda and South Africa (discussed below) amongst others, it is certainly not a Commonwealth practice and should not become one.[28]

Obtaining the views of the people on the contents of the new Constitution is now an integral part of the constitution-making process in Commonwealth Africa and is in sharp contrast to the pre-1990 position. Constitutional commissions have played an important role in this process. However, the Zambian experience, in particular, demonstrates that they can only have a meaningful role if they are demonstrably independent and report to a demonstrably independent constitution-making body. This means that whilst the views of government and all other political parties must also be heard and given due weight, these should form only a part of the consultative process.

B. The Adoption of the New Constitution by a Fully Representative Body

The new Constitutions in the majority of Commonwealth African countries have been adopted by a constituent assembly, with the national legislature normally doubling as this body. For example, in Namibia, the Independence Constitution of 1990 was drawn up by a constituent assembly comprising members of the seven political parties which had mustered sufficient support in the United Nations-supervised elections. Although based on a draft produced by the South West Africa Peoples Organisation, which won most seats in the elections, the results gave no party the necessary two-thirds majority required to adopt the Constitution alone. Thus the other parties played an important part in the preparation of the document and as a result there was consensus as to the final Constitution. Indeed this

---

[26] For details see Ndulo and Kent, above, 271.
[27] Ministry of Legal Affairs *Constitutional Reform '96: The Public Debate - Adopting the Constitution: Topic 1 The Constituent Assembly* Lusaka, 1996.
[28] In 1999 the President of Zimbabwe, Robert Mugabe, went even further and *added* a controversial provision relating to land acquisition to the draft Constitution submitted to him by a constitutional commission. The Zimbabwean People were not prepared to accept this blatant interference in the constitution-making process and rejected the draft in a February 2000 referendum.

document is widely regarded as something of a model Constitution and has been extremely influential in developing a high regard for fundamental rights and freedoms within the country.[29] Even so, it is worth noting that the process was criticised because of the absence of any true popular participation. For example, the National Union of Namibian Workers, the country's trade union federation, called for the promotion of public debate on the draft Constitution whilst resentment was expressed in the press that there was seemingly no genuine attempt on the part of the Constituent Assembly to involve the public in finalising the Constitution.[30]

Restricting membership of the constitution-making body to parliamentary representatives has important limitations. For example, in 1992 the Seychelles returned to a multi-party state. Following the holding of a general election, the constituent assembly (known as the Constitutional Commission), which was charged with drawing up the new Constitution, was made up overwhelmingly of representatives of the two main political parties, the Seychelles People's Progressive Front (SPPF) led by President René and the Seychelles Democratic Party (SDP) led by James Mancham. This was because President René considered that the drafting of the new Constitution was essentially a party political matter. Given the past history of the two main political parties,[31] not surprisingly the Constitutional Commission split on party lines and agreement became impossible. It was left to René's ruling party to draw up the document which was widely perceived as being unsatisfactory in several respects. It was only thanks to the need for a referendum on the document (see below) that the position was remedied.[32]

The Zambian position is also interesting. Following the submission of the Mwanakatwe Report to the Government, a Government white paper[33] was published setting out its reaction to the Report. This was followed by the publication of the 'Government's draft Constitution' which was to be submitted to the legislature for adoption by statute. Some opposition parties, church leaders and non-governmental organisations insisted that the revised Constitution must be adopted through a constituent assembly. A 'Green Paper' attacking government proposals was published and a highly-publicised conference held to raise public

---

[29] For a useful discussion on the process see: D Van Wyk, 'The Making of the Namibian Constitution: lessons for Africa' *Comparative and International Law Journal of Southern Africa* 341. See also John Hatchard and Peter Slinn 'Namibia: The Constitutional Path to Freedom' (1990) X *International Relations* 137, 144-146.

[30] See *The Namibian* 11 and 19 January 1990 and the discussion in Hatchard and Slinn, above, 145-6.

[31] At independence in 1976 Mancham became the first President of the Seychelles with René as Prime Minister. In 1977 a coup led to René seizing power and the country later became a one-party state with the SDP banned. See generally, John Hatchard, 'Re-establishing a Multi-Party State: Some Lessons from the 1992 Constitutional Developments in the Seychelles' (1993) 31 *Journal of Modern African Studies* 601.

[32] Similarly the constitutional commission in Zimbabwe established by President Mugabe was overwhelmingly made up of his own supporters. In 2000 their attempt to force through an unsatisfactory document was aborted due to its rejection in a national referendum.

[33] Government Paper No 1 of 1995.

outside of parliament. The key to final success was the multi-party constitutional talks which were attended by delegates from twenty-six parties and political groups that spanned the political spectrum. Under the name of the Multi-Party Negotiating Process (MPNP) it was agreed that all groups would participate on the basis of formal equality and that decisions would be taken on the basis of 'sufficient consensus'. The whole process was notable for the willingness on the part of participants to reach a consensus through compromise and led to agreement on the transitional process, the adoption of a draft interim Constitution and the setting of a date for all-racial elections. In order to meet concerns that the new Constitution might not sufficiently address the anxieties and fears of all groups, it was agreed that there would be a two-stage transition. An interim government, established and functioning under the interim Constitution, would govern the country on a coalition basis while the final Constitution was being drafted. It was agreed that a national legislature, elected by universal adult suffrage, would double as the constitution-making body.

Given the political history of the country, it was hardly surprising that there were concerns that the final Constitution might not sufficiently address the anxieties and insecurities of all interested groups. Thus it was agreed that its text must comply with certain principles, as the Preamble to the Interim Constitution stated:

AND WHEREAS in order to secure the achievement of this goal, elected representatives of all the people of South Africa should be mandated to adopt a new Constitution in accordance with a solemn pact recorded as Constitutional Principles.

The adoption of the '34 Constitutional Principles' (CPs) as they became known (although in reality they covered many more issues) was the key to the adoption of the new Constitution. To ensure that it complied with the CPs, the process called for an independent determination of the issue by the Constitutional Court. As section 71(2) of the interim Constitution provided:

The new constitutional text passed by the Constitutional Assembly, or any provision thereof, shall not be of any force and effect unless the Constitutional Court has certified that all the provisions of such text comply with the Constitutional Principles....

On 8 May 1996 the Constitutional Assembly adopted the new Constitution and the matter was then duly referred to the Constitutional Court. In undertaking its task of certification, the Court invited political parties and any other body or person wishing to object to the certification of the new Constitution to submit a written objection (the latter being restricted to one thousand words). In the event, notices of objection were submitted on behalf of five political parties and a further eighty-four private individuals and groups. A right of audience was granted to the political parties as well as to twenty-seven other bodies or persons.

On 6 September 1996 the court delivered its judgment in *Certification of the*

*Constitution of the Republic of South Africa, 1996*.[36] It recognised that the new Constitution represented a 'monumental achievement', particularly given the circumstances of South Africa, and concluded that the document complied with the overwhelming majority of the requirements of the CPs. However it identified several areas for re-consideration by the Constituent Assembly before it could certify the Constitution. Of particular interest here were the constitutional amendment provisions. The original section 74 of the 1996 document provided that most constitutional provisions could be amended by a vote in the National Assembly of at least two-thirds of its members. This was extraordinary because, as the Association of Law Societies noted, it meant that although the Court was required to check the new constitutional text with the CPs, the section left 'Parliament free the following day (by a mere two-thirds majority) to amend the new Constitution in a way which violates the Constitutional Principles'.[37] The Court itself focused on the requirement that the amendment procedure have 'special procedures involving special majorities' (CP XV) which it found the wording of section 74 did not satisfy. The matter was referred back to the Constituent Assembly which speedily approved a new provision and this was accepted by the Constitutional Court.[38] The Final Constitution then received presidential assent on 18 December 1996. This complex process proved remarkably successful (aided by almost uncannily helpful election results which gave the ANC a healthy parliamentary majority but not sufficiently large to draft the new Constitution alone).

*Overview*

One of the reasons for the adoption of the two-stage process in South Africa was the fact that those involved in the MPNP were, of necessity, not elected to their positions as a result of any free and fair elections. Thus it was thought desirable that the final Constitution was adopted by a 'credible body properly mandated to do so in consequence of free and fair elections based on universal adult suffrage'. In the special circumstances of South Africa, this approach was understandable. However, whilst the adoption of a new Constitution by a constituent assembly is certainly desirable, the use of the legislature as a 'credible' constitution-making body is arguably still unsatisfactory, for in many Commonwealth African States they remain largely rubber-stamp bodies. This means that there is considerable potential for the politicisation of the constitution-making process, a fact epitomised by the submission in 1996 of the 'Government's draft Constitution' to the Zambian parliament for its approval (which was obtained without amendment).

---

[36] 1996 (10) *BCLR* 1253 (CC).
[37] See ALS written submissions to the Constitutional Court, 31 May 1996, paras 3.2-3.
[38] See 'Certification of the Amended Text of the Constitution of the Republic of South Africa', 1996 1997 (1) *BCLR* 1. The revised section is discussed below.

This suggests that a body that represents a wider spectrum of civil society than that covered by parliamentarians should form the constituent assembly. The point is crucial for if a Constitution is to be 'popular and durable' its making must be above partisan politics. It is argued that, in order to give a voice to those who might not figure in the parliamentary process, a constituent assembly should consist of a representative cross-section of civil society which includes parliamentarians and representatives of all political parties. In this respect, the approach in Ghana, Nigeria and Uganda is well worth considering.

C. Securing the Approval of the People in a Referendum

Arguably, decisions by referendum are the most legitimate of all because they encourage the full participation of the people and give a 'seal of approval' to the document.[39] Indeed this was the very reason for the proposal by the Constitutional Review Committee in Nigeria that the new Constitution be put to a national referendum. Holding a national referendum on the proposed Constitution can generate wide publicity and engender full public debate, thus increasing the chances of the document receiving the sort of critical and objective consideration which it deserves. Further, a referendum can counterbalance the influence of the executive over a compliant parliament. A related question is whether a simple majority is sufficient or, given the importance of the subject-matter, an increased majority is needed. These issues are usefully illustrated by the experience of the Seychelles and Zambia.

In the Seychelles there was a requirement for the submission of the 1992 draft Constitution to a referendum and that it obtain at least a 60 per cent affirmative vote. The unsatisfactory nature of the adoption process was noted earlier and led to claims by opposition groups that the draft document would perpetuate one-party rule. Thus the referendum gave them an opportunity to campaign strongly for a 'No' vote. Their cause was assisted by the influential Catholic Church which particularly objected to a provision in the draft document that permitted abortion. In the event the 1992 referendum produced only a 53.7 per cent affirmative vote and, as a result, the Constitutional Commission resumed its work but this time with all parties participating. This led to the adoption of a new and thoroughly revised bi-partisan document which received a 73.6 per cent affirmative vote in the ensuing referendum.[40]

The controversy over the making of the 1996 Constitution of Zambia was also noted earlier. It is particularly interesting that Part III of the 1991 Constitution governing the protection of fundamental rights was not repealed because any such alteration required approval by a national referendum.[41] Whilst the government

---

[39] A point emphasised by Butler & Ranney in D Butler and A Ranney (eds) *Referendums: A Comparative Study of Practice and Theory* Washington DC, 1978, at 226.
[40] See J Hatchard, above, 601-612.
[41] See Art 79(3) Constitution of Zambia 1991.

could rely on a compliant legislature to replace the rest of the 1991 Constitution, it seems it did not believe it enjoyed sufficient support for its proposals in a referendum and did not pursue the matter.

Referendums inevitably have their own drawbacks: in particular the actual wording of the question(s) may greatly influence the result; they are expensive and time-consuming;[42] and, according to the Nigerian government when rejecting the views of the Constitution Review Committee, they are too 'formal and static'.[43] Certainly these are important concerns but the experience of the Seychelles and Zambia amply demonstrate that they can play a key role in ensuring that the wishes of the executive remain subordinate to those of the people.

D. Conclusions

The significance of a national Constitution means that establishing a satisfactory procedure for making it is of vital importance. This discussion has not sought to provide a detailed, country by country, analysis of the situation in Commonwealth Africa but rather to emphasise the importance of getting the procedure 'right' so that the ultimate product has a chance of being a popular and durable Constitution, one that is above partisan politics and one that can help develop an ethos of constitutionalism. Certainly, the constitution-making process of the 1990s in Commonwealth African countries was ostensibly designed to give them a fresh start, whilst the experience of some countries still discloses an unwarranted intrusion on the part of governments into the process.

It is argued that as the Constitution is the supreme law, the constitution-making process is neither the responsibility of government nor parliament. A Constitution belongs to the people and they must be intimately involved throughout the process. This requires (a) full public consultation on the contents of the document through the medium of an independent constitutional commission or the like which reports directly to the constitution-making body;[44] (b) the adoption of the Constitution by a popularly selected body that includes parliamentarians and delegates from political parties but one that is fully representative of civil society; and (c) that the document is ratified by the people in a referendum.

---

[42] Although this might also inhibit efforts to make frequent amendments to the Constitution.
[43] See Read, above, 175. In addition, as the result of the referendum on the draft Constitution of Zimbabwe in February 2000 demonstrates, a 'No' vote may also reflect widespread dissatisfaction with the Present as much as a rejection of the document itself.
[44] This should include giving people guidance as to the sort of choices they have to consider - a task successfully accomplished in Uganda by the Constitutional Commission.

## IV. AMENDING THE CONSTITUTIONS OF COMMONWEALTH AFRICA

A. Why a Power to Amend?

The need to make a Constitution that is transgenerational and promotes an ethos of constitutionalism was noted earlier. Some have also argued that a Constitution should therefore be unamendable[45] and certainly some provisions in, for example the Namibian Constitution (see below) fall into this category. The 'unamendable Constitution' overlooks the fact that however rigorous the procedure for making the Constitution, the document may still contain imperfections. As George Washington himself noted in 1787, 'The warmest friends and the best supporters the [US] Constitution has do not contend that it is free from imperfections; but they found them unavoidable and are sensible that if evil is likely to arise there from, the remedy must come hereafter'.[46]

In the African context, the experience of Ghana neatly illustrates a potential problem with the unalterable Constitution, in this case where the 'imperfection' was deliberately inserted by the outgoing military government.[47] The Constitution of Ghana 1979 came into effect following the handover of power by the Armed Forces Revolutionary Council (AFRC) to a civilian government. Shortly before promulgating the Constitution, the AFRC inserted certain unamendable 'Transitional Provisions', the net effect of which was to ensure that neither the incoming administration nor the courts could disturb certain decisions taken by the Council. This struck at the balance of the whole document itself and provoked a storm of protest, both within and without Parliament, against the deprivation of the people's inherent right to amend any provision of the Constitution under which they were democratically governed.[48]

The very real difficulties inherent in the creation of an 'unamendable' Constitution means that in practice the need for a formal procedure to 'perfect the imperfections' is recognised throughout Commonwealth Africa.[49]

---

[45] For example, John Locke's draft of the 1669 Fundamental Constitutions of Carolinas provides that 'these fundamental constitutions shall be and remain the sacred and unalterable form and rule of government ... forever': quoted in S Levinson (ed) *Responding to Imperfection: The Theory and Practice of Constitutional Amendment* Princeton University Press, Princeton, 1995, at 4.

[46] Quoted in Levinson, above, at 1.

[47] In fact the Constitution of Ghana 1969 also had provisions that were declared unalterable for all time. These included matters such as the Supremacy of the Constitution, judicial power to interpret and enforce the Constitution and a specific provision that 'Parliament shall have no power to pass a law establishing a one-party state'. This Constitution lasted little more than two years before the country experienced another military takeover.

[48] In fact the situation in Ghana was never resolved because at the height of the national debate on the subject, the Government and Constitution were overthrown in a military coup.

[49] Of course Constitution may also be 'amended' by judicial interpretation, a situation that is becoming increasingly a feature of Commonwealth African states.

## B. Getting the Balance Right: The Present Position

Devising a satisfactory amendment procedure requires a tricky balancing act. An over-rigid procedure may prevent or deter efforts to strengthen constitutional provisions whilst a Constitution that has 'weak' amendment provisions carries with it the possibility of its wholesale amendment and the resultant undermining of key provisions. As Brandon rightly notes: 'A Constitution, which is to some extent a device for *preserving* certain states of affairs, might become a device for *undermining* the very states of affairs it is designed to preserve'.[50] Certainly the amendment of many Constitutions in Commonwealth Africa prior to 1990 resulted in a further entrenching of executive power and the curtailment of fundamental rights and freedoms. Once again, this calls for the drafters of a Constitution to get the amendment procedure 'right'.

In practice the amendment procedure contained in the Westminster model still exerts a considerable influence in Commonwealth Africa. This provides the legislature with the role of 'guardian of the Constitution'. Thus any constitutional amendment Bill required approval by a specially enhanced parliamentary majority. This is often linked to a requirement for the publication of the text of any constitutional amendment Bill in the Government *Gazette* for 30 days before the First Reading in Parliament. Ibrahima Fall, a senior UN official suggests that legislatures have this guardianship role because they are:-

one of the crucial elements in a democratic society and essential in ensuring the rule of law and protection of human rights. In fact, in their daily work of transforming the will of the people into law and in controlling the Executive and public administration, parliaments and parliamentarians are often the unsung heros of human rights.[51]

However, grave doubts remain as to whether the legislature alone should have responsibility for amending the Constitution. Here the experience of Zimbabwe is particularly valuable.

### *The Zimbabwe experience*

Since independence in 1980, fifteen separate Amendment Acts (all of which made multiple changes) completely re-shaped the Constitution of Zimbabwe. Given the circumstances of its birth, some amendments were inevitable and entirely

---

[50] M Brandon 'The 'Original' Thirteenth Amendment and the Limits to Formal Constitutional Change' in Levinson, above, at 215 (emphasis in the original). See also John Hatchard 'Undermining the Constitution by Constitutional Means: Some Thoughts on the New Constitutions of Southern Africa' (1995) XXVII *Comparative and International Law Journal of Southern Africa* 21-35.
[51] See *Parliament: Guardian of Human Rights* Inter-Parliamentary Union, 1993, 5. At that time Fall was the UN Assistant-Secretary-General for Human Rights.

desirable.[52] The same cannot be said for some of the others. Thus constitutional amendments have, amongst other things, specifically sought to oust the jurisdiction of the courts;[53] to prevent the Supreme Court from hearing a case relating to the scope of the fundamental rights provisions; and to overturn its decisions thereon.[54] For example, in 1990 in *Chileya v S*[55] the Supreme Court asked for full argument on the issue of whether the use of hanging constituted inhuman or degrading treatment or punishment contrary to section 15(1) of the Constitution, and a date was set down for the hearing. The response of government was immediate. Shortly before the hearing, a Constitutional Amendment Bill was published which included a provision specifically upholding the constitutionality of executions by hanging.[56] The Minister of Justice, Legal and Parliamentary Affairs informed Parliament that any holding to the contrary 'would be untenable to government which holds the correct and firm view ... that Parliament makes the laws and the courts interpret them'. He added that the abolition of the death sentence was a matter for the executive and legislature and that 'government will not and cannot countenance a situation where the death penalty is *de facto* abolished through the back door...'.[57] As discussed below, there was little parliamentary debate on this aspect of the Bill and members overwhelmingly approved the measure.

A second example concerns the case of *Catholic Commission for Justice and Peace in Zimbabwe v Attorney-General*[58] where the Supreme Court held that the dehumanising factor of prolonged delay, viewed in conjunction with the harsh and degrading conditions in the condemned section of the holding prison, meant that executing four condemned prisoners would have constituted inhuman and degrading treatment contrary to section 15(1) of the Constitution. Accordingly, the court directed that the death sentences be replaced by sentences of life imprisonment. It also gave a series of directions on the procedure for dealing with condemned prisoners and suggested that petitions of mercy should be dealt with expeditiously by the executive, recommending three months as a possible timeframe. This landmark decision was later followed by the Judicial Committee of the Privy Council in *Pratt and Morgan v Attorney-General for Jamaica*[59] and received

---

[52] For example, the removal of the parliamentary seats reserved for non-Africans. See generally the discussion in John Hatchard 'The African-Zimbabwe Constitution: A Model for Africa?' (1991) 35 *Journal of African Law* 79-101.
[53] Constitution of Zimbabwe Amendment (No 12) Act, 1993, section 2 which amended section 16(1)(e) of the Constitution.
[54] Section 24 of the Constitution gives the Supreme Court original jurisdiction to 'hear and determine' issues relating to fundamental rights and to 'make such orders ... and give such directions as it may consider appropriate for the purpose of enforcing or securing the enforcement of the Declaration of Rights'.
[55] Supreme Court of Zimbabwe SC 64/90 unreported.
[56] This later became section 15(4) of the Constitution.
[57] Parliamentary Debates 6 December 1990.
[58] 1993 (4) SA 239. The decision of the five-man bench was given by Gubbay, CJ
[59] [1993] 4 All ER 769.

warm approval from commentators.[60] Even so, it drew a critical response from the government and within weeks the Constitution of Zimbabwe Amendment (No 13) Act 1993 was passed which retrospectively exempted the death penalty from the scope of section 15(1). Once again Members of Parliament overwhelmingly approved the Bill.

Whilst the Acts were passed in accordance with the Constitution, the Zimbabwean experience highlights some of the potential weaknesses of centring the amendment procedure around the legislature. Thus Zimbabwe, in line with several other Commonwealth African States, has one dominant political party, ZANU(PF) which controls 147 of the 150 seats in Parliament.[61] This inevitably means that the requirement for a two-thirds majority is so easily met that it has no practical value. Of course it is arguable that a party with a two-thirds majority in the legislature enjoys sufficient popular support to be allowed to pass constitutional amendments. This overlooks reality, as illustrated in Zimbabwe where the Executive (and the Central Committee of the ruling party) has exercised and continues to exercise complete control over Members of Parliament with the resultant rubber-stamping of all constitutional amendments.

Further, it is questionable whether all Members of Parliament are able and/or prepared to undertake a critical and informed view of proposed constitutional changes. For example, in the parliamentary debate on the 1993 Act, the few Members of Parliament who did speak seemingly did not understand the Supreme Court decision in the *Catholic Commission* case and believed its effect was to abolish the death penalty itself.[62] Indeed just one Member managed to state and analyse the ruling accurately.[63] Regrettably, Members were not assisted by the Minister of Justice, Legal and Parliamentary Affairs who informed them that the decision 'allowed the *de facto* abolition of the death sentence by the judiciary' and that the judgment 'was to the effect that from the day a person is sentenced to death by the High Court, three months should be the maximum. If three months pass before he is executed ... then there is a delay, which in the opinion of the Supreme

---

[60] See, for example, W A Schabas '*Soering*'s Legacy: the Human Rights Committee and the Judicial Committee of the Privy Council Take a Walk Down Death Row' (1994) 43 *ICLQ* 913. It is also worth noting that Zimbabwean government criticism of the judgment ceased after the decision in *Pratt and Morgan*.

[61] As at December 1999 Commonwealth African countries where the ruling party holds at least two-thirds of the parliamentary seats (% in brackets) include: Tanzania (79%), Zambia (85%), Seychelles (81%), Namibia (73%), Mauritius (90%) and Ghana (67%). Source: *Democracy Still in the Making* Inter-Parliamentary Union, Geneva, 1997, Annex 1.

[62] Just 26 of the 150 members made any contribution to the debate on the Second Reading and, seemingly, only five of these were not in favour of the Bill although their contributions on the matter were not always very clear. Thus one member asserted that 'the proposal should be supported and we should remove [the] death sentence for the democratic development of our nation' (Mr Nyashanu, *Parliamentary Debates*, 28 September 1994).

[63] See the contribution of Mr Malunga in *Parliamentary Debates* 22 September 1994.

awareness and elicit public resistance to the new Constitution. The Government was not swayed by this and asserted that Parliament was a 'more democratic' forum for the adoption of the Constitution than a constituent assembly. Thus the new Constitution was brought into force, like its predecessors, by an Act of Parliament passed by a legislature that was totally dominated by its own supporters. Members of the major opposition party in Parliament walked out in protest at the Bill.

Efforts to convene a more representative body were made in Ghana, Nigeria and Uganda. In Uganda there was considerable debate over the composition of the Constituent Assembly. The idea that the National Resistance Council (NRC) should take over that role proved controversial, particularly on the ground that it was not a directly-elected body and thus did not enjoy a mandate from the electorate. In the event, the Constituent Assembly Statute of 1993 provided for the holding of elections to a Constituent Assembly. These were successfully held in April 1993 and as a result a popularly elected Assembly of 214 members met to approve the Constitution. They were joined by representatives from, amongst others, the army, trades unions, political parties, youth and the disabled together with thirty-nine women (one from each of the thirty-nine districts). Indeed one notable aspect was the involvement of women and women's groups throughout the entire process. After sixteen months of sometimes acrimonious debate, the Constituent Assembly produced the new Constitution which was promulgated in October 1995.

In Nigeria the draft Constitution [of 1989] was referred to a Constituent Assembly consisting of 567 members, the majority of whom were indirectly elected by local government councillors with additional members being appointed by the government to represent particular interest groups, including women, business, trade unions and traditional leaders.[34] The Assembly deliberated for nearly one year and finally produced a draft Constitution which formed the basis of the final document.[35] In Ghana a Consultative Assembly made up of some 250 Ghanaians representing a broad spectrum of society was established in 1991 to prepare a draft Constitution which was later approved in a referendum.

A brief examination of the Constitution-making process in South Africa is helpful for, whilst the procedure inevitably included some unique features, it emphasises the importance of seeking a broad consensus. The entire negotiating process leading to the making of the interim Constitution of 1994 took place

---

[34] That is not to say that the membership of the Assembly was wholly representative because, amongst other things, candidates were vetted by the government to avoid 'extremists'.

[35] Even so, the government retained the final say on the document and later made important changes thereto. Thus recommendations on the length of term of the President and State Governors were rejected, as were proposals on limiting the presidential power of appointment of Ministers and reducing the size of the Senate. For a useful account of the constitution-making process see J Read 'Nigeria's Constitution for 1992: The Third Republic' (1991) 35 *Journal of African Law* 174, 175-77. For an in-depth discussion on the work of the 1992 Constitution see A N Aniagolu *The Making of the 1989 Constitution of Nigeria* Spectrum, Lagos, 1993.

Court, vitiates the execution'.[64] As noted above, that was certainly *not* the ruling of the Supreme Court. A failure to appreciate the importance of constitutional amendments was also demonstrated when the final vote on the Bill had to be nullified and retaken because of an oversight that it required a two-thirds majority. Such actions do not reflect well on the role of parliamentarians of:-

not allowing amendments to fundamental rights provisions in the Constitution to be rushed through Parliament. The people should expect their Parliamentarians to consider with great care the implications of any measures which will have the effect of diluting fundamental rights provisions. The people expect Parliament to uphold fundamental rights and not to acquiesce in a process which weakens these rights.[65]

In addition, several of the Constitutional Amendment Bills have contained multiple changes which may well have contributed to inadequate discussion and consideration of some of their provisions. For example, the provision pre-empting the Supreme Court from hearing the appeal in *Chileya* was included in a Bill which also amended the highly sensitive and emotive land provisions and in the debate was thus almost entirely neglected by Members in their eagerness to discuss the land issue.

The Zimbabwean experience is not unique and the perceived widespread weakness of opposition parties and the strict hegemony of the ruling party elsewhere in Commonwealth Africa does not hold out the promise of parliament being an effective 'guardian of the Constitution'. This raises the question of how best to provide for special procedures and special majorities. The approach in other Commonwealth African countries provide some useful alternatives.

C. Getting the Balance Right: Some Alternatives

*1. Special procedures: the role of the legislature in the amendment process*

Concern about the performance of legislatures in Commonwealth Africa is not the only consideration when considering the amendment procedure. As argued earlier, the Constitution belongs to the People and must be made by them. It follows that any substantive constitutional amendment to it requires a similar process, i.e. approval by a constituent assembly plus approval in a national referendum.

Some Commonwealth African countries come close to this approach. The Constitution of Malawi provides that any amendment to the 'Fundamental Principles' or Human Rights provisions enshrined in the Constitution requires a simple parliamentary majority provided that the proposed amendment has received the support of the majority of those voting in a national referendum. A similar

---

[64] Parliamentary Debates 22 and 28 September 1993
[65] See the Editorial entitled 'A Regrettable Amendment' in (1994) 6 *Legal Forum* 1-2.

approach is adopted in Lesotho[66] where a Constitutional Amendment Bill cannot be submitted to the King for assent unless between two and six months after the Bill has received parliamentary approval it is approved in a national referendum. In Sierra Leone, a two-thirds parliamentary majority is required as well as approval in a national referendum.

Enhanced majorities in the referendum are also provided for in some cases. Thus the 1991 Constitution of Sierra Leone specifically lists provisions, including those relating to the protection of fundamental rights, which can only be amended if approved in a referendum where the approval must be by not less than two-thirds of all the votes cast.[67] Similarly, in the Seychelles, proposed amendments to specific provisions require the approval of not less than 60 per cent of the votes cast.

Requiring approval of constitutional amendments by the legislature and by the people in a referendum is attractive because it carries with it a greater chance of proposed constitutional amendments receiving the sort of serious, critical and objective consideration which they deserve and counters executive attempts to undermine constitutional rights through the use of a compliant legislature. In view of the experience of Zambia and the Seychelles discussed earlier, the requirement for an enhanced majority is also welcome.

There are two arguments against the use of a referendum. Firstly, the procedure may lead to some delay in the coming into effect of provisions that strengthen fundamental rights provisions: however this is a small price to pay for protecting the Constitution. Secondly, it is an inconvenient procedure if the constitutional amendment is of a minor nature. Here the Constitution of Malawi provides a helpful solution in that where the 'amendment would not affect the substance of [*sic*] effect of the Constitution' and the Speaker has so certified, then the Bill may be passed with a two-thirds majority of the National Assembly.[68]

The inclusion of a referendum in the amendment process is certainly an improvement on relying on the legislature alone. Even so, it is argued that a constituent assembly that represents a genuine cross-section of civil society remains the preferred option.

## 2. *Providing special majorities*

If parliament is to remain the 'guardian of the Constitution' it raises the question as to the 'ideal' super-majority required to pass a constitutional amendment. Should it be a two-thirds majority as required for amending parts of the Constitution of Zambia? a 65 per cent majority as required for amending the Constitution of Kenya? a 75 per cent majority, as required for amending parts of the new South

---

[66] Chapter VII of the Constitution of Lesotho.
[67] See s. 108(3) and (4). At least 50% of registered voters must also have participated.
[68] See ss. 195-197.

African Constitution? or a 100 per cent affirmative vote, as required for amending parts of the Constitution of Zimbabwe up to 1990?[69] What happens if the ruling party breaks up so that even a two-thirds majority becomes impossible to achieve? With different political conditions in different countries it is surely unrealistic to expect to devise a satisfactory numerical formula.

In considering an alternative approach, one must consider two of the basic concerns underlying the special majority procedure: i.e. the need to ensure that no political party has the sole right to amend the Constitution and the need to protect the position of minorities. Thus if a 'special majority' provision is desired, a more flexible approach is needed to satisfy these concerns. It is suggested that this is done by providing that any Constitutional Amendment Bill obtains the support of the majority of the members of the ruling party together with a majority of the members of the main opposition party(ies). This has the advantages of involving a wider range of political opinion, raising the level of parliamentary debate with Ministers having to persuade more than just their own Parliamentary supporters of the merits of the Bill, developing a more consensual approach to the amendment process and eliminating the inflexible and undesirable numerical approach.

*3. Other special procedures*

The requirement that the text of any Constitutional Amendment Bill be published in the Government *Gazette* for thirty days before the first reading in the legislature for public comment is retained in several Constitutions, including Zimbabwe, South Africa and Zambia.[70] In South Africa there is provision for a further 'cooling-off' period so that an amendment cannot be put to the vote in the National Assembly within thirty days of its introduction/tabling in the Assembly.[71]

Some have questioned whether this is a 'special procedure' that makes a Constitution less vulnerable to amendment and this concern may have persuaded some constitutional drafters to exclude it in favour of holding a referendum. Certainly a 'cooling-off' period, on its own, hardly provides a check on amending the Constitution but it is a potentially useful means of stimulating public awareness and of giving an early warning sufficient to allow for lobbying on the issue. Given the potential lack of any critical analysis of the proposed amendment by parliamentarians, this process at least allows the NGO community in particular to

---

[69] Certainly this deterred attempts to amend the Constitution for it was only after the requirement fell away that the protected provisions were amended.

[70] See Art 79(2) Constitution of Zambia and s.52 Constitution of Zimbabwe. In South Africa, the person or committee introducing the Amendment Bill must submit any written comments received from the public and the provincial legislatures to the Speaker for tabling in the National Assembly: see s.74(6) Constitution of South Africa.

[71] S.74(7).

engage government in dialogue.[72] However to enhance its value, wide publicity of the Bill is essential and this is not achieved by merely publishing it in the official government organ. To be effective the proposed amendment(s) must be published by law in the major news media including those in the vernacular.[73]

D. Prohibiting any Weakening of Fundamental Rights Provisions

As noted earlier, a power to amend a Constitution opens up the possibility of key provisions being undermined. In Namibia, concern over this led to the drafters of the Constitution including a provision that prohibits any repeal or amendment of any provision of the Constitution in so far as this

> diminishes or detracts from the fundamental rights and freedoms contained in [the Constitution] and no such purported repeal or amendment shall be valid or have any force or effect.[74]

The advantage of this approach is that fundamental rights can be strengthened as appropriate but not weakened, thus preventing the possibility of a repeat of the Zimbabwe experience. Of course its very rigidity could prove troublesome if a widely-held public view developed that a fundamental human rights provision required amendment: for example, overwhelming public support for the reintroduction of the death penalty which, at present, is outlawed in the Namibian Constitution. Perhaps the way to tackle this potential problem is to ensure that the fundamental rights provisions in the Constitution meet the aspirations of the people and the international human rights obligations of the country in the first place.

The provision remains unique to Namibia and seemingly will remain so. It certainly highlights the importance of protecting a Constitution against 'retrogressive' amendment, but its very inflexibility could pose problems in the future.

*Overview*

This discussion has highlighted the importance of putting in place effective safeguards against the erosion of constitutional rights by means of the amendment

---

[72] This is well illustrated by the critical response of human rights NGOs in Zimbabwe to plans to amend the Constitution to abolish the right of a non-citizen husband to reside in Zimbabwe with his citizen wife. As a result of their pressure, changes were made to the proposed Amendment Bill.

[73] The Land Acquisition Act 1992 in Zimbabwe provides a useful precedent. Section 5 states that an intention to acquire any land other than by agreement must be signified by a notice to this effect published once in the Government *Gazette* and twice 'in a newspaper circulating in the area in which the land is to be acquired is situated and in such other manner as the acquiring authority thinks will best bring the notice to the attention of the owner'.

[74] Art 131.

process. What is striking about the post-1990 Constitutions of Commonwealth Africa is that so many still follow the Westminster model with its emphasis on the role of parliament as the guardian of the Constitution. In view of the weakness of many Commonwealth parliaments, arguably that 'trust' is largely misplaced. Perhaps more importantly it highlights the continued failure to recognise that the process of *amending* a Constitution is just as much the business of the People as is the *making* of the document and it is they who must be consulted and they who must give their consent. On this point the views of George Washington are as relevant today as they were in 1787 when they were written:

The People (for it is with them to judge) can, as they will have the advantage of experience on their side, decide with as much propriety on the alterations and amendments which are necessary.[75]

Overall the key test is whether a Constitution provides for a special amendment procedure that makes a clear distinction between constitutional matters and normal legislation and one that provides for a high level of public debate and participation. It is argued that the present provisions in Commonwealth African Constitutions do not satisfy this test, and amendment via a broadly-based constituent assembly and national referendum is the way forward. Further, if it is desired to retain the legislature as 'the guardian of the Constitution', then the current unsatisfactory provisions relating to special majorities need replacing by a process that better reflects the views of all parliamentarians.

## V. CONCLUSION

Constitutions are delicate creatures and their history in the African context is one of abrogation, derogation and retrogressive amendment. The 1990s saw a fresh start with efforts taking place to provide popular and durable national Constitutions in many Commonwealth African countries. This chapter has demonstrated the importance of providing appropriate procedures for both the making and amending of these documents so as to help establish and retain an ethos of constitutionalism that can, hopefully, help maintain constitutional stability.

The common theme running through the discussion is that a Constitution belongs to the People and that it is they who must have the final say on its content. Further, legislatures cannot play the role of guardians of the Constitution satisfactorily and other mechanisms and strategies are required.

---

[75] Letter of George Washington to Bushrod Washington, 10 November 1787, referred to in Levinson, above, 3.

Chapter Two

# THE JUDICIAL ENFORCEMENT OF CONSTITUTIONAL HUMAN RIGHTS IN COMMONWEALTH COUNTRIES: THE RIGHT TO PARTICIPATION IN PARLIAMENTARY PROCESSES

Peter Slinn

## I. INTRODUCTION

At national and international level, human rights instruments seek actively to protect the right to democratic participation in the political process. The effective protection of such democratic entitlements is a vital element in human rights discourse for the new millennium. However, the development of a secure democratic culture is a complex and hazardous process in which the legal environment is but one factor. The Commonwealth as an organisation has been much concerned with the promotion of fundamental political values of democracy and the rule of law, as the Harare Declaration and the Millbrook Action Programme bear witness.[1] Yet fifty years after the Declaration of London provided the foundation of the modern Commonwealth, the association is a painful witness to the difficulty experienced by Member States in sustaining those values. Recent events in Pakistan, Sierra Leone, Sri Lanka, Fiji, the Solomons and Zimbabwe have demonstrated the problem of the sustainability of parliamentary government. In Fiji a gang of gun-waving desperadoes was able to kidnap the elected Prime Minister and compel the resignation of the Head of State; in Zimbabwe, the ruling party appeared willing to go to any lengths to avert the possibility of defeat at the polls. The Supreme Court of Pakistan, when faced with a constitutional challenge to the take-over of the government by the armed forces, found that the conduct of the democratically elected government had been such in terms of corruption and mismanagement so as to justify the soldiers' action on the basis of the doctrine of state necessity.[2]

---

[1] Alison Duxbury, 'Rejunevating the Commonwealth - The Human Rights Remedy', 46 (1997) ICLQ 344.
[2] Constitutional Petitions under Article 184(3) of the Constitution of the Islamic Republic of Pakistan, provisional judgment delivered by Irshad Hasan Khan, CJ, 12 May, 2000.

Against this depressing background, a far cry from the bright new dawn of Francis Fukayama's triumph of democracy[3], the purpose of this short chapter is to attempt some assessment of the role of the judicial process in enforcing democratic entitlements. The issues concern not only the rights of voters but also those of elected representatives who should (but sadly often fail to) play a crucial role in ensuring democratic accountability.

## II. INTERNATIONAL INSTRUMENTS

The familiar human rights instruments contain provisions protective of the individual's right to democratic participation. For example, article 21 of the Universal Declaration of Human Rights declares that everyone has the right to take part in the government of his country, directly or through freely chosen representatives and -

The will of the people....shall be expressed in periodic and genuine elections which shall be by universal and equal suffrage and shall be by secret vote or by equivalent free voting procedures.

Article 25 of the International Covenant on Civil and Political Rights contains similar provisions. Article 3 of Protocol I of the European Convention on Human Rights provides that the parties -

..undertake to hold free elections at reasonable intervals by secret ballot, under conditions which will ensure the free expression of the opinion of the people in the choice of the legislature.

The Strasbourg Court recently held that this right was violated by the failure of the United Kingdom to ensure that a British citizen resident in Gibraltar could participate in elections to the European Parliament.[4] Other fundamental rights are obviously relevant to the political process such as freedom of expression, freedom of association and freedom from discrimination.

Aside from specific instruments, it has been argued forcefully by Professor Thomas Franck and others that -

Both textually and in practice the international system is moving towards a clearly defined democratic entitlement, with national governance validated by international standards and systematic monitoring of compliance.[5]

---

[3]  *The End of History and the Last Man* (1992).
[4]  *Matthews v. United* Kingdom, *Times,* 3 March 1999.
[5]  Franck, *Fairness in International Law and Institutions,* Oxford, 1997, chapter 4, 'Fairness to Persons: The Democratic Entitlement', p.139.

As far as the Commonwealth is concerned, the principal instrument is the Harare Declaration of 1991. This is not of course not binding on Member States in the same way as an international treaty, but it does embody the shared commitment to certain fundamental principles, including -

> the individual's inalienable right to participate by means of free and democratic political processes in framing the society in which he lives.

At the Heads of Government Meeting in Auckland in 1997, the Millbrook Action Programme was adopted. This attempted to give some teeth to the Harare Declaration by providing for measures to be taken when a member country was misperceived to be clearly in violation of that Declaration. This has led to the suspension from the councils of the Commonwealth of Fiji and Pakistan, following the forceful overthrow of democratically elected governments. However, measures taken by governments against each other are likely to be of limited scope and effectiveness, given the dubious democratic credentials of a number of Commonwealth countries which have not witnessed the unconstitutional overthrow of government. Civil society throughout the Commonwealth has an important part to play in ensuring democratic entitlements. This role has been articulated in the 'Latimer House Guidelines' adopted in 1998 by a gathering of members of the Commonwealth professional legal associations and of the Commonwealth Parliamentary Association. These Guidelines on 'good practice governing relations between the executive, parliament and the judiciary in the promotion of good governance, the rule of law and human rights' are designed to ensure the effective implementation of the Harare Principles. In dealing with matters relating to the independence and accountability of the judiciary and of parliamentarians, the Guidelines are central to the theme of the effective judicial enforcement of democratic rights in the Commonwealth.[6]

## III. NATIONAL IMPLEMENTATION

A. Protection of Political Rights

Political rights can be expressed in straightforward human rights terms in the protective provisions of the domestic bill of rights. Thus in the South African Constitution, 1996, article 19 (headed 'political rights') provides:

> (1) Every citizen is free to make political choices, which includes the right -

---

[6] The Guidelines are attached to this chapter. The author must declare an interest in that he was one of those closely involved with the production of the Guidelines. For the full story, see J Hatchard & P Slinn, *Parliamentary Supremacy and Judicial Independence: A Commonwealth Approach*, London, Cavendish, 1999.

(a) to form a political party
(b) to participate in the activities of, or recruit members
(c) to campaign for a political party or cause.

(2) Every citizen has the right to free, fair and regular elections for any legislative body established in terms of the Constitution.

(3) Every adult citizen has the right -
(a) to vote in elections or any legislative body established in terms of the Constitution, and to do so in secret, and
(b) to stand for public office and, if elected, to hold office.

This detailed expression of the democratic entitlements is to be expected in a modern constitution, drafted in the light of a legacy of denial of democratic rights to the vast majority of the population. However, a number of attempts have been made to restrict freedom of political choice. Apart from Uganda, where political activity outside the 'movement system' is severely restricted,[7] a constitution may prescribe the limitation of political activity to registered political parties satisfying certain criteria. This device is justified on the basis of the elimination of political parties operating on a tribal or ethnic basis, but may be open to abuse.[8]

A number of other factors may affect the effective delivery of the democratic entitlement. Restrictive electoral registration measures may deprive persons otherwise entitled of the franchise.[9] Citizenship qualifications or other restrictions may be used to restrict eligibility to stand for political office or even participate in the political process.[10] In such cases, the courts may intervene to protect fundamental rights. Thus the Privy Council, reversing a decision of the Court of Appeal of Antigua and Barbuda, held that the imposition of a blanket prohibition on all civil servants from communicating to anyone any expression of view on any matter of political controversy was an excessive restriction on the freedom of expression and assembly of public officers.[11]

The electoral process itself may be marred by bribery, intimidation or typically government control of access to party funding or the media. Election monitoring by independent international agencies plays an important role in limiting such abuses and the Commonwealth itself has played a major part in these observations.[12] The courts may intervene in such cases in a number of ways.

---

[7] Constitution of Uganda, articles 69-75.
[8] See, for example, article 55 of the Constitution of Ghana.
[9] For example, the 'bar code' controversy surrounding the South African General Election of 1999, *The Times*, 4 March 1999.
[10] As was done in Zambia by the 1996 Constitutional amendment: see M Mbao, 'Human Rights and Discrimination: Zambia's Constitutional Amendment, 1996' [1998] 42 Journal of African Law, 1-11.
[11] *de Freitas v. Permanent Secretary of Agriculture, Fisheries and Housing* [1998] 3 LRC 62.
[12] See, for example, the Commonwealth Secretary-General's Report, 1997, which recorded that between 1995 and 1997, Commonwealth Observer groups had monitored seven elections in Tanzania, Sierra Leone, Bangladesh, Ghana, Pakistan, Cameroon and Papua New Guinea.

Election petitions may succeed in nullifying election victories achieved by bribery or intimidation.[13] In Zimbabwe, an Act authorised funding for political parties in proportion to their representation in Parliament, provided that they had at least 15 elected members. In the 1995 election the ruling party won 118 out of the 120 seats filled by election. The Supreme Court upheld a challenge to the validity of this provision on the basis that it was violative of the right of freedom of expression of members of a party which had no members in Parliament. [14]

One issue which appears outside the jurisdiction of the courts is the question of the composition of the legislature. The principle of popular representation may be diluted by the presence of unelected members in the 'people's' chamber. This presence may be justified on the grounds of the need to ensure the participation of otherwise under-represented groups such as women or religious minorities. However, such members may have a decisive effect on the political process. Thus in Zimbabwe, 30 of the 150 members of the unicameral legislature are nominated, *ex officio* or chosen by electoral colleges of traditional chiefs. In the 2000 election, opposition parties won 58 seats, but the unelected members ensure ZANU/PF of a comfortable if not quite two/thirds majority.[15]

The problem of gender and other social imbalance of course remains.

There is chronic under-representation of women in Commonwealth elected legislatures. In 1995, the Commonwealth average of parliamentary seats held by women was 7.2 per cent; compared with a global average of 11.4 per cent.[16] For good reason, therefore, the Latimer House Guidelines contain a section devoted to 'Women in Parliament', with strategies designed to redress gender imbalance .[17]

B. Rights of Elected Representatives

The Latimer House Guidelines recognise that parliamentarians also require the protection of the law in the context of the preservation of the right of free speech and security of tenure.[18] Regarding the former, the role of the courts is to *abstain* from any intervention in the conduct of parliamentary business in accordance with the venerable words of the Bill of Rights of 1688:

That the Freedome of Speech and debates or Proceedings in Parlyement ought not to be impeached or questioned in any court or place out of Parlyement.

---

[13] At the time of writing (August, 2000), the result of a number of election petitions challenging ZANU/PF victories in the recent Zimbabwe election is awaited.
[14] *United Parties v. Minister of Justice* [1998] 1 LRC 614.
[15] For details of the composition of African legislatures, see D Nohlen, M Krennerich & B Thibaut, *Elections in Africa: A Data Handbook,*Oxford, 1999.
[16] Yasmin Tambiah, 'Promoting Women's Political Participation in Commonwealth Asia', *Commonwealth Currents,* 2 1998 18-19.
[17] See Guideline IV, below, p.36.
[18] Guideline II, 'Preserving the Independence of Parliamentarians', below, p.34.

A balance has always to be struck between protecting the privileges of parliamentarians and the protection of freedom of expression, for example, the freedom of newspapers to criticise politicians and question their fitness to hold office.[19]

The question of security of tenure of members, once elected, raises the issue of the constitutionality of 'anti-defection clauses', which deprive a member of her seat if she ceases to be a member of the party on whose ticket she was elected. The discussions which led to the adoption of the Latimer House Guideline III 2(a) revealed a deep division of opinion between those who regarded such a measure as an essential safeguard against corruption and those who regarded any restriction on floor-crossing as a severe threat to the independence of members. Faced with challenges to such provisions, the courts have differed in their approach. In Malaysia, the Supreme Court held that legislation against floor-crossing was violative of the fundamental right to freedom of association.[20] In Zambia, the Supreme Court upheld a provision in the constitution dealing with vacation of seats by members even if a member left a political party in order to sit as an independent.[21]

The inclusion of an anti-defection provision in the interim Constitution of South Africa was intensely controversial. However, the Constitutional Court sanctioned the retention of such a clause in its certification of the draft permanent constitution as being in compliance with fundamental constitutional principles. The court was apparently influenced by the nature of the electoral system: under a list system of proportional representation, it was parties that the electorate voted for and it was those parties, not individual members, which were accountable to the electorate.[22] Nevertheless, the unqualified anti-defection clause has been subject to fierce academic criticism as

...a patent and indefensible violation of freedom of political expression which is at variance with both the letter and ethos of parliamentary democracy.[23]

---

[19] See, for example, the discussion by the High Court of Australia in *Theophanous v. The Herald and Weekly Times Ltd* [1994] 3 LRC 446. The Court was deeply divided on the question of the availability of a defence of implied freedom of political discussion to an action for defamation.. Australia of course is one of the very Commonwealth states without an explicit guarantee of freedom of expression.

[20] For an analysis of the relevant caselaw, See A J Harding, 'When is a resignation not a resignation? A crisis of confidence in Sabah', (1995) The Round Table 335 at 353.

[21] *Attorney-General v. Kasonde* [1994] 3 LRC 144. For fuller discussion, see my case-note in [1996] 40 Journal of African Law 115-118.

[22] *In re Certification of the Constitution of the Republic of South Africa, 1996*, 1996 (10) BCLR 1253 (CC) paras 14-186.

[23] G E Devenish, *A Commentary on the South African Constitution*, Butterworths, Durban, 1998, p.120.

## IV. CONCLUSION

This chapter has sought to demonstrate that, although the right to political participation is universally recognised at both national and international levels, its effective enjoyment requires constant vigilance. The courts are essential watchdogs in this process. However, the courts cannot play an effective role where the independence of the judiciary is itself in question or where the political process is fundamentally flawed. Unfortunately, although the Commonwealth has taken the lead in setting standards, the enforcement of democratic entitlements in many Commonwealth jurisdictions is weak, as the references in the first paragraph of this brief discussion illustrate.

## LATIMER HOUSE GUIDELINES FOR THE COMMONWEALTH

### 19 June 1998

A Joint Colloquium on *"Parliamentary Supremacy and Judicial Independence ... towards a Commonwealth Model"* was held at Latimer House in the United Kingdom, from 15 - 19 June 1998. Over 60 participants attended representing 20 Commonwealth countries and three overseas territories.

The Colloquium was sponsored by the Commonwealth Lawyers' Association, the Commonwealth Legal Education Association, the Commonwealth Magistrates' and Judges' Association and the Commonwealth Parliamentary Association with the generous support of the Commonwealth Foundation, the Commonwealth Secretariat and the United Kingdom Foreign and Commonwealth Office.

The following Guidelines for the Commonwealth are a result of deliberations during the Colloquium.

The Commonwealth Statement on Freedom of Expression has been reproduced with the kind permission of the Commonwealth Media Laws Project.

**Copyright**

Copyright is retained by the four sponsoring associations but the Guidelines can be reproduced providing the source of the documents is acknowledged.

----------------------------------

# THE CREATION AND AMENDMENT OF CONSTITUTIONAL NORMS

*Guidelines on good practice governing relations between the Executive, Parliament and the Judiciary in the promotion of good governance, the rule of law and human rights to ensure the effective implementation of the Harare Principles.*

## PREAMBLE

RECALLING the renewed commitment at the 1997 Commonwealth Heads of Government Meeting in Edinburgh to the Harare Principles and the Millbrook Commonwealth Action Programme and, in particular, the pledge in paragraph 9 of the Harare Declaration to work for the protection and promotion of the fundamental political values of the Commonwealth:

- democracy;
- democratic processes and institutions which reflect national circumstances, the rule of law and the independence of the judiciary;
- just and honest government;
- fundamental human rights, including equal rights and opportunities for all citizens regardless of race, colour, creed or political belief;
- equality for women, so that they may exercise their full and equal rights.

Representatives of the Commonwealth Parliamentary Association, the Commonwealth Magistrates' and Judges' Association, the Commonwealth Lawyers' Association and the Commonwealth Legal Education Association meeting at Latimer House in the United Kingdom from 15 to 19 June 1998

HAVE RESOLVED to adopt the following Principles and Guidelines and propose them for consideration by the Commonwealth Heads of Government Meeting and for effective implementation by member countries of the Commonwealth.

## PRINCIPLES

The successful implementation of these Guidelines calls for a commitment, made in the utmost good faith, of the relevant national institutions, in particular the executive, parliament and the judiciary, to the essential principles of good governance, fundamental human rights and the rule of law, including the independence of the judiciary, so that the legitimate aspirations of all the peoples of the Commonwealth should be met.

Each institution must exercise responsibility and restraint in the exercise of power within its own constitutional sphere so as not to encroach on the legitimate discharge of constitutional functions by the other institutions.

It is recognised that the special circumstances of small and/or under-resourced jurisdictions may require adaptation of these Guidelines.

It is recognised that redress of gender imbalance is essential to accomplish full and equal rights in society and to achieve true human rights. Merit and the capacity to perform public office regardless of disability should be the criteria of eligibility for appointment or election.

## GUIDELINES

### I  PARLIAMENT AND THE JUDICIARY

1. The legislative function is the primary responsibility of parliament as the elected body representing the people. Judges may be constructive and purposive in the interpretation of legislation, but must not usurp Parliament's legislative function. Courts should have the power to declare legislation to be unconstitutional and of no legal effect. However, there may be circumstances where the appropriate remedy would be for the court to declare the incompatibility of a statute with the Constitution, leaving it to the legislature to take remedial legislative measures.

2. Commonwealth parliaments should take speedy and effective steps to implement their countries' international human rights obligations by enacting appropriate human rights legislation. Special legislation (such as equal opportunity laws) is required to extend the protection of fundamental rights to the private sphere. Where domestic incorporation has not occurred, international instruments should be applied to aid interpretation.

3. Judges should adopt a generous and purposive approach in interpreting a Bill of Rights. This is particularly important in countries which are in the process of building democratic traditions. Judges have a vital part to play in developing and maintaining a vibrant human rights environment throughout the Commonwealth.

4. International law and, in particular, human rights jurisprudence can greatly assist domestic courts in interpreting a Bill of Rights. It can also help expand the scope of a Bill of Rights making it more meaningful and effective.

5. While dialogue between the judiciary and the government may be desirable or appropriate, in no circumstances should such dialogue compromise judicial independence.

6. People should have easy and unhindered access to courts, particularly to enforce their fundamental rights. Any existing procedural obstacles to access to justice should be removed.

7. People should also be made aware of, and have access to, other important fora for human rights dispute resolution, particularly Human Rights Commissions, Offices of the Ombudsman and mechanisms for alternative dispute resolution.

8. Everyone, especially judges, parliamentarians and lawyers, should have access to human rights education.

## II  PRESERVING JUDICIAL INDEPENDENCE

1. Judicial autonomy

In jurisdictions that do not already have an appropriate independent process in place, judicial appointments should be made on merit by a judicial services commission or by an appropriate officer of state acting on the advice of such a commission.

Judicial appointments should normally be permanent; whilst in some jurisdictions, contract appointments may be inevitable, such appointments should be subject to appropriate security of tenure.

The judicial services commission should be established by the Constitution or by statute, with a majority of members drawn from the senior judiciary.

Appointments to all levels of the judiciary should have, as an objective, the achievement of equality between women and men.

Judicial vacancies should be advertised. Recommendations for appointment should come from the commission.

2. Funding

Sufficient funding to enable the judiciary to perform its functions to the highest standards should be provided.

Appropriate salaries, supporting staff, resources and equipment are essential to the proper functioning of the judiciary.

As a matter of principle, judicial salaries and benefits should be set by an independent commission and should be maintained.

The administration of monies allocated to the judiciary should be under the control of the judiciary.

3. Training

A culture of judicial education should be developed.

Training should be organised, systematic and ongoing and under the control of an adequately funded judicial body.

Judicial training should include the teaching of the law, judicial skills and the social context. including ethnic and gender issues.

The curriculum should be controlled by judicial officers who should have the assistance of lay specialists.

For jurisdictions without adequate training facilities, access to facilities in other jurisdictions should be provided. Courses in judicial education should be offered to practising lawyers as part of their ongoing professional development training.

### III PRESERVING THE INDEPENDENCE OF PARLIAMENTARIANS

1. Article 9 of the Bill of Rights 1688 is re-affirmed, This article provides:

> *"That the Freedome of Speech and Debates or Proceedings in Parlyement ought not to be impeached or questioned in any court or place out of Parlyement."*

2. Security of members during their parliamentary term is fundamental to parliamentary independence and therefore:

(a) the expulsion of members from parliament as a penalty for leaving their parties (floor-crossing) should be viewed as a possible infringement of members' independence; anti-defection measures may be necessary in some jurisdictions to deal with corrupt practices;

(b) laws allowing for the recall of members during their elected term should be viewed with caution, as a potential threat to the independence of members;

(c) the cessation of membership of a political party of itself should not lead to the loss of a member's seat.

3. In the discharge of their functions, members should be free from improper pressures and accordingly: -

(a) the criminal law and the use of defamation proceedings are not appropriate mechanisms for restricting legitimate criticism of the

government or the parliament;
- (b) the defence of qualified privilege with respect to reports of parliamentary proceedings should be drawn as broadly as possible to permit full public reporting and discussion of public affairs;
- (c) the offence of contempt of parliament should be drawn as narrowly as possible.

## IV WOMEN IN PARLIAMENT

1. To improve the numbers of women members in Commonwealth parliaments, the role of women within political parties should be enhanced, including the appointment of more women to executive roles within political parties.

2. Proactive searches for potential candidates should be undertaken by political parties.

3. Political parties in nations with proportional representation should be required to ensure an adequate gender balance an their respective lists of candidates for election. Women, where relevant, should be included in the top part of the candidates lists of political parties. Parties should be called upon publicly to declare the degree of representation of women on their lists and to defend any failure to maintain adequate representation.

4. Where there is no proportional representation, candidate search and/or selection committees of political parties should be gender balanced as should representation at political conventions and this should be facilitated by political parties by way of amendment to party constitutions; women should be put forward for safe seats.

5. Women should be elected to parliament through regular electoral processes. The provision of reservations for women in national constitutions, whilst useful, tends to be insufficient for securing adequate and long term representation by women.

6. Men should work in partnership with women to redress constraints on women entering parliament. True gender balance requires the oppositional element of the inclusion of men in the process of dialogue and remedial action to address the necessary inclusion of both genders in all aspects of public life.

## V JUDICIAL AND PARLIAMENTARY ETHICS

1. Judicial ethics

   (a) A Code of Ethics and Conduct should be developed and adopted by each judiciary as a means of ensuring the accountability of judges;

(b) The Commonwealth Magistrates' and Judges' Association should be encouraged to complete its Model Code of Judicial Conduct now in development;
(c) The Association should also serve as a repository of codes of judicial conduct developed by Commonwealth judiciaries, which will serve as a resource for other jurisdictions.

2. Parliamentary ethics

(a) Conflict of interest guidelines and Codes of Conduct should require full disclosure by ministers and members of their financial and business interests;
(b) Members of parliament should have privileged access to advice from statutorily-established Ethics Advisors;
(c) Whilst responsive to the needs of society and recognising minority views in society, members of parliament should avoid excessive influence of lobbyists and special interest groups.

## VI ACCOUNTABILITY MECHANISMS

1. Judicial Accountability

   (a) Discipline:

   (i) In cases where a judge is at risk of removal, the judge must have the right to be fully informed of the charges, to be represented at a hearing, to make a full defence, and to be judged by an independent and impartial tribunal. Grounds for removal of a judge should be limited to:

   (A) inability to perform judicial duties; and
   (B) serious misconduct.

   (ii) In all other matters, the process should be conducted by the chief judge of the courts;
   (iii) Disciplinary procedures should not include the public admonition of judges. Any admonitions should be delivered in private, by the chief judge.

   (b) Public Criticism:

   (i) Legitimate public criticism of judicial performance is a means of ensuring accountability;
   (ii) The criminal law and contempt proceedings are not appropriate mechanisms for restricting legitimate criticism of the courts.

2. Executive Accountability

(a) Accountability of the Executive to Parliament:

Parliamentary procedures should provide adequate mechanisms to enforce the accountability of the executive to parliament. These should include:

(i) a committee structure appropriate to the size of Parliament, adequately resourced and with the power to summon witnesses, including ministers. Governments should be required to announce publicly, within a defined time period, their responses to committee reports;
(ii) standing orders should provide appropriate opportunities for members to question ministers and full debate on legislative proposals;
(iii) the Public Accounts should be independently audited by the Auditor General who is responsible to and must report directly to parliament;
(iv) the chair of the Public Accounts Committee should normally be an opposition member;
(v) offices of the Ombudsman, Human Rights Commissions and Access to Information Commissioners should report regularly to parliament.

(b) Judicial Review

Commonwealth governments should endorse and implement the principles of judicial review enshrined in the Lusaka Statement on Government under the Law.

## VII THE LAW-MAKING PROCESS

1. Women should be involved in the work of national law commissions in the lawmaking process. Ongoing assessment of legislation is essential so as to create a more gender balanced society. Gender-neutral language should be used in the drafting and use of legislation.

2. Procedures for the preliminary examination of issues in proposed legislation should be adopted and published so that:

(a) there is public exposure of issues, papers and consultation on major reforms including, where possible, a draft bill;
(b) standing orders provide a delay of some days between introduction and debate to enable public comment unless suspended by consent or a significantly high percentage vote of the chamber; and
(c) major legislation can be referred to a select committee allowing for the detailed examination of such legislation and the taking of evidence from members of the public.

3. Model standing orders protecting members rights and privileges and permitting the incorporation of variations, to take local circumstances into account, should be drafted and published.

4. Parliament should be serviced by a professional staff independent of the regular public service.

5. Adequate resources to government and non-government back benchers should be provided to improve parliamentary input and should include provision for:

   (a) training of new members;
   (b) secretarial, office, library and research facilities;
   (c) drafting assistance including private members' bills.

6. An all party committee of members of parliament should review and administer parliament's budget which should not be subject to amendment by the executive.

7. Appropriate legislation should incorporate international human rights instruments to assist in interpretation and to ensure that ministers certify compliance with such instruments, on introduction of the legislation.

8. It is recommended that "sunset" legislation (for the expiry of all subordinate legislation not renewed) should be enacted subject to power to extend the life of such legislation.

## VIII THE ROLE OF NON-JUDICIAL AND NON-PARLIAMENTARY INSTITUTIONS

1. The Commonwealth Statement on Freedom of Expression provides essential guarantees to which all Commonwealth countries should subscribe.

2. The Executive must refrain from all measures directed at inhibiting the freedom of the press, including indirect methods such as the misuse of official advertising.

3. An independent, organised legal profession is an essential component in the protection of the rule of law.

4. Adequate legal aid schemes should be provided for poor and disadvantaged litigants, including public interest advocates.

5. Legal professional organisations should assist in the provision, through pro bono schemes, of access to justice for the impecunious.

6. The executive must refrain from obstructing the functioning of an independent legal profession by such means as withholding licensing of professional bodies.

7. Human Rights Commissions, Offices of the Ombudsman and Access to Information Commissioners can play a key role in enhancing public awareness of good governance and rule of law issues and adequate funding and resources should be made available to enable them to discharge these functions. Parliament should accept responsibility in this regard.

Such institutions should be empowered to provide access to alternative dispute resolution mechanisms.

## IX MEASURES FOR IMPLEMENTATION AND MONITORING COMPLIANCE

These guidelines should be forwarded to the Commonwealth Secretariat for consideration by Law Ministers and Heads of Government.

If these Guidelines are adopted, an effective monitoring procedure, which might include a Standing Committee, should be devised under which all Commonwealth jurisdictions accept an obligation to report on their compliance with these Guidelines.

Consideration of these reports should form a regular part of the Meetings of Law Ministers and of Heads of Government.

Chapter Three

# THE CONSTITUTION OF THE COMMONWEALTH OF AUSTRALIA

Leslie Zines[*]

## I. INTRODUCTION

The Constitution of the Commonwealth of Australia is contained in the Commonwealth of Australia Constitution Act of the United Kingdom Parliament (63 & 64 Vict. ch. 12). The Act was assented to on 9 July 1900; however, the Commonwealth of Australia was established, and the constitution took effect, on 1 January 1901 by virtue of a proclamation made under section 3 of the Act.

The principal object of the constitution was the union of six British colonies, namely New South Wales, Victoria, Queensland, South Australia, Western Australia and Tasmania. By virtue of the constitution these colonies were converted into States of a new federal polity, the Commonwealth of Australia. The preamble to the Act states that the people of the named colonies 'have agreed to unite in one indissoluble Federal Commonwealth under the Crown of the United Kingdom of Great Britain and Ireland and under the Constitution hereby established'.

The Commonwealth of Australia thus began life as a colony of Great Britain.[2] The Imperial Conference of 1926 declared that Britain and the Dominions (including Australia) were equal in status in all matters of internal and external affairs. The Statute of Westminster 1931 (UK), in order to give effect to this principle, empowered the Dominion Parliaments to override Imperial legislation (but not the Australian or Canadian Constitutions) and to make laws that operated extra-territorially. The Australian Parliament adopted the Statute of Westminster in 1942[3] retrospectively from 3 September 1939. The two restrictions on Dominion power which the Statute abolished were not stated in the Australian Constitution but were regarded as inherent in the status of a British dependency. The paramount effect of any United Kingdom statute applying to a colony had been further affirmed

---

[*] Professor Emeritus, The Australian National University.
[2] In order to distinguish the major self-governing colonies of the Empire from other dependencies, the Imperial Conference of 1907 bestowed on them the title of 'Dominions'.
[3] Statute of Westminster Adoption Act 1942 (Cth).

by the Colonial Laws Validity Act 1865 (UK).[4]

Between the world wars the Dominions were accepted by the international community as independent sovereign States of the world. None of these developments required any change to the wording of the Constitution of Australia, but they resulted in its provisions being given a full interpretation unrestricted by reference to colonial status. For example, in 1901 it was assumed that the executive power exercisable by the Governor-General under section 61 did not include the power to enter into treaties because it was not consistent with colonial status. Thirty years later it was interpreted to include that power,[5] although the wording of the provision had not changed.

Much of the change of status was achieved by alteration of constitutional conventions rather than by statute or constitutional amendment. It was agreed, for example, at Imperial Conferences in 1926 and 1930 that when the sovereign acted in respect of, for example, Australia, he would act on the advice of his Australian Ministers, rather than, as was the case previously, United Kingdom Ministers. This eventually resulted in the disintegration of the Imperial Crown into a series of national Crowns. This in turn affected the meaning of terms in the constitution. For example, the expression 'subject of the Queen' in the constitution now means a subject of the Queen of Australia, i.e., an Australian citizen. It does not include, as it once did, a British or Canadian subject.[6]

Many of these changes did not affect the States, which remained, to a degree, dependencies in law, if not in fact. Until 1986 the States remained unable to override British legislation such as the Merchant Shipping Act 1894. The State Governments could not advise the Queen directly, but had to go through a British Secretary of State. To rectify this situation, the Australian Parliament, with the consent of the State Parliaments, enacted the Australia Act 1986 (Cth), and the United Kingdom Parliament, acting on the request and consent of the Australian Parliament, enacted the Australia Act 1986 (UK). The two Acts are in the same terms and came into force at the same moment. Each Act removes restrictions on State power, but does not affect the overriding force of the Australian Constitution. It is declared that the United Kingdom Parliament has no legislative power in Australia (section 1) and that the United Kingdom Government has no responsibility for the government of any State (section 10).

## II. THE ORIGIN OF THE CONSTITUTION

In the 1850s all the Australian colonies other than Western Australia were granted, under Imperial statutes, that form of self-government known as 'responsible government' in respect of their internal affairs. Western Australia achieved that status in 1890.

---

[4] Zines, 'The Growth of Australian Nationhood and its Effect on the Powers of the Commonwealth' in Zines (ed.), *Commentaries on the Australian Constitution*, 1977, Ch.I.
[5] *Rex v. Burgess, Ex parte Henry* (1936) 55 *Commonwealth Law Reports* 608 (hereafter '*CLR*').
[6] *Nolan v. Minister for Immigration and Ethnic Affairs* (1988) 165 *CLR* 178.

A future union of the Australian colonies had been discussed for many years, but few practical steps to that end were taken. In 1889, however, the premier of New South Wales, Sir Henry Parkes, called upon the governments of the other colonies to agree to a conference to consider a union of the colonies. Such a conference took place in 1890, where it was resolved that the several Parliaments should elect delegates to a convention to draft a federal constitution.

Historians debate the causes of the Australian federal movement.[7] It is clear, however, that despite differences among the colonies as to the virtues of free trade and protectionism, they all wished to see the end of customs barriers between them and, also, the establishment of a common external tariff.[8]

Another important factor was the defence of the colonies. Australians were concerned at the interest shown by Continental powers, including France and Germany, in annexing islands in the Pacific, such as New Guinea and New Caledonia. There was a feeling in the colonies that Britain was not showing sufficient interest in the defence of their part of the world. By uniting, the colonial governments hoped to persuade the British Government to devote more resources to the defence of the south Pacific region.

It had originally been thought that the new union would be modelled on that of Canada, which was the sole British federation and which also provided for a monarchial and Westminster form of government. The delegates to the convention, however, quickly turned their attention, instead, to the United States Constitution. The major difference between the two was as follows. The British North America Act endeavoured to divide all (or nearly all) subjects of legislative power into two lists, each within the exclusive authority of the provincial legislatures and Canadian Parliament respectively. Any residuary authority belonged to the latter. The United States Constitution, on the other hand, confined the power of Congress to specified subjects and left all the residue of power to the States.

The Australian delegates at the 1891 convention, and later, adopted the American scheme, because they considered that it left the States with greater power. They desired a union only in respect of certain named subjects, such as defence, currency, interstate and overseas trade, immigration, external affairs, various commercial and financial matters (such as banking, insurance, intellectual property, and bills of exchange), postal services, and marriage and divorce. All other matters, which were thought to include the vast bulk of laws that affected the day-to-day life of the citizen, were to be left within State authority.

Other important features of United States constitutional law were, however, rejected, namely, presidential government and the bill of rights. Most of the delegates desired the preservation of the form of government with which they were familiar, that is, parliamentary government on the British model. A general list of entrenched rights was rejected, although a few specific limitations on federal power in the nature of rights were inserted, such as provision for trial by jury (section 80),

---

[7] Martin (ed.) *Essays in Australian Federalism* (1969).
[8] La Nauze, *The Making of the Australian Constitution* (1971) 34.

freedom of religion (section 116) and requiring the acquisition of property to be on 'just terms' (section 51 (xxxi)). These restrictions do not apply to the States. A proposed provision using such terms as 'due process of law' and 'equal protection of the laws', taken from the Fourteenth Amendment to the United States Constitution, was rejected.[9]

In relation to the Westminster system of responsible government, there was some tension between the principle that the executive is responsible to the lower House (the House of Representatives) and the federal principle that the Senate should have near-equal powers with the House of Representatives and should comprise an equal number of senators from each State. The tension was dramatically evidenced in the dismissal by the Governor-General in 1975 of a federal government which had the confidence of the House of Representatives. The dismissal came about because the Senate would not assent to appropriation bills (necessary to enable the government to carry on public services) unless the government agreed to a general election.[10] The Prime Minister had refused to resign or advise a dissolution and a general election.

After the Constitutional Convention had completed its work, the draft constitution was presented to the Parliaments of the colonies. The draft was in fact put aside for years as the country experienced a severe economic depression. Another cause was the rise of what became the Australian Labor Party. Labour members appeared for the first time in 1893 in the New South Wales Parliament in substantial numbers. They were inclined to be suspicious of the federation proposal as a capitalist conspiracy and, in any case, of less urgency than issues of social welfare and industrial terms and conditions of employment. The federal cause languished.

The next few years saw many popular groups formed to push the idea of federal union. Some leading figures felt it was necessary to take the issue out of the hands of the politicians and give the people the final say. Finally, as a result of considerable agitation and pressure, New South Wales, Victoria, South Australia and Tasmania passed Acts under which the electorate directly elected delegates to a 'people's convention' to draft a constitution. Instead of requiring that the convention's proposals go to the colonial Parliaments for approval, the Acts provided that the final draft constitution be put to the electors of the respective colonies for approval. Western Australian legislation preserved parliamentary appointment and approval, while Queensland delegates did not attend because of internal troubles. In fact, however, the electors of those two colonies, like the other four, did eventually approve the draft constitution.

The convention met in 1897 and 1898 and, after much debate and compromise, the delegates resolved on a draft constitution which was substantially based on the 1891 draft. After a number of vicissitudes, including a premiers' conference to make some changes after the failure of the first referendum in New South Wales,

---

[9] *Australian Constitutional Convention Debates* (Sydney, 1897) 149.
[10] Sawer, *Federation under Strain* (1977).

the proposed constitution received in 1899 and 1900 the approval of voting majorities in all six Australian colonies.

The draft bill was taken to London by representatives of the colonies for enactment by the British Parliament. There was an attempt by the Colonial Office and by the Secretary of State, Sir Joseph Chamberlain, to alter some of the provisions with a view to protecting Imperial interests. The attempts were resisted. In the upshot only one provision - section 74 - was changed after discussion with the colonial authorities. The change preserved in certain circumstances appeals to the Judicial Committee of the Privy Council. This remains the only provision not approved by the electorate. It is now defunct.[11]

## III. CONTINUATION OF PRE-EXISTING LAW

Because it was an enactment of the British Parliament, the Australian Constitution came into existence as part of an Imperial legal system. The same is true of the State constitutions, which are derived from the same source. Under section 106 of the Australian Constitution each of the State constitutions was preserved, subject to the federal constitution, and until altered in accordance with the State constitution. The status as law of the several constitutions in Australia depended therefore on a grundnorm or fundamental rule of obedience to the Imperial Parliament. Judicial review of legislation, whether federal or State, followed appropriately from that rule. The courts were simply enforcing an enactment of the supreme legislature.

Other Imperial Acts also remained binding in Australia, such as the Colonial Laws Validity Act 1865 and the Merchant Shipping Act 1894.[12] Section 108 of the constitution provided for the continuation in force of pre-existing State laws that were not inconsistent with the Australian Constitution.

The common law is a general assumption of the constitution.[13] Common law rules of interpretation provide the basis of constitutional construction. Common law principles of public law, including principles derived from British constitutional history, are also readily resorted to in interpreting and applying the constitution. Indeed, much of the constitution would be incomprehensible without it. For example, the constitution vests legislative power in the Parliament (section 1), executive power in the Queen, exercisable by the Governor-General (section 61) and judicial power in specified courts (section 71). It is from pre-existing common law principles, derived from British constitutional development, that one knows that the treaty-making and war-declaring powers are held by the executive government, that the levying of taxation is a purely legislative function, and that the making of rules of court, while analytically legislative, is exercisable by the judiciary as well. The common law operates to give the executive government the prerogative powers and immunities of the Crown. It also gives meaning to words and phrases in the

---

[11] La Nauze, *op.cit. supra* n.7, ch.16.
[12] *China Ocean Shipping Co. v. South Australia* (1979) 145 CLR 172.
[13] Dixon, *Jesting Pilate* (1965) 174, 198-202, 203-213.

constitution such as 'trial' and 'jury' (section 80). Similarly the jurisdiction of the High Court in matters 'in which a writ of Mandamus, prohibition or an injunction is sought against an officer of the Commonwealth' (section 75(v)) is explicable only in relation to pre-existing law.

## IV. CONVENTIONS

The constitution also assumes, but does not expressly refer to, most British constitutional conventions. A literal reading of the Australian Constitution would lead to the conclusion that it establishes a royal autocracy, with the Crown possessing most of the powers sought by the Stuarts in the early 17th century. For example, as mentioned earlier, the constitution vests all federal executive power in the Queen, exercisable by the Governor-General. The Governor-General is empowered to appoint members of the Federal Executive Council, to advise him, and Ministers of State. They hold office 'during his pleasure' (sections 62 and 64). He decides 'according to his discretion' whether to assent or withhold assent to, or to reserve 'for the Queen's pleasure', bills that have been passed by the Houses of Parliament (section 58). The Governor-General is declared to have vested in him the command-in-chief of the naval and military forces (section 68). All these provisions look like a travesty of the Australian system of government. What is missing are those principles, not enacted in the constitution, which require that the Governor-General shall choose Ministers that have the 'confidence' of a majority of the House of Representatives and that (except in rare circumstances) the Queen and the Governor-General shall exercise power on the advice of those Ministers.

Because of the practice of not enacting principles that depend on convention, the Australian Constitution contains no reference to its most important political officers and institutions, such as the Prime Minister and the cabinet.

## V. MEANS OF AMENDMENT OF THE CONSTITUTION

Section 128 of the constitution provides for its alteration  Subject to a few exceptions, dealt with later, the method of alteration is as follows.

1. An amendment can be initiated only in the federal Parliament. The proposal must be passed by either:

(a) an absolute majority of each House of Parliament, or
(b) by an absolute majority of one House on two separate occasions where the other House does not pass it on either occasion. The second proposal must be passed not less than three months after the other House's first failure to pass.

2. The proposed amendment must then be submitted to the electors and approved by:

(a) a majority of all electors voting, *and*

(b) a majority of electors in a majority of States. At present that means at least four of the six States

There is an exceptional procedure in three prescribed cases. The relevant provision is as follows:

No alteration diminishing the proportionate representation of any State in either House of the Parliament, or the minimum number of representatives of a State in the House of Representatives, or increasing, diminishing, or otherwise altering the limits of the State, or in any manner affecting the provisions of the Constitution in relation thereto, shall become law unless the majority of the electors voting in that State approve the proposed law.

The electorate for the purpose of constitutional alteration comprises all persons who have a right to vote for the election of the House of Representatives. Qualifications for voting are prescribed by Parliament. Generally speaking, the electors include all persons who are at least 18 years of age. Since 1924 voting at federal elections and constitutional referenda has been compulsory. That, however, is not an entrenched constitutional requirement.

The method of constitutional alteration was taken from Article 118 of the Swiss Constitution. The provision for referendum reflected both the method used to approve the constitution and the relatively democratic nature of Australian society. (I say 'relatively' because only Western Australia and South Australia then permitted women to vote; however, the Australian Parliament introduced female suffrage in 1902.) The provision for 'double majority' was required to deal with the fears of the four smaller States that they would be dominated by New South Wales and Victoria, which had about two-thirds of the total population.

There have been forty-three proposals for constitutional alteration put to the electors by referendum. Only eight were approved. Only three of these had any significant effect on Commonwealth-State relations and balance of power.[14] None related to entrenched rights and freedoms.

All eight proposals accepted by the electorate had bipartisan political support. This is generally regarded in Australia as a pre-requisite for a successful constitutional alteration. It is not, however, sufficient; some proposals supported by both sides of federal politics have failed. Active opposition by one or more State governments seems at times to have been a relevant consideration.[15]

---

[14] Section 51(xxiiiA) was inserted in 1946 conferring power on the Australian Parliament to provide for various forms of social security benefits and payments. In 1967 s.51(xxvi) was amended to enable that Parliament to make laws with respect to the people of the Aboriginal race. In 1929 s.105A was inserted to give constitutional force to agreements between the federal and state governments relating to the control of government borrowing. A national body, the Loan Council, was created on which all governments were represented.

[15] E. Campbell, 'Changing the Constitution - Past and Future' (1989) 17 *Melbourne University Law Review* 1 at 6.

## VI. THE SCOPE OF THE AMENDING PROVISION

Section 128 of the constitution has not as yet given rise to any legal problems. Some legal writers suggest, however, that there may be some limits to its reach. The High Court of Australia has made no pronouncements on that issue.

Parliament and the legal community have acted on the basis that section 128 itself may be altered in accordance with the existing provisions of that section. This occurred in 1977 when a referendum approved an amendment to section 128 giving the people of certain federal Territories the right to vote at referenda for the purpose of determining whether there is a national majority in favour of a proposed amendment. (The second element of the amending formula remains that of a majority of electors in a majority of *States*.)

If this alteration were ever challenged in the High Court, I am of the view that it would be upheld. Section 128 refers to alteration of 'the Constitution'. Clearly section 128 is itself a provision of the constitution. The democratic nature of the amending process and the Australian social and political context also tend towards a broad and literal construction of the provision.

Other difficulties in respect of constitutional alteration could arise because of the form of the Commonwealth of Australia Constitution Act. The Act has nine sections and the entire constitution of 128 sections is set out in section 9 of the Act. The other eight sections are usually referred to as the 'covering clauses'. Section 128 refers only to the alteration of 'this Constitution'. As the covering clauses are outside the provisions referred to as 'the Constitution' it is argued by some that they cannot be altered in accordance with section 128. In the past the orthodox view was that they could be altered only by the Parliament of the United Kingdom. (That was the position with respect to many important provisions of the British North America Act 1867 before the enactment of the Canada Act 1982 (UK).) Under the Australia Acts 1986 of the United Kingdom and Australian Parliaments, the United Kingdom Parliament has no longer any legislative power over Australia. It would be possible, therefore, to argue that the covering clauses have become unalterable. Few people believe that the High Court would so decide, but views differ as to how the matter might be dealt with should the need arise.

The issue has been discussed in the context of the present debate as to whether Australia should become a republic. As mentioned above, the preamble to the constitution Act declares that the people of the various colonies 'have agreed to unite in one indissoluble Federal Commonwealth under the Crown of Great Britain and Ireland'. It is argued by some that the preamble (which precedes the covering clauses and is not therefore in section 9 which sets out 'the Constitution') prevents use of section 128 to abolish the monarchy.

It is unlikely, in my view, that the preamble would be held to control a substantive provision of the constitution. The High Court has frequently stated that the constitution must be construed in a broad and liberal manner because it is an instrument intended to endure for ages and to govern in circumstances that could not be conceived by those who framed it. There is no reason why this principle should not extend to the provision for constitutional amendment.[16]

Another relevant provision in the covering clauses is section 2, which provides that references in the constitution to the Queen 'shall extend to Her Majesty's heirs and successors in the sovereignty of the United Kingdom'. This provision would not prevent the omission of all references to the Queen in the constitution. In that event it would simply be a provision that had no operation; but its presence in those circumstances could create confusion.

The Constitutional Commission in 1988 expressed the opinion that all the covering clauses could, since the Australia Act 1986 ended the sovereignty of the United Kingdom Parliament, be repealed or altered in accordance with the process prescribed in section 128.[17] Some argue that it would also be desirable to adopt additional procedures such as an Act of the Australian Parliament passed with the consent of all the State Parliaments. It is unnecessary to set out the reasons for that view.[18] Nearly everyone, however, agrees that a referendum under section 128 is necessary.

## VII. SUGGESTED CHANGES TO THE AMENDMENT PROCESS

In the early days of federation it was expected that section 128 would prove to be a fairly easy means of constitutional alteration. Contrasts were often made with the amendment provision in the United States Constitution. Indeed, in a book published in 1902, an eminent professor of constitutional law at the University of Melbourne said that:

The great facility with which the Australian Constitution may be altered makes it probable that its development will be guided less by judicial interpretation and more by formal amendment than the development of the United States.[19]

The opposite occurred. The referendum has proved to be a considerable barrier to constitutional change. For whatever reason, the Australian electorate has been more conservative than was originally expected.

From time to time it has been suggested that section 128 be altered by reducing the number of States in which a majority of electors is required from a majority of States (at present four) to half (at present three). Such a proposal was put to referendum in 1974 and it failed. It was also recommended by a majority of the Constitutional Commission in 1988. Had this been the rule from the beginning it

---

[16] The argument which relies on the preamble neglects the fact that there has not been a Crown of the United Kingdom of Great Britain *and Ireland* for about 70 years. That reinforces the view that the preamble is merely an historical statement rather than intended as an overriding principle.

[17] *Final Report of the Constitutional Commission* (1988) para. 3.113-123.

[18] See Gageler and Leeming, 'An Australian Republic: Is a referendum enough?' (1996) 7 *Public Law Review* 143; Lindell and Rose, 'A Response to Gageler and Leeming' 7 *Public Law Review* 155.

[19] Harrison Moore, *Constitution of the Commonwealth of Australia* (1902) 332 quoted in La Nauze, *The Making of the Australian Constitution* (1971) 287.

would have altered the result in only three past proposals.[20]

Some believe that the tendency of the electorate to vote against change has been strengthened by the statutory provisions for compulsory voting which were introduced for federal elections and referenda in 1924. It is said that persons who are compelled to vote and who are otherwise uninterested in or ignorant of the issues tend to vote against a proposal.[21] The fact is, however, that a larger percentage of referenda succeeded after compulsory voting was introduced than before.

One factor emphasised by the Constitutional Commission in its 1988 Report is that the initiation of a referendum is confined to one of the federal partners, namely the national Parliament. The Commission recommended that the Parliaments of three States be given the opportunity to initiate a referendum if they represent a majority of the national electorate.[22] The proposal required that the Parliaments concerned should each propose the same alteration within a twelve-month period. Such an alteration would certainly increase the possibility of more changes to the constitution, but in a manner that could lead to more centrifugal results. On the other hand it is possible that the electorate might react in the same way to State proposals as they have done hitherto to those put forward by the Australian Parliament, that is in favour of the status quo.

A minority of the Commission (Sir Rupert Hamer and myself) were in favour of citizens' initiative for proposals for constitutional amendment. The minority view was that a proposal should be put to a referendum if it was supported by 5 per cent of the national electorate and at least 5 per cent of the electorate in at least three States. This suggestion was put forward as a means of overcoming the frequent expression of 'alienation' of individual citizens from the political process. It was argued that there was often a feeling of remoteness and impotence by individuals in respect of political affairs. The minority who argued this way, however, did not expect the proposed method of alteration to be used successfully very often. The minority's view was opposed by a majority of the Commission on grounds related to responsible government, representative and deliberative democracy and the protection of minorities.[23]

No action has been taken on the Commission's recommendations for alteration of section 128. As it would involve taking away the monopoly of the federal Parliament in initiating constitutional amendments it might, perhaps, be optimistic to expect any action in this respect.

It has also been argued that the result of the referenda held since the beginning of federation showed that Australians have remained, generally speaking,

---

[20] These comprise two referenda in 1944 related to agricultural marketing schemes and industrial relations laws, and one referendum in 1977 relating to simultaneous elections of the two Houses.
[21] Sampford, 'Some Limitations on Constitutional Change' (1979) 12 *Melbourne Law Review* 210; Rydon, 'The Case for Voluntary Voting in Referenda' (1976) 11 *Politics* 209, and 'Australian Constitutional Change and Referenda' (1977) 12 *Politics* 94.
[22] *Final Report of the Constitutional Commission*, para. 13.19.
[23] *Supra* n.21 para 13.75-13.89.

reasonably contented with their constitutional framework of government. If that were so, it would not be possible to say that the amendment process has been unsuccessful in balancing stability and certainty with the need to be responsive to changes in society. That, of course, assumes that being 'responsive' is related to what the population of a democratic country apparently desires.

There is, however, much debate in Australia as to whether the tendency to vote 'No' in referenda is an instinctive reaction against entrenching in the constitution changes that are the subject of political dispute, or whether it reflects the considered judgment of the Australian people.

Much of this argument ignores the fact that, as a practical matter, there has been a great deal of change in Australian constitutional law as a result of judicial review. Although there has been little formal change to the constitution in nearly a century, that has not caused any crises in Australian society because of the part played by the High Court of Australia in interpreting the constitution.

## VIII. THE RECORD OF JUDICIAL CONSTITUTIONAL REVIEW

The High Court of Australia has been the chief vehicle for ensuring that the Australian Constitution has responded to the needs of the nation.

It was assumed by the framers and accepted by all courts and governments since the beginning of federation that the judiciary must enforce the constitution as the supreme law and that legislation and executive acts inconsistent with it must be held invalid. On many hundreds of occasions the High Court has had to consider the constitutional validity of federal and State laws and governmental actions.

The main effects of judicial review have been as follows:

a) Different approaches to interpretation have from time to time been taken by judges of the Court. Since 1920, however, the general tendency has been to increase the powers of the Australian Parliament at the expense of those of the States.

The most controversial cases in relation to this aspect of the Court's work have involved the construction of the power given to the Parliament to make laws with respect to 'external affairs'. In 1983 it was held[24] that under this power the Australian Parliament could enact laws to implement any international agreement ratified by Australia on any subject, even if the subject-matter of the treaty did not come within any other federal power.[25] Under this interpretation laws have been upheld relating to racial discrimination, the protection of the environment and labour relations - all subjects which generally would otherwise not be within the power of the Australian Parliament.[26] To be valid under this aspect of the external

---

[24] *The Commonwealth v. Tasmania* (1983) 158 *CLR* 1.
[25] In Australia, as in Britain, treaties do not change domestic law. Legislation is necessary for that purpose. Treaty-making power is vested exclusively in the federal government.
[26] *Koowarta v. Bjelke-Petersen* (1982) 153 *CLR* 168; *Commonwealth v. Tasmania* (1983) 158 *CLR* 1.

affairs power, however, the Act must be one that can reasonably be regarded as a means of achieving the purpose of the treaty.

There have been many demands to override the principle of these decisions by constitutional amendment, but the major political parties have been unable to agree. The Constitutional Commission said it was unable to formulate any alteration to the scope of the power that would nevertheless ensure that the federal government and Parliament retained sufficient power to protect and advance Australia's international interests and ensure that Australia could contribute to, and benefit from, the burgeoning growth of international relations, agreements and institutions. The Commission instead recommended that the States and the federal Parliament be given a greater role in assisting in the negotiation of treaties and in recommending whether they should be ratified. Final legal responsibility, however, would remain with the federal authorities.[27]

b) The High Court has found implied in the constitution a principle of the separation of judicial power in the federal sphere. This means that only courts can determine conclusively controversies relating to legal rights and duties. A great many cases have involved the issue whether particular functions can be conferred only on courts exercising federal jurisdiction, or only on administrative tribunals, or on both.[28] In recent years there have been numerous judicial pronouncements that this implied principle also prevents Parliament from impairing procedural due process or preventing the courts from providing a fair trial. For example, in *Dietrich v. The Queen*[29] the High Court laid down a common law rule that where an indigent defendant is prosecuted for a serious offence the court should grant a stay of proceedings until such time as the defendant is provided with counsel. This decision was based on the common law notion of a fair trial. It is likely that any attempt to alter this rule by statute in relation to federal offences would be found to be unconstitutional as interfering with the exercise of federal judicial power which is exclusively vested in the judiciary. It is likely that those common law rules of evidence and procedure that the High Court considers fundamental will also be regarded as entrenched.

It has also been held that an Act of Attainder, or of pains and penalties, would be invalid because of the separation of judicial power.[30] These are laws which judge a person or member of a group to be guilty of an offence or which punishes such persons. The result is that by implication Australia seems to be acquiring a number of constitutional rights in relation to the administration of justice that in the United States are express guarantees.

c) Other freedoms implied from the constitution by the High Court have been more controversial. Sections 7 and 24 provide that members of the Senate and the

---

[27] *Final Report of the Constitutional Commission* (1988) para. 731.
[28] Zines, *The High Court and the Constitution*, 4th edn (1997) ch.10.
[29] (1992) 177 *CLR* 292.
[30] *Polyukhovich v. Commonwealth* (1991) 172 *CLR* 501.

House of Representatives, respectively, shall be 'directly chosen by the people'. The Court has inferred from these sections and other provisions that the constitution requires a system of representative government and that essential to such a system is freedom of communication on matters of political and governmental affairs. The Court held invalid, under this principle, federal legislation prohibiting political advertising on radio and television during election periods, subject to some exceptions.[31] It would seem to follow that other freedoms associated with political or governmental affairs are likewise guaranteed, such as freedom of assembly and association.

The implied freedom of communication on governmental matters was held to limit the common law and statutory law of defamation where such communication is involved.[32] Recent decisions have affirmed that position.[33] Once again, as a result of judicial decision, Australia seems to have acquired constitutional rights even though not expressly provided.

d) The demise of the principle of sovereignty of the British Parliament had led some to search elsewhere for a 'sovereign'. A number of judges have said that sovereignty is now possessed by 'the people'[34] which, as mentioned above, are referred to in the preamble as having agreed to the creation of the Commonwealth of Australia. There is of course considerable political basis for this view having regard to the substantial popular element in the method of creation and amendment of the constitution. Apart from the object of representative government it is not clear, however, what follows from the notion of popular sovereignty as a legal proposition. It could perhaps, as some judges have suggested, lead to an implication of equality.[35] It is, in my opinion, extremely unlikely that a majority of the present High Court would uphold that view.

e) For the past decade the High Court has been active in developing an Australian common law and in giving new interpretations to many provisions of the constitution. In respect of both private law and public law, the Court has shown great willingness to have regard to developments in other common law countries, in the European Union and in international law, particularly where Australia is party to an international convention.[36] This increased 'activism" has made the Court a subject of political controversy to a greater degree than in the past, although it has not been free of controversy throughout its history.

---

[31] *Australian Capital Television Pty Ltd v. Commonwealth* (1992) 177 *CLR* 106.
[32] *Theophanous v. Herald & Weekly Times Ltd* (1994) 182 *CLR* 104; *Stephens v. West Australian Newspapers Ltd* (1994) 182 *CLR* 211.
[33] *Levy v. Victoria* (1997) 189 *CLR* 579; *Lange v. Australian Broadcasting Corporation*, (1997) 189 *CLR* 520.
[34] *Australian Capital Television Ltd v. Commonwealth* (1992) 177 *CLR* 106 at 137-8; *Nationwide News Pty Ltd v. Wills* (1992) 177 *CLR* 1 at 70.
[35] E.g. *Leeth v. Commonwealth* (1992) 174 *CLR* 455 per Deane and Toohey JJ.
[36] Walker, 'Treaties and the Internationalisation of Australian law' in Saunders (ed.), *Courts of Final Jurisdiction* (1996), 206.

Chapter Four

# THE CREATION AND AMENDING PROCESS IN THE BRAZILIAN CONSTITUTION

Luciano Maia

The Brazilian Constitution 1988 came into force on 5 October 1988. The constitution, which represents the recommitment of the Brazilian people and Brazilian State to constitutionalism and to the rule of law, is a direct response to the military regime, which ruled the country from March 1964 to January 1985 as a dictatorship.

Brazil was, in March 1964, governed by President Joao Goulart, who was seen by the rightist military as communist, and unreliable. Structural social reforms were then on the agenda which included agrarian reform, reform of the educational system, reform of the banks, and many other fundamental matters. These reform proposals involved a deep change to the developmental model in force. Jango found it difficult to achieve a compromise which could make his reforms acceptable to conservative forces within the country. The government had no political support to carry on such basic reforms. According to Chacon, the decline of the main centrist parties at this time led to governmental instability caused by fragmenting coalitions.[1] The process led to the disintegration of representative democracy, with the emergence of chaotic decision-making. With the internal dissolution of the political parties, powerful unrepresentative interest groups exercised strong pressure on the government.[2]

On 13 March 1964, in a public meeting, the President by decree nationalised oil refineries, and instituted a state agency to deal with agrarian reform. This was regarded as highly provocative in right wing circles.

A coup d'etat took place on 31 March 1964 with the support of the Catholic Church, right wing and centre-right politicians, and the American government. The press also favoured the removal of the President.[3]

A military junta, which gathered the top officials from the three branches of the armed forces, took power, and issued what was called the 'Institutional Act', by virtue of which they established a revolutionary government with power to change and amend the constitution. The constitution only applied insofar as it was

---

[1] Chacon, Vamireh [1996]: *História Institucional do Senado Federal.* Brasília: Senado Federal at page 171-173.
[2] Afonso Arinos, quoted by Chacon. See Note 1, *supra*, at page 171.
[3] [1996].*O Senado na História do Brasil.* Brasília: Senado Federal. P. 59.

compatible with the Acts of the new regime. Right wing politicians were in dismay. The Act made clear that the coup did not seek to legitimise through Congress, but the other way round: Congress received its legitimisation from the new rulers.

The first Act deposed the President, establishing the military rulers, but the constitution was kept in force. States within the federation still had free elections for governors, senators, members of the Chamber of Deputies, and State Legislative Assemblies, as well as local councils and mayors.

In 1965, however, Institutional Act 2 was enacted, with retrospective power to deny political rights to top opposition leaders—'enemies of the regime'. Judicial guarantees of access to the courts, life tenure and irremovability of judges were suspended. A 'bill of indemnity' was included in the Act, barring judges from reviewing 'revolutionary acts'.

Justices from the Federal Supreme Court (Supremo Tribunal Federal) were dismissed; politicians were deprived of their political rights. National Congress had its functions suspended. Civil and political rights, like freedom of the press, freedom of speech and assembly were curtailed.

Politicians, union workers, students, and scholars were persecuted and punished by the regime, and labelled as its enemies. Torture, as a means of obtaining information, confessions, imposing punishment, or simply as intimidation, was a widespread practice, particularly from 1968 to 1973. Many disappeared, and many others were forced into exile.

The opposition party won the 1974 elections for the Senate, and step by step civil society started to recover its civil and political rights. Union workers and students rallied in 1978, with strikes and mass movements spreading all over the country. In 1982 people recovered the right to vote for State Governors again and the opposition parties made a move to force the military rulers not to run for the 1985 indirect presidential elections. Two civilians ran for that election. Tancredo Neves, a traditional opposition leader of the centre, won the elections, being backed by José Sarney, former leader of the military rulers, but died before he could take power. However Sarney inaugurated the new civilian government, and immediately put forward an Amendment Proposal, restoring the direct vote for presidential elections, and convoking a National Constituent Assembly. The downfall of the military regime did not come from a national uprising but rather from a gradual loss of support and reassertion of civil rights.

## I. THE NATIONAL CONSTITUENT ASSEMBLY

Members of the National Constituent Assembly were elected with the dual function of writing the new constitution while at the same time performing the ordinary functions of the national congress. Thus, senators, who represent on an equal basis each state of the Federation, and federal deputies, the number of which representing each State depends on the size of the electorate of each State, would sit separately in their chambers, when enacting ordinary legislation, and would sit as one chamber, when discharging their constituent duty.

The inaugural session of the National Constituent Assembly took place on 2

February 1987, and was chaired by the Chief Justice of the Federal Supreme Court. The final text of the constitution was promulgated on 5 October 1988, and endorsed by all.

The National Constituent Assembly split into eight thematic commissions, and each of these split into three sub-commissions, aiming at drafting the new text. After draft proposals were finalised by each sub-commission, they were submitted to the commission. A general rapporteur was in charge of drafting the general blueprint, based upon the contributions of the several commissions.

At every stage it was open to receive proposals from the public for amendment to the draft constitution and several articles of the final version were based on these proposals.

The 1988 Constitution clearly marked a break with the previous constitutional order. It was a reassertion by the people of their sovereignty, which had been usurped by the military since 1964. Thus, the constitution is a legitimate outcome of the exercise of popular sovereignty, with all the virtues and vices thereof. [4]

## II. CONTINUANCE IN EFFECT OF THE PREVIOUS LEGAL ORDER

Not all Brazilian constitutions dealt with the continuance in effect of the previous legislation which was not incompatible with the new legal system. The first to mention such a circumstance was the 1891 Constitution, of which article 83 provided that the laws of the previous regime were to continue in force insofar as they were not inconsistent implicitly or explicitly with the system of government established by the constitution and with the principles of the constitution. A similar provision is found in article 183 of the 1937 Constitution, and in article 1 of the Institutional Act 9 of April 1964 (which institutionalised the coup d'etat in Brazil). The only express reference in the 1988 Constitution is confined to taxation. According to article 34 of the Temporary Constitutional Provisions Act:

the national tax system shall become effective on the first day of the fifth month following the promulgation of the Constitution, and until then the system set forth in the 1967 Constitution, with the wording provided by Amendment number 1 of 1969 and by the subsequent ones, shall be maintained.

No other Brazilian constitution or constitutional document contained any provision concerning the continuance in effect of the previous legal order considered to be compatible with the new constitution. Horta argues that absence must not mislead the interpreter as meaning a denial. The reception of previous legislation does not require express recognition, as it is a principle that derives from the political and constitutional regime.[5] On the other hand, the introductory act to the Brazilian Civil

---

[4] Barroso, Luís Roberto [1996]: *Interpretação e Aplicação da Constituição*. São Paulo: Saraiva at page 61.
[5] Horta, Raul Machado [1995]:*Estudos de Direito Constitucional*. Belo Horizonte: Del Rey at page 230.

Code has a provision which is considered to be paramount, as it sets down general principles of law that apply to all legislation. According to article 2 paragraph 2 of the introductory act to the Civil Code, a law is revoked by new legislation only insofar as it is incompatible with the new legal order, or the matter is entirely dealt with by the new legislation.

Constitutional doctrine in Brazil recognises the phenomenon of 'reception' of previous legislation which is compatible with the new constitution.[6] But there has been doctrinal dispute concerning the possibility of reception of former constitutional provisions, compatible with the new constitution, but not expressly mentioned in the new text. The contention is that a new phenomenon would have occurred: the 'deconstitutionalization' of a constitutional norm, by virtue of which previous constitutional norms, although losing their higher rank in the hierarchy of norms, would be kept in force as ordinary law.[7] The Federal Supreme Court, however, did not accept this theory, contending that a constitution, as a whole system, when coming into force would abrogate the previous constitution as such.[8]

## III. PROCEDURES IN PLACE FOR AMENDING THE CONSTITUTION

All Brazilian constitutions have been written, solemn documents, that accept changes only in accordance with their own rules. It has long been established under Brazilian constitutionalism that a constitution is the body of rules that determines the structure and operation of public powers and guarantees freedom to citizens. Thus, a constitution must adapt itself to the environment in which it is in force. The underlying assumption is that either the supreme law is adapted to new social conditions, or it turns into an obstacle to the development of national life. That seems to be the reason why all written and rigid constitutions must organise the process by virtue of which they can be reformed and modified.[9]

The 1988 Constitution is not an exception, and article 60 sets down procedures and requirements to be followed, and limits to be respected, in order to introduce constitutional changes. Article 60 reads as follows:

> Article 60. The Constitution may be amended on the proposal of:
>
> I - at least one-third of the members of the Chamber of Deputies or of the Federal Senate;
> II - the President of the Republic;
> III - more than one half of the Legislative Assemblies of the units of the Federation, each of them expressing itself by the relative majority of its members.

---

[6] See, e.g., Habeas Corpus (HC) 68210/91 RS. Revista Trimestral de Jurisprudência (hereinafter RTJ) 142/3, at page 832.
[7] Barroso, *op. cit.* at page 56.
[8] Representação (RP) 753 SP. RTJ 46/2, at page 441.
[9] Maximiliano, Carlos [1918]:*Commentarios à Constituição Brasileira*. Rio de Janeiro: Jacintho Ribeiro dos Santos, Editor. at pages 126 and 801.

Paragraph 1 - The Constitution shall not be amended while federal intervention, a state of defence or a state of siege is in force.

Paragraph 2 - The proposal shall be discussed and voted upon in each House of the National Congress, in two readings, and it shall be considered approved if it obtains, in both readings, three-fifths of the votes of the respective members.

Paragraph 3 - An amendment to the Constitution shall be promulgated by the Directing Board of the Chamber of Deputies and the Federal Senate with its respective sequence number.

Paragraph 4 - No proposal of amendment shall be considered which is aimed at abolishing:

I - the federative form State;
II - the direct, secret, universal and periodic vote;
III - the separation of government Powers;
IV - individual rights and guarantees.

Paragraph 5 - The matter dealt with in a proposal of amendment that is rejected or considered impaired shall not be the subject of another proposal in the same legislative session.

The new constitution is a rigid one, with a complex revision procedure, purportedly making future changes to its text more difficult. Nevertheless, it can be amended. The intention of the constituent is to let it be perennial to a certain degree.[10]

The 1988 Constitution amending system preserves the same initiative procedures as were present in previous documents. Members of the Chamber of Deputies have had the same power to initiate the amendment procedure since the first constitution; members of the Federal Senate have had a power of initiative since the 1891 Republican Constitution (except during the Estado Novo regime, when the Federal Senate was renamed 'Conselho Federal'—Federal Council); presidential initiative has been in Brazilian constitutions since 1937.(Although suppressed by the 1946 Constitution, it was reintroduced in 1967, maintained by Constitutional Amendment 1 (1969), and the 1988 Constitution.) A power of initiative by at least half of States Assemblies has existed since the first Republican constitution, due to the establishment of the Federation. This latter power has never been exercised.

The immutability clause, barring changes on the Republican form of government, and on the Federative form of State, was inherited from the 1891 Constitution, and kept in all other constitutions since.

As for the circumstantial entrenchment, the 1934 Constitution introduced the state of siege element, suppressed by the 1937 Constitution, reintroduced by the 1946 one, and also maintained by the 1967 Constitution. Under the 1988 Constitution, state of siege is decreed by the President, upon authorisation requested from the National Congress, and following consultation with the Council of the

---

[10] Ferreira, Pinto [1992]:*Comentários à Constituição Brasileira*. São Paulo: Saraiva at page 190.

Republic and the National Defence Council. State of siege may be decreed in the event of serious disturbance with nationwide effects that evidence the ineffectiveness of a measure taken during the state of defence, declaration of state of war or response to foreign armed aggression (article 137).

The state of emergency factor introduced in the 1967 Constitution as a bar to use of the amendment procedure by Amendment 11 (January 1979), and unique to it, was replaced by the state of defence in the 1988 Constitution.

During a state of siege and a state of defence certain civil and political rights may be restricted.

Another form of circumstantial entrenchment, introduced by the 1988 Constitution, is federal intervention in matters within the jurisdiction of States. Since Brazil became a Federation, all constitutions have contained provisions regarding Federal intervention in State matters. However these powers can only be invoked in exceptional circumstances.

The 1891 Constitution provided for Federal intervention in the States, when necessary, to repeal foreign invasion; to preserve the Federation; to preserve peace and order, at the request of States; and to ensure the implementation and enforcement of the law (article 6). These seem to be the core elements present ever since.

Commenting on such circumstantial entrenchment, Martins supports the view that the principle is a healthy one because at a time of federal intervention, state of defence or state of siege there is no political environment in which a constitutional amendment can be properly discussed, and the three occurrences show the existence of an acute political crisis, which may threaten institutions.[11]

There is also an immutability clause in the 1988 Constitution but it is much different from the first one, introduced by the 1891 Constitution, by virtue of which no amendment proposal attempting to abolish the Republic or the Federative form of State could be discussed. The new formula protects the Federative form of State, but excludes the republican form of government as non-amendable. The change to monarchy was even allowed by the constitution, as article 2 of the Temporary Constitutional Provisions Act provided for a plebiscite, through which voters could define the form (republic or constitutional monarchy) and system of government (parliamentary or presidential) to be in force in Brazil. The plebiscite took place in April 1993, and people decided to keep the presidential republic.

The 1988 immutability clause, however, is broader than previous clauses. Unlike other Brazilian constitutions, this one says that no proposal of amendment shall be considered which is aimed at abolishing the federative form of State; the direct, secret, universal and periodic vote; the separation of government powers; and individual rights and guarantees.

A republic has always been seen, under Brazilian constitutionalism,

---

[11] Bastos, Celso Ribeiro and Ives Gandra da Silva Martins [1995]:*Comentários à Constituição do Brasil*. São Paulo: Saraiva. Volume IV, at page 340.

essentially as a form of government elected by the people.[12] Electability of the legislature is the essence of the democratic regime, and what is specific within a republic is electability and temporality of the legislative and executive power.[13] As Ferreira recalls, previous Brazilian constitutions presented as inalterable the constitutional nucleus of the federation and the republic. The federation was maintained but the republic became a mere constitutional illusion. The Third Republic (1937 to 1945) suppressed the vote. The Fifth Republic (1964 to 1988) generalised the indirect vote and suppressed individual rights and guarantees.[14]

Congress may alter the constitution, within limits imposed by the entrenchment mechanisms within the constitution.[15] Entrenchment mechanisms include a temporal one, by virtue of which an amendment proposal is discussed and voted upon in two readings, in both the Federal Senate and the Chamber of Deputies. Internal rules of both Houses provide that once approved on first reading, a time delay of five sessions must follow before a second reading takes place. After approval on second reading in one House, the proposal is sent to the other House.

Entrenchment mechanisms also encompass a qualified majority of three-fifths of the votes of the respective members of both Houses for approval.

The Temporary Constitutional Provisions Act introduced a special mechanism for revision of the 1988 Constitution. Article 3 of the Act provided for a revision that should 'be effected after five years as of its promulgation, by the vote of the absolute majority of the members of the National Congress in a unicameral session'.

Bonavides contended that such constitutional revision was linked to the result of the plebiscite favouring monarchy and the parliamentary form of government, as mentioned in article 2 of the Temporary Constitutional Provisions Act.[16] The Governor of the State of Paraná brought a direct action of unconstitutionality against a joint resolution of the Federal Senate and the Chamber of Deputies, setting down rules on the joint sitting of both Houses for the 1993 constitutional revision. He argued (as per Bonavides) that as the vote in the plebiscite went in favour of the maintenance of the republic and of the presidential form of government, no revision was required. The Supreme Court, however, concluded that the result of the plebiscite did not alter the possibility and eventually the need for a constitutional revision, the rules for which were more flexible and loose than those of the ordinary procedure to amend the constitution.[17]

To date, 22 constitutional changes to the 1988 Constitution have been effected. Only six of them were under the constitutional revision rules, which, at the end of the day, did not bring about as many changes as expected.

---

[12] Cavalcanti, Themistocles B. [1949]:*Constituição Federal Comentada*. Rio de Janeiro: José Konfino. Volume IV, at page 250.
[13] Dória, Sampaio [1960]: *Comentários à Constituição de 1946*. São Paulo: Max Limonad at page 878.
[14] Ferreira, *op. cit.*, at page 211.
[15] Martins, *op. cit.* See note 13, at page 325.
[16] Bonavides, Paulo [1996]: *São Paulo: Malheiros*. 6th Ed. at page 186.
[17] ADIMC 981/PR, Néri da Silveira, J.; Judgment Dec. 1993; DJ 5 Aug. 1994, at page 30.

## IV. THE 1824 IMPERIAL CONSTITUTION

Brazil's first constitution, that proclaimed by Emperor Peter I in 1824, provided for a special amendment procedure. Proposals for amendment were discussed by the legislature and if desired the voters were asked to approve the proposals at the next election. If approved by the electorate the amendment was then effected by ordinary legislation during the life of the next parliament.

## V. THE 1891 REPUBLICAN CONSTITUTION

With the proclamation of the Republic in 1889, the provisional government issued an interim constitution, while at the same time convoking a Constituent Assembly to discuss this constitution. The 1891 Constitution was inspired by both the French and American Constitutions. The American Constitution influenced the provisions on the equal representation of States at the Senate; the French one (1884, article 8) inspired the republican form of government: 'the republican form of government cannot be the subject of a revision proposal'.[18] Barbosa, a closer commentator, is more critical. Barbosa considered the 1891 Brazilian Constitution to be a transplantation of the 1787 American Constitution.[19]

Article 85 of the interim constitution and article 90 of the 1891 Constitution provided for constitutional reform. A proposal for amendment could be initiated by members of the Federal Senate or the Chamber of Deputies. A previous stage consisted of the acceptance of the proposal for discussion, after it had been submitted to three readings, and voted upon by a majority of two-thirds of each House.

The amendment procedure could also be initiated by two-thirds of the State Assemblies. An amendment proposal initiated in this manner would have to be approved by two-thirds of the members of each House of Congress.

Perhaps it is important to mention that Brazil as an empire was a unitary State until it became a Republic. When the empire collapsed, its former provinces were transformed into State members of the new Federal Republic. This impacted upon the procedure for making amendment proposals in that the 1891 Constitution provided that constitutional changes might be proposed by a majority of State Assemblies.

The 1891 Constitution introduced an immutability clause, by virtue of which Congress could not deliberate upon proposals to abolish the Republic or the Federal form of State, or impair the parity of States' representation in the Senate. This constitution was amended once (although several articles and provisions were amended at the same time) in its 39 years of existence.

According to Barbosa, under the 1891 Constitution constitutional revision of the provisions dealing with the following matters were not permissible: the republican and federal nature of the State; the territory of States of the Federation;

---

[18] Horta, *op. cit.* at page 170.
[19] Barbosa, *op. cit.*, at page 460.

equal representation of States in the Senate; religious freedom and the separation of Church and State; judicial power to decide on the constitutionality of legislative acts; the prohibition on inter-State taxation; the prohibition on retroactive legislation; and the autonomy of States to write their own constitution in conformity with the federal constitution.[20] As though anticipating what would become part of an immutability clause of the 1988 Constitution, he also held the view that the Constitutional Bill of Rights could not be subjected to reform, except for the purpose of including new rights.[21]

## VI. THE 1934 CONSTITUTION

The 1930 Revolution in Brazil was a major movement against rural oligarchies, which had been in power for decades. A National Constituent Assembly promulgated a new constitution in July 1934. This fundamental document set down different rules for constitutional amendment and for constitutional revision. Changes in the political structure of the State (Federal State, with separation of power, partition of competence between the federal union and the states) could only be revised, not amended. All other issues could be the subject of constitutional amendment.

The power of initiative could be exercised by one quarter of the members of any of the two Houses, and by the majority of the State Assemblies.

An amendment would be considered approved when supported and voted upon, following two debates, by an absolute majority of both Houses of Congress (Federal Senate and Chamber of Deputies) within two years.

A revision could be initiated by a proposal of two-fifths of the members of any House of Congress, or two-thirds of the State Assemblies, then submitted for the deliberation of each House. The proposal would have to receive the support of the majority of each House. Once approved, a draft would be prepared to be submitted to the forthcoming Legislature. The revision would only be concluded after being approved twice in each house.

Besides keeping the immutability clause introduced into the Brazilian legal system by the 1891 Constitution (proposals to abolish the Republic or the Federal State could not be considered) the 1934 Constitution introduced a 'circumstantial' entrenchment: no constitutional reform would proceed during a state of siege. This was in response to the 1926 constitutional changes, which took place when a state of siege was in force.

The 1934 Constitution was the shortest one to stay in force. It lasted only three years and was superseded by the 1937 Constitution, decreed by the civilian President Getulio Vargas, who instituted the 'New State' (Estado Novo), a fascist-like model of dictatorship and governance.

---

[20] Barbosa, *op. cit.* at page 461.
[21] Barbosa, *op. cit.*, at page 462.

## VII. THE 1937 CONSTITUTION

The 1937 Constitution provided for the holding of elections soon after it came into force but these elections were never held. From 1937 to 1945 Vargas ruled the country, without Parliament, and with the judicial branch of government severely restricted. Article 170 provided that during a state of emergency or a state of war the courts could not entertain any challenge to official acts. Article 186 declared that the whole country was under a state of emergency.

Vargas' dictatorship lasted until 1945. As National Congress was not assembled, he issued what he called 'constitutional laws' introducing changes to the constitution, 21 of which were issued from 1937 to 1946.

In 1945, under pressure from the opposition, the President agreed to hold a general election. A Constituent Assembly was elected to vote upon a new constitution.

## VIII. THE 1946 (LIBERAL DEMOCRAT) CONSTITUTION

The Directing Board of the Constituent Assembly promulgated the 1946 Constitution on 18 September of that year. It was a liberal-democrat document which restored the 1891 core provisions concerning the amendment process, with minor changes. The amendment procedure could be initiated by one quarter of members of the Chamber of Deputies or the Federal Senate, or by the majority of the State Assemblies (Article 217, paragraph 1). Such proposals had to be submitted to two readings and voted upon by the majority of each of both houses, in two ordinary and consecutive legislative sessions.

Unlike previous constitutions, or perhaps because of them, the Executive Power has no role in constitutional reforms. The President could not initiate, had no veto, did not promulgate amendments.[22] An immutability clause, barring Congress from changing the federal or republican nature of the State, was restored. The constitution also restored the circumstantial entrenchment provisions which prohibited change to the constitution during a state of siege.

## IX. THE MILITARY TAKEOVER AND THE 1967 CONSTITUTION

The 1946 Constitution was amended six times until, in April 1964, the military junta took power. The President was overthrown and a new President was elected indirectly by the National Congress (and not by direct vote as provided for in the constitution) within two days

At the beginning the junta tried a kind of compromise with the previous legal order, expressly establishing the maintenance in force of the constitution, except insofar as it had been changed by the Institutional Act mentioned earlier.

Nine new amendments were approved by Parliament, until Institutional Act

---

[22] Dória, *op. cit.*, at page 877.

2 (October 1965) was issued, which itself effected constitutional amendments, and which also provided a new procedure for future amendments. The requirement that a proposal for amendment be submitted to two readings in subsequent legislative sessions was replaced by provisions whereby the two readings and two round ballots could be held in the same legislative session.

Among other relevant constitutional changes, Institutional Act 2 enlarged the Supreme Court, increasing its number from 11 to 16. It also strengthened powers to deny political rights, and introduced new situations that would be immune from judicial control.

Amendments 16 to 19 were passed according to the new rules. Institutional Act 3 introduced indirect elections for Governors (February 1966). Two new amendments were approved until Institutional Act 4 was issued, presenting Congress with the draft of a new constitution which was approved and came into force as the 1967 Constitution, thereby institutionalising and consolidating Brazilian military dictatorship.

The 1967 Constitution, formally approved by Congress, 'legalised' all 'revolutionary' acts. Article 173 approved all such acts, plus all 'complementary acts' issued on the basis of these Institutional Acts, excluding all of them from judicial review. This bill of indemnity was tested by the Supreme Court which was under extreme pressure because it could not rule with full independence. 3 Justices had already at this stage been removed by the military. The Court had to accept this bill of indemnity barring legal challenges to the acts issued on the basis of the Institutional Acts. However it did try to limit the scope of the indemnity.[23]

The amending system introduced by 1967 Constitution was not different from previous constitutions. One-fourth of the members of any of the Houses, the President of the Republic, and the majority of State Assemblies had initiative of amendment proposals. But unlike previous constitutions, the debate and the voting took place with both Houses assembled together as Congress, and the proposal being considered was deemed approved when supported by the majority of its members, in two rounds, in the same legislative session. The 1967 Constitution included the immutability clause protecting the Republic and the Federal form of State, and the circumstantial entrenchment clause prohibiting changes to the constitution during a state of siege.

The 1967 Constitution amending process was reformed four times, twice by the President (Amendments 1 and 8) invoking his revolutionary powers. Constitutional Amendment 1 (October 1969), which changed the whole constitution, increased the necessary support for approving a change - from unqualified majority to two-thirds majority -, and removed States Assemblies power

---

[23] RE 67843/70 DF; Luiz Gallotti, J.. 'Decrees issued by the President, while Congress was in recess, are not immune from judicial review under article 173, III of the 1967 Constitution (bill of indemnity). Legislative power conferred upon the President, during recess of the Congress, is the same power Congress has while not in recess. And Congress may not pass legislation which conflicts with the Constitution. Neither, therefore can the President, while substituting Congress, during its recess.' RTJ 54-3/610.

to initiate the constitutional amendment procedure. Constitutional Amendment 8 (April 1977) increased the necessary numbers of members of parliament to initiate a proposal: from one-fourth to one-third. And reduced the approval requirement: from two-thirds majority to absolute majority.

Constitutional Amendment 11 (January 1979) expanded the circumstantial entrenchment. The constitution could not be amended during a state of siege or a state of emergency. A State of Emergency, according to Amendment 11, could be decreed by the President, when necessary to combat subversive activities. Constitutional Amendment 22 (June 1982) increased the support required for approval, establishing a two-third majority again.

One should be so naïve as to believe that the constitutionalisation of the military regime meant that the dictatorship would give place to a rule of law. It did not. In fact, there was a coup within the coup and the extreme right wing within the military took power. Institutional Act 5, the darkest instrument of all, was issued on December 13th 1968. It allowed the suspension of the National Congress, State Assemblies or local councils to be ordered by decree; intervention in the exercise of power by the Executive branch of State governments; removal of civil and political rights; suspension of judicial guarantees of life tenure, irremovability, and stability; confiscation of properties; all without due process of law, constitutional restraints, or submission to judicial review.

Following the Institutional Act 5, 'Complementary Acts' were enacted, introducing changes to the constitution. Such changes were considered to be constitutional amendments, which were ratified as such by article 3 of Institutional Act 6, of February 1969.

Direct constitutional changes were still introduced by Institutional Acts 7, 9, 14, and 16, whereas Institutional Acts 8, 10, 11, 12, 13 and 17 introduced implied changes, as its provisions affected or impaired constitutional rights.

As Congress was in recess since December 13th 1968, the military junta had power to pass legislation, which its view it included effecting constitutional amendments. During this recess the junta decided to promulgate constitutional Amendment 1, which changed the whole 1967 Constitution, and is considered in fact to be another constitution.

As late as 1977, the President decreed the recess of Congress, and promulgated two more constitutional amendments. Constitutional Amendment 7, introducing major reform of the Judiciary; and constitutional Amendment 8, defining rules for indirect balloting for the election of Governors of States.

From 1967 to 1985, Congress passed 24 constitutional amendments. The 26th Amendment was proposed by the first civilian President after two decades of military regime. It convened a National Constituent Assembly to write a new constitution.

The convening of the National Constituent Assembly signalled a recommitment to democracy and the rule of law. As Reale has noted the military government focused only on economic issues.[24] When the economy was no longer able to provide an argument for military government it could no longer justify itself. The people reasserted their right to a representative government.

## X. SIGNIFICANT PROBLEMS WHICH HAVE ARISEN AS REGARDS THE OPERATION OF THE PROCEDURES FOR CONSTITUTIONAL AMENDMENTS

Perhaps the most significant problem concerning the operation of the procedures for constitutional amendments in Brazil is when such procedures are not followed, and changes are introduced by means of political power of the Executive, sidestepping the constitution, and suppressing the powers of the legislature and judiciary.

When Brazil was under a fully democratic government, all constitutional changes were introduced by constitutional amendments, effected according to specific procedures laid down by the basic document. But when governed by a civilian dictator, such as Getulio Vargas, or by a military junta dictatorship, and afterwards by military Presidents, the constitution and its amending procedures had no importance at all, as 'constitutional laws', 'constitutional amendments', 'institutional acts', 'complementary acts', and the like, were passed by a stroke of a pen, and supported by many strokes of sticks. These 'laws' found their source in the effective control of power by the dictatorship and they were implemented through the use of intimidation, violence and threats.

After 12 years of civilian Presidents, and the restoration of civil and political rights, Congress is the sole institution to have a last say on which changes are to be introduced and which changes are not. That is not to say that the President has no power to influence Congress. He has. But to influence, not to substitute. That's the main difference between democracy and dictatorship.

We return to that later, but significant problems that may be rising on procedures to amend the constitution may be due to a lack of convergence of political interest or political will than to any other internal or external cause. As consensus cannot be easily found under the three-fifths majority rule, there is now a claim for a new constitutional revision in 1999, with the same relaxed rules of the 1993 revision (joint sitting, absolute majority rule). Many argue that such revision, which is not expressly mentioned under 1988 Constitution, would have to follow ordinary amending procedures rule, unless a plebiscite is voted allowing a revision in such conditions.

---

[24]  Reale, Miguel [1977]: *Da Revoluçao à Democracia*. Rio de Janeiro: Forense. at p. 21.

## XI. BALANCING THE NEED FOR STABILITY AND CERTAINTY IN THE CONSTITUTION WITH THE NEED FOR THE CONSTITUTION TO CHANGE IN RESPONSE TO THE CHANGING NEEDS OF SOCIETY

The issue on the agenda now is governability. Since President Cardoso stepped into power he ignited a process of 'reforms'. He did not mention social reforms, widely required by Brazilian society. He mentioned constitutional reforms. 1994 presidential campaign coincided with the sitting of the revising Congress. But the revising Congress did not gather enough consensus to pass constitutional amendments meeting the needs of the so said required reforms.[25]

Martins holds the view that, on discussing governability on the light of the 1988 Constitutions, consensus is reached on the conclusion that the 1988 Constitution not being revised in 1993 is the main cause of political instability in the country.[26]

Ferreira Filho shares the same opinion, and states that 1988 Brazilian Constitution is responsible for aggravating the governability crisis in the country. He argues that the constitution imposes so many tasks and duties upon the State, that it is overburdened by such unlimited State obligations.[27]

To tackle these issues, President Cardoso's strategy is to implement a reform of the State. By this he means focus State activities on basic social demands, shifting from executing to fostering social and economic development, all this supported by a new managerial model of administration.[28]

To achieve these goals, some constitutional changes have already been introduced, envisaging bringing the country to a free market economy (amendments 6, 7, 8, 9 and 13), or aiming at increasing revenues for the State, to fund health and educational services (amendments 10, 12 and 14). And some other constitutional amendment proposals were sent to Congress, to deliberate upon welfare system reform, and on State administration reform, this latter basically dealing with removal of life tenure for civil servants; removal of public exams as a means of recruitment of civil servants; and limits of pay for civil servants, and members of all branches of the government.

Although federal government urges for these constitutional amendment proposals, they are under discussions for more than 2 years. Yet, government is not sure its parliamentary basis will be strong enough to meet the required majority.

On the other hand, as late as January 1997, a constitutional amendment proposal, inspired (if not instructed) by the President was sent to Congress, allowing chiefs of the Executive - President, Governors and Mayors -, to run for a re-election. The proposal has already been approved by both Houses, and turned to be Constitutional Amendment 16, dated 4 June 1997.

---

[25] See revision amendments on Table of Constitutional Amendments, p.81.
[26] Martins, See note 13, *op. cit.*, at page 346.
[27] Ferreira Filho, Manoel Gonçalves [1995]: *São Paulo: Saraiva.* at page 34 and 37.
[28] Green Paper on the Reform of the State, MARE Ministério da Administração e Reforma do Estado.

Nóbrega tries to understand why such re-election constitutional amendment has already been approved, whilst administrative and welfare system constitutional reforms have not yet. He came to the conclusion that, under Brazilian presidential system, parliamentary majorities are reached in a case by case basis. Thus, it is far easier to gather members of parliament to support a re-election constitutional amendment, which is just like a plebiscite, whereas other reforms would demand a deeper analysis, when electoral interests speak louder, as such reforms would impact more intensively on voters.[29]

The explanation given by Nóbrega seems to be feasible, whereas the arguments that the constitution in itself is the main source of ungovernability seems to be ill-conceived and misdirected.

As Bradley says, constitution in its wider sense refers to 'the whole system of government of a country, the collection of rules which establish and regulate or govern the government'.[30] The role of the government is not confined to civil and political rights. It also encompasses tasks and duties on social, economic and cultural rights. Laubadère realised that, unlike ancient constitutions, recent constitutions almost always contain, in different degrees, articles regarding economic institutions.[31]

Brazilian constitution encompasses economic, social and cultural rights as part of fundamental rights and guarantees. These programmatic or directive principles and dispositions are binding on all branches of the government, and on society as a whole. They are, in different degrees, justiciable. Portuguese modern constitutionalism influenced Brazilian 1988 Constitution. Canotilho, discussing upon programmatic norms, asserts that the programmatic, the principles and the constitutional directives are nothing but proposals to materially legitimise a Magna Chart of a country. A programme seeks to be just and not only true; aspires a practice not only a theory.[32]

Unlike 1946 Constitution, which was a liberal democratic document, Brazilian 1988 Constitution is a social democratic document (welfare State document), that entails not only negative rights, but also right to positive measures from the State.[33] Constitutional Bill of Rights encompasses civil and political rights, that's true. But it also includes economic, social and cultural rights, like right to education, right to health, right to welfare benefits, right to welfare assistance, right to housing, right to an agrarian reform, right to an adequate standard of living, etc.

Despite having acceded to the International Covenant on Economic, Social and Cultural rights of the United Nations, with due ratification of the instrument, and it internalisation in the domestic level by means of formal approval by the

---

[29] Nóbrega, Maílson da, *Razões da demora nas reformas*. Article published on 30 May 1997, in Brazilian newspaper *Folha de São Paulo*. 2/2.
[30] Bradley, A. W. and K. D. Ewing [1994]:*Constitutional and Administrative Law*. 11th Edition. London: Longman. at page 77.
[31] Laubadère, André de [1981:*Direito Econômico*. Coimbra: Almedina. at page 69
[32] Canotilho, J.J. Gomes [1982]:*Constituição Dirigente e Vinculação do Legislador*. Coimbra: Editora Coimbra. at page 22.
[33] Canotilho, J.J. Gomes [1991]:*Direito Constitucional*. Coimbra: Almedina. at page 78.

Federal Senate, and promulgation by Executive decree, Brazil has not properly understood what is the nature of State obligations concerning economic, social and cultural rights, and the positive measures thereof.

If one considers that Brazilian 1988 Constitution is attuned with the ICESCR, one may be able to find guidance on studies carried on when interpreting the UN document. Trubek remembers that the Economic Covenant is oriented around the principle of 'progressive realization'.[34] The language of the Covenant commits States to take steps, with a view to achieving progressively the rights recognised, to the maximum of its available resources. In article 2 progressive realization indicates that the rights must be implemented over time, by a program of activities. The framers of the Covenant were aware that the implementation of social rights would require states to allot money on them, thus conditioning the rate of progress towards the goals established.[35]

If States obligations are to be implemented over time, depending on available resources, one cannot talk about an overburden of tasks and activities. Conversely, one can conclude, with Craven, that the failure of many States fully to implement economic, social and cultural rights can often be more clearly attributed to a lack of political will than any matter of resource scarcity.[36]

## XII. TESTING CONSTITUTIONALITY OF CONSTITUTIONAL AMENDMENTS

A constitution is the supreme law of the country; against its letter or its spirit neither federal power resolutions, nor state constitutions, decrees or decisions, nor treaties or any diplomatic acts prevail.[37] Within the constitution, there is no rank order of constitutional norms. But constitutional norms introduced by constitutional amendments may be subject to control of constitutionality. It's unconstitutional every constitutional change that does not respect the established special procedure (initiative, ballot, quorum, etc.), or does not respect a disposition not subject to constitutional amendment. Such constitutional changes can be tested by the Judiciary.[38]

Constitution rigidity lays on reform technique, imposing a more difficult process to change it, [39] or a non-amendable clause, and on the establishment of organs and mechanisms to test and control constitutionality. The underlying principle is constitutional supremacy, based on formal and material superlegality. Constitutional reform or revision laws, introducing changes to the original

---

[34] Trubek, David M. *Economic, Social and Cultural Rights in the Third Word*, in Meron, Theodor [1992]:*Human Rights in International Law*. Oxford: Clarendon Press.
[35] Trubek, *op. cit.*, at page 213.
[36] Craven, Matthew [1995]:*The International Covenant on Economic, Social and Cultural Rights*. Oxford: Clarendon Press. at page 106.
[37] Maximiliano, [1918], *op. cit.*, at page 108.
[38] Da Silva, José Afonso [1996]:*Direito Constitucional Positivo Brasileiro*. São Paulo: Malheiros. 12nd Edition. at page 70.
[39] Da Silva, *op. cit.* at page 65.

constitution, may be rendered unconstitutional as violative of procedural rules as well as temporal and material revision limits or entrenchment. [40]

In Brazil, the constitutionality control system in force is the judicial one, accommodating both American diffuse system and Austrian concentrated system. As the diffuse constitutionality control method is admitted, it is possible to any organ invested with judicial power to express its view concerning constitutional dispositions.[41]

Abstract judicial control of laws, by means of direct action, was introduced in Brazilian legal system in November 1965, when Constitutional Amendment 16 to the 1946 Constitution established the Supreme Court as originally competent to sentence representation filed by the Procurator-General of the Republic.

All norms are subject to judicial scrutiny, as far as control of constitutionality is concerned. Constitutionality control encompasses even the revision prerogative recognised to the derived constituent power.[42] An act of the Legislature, which includes a constitutional amendment, repugnant to the constitution is void. Mendes recollects that aafter the wide constitutional reform that took place in 1925/1926, the Federal Supreme Court by majority declared the constitutionality of the revision process, thus also recognising its competence to assess if a revision constitutional law is compatible with the constitution.[43]

There are two ways of controlling constitutionality of a law or of a normative act. Firstly, incidentally, in a lawsuit, when the declaration of unconstitutionality is not the object of the litigation in itself, but the judge has to decide to apply the constitution, and to repeal the law or normative act. If a law be in opposition to the constitution, if both the law and the constitution apply to a particular case, so that the Court must decide the case conformably to the constitution, disregarding the law.[44] In such situation, the Court does not strike down legislation, nor abrogates it. It simply declares it inapplicable to that particular case, and to those particular petitioners and respondents. The law stays in force until the Federal Senate decides to stop the application of such a unconstitutional law, so declared by final decision of the Supreme Federal Court.[45] Such final decision is delivered by the Supreme Court sitting as an ordinary or extraordinary appeal Court.[46]

Secondly, in a main action, by means of an autonomous constitutional proceeding. Constitutional proceedings to test in abstract constitutionality of laws or normative acts under 1988 Constitution are laid down in Article 102, I, 'a', which defines competence of the Supreme Court to institute legal proceedings and trial, in the first instance, of direct actions of unconstitutionality of a federal or state law

---

[40] Canotilho (1991), *op. cit.* at page 972, and 1009.
[41] Federal Supreme Court, AG 149241-4 (AgRg), Mauricio Correia, J.; Informativo STF 72; 28 May 1997.
[42] Mendes, Gilmar Ferreira [1990]:*Controle de Constitucionalidade de Leis*. São Paulo: Saraiva. at page 95.
[43] Mendes, *op. cit.*, at page 103.
[44] The Doctrine announced in *Marbury v. Madison* is applied.
[45] Da Silva, *op. cit.*, at page 56.
[46] 1988 Constitution, article 102, sections I and II.

or normative act, and declaratory actions of constitutionality of a federal law or normative act.

These two instruments of abstract control of norms, direct action of unconstitutionality, and declaratory action of constitutionality, have the same aim, but with distinctive assumptions. The former assumes that the norm is unconstitutional; the latter, that it is constitutional.

The Supreme Court itself, deciding the *ADIN (AgReg) 203-1 DF*, laid down a definition as to the aims of the remedy, and its object:

Direct action of unconstitutionality is a remedy to preserve the integrity of the legal order established by the constitution in force. It acts as an instrument which activates constitutional jurisdiction, concentrated on the Federal Supreme Court, giving occasion to the Court, in the abstract control of a juridical norm, to perform a typical political or governmental function.

The law and normative acts emanated from the Union, the Member-States and the Federal District, are object of the concentrated control of constitutionality.

Abstract control of norms envisages the protection of the constitutional order, without reference to any individual or concrete legal situation.[47]

A decision that declares the unconstitutionality of a law has effects 'ex tunc' (ab initio). Thus, a representation of unconstitutionality is not ruled prejudiced if the law which is tested is revoked in the course of action, when there are still lasting effects.[48]

The constitutionality test must be one of direct confrontation with the constitution. So, when infra constitutional norms regulate a matter in a manner which is ultra vires a law, there is a crisis of legality, not one of constitutionality. Only when there is no law preceding a regulatory norm can this latter be tested against the constitution.[49]

The abstract and concentrated constitutionality control encompasses only existing norms. Neither bills, nor proposals. The Supreme Court declared:

Brazilian constitutional positive law, throughout its historical evolution, has never authorised - as the 1988 does not do - a preventive judicial control of constitutionality, in abstract.

Concentrated control of constitutionality requires the existence of a norm.[50]

Among norms subject to judicial scrutiny, no doubt constitutional amendments are included. Not only to test compliance with procedural rules, or temporal or circumstantial entrenchment. Also the immutability clause bars constitutional amendment proposals. Thus, if such immutability clause is violated, the

---

[47] ADIN (AgReg) 203-1 DF, June 1990; Celso de Mello, J.; Lex Jurisprudência do Supremo Tribunal Federal, hereinafter Lex JSTF 140/74.
[48] RP 971/77 RJ; Djaci Falcão, J.; RTJ 87-3/758.
[49] ADIMC 1253/94 DF; Carlos Velloso, J.; published in Diário da Justiça [official daily publication of Courts decisions] (hereinafter DJ) 25 Aug 95, at page 26.022.
[50] ADIMC 466/91 DF; Celso de Mello, J.; RTJ 136/1 at page 25

constitutional change may be declared null and void.

The constitution imposes express material limits to a reform to the fundamental law. Such are the petrous clauses or eternity guarantee (Ewigkeitsgarantie), which limit reform power upon certain matters. Such clauses impede not only a constitutional order suppression, but also any changes that alter fundamental elements of its historical identity.[51]

The Supreme Court had no difficulty on defining that such petrous clause were binding on constituent derived power. In the already referred *ADIMC 466/91 DF*, Celso de Mello J. leading opinion held:

The juridical impossibility of an abstract preventive control of mere amendment proposals does not bar testing them once converted in constitutional amendments. These latter, not being original constitutional norms, are not excluded from the ambit of a successive or repressive control of constitutionality.

National Congress, when exercising its derived constituent power, and performing its reforming function, is legally bound by the original constituent power, which has laid down, besides circumstantial entrenchment to reform, an immutable clause, immune to parliamentary revision.

Explicit material limitations, defined by paragraph 4 of article 60 of the constitution, constrain reforming power conferred upon the legislative. The immutability of such thematic nucleus, eventually violated, may render legitimate an abstract normative control and even a concrete control of constitutionality.[52]

In a previous judgment, *ADIMC 981/93 PR*, the Supreme Court had reached the conclusion that any constitutional reform, be it by means of ordinary amending procedures, or by revision procedures referred to by the Transitory Constitutional Dispositions Act, had to conform to the constitution. The Court held:

Revision and amendment, as procedures to introduce constitutional changes, are expression of an instituted constituent power, thus, limited by nature.

The revision referred to by article 3 of the Temporary Constitutional Provisions Act is subject to the limits established by article 60, paragraph 4, of the Constitution. Constitutional changes deriving from a revision are subject do judicial control and scrutiny, as regard the petrous clauses.[53]

Direct actions of unconstitutionality have been filed against 7 of the 16 Constitutional Amendments and 6 Revision Constitutional Amendments. On deciding the *ADIN 939-7 DF*, challenging constitutionality of Constitutional Amendment 3, the Supreme Court held:

---

[51] Mendes, *op. cit.*, at pages 96 and 98.
[52] See note 61 *supra*.
[53] ADIMC 981-8/600/93 PR; Néri da Silveira, J.; Dec 93; Lex JSTF 192/56.

A constitutional amendment, which is emanated from a derived constituent, when violative of the original constitution, may be declared unconstitutional by the Supreme Court, which is the guardian of the constitution.

Constitutional Amendment 3, of 17 February 1993, whose article 2 authorised the Union to institute a tax on the transaction or transfer of securities and of credits and rights of a financial nature, is held to be unconstitutional, since paragraph 2 of this disposition states that article 150, III, b, and VI, of the Constitution does not apply to the tax mentioned, thus violating the following principles and immutable norms:

1. The principle of preceding legislation, which is an individual guarantee of the tax-payer;
2. The principle of reciprocal tax immunity (which prohibits the Union, the States, the Federal District and the Municipalities to institute taxes on the property, income, and services from one another), which is a guarantee of the Federation;
3. The norm that, imposing other immunities, forbids the institution of taxes on temples of any denomination; books, newspapers, periodicals; on the income, property, and services of political parties, trade unions, educational and welfare institutions.'[54]

In both decisions, the Supreme Court decided that the constitutional supremacy required from constitutional amendments compliance with its petrous clause.

A decision in a direct action of unconstitutionality or in a direct action of constitutionality has its effects 'erga omnes', and not only between the parties. The norm is either repealed or maintained, totally or partially, and the decision is binding on all State powers, and private individuals. Conversely, a decision on a concrete case, with individual petitioners, when the norm is held to be non applicable because of being unconstitutional, binds only on the parties. If such decision is delivered by the Supreme Court, the Federal Senate must be notified to *'stop the application, in full or in part, of a law declared unconstitutional by final decision of the Supreme Federal Court'.*[55]

A direct action of unconstitutionality may be filed by the President of the Republic; the Directing Boards of the Federal Senate, of the Chamber of Deputies, and of any State Legislative Assembly; a State Governor; the Procurator-General of the Republic[56]; the Federal Council of the Brazilian Bar Association; a political

---

[54] ADIN 937-7 DF; Sydney Sanches, J.; RTJ 189-1/69.
[55] 1988 Constitution, article 52, Section X.
[56] The Procurator-General is the head of the Public Ministry, a quasi-judicial body, which duty is to defend the juridical order, the democratic regime and the inalienable social and individual rights (1988 Constitution, article 127). Sometimes there is confusion with the Attorney-General, which represents the Federal Union judicially. The Attorney-General, according to certain translation, is then

party represented in the National Congress; a confederation of labour unions or a professional association of a nationwide nature.[57]

A declaratory action of constitutionality may be filed by the President of the Republic; the Directing Board of the Federal Senate or of the Chamber of Deputies, or by the Procurator-General of the Republic.[58]

## XIII. FEDERAL CONSTITUTION *VIS-À-VIS* STATES' CONSTITUTIONS

Brazilian Federation results from the proclamation of the Republic, and the transformation of former provinces into Federate States. Unlike American federalism, Brazilian one derives from the decentralisation of the former unitary Imperial State. Article 63 of the Constitution of the Republic prescribed that each State should be ruled by the constitution and laws they adopted, with due respect to the constitutional principles of the Union.[59]

Mello holds the view that the States received constituent competence by delegation of the provisory government of the republic. States self-organisation was neither by own initiative, nor because of being vested by an organisational power. Instead it was a compliance with a revolutionary command, which had instituted the republican regime, and had opted to integrate Brazil in a federative model.[60]

Trying to apply American experience, Brazilian 1891 Constitution, and all following republican documents, have reserved to States residual power. Although this is a relevant principle, in Brazil residual competence is an illusory one.[61]

State Constituent power derives from and is subject to the principles laid down by the federal constitution.[62] It is so since 1891 Constitution. Article 11 of the Transitory Constitutional Dispositions Act 1988 reads as such:

Article 11. Each Legislative Assembly endowed with constituent powers, shall draft the State Constitution within one year as from the promulgation of the Federal Constitution, with due regard for the principles of the latter.

Thus, not only State constitutional amendments, but even State constitutions are subject to constitutionality control, as regard the federal constitution. This latter is hierarchically superior to the former.

The Supreme Court, deciding upon the *ADIMC 568/91 AM*, proclaimed:

---

christened the Advocate-General.
[57] 1988 Constitution, article 103.
[58] 1988 Constitution, article 103, paragraph 4.
[59] Barbosa, *op. cit.*, at page 467.
[60] Mello, Oswaldo Trigueiro de Albuquerque [1980]:*Direito Constitucional Estadual*. Rio de Janeiro: Forense. at page 49.
[61] Melo, *op. cit.* at page 84.
[62] RMS 9558/62 GB; Pedro Chaves, J.; DJ 16 Aug 63, at page 2623.

Transitory Constitutional Dispositions Act 1988, in article 11, imposed State Members, when exercising their constituent power, strict conformity to the Charter of the Republic.

Constituent Power ensured to federate units is essentially an institutional prerogative juridically limited by the subordinating normativeness emanated from the fundamental law.[63]

From the beginning, Melo concluded, state constitutions are federal constitution inspirations, and inevitable miniatures.[64]

One basic principle, present in all Brazilian constitutions, and imposed upon State constitutions is separation of powers. How the Supreme Court applied such principle, as regard State Constituents, is well illustrated in the judgment of the direct action of unconstitutionality 18/AL.

Fernando Collor de Mello, who became President of the country, was the Governor to the State of Alagoas. He sued the *State Constituent Assembly* for promulgating, prior to the promulgation of the new State constitution, the *Constitutional Act 1,* by virtue of which it was declared that all enactment of the new government, since the inaugural session of the State Constituent Assembly, that had dismissed civil servants, or that had extinguished administrative bodies and institutions were held to be null and void.

The Supreme Court held that

it conflicts with the Federal Constitution an act issued by the Directing Board of the State Constituent Assembly which struck down Decree by the Governor, by virtue of which, in the ambit of the administration of the State, he disposed about dismissals of civil servants.

Article 11 of the transitory constitutional norms authorises the State Constituent Assembly to write down the new Constitution. Such power derived from a delegation of the federal constituent power, as the holder of national sovereignty. Such derived power was a limited one. Thus, such act by the Directing Board of the SCA exceeded the powers conceded.

In his leading opinion, Marco Aurélio J. held the view that:

Federal Constitution, as regard State powers, is based upon the notion of independence and harmony. In the case under judgment, the Legislative Assembly decided to edit a constitutional act, repealing a Decree from the chief of the Executive. Doing so, the Assembly acted as a reviewing power, replacing, by means of an extravagant act, measure within the competence of the Governor. Such attitude conflicts with power conferred upon State Assemblies.[65]

The Supreme Court came to a same conclusion, when having to decide upon the case *EDADI 348/95 MG,* with Ilmar Galvão, J., delivering the opinion of the Court:

The norm was declared formally unconstitutional because it dealt with a matter which

---

[63] ADIMC 568-5/600/91 AM; Celso de Mello, J.; Sep 1991; Lex JSTF 160/32.
[64] Melo, *op. cit.*, at page 62.
[65] ADIN 18 AL; Marco Aurélio, J.; RTJ 135-3/860.

initiative was not encompassed by derived constituent's one, conversely, legislative initiative belonged to the chief of the executive.[66]

As for the extension of such *principles* underlying federal constitution, the Supreme Court held that the phenomenon of 'deconstitutionalisation', with reception as ordinary laws of previous constitutional norms which did not contravene the new constitution was not compatible with the federal constitution system. Djaci Falcão, delivering the Court's opinion, held:

Article 147 of the Constitution of the State of São Paulo - which establishes that stay in force, albeit holding a character of only ordinary law, norms from the 1947 State Constitution which do not contravene the new document -, besides being ultra vires the limits of adaptation, is incompatible with the system instituted by the Magna Charter.[67]

Constitutional innovation in the State level is, in fact, a not very safe ground. Nevertheless, States have introduced slight differences in their systems, some of which have been held constitutional. Quite recently the Supreme Court held that

The rule of article 57, paragraph 4, of the Federal Constitution, which deals with election of the Directing Board of the Federal Legislative Houses, and forbids re-election for the same office in the immediately subsequent term, has not to be compulsorily adopted by States Constitutions, because it is not an established constitutional principle.[68]

Sometimes the Supreme Court has had difficulty on drawing the line between constitutional principles and constitutional dispositions. Thus, there is not a clear cut between a principle underlying a disposition and the disposition itself, and if the State constitution does not repeat the Federal constitution disposition, it is very likely that it may be held to be unconstitutional.

## XIV. JUDICIAL INTERPRETATION AND CONSTITUTION MAKING

It is a long established assumption, under Brazilian jurisprudence, that the laws are to be interpreted according to the constitution, not conversely.[69] Also, and according to the Supreme Court, if it is true that all interpretation encompasses a certain amount of legal construction, it is not less true that it is bound to the juridical-constitutional order. The phenomenon is based on norms in force, varying according to the interpreter's professional and humanistic background. Performing its duty, it is not left to the interpreter to insert in the norm his own judgment, as to

---

[66] EDADI 388/95 MG; Ilmar Galvão, J.; DJ 29 Sep 95, at page 3.190.
[67] RP 753 SP, Djaci Falcão, J.; RTJ 46-2/441.
[68] ADIN 793-9 DF, Carlos Velloso, J.; Informativo STF 71, 16 May 97.
[69] AgrPet 423/91 SP; Sepúlveda Pertence, J.; Apr 91; RTJ 136-3/1034.

the aims that the rule should pursue.[70]

The Supreme Court has always admitted its power to entertain and decide upon political questions, when constitutional matters being involved. In its view, political decisions are discretionary only in the sense that they pertain the discretion power of congress or of government as regard opportunity and convenience, or the exam of circumstances that may authorise them. But legislative or administrative discretion cannot be exercised outside constitutional or legal boundaries. Therefore, ancient American jurisprudential criterion (merely, purely, exclusively political questions) has been overruled. [71]

Brazilian Supreme Court has been regarded as one of the essential elements of political stability. Gomes remarks that in a country which is illustrated by successive changes from institutional normality to abnormality, it is astonishing that the theoretically so considered the weakest branch of government has been able to stay almost immune to all political crises, with the Executive and the Legislative paying due regard to its role.[72]

The following cases may show the political role performed by the Supreme Court, in very important institutional events. The first two cases dealt with the activities of the democratic National Constituent Assembly elected in 1986, which promulgated the 1988 Constitution.

A Member of Parliament licensed from his functions, with leave to be in charge of the Secretary of Transports, to the State of Rio de Janeiro, was charged of having committed the criminal offence of defamation against a civil servant.

As defence, the member of parliament alleged *absolute privilege,* based on *Internal Rules of the National Constituent Assembly,* by virtue of which the constituents enjoyed inviolability on account of their opinions, words and votes.

The Court agreed with the opinion delivered by the *Procurator-General,* according to which the *National Constituent Assembly* had power to write a new constitution without limitations. But such new constitution would only come into force after it had been promulgated, after having been voted and approved according to the rules of its convocation. Nevertheless, it had no power to introduce immediate changes in the constitution that was in force.

The Court found that the acts attributed to the Member of Parliament took place while he was licensed from his functions. Thus, he could not argue, as a defence, *absolute privilege,* as despite being a member of parliament the offensive libel was not in the course of the mandate, nor related to it.

Besides, constitutional rule establishing criminal responsibility for crimes against the honour committed by members of parliament was still in force, and had not been abrogated by *National Constituent Assembly Internal Rules.* The Chamber of Deputies, however, could suspend the course of the criminal action.[73]

The second case is a *Writ of Mandamus* sued by a journalist, allegedly in the

---

[70] RE 148304 MG; Marco Aurélio, J.; Jun 1994; DJ 12 May 1995, at page 12993.
[71] MS 1423/51 DF; Jun 1951; DJ 14 Jun 1951, at page 5287.
[72] Gomes, *op. cit.,* at pages 210/211.
[73] Inquérito Policial 273-RJ (Criminal Inquiry); Sidney Sanches, J. RTJ 134-2/501.

position of chairman of a political party, aiming at excluding from taking part on constitutional debates and activities - thus denying to them the condition of constituents - Senators who had been elected in 1982 general elections, for a 8 eight years mandate, and had not been specifically voted for being a constituent. [In 1986 only 2/3 of the Senators had their mandate renewed].

At the inaugural session of the *National Constituent Assembly,* which was chaired by the *Chief Justice of the Supreme Court*, it had been decided that those Senators could take part in all activities, on an equal basis as the other 2/3 members of the Senators could.

The Court did not decide on the merit. The Court found that the plaintiff did not substantiate his condition of chairman of a political party. The case had to be heard taking into account his individual capacity as a journalist. And there was no individual right in dispute. Thus, he had no standing for such a claim. The petition was dismissed.[74] And all Senators could take part in the constituent activities on an equal basis.

On the other hand, an illustration of the political role of the Court is the decision on MS 21.564/92 DF, concerning the 1992 impeachment process of President Collor de Mello. The issue involved the discussion upon the reception, by the constitution, of article 23 of the 1079 Act 1950.

Constitutional Amendment 4 of 1961, which introduced changes to the 1946 Constitution, instituted a parliamentary regime of government. Thus it abrogated crimes of responsibility committed by a President. Nevertheless, Constitutional Amendment 6, of 1963, repealed Constitutional Amendment 4, restoring the presidential regime instituted by 1946 Constitution. The issue was: being restored the presidential regime, the 1079 Act 1950, which laid down crimes of responsibility would be in force again? If the Supreme Court said 'no', there would be no impeachment process. But the Court said 'yes', considering that all the presidential regime was restored, with express representation of the whole system. Implicitly, 1079 Act 1950, which was a norm that was required to compound such regime.[75]

On the other hand, Supreme Court decisions on constitutionality control has often led to resort to constitutional amendment proposals. Although it is out of the scope of this work to bring in depth the impact of those decisions, some may just be referred, as obvious references.

The decision on the direct action of unconstitutionality *ADIMC 353-DF* gave room to Constitutional Amendment 4. The Court had to decide on the constitutionality of a Complementary Act, 64/1990, which introduced ineligibility situations. It was contended that the law could not be enforced on the 1990 election, as article 16 of the constitution required a law to be in force one year prior to being introduced an alteration to the electoral process. The Court held that it was still opened to the Supreme Court to define the meaning of 'electoral process' and its

---

[74] MS 20.692-DF; Aldir Passarinho, J. RTJ 127/451.
[75] MS 21.564/92 DF; Carlos Velloso, J.; Sep 1993; in [1995] *Impeachment.* Brasília: Imprensa Nacional at page 104.

reaching effects. That particular case was dismissed on procedural rules. But Constitutional Amendment 4 changed article 16. The new wording states that 'the law that alters the electoral procedure shall come into force on the date of its publication, and shall not apply to the elections that take place within one year of it being in force'.

Constitutional Amendment 8 seems to be a response to a decision delivered on the direct action of unconstitutionality 432-DF. A regulation of the Ministry of Infra-Structure abrogated previous norms on telecommunications, ordering studies to be carried on, concerning privatisation of cellular mobile services, and other telecommunications services. The Court held that the act was not a norm as to be subject to abstract control of constitutionality. But it also anticipated that a prospective regulation, aiming at implementing such deregulation, and authorising private individuals or companies to explore telecommunications would be held to be unconstitutional, because of being violative of state monopoly.[76] Then constitutional amendment 8 was passed, braking State monopoly on that issue.

One can also mention that Constitutional Amendment 15, which changed article 18, paragraph 4, dealing with creation, merger and dismemberment of municipalities, is a reply to *ADIN 1034/TO* and *ADINMC 1262/TO*.[77]

Having said that the Executive and the Legislative have a due regard to the Supreme Court decisions, does not mean that there are not tensions between these branches of government. In fact, a very serious and worrisome tension is under process, involving constitutional changes on the role and prerogatives of the Judiciary as a whole. A ample reform of the Judiciary is being advocated, including the introduction of a mechanism to exercise an external control upon it. The contention is that the Judiciary controls the two other branches of government, but does not control itself, as no one does.

Another contention is that the Brazilian model of control of constitutionality, accommodating both a diffuse control with a concentrated control, is not very operative, producing stunning perplexity. Judges and Courts, holding competence to declare incidentally the unconstitutionality of any norm, often have been delivering conflicting opinions. And as higher Courts decisions do not have binding effects upon lower Courts, there is an overburden of cases upon the Supreme Court. In fact, according to the constitution only opinions delivered by the Supreme Court on declaratory actions of constitutionality have such binding effects. This lawsuit, which was introduced in Brazilian legal system by Constitution Amendment 3, to the 1988 Constitution, was itself challenged in its constitutionality. When the very first direct action of constitutionality was filed before the Supreme Court, a preliminary issued to be decided upon was that. And the Court held that Constitutional Amendment 3, as regard the introduction of declaratory action of constitutionality, was constitutional.[78]

---

[76] ADIN 432 - DF; Celso de Mello, J.; May 1991; RTJ 136-2/495.
[77] ADIN 1034/TO, DJ 15 Apr 1994, at page 8047; ADIMC 1262/TO, Sydney Sanches, J.; DJ 16 Jun 1995, at page 18214.
[78] ADC 1-1 DF; Moreira Alves, J.; June 1995. Lex JSTF 214/24.

As part of the political system, the Judiciary has to be opened to the required changes of the system, to make it be more operative. Also, to make tensions be solved, without ruptures. The smooth operation of a constitution is not the work of its wording alone. And, as Bradley says, if a written document has no greater force than that which persons in authority are willing to attribute to it, the Judicial Power, the most authorised to express the constitutional will, must stay attuned.[79]

---

[79] Bradley, *op. cit.*, at page 5.

# ANNEX I

# TABLE OF AMENDMENTS TO THE 1988 CONSTITUTION

| Amendment | Articles Modified | Content of Change |
|---|---|---|
| 1/92<br>Mar 92 | 27 and 29 | Limiting the remuneration of the State Deputies and Councilmen |
| 2/92<br>Aug 92 | 2 of the Temporary Constitutional Provisions Act TCPA | Defining rules for the plebiscite on form (Republic or Monarchy) and system of government (Presidential or Parliamentary) |
| 3/93<br>Mar 93 | 40, 42, 102, 103, 150, 155, 156, 160, 167, | Rules of retirement of civil servants, and servicemen; institution of declaratory action of constitutionality and its initiative; rules for tax exemption; states competence to institute taxes on transfer by death and donation; municipal taxation; tax revenue sharing and remittance; budget and bound tax revenues. |
| 4/93<br>Sep 93 | 16 | Legal time delay to alter the electoral process |
| RCA 1/94<br>Mar 94 | 71, 72 and 73 of the TCPA (inclusion) | Institution of an emergency social fund, aiming at the recuperation of the Federal Public Finances and the economic stabilisation, and to fund health, education and welfare benefits and welfare assistance systems |
| RCA 2/94<br>Jun 94 | 50 | Enlarges the Congress power to summon or to forward written requests for information to any Minister of State or any chief officers of agencies directly subordinate to the Presidency of the Republic to personally render information |
| RCA 3/94<br>Jun 94 | 12 | Nationality by birth and by naturalisation |
| RCA 4/94<br>Jun 94 | 14 | Political rights; new bases for ineligibility |
| RCA 5/94<br>Jun 94 | 82 | Reduction of presidential term of office from 5 to 4 years |
| RCA 6/94<br>Jun 94 | 55 | Resignation of a Congressman and its effects when in course a lawsuit aimed at loss of mandate |
| 5/95<br>Aug 95 | 25 | States power to operate the local services of piped gas |
| 6/95<br>Aug 95 | 170, 176, 246 (inclusion) | Preferential treatment for small Brazilian enterprises; prospecting and mining of mineral resources; prohibition of adoption of "provisional measures" to regulate enforcement of constitutional amendments passed by Congress after 1995 |
| 7/95<br>Aug 95 | 178 | Regulation of air, ocean and land transportation |
| 8/95<br>Aug 95 | 21, XI | Power of the Union to operate the telephone, telegraph and data transmission services; the services of sound |

|  |  |  | broadcasting and of sound and image, excluding other telecommunications services |
|---|---|---|---|
| 9/95 Nov 95 |  | 177 | Exercising its monopoly on prospecting and exploitation of deposits of petroleum, the Union is allowed to hire public or private corporations |
| 10/96 Mar 96 |  | 71 and 72 of the TCPA | Institution of an emergency social fund, to face financial imbalance, and to fund health, education and social security systems |
| 11/96 May 96 |  | 207 | Allowing universities to hire foreign lecturers, technicians, and scientists |
| 12/96 Aug 96 |  | 74 TCPA (inclusion) | Empowers the Union to institute provisory contribution on transmission and movement of financial assets, credits and rights |
| 13/96 Aug 96 |  | 192 | National financial system; regulation of insurance and re-insurance |
| 14/96 Sep 96 |  | 34, 208, 211, 212; and 60 of the TCPA | To ensure compliance with the required minimum application of tax revenues in education is introduced as a reason to federal intervention; compulsory and free elementary school, and progressive universalization of free secondary school; introduction of a national education quality standard; re-definition of the role of States and municipalities in matters of education; creation of an educational fund |
| 15/96 Sep 96 |  | 18 | Establishment, merger, fusion and dismemberment of municipalities |
| 16/97 Jun 97 |  | 14, 28, 29, 77, 82 | Allows Presidents, Governors, and Mayors to run for a re-election |
| 17/97 Nov 97 |  | 71, 72 of the Temporary Constitutional Provisions Act TCPA | Extends the deadline of validity of the Emergency Social Fund, set forth by Constitutional Amendment 10, of March 1996, and increases the rate of contribution. |
| 18/98 Feb 98 |  | 37, 42, 61, 142 | Public servants and armed forces servicemen guarantees and wages |
| 19/98 Jun 98 |  | 21, 22, 27, 28, 29, 37, 38, 39, 41, 48, 51, 52, 57, 70, 93, 95, 96, 127, 128, 132, 135, 144, 167, 169, 173, 206, 241, 247 (includes) | *The Administrative Reform.*<br><br>"Flexibilizes" constitutional norms of recruitment and dismissal of tenured civil servants; allows managerial, budgetary and financial autonomy to be granted to agencies, based on goals and performance assessment. |
| 20/98 Dec 98 |  | 7, 37, 40, 42, 73, 93, 100, 114, 142, 167, 194, 195, 202, 248, 249, 250, | *The Social Security Reform.*<br><br>Requirements of age and years of service are expanded, in order to get retirement; pension values are limited. |
| 21/99 Mar 99 |  | 75 TCPA (inclusion) | Extends the term of validity of the provisory contribution on transmission and movement of financial assets, credits and rights, and increases its rate. |

| | | |
|---|---|---|
| 22/99<br>Mar 99 | 98, 102, I, 105, I,c, | Creation of special court of civil suits of lesser complexity and criminal offences of lower offensive potential, in the Federal Justice; redefines competence of the Supreme Court and the Superior Court of Justice to trial habeas corpus |
| 23/99<br>Sep 99 | 12,VII, 84, XIII, 91, V, VIII, 102, I, 105, I | Adapts constitutional provisions to introduce powers granted to the newly created Ministry of Defence |
| 24 99<br>Dec 99 | 111, 112, 113, 115, 116 | Introduces changes to the composition of labour courts, extinguishing temporary judges, which represented professional categories |
| 25 2000<br>Feb 2000 | 29, VI; includes 29-A | Deals with subsidies for Councilmen, defining criteria to the applied, according to the size of the municipality, and imposes limits of expenses |
| 26 2000<br>Feb 2000 | 6 | Includes right to housing as a fundamental right |
| 27 2000<br>Mar 2000 | 76 TCPA (inclusion) | Asserts that, from 2000 to 2003, 20% of the collection of all taxes already instituted, or to be instituted, are not bound to any agency, fund or expense. |

84  THE CREATION AND AMENDMENT OF CONSTITUTIONAL NORMS

| State Member | Initiative | | | | Immutability clause (tending to abolish...) | | | | | Circumstantial entrenchment | | | Quorum requirement and time delay | | |
|---|---|---|---|---|---|---|---|---|---|---|---|---|---|---|---|
| | Governor | State Deputies | Local Councils | Citizens (electorate) | Federation membership | Direct, secret, periodic vote | Separation of powers | Individual rights and guarantees | Federal intervention | State of defence | State of siege | Two rounds | Legislative session delay for rejected or impaired amendment proposal | Majority required |
| Acre | Y | 1/3 | No | Y | No | No | No | No | Y | Y | Y | Y | Y | 3/5 majority |
| Alagoas | Y | 1/3 | >half | 1% | No | No | No | No | Y | Y | Y | Y | Y | 3/5 majority |
| Amazonas | Y | 1/3 | >half | 5% | No | No | No | No | Y | Y | Y | Y | Y | 3/5 majority |
| Bahia | Y | 1/3 | >half | 1% | No | Y | Y | No | Y | Y | Y | Y | Y | 3/5 majority |
| Ceará | Y | 1/3 | >half | 1% | local autonomy | No | No | No | Y | Y | Y | Y | Y | 3/5 majority |
| Espírito Santo | Y | 1/3 | 1/3 | Y | No | No | No | No | Y | Y | Y | Y | Y | 3/5 majority |
| Goiás | Y | 1/3 | >half | 1% | Y | Y | Y | Y | Y | Y | Y | Y | Y | absolute majority |
| Maranhão | Y | 1/3 | >half | No | No | No | No | No | Y | Y | Y | Y | Y | 3/5 majority |
| Mato Grosso | Y | 1/3 | >half | No | Y | Y | Y | Y | Y | Y | Y | Y | Y | 3/5 majority |
| Mato Grosso do Sul | Y | 1/3 | >half | No | Y | Y | Y | Y | Y | Y | Y | Y | Y | 2/3 majority |
| Minas Gerais | Y | 1/3 | >half | No | No | No | No | No | Y | Y | Y | Y | Y | 3/5 majority |

# THE CREATION AND AMENDING PROCESS IN THE BRAZILIAN CONSTITUTION

| State Member | Governor | State Deputies | Local Councils | Citizens (electorate) | Federation membership | Direct, secret, periodic vote | Separation of powers | Individual rights and guarantees | Federal intervention | State of defence | State of siege | Two rounds | Legislative session delay for rejected or impaired amendment proposal | Majority required |
|---|---|---|---|---|---|---|---|---|---|---|---|---|---|---|
| Pará | Y, and the High Court of Justice | 1/3 | >half | Y | Y | Y | Y | Y | Y | Y | Y | Y | Y | 3/5 majority |
| Paraíba | Y | 1/3 | No | No | Y | Y | Y | Y | Y | Y | Y | Y | Y | 3/5 majority |
| Paraná | Y | 1/3 | 1/3 | No | No | No | No | No | Y | Y | Y | Y | Y | 3/5 majority |
| Pernambuco | Y | 1/3 | >half | 1% | No | No | No | No | Y | Y | Y | Y | Y | 3/5 majority |
| Piauí | Y | 1/3 | 1/3 | No | No | No | No | No | No | No | No | No | No | 3/5 majority |
| Rio de Janeiro | Y | 1/3 | >half | No | No | No | No | No | Y | Y | Y | Y | Y | 3/5 majority |
| Rio Grande do Norte | Y | 1/3 | No | No | Y | Y | Y | Y | Y | Y | Y | Y | Y | 3/5 majority |
| Rio Grande do Sul | Y | 1/3 | >1/5 | Y | No | No | No | No | Y | Y | Y | Y | Y | 3/5 majority |
| Rondônia | Y | 1/3 | >half | No | No | No | No | No | Y | Y | Y | Y | Y | 2/3 majority |
| Santa Catarina | Y | 1/3 | >half | 2,5% | Y | No | Y | No | Y | Y | Y | Y | Y | 3/5 majority |
| São Paulo | Y | 1/3 | >1/3 | 1% | No | No | No | No | No | Y | Y | Y | Y | 3/5 majority |

86   THE CREATION AND AMENDMENT OF CONSTITUTIONAL NORMS

| State Member | Governor | State Deputies | Local Councils | Citizens (electorate) | Federation membership | Direct, secret, periodic vote | Separation of powers | Individual rights and guarantees | Federal intervention | State of defence | State of siege | Two rounds | Legislative session delay for rejected or impaired amendment proposal | Majority required |
|---|---|---|---|---|---|---|---|---|---|---|---|---|---|---|
| Sergipe | Y | 1/3 | > half | 1% | No | No | No | No | Y | Y | Y | Y | Y | 3/5 majority |
| Tocantins | Y | 1/3 | 60% | No | No | No | No | No | Y | Y | Y | Y | Y | 2/3 majority |

Chapter Five

# THE ONGOING SEARCH FOR AN ACCEPTABLE AMENDING FORMULA IN CANADA

Christopher Ram[*]

## I. INTRODUCTION

In recent years, attempts by Canadians to restructure their constitution have begun to attract attention from abroad. The near-victory of the pro-sovereignty 'yes' side in the 30 October 1995 referendum on the secession of Quebec from Canada gained world-wide media coverage, prompting people around the world to voice their surprise that citizens of a country with an established constitution and a well-developed, stable political and economic structure would seriously contemplate such radical changes.

Canadians themselves were surprised at the closeness of the referendum result, but the national debate on fundamental constitutional issues itself came as neither a surprise nor a novelty. Nor is the status of Quebec the only major constitutional subject currently in issue in Canada. As will be seen in this chapter, Canada is faced with the challenge of balancing between its past and its future, and between major pressures for constitutional change based on historical, language, ethno-cultural, regional and aboriginal criteria. Quebec federalists seek constitutional status which will protect their language and culture and Quebec's historical position as a founding element of Canada, while sovereignists seek autonomy to the point of complete secession. Individually, the various regions and provinces seek a satisfactory balance of political power and influence among themselves. Collectively they seek a balance between themselves and Quebec, and between themselves and the federal government, taking into account population, geographical, economic and other pressures. Canada's aboriginal population seeks greater constitutional status, particularly with respect to constitutional amendments and self-government powers, as well as the redress of its historical grievances over land-claims and other matters. In addition to these areas of substantive debate, the

---

[*] The author is employed as legal counsel by the Canadian Federal Justice Department (on leave). Any opinions or conclusions herein reflect the views of the author and are not necessarily those of the Department or of any government of Canada, past or present. The author wishes to thank Messrs. Padraic Taylor and Stephen Zaluski for their advice and assistance.

complexity of the agenda for constitutional discussions and the competition among various interests for priority and bargaining power has itself become a major factor in the process.

Issues going to the very foundation of Canadian federalism have been unresolved since the first constitution of 1867 was adopted. Many of these same issues have generated open and often intense public debate since the 1970s, when reform pressures leading to the 1982 constitutional reforms began to gain momentum. Canada's major population groups - the Anglophone majority, Francophone minority, and more recently, aboriginal peoples have been competing for constitutional influence for much of this period. At the same time, a second layer of debate has developed among the various provinces and between the provinces as a group and the federal government. The intensity of these debates and the inability of participants to achieve consensus in support of a new model of Canadian federalism led to a state of what has been described as 'constitutional fatigue' for much of the 1990s. The present governments of Canada and most provinces have taken the position that restructuring by non-constitutional means is needed to relieve pressures while allowing passions to cool, concerns to be addressed and consensus to be built, before formal constitutional changes will become possible.

The potential secession of Quebec is clearly a major constitutional concern for all Canadians and has raised some eyebrows among Canada's allies and trading partners, but it is important that it be kept in perspective. To some degree, the fact that such matters can be discussed openly in Canada attests to the strength of its constitution and fundamental political and social values. Where the constitutions of many countries prohibit secession or the surrender of territory, the present Government of Canada takes the view that the norm in embodied in Canada's constitution is that '...our Canadian identity is too precious to be based on anything other than voluntary adherence.'[1] Faced with circumstances which in many countries would have led to armed conflict, Canadians have spent the years since the 1995 referendum addressing their various constitutional differences through legal and political means.

Constitutional issues have been kept very much alive by developments since October 1995. Quebec and the federal government continue to debate the legal, social and political consequences of sovereignty or secession options. A year after the referendum, the federal government referred questions relating to the constitutional and legal rules governing secession of Quebec to the Supreme Court of Canada, proceedings which were boycotted by Quebec. The Court found that

---

[1] *Who's Afraid of Clarity?*, brief of federal Intergovernmental Affairs Minister Stéphane Dion to the House of Commons Legislative Committee on Bill C-20, February 16, 2000, p.9. Available from the Government of Canada, Privy Council Office, or on-line at http://www.pco-bcp.gc.ca. See also the *Minutes of Proceedings and Evidence* of the Committee for February 16, 2000, available on-line at: www.parl.gc.ca/36/1/parlbus/commbus/house/CommitteeMinute.asp?Language=E&CommitteeID=116.

there would be a constitutional obligation to negotiate constitutional amendments to effect secession, but only after a clear expression of the desire to secede by the population of the province, a ruling promptly claimed as a victory by both sides. The federal government responded with legislation giving the federal House of Commons a mandate to review any further referendum questions to determine whether they were clear enough to give rise to an obligation to negotiate secession, to which Quebec in turn responded with legislation claiming exclusive powers over referenda for itself. During the same period, the nationalist government of Quebec was re-elected, but with an overall minority of votes cast and no mandate to hold further secession referenda in the forseeable future. Ministers and spokespersons, official and unofficial, maintained a vigorous (and continuing) debate in the public media throughout.

Aboriginal issues also remained prominent during this period. Significant progress towards meaningful aboriginal self-government was made with the conclusion of a modern treaty between the Nisga'a band of British Colombia and the federal and provincial governments dealing with both land-claims and government issues in 1998, but other aboriginal groups publicly renounced negotiations in favour of litigation. The social, political and constitutional implications of the Nisga'a agreement have drawn some controversy, but it is seen as progress by the three governments involved and most experts in aboriginal and constitutional matters. The constitutional interests of Quebec's aboriginal population, which wants no part of any proposal to secede, also remain a matter of significant controversy within the context of the larger question of Quebec's status.

The ongoing Canadian debate is about process as much as substance. Throughout much of the 20th Century, federal and provincial governments discussed a range of substantive constitutional proposals. In the decades prior to the 1982 'patriation' of the Constitution (by extinguishing the role of the U.K. Parliament), however, negotiations heated up, as various factions withheld their consent to changes until their own needs were met. For provinces, this represented a struggle for negotiating time and constitutional priority; for Canada's aboriginal people, it was a struggle simply for basic status in the negotiations and a seat at the table.

Underlying all of the substantive debates has been the fundamental question of the amending procedure. The amending formula is both substantive and procedural: it is about procedures for amending the constitution in the future, but also about what the constitution itself says about balancing of a complex network of interests and relationships within the Canadian federation. It has come to be seen by those involved as an indication of their present status and future prospects within the federation, and together with a few other key issues, as a lightning rod for public and political debate about constitutional reform. Participants regard the amending rules as crucial to achieving and protecting their interests and their status within Canadian federalism. Some fear that increased influence for others will lead to an erosion of their own. Many experts fear that rules which attempt to satisfy all of these pressures will ultimately result in a constitution which is virtually impossible to amend. The question of amending formulae lies at the very heart of the greater constitutional debate in Canada and is an essential key to understanding that debate and how it may be resolved in future. This chapter will examine the debate over how the Constitution of Canada should be amended: the origins of the debate, why it has become such a difficult problem for Canada, and where it may ultimately lead Canada and its constitution.

## II. HISTORICAL AND CONSTITUTIONAL BACKGROUND: 1867-1982

The modern-day population of Canada includes immigrants and descendants of immigrants from almost every part of the world, but three major groups have significant constitutional status as a result of the country's immigration history prior to Confederation.[2] The three main groups are aboriginal peoples, Francophones and Anglophones. The population was entirely aboriginal until a period of colonisation by the French in the 16th Century[3] followed by an influx of Anglophone immigrants from the British Isles and United States. Most Francophones live in what is now Quebec and the adjoining regions of Eastern Ontario and the Atlantic provinces. Aboriginal Canadians are distributed throughout the country, some interspersed in the populations of large communities, others in smaller, predominantly aboriginal reserves.

Most of the residents of Canada's northern regions are aboriginal or have significant aboriginal ancestry.

The majority of Canadians are Anglophone but no longer of exclusively British origin. Immigrants from almost every part of the world and their descendants can be found in Canada's present population, a fact which has added multiculturalism and minority-rights issues to the constitutional agenda.

Politically, the country is now a federation of ten provinces and three northern regions, the Yukon and Northwest Territories and Nunavut, the last created by Act of Parliament on April 1, 1999. Provincial populations vary widely, the number of inhabitants ranging in size from 136,000 (Prince Edward Island) to about 11.1 million (Ontario). Provinces are governed by their own autonomous legislative assemblies within a federal constitution which allocates legislative powers between the two federal and provincial legislatures. The three territories have limited self-government, including elected assemblies, created by federal statute.

---

[2] Canadians generally refer to 'confederation', and the term will be used in this paper, but Canada is not a confederation in the conventional sense. In a true confederation, national government is subordinate to those of the provinces, as was the case with the original 1777 union of the United States. The legislatures of Canada and its provinces are equal and autonomous within defined constitutional spheres. Thus Canada, in modern terms, is more properly regarded as a federation.

[3] For a breakdown of the various groups, see Statistics Canada, *Canada Yearbook 1997*, p.33 and tables 3.15-3.17, pp.88-90.

Canada shares constitutional history and convention and many of its political and legislative practices with the United Kingdom, but in many ways, it is constitutionally quite different. Where the British constitution has been described as 'indeterminate, indistinct and unentrenched,'[4] Canada's constitution has always been at least partly codified, first as an enactment of Westminster in 1867 and later as an autonomous constitution,[5] and has always been justiciable. The federal Parliament is based on the Westminster model and incorporates many of the procedures and conventions of that body, including government by a cabinet which must enjoy the confidence of the House of Commons, which is in turn responsible to voters in a 'first past the post' constituency system. As in the UK, loss of confidence results in either the replacement of the government by the House, or replacement of the House itself in a federal election. The Upper House, the Senate, is based on the House of Lords, but members are appointed and serve until age 75; seats are not inherited. Both levels of government recognise the British sovereign as the constitutional monarch of Canada.[6]

The constitutional history of Canada between 1867 and 1982 reflects a gradual transfer of sovereignty from the UK. As the federation expanded from the original four members to ten provinces and two territories, control of economic, legal, political and constitutional powers gradually devolved from Westminster to Ottawa and the provinces. A major function of the original enactment, the British North America Act 1867,[7] was to allocate legislative powers and generally structure the relationship between the federal and provincial orders of government. There have been a few formal amendments to the division of powers provisions, but the primary mechanism of adjustment has been judicial interpretation.

The BNA Act remained an Act of Westminster and amendable as such until 1982. The substantive role of Westminster effectively ended with the Imperial Conferences of 1926-31, in which Britain responded to the concerns of Dominion governments by adopting a constitutional convention that Westminster would not make laws affecting the dominions without their request and consent, followed by the 1931 Statute of Westminster, providing that ordinary acts of the English

---

[4] Finer, Bogdanor, and Rudden, 1995, pp.40-43.
[5] On the question of whether Canada's modern constitution is fully autonomous, see Hogg, 1997, ch. 3.5 at pp.55-60.
[6] The Queen is the Head of State, but by convention governs on the advice of HM Privy Council for Canada. Functions of the Head of State in Canada are carried out by a Governor-General, also appointed by the Queen on advice. Comments about the U.K. House of Lords pre-date the 1999-2000 reforms, which were still in progress at the time of writing.
[7] UK 30 & 31 Vict. c.3. This Act, commonly referred to in Canada as the 'BNA Act', remains in force but was re-named the Constitution Act 1867 as part of the 1982 constitutional reforms. It now operates in Canada as part of the Schedule to the Constitution Act, 1982. The division of powers provisions are in Part VI (ss.91-95) of the 1867 Act.

Parliament did not apply elsewhere unless so specified.[8]

Basic rights were not entrenched or justiciable as part of the Constitution until the inclusion of the Canadian Charter of Rights and Freedoms in 1982, but other elements of the constitution have always been justiciable and superior to ordinary laws. Federalism requires a third party to arbitrate with respect to the jurisdictions of two semi-sovereign levels of government, and Canadian courts have always had the power to strike down legislation as *ultra vires* of the enacting legislature in disputes between the federal and provincial levels. This included appeals to the Judicial Committee of the Privy Council until 1949, and early House of Lords decisions played a significant role in structuring Canadian federalism.[9] The role played by the UK in determining Canada's constitution through amendments and appeals to the Judicial Committee was increasingly regarded as an affront to Canadian sovereignty after 1930, as links to the UK grew attenuated and the population of Canada grew more cosmopolitan.[10]

Westminster's role in amending Canada's constitution represented a significant and growing problem for Canadian governments in terms of sovereignty, but it also served as a means of entrenchment, stabilising the constitutional law of Canada during that period. The fact that governments had to approach the Parliament of another country to ask for amendments did not always stop them from doing so, but it did keep the number of amendments to a minimum, and may have blocked a course of gradual constitutional evolution that might otherwise have taken place.[11] The situation was described by one writer as '...an affront to Canadian nationalism' and another as 'gradual embarrassment.'[12] At the end of the period, speaking in the debate on the introduction of what would eventually become the Constitution Act

---

[8] This raised concerns at the time about the supremacy of the UK Parliament, but in practical terms largely ended the legislative role of the UK in everyday Canadian affairs. See: Hogg, 1997, ch. 3.3, pp.50-53 and De Smith and Brazier, 1990, pp.76-78.

[9] House of Lords decisions are credited with a general shift of powers to the provinces during the first six decades of Confederation. See Hogg, 1997, ch.5.3 at pp. 118-120 and authorities there cited, including *Hodge v. the Queen* (1883) 9 App.Cas.117 (PC) and *Attorney General of Canada v. Attorney General of Ontario* [1937] AC 326 (PC). After an unsuccessful attempt to abolish criminal appeals to the Judicial Committee in 1888, Canada's Parliament successfully enacted such legislation after the 1930 Statute of Westminster. Legislation abolishing all appeals followed in 1939, but this was not itself held to be valid (by the Judicial Committee) until 1947. Abolition was not retroactive: the last appeal was heard in 1959, on a case which arose in 1949. See Hogg, 1997, ch. 5.3(c), 17.3(a), 8.2 and 17.4(a), and *Nadan v. The Queen* [1926] AC 482 (striking down abolition of criminal appeals), *British Coal Corp. v. The King* [1935] AC 500 (upholding abolition of criminal appeals), and *A-G of Ontario v. A.G. of Canada* [1947] AC 127 (upholding Supreme Court Act provision abolishing all appeals).

[10] See Scott, 1954 (1977 reprint) pp.142-56 at p.145.

[11] The Schedule to the Constitution Act 1982 now lists 29 amendments made between 1867 and 1975. Of these, 14 were made with or after the 1931 Statute of Westminster, including the consequential amendments implementing the Statute itself.

[12] Hogg, 1997, p.54, and Lederman, 1984, at pp.339-40, respectively. As Prof. Hogg points out, however, the power of Westminster to amend Canada's constitution was also necessary during this period, since there was no power for the federal and provincial legislatures of Canada to do so until one was created in 1982. Similar issues have arisen in the relationship between Australia, its states, and the UK See Zines, 1991, pp.15-18.

1982, Canada's Justice Minister said:

Once we have succeeded in bringing our constitution home with an amending formula, we will have created a mechanism to permit constitutional change as and when necessary. We will no longer have to hesitate because of the humiliation of having to go to London every time we want to change our constitution.[13]

While Canada's political leaders generally agreed that this situation was unsatisfactory, it continued for five decades, largely because they were never successful in arriving at a completely Canadian amending process. Attempts were made in 1927, 1935-36, 1950, 1960-61, 1964, 1968-71, 1975-76, 1978-79, 1980 and 1981, and were nearly successful in 1964 and 1971, but were ultimately frustrated by the inability to reconcile issues raised between the federal and provincial levels and between Quebec and the rest of Canada as a group.[14] Each of the federal and provincial governments sought substantive changes and an amending formula which were consistent with its own views on federal structure and balance, but the various views could not be reconciled or compromised. Aboriginal people as a distinct group were not a significant part of the process until very end of this period, during the proceedings leading to the adoption of the 1982 constitution. At about this time, the question of adopting a constitutional bill of rights also arose, and this too became an obstacle. While the provinces were not philosophically opposed to basic rights, the proposal to make what would later become the Canadian Charter of Rights and Freedoms both justiciable and superior to ordinary federal or provincial enactments was opposed by the provinces, and particularly Quebec, as a potential erosion of their powers.

By the mid-1970s, the adoption of a fully-Canadian constitution had become a major goal of the Liberal government of Pierre Elliott Trudeau (1968-84).[15] After several failed attempts to arrive at a satisfactory package, the government decided to force the issue. It introduced a resolution in the Canadian House of Commons on 6 October 1980 calling on Westminster to amend the British North America Act without provincial consent, based on the amending formula which had thus far come the closest to a negotiated agreement. This was seen as a way of breaking the deadlock by imposing a temporary amending formula on the provinces in order to remove amendment rules as an obstacle to agreement on other substantive issues, but it re-opened the long dormant question of whether or not the provinces had any role in formal amendment and if so, what it was.

---

[13] House of Commons Debates, 6 October 1980, pp.3283.
[14] Government of Canada, Federal-Provincial Relations Office, *Amending the Constitution of Canada: A Discussion Paper*, FPRO, Ottawa, December 1990, pp.3-4.
[15] A great deal has been written about the period leading up to the 1982 constitutional reforms. See, for example, Lederman, 1982 and 1984, Hogg, 1997, ch.3-4, Russell, 1992, ch. 8, Sabetti, 1982, Scott, S.A., 1982, and Cairns, A. 'The Politics of Constitutional Renewal in Canada', in Cairns, 1991, pp.66-107.

The resolution was vigorously resisted in Parliament, and debates continued in parallel with further talks with the provinces.[16] When the federal government nonetheless proceeded, several provinces brought references in their courts of appeal asking whether this was constitutional. The appeals which resulted were eventually decided by the Supreme Court of Canada. It ruled, in a landmark 1981 decision, that while convention required a 'substantial degree' of provincial concurrence before an amendment could be placed before Westminster, there was no conventional requirement that every province consent, and no legal requirement of any kind.[17] Quebec, which contended that it had always had a veto over amendment proposals, then brought a further reference asking whether the Supreme Court's 'substantial degree' of provincial support necessarily included the approval of Quebec, a proposition which, on appeal, the Court also rejected.[18]

The rulings broke the long-standing deadlock and negotiations resumed on a fresh footing. At the end of a federal-provincial meeting between 2-5 November 1981, nine of the ten provinces reached agreement on a package which included a compromise amending formula, the Canadian Charter of Rights and Freedoms, and the original 1867 provisions governing federal and provincial legislative powers. The federal government had succeeded in producing the substantial degree of consent the Supreme Court had said was required, but only after making several major concessions. A provision in the original package which would have allowed the use of popular referendums on amendments as an alternative to ratification by provincial legislatures was dropped, and a 'notwithstanding' provision allowing legislatures to temporarily exempt specific enactments from certain Charter provisions was added. Quebec was the sole dissenter, but after the Supreme Court ruling, the process went forward without it.

Quebec's failure to agree to the reform package remains a matter of some controversy. The provincial government at the time was composed of the sovereignist Parti Québécois, and federalists have claimed that its leader, René Levesque, would not have agreed to any measure which would have led to a viable federal constitution and thereby made Quebec independence less likely.[19] This may

---

[16] See Manfredi, 1996, at pp.42-43 and *Amending the Constitution of Canada: A Discussion Paper*, FPRO, Ottawa, December 1990, pp.3-7.

[17] *Re Resolution to Amend the Constitution* [1981] 1 SCR 753, 120 DLR (3d) 1 (SCC). The judgment is unusual in that it runs contrary to Dicey's view that conventions were not legal rules and were therefore not justiciable. It also combines English, Imperial and Canadian conventions. A great deal, some of it critical of the Court's use of conventions, has been written about the case. See, for example Hogg, 1997, ch.1.10(b) and 4 and 1992B, pp.253-60, Lederman, 1982 and 1984, and Sabetti, 1982.

[18] *Re: Objection by Quebec to Resolution to Amend the Constitution* [1982] 2 SCR 793. See also Lederman, 1982, Petter, 1984, and Russell, 1992, pp.127-30.

[19] For the federalist version of this argument, see Pierre Elliott Trudeau: 'J'Accuse', *Montreal Gazette*, Saturday February 3, 1996. Trudeau, who oversaw the 1982 process as Prime Minister, argues that the Parti Québécois government of Quebec deliberately misrepresented the events of 1982 in its 1995 referendum campaign. Trudeau's version has been supported by other provincial premiers who took part. Premier Levesque, who would possibly have disagreed, has since died.

be partly accurate, but the 1982 constitution has not been ratified by subsequent federalist Quebec governments, either. Levesque and his supporters have always claimed that he was been betrayed by the premiers of the other provinces in the final stages of negotiations, in what sovereignists still refer to as '..the night of the long knives'.[20] The view that Quebec was the victim of a constitution imposed on it against its will has been re-stated on many occasions since by sovereignists, and remains the position of the present government of the province.[21] Whatever the truth, it is clear that a major obstacle to Quebec's concurrence in 1982 and subsequently, is the amending formula, and in particular what it considered the loss of its veto over future amendments.

The new constitution was formally adopted as a resolution by Canada's Parliament and subsequently, upon request, enacted by Westminster as the Canada Act 1982.[22] The Act itself contains only a preamble and four sections, providing for the interpretive equality for the French and English texts, citation, the effect of schedules, and extinguishing the powers of Westminster by providing that no future act of that body would extend to Canada. Most of the substantive content is found in the schedules, which were produced in Canada and transmitted to Westminster. These contain the original British North America Act, as amended,[23] and the Canadian Constitution Act 1982, which itself contains the Canadian Charter of Rights and Freedoms. Thus the post-1982 constitution was in fact produced in Canada, but was and remains an enactment of the legislature of the United Kingdom. The Canada Act package was formally proclaimed by Queen Elizabeth II (as Head of State of Canada) in Ottawa on 17 April 1982.

---

[20] See, for example, Fraser, G., 'Long Knives Hone Bouchard's Message: Vision of Betrayal by Other Provinces in 1981 Constitutional Deal Underpins Nationalist Narrative', *Canada Globe and Mail*, October 27, 1995, p.A8.

[21] For a summary of the sovereignist position on the events of 1982 and the position of the present government of Quebec, see 'The Parti Quebecois Government Sovereignty Plan', on-line at http://www.premier.gouv.qc.ca/projet/historia.htm.. See also Canada House of Commons Debates, 29 November 1995, pp.16971 *et seq*, which contains the final speech of Lucien Bouchard, the present Quebec Premier, shortly after the 1995 referendum, and just before he left the federal House of Commons to take up provincial office. More recently, the argument that the 1982 Constitution and its amending formula were imposed on Quebec and have no legitimacy there was raised by the province's Intergovernmental Affairs Minister in opposition to the 1999-2000 federal 'clarity' legislation, Bill C-20. See: Canada House of Commons, Legislative Committee on Bill C-20, *Minutes of Proceedings and Evidence*, appearance of the Hon. J. Facal, February 24, 2000 (meeting #10) available on-line at: www.parl.gc.ca/36/1/parlbus/commbus/house/CommitteeMinute.asp?Language=E&CommitteeID=116.

[22] UK, 1982, c.11.

[23] The original British North America Act was re-named the Constitution Act 1867. One of the major effects of retaining the old constitution as part of the new, was the retention of the federal-provincial allocation of legislative powers in ss.91 and 92, and with it, 115 years of case law from the Judicial Committee and Supreme Court. One change was made: s.92A, transferring some powers to deal with natural resources to the provinces, was added.

## III. 1982-1997: FAILED ATTEMPTS AT CONSTITUTIONAL RENEWAL

The 1984 general election ended the Trudeau era and saw the election of the Progressive Conservative Party headed by Brian Mulroney to two successive majority governments. Under the Conservative Government two attempts were made at constitutional reform, both unsuccessful. The first attempt, an agreement reached at Meech Lake, Quebec, in April 1987, initially met the approval of all eleven first ministers, but subsequently lapsed when not ratified by two of their legislatures by June 1990. The second attempt, an expanded package produced at Charlottetown, was overwhelmingly defeated in a national referendum held on 26 October 1992. The sovereignist Parti Québécois returned to power in Quebec in the following year, elected on a platform which committed it to the holding of a referendum on sovereignty during its first year in office. This was held on 30 October 1995, and won by the federalist side, but by a margin of only about 1.2 per cent of a vote in which over 95 per cent of eligible voters cast ballots.

### A. The 'Meech Lake Accord' of 1987-90[24]

As part of its commitment to constitutional renewal, the new Conservative government called a series of meetings between the Prime Minister and provincial premiers which produced an agreed package of constitutional changes at Meech Lake, Quebec, on 30 April 1987. Its signing on 3 June 1987 was an undertaking on the part of the federal government and the provincial leaders to submit resolutions to Parliament and the provincial legislatures as required to amend the Constitution.[25] The Accord centred on bringing Quebec into the constitution. It was based on the position taken by its federalist Premier, Robert Bourassa, since his election in 1985, with one exception: it contained a unanimous-approval requirement for some amendments, but not the sought-after Quebec veto. Major elements of the Accord included the following:[26]

- a constitutional amendment recognising Quebec as a 'distinct society' within Canada,[27]

---

[24] For a brief chronology, see 'Meech Lake Documents', 1992 at pp.147-55.
[25] The amending procedure is set out in detail at page109 below.
[26] For a detailed analysis of the proposed changes, see Hogg, 1988. The text of the Accord and other relevant information can also be found in 'Meech Lake Documents', 1992.
[27] Section numbers refer to the Proposed Constitutional Amendment 1987. The idea of Quebec as a 'distinct society' has proved a major point of contention, then and since. Quebec sought 'distinct society' status for both symbolic and interpretive reasons, to be used by the courts to consider the protection of its language and culture, especially in applying the Charter of Rights. Most other provinces were willing to acknowledge Quebec's distinctiveness in symbolic terms, but argued that the constitutional rules, and especially fundamental rights, should be universally and equally applied in all provinces. In an effort to reassure both sides, the government obtained a legal opinion, endorsed by six leading constitutional experts, to the effect that Charter rights would not be eroded. See 'Meech Lake

- a provincial role in appointing justices to the Supreme Court of Canada,[28]
- greater control for Quebec (or any other province) over immigration into the province,[29] and
- controls on the use of the federal spending power to limit federal influence over areas of exclusive provincial constitutional jurisdiction.[30]

The amending rules in the 1982 constitution prescribe different procedures depending on the nature of a proposed change, which made individual elements of the Meech Lake package subject to different amending requirements. Some changes required ratification by all provinces, and others required ratification by a specified number of provinces within three years. The elements of the package may have been constitutionally distinct, but the extensive negotiations leading to the Accord meant that all of its elements were politically linked: the failure of an element supported by any one province would have caused it to withdraw support for other elements. This combination of politics and the entrenched amending formula effectively made the package an all-or-nothing agreement, subject to the highest procedural amending requirements for each of its elements. The time period began soon after the Accord was signed, when Quebec became the first provincial legislature to ratify it on 23 June 1987. From this point, the Accord could only succeed if approved within three years by all eleven legislatures.[31]

All provincial premiers initially supported the Accord, but during the ratification period, elections changed governments in several provinces, and grass-roots political opposition mounted. Interest groups opposed specific elements of the package, and the entire Accord was attacked as a product of 'executive federalism', in which most of the negotiations had taken place between first ministers behind closed doors. Three weeks before time ran out, in an attempt to obtain support from hold-out provinces, another, supplementary agreement was reached (in marathon negotiations) to the effect that the parties would assemble by the end of 1990 to

---

Documents' 1992, at pp.192-93.

[28] S.6. This would have made two changes. It proposed to constitutionally entrench the existing statutory requirement that at least three of the nine justices be appointed from the Quebec Bar, ensuring a civil law background and French-language ability. It would also have given the provinces a role in appointments by requiring the federal government to choose justices from lists of candidates prepared by the provinces.

[29] S.3. Immigration controls would also have required changes to subsection 91(25) of the Constitution Act 1867, which gives the federal government exclusive jurisdiction over 'naturalization and aliens'.

[30] Ss. 7, 9. These would have required the federal government to pay compensation to any province which opted out of any new national programme funded by the federal government, if that programme involved a matter of exclusive provincial legislative jurisdiction under the constitution.

[31] See Hawkins, 1989.

consider western proposals for a 'Triple E' Senate.[32] In Manitoba, a last-minute attempt at ratification was blocked by a single aboriginal member of that province's assembly, who refused the unanimous consent needed to introduce the measure on short notice. On learning of this development, Newfoundland, which had been reluctantly preparing a last-minute ratification resolution, declined to introduce it in the legislature. The Accord lapsed for want of ratification in these two provinces on 23 June 1990.

B. The Charlottetown Accord[33]

The failure of the Meech Lake Accord was widely attributed to the fact that it had been produced by first ministers who focussed on the need to bring Quebec into the constitution, but in so doing had excluded other issues and agendas and any real opportunity for broad-spectrum popular input or consensus-building.[34] The Mulroney government's second attempt sought to respond to these concerns by allowing for a more open process of formulation, including public deliberations by a joint House of Commons and Senate committee which conducted proceedings on-camera, rather than *in camera* and which heard witnesses from a variety of governmental and non-governmental interests. A series of 'Citizens Forums' were convened in regions across Canada to solicit input and discuss options. The resulting Charlottetown Accord included measures to secure constitutional ratification in Quebec, and added Senate reform to address western concerns, and proposals to address aboriginal concerns about self-government.

Major elements of the Charlottetown package included:

- a clause recognising Quebec as a 'distinct society' and a 'Canada clause' stating the fundamental characteristics of Canada,

- a guarantee that Quebec's representation in the House of Commons would not fall below 25 per cent of the seats,

- a recognition of the 'inherent right of self-government' for aboriginal Canadians,

- a shift of the federal-provincial power balance to a more devolved or decentralised federalism,

---

[32] The western provinces had sought to replace the Upper House with one more representative of regional interests. The 'Triple E' model was to be: chosen by *election*, having an *equal* number of Senators from each province, and *effective* in using its powers to balance those of the House of Commons.

[33] See Hogg, 1993. More detailed discussion can be found in McRoberts and Monahan, 1993, and Cook, 1994.

[34] Almost every author who has written about the Accord has made this observation. See: Bakan and Pinard, 1989, at pp.247-50, Johnson, 1994, at pp.511-16, Schwartz, 1987, at pp.1-3 and Swinton, 1992.

- entrenchment of provisions concerning the Supreme Court of Canada,
- a 'Triple E' Senate,
- a non-justiciable social and economic union committing the federal and provincial governments to basic policy objectives, and
- replacement of much of the 1982 amending procedures with a rule that would require ratification of most proposed amendments by both Parliament and all of the provincial legislatures.

Politically, the failure of the Charlottetown Accord can be ascribed to a number of different factors. In seeking a comprehensive package, the drafters had managed to include something for everyone, but also something to which almost everyone objected. Those who supported a strong central government objected to decentralisation. Quebeckers felt it did too little in securing the place of Quebec within the federation and future constitution-making. Constitutional experts argued that the proposed amending formula was too rigid and would make future constitutional change almost impossible. Quebec had already enacted provincial legislation requiring that a provincial referendum be held on any new federal proposals, or if none were forthcoming, on secession. In an attempt to salvage the agreement, the federal government moved to hold a national referendum in the rest of Canada at the same time as Quebec.[35] The referendum was held on 26 October 1992, and lost decisively, 54.4 per cent to 44.6 per cent. Regionally, it was rejected by Quebec, the western provinces, and among aboriginal people, with Ontario voting only 50.1 per cent in support.

## IV. THE 1995 QUEBEC REFERENDUM AND ONGOING CONSTITUTIONAL DEVELOPMENTS

The failure of two successive attempts at constitutional change significantly altered the Canadian political landscape. A year after the national referendum, a federal election (October 1993) reduced the federal Conservative Party from a position of majority government to only two of the 301 seats in the federal House of Commons, elected a strong Liberal majority government and produced an opposition almost exactly split between western conservatives and sovereignist Quebeckers. Non-constitutional political developments contributed to this change, but the interplay of various constitutional issues and the failure of the incumbent government to deliver its proposed constitutional reforms were clearly a major factor. In the west, dissatisfaction with negotiations on the status of Quebec and

---

[35] For discussion, see below and Johnson, 1994. See also *Haig v. Canada (Chief Electoral Officer)* [1993] 2 SCR 995, 105 DLR (4th) 577 (SCC) ruling on voting rights and discrepancies between Quebec and federal voting laws.

the failure of reforms to the Senate of Canada contributed to the development of the Reform Party. In the western provinces of Manitoba, Alberta, Saskatchewan and British Colombia, the new party drew support from both the right and the left and took most of the Parliamentary seats. It did not attract sufficient support in central and eastern Canada to capture seats there because of its association with western grievances and the fact that its policies were too far to the political right, but the support it did attract split the traditional right-wing vote, electing candidates from the Liberal Party in many constituencies. In Quebec, the support of the Conservatives had been based on a coalition of political conservatives and moderate nationalists. The latter abandoned Conservative candidates in favour of another new party, the Bloc Quebecois, created to represent sovereignist interests in Ottawa. With the combined support of moderate and extreme nationalists and other Quebeckers discouraged by the lack of constitutional progress and perceived rejection of Quebec's constitutional and other aspirations within Canada, the Bloc captured most of the constituencies in Quebec.

In September of 1994 the sovereignist Parti Quebecois, drawing increased support from the same sources, was elected as the new government of Quebec. On 30 October 1995, the new provincial government made good its campaign promise to hold a referendum on sovereignty within the first year of its mandate.[36] In choosing the wording of the referendum question, pragmatism won out over ideology: it did not ask for a direct mandate for outright secession, but for approval of secession should proposals for a restructured political and economic relationship with Canada fail:[37]

Do you agree that Québec should become sovereign, after having made a formal offer to Canada for a new Economic and Political Partnership, within the scope of a Bill respecting the future of Québec and of the agreement signed on 12 June 1995?

This was attacked by federalists as misleading and unclear. Subsequent developments suggest that the question and other conditions during the referendum campaign caused confusion among voters, although this is disputed by the Government of Quebec. Significant numbers of those who voted 'yes' appear to have believed that a 'sovereign' Quebec would remain a province of Canada and continue to elect members to the federal House of Commons, for example. Others read the question as an option offering voters elements of partnership between Quebec and Canada which could not have been provided by a sovereign Quebec and would not have been offered by Canada following any secession.[38] In some

---

[36] In actual fact, the election was held on 12 Sept. 1994, and the referendum on 30 October 1995.
[37] Motion of Quebec Premier Jacques Parizeau, Quebec National Assembly, 7 Sept. 1995.
[38] The question of clarity in future referenda arose during the subsequent Supreme Court reference on secession. Regarding the degree to which voters may have misunderstood key elements of the 1995 referendum question, see evidence of Prof. M. Pinard, Canada House of Commons, Legislative Committee on Bill C-20, *Minutes of Proceedings and Evidence* for February 24, 2000 (Meeting #10). Prof. Pinard cites confusion about the meaning of terms, particularly 'sovereignty', confusion about the

cases, the juxtaposition of elements dealing with secession and partnership may also have led to strategic voting, in the form of 'yes' votes from those who did not seek sovereignty, but thought that such a vote would strengthen Quebec's position in any negotiations on a renewed federal structure.[39]

A victory for the 'yes' side would have given control of subsequent negotiations to a provincial government committed to secession and could have been construed as a mandate for secession if those negotiations were unsuccessful.

Disclosures in the months following the referendum call into question the intention on the part of the Province's government, or at least some members thereof, to seriously negotiate within the Canadian federation prior to declaring an independent state.[40] The federalist 'no' side held a strong lead for much of the campaign, but this changed dramatically after the hard-line separatist Premier of Quebec, Jacques Parizeau, was replaced by the more moderate Lucien Bouchard as spokesperson for the 'yes' side late in the campaign. After furious last-minute efforts (and accusations of electoral misconduct) by both sides, the vote was won by the federalist 'no' side by only the narrowest of margins: over 96 per cent of eligible voters cast ballots, and the margin of victory was only 1.2 per cent of the total vote.

The close result raised serious concerns in Canada and abroad, but probably does not represent the degree of support for actual secession that many believe. It

---

nature of any partnership or relationship with Canada following a 'yes' vote, and confusion about the course of post-referendum negotiations as significant factors. Professors Monahan and Hogg, appearing before the same Committee (meetings #5 and 6, 21 and 22 February 2000, respectively) voice similar concerns. Both raise the lack of clarity as a factor eroding the legitimacy of any referendum result, particularly where the issue involves secession, a serious and irrevocable constitutional change. Prof. Hogg also points out that the question may have further confused some voters by offering elements of partnership (e.g. boundary guarantees, use of the Canadian currency etc.) between Quebec and Canada that were either inconsistent with political secession or sovereignty or were not within the powers of a sovereign Quebec and unlikely to be agreed to by Canada following secession. For its part, the Government of Quebec maintained that the high turnout in the vote and information disseminated during the campaign, including the message of federalists that a 'yes' vote meant irreversible change, meant that voters '...were perfectly aware of what was at stake.' For the Province and its sovereignists, any attempt by the federal Parliament to influence the conduct of future references in any way amounts to an interference with the political prerogative of Quebec. See evidence of the Hon. J. Facal, Quebec Minister of Intergovernmental Affairs (meeting #10, February 24, 2000).

All of the Committee's proceedings are available on-line at www.parl.gc.ca/36/1/parlbus/commbus/house/CommitteeMinute.asp?Language=E&Committee ID=116.

[39] One of Prof. Pinard's conclusions, based on his review of polling data, is that there were many more confused voters than strategic ones, since the latter were limited to a relatively small portion of the population which was both well-educated and politicised.

[40] See MacLauchlin, 1997 at pp.165-66 and sources there cited. The actions of then-Premier Jacques Parizeau and Deputy-Premier Bernard Landry suggest that a very quick unilateral secession would have been attempted. These were later repudiated by the more-moderate Lucien Bouchard, who assumed leadership of the 'yes' faction in mid-campaign and the leadership of the Parti Quebecois and Premiership of Quebec several months after the vote. The legal issues surrounding a unilateral declaration and the views of experts on the federalist and sovereignist sides are set out in Webber, 1997 and in the 1998 Supreme Court opinion in *Reference re: Secession of Quebec*.

seems clear that most Quebeckers want a constitutional structure which would give the province greater autonomy and protect its language and culture, but the result was limited as an indication of support for outright secession by the ambiguity of the question put to voters and the relatively moderate position taken by M. Bouchard in the late stages of the campaign. Generally, the support for Quebec nationalist options, of which complete secession is the most extreme, has been attributed to a combination of factors, including the fear of Quebeckers for the survival of their language and culture as distinct from that of the rest of Canada and Quebec's southern neighbour, the United States, confidence in the ability of Quebec to thrive as an independent country, and a sense of constitutional impasse or rejection of Quebec's constitutional and other aspirations by the rest of Canada.[41] These factors, and their perception in Quebec, remain in flux, and consequently, popular support for sovereignty depends not only on exactly what is on offer, but also on the social and political conditions which exist whenever the question is asked.

The immediate aftermath of the referendum was a *de-facto* moratorium on constitutional developments. Quebec's sovereignist government was constrained from quickly holding another vote by provincial referendum legislation[42] and the distaste of moderate nationalists, whose 'swing' vote is crucial to both sides, for another vote. For its part, the federal government initially decided to attempt to address the concerns of Quebec and the other provinces piecemeal and within the framework of the existing constitution, where possible, in what was termed a 're-balancing' of the Canadian federation. On 3 June 1997, a federal election returned the Liberal Party to power with a much smaller majority. The position of the governing Liberals remained that formal constitutional change was desirable, but should not be attempted until it was clear that sufficient popular consensus had developed in support of both the need for change and the substance of the changes themselves.

In the interim, the government proposed to achieve as much as possible by non-constitutional means. Between 1997 and 1999 this approach included the transfer of funding and formerly-federal programs to the provinces,[43] the adoption of a House of Commons resolution recognising Quebec as a 'distinct society' within

---

[41] See Dion,1992, and MacLauchlin, 1997 at p.156. M. Dion was subsequently elected to Canada's House of Commons and is presently the federal Minister for Intergovernmental Affairs, a portfolio which includes responsibility for constitutional reform and what is referred to in government as the 'national unity' question.

[42] Quebec's legislation on consultative referenda limits governments to holding one vote on a particular issue per mandate. See *Loi sur la consultation populaire*, R.S.Q. c. 64.1, s.12. Since this is not superior to other enactments of the Quebec legislature, it forms more of a political constraint than a legal or constitutional one, however. The sovereignty referenda thus far have been set by legislative enactments, and any future bill need only be worded as an exception to or amendment of the existing legislation to avoid this restriction.

[43] 'Chrétien steps back from unity issue: Prime Minister refocusing on economy as constitutional veto bill passes, Parliament prorogues', Canada *Globe and Mail*, 3 Feb. 1996, pp. A1, A3.

confederation,[44] and the enactment of *An Act Respecting Constitutional Amendments*, an attempted response to Quebec's demand for a veto on constitutional amendments.[45]

A similar approach was taken to addressing some of the constitutional concerns of aboriginal peoples. The negotiation of land-claims, self-government and other issues, ongoing for decades in aboriginal communities across Canada, continued throughout the period, and some progress has been made. With the exception of the occasional public demonstration in support of aboriginal positions, these negotiations have generally been low-profile affairs, attended only by negotiators representing the aboriginal band or community involved and the appropriate federal and provincial government departments. This changed in 1998 with the conclusion of an agreement between the Nisga'a people of British Colombia, and the provincial and federal governments, which contained a significant self-government component, providing for a Nisga'a constitution and some law-making powers. The quasi-constitutional elements of the agreement and whether it amounted to an amendment to the Constitution of Canada were a matter of controversy, and its ratification by all three parties drew considerable public attention.[46]

The non-constitutional approach to reforms continued for two years after the referendum, but confronted with criticism for its inaction on secession and supported by lower popular support for secession within Quebec, the federal government eventually decided to take a harder line on this question, in what has popularly become known as 'Plan B'. While it continued to try to address some of Quebec's concerns within the existing constitutional and political structure, it also began to challenge that province's position that Quebeckers and only Quebeckers

---

[44] Canada House of Commons Debates, 29 November 1995, pp.16971 *et seq.*

[45] SC 1996 c.1. The Act is discussed in more detail below. See also Hogg, 1997, chapt.4.3(h).

[46] Following ratification by the Nisga'a and legislature of British Colombia, the Parliament of Canada considered Bill C-9, *An Act to Implement the Nisga'a Final Agreement* during the spring of 2000. The legislation was enacted, receiving Royal Assent on April 13, 2000. It is now published as S.C. 1999-2000, c.7. Much of the controversy surrounded the question of the extent of self-government powers given to the Nisga'a, whether these would be entrenched by the Canadian constitution, and if so, whether adoption of the Agreement required approval under the constitutional amending formula. While the Agreement is clearly of a constitutional nature, the predominant opinion of experts is that it is not a formal amendment to the 'Constitution of Canada' such as to invoke the requirements of the amending formula of Part V of the *Constitution Act, 1982*. This implications of this are discussed below. The position of the federal government had previously been that any new self-government agreements should specify that any governance provisions did not create rights under s.35 of the *Constitution Act*. At the present time, the government takes the position that the Nisga'a Final Agreement does create such rights and it has begun a process to bring the same status to older agreements from which it had previously been excluded. See evidence of Prof. P. Hogg and Prof. P. Monahan, *Minutes of Proceedings and Evidence of the Standing Committee on Aboriginal Affairs and Northern Development*, Canada House of Commons, November 23, 1999, pp.1304-1400 at 1350, available at: http://www.parl.gc.ca/36/1/parlbus/commbus/house/CommitteeDocument.asp?DocumentID=13957&Language=E.

should have a substantive or procedural influence on any decision to secede. During the 1997 federal election campaign the Liberal Party committed the government to ensuring that:[47]

... any future debate that puts into question the continuing existence or unity of Canada will be characterized by clarity and frankness ...

Prior to the election, the federal government sought the advice of the Supreme Court of Canada in the form of a Reference. On September 26, 1996, the federal Justice Minister announced that the Court would be asked to respond to three questions:[48]

- Within the constitution, can the government of Quebec unilaterally secede from Canada?

- Does Quebec have right of unilateral secession under international law, based on the right of self-determination or any other principle?

- Is there a conflict between domestic and international law on the question of unilateral secession, and if so, which takes precedence in Canada?

In response, the government of Quebec took the position that secession is a political, not legal, question and as such not a matter for the courts. It did not appear in the case, and the pro-secession arguments were made by counsel appointed by the Court.[49] While the case was pending, both sides maintained a vigorous public debate about the legal, social and economic merits of secession or various forms of sovereignty. The Government of Quebec argued that the hard line of the federal government was an infringement on the democratic right of Quebeckers to determine their own future, and the Government of Canada focussed on the adverse

---

[47] Campaign document *Securing Our Future Together*, Liberal Party of Canada 1997, p.23.
[48] *Factum of the Attorney General of Canada in the Matter of a Reference by the Governor in Council concerning certain questions relating to the secession of Quebec from Canada*, filed 28 February 1997, Supreme Court of Canada docket 25506.
[49] *Amicus Curiae* may be appointed pursuant to the Supreme Court Act, RSC 1985, c. S-26, subs.53(7). As with almost every aspect of the case, this was controversial. Unlike conventional litigation, in which adversaries must appear, the Reference is in effect a request from only one party, the federal government, for a legal opinion from the Court. The granting of status to any other parties is at the discretion of the Court, based on its assessment of whether they will contribute evidence or argument relevant to the questions posed by the government. Quebec could not be compelled to appear, but neither it could it interfere with the Court's decision to appoint counsel to represent the sovereignist position. Quebec's attempts to discourage counsel from accepting the brief have been criticised as an attempt to prevent the Court from giving judgment on the threshold question of whether the matter was justiciable or not by boycotting the proceedings. See MacLauchlin, 1997, pp.162 and 174-75.

effects of secession on Quebec's territory and aboriginal minority.[50]

On August 20, 1998, the Court released its opinion in the *Secession Reference* case.[51] It found that the Constitution applied to the secession of a province and that while there was no right to secede as such, there was a right to pursue secession and an obligation on all parties to negotiate this if certain conditions were met.[52] It also held that the right to secede at international law, if any, lay in the right of self-determination, which did not apply to Quebec because it was able to exercise sufficient self-determination within Canada.[53] This made it unnecessary to answer the question of whether Quebeckers were a 'people' capable of exercising self-determination under international law, and the Court declined to do so.[54]

The Court found that the legal means of secession required a constitutional amendment, developed not only in accordance with the formal amending process, but also the underlying principles of federalism, democracy, the rule of law and respect for minorities.[55] The judgment does not specify which of the amending procedures under Part V of the Constitution Act, 1982 would apply to secession because it was not necessary to determine this to answer the reference questions and because it would depend on specific facts not known or before the Court.[56] The Court declined to address most of the issues argued by aboriginal interests on the

---

[50] Popular debate about partition has been characterised by the phrase 'if Canada is divisible, so is Quebec'. The debate included open letters from the Minister, Stéphane Dion, and to the Deputy Premier of Quebec, Bernard Landry. See Canada *Globe and Mail* 28 Aug. 1997, p.A17 (text of letter), p.A16, 'Weighing Dion's arguments on the nightmarish topic of partition', and p.A3, 'Ottawa plays tough guy with provinces'.

[51] *Reference re Secession of Quebec*, [1998] 2 S.C.R. 217, posted on-line at: http://www.droit.umontreal.ca/doc/csc-scc/en. References in the following notes are to numbered paragraphs of the on-line text. For discussion of the legal issues involved in the Reference and judgment, see Haljan, 1999, Howse and Malkin, 1997, MacLauchlan, 1997, Millard 1999, Monahan, 1996, and Webber 1997.

[52] Paragraphs 88-97. While it notes that referenda have no legal effect, the Court states that there would be an obligation to negotiate constitutional changes to respond to the desire to secede if clearly expressed in such a vote. The Court is careful not to prejudge the outcome of any negotiations or to impose a constitutional requirement that they conclude with secession or any other outcome, however. It notes (para.97) that there is no legal entitlement to secede, that many outcomes, including impasse, are possible, and expressly refuses to speculate as to what would follow if this occurred. See also paras. 150-51, quoted below.

[53] Paragraphs 135-39.

[54] Paragraphs.123-25.

[55] Paragraphs 84-90.

[56] Paragraph 105. Which specific section of Part V of the Constitution Act, 1982 would apply is a significant political and constitutional issue because this would determine how many provinces other than Quebec would have to ratify the necessary amendments. See Webber, 1997, pp.287-94 and Howse and Malkin, 1997, pp.191-96. In its Opinion, the Supreme Court suggests that all provinces would be involved in any secession negotiations, but not necessarily in any subsequent constitutional amendments. See discussion between Prof. Hogg and Daniel Turp, M.P., Canada House of Commons, Legislative Committee on Bill C-20, meeting #6, February 22, 2000. Available on-line at: http://www.parl.gc.ca/36/1/parlbus/commbus/house/CommitteeMinute.asp?Language=E&CommitteeID=116.

basis that their concerns only arose if there was a right to secede unilaterally. Since the Court found that there was no such right, it simply noted that the status of Quebec's aboriginal population would be one of the issues that would have to be resolved as part of the larger process of negotiating a package of appropriate constitutional amendments to effect secession, should this occur.[57]

On the key question of exactly what conditions would give rise to an obligation to negotiate amendments, the nature of such negotiations and the relationship between constitutional referenda and constitutional amendments, the Court found that referenda *per se* have no status as part of the formal amending process, but that a mutual obligation to negotiate would arise if the vote of a 'clear majority' of Quebeckers on a 'clear question in favour of secession' expressed the will to secede.[58]

...While it is true that some attempts at constitutional amendment in recent years have faltered, a clear majority vote in Quebec on a clear question of secession would confer democratic legitimacy on the secession initiative which all of the other participants in Confederation would have to recognize.

The democratic vote, by however strong a majority, would have no legal effect of its own and could not push aside the principles of federalism and the rule of law, the rights of individuals and minorities, or the operation of democracy in the other provinces or in Canada as a whole. Democratic rights under the Constitution cannot be divorced from constitutional obligations. Nor, however, can the reverse proposition be accepted. The continued existence and operation of the Canadian constitutional order could not be indifferent to a clear expression of a clear majority of Quebeckers that they no longer wish to remain in Canada. The other provinces and the federal government would have no clear basis to deny the right of the government of Quebec to pursue secession, should a clear majority of the people of Quebec choose that goal, so long as in doing so, Quebec respects the rights of others...There would be no conclusions predetermined by law on any issue. Negotiations would need to address the interests of the other provinces, the federal government, Quebec, and indeed the rights of all Canadians both within and outside Quebec, and specifically the rights of minorities. No one suggests that it would be an easy set of negotiations.

In November 1998, the Sovereignist government of Quebec was re-elected, removing the legal barriers to another referendum, but not the political ones. The federalist Liberal Party campaigned on an undertaking not to hold a further referendum under any circumstances, and won a small overall majority of votes cast. The incumbent sovereignist Parti Quebecois campaigned on the undertaking than no referendum would be held until what it described as 'winning conditions' existed. The sovereignist side won the majority of seats, and a further term in

---

[57] Paragraph 139.
[58] Quotes are from Paragraphs 150 and 151, respectively.

government, because much of the federalist vote is concentrated in a few large urban constituencies in the Montreal area. The new government turned away from sovereignty and towards more practical governance matters, and popular support for further discussions about overeignty have further declined from the levels of October 1995.

The federal government has continued to pursue its policy of clearly establishing the precise legal conditions for secession by introducing Bill C-20, legislation setting criteria by which the federal House of Commons would determine, prior to any voting, whether a proposed referendum question was sufficiently clear and following any vote favouring secession, whether a sufficient majority had been obtained.[59] The legislation does not dictate specific referendum questions or set a minimum percentage of votes cast, but it creates a federal power to review and consult on these questions before or after a referendum is held. If the federal House of Commons concludes that either the question or the majority result was not sufficiently clear, federal ministers, who would normally introduce any constitutional amendments needed to accomplish secession, are barred from doing so. Quebec responded promptly with legislation of its own setting the majority required to win any secession at the minimum 50 per cent +1 of the votes cast and claiming for itself the exclusive power to fix the question and other conditions in such a referendum.[60]

The apparent belief on the part of the federal government is that, while many of the people of Quebec may vote for sovereignty in general terms out of simple confusion about the implications or to strengthen the province's negotiating position, a majority will not support secession if confronted with a clear and unequivocal choice.[61]

The wording of the [referendum] question ought not to be part of the secessionist arsenal of winning conditions. Rather than 'winning,' the question must be clear, allowing the

---

[59] Bill C-20, *An Act to give effect to the requirement for clarity as set out in the opinion of the Supreme Court of Canada in the Quebec Secession Reference*, introduced December 10, 1999. As this chapter was last revised, in May 2000, the Bill was still before a Special Committee of the Senate. It was passed by the House of Commons March 15, 2000, with two amendments. Parallel changes to subsections 1(5) and 2(3) include aboriginal peoples within the list of those who must be consulted in determining whether any referendum question or majority vote was sufficiently clear. The text of the Bill and transcripts of legislative debates in both Houses and their respective committees are available on-line at: http://www.parl.gc.ca. Editor's note: Bill C-20 was passed by the Senate of Canada and given the Royal Assent on the same day, June 29, 2000. It is now S.C. 2000, c.26.

[60] *An Act Respecting the Exercise of the Fundamental Rights and Prerogatives of the Québec People and the Québec State*, introduced December 15, 1999. The legislation is available on-line at: http://www.assnat.qc.ca/eng/publications/Projets-loi/publics/99-a099.htm. The Premier of Quebec set out his government's position on the federal law and Quebec's response in a public broadcast when the Quebec law was introduced. See: http://www.premier.gouv.qc.ca/projet/indexa.htm.

[61] *Who's Afraid of Clarity?*, brief of federal Intergovernmental Affairs Minister Stéphane Dion to the House of Commons Legislative Committee on Bill C-20, February 16, 2000, p.5. Available from the Government of Canada, Privy Council Office, or on-line at http://www.pco-bcp.gc.ca.

population to state unambiguously whether or not it wants to cease to be part of Canada and make its province an independent country.

For some time, one of the fundamental political gaps between Quebec and the rest of Canada has been the political frame of reference within which any decisions about Quebec's constitutional status or sovereignty should be made. While many Canadians support the proposition that such a decision affects all of Canada and would have to involve input at the national level, most Quebeckers, and in particular those at the nationalist or sovereignist end of the political spectrum, take the view that this is a matter for Quebeckers alone. The ongoing federal strategy, including both the *Quebec Secession Reference* and the follow-up clarity legislation, is seen as risky by some federalists (and is welcomed by some sovereignists) because it may be seen by the people of Quebec as an attempt to restrict their democratic rights and provoke a backlash in support of secession.[62] Mr. Claude Ryan, long-time Quebec federalist, senior minister in several previous provincial governments and campaigner for the 'no' side in the 1980 and 1995 referenda, expressed the conflicting sentiments when asked how the 1980 'no' committee would have reacted to Bill C-20:[63]

I will tell you quite honestly that there would be disagreement in my caucus. Half would call for submission to the federal bill and the other half would call for the defence of Quebec. If I were the leader, I would say that Quebec comes first in this case.

## V. RIGIDITY, FLEXIBILITY AND THE PRESENT CONSTITUTION

As noted above, from 1867-1982 Canada's constitution was unofficially entrenched by the requirement for amendment by Westminster and not the Parliament of Canada. Convention required that Ottawa develop the substance of amendments and request that the changes be made, but all changes, including the extinction of Westminster's powers in 1982, were formally enacted in London. The conflict between Canadian sovereignty on the one hand and the need for constitutional evolution on the other during this period can be seen as a significant factor contributing to the present constitutional problems in Canada. Changes to address strains in the federal-provincial balance and between Quebec and the Anglophone provinces might well have been made incrementally and much sooner, had there

---

[62] A good summary of the chronology of events leading up to the federal legislation and the political positions of the various parties has been prepared by the Canadian Broadcasting Corporation. See Kennedy, T., 'The 'Clarity Bill', CBC News in depth, 'The Clarity Conflict', on-line at: http://cbc.ca/news/indepth/clarity.

[63] Appearance of Mr. Claude Ryan (official translation from French), Canada House of Commons, Legislative Committee on Bill C-20, meeting #5, February 21, 2000, available on-line at http://www.parl.gc.ca/36/1/parlbus/commbus/house/CommitteeMinute.asp?Language=E&CommitteeID=116.

been more flexibility during this period.

The adoption of the 1982 constitutional reforms, and the debates which preceded it, focussed a great deal of attention on the Constitution and its amending formulae not just as constitutional instruments, but as symbols of the relative importance and status of the major constituent elements of Canada. The adoption of the 1982 amending formula created practical rules for changing the constitution, but it did nothing to bring about national consensus, or the consent of those constituent elements, for further constitutional change. Indeed, the dissatisfaction of Quebec, which has never accepted the amending procedures, and the quest of both Quebec and Canada's aboriginal peoples for greater status in the amending process, have made the amending formula a major point of contention, rather than a mechanism for resolving constitutional problems in other areas.

A. The 1982 Amending Formula[64]

The amending formula itself was a major issue in the negotiations leading to the 1982 constitution. The compromise result was a formula which required both federal and provincial ratification as a basic means of entrenchment, and fixed a degree of provincial ratification which varied according to the nature of the change being proposed and the interests it affected. The procedures may be summarised as follows:[65]

- General amending formula (S.38). Any constitutional provision to which a more specific amending rule does not apply can be amended by a simple (i.e. 50 per cent + 1) majority in each of the two federal Houses, plus resolutions of the legislatures of at least seven provinces representing at least 50 per cent of the total provincial population.[66]

- Unanimity requirement (S.41). Major changes affecting the monarchy, guarantees of provincial representation in the federal House of Commons, two official languages, Supreme Court, or the amending formula itself require a simple majority in each of the two federal houses, plus resolutions of the legislatures of all ten of the provinces.

---

[64] For discussion of the amending formula and its adoption, see: Cheffins, 1982, Hogg, 1997, chapt.4.2-4.8, Lederman, 1984, and Scott, 1982.

[65] All references are to sections of the Constitution Act 1982, being Schedule II to the Canada Act 1982, UK, 1982, c.11. The amending formula is Part V of the Constitution Act.

[66] At present, this gives Ontario, with 37% of the population, and Quebec, with 25%, a combined veto over changes, but neither could act alone. 1991 Census figures list the following provincial populations: Newfoundland - 2.08%, Prince Edward Island - 0.46%, Nova Scotia - 3.30%, New Brunswick - 2.65%, Quebec - 25.26%, Ontario - 36.9%, Manitoba - 4.00%, Saskatchewan - 3.62%, Alberta, 9.33%, British Columbia - 12.02%, and the two territories (total) - 0.31%. The population in both Ontario and British Columbia has been increasing faster than the national rate since 1961, making it likely that these two provinces will also acquire a combined veto, if this has not already occurred. Source: 1991 federal census, as summarised in *Canadian Almanac, 1994*.

- Changes affecting some but not all provinces (S.43). These changes require a simple majority in each of the two federal Houses, plus resolutions of the assemblies of the provinces affected.

- Changes affecting only the federal government (S.44). These changes require only an ordinary federal enactment, accomplished by a simple majority in each of the two federal houses and Royal Assent.

- Changes affecting only one province (S.45). Changes to provincial constitutions can be made by the provincial legislature acting alone, in accordance with ordinary legislative process.

- Changes to provisions which directly affect aboriginal rights (S.35.1). These would be made under whichever of the foregoing rules otherwise applied, but also require the holding of a constitutional conference to which aboriginal representatives must be invited.

Absent from this formula is any formal legislative role for the three territories, which have legislatures created by Acts of Parliament. The populations (0.31 per cent of the national population) are represented in the process only through their elected Members of Parliament and Senators.

This approach to federal constitution-making has much to recommend it, but as the events discussed in this chapter illustrate, it has not solved Canada's constitutional difficulties, nor has it made possible substantive constitutional changes which would do so. One major advantage is that areas of the Constitution which are of fundamental importance to the country as a whole and unlikely to require frequent changes can be most deeply entrenched, while greater flexibility can be given to less-critical subject areas, while still entrenching them beyond the reach of ordinary legislation. Rigidity also need not be evenly distributed in such a formula: in some cases, provinces are given an effective veto over amendments which directly affect them, while they may have no say in changes which affect only other provinces.

There are drawbacks, however. One major problem is that it is necessary to classify each amendment under the amending formula to determine which rule applies. This may be a straightforward determination for single-issue changes which fit neatly within the framework, but more abstract, compound or complex policy changes represent greater problems. Some of the more complex issues on the current agenda, such as aboriginal self-government or the secession of Quebec could not be accomplished by single stand-alone amendments. They would trigger numerous consequential amendments, each of which may have its own procedural amending requirements.[67] It will not always be clear which requirements apply, nor

---

[67] The classification of possible subjects in the present amending formula does not specifically include the secession of a province, which arguably brings secession within the general amending formula (s.38), requiring resolutions of Parliament and seven provinces having at least 50% of the total provincial population. On the other hand, some of the consequential changes, such as abolishing the

will it be free of controversy. As will be seen, this is both a legal and a political problem: the elements of recent constitutional reform packages which were legally distinct under the amending formula nevertheless became linked by political negotiations.

B. The 1996 Attempt to Provide *de facto* Rigidity by Statute

One further development may have changed the amending formula since 1982, depending on one's characterisation of events. After the narrow margin in the October 1995 referendum, the federal government attempted to address Quebec's demand for a constitutional veto, not by changing the constitution but by ordinary statute. It produced legislation, *An Act Respecting Constitutional Amendments*, which bars federal ministers from introducing constitutional resolutions without the consent of each of five defined regions of the country.[68] As the formal amending process requires the resolutions of both federal Houses, this effectively creates a veto for each of the five regions, at least with respect to government-sponsored amendments.[69]

The legislation was contentious. Federalist opponents argued that it was an unconstitutional change to the amending formula. In their view, its real purpose, or 'pith and substance,' was to alter the process whereby constitutional amendments could be made.[70] It has also been argued that the creation of regional vetoes would

---

office of Lieutenant-Governor of Quebec, the provisions dealing with the status of English and French as official languages of Canada and the removal of Quebec's guarantee of three justices on the Supreme Court, invoke the unanimity requirement of s.41. See Hogg, 1997, p.135-36 and Monahan, 1995, at pp.5-15. On the question of which section(s) of Part V would apply to the secession of a province or whether some alternative amendment (e.g. by referendum) could accomplish this, see Webber, 1997. The 1998 judgment of the Supreme Court in *Reference re Secession of Quebec* answers the second question, holding that secession must be accomplished under Part V. The Court refused to address the first question as unnecessary to the issues in the Reference. See above and para.105 of the judgment.

[68] Bill C-110, introduced 29 November 1995 and assented to on 2 February 1996, becoming SC 1996, c.1.

[69] The wording of subsection 1(1) of the Act provides that 'No Minister of the Crown shall propose a motion for a resolution to authorise an amendment to the Constitution of Canada ...' which would appear to leave open the possibility that a future government might circumvent this requirement by inducing a 'back-bencher' to introduce such a motion as a Private Member's Bill. The Act was probably worded this way in order to address concerns that it was a violation of parliamentary supremacy or an infringement of the privileges of Members of Parliament. The same issue arises with respect to Bill C-20, discussed above. In that case, any Member of Parliament other than a Minister could presumably introduce a resolution to amend the Constitution in order to achieve Quebec secession following a referendum vote. Indeed, given the representation of Quebec sovereignists in the House of Commons, this could well occur. The mechanics of the House of Commons make it unlikely that such a resolution would be allowed to proceed or be adopted by the House without government support, however.

[70] See Prof. Andrew Heard, Simon Fraser University, *Proceedings of the Special Committee of the Senate on Bill C-110*, Issue No. 6, pp.11-12, 31 January 1996; Prof. Patrick Monahan, Osgoode Law School, York University, *Proceedings of the Special Committee of the Senate on Bill C-110*, Issue No. 4, p.31, 25 January 1996.

entrench existing constitutional provisions more deeply, with the effect of making amendment more difficult and adding further legal obstacles to the existing political obstacles to constitutional reform.[71] Proponents of a federation of ten equal provinces also objected on the basis that the Bill created separate classes of province or amounted to discrimination based on population.[72] Quebec sovereignists sought to play down any significance of the Bill as a political gesture and pointed out that it fell far short of the province's demands for a veto entrenched in the amending formula itself. Supporters of the Bill argued that it was a significant recognition of Quebec's concerns and that it did not amend the constitution, but only regulated the conditions under which the federal government could exercise its powers to put forward constitutional amendments[73]

C. The Role of Referenda in Canadian Constitutional Amendments

Despite the October 1995 Quebec referendum on sovereignty, which received extensive international media coverage, referenda are not mentioned in Part V of the Constitution Act 1982, and are not part of the formal amending process.[74] In the UK, the supremacy of Parliament makes a truly binding referendum requirement impossible. In Canada, Parliamentary supremacy is subject to the codified constitution, but since this makes no provision for referenda, binding constitutional votes cannot be held in Canada either. Federal negotiators proposed national referenda as an alternative to the requirement for provincial ratification of proposed constitutional amendments in discussions leading up to the 1982 package and again in 1990 talks, but these were rejected by the provinces as an erosion of their constitutional powers in the amending formula.[75] The difficulties faced by the

---

[71] Hogg, 1997, chapt.4.3(h). Prof. Hogg describes the law as '...probably an unwise initiative, since it makes the Constitution even more difficult to amend, and further reduces the faint hope of genuine constitutional change.'

[72] See generally, the evidence of the Hon. Andrew Petter, Minister of Forests, representing the Government of British Columbia, *Proceedings of the Special Committee of the Senate on Bill C-110*, Issue No. 2 at pp.22-25.

[73] The Hon. Alan Rock, Minister of Justice, on the Second Reading of Bill C-110, An Act Respecting Constitutional Amendments, House of Commons Debates, 30-11-1996, pp.17000-17003 at 17002.

[74] Two provinces, Alberta and British Columbia, have enacted statutes requiring that a provincial referendum be held on any proposed constitutional amendment, but these are not entrenched and are not part of the formal amending requirements. Opponents of the 1998 *Nisga'a Final Agreement*, discussed below, argued that, since the *Agreement* would be constitutionally-entrenched once ratified by the parties, it amounted to a constitutional amendment and must therefore be put to a referendum under the British Colombia law. Quebec has more general legislation on the use of consultative referenda, under which the 1980 and 1995 constitutional questions were put. In setting out general conditions for referenda, this provides that only one referendum can be held on a particular topic during the term of a provincial government.

[75] Scott, S.A., 1982, at pp.266-69. See also Hogg, 1981, pp.348-51, and 1997, chapt.4.8(d), supporting such a proposal as a means of additional flexibility, and *Amending the Constitution of Canada: A Discussion Paper*, FPRO, Ottawa, December 1990, pp.15-18.

Australian and Irish governments in obtaining referendum approval, particularly where (in Australia) state governments opposed the changes, suggest that referenda may not be very effective in breaking deadlocks in any event.[76]

The 1998 judgment of the Supreme Court of Canada in the Quebec secession reference case confirms that referenda have no formal role in amending the constitution, even where the issue in question is the secession of a province, but it also recognises that they may have an informal role in some circumstances. The Court found that federalism, democracy, constitutionalism and the rule of law, and the protection of minorities are 'underlying constitutional principles' which have full legal force. As an expression of democratic will, referenda do not have priority over any or all of the other three principles, but they can give rise to a legal obligation to open negotiations leading to constitutional amendment, providing that the nature of the referendum and the answer obtained amount to a clear expression of such will.[77]

There appears to be continuing popular support for the use of referenda in Canada, which is somewhat surprising, given the conspicuous lack of success with them thus far.[78] Three non-binding votes on constitutional issues have been held since 1980, and none of them has resolved the issues out of which they arose. In two, Quebec voters rejected sovereignty options, but the province's separatist politicians have repeatedly indicated that they plan to keep trying until they achieve what they consider to be a favourable result. In the third, federal constitutional proposals were rejected as a package, but virtually all of the elements of that

---

[76] Regarding Australia's problems with constitutional referenda, see Campbell, 1989, Ford, 1988, Rydon, 1976 and 1977, and Sampford, 1979.

[77] *Reference re Secession of Quebec*, [1998] 2 S.C.R. 217, at para.. 49-97, posted on-line at: http://www.droit.umontreal.ca/doc/csc-scc/en. See in particular paras. 49, 66, 87-88 and 91. The judgment emphasizes that referenda proposing constitutional changes must be taken in the context of the constituency which expresses that will, existing constitutional or legal requirements (including the rules for amendment), the protection of minorities and other factors. At para.91, the Court sums up its findings as follows: 'The democracy principle, as we have emphasized, cannot be invoked to trump the principles of federalism and the rule of law, the rights of individuals and minorities, or the operation of democracy in other provinces or in Canada as a whole.'

[78] Apart from Quebec sovereignists, who seek to use referenda to either secede or generate pressure in constitutional negotiations, much of the popular support is from the political right, which prefers more direct democracy than is afforded by the election of representative Members of Parliament. For the latter, referenda would be used not only for constitutional questions, but for more routing political decision-making as well. At least one prominent constitutional expert also supports referenda, albeit with some important qualifications. Prof. Hogg has consistently advocated the use of 'initiative and referendum' as an alternative to the existing means of constitutional amendment. By this, he means a process in which a proposal would be put forward directly by a large number of voters in a petition. Governments could campaign for or against the proposal, but would have to do so on the merits, and would not be able to use their approval as a bargaining-chip for other proposals, as occurs at present. See Hogg, 1981, pp348-51, and 1997, chapt.4.8(d). The incorporation of a petition, and the exercise of gathering the required number of signatures would reduce the political risks by screening out many of the proposals for which the referendum exercise might do more harm than good, but some of the risks could simply be displaced to the petition stage of the process.

package remain on the constitutional waiting-list and are still supported by significant elements of the population.[79]

Referenda can establish popular support or consensus, but they are unlikely to create it, and may destroy it in cases where it already exists.[80] The need to convince voters to support or oppose amendment proposals tends to politicise the process and polarise ideas and ideologies. Reflecting on Canada's experience with referenda, many politicians and observers believe that the campaigns may have caused significant and lasting damage to prospects for national consensus-building on constitutional reform proposals and the status of Quebec in Canada. Clearly, at least for Canada, the referendum is a high-risk strategy, vulnerable to undue influences from accidental and intentional sources.[81]

D. The Present Balance of Constitutional Interests in Canada

In addition to providing a suitable balance of stability and flexibility, a key function of federal constitutions is to balance the interests of the country as a whole against those of the regions, and the interests of the regions against one another. Unfortunately, Canada's attempts to balance rigidity and flexibility among the various interests thus far have not been entirely successful. This may be attributed in part to the formal requirements for amending the constitution, but underlying social and political factors have posed a more significant problem. The 1982 amending formula was a brilliant innovation in that it attempted to set several different degrees of entrenchment, in accordance with the concerns of the parties who negotiated it. The number of provinces which must approve an amendment resolution varies depending on the nature of the amendment proposed. As the failed attempt of Meech Lake illustrates, however, this variable entrenchment can be partly frustrated because the various elements of the package become linked by

---

[79] On 20 May 1980 the Quebec government held a vote which rejected 'sovereignty-association' by margin of 60%-40%. On 26 October 1992 voters in two separate but identical votes in Quebec and the rest of Canada decisively rejected the 1991 Charlottetown amendment package 54%-46%. On 30 October 1995 a second Quebec referendum, this time asking for a mandate to secede if constitutional negotiations failed, rejected secession, but only by a margin of about 1.2% of the 96% of eligible voters who participated. The present Government of Quebec has pledged to hold another referendum, but not until what it considers 'winning conditions' exist.

[80] A recent narrow escape in this regard is the 1998 *Nisga'a Final Agreement*, which opponents argued should be put to a referendum in British Colombia. Support for the agreement was high among the province's aboriginal population, but the sentiments of the non-aboriginal majority were not clear. Had a referendum been held, one possible outcome would have been a devastating rejection of aboriginal aspirations by the general population, a severe setback for any further negotiations in the province, and potentially in other parts of Canada as well. The vote was not held because it was concluded that the *Agreement* was not a constitutional amendment and therefore not within the province's law requiring referenda in such cases.

[81] At the time of the 1992 referendum, it was described by the Prime Minister as 'rolling the dice', a remark which drew heavy criticism in the media. The attempts to tailor the 1995 Quebec referendum question to produce a 'yes' outcome and the subsequent fallout from this are discussed in Part IV, above.

political bargaining, with the effect of attaching the highest degree of entrenchment, that of unanimous provincial approval, to the entire package.

There also still remains the problem that the entrenchment formula arrived at in 1982 is not satisfactory to everyone: Quebec seeks greater entrenchment in the form of a provincial veto, and aboriginal peoples still seek some as yet undefined formal role in the process. The 1996 regional veto legislation, intended to partially address the second problem, will probably serve only to aggravate the first, should further amendment packages be proposed.

For both of these problems, as well as for the more general questions of how constitutional influence should be distributed among the various constituent groups in Canada, the amending formula itself is only the tip of the iceberg. It is important as a codification of the constitutional relationships which make up the Canadian federation and, a symbol of the consensus of Canadians about what those relationships are, if such a consensus can be reached, but a successful amending formula must follow compromise and consensus; it is unlikely to produce it. This fact is not lost on the more militant elements seeking Quebec secession, who consistently portray such consensus as impossible to achieve in order to advance their cause. Constitutions have been described as a form of 'power map' of the underlying elements of government and society, identifying centres of power and the distance, directions or relationships between them.[82] It is this function of the Canadian Constitution that is most in issue, and while other elements of the map, such as the constitutional lists allocating legislative powers between the federal and provincial governments are also on the table, it is the amending formula which has become the most contentious element of the debate.

Generally, the post-1982 constitutional developments in Canada reflect attempts to balance stability and flexibility in four major distinct but inter-related contexts.

- The need to strike a viable balance of power between the federal government and the provinces collectively.

- The need to strike a balance between the degree of influence accorded to the various provinces, taking into account relative populations, affluence and similar factors.

- The need to find a balance between Quebec and the rest of Canada which secures Quebec's French language and culture without giving the province undue influence over the constitution or the national political or economic agendas.

- The need to accommodate aboriginal interests socially, politically and in respect of future constitutional amendments.

---

[82] Duchacek, 1973 and Banting and Simeon, 1985, p.3.

## 1. The balance between provincial and federal governments

The overall federal-regional balance of power is a critical element of any federal constitution, and Canada is no exception. Confederation and the 1867 constitution were based on the assumptions that both levels of government would be subordinate to Westminster in constitutional matters and that the federal level would be dominant within Canada.[83] As the country matured and became more autonomous, this gradually changed, but the changes were effected more by evolving conventions in Ottawa and London and judicial interpretation than formal constitutional amendments.

The application of conventions and case-law permitted some adjustments in the federal-provincial balance, but a more accessible formal amending process might have generated more public discussion about the structure and balance of federalism, forcing the developing nation to deal with some of the key issues earlier. Those familiar with the historical record may well note, with some support, that prior to the 1960s, neither Quebec nor aboriginal interests would have been represented very effectively. It is true that the political positions of these factions, and much of their ability to express them, have evolved significantly since then. It is not suggested here that those positions would have developed sooner, although this is certainly possible. However, incremental changes made earlier may have avoided the problems which arose when all of these groups later sought constitutional reforms at the same time, once a domestic amending formula became available. Had formal amendments adjusting the federal structure been made earlier, some of the pressure for change might have been relieved, some grievances addressed, and both a precedent and a platform for addressing contemporary reform issues might have been established.

In recent years, the provinces have collectively sought to reassert their influence over areas seen as federal matters. Pressure for greater provincial powers was a factor in much of the negotiation process which led to the 1982 Constitution Act, and several provinces expressed concerns were expressed about the impact that adopting a justiciable Charter of Rights would have on their powers and the federal-provincial balance. One element of the 1982 constitutional reform package did expand provincial influence in the area of natural resources, an area of major concern, particularly in the west. Another major provincial concern has been the growth of federal influence through the use of the federal spending power. Since many provincial projects require federal funding, the federal government can exert influence by imposing conditions on funding or funding only those projects of

---

[83] Ss.91-92 of the Act set forth two distinct lists of legislative competencies, but Parliament has residual powers to make laws for the 'Peace, Order and Good Government' of Canada under the preamble to s.91, and the doctrine of federal paramountcy gives priority to federal enactments in respect of any concurrent subject matter. S.90 gave the federal government powers to disallow provincial statutes, but these have not been used since 1948, having been abandoned in favour of judicial means of distinguishing federal and provincial matters in legislation. See Hogg, 1997, ch.3.1 and 5.3(e).

which it approves. This has made the spending power a major issue in post-1982 negotiations as provinces have sought to limit federal influence in key areas such as education, occupational training and health-care.[84]

With respect to formal constitutional amendments, there has never been any question that the provinces should have a substantial role to play in developing and ratifying proposed changes. The 1982 amendments and all of the proposals which preceded them envisaged some formula whereby provinces would have input, either legislatively, or in the 1981 referendum proposal, by requiring referendum majorities in provinces as well as nationally. What has occupied most of the negotiations, before and after 1982, has been conflicting views with respect to how influence over the constitutional amendment process should be distributed among the various provinces, and it is to this issue we now turn.

*2. The balance among the ten provinces*

The recent constitutional discussions in Canada have been dominated by two conflicting provincial models of confederation and their implications for constitutional amendment. These may be characterised as equality models, which perceive Canada as a union of ten equal provinces, and majoritarian models, which argue that the degree of influence accorded to each province or region should be more or less in accordance with the numbers of Canadians who live there. Not surprisingly, the former model tends to be favoured in the smaller and less densely-populated provinces of the east and west, while the latter are favoured in Ontario and Quebec, which have, respectively 36 per cent and 25 per cent of the total national population. Added to this is a third model, espoused by Quebec, which sees Canada as a union of two founding peoples, each of which should have equal constitutional influence. Further complicating matters is the opposition of aboriginal Canadians, who were on the land before anyone else and who subscribe to none of the foregoing models and take particular exception to the 'two founding peoples' concept. The positions of Quebec and aboriginal Canadians will be considered in the following two segments.

The strain between equality and majoritarian models of Canada is not new. The English drafters of the Constitution Act 1867 structured the House of Commons on

---

[84] This influence has been reduced in the 1990s by reductions in federal spending brought about by scarce resources and federal attempts to reduce the national debt. See: 'Premiers divided on federal role' and 'Ottawa must revise attitude, premiers say', Canada *Globe and Mail*, 24 August 1995, p.A-4. Concerning the constitutional question of the federal spending power, see Phillips, S., ed., *How Ottawa Spends: A More Democratic Canada...?* Carleton Univeristy Press, Ottawa, 1993, and Hogg, 1997, chapt.6.8, and sources there cited. Prof. Hogg is of the view that conditional federal funding in areas of provincial jurisdiction involves no constitutional infringement on provincial powers, since the provinces are free to proceed without the funding if they choose. Most provinces would probably agree, but they seek some limitation on the practice anyway, either in the form of a constitutional constraint or a political agreement.

a majoritarian basis and the Senate on a regional basis.[85] The proposals of the 1960s and 70s and the 1982 amending procedures all allocate influence based on some compromise between population and provincial equality.[86] More recently, the regional vetoes of the 1996 *Act Respecting Constitutional Amendments* are a product of the same reasoning.

Majoritarian models allow amendments based on the approval of provinces representing a majority (or special majority) of the national population, which raises concerns among the smaller provinces that Ontario and Quebec, with about 62 per cent of the population (and almost 60 per cent of House of Commons seats) between them, could amend the constitution by themselves. Equality models, on the other hand, would allow amendments by a majority of equal provinces, regardless of population. This could lead to a constitutional amendment being made even though it was opposed by provinces representing a majority of the national population: an amendment opposed by both Ontario and Quebec could still be made by a provincial 'vote' of 8-2 in favour.

Attempts to meet the requirements of proponents of both models have led to occasional suggestions that the ratification of every single province, regardless of population, be required. Unanimity requirements meet both of these concerns, since any single province could defeat an amendment, but raise concerns about excessive rigidity and in some cases concerns about giving regional interests the power to veto changes which do not involve their interests. The major objection to these is that they would amount to 'an agreement not to agree',[87] making the constitution so rigid and amendment so difficult that the text would gradually fail to reflect changes in national circumstances.

The conflict between equality and majoritarian models of confederation has been fed by the perception, particularly in the western provinces, that the legislative agenda is dominated by central Canada, and has led to calls for changes to the Senate to ensure that Canada's less-populous regions are represented more effectively. Reform proposals have included suggestions that Senators be either elected or appointed on a provincial basis and accountable either to provincial legislatures or to voters on a provincial basis. Proposals for a 'Triple E' Senate, with equal numbers of Senators chosen by election from each province and significant powers to block or amend legislation were advanced as part of a last-minute attempt to salvage the 1987 Meech Lake proposals in 1990 and were incorporated into the failed Charlottetown Accord of 1992. What has been described as 'western

---

[85] Constitution Act 1867, s.26.
[86] See Hogg, 1997, ch.4.1(b). One example is the unsuccessful 1970 Victoria agreement, which would have required ratification by any province having at least 25% of the population, any two of the four Atlantic provinces, and at least two of the four western provinces having at least 50% of the total western population. The major obstacles to their adoption were the conflict with Quebec, which wanted a veto in recognition of its equality with the rest of Canada, and concerns that influence would erode as populations increased or decreased in different regions.
[87] Hogg, 1997, p.65. Prof. Hogg uses the words to describe an early unanimity proposal, the 'Fulton-Favreau' proposal, put forward in 1964.

disaffection' with the dominance of central Canada and the prolonged constitutional wrangling with Quebec remain a sore point with residents of Alberta, British Columbia, Manitoba and Saskatchewan, and Senate reform is likely to remain on the agenda for the foreseeable future.[88]

Senate reform does not require changes to the amending formula, but may trigger such changes because of the role allocated to the Senate by the existing formula. Under the existing amending formula, a 'Triple E' Senate which represented provincial interests would effectively give the provinces influence at two stages of the amendment process: the adoption of resolutions in their own legislatures, and during Senate review of the House of Commons resolution.[89] The constitutions of Australia and Germany are sometimes suggested as precedents for this, but neither requires this degree of influence. In Australia, the states participate through the Senate (six elected members per state) and the referendum, which requires both state and national majorities, but the state legislatures have no direct input. In Germany, the *Bundesrat* (from 2-6 members appointed by *land* governments) must ratify amendments, but the states have no formal input from their own legislatures. The closest model is probably that of the United States, where the elected Senate and state legislatures both have direct influence.

It has also been suggested that a powerful Canadian Senate might not achieve the goals sought by its provincial supporters. An elected Senate would divide itself along partisan political lines and Senators would more likely vote along party lines than in accordance with provincial wishes. Also, Canada's Senate is sometimes at odds with its House of Commons, but seldom exercises its powers to block legislation because it lacks an electoral mandate. This would not continue if the Senate were elected. If the new rules created a Senate dominated by the same party as that which controlled the House of Commons, its input would generally be redundant. If they created a Senate dominated by the opposition, the result could be legislative and constitutional paralysis. If the powers of an elected Senate were curtailed to reduce the potential for deadlock, its effectiveness in representing

---

[88] For a discussion of Senate reform proposals, see Francks, 1987, Crommelin, 1989, Woehrling, 1992, and Resnick, 1993. Many of the House of Commons and Senate committee proceedings on constitutional reform over the past four decades also consider the question of Senate reform. The other proposal often advanced is to simply abolish the Senate in favour of a unicameral system.

[89] The Senate cannot block constitutional amendments, but has a suspensive veto. If an amendment resolution is not adopted by the Senate within 180 days of an equivalent resolution from the House of Commons, the Commons may proceed alone by passing a second resolution (Constitution Act 1982, s.47). The Senate could also exert influence by introducing amendment resolutions of its own under s.46, and it has the same powers to conduct public hearings into matters before it as does the lower House. Historically, the Canadian Senate has served as a repository of constitutional expertise, and its deliberations on constitutional issues carry considerable political influence, although this could change if its composition was altered by the election of its members.

regional or provincial interests would be curtailed.[90]

## 3. The balance between Quebec and Anglophone Canada

Quebec, while bound by the 1982 constitution, has never ratified or signed it. The views of Quebeckers today range from extreme nationalism to satisfaction with the status quo, but there is substantial consensus that the province requires greater autonomy and constitutional influence than at present. For hard-line separatists, this entails secession and full sovereignty. Moderate separatists seek constitutional independence but some continued social and economic ties, a model described as 'sovereignty-association'. Federalists seek some form of restructuring or renewal within the existing constitutional framework, but many of their demands would still require fairly fundamental constitutional changes to decentralise and devolve powers.

The pressure for greater autonomy in Quebec is driven, in part, by the fear of Francophones that their language and culture will be gradually eroded if not protected in some way. This arises from the province's minority position within Canada and within North America: where Quebec Francophones number somewhat less than seven million, they live in close proximity to about 225 million Canadians and Americans, in what is often referred to as a 'sea of Anglophones'. Culturally, this can be seen as a conflict between the quest for a political state based around a distinct language and culture, and the realities of modern-day Canada, including Quebec, as a state with a heterogenous, multicultural population produced by over a century of immigration.[91] The gap has been widened by the sense of historical grievance of Francophones, who were politically and economically dominated by the Quebec's Anglophone minority and culturally dominated by the Catholic Church until the early 1960s.

The constitutional debate has become a lightning-rod for these controversies in Quebec, where either progress or secession is seen by many as an essential to cultural survival. The debate also turns on a conflict between Quebec's view of federalism and both the equality and majoritarian models supported by the other provinces. Quebec nationalists view confederation as a union of two founding peoples and tend to seek constitutional influence on that basis. This is resisted by other provinces, who argue that influence should be allocated to provinces based on either population or provincial equality. It is also strongly opposed by aboriginal

---

[90] Hogg, 1993 at pp.52-53 and 1997, at chapt.9.4(c). The potential for deadlock exists in the present system. Senators serve until age 75, and frequently outlast the governments which appointed them. Governments which serve for extended periods, notably the Liberal regimes of Lester Pearson and Pierre Trudeau (1962-84) and the Conservative regimes of Brian Mulroney (1984-93), produced majorities in the Senate which confronted their successors in office. The problem is a variation of that with the UK House of Lords, except that instead of having what Profs. Wade and Bradley (1992, pp.194-96) describe as a 'permanent Conservative majority', the majority in Canada's Senate shifts back and forth (usually out of phase with the Commons) because members are chosen by politics and not heredity.
[91] See MacDonald 1996.

groups, who resent the contention that Canada was founded by only two peoples when they were there first.

Quebec governments have consistently demanded a veto over constitutional amendments. Until the Supreme Court held otherwise in its 1981 and 1982 decisions, Quebec believed it had such a veto by convention, and it previously rejected proposals which did not include a veto or which included one only as part of a package of regional vetoes or vetoes for every province. When it did so, in 1964 and 1970, the proposals were dropped, which suggests some recognition of a conventional veto by the other parties.[92] While Quebec has seen a veto as necessary for its security, the rest of Canada is concerned about giving the province too much leverage in future constitutional developments, or, if everyone has a veto, making the constitution too rigid. If unanimous support for amendments is required, there is little incentive for the parties to negotiate or compromise, and incentives are created to withhold consent, as the last hold-out gains the most bargaining-power.[93] Unanimity requirements also tend to produce packages which include something for everyone in exchange for not using the veto. This can produce political consensus, but works against achieving the high degree of popular support seen as necessary for constitutional change. In Canada's 1992 referendum, voters objected to the entire package based on their dislike of individual elements.[94] It also results in the linking of proposals by politics rather than policy, which is not necessarily conducive to the development of a viable constitution.[95]

Another major issue affecting the Canada-Quebec problem has been the effects, real, perceived and feared, of the fully-justiciable Canadian Charter of Rights and Freedoms on Quebec's powers to manage its own affairs. Efforts by nationalists to protect the French language and culture have come into conflict with the basic rights guarantees of the Charter. This has provoked a reaction among Quebec's non-Francophone minorities, who fear exclusion from a state intent on protecting a culture to which they do not belong, and among Canadians from other provinces, over whether Charter values should be given priority over policies many Quebeckers see as a matter of cultural survival. In the late 1980s, what has been described as a 'language crisis' occurred after the Supreme Court struck down laws enacted to protect the French language in Quebec as violations of the freedoms of

---

[92] Hogg, 1997, ch.4.1(b) and (c). The position taken by Quebec during the 1971-82 period is not entirely consistent either. Quebec rejected a proposal which would have given a veto to provinces with at least 25% of the national population (i.e. Ontario and Quebec) in 1971. Subsequently it approved a formula without a veto in 1981, and then refused to agree to a similar formula eventually used in the Constitution Act 1982 a few months later. Whether the sudden change of position resulted from the negotiations or political opposition in Quebec remains a matter of controversy.

[93] These problems are by no means unknown in Canadian constitutional discussions. See Sabetti, 1982, at pp.28-32.

[94] Similar problems have been encountered in Australia and Ireland. See Campbell, 1989, at p.10 and *Report of the Constitutional Review Group*, (Government of Ireland), 1996, pp.399-400.

[95] See Forsey, 1988 (as reprinted, 1989).

expression and association. This generated a backlash against the Charter and the Supreme Court as instruments of federal domination.[96]

The 1982 amending rules make it unlikely that a Quebec veto over all constitutional amendments will be created, since this now requires provincial unanimity. There may be room for some progress towards Quebec's goal of greater influence, but the symbolic importance of the recognition of equal status with the rest of Canada will probably prove elusive, at least within the present constitutional framework. Giving Quebec an exclusive veto is unacceptable to many of the other provinces on basic democratic grounds and out of concern for the imbalance of constitutional power which would result. A Quebec veto as part of a unanimity rule for all amendments is opposed by much of Canada as making the constitution too rigid and by many Quebeckers as a rejection of its 'two founding partners' model of Confederation.

*4. The inclusion of aboriginal peoples*

The fourth critical issue for future constitutional amendment involves Canada's aboriginal population, which is composed of several distinct groups and numerous smaller bands and communities, often with divergent political and constitutional agendas.[97] Generally, aboriginal Canadians have grown increasingly militant since the 1982 constitution was adopted, and have become unwilling to allow other constitutional changes to proceed until their own concerns are met. Key issues on the aboriginal agenda arise at three levels.

- Questions relating to constitutional amending procedures, including both the existence, nature and extent of aboriginal rights to participate formally in making constitutional amendments and the substantive and procedural details of what such participation would consist of and how it would be exercised in the context of specific proposals.

- Questions about substantive constitutional matters, including self-government, aboriginal participation in Parliament, the constitutional protection of aboriginal traditional and treaty rights, conflicts between the 1982 Charter of Rights and aboriginal rights or self-government, and the

---

[96] See Veitch, E., 1990, *Devine v. Quebec (Attorney General)* [1988] 2 *SCR* 790, (1987) 55 DLR (4th) 641, *Ford v. Quebec (Attorney General)* [1988] 2 SCR 712, 54 DLR (4th) 577 and *Quebec (Attorney General) v. Quebec Protestant School Boards* [1984] 2 SCR 66. The Supreme Court has also acted to protect the rights of the Francophone minorities outside of Quebec. See *Re: Manitoba Language Rights* [1985] 1 SCR 721, in which the Court struck down every enactment made by the province of Manitoba since 1870 on the basis that none had been enacted in French as well as in English as required by the province's constitution.

[97] The three major groups are the Inuit, who inhabit the northern regions of most provinces, the Métis, who are descended from French fur-traders and Indians and who are found mostly in Manitoba and Saskatchewan, and North American Indians who make up the remaining aboriginal population and are found everywhere in Canada.

status of Quebec's aboriginal population in the context of any attempt by the province to secede from Canada unilaterally or by constitutional amendment.

- Non-constitutional problems, such as the settlement of land-claims, problems of corruption and accountability in bands and municipalities, status and membership issues and similar matters.

Both the 1982 constitutional package and the 1987 Meech Lake Accord were bitterly attacked for lack of indigenous input. Some concessions were made in 1982, but a provision reaffirming aboriginal and treaty rights was nearly removed at the last minute, and was only restored after a wave of aboriginal protest.[98] Indigenous groups travelled to London to urge Westminster not to enact the package. The 1982 Act itself protects pre-existing rights (s.35) and guarantees that the Canadian Charter of Rights and Freedoms will not abrogate or derogate from aboriginal rights (s.25). It also provided for First Ministers' conferences on further constitutional amendments (s.37), with agendas to include aboriginal issues, and aboriginal representatives to be invited. Meetings were held in 1983, 1984, 1985 and 1987, but agreement on a constitutional package could not be reached, leaving s.37 exhausted without any changes to the constitution. One major advance has been made, by amendment in 1983. S.35.1, adopted under the general amending procedure, declares that the federal and provincial governments are 'committed to the principle' that before constitutional changes are made which affect aboriginal interests, a conference will be held to discuss the proposed changes and aboriginal representatives will be invited.[99] This clearly recognises the unique constitutional position of indigenous Canadians, but falls short of a role in the formal amending procedure.

All of this led to a growing consensus of both indigenous and non-indigenous Canadians in support of some form of self-government and a more formal role in constitutional amendment, but until recently only modest progress was made in defining either. In June 1991, a Joint Parliamentary Committee linked the issues of self-government and constitutional participation on the basis that a requirement for constitutional consent implied a government-to-government relationship.[100] It also concluded that some form of governance framework would be needed to formally develop a position and articulate it. It recommended that any future constitutional amendments affecting aboriginal interests require 'the consent of the aboriginal peoples of Canada', that aboriginal peoples be invited to participate in all future

---

[98] See Hall, 1989 at pp.425-27. The provision is now s.35 of the Constitution Act 1982.

[99] Constitution Act 1982, s.35.1, adopted by the Constitution Amendment Proclamation 1983, RSC, 1985, Appendix II, No.46, discussed in Hogg, 1997, ch.27.10. A consent requirement for some constitutional changes may also exist by convention or as a result of the federal fiduciary obligation to aboriginal peoples. See Monahan, 1995, at pp.15-16, and sources there cited.

[100] This is often described as a 'third order of government' to distinguish aboriginal government from the federal and provincial levels.

constitutional conferences, and that a regular series of biennial conferences be set up. It also noted the popular support for this.[101]

In developing the Charlottetown package during the following autumn, the federal government expressed general support for self-government, but placed some limits on how far it could go in recognising sovereignty. It opposed any change which would not have made aboriginal governments subject to the Charter of Rights, which presently only applies to the acts of Parliament, the provincial legislatures and their dependent bodies.[102] The Charlottetown proposals attempted to break the earlier deadlock over self-government issues by adding general guarantees to the constitution which would be inert for up to ten years to give time for details to be worked out and enacted, but with the threat of full force and justiciability at the end of that time-frame. Specific amendments proposed included the following:[103]

- a reference to the fact that aboriginal peoples were historically self-governing and that their rights are recognised in Canada,

- immediate entrenchment of a right to self-government, to have effect after ten years, during which period the necessary constitutional underpinnings would be developed and, it was hoped, adopted,

- entrenchment of a process for developing and reviewing constitutional provisions dealing with aboriginal matters, and

- the representation of aboriginal peoples in the Senate as part of a larger process of Senate reform.

The Charlottetown Accord was supported by aboriginal leaders, and their interests received a major setback when it was rejected by Canadians (including a majority of aboriginal Canadians) in the ensuing referendum.

If developments since 1982 are any indication, it seems clear that some form of participation in constitutional deliberations and amendment will eventually be added to the constitution. Having been offered this in the 1992 proposals, aboriginal representatives are unlikely to settle for anything less, and the moral claim to some form of special constitutional status is strong. This endeavour raises a number of practical problems, however. Canada's aboriginal population is not homogenous in language, culture, ethnicity or territory. The constitutional status of bands is often

---

[101] See *The Process For Amending the Constitution of Canada*, 1991, Part 'C', pp.16-1, paras. 26-33 and recommendations 1-3.
[102] Canadian Charter of Rights and Freedoms, s.32.
[103] See *Aboriginal Peoples, Self-Government, and Constitutional Reform*, 1991, pp.19-2, *Shaping Canada's Future Together: Proposals*, 1991, pp.7-9, and Hogg, 1997, chapt.4.1 (c) at pp.69-70 and chapt.27.11.

site- and band-specific,[104] which means that it is by no means clear that every band would have the same substantive or procedural rights to input. The intermingling of populations raises both logistical and political problems in gathering and assessing aboriginal input into the constitutional process. Aboriginal people, particularly those living in the general population, participate in federal and provincial elections, raising the question of whether they are represented in the amendment process in the same way as other Canadians or whether leaders selected in more traditional fora should speak for them.[105]

The fragmentation of the aboriginal population also makes it unlikely that aboriginal people will speak with a single voice in any amendment process. Individuals and groups can and do disagree about priorities and how to proceed. This is, of course, the same with other constituent groups, but it raises the need to establish consensus-building and decision-making structures within the aboriginal community as a whole so that its positions, once determined, are coherent and can be put authoritatively.[106] Canada's non-aboriginal community speaks through federal and provincial legislatures which have established procedural rules for debate and decision-making. Aboriginal self-governance methods, on the other hand, vary from one community to another. Some communities have faced conflicts between band councils chosen by conventional elections and chiefs or councils chosen by heredity or other traditional means. Many aboriginal people live interspersed in non-aboriginal communities and have no mechanisms for consultation or input at all. There may also be problems determining status at the individual level. Whether a person who has some aboriginal ancestry has legal status as an 'indian' or aboriginal person in Canada can be difficult to determine, and may depend on the statutory or constitutional provision in question.[107] The question of who should have such status with respect to the right to participate in

---

[104] *R. v. Sparrow* [1990] 1 SCR 1075. On aboriginal traditional and treaty rights and the factors which determine whether they still apply in individual cases, see Hogg, 1997, chapt. 27.5-27.8. Statistical estimates of Canada's aboriginal population vary from about 500-650,000 individuals with formal status under the federal *Indian Act*, with an additional 500,000 Métis and non-status Indians: Hogg, 1997 chapt 27.1(b) *Canada Yearbook, 1997*, page 33 and tables 3.15-3.17, pp.88-90 (1991 census figures). Of the total population, only about 59% live in aboriginal 'reserve' communities; the rest are distributed throughout the general population. See statistical report *Facts on Stats*, Issue #11, March-April 1996, Canada Dept. of Indian and Northern Affairs.

[105] Cairns, 1997, pp.85-86. Given the small percentage of aboriginal people in all but a very few northern constituencies, most aboriginal Canadians maintain that the legislatures do not speak for them, and that they therefore require a more direct form of representation.

[106] See, for example, Hall, Tony 'AFN's reckoning with self-rule', *Ottawa Citizen*, July 19, 1997, p.A-11, which discusses the 1997 election of a new Grand Chief by the Assembly of First Nations. The very existence of the AFN, which has become the predominant focus for the development and articulation of aboriginal positions on a Canada-wide basis, testifies to the recognition by aboriginal people that such a forum is needed and to their substantial progress in developing it.

[107] Hogg, 1997, chapt. 27.1(b). See also Frideres, 1988, pp.6-17. Frideres discusses the question of legal status and estimates that more than one million of Canada's present inhabitants have some aboriginal ancestry.

the formal amendment of the constitution has not yet arisen.

There is also the question of whether aboriginal peoples would have input in the same form and degree for all proposed amendments, or whether the degree of input would be greater for changes which directly affected aboriginal interests. The structure of the 1982 amending formula and s.35.1 of the *Constitution Act, 1982* suggest that some form of variable input would be appropriate, but the details would have to be worked out and agreed. As with constitutional amendments affecting other constituent interest groups, there would also be the legal and political question of whether a particular proposal (such as amendments to effect the secession of Quebec) indirectly affected aboriginal interests to a degree sufficient to invoke any special consultation or consent requirements.[108]

Many of the past conflicts between Canada's aboriginal and majority populations arise, in part, from the fact that traditional forms of governance of Canada's First Nations are inherently informal by European legal standards. Aboriginal demands for self-government powers have been rejected in the past by provincial governments because proponents could not provide detailed information on how they would work and how they would interact with the established orders of government. This conflict is to some degree being addressed by the development of people and institutions within the aboriginal community who are capable of developing, articulating an ultimately of implementing, models of self-government. There is also a growing acceptance of both the legitimacy of self-government itself and the practical viability of some of the proposals being proposed. Where self-governance is concerned, institution-building has been seen as a problem for aboriginal peoples to deal with among themselves, but the amendment of the Constitution of Canada is another matter. Constitutional change affects everyone, and aboriginal input will be expected to stand up to the scrutiny of the population as a whole, a reality which is by no means free of controversy.[109] The progress of Canada's aboriginal and non-aboriginal communities towards practical self-government gives substantial grounds for optimism, but reconciling the unstructured and informal realities of aboriginal life and self-government in Canada with the process of amending the Constitution, the most formal and structured of legal and political exercises, is likely to represent a significant challenge for the foreseeable future.

---

[108] S.35.1 commits the federal and provincial governments to the principle of consultation before any amendment to the federal power to legislate in respect of 'Indians, and land reserved for Indians' (subs.91(24) of the 1867 *Act*) or Part II of the 1982 *Act* which establishes aboriginal rights. This principle might well be carried forward in any further change to the 1982 amending formula, but this would still leave open the question of aboriginal input into constitutional amendments in general, and to amendments to other parts of the constitution which directly affected aboriginal interests in some way. See Monahan, 1995, pp.15-17, where it is argued that the federal government would be in breach of its fiduciary obligation to Quebec's aboriginal population, were it to agree to secession without their consent. As noted elsewhere in this chapter, the Supreme Court declined to address this question in the 1988 *Secession Reference* case.

[109] Cairns, 1997, pp.80-82.

While there has been no change to the status of aboriginal people in the constitutional amendment process since the 1982 Charlottetown proposals, some recent developments do affect the constitutional status of aboriginal people and their relationships with the non-aboriginal majority outside of that process. Two of these, the question of the interests and status of Quebec's aboriginal population, and the recent completion of a comprehensive agreement concerning the land-claims and self-government demands of the Nisga'a people of British Colombia, warrant comment here.

Aboriginal interests continue to complicate the question of restructuring the constitutional relationship between Quebec and the rest of the country, and constitute a significant legal and political obstacle to those who advocate secession. Quebec's aboriginal population contends that it has an historical relationship with the federal government deriving from sovereign dealings with the British Crown, and vigorously opposes any change which would limit aboriginal rights and interests.[110] In response to Quebec's provincial referenda on sovereignty, it's aboriginal groups have held referenda of their own, with 'overwhelmingly federalist results', raising questions about whether any secession would include the large portion of aboriginal lands, particularly in the north.[111] Quebec sovereignists dispute this. They acknowledge the need to protect minority rights, but argue that any secession would take with it the entire territory of the present province and that aboriginal rights can only be exercised within the context of national constitutions, including that of a sovereign Quebec, should it secede.[112]

Five aboriginal groups intervened in the 1998 case *Reference re Quebec Secession*, four of them arguing that their essential interests would be profoundly affected by secession and that it could not be brought about under the Constitution without their consent. The Supreme Court found that secession required one or more constitutional amendments and, hence, negotiations to produce the necessary changes, but it declined to address the specific amending mechanisms or the status or roles of aboriginal groups in the process.[113] The concerns of aboriginal groups were also expressed in the consideration of the 1999-2000 federal legislation dealing with referendum clarity, where the only amendment to the Bill added aboriginal groups to the list of parties who must be consulted by the House of

---

[110] The views of the Cree people of Quebec are set out at length in *Sovereign Injustice: Forcible Inclusion of the James Bay Cree Territory into a Sovereign Quebec*, Grand Council of Quebec Crees, Nemaska, Quebec, 1995. On the question of territory, see also 'Crees use [Quebec Premier] Bouchard argument on division', *Canada Globe and Mail*, January 30, 1995, p.A5.

[111] Cairns, 1997, p.86.

[112] Hon. J. Facal, Quebec Minister of Intergovernmental Affairs, Legislative Committee on Bill C-20, meeting #10, 24 February, 2000, available on-line at: http://www.parl.gc.ca/36/1/parlbus/commbus/house/CommitteeMinute.asp?Language=E&CommitteeID=116.

[113] The positions of the groups are summarised by MacLauchlan, 1997, at pp.171-73. The judgment of the Supreme Court discusses the constitutional position of minority rights, including those of aboriginal peoples, at paras.79-82. See also paras. 105 (no finding as to what amendment process would apply) and 139 (aboriginal interests to be taken into account in constitutional negotiations).

Commons before deciding whether a referendum question and vote in favour of secession were sufficiently clear.

Developments on Canada's west coast are of a more positive nature. In July 1998, after a Supreme Court decision[114] and 22 years of on and off negotiations, a modern treaty was agreed between the Nisga'a people of British Columbia, the Government of British Colombia, and the Government of Canada. This agreement contains an extensive package of changes, providing not only for the settlement of long-standing claims to land rights and natural resources, but also a system of self-government for the Nisga'a.[115] Once the treaty is implemented, the Nisga'a will draft and adopt their own constitution (by referendum), and will gain legislative powers in areas which are of direct concern to them. Some of these powers will be concurrent with those exercised by the federal and provincial legislatures under the Constitution of Canada. In a few specific areas, Nisga'a laws will have priority over those of the other legislative bodies insofar as they apply to Nisga'a lands and people.

As with the 1996 regional veto legislation and 1999-2000 referendum clarity Bill, the self-government elements of the Nisga'a agreement represent an attempt to bring about changes which affect constitutional status and relationships without formal amendments to the constitution itself. As a modern aboriginal treaty, the Nisga'a agreement automatically has constitutional status and protection under s.35 of the *Constitution Act, 1982*. This has given rise to questions about its exact constitutional status, how it would be amended once adopted, and arguments that it amounted to a formal constitutional amendment. Opponents of the agreement took the position that, in creating what amounted to a new, partially sovereign order of government, it altered the existing constitutional allocation of legislative powers between the federal and provincial governments. In their view, such a change could not be validly made without recourse to the formal amending procedures of Part V of the *Constitution Act, 1982*. Since the agreement involved the Government of British Colombia, this would also have necessitated a referendum under provincial law.[116]

The federal and provincial governments, backed by most constitutional experts, argued that, while the agreement would attain entrenched constitutional status once ratified, this did not make it a constitutional amendment. In their view, s.35 of the *Constitution Act, 1982* recognised and affirmed aboriginal and treaty rights, including both those which existed as of 1982, and those which might

---

[114] *Calder v. British Colombia (Attorney General)* [1973] S.C.R. 313.

[115] *Nisga'a Final Agreement*, August 4, 1998. The full text and related documents are available from the Government of British Colombia at: http://www.aaf.gov.bc.ca/aaf/treaty/nisgaa/docs/nisga_agreement.html. The Nisga'a also maintain a web-site with the text, their views and other information about the Agreement and ratification process. See http://www.ntc.bc.ca.

[116] See evidence of Gordon Campbell, opposition leader of British Colombia, *Minutes of Proceedings and Evidence of the Standing Committee on Aboriginal Affairs and Northern Development*, Canada House of Commons, November 18, 1999, pp.1514-1515, available at: http://www.parl.gc.ca/ InfoComDoc/36/2/AAND/Meetings/Evidence/aandev12-e.htm#T1450.

be created later by agreements such as that involving the Nisga'a. In that sense, the land and self-government interests of the Nisga'a had always been constitutionally protected, and the 1998 agreement and the federal and provincial legislation implementing it simply clarified the nature and extent of the interests involved.[117]

The final legislative hurdle to Nisga'a self-government was cleared on April 13, 2000, when federal legislation implementing the *Agreement* became law, and aboriginal and non-aboriginal Canadians alike look to the Nisga'a with interest, and some optimism, to see what they will make of their new powers.

## V. THE WAY FORWARD: CAN AN ACCEPTABLE AMENDING FORMULA BE FOUND?

The adoption of Canada's present constitution in 1982 reflected consensus that it was time to end the formal role of Westminster, but not much else. Since then, deliberations have not resolved fundamental differences with respect to how the Canadian federation should be structured and how power should be balanced and allocated within it. The amending formula lies at the heart of a delicate balance not only of the constitutional influence accorded various interests, but also overall rigidity and flexibility. As the principal mechanism of entrenchment, the formula has been a key element of all recent constitutional deliberations. It was at the heart of the 1982 patriation debate, and has figured prominently in the demands of the provinces, Quebec and aboriginal people since then. The provinces collectively seek to preserve their political powers against federal encroachment and individually to protect or expand their constitutional influence. Quebec and aboriginal peoples, the two most polarised factions, both seek to place minority protections, which they see as critical to their survival, beyond the reach of easy amendment. More fundamentally, both groups seek constitutional status as a symbol of respect, dignity, and recognition of their own models of what the Canadian federation has been in the past and should be in the future. Their demands have become more nationalistic and deeply entrenched.[118] Since these demands are

---

[117] See legal opinions of Prof. P. Hogg and R.V. Farley to the effect that the agreement was not an amendment to the Constitution of Canada and therefore did not trigger the referendum requirement of the provincial *Constitutional Amendment Approval Act*, available at: http://www.aaf.gov.bc.ca/aaf/treaty/nisgaa/docs/nisga_agreement.html and http://www.aaf.gov.bc.ca/aaf/news/1998/Farley.htm, respectively. See also evidence of Prof. Hogg and Prof. P. Monahan, *Minutes of Proceedings and Evidence of the Standing Committee on Aboriginal Affairs and Northern Development*, Canada House of Commons, November 23, 1999, pp.1304-1400, available at: http://www.parl.gc.ca/36/1/parlbus/commbus/house/CommitteeDocument.asp?DocumentID=13957&Language=E. On the nature of aboriginal rights and the need for constitutiona protection of those rights, see Hogg, 1997, chapt.27.5-27.7.

[118] See Cairns, 1997 suggesting that the increasing nationalism of both Quebeckers and aboriginal people has become a major impediment to the sort of civil dialogue likely to bring about constitutional reforms.

inconsistent with each other and with those to which other Canadians subscribe, political and social reconciliation and compromise will be needed before any legal changes to the amending formula can be agreed.

The more extreme Quebec nationalists have expressed the view that, at least insofar as the question of the status of Quebec is concerned, such reconciliation and compromise is impossible. Leaving aside the tactical motives for making such claims, the constitutional way forward will be shaped to a large degree to the extent to which they are borne out. To some degree, such pessimistic views ignore the political reality that, while compromise and popular consensus must be substantial for constitutional reform, it need not be unanimous or universal. While the demands of some Quebeckers will not be satisfied with anything short of secession and sovereignty, the more moderate views of most Quebeckers, whether nationalist or federalist leave room for both movement and optimism. The same is true for the other contentious issues of Canadian federalism and the factions presently involved in the debate.

The challenge of making further progress may have more to do with procedure than substance. The positions of the key players have all been clearly established, and identifying areas where compromise is needed is not difficult. What will be difficult, and is clearly the major challenge facing the players, is finding a procedure which encourages compromise and a realistic assessment of what is possible, on the part of both negotiators and of the constituencies they represent. The attempts of the 1980s and '90s established that populations will not accept compromises if they are excluded from the process, which makes some degree of direct involvement on the part of the various constituencies both necessary and inevitable.

Developing a realistic constitutional dialogue will take time, both for the 'cooling off' of constitutional passions and the education of population groups. Canadians are probably better informed than most about their constitution and its problems, but there is a need for a realistic assessment of the possibilities for constitutional compromise. The constant negotiations of the 1970's, '80's and '90's led to some inflated expectations about the prospects for constitutional change and the potential impact of such changes had they been made. There is also a need for realistic assessment of what constitutional reforms can and cannot be expected to achieve in the real world. A compromise amending formula and future substantive amendments may well lay the groundwork for addressing the historical problems of Canada's aboriginal peoples, protecting the French language and culture of Quebec, or addressing other current or future issues, but constitutional measures alone will solve none of these problems. Constitutional rules function as a constraint on the making and application of ordinary laws, and can have substantial importance as symbols of the way in which the state and its citizens should conduct themselves, but they do not have the direct and profound impact that many Canadians suppose. In the case of Quebec, many of the pressures on language and culture are social or economic developments, making the assumption that language and culture would be better protected in a sovereign state than in the Canadian federation particularly open to question.[119] Similarly, constitutional changes may have little impact on the profound social problems confronting aboriginal Canadians.

In this context, the strategy of moving the agenda forward through piecemeal changes made by non-constitutional means may provide the necessary time, but it is not without risks. Not everyone seeks compromise, and slow changes create opportunities for more extreme factions in Quebec to create the impression of a complete *impasse*, in which Quebec's demands could only be met by secession. It may also open opportunities for sovereignists to create what they characterise as 'winning conditions' for secession, or to take advantage of randomly-occurring events or unrelated social or economic developments.

In the interim, the use of judicial and administrative measures and ordinary statute legislation can compensate to some degree for excessive constitutional rigidity, but there are risks here as well. Accomplishing piecemeal changes when formal ones are blocked may be preferable to not having changes at all, but attempting systematic constitutional changes by this means ignores the fundamental role of constitutions in allocating powers and status and as a safeguard against instability. The entrenchment of constitutions is intended to make amendment difficult, time-consuming and subject to greater consultation and deliberation than ordinary law-making, and the use of ordinary statutes to make constitutional changes in Canada sets a dangerous precedent, even if it is constitutionally valid.

The need for a constitutional balance between stability and flexibility is a critical issue which tends to be obscured in this debate. There is concern on the part of Canadian constitutional experts that further changes to the amending formula in the present constitutional climate would lead to even more excessive rigidity. All of the major players seeking constitutional change include demands which would have this effect. Quebec wants a veto, aboriginal people want a consent requirement, at least over some changes, and other provinces want vetoes of their own if Quebec has one. Not surprisingly, those same interests are reluctant to concede greater constitutional influence to others, since their own needs are not met and would become more difficult to meet if such influence was granted. Meanwhile, the constitution becomes more and more deeply entrenched as the political positions of the players do. Concessions will be required not only to break

---

[119] Quebec sovereignists have consistently maintained that the linguistic and other rights of minorities in the province would be protected, which would leave essentially the same internal relationship between francophones and anglophones that now exists intact. Even if the government of a sovereign Quebec was prepared to restrict the use of English and other languages to a greater degree than is possible under the present Canadian Constitution and the *Canadian Charter of Rights and Freedoms*, it still seems arguable that most of the pressures on the French language and culture arise from the Province's social and commercial relationships with the United States and the rest of Canada. Over the long term, secession would probably have little impact on social or commercial links with other countries, and a negative impact on the willingness of other Canadians to respect or preserve Quebec's language and culture.

the deadlock, but to produce a constitutional product which retains sufficient flexibility to permit the federation to evolve in the future.

Certain elements of the Constitution have been made more rigid, or at least their rigidity has been made more apparent, by judicial and legislative efforts after the 1995 Quebec referendum to establish the constitutional ground-rules for the secession of Quebec from Canada. From the perspective of some, clarity is a good thing in this area because the lack of it thus far has been exploited by sovereignists, who seek to exploit the lack of any reference to secession anywhere in the formal Constitution to declare independence simply because 50%+1 of Quebeckers vote for it. It is significant that those who disagree include both sovereignists and some Quebec federalists, who agree that the potential effect will be a shift of moderate Quebec nationalists from the federalist to the sovereignist camps, should another referendum be held. This also illustrates a central conflict between those who rely on adherence to the formal constitution and the rule of law and those who advocate more fluid (and faster), political solutions.[120] Leaving aside the views of militant sovereignists, who oppose the formal rules because they do not favour the outcome of secession, there is still a very real division among other Quebeckers, which arises from the political failure to obtain Quebec's consent to the 1982 Constitution, then or since. Whether politics or the rule of law prevail remains to be seen.

Finally, the political linkages between the different agendas, and not constitutional rigidity, defeated the 1987 and 1992 amendment proposals. The breaking of these linkages - a generosity of spirit which would allow each of the parties to allow one another's needs to be met, and the confidence of the parties in the generosity of others in allowing their own needs to be met - is an important, and probably essential, element of further constitutional evolution in Canada. Part of this generosity lies in the recognition that constitution-making is an open-ended, ongoing, and probably never-ending process, and in the willingness to keep talking for as long as it takes.

---

[120] See MacLauchlan, 1977, pp.156-57, which points out the conflict between the intentionally slow pace of constitutional change and the political pressures which would lead Quebec sovereignists to try to accomplish secession quickly after any referendum vote in favour of this.

## Chapter Six

# FROM ABOLITION TO AMENDMENT: LIFE AND DEATH OF CONSTITUTIONS IN FRANCE

### Sophie Boyron[*]

In any given constitutional system, the choice of processes for changing or amending constitutional norms will determine the type, pace and extent of constitutional change. It might also settle other fundamental questions for the regime such as its survival, its efficiency, its legitimacy etc. In fact, it could easily be argued that the regulation of constitutional change is the very basis for the existence of constitutional law.

France does not escape these broad generalities; moreover, the process of creation and amendment of constitutional norms in France is rich and revealing. On the one hand, there have been seventeen different regimes and fifteen constitutional instruments since the revolution of 1789.[1] On the other, constitutional change in the present regime is particularly interesting: not only has the formal amendment procedure not always been respected but the regime established in the written document has been substantially 'changed' by constitutional practice.

## I. A CHEQUERED CONSTITUTIONAL HISTORY

For a long while constitutional change took the systematic form of new constitutional instruments. It was often felt necessary that a totally different constitutional document be adopted in order to wipe out the effects of the previous regime. For instance, the 1958 constitution was drafted in reaction to the regime of the fourth Republic.

### A. A Triumph of Optimism over Experience

France's fifteen written constitutional instruments represent a prodigious experience of constitutional drafting: French constitutions have covered most types of regimes from constitutional monarchy to presidential regimes etc., and

---

[*] Lecturer in Law, University of Birmingham.
[1] France has been described by one writer as a "constitutional laboratory".

from empires to parliamentary regimes. Indeed, most forms of government that exist have been covered at some point of French constitutional history. Moreover, the choice between amending and abolishing the Constitution is generally made in favour of abolition.

*1. Choosing abolition over amendment: a traditional choice*

It is clear, as has been emphasised above, that French lawyers, politicians and even the electorate[2] often chose to start afresh. However, this does not mean that this process of creation of new constitutional norms is chaotic or random.

It has been suggested that since 1789 a French constitutional law tradition has emerged.[3] To understand this, it is important to draw a line between substantive constitutional values (such as fundamental rights and civil liberties) and institutional values (such as form and structure of government and political institutions). If a strong tradition can be recorded with regard to the first category[4], it is doubtful whether a tradition as regards a specific form of government or structure of the institutional organisation was ever created.

However, this is not to say that the institutional choices have always occurred by chance. A number of writers have pointed out that France knows some sort of constitutional cycle: in the first period of the cycle, the legislative branch is predominant; this is followed by a period of reaction, during which the executive branch dominates the political system; lastly, a third period of conciliation between the various branches is established for a while until the cycle starts again. Although some people might query the systematic simplicity of such an exposition, it is clear that there is some truth in this presentation.

In terms of creation of constitutional norms, this is often translated into a clear disavowal of the former regime. The constitution of the fifth Republic in that sense is not much different to most previous constitutional instruments. It could be argued that this recurring choice is itself part of the tradition that makes French constitutional law.

*2. A certain understanding of constitutionalism*

There is a certain assumption in France that political reality can be controlled by a written text and that political change can be engineered by written constitutional change. This belief is common to politicians, public lawyers and as far as it is possible to ascertain, the electorate. All share the belief that 'bad' political behaviour and practices can be corrected by 'good' and effective constitutional provisions. For instance, the Constitution of 1946 contained very detailed

---

[2] In 1945, the electorate took the decision by referendum to terminate the third Republic and to have a new constitution drafted.
[3] See J. Bell, *French Constitutional Law*, OUP, 1992, at p. 2.
[4] Although some regimes did not really respect them.

mechanisms for withdrawing confidence from the government and it was hoped that these provisions would eradicate the governmental instability which dominated the end of the third Republic.

Moreover, some institutional structures or forms of government are regarded by all as being more likely to attract 'bad' behaviour and practices. A clear example of this is the question of a single chamber parliament. The French electorate has twice rejected the option of having a unicameral regime: in 1945, the draft for a new Constitution which created a single chamber regime was rejected by the people,[5] and in 1969 de Gaulle's wish to abolish the *Sénat* failed to meet with the support of the electorate. The deep-seated dislike of single chamber parliaments can itself be explained by history: many have argued that Robespierre's dictatorship and the *Terreur* were due to the fact that the Convention, the only chamber of that regime, was not controlled by another. In turn this means that in France, constitutional history, or more accurately the perception that people have of constitutional history, has often determined fundamental aspects of new regimes at any given time.[6]

However, it important to distinguish between the difference in impact which recent history has as against more remote history: in the first case, weaknesses and failures of the previous regime are present in the mind of the drafters and they will attempt to correct them systematically; while in the second lessons are drawn and traditions established; in time they construct a certain understanding of constitutionalism.

*3. The need for a new regime: a case study*

When the present Constitution, that of the fifth Republic, came into force on 4 October 1958, it was impossible to foresee the constitutional and political changes that the new regime would bring. However change was wished for and necessary. The fourth Republic is known to constitutional lawyers more for its political and constitutional problems than anything else. French political life had been perturbed for quite some time when the 1958 change occurred. One of the more obvious disturbances was the notorious government instability: between 1946 and 1958, twenty-one governments came and went, an average of less than seven months for each government. There was more than one reason for this situation. First of all, instability was already endemic in the previous Republic: during the second part of the third Republic, governments were easily dismissed.[7] Article 51

---

[5] It has been said that the vote was based on the rejection of two elements of the regime: Parliament had only one chamber and, moreover, there was no mention of the Declaration of the Rights of Man of 1789.

[6] One of the best examples might be the question of a single chamber constitution.

[7] Between 1870 and 1940, there were 104 governments, which gives an average of eight months each. Even then, the system was clearly perverted: one government (Blum's in 1937) resigned although no vote had taken place, and twice governments resigned, although each had just obtained a vote of confidence (Briand's in 1910 and Daladier's in 1934).

of the 1946 Constitution was therefore drafted so as to put a stop to the problem: the government was only responsible before the lower chamber; only the Président du Conseil could request a vote of confidence, the withdrawl of which required an absolute majority; lastly, dissolution (a deterrent) was open to the President of the Republic if two such governmental crises intervened within 18 months of each other.[8]

However, the protection provided by the Constitution in this area remained a dead letter: governments went on resigning on simple majority votes.[9] As a result, although governments kept resigning, no dissolution was possible since the constitutional conditions were never met.[10]

Political circumstances led to this situation in the *Assemblée Nationale*: first of all, politics became concentrated at the centre of the political spectrum since parties at each end were discredited, the extreme right because of the recent fascist experiences and the Communist Party from the beginning of the Cold War in 1947.[11] As a result, the *troisième force* which was posited at the centre of the political spectrum and included both socialists and *radicaux* formed most coalition governments. Secondly, the electoral system, proportional representation, strengthened the existence of small parties and led to the main parties being split into numerous factions. Any given government needed the support of many parties and factions to stay in power. When agreement between the coalition parties ceased, governments would fall.[12] Since political practice ensured that dissolution of the Assemblée Nationale was not a likely result of the fall of a government, the fear of dissolution did not therefore deter coalition parties from withdrawing support from government.

Consequently, no coalition managed to stay in power long enough to implement new policies. In effect, political choices, especially difficult ones, were never made since these are in essence controversial and would have resulted in the fall of the coalition of the day. Therefore and paradoxically the fourth Republic suffered from a second evil: Parliament was paralysed and found it difficult and even impossible to pass legislation on the most innocuous of subjects; substantial legislative powers ended up delegated to the executive, although this move in itself was unconstitutional. The third Republic had encountered the same problem and the 1946 Constitution attempted to reinstate the sovereignty of Parliament; Article 13 specified that only the *Assemblée Nationale* could pass legislation and that the right to legislate could not be delegated. However as early as 1948, two mechanisms were resorted to in order to get round this provision;

---

[8] During the third Republic, it was possible for any minister to request a vote of confidence which could be withdrawn with a simple majority in either of the two legislative chambers.

[9] These votes were achieved after careful calculations: they were meant to show the government a clear majority of discontents but fall just short of the number for an absolute majority so that the effects of Article 51 were paralysed.

[10] Only once was such a dissolution possible in 1955.

[11] At the time, the Communist Party was a much larger party than it is today.

[12] Each MP would hope to gain a portfolio in the process.

firstly, the *loi-cadre*[13] and secondly, an extreme form of delegated legislation: matters were delegated to the executive on a quasi-permanent basis.[14]

Soon, the defects of the third Republic became the failures of the fourth. One is forced to recognise a rather strong resistance of political reality to change.[15] If constitutional change is to be achieved, a purely textual change is unlikely to be sufficient; political behaviour and tradition need to evolve or change as well.

B. Adopting the New Constitution

The arrival of de Gaulle in power was very similar to that of Pétain in 1940 (and the latter soon headed a fascist regime). The country was not invaded by foreign powers but it was on the brink of a civil war. Moreover, the condition of drafting a new constitution which de Gaulle imposed before agreeing to become Prime Minister could easily have led to great abuse.

To counteract this, several mechanisms were created to ensure that de Gaulle did not stray: the statute of 3 June 1958 was voted by Parliament to imposecertain principles to be respected in the new Constitution and also to establish a procedure by which the text was to be drafted.[16]

---

[13]  A statute contains some rough political orientations and the executive legislate by filling in the details.
[14]  Although this could be changed by statute at any time.
[15]  In order to explain fully the experience of the adoption of the Constitution of the fifth Republic it is necessary to understand that in-depth constitutional reform had in effect been necessary since the third Republic, and that the fourth Republic was already an attempt to achieve such reform (even though it failed).
[16]  Loi constitutionnelle du 3 Juin 1958:
L'Assemblée nationale et le Conseil de la République ont délibéré, L'Assemblée nationale a adopté, Le Président de la République promulgue la loi dont la teneur suit:
Article unique - Par dérogation aux dispositions de son article 90, la Constitution sera révisée par le Gouvernement investi le 1er juin 1958 et ce, dans les formes suivantes:
Le Gouvernement de la République établit un projet de loi constitutionnelle mettant en oeuvre les principes ci-après:

1. Seul le suffrage universel est la source du pouvoir. C'est du suffrage universel ou des instances élues par lui que dérivent le pouvoir législatif et le pouvoir exécutif;

2. Le pouvoir exécutif et le pouvoir législatif doivent être effectivement séparés de façon que le Gouvernement et le Parlement assument chacun pour sa part et sous sa responsabilité la plénitude de leurs attributions;

3. Le Gouvernement doit être responsable devant le Parlement;

4. L'autorité judiciaire doit demeurer indépendante pour être à même d'assurer le respect des libertés essentielles telles qu'elles sont définies par le préambule de la Constitution de 1946 et par la Déclaration des droits de l'homme à laquelle elle se réfère;

5. La Constitution doit permettre d'organiser les rapports de la République avec les peuples qui lui sont associés.

Pour établir le projet, le Gouvernement recueille l'avis d'un comité consultatif où siègent notamment des membres du Parlement désignés par les commissions compétentes de l'Assemblée nationale et du Conseil de la République. Le nombre des membres du comité consultatif désignés par les commissions est égal aux deux tiers des membres du comité.

Le projet de loi arrêté en Conseil des ministres, après avis du Conseil d'Etat, est soumis au

## 1. An attempted coup: the fatal blow

Beyond the long term constitutional problems mentioned, in 1958 the fourth Republic was faced with an immediate crisis: the Algerian war. The decolonisation of Algeria represented an extremely difficult political problem for which no easy solution could be found. Considering that most solutions would be heavily criticised and lead almost most certainly to the downfall of the government, no administration felt able to take any decision as regards the future of Algeria. As a result, the situation there, which became more untenable by the day, precipitated the fall of the fourth Republic. However, it is difficult to believe that absent the Algerian question the fourth Republic would have survived. It is more likely that another problem would have achieved the same result later.

The end of the fourth Republic can be easily dated: on 13 May 1958, a crowd invaded government headquarters in Algiers (supported by the neutrality of both police and army) and created a *Comité de salut public*. This in itself should not have affected the regime, however, the political system was going through its twentieth ministerial crisis and no one was assuming governmental power at the time. Moreover, the army was supporting the rebellion openly. The depth of the problem can be evidenced by two incidents: the President of the Republic, René Coty, called on the Army to cease its insubordination, but to no avail; the Minister for Algeria was also unable to travel there, since the *Comité de salut public* had served an exclusion order against him! The metropolitan government had lost control over Algeria. Furthermore, politicians in Paris were quite content with the coup: they wanted to stop the creation of a new government headed by Pierre Pflimlin whom they suspected of wanting Algeria's independence.[17]

On 14 May, General Massu called on de Gaulle to come back to power, a call repeated by General Salan on 15 May. In a press conference on the same day, de Gaulle declared himself ready to do so.[18] On 24 May, the rebellion spread to Corsica and from then on, power was clearly divided between the legal power of the Government in Paris, the *de facto* power of the insurrection in Algiers, and the moral authority of de Gaulle.

As time passed, the government's authority and legitimacy decreased even further and finally, on 28 May, Pflimlin resigned. The President of the Republic increased the pressure on Parliament by addressing an ultimatum: 'Call de Gaulle to office or I will resign'.

---

référendum. La loi constitutionnelle portant révision de la Constitution est promulguée par le Président de la République dans les huit jours de son adoption.

[17] However, the coup had the opposite effect: a large parliamentary majority supported his new government on the very day of the coup.

[18] 'Naguère le pays, dans ses profondeurs, m'a fait confiance pour le conduire tout entier jusqu'à son salut. Aujourd'hui, devant les épreuves qui montent de nouveau vers lui, qu'il sache que je me sens prêt à assumer les pouvoirs de la République'.

On 31 May de Gaulle was asked to form his government. It received the confidence of the *Assemblée Nationale* on 1 June 1958 by 329 votes to 224.[19] However, this quasi-insurrection revealed a deep crisis due to strong divisions among the population.[20]

## 2. A legitimised process?

De Gaulle had accepted to become the last Prime Minister of the fourth Republic on the condition that he would put forward the draft for a new Constitution. He had attacked the institutions of that regime consistently since the beginning, and had already made known his constitutional ideas in one significant speech - 'the *Discours de Bayeux*' - in June 1946.[21] Even though the political circumstances were rather pressing, it is interesting that the people were not consulted by referendum about the fate of the 1946 Constitution as had been done with the Third Republic[22]. It is clear, however, that the population had long ago ceased to support the regime.

The draft was to be examined first by a *Comité consultatif*, two thirds of the members of which were appointed by each chamber of Parliament and the remaining third by the *Conseil d'Etat*. Once adopted by the *Conseil des Ministres*,[23] it was to be submitted to a referendum.

An *avant-projet* was drafted by a working group of civil servants who met under the chairmanship of Michel Debré as early as 12 June 1958. This was followed by a number of constitutional meetings under the chairmanship of de Gaulle with the following in attendance: Guy Mollet, Pierre Pflimlin, Félix Houphouet-Boigny, Louis Jacquinot, René Cassin, Michel Debré.[24] A first draft was ready by the end of July 1958. At this point the opinion of each minister was sought and the text was submitted to the *Conseil de cabinet*.[25] The draft Constitution was then examined by the *Comité consultatif* provided for in the

---

[19] The Communists and some socialists (mendesists, a faction who supported Mendès France) voted against his investiture.
[20] Three clear divisions could be drawn at the time: French population in Algeria v French population in Metropolitan France, government v. army and lastly, politicians v. population. Also, one should not forget that a strong anti-parliament feeling had already been voiced through the success encountered by the Poujadist movement earlier on.
[21] Although it was after the rejection of the first 1946 draft Constitution, it had no influence on the Constitution finally adopted on 27 October 1946.
[22] See the referendum of 21 October 1945 which required a new Constitution: 18,584,764 were in favour while 699,136 were not.
[23] The *Conseil des Ministres* is the equivalent of the Cabinet in French constitutional law.
[24] Half these personalities were important figures in the fourth Republic (Guy Mollet, Pierre Pflimlin, Félix Houphouet-Boigny) while the others were de Gaulle's men (René Cassin, Michel Debré, Louis Jacquinot).
[25] Which comprised de Gaulle and all the ministers of his government. In fact his government was itself composed of a great number of prominent political figures of the fourth Republic. This might explain the conclusion we have reached that the text of the 1958 Constitution in appearance instituted nothing more than another parliamentary regime.

statute of 3 June 1958. The amendments to the draft put forward by the *Comité* were finalised on 14 August 1958. Finally, the *Conseil d'Etat*[26] examined the text forwarded on 21 August 1958, and the *Conseil* acted with great efficiency. Its amendments were presented on 28 August. A final text was adopted by the *Conseil des Ministres* on 3 September 1958 and a referendum was held on 28 September. The Constitution was adopted by 82.6 per cent of the votes cast and promulgated on 4 October 1958.

It is worth pointing out that the 1958 Constitution does not contain any provisions as regards the continuance of elements of the previous legal order (legislation,[27] constitutional conventions etc). There were transitory provisions in the last title of the Constitution which aimed at achieving two different things: Article 91 organised the passage from one set of institutions to the other while Article 92 gave rather large powers to the Government to implement the new Constitution and to legislate in general.[28]

## II. BY-PASSING THE FORMAL PROCEDURE

One of the most interesting features as regards the revision process of the fifth Republic lies in the fact that the formal process was not always used in order to revise the Constitution. Constitutional practice has in fact increased the number of procedures which can be used in order to achieve this aim. In particular Article 11 was used on a number of occasions to effect changes, although not originally intended to be used for this purpose. One might wonder however about the likelihood of Article 11 being used in this manner again.

A. The Formal Process of Revision

The very question of the procedure to be used to amend the 1958 Constitution is itself a controversial subject. Article 89, the only article included in Title XIV 'Revision', was obviously the article which should have been systematically resorted to in order to amend the 1958 Constitution. However, in practice it was not.

---

[26] The *Conseil d'Etat* both advises the government on legislative matters and questions of drafting and is the highest of the administrative courts.

[27] France has had seventeen different regimes since the first revolution of 1789. It might seem paradoxical, but the changes in regimes were rarely followed by a similar upheaval in legislation: the Code Civil adopted in 1804 has survived all these regimes to this day, albeit somewhat amended.

[28] For instance, Article 91 specifies that the new institutions must be in place within the four months of the promulgation of the Constitution. Meanwhile, Article 92 gives the Government legislative power subject to various conditions.

## 1. The procedure of Article 89

Article 89 contains two procedures: one which requires the intervention of the electorate and one which is mainly parliamentary. The initiative for revision lies either with the President of the Republic (on a proposal from the Prime minister) or with parliamentarians.[29] Both procedures begin in the same manner, an identical draft of the proposal having to be adopted by the two chambers. Then the President has the choice of submitting the draft to either a referendum or the *Congrès*[30]. If it is submitted to the *Congrès*, it needs to be adopted by a three-fifths majority.

Furthermore, Article 89 contains three important restrictions: no revision can take place when the integrity of the (French) territory is in jeopardy[31] or when the Presidency of the Republic is vacant, and the republican nature of the regime cannot be abolished.[32] These limitations can be explained by constitutional history: on 10 July 1940, the Parliament passed to Pétain all powers of government while part of France was occupied by Germany. This resulted in the creation of a fascist dictatorship in the France of Vichy.[33] Moreover, France has not only known five republics[34] but also three constitutional monarchies, two empires, and other dictatorial regimes; it was a wise reminder (if of doubtful effect)[35] that the republican nature of the regime must not be altered.

In essence, the procedure is relatively simple. Lessons had been learnt from the fourth Republic; the procedure contained in Article 90[36] of the 1946

---

[29] In reality no proposal has ever been started on the initiative of MPs.
[30] The Congress is made up of both chambers (*Assemblée Nationale* and *Sénat*) convened together.
[31] See Article 89 Paragraph 4: 'No procedure for revision may be instituted or continued when the integrity of the territory is in jeopardy'.
[32] See Article 89 paragraph 5: 'The republican nature of the regime cannot be revised'.
[33] The regime of Vichy was the part of France which was not occupied by the Germans from July 1940 until 1943.
[34] Even the regime which led to the third Republic hesitated for a while between a republic or a constitutional monarchy.
[35] In reality it will be shown later that a study of French constitutional history reveals that Constitutions rarely get amended in depth: they are simply abolished and replaced to facilitate the birth of another regime.
[36] 'La révision a lieu dans les formes suivantes.

La révision doit être décidée par une résolution adoptée à la majorité absolue des membres composant l'Assemblée nationale.

La résolution précise l'objet de la révision.

Elle est soumise, dans le délai minimum de trois mois, à une deuxième lecture à laquelle il doit être procédé dans les mêmes conditions qu'à la première, à moins que le Conseil de la République, saisi par l'Assemblée nationale, n'ait adopté à la majorité absolue la même résolution.

Après cette seconde lecture, l'Assemblée nationale élabore un projet de loi portant révision de la Constitution. Ce projet est soumis au Parlement et voté à la majorité et dans les formes prévues pour la loi ordinaire.

Il est soumis au référendum, sauf s'il a été adopté en deuxième lecture par l'Assemblée nationale à la majorité des deux tiers ou s'il a été voté à la majorité des trois cinquièmes par chacune des deux assemblées.

Constitution was so complex that it was nearly impossible to use. Only once was such a revision successful[37] and it took four years to realise.[38] It proved impossible to achieve the necessary corrections which might have allowed the institutions of the fourth Republic to survive. Two other constitutional reforms were being processed when de Gaulle came to power. The second revision had been started in 1955 and had already been judged too restrictive as to the list of articles to be redrafted; therefore, another and third revision was also started in May 1958, and was to run parallel to the second one!

In effect, Article 89 remedied two major defects of the amendment procedure of the 1946 Constitution: the length of the procedure and the lack of right of initiative for the Government.

The idea of the *Congrès* is attributed to Guy Mollet. He certainly aimed to protect the declining powers of Parliament and to create a quicker and easier way of revising the Constitution.

*2. The use of Article 89*

Article 89 has been used 11 times:

- 1963: date of parliamentary sessions
- 1974: right given to MPs to refer a statute to the *Conseil constitutionnel*
- 1976: death or incapacitation of a candidate in presidential elections
- 1992: reform necessitated by the Maastricht Treaty
- July 1993: reform of the *Conseil Supérieur de la Magistrature*, creation of the *Cour de Justice de la République*, and criminal liability of Government
- November 1993: reform necessitated by the Schengen Agreements (right of political asylum)
- 1995: extension of the referendum, length of parliamentary session, parliamentary privilege
- 1996: extension of the jurisdiction of Parliament to matters of social security (financial arrangements)
- 1998: status of New Caledonia

---

Le projet est promulgué comme loi constitutionnelle par le président de la République dans les huit jours de son adoption.

Aucune révision constitutionnelle relative à l'existence du conseil de la République ne pourra être réalisée sans l'accord de ce Conseil ou le recours à la procédure de référendum'.

[37] It was concluded in 1954.
[38] The important dates of the revision of 1954:
- the resolution was adopted by the *Assemblée Nationale* on 30 November 1950
- the resolution was adopted by the *Conseil de la République* on 25 January 1951
- the bill was adopted by the *Assemblée Nationale* on 22 July 1953
- the bill was adopted by the *Conseil de la République* on 17 March 1954
- the final adoption of the revision by the *Assemblée Nationale* occurred on 30 November 1954

- January 1999: reform necessitated by the Amsterdam Treaty
- July 1999: sexual equality in political life and reform necessitated by the Treaty on the International Criminal Court.

It is possible to organise these amendments into three categories: minor institutional changes, consequential institutional changes, implementation of international agreements.

*a. Minor institutional changes*

Two reforms can be entered in the category of minor institutional changes: the first reform of 1963 which aimed only at changing the dates of the spring session of the Parliament, and the 1976 reform which aimed at closing a loophole in the organisation of presidential elections.[39]

The situation in New Caledonia, which necessitated a constitutional revision so as to take the first steps towards independence for those territories[40], is not a minor political matter. However, in institutional terms, it could not be regarded as leading to fundamental changes in the regime. It is a revision with important political significance but little institutional impact.

*b. Consequential institutional changes*

A number of amendments of the Constitution were quite important either because they led to fundamental changes in the working of the institutions or because they are evidence of a general move to alter the basis of the regime.

For instance, the amendment of 1974 which gave a right to MPs to refer draft legislation to the *Conseil constitutionnel* might not have been seen to be a fundamental revision at the time. However, in practice, reference by MPs has led the *Conseil* to give its opinion on numerous occasions and to create an important body of case law. Moreover, the *Conseil constitutionnel* modified the very role it assumed in the institutional balance of the fifth Republic: it moved away from being a protector of the prerogatives of the government to being the guardian of rights and civil liberties.

As the 1990s have seen a general constitutional move away from the executive, various revisions have attempted to give more power and legitimacy to the other two branches and to the electorate in general: for instance, the revision of July 1993 which altered the membership of the *Conseil Supérieur de*

---

[39] The *Conseil constitutionnel* pointed out that there was no provision in case a candidate were to die or to become incapacitated during the presidential election.

[40] The redrafting of Article 77 was part of a package which was the result of arduous negotiations with all the populations of the island. It culminated in a referendum which underwrote the negotiations and allowed constitutional change.

*la Magistrature*[41] and created the *Cour de Justice de la République* increased the independence of the judiciary. Furthermore, the reform of 1996 and some aspects of the reform of 1995 aimed at reinforcing the status of Parliament; this was achieved by creating one annual session of Parliament (1995) and by extending the jurisdiction of Parliament to financial legislation for social security matters (1996). Again, two versions aimed at strengthening the elements of popular sovereignty in the Constitution to counterbalance the negative effects of representative democracy: the field of the referendum was extended (1995), and more recently the Constitution was amended so as to promote equal access of women to political life (July 1999).[42]

*c. International treaties*

Four international treaties have required that the Constitution be amended: the Maastricht Treaty, the Schengen Agreements, the Amsterdam Treaty and the Treaty on the International Criminal Court. In all cases the necessity to amend the Constitution was declared by the *Conseil constitutionnel*.[43]

Three aspects of the Maastricht Treaty wwere not compatible with the 1958 Constitution: the right for all EU citizens to vote in municipal elections, some decisions of the European Central Bank and the granting of visas to non-European nationals. All these would found to run contrary to French national sovereignty.

Furthermore, the Schengen Agreements which allow a request for asylum to be treated by another Member State were considered incompatible with the provisions of the 1946 Preamble providing political asylum to anyone persecuted for his/her actions in favour of freedom.

Again, Title IV of the EC Treaty on 'Visas, asylum, immigration and other policies related to the free movement of persons', which was introduced by the Amsterdam Treaty, required another revision of the Constitution. The new Title contained further transfers of competence which had not been included in the Maastricht Treaty but which needed to be authorised by the Constitution.[44]

---

[41] Another constitutional reform was abandoned recently which aimed at reforming once again the *Conseil Supérieur de la Magistrature*.

[42] In a decision of 1982, the *Conseil constitutionelle* had decided that the compulsory requirement of a female quote on electoral lists was not compatible with the principle of equality (C.Cons.82-146 DC, 9 November 1982, Municipal Elections, Rec. 66). It was therefore necessary to amend the Constitution before such legislation could be passed. This was finally done in July 1999.

[43] Although in the case of the Schengen Agreements this finding was somewhat surprising. Normally under Article 54, treaties or international agreements are referred to the *Conseil constitutionnel* before ratification. However, the Schengen Agreements were not thought to be incompatible with the Constitution and were never referred. The question of compatibility arose when a statute seeking to implement the Schengen Agreements was struck down by the *Conseil constitutionnel*. See C.Cons. 92-308 DC, 9 April 1992, Maastricht I, Rec. 55; C.Cons. 93-325 DC, 12-13 August 1993, Immigration control, Rec. 224.

[44] C.Cons 97-394 DC, 3 December 1997, Rec. 334.

More recently, the Treaty on the International Criminal Court led to the latest revision of the Constitution. Both the rules allowing a person to be arrested and transferred to the jurisdiction of the International Criminal Court regardless of rules on amnesty or limitation and the considerable investigative powers granted to the public prosecutor were not compatible with the French Constitution.[45]

## B. The Use of Other Constitutional Provisions

Three attempts have been made to evade Article 89, two of which were successful. Article 85 has been used once to revise the Constitution while Article 11 has been used twice, although the last attempt failed.

### 1. Article 85

Any discussion of Article 85 is rather obsolete since the part of the Constitution which contained it was abolished in the constitutional revision of 1995.

Part XII of the 1958 Constitution contained a number of provisions which organised the relationship between French colonies and Metropolitan France within an organisation called the Community.[46] Once a colony had become independent it had to leave the Community. However, some of the new States had asked to remain in the Community after having acceded to independence. It was therefore necessary to revise the Constitution. Article 85 itself contained a specific procedure to revise the institutions of the Community; it only required that a text be voted in identical terms by the French Parliament and the *Sénat* of the Community.

In 1960, the revision of Article 86 allowed independent States to be part of the Community and more importantly added another mechanism to revise Part XII of the Constitution: these provisions could be amended by agreements concluded between all the members of the Community.

At the time of the revision it was felt that the amendments were such that they warranted the use of Article 89 rather than Article 85. For instance, the *Conseil d'Etat* in an opinion[47] pointed out that the revision changed the very nature of the Community and for that reason went beyond the scope of Article 85. However, this was never the subject of a real controversy, unlike what happened with Article 11.

### 2. Article 11

The use of Article 11 proved at the time to be extremely controversial. It was used in order to by-pass the procedure of Article 89. De Gaulle knew that

---

[45] C.Cons. 98-408 DC, 22 January 1999, JO 24 January 1999 p.1317.
[46] Not to be confused with the European Community.
[47] Opinion of 26 April 1960.

Parliament would not have approved the two reforms that he wanted to see adopted. Therefore he decided to invoke Article 11, which provides the President of the Republic with a right to submit a number of questions (for instance, the organisation of the institutions or the ratification of a treaty) to a referendum.[48]

In reality, the potential competition between Article 89 and Article 11 had already been raised during the discussions which led to the adoption of the new Constitution. On 9 July 1958 a debate took place about the potential overlap between these provisions and the possibility of undertaking a revision of the Constitution using Article 11.

De Gaulle, first President of the fifth Republic, had adopted a reading of the Constitution which was heavily presidential. Unfortunately, the electoral system which chose the President of the Republic was indirect and therefore would give little legitimacy to the next incumbent. If the presidential reading favoured by de Gaulle was to be preserved, it was necessary to endow the presidency with more legitimacy. Not everyone would have de Gaulle's historical and moral authority. Parliament was obviously opposed to any such change (more particularly the *Sénat* which opposed de Gaulle's policies throughout his mandate). De Gaulle therefore resorted to a simple referendum and linked his fate to the result of the referendum. He would resign if the result was negative. The referendum which took place on 28 October 1962 showed that 62 per cent of the population agreed that the President be directly elected. Articles 6 and 7 of the 1958 Constitution were amended accordingly.

However, in 1969, a second revision using Article 11 was not successful. De Gaulle wanted to create regions in France and at the same time to curb considerably the powers of the second chamber, the *Sénat*.[49] The result of the referendum of 27 April 1969 was negative: 52 per cent of the population did not support the reform. De Gaulle resigned from office.

Although the referendum statute was referred to the *Conseil constitutionnel* for scruniny, it decided that it did not have jurisdiction to decide on the matter.[50] It was made clear in a later decision that it was impossible to contest legislation once it had been endorsed by a referendum, since a referendum constitutes 'the direct expression of popular sovereignty'.[51] It is an interesting question whether the use of a procedure which seems clearly unconstitutional is rendered

---

[48] See the original drafting of Article 11: 'On the recommendation of the Government during sessions [of Parliament], or on joint recommendation of both chambers published in the *Journal Officiel*, the President of the Republic may submit to a referendum any bill concerning the organization of public authorities, or requiring the approval of a Community agreement, or providing for authorization to ratify a treaty that, without being contrary to the Constitution, would affect the functioning of its institutions.

Where a referendum has decided in favour of the bill, the President of the Republic shall promulgate it within the time limit set out in the preceding article'.

[49] It was not part of the legislative process any more: it could only be consulted.

[50] C.Cons. 62-20 DC, 6 November 1962, Rec. 27.

[51] C.Cons 92-313 DC, 23 September 1992, Rec. 94.

constitutional once it has received the assent and legitimacy of the electorate. Perhaps the answer lies in Article 3 of the 1958 Constitution which emphasises that national sovereignty belongs to the people, and that it finds its expression through elected representatives and by means of referenda.

## C. The Role of the *Conseil constitutionnel*

The issue of the validity of the referendum raises the question of reviewl by the *Conseil constitutionnel*.

### 1. Little control over the revision process

Generally, it can be said that there is no mechanism by which the constitutionality of an amendment or its consistency with the rest of the Constitution can be tested. However, there might be some circumstances in which such a review of constitutionality could be envisaged.

It was mentioned above that the referendum of 1962 was referred to the *Conseil constitutionnel*. Although it declared that it did not have jurisdiction to undertake such a review, the *Conseil constitutionnel* explained that a reform accepted by popular sovereignty could not be questioned.[52] It would be interesting to see if the *Conseil constitutionnel* dealt differently with wholly 'parliamentary' revisions.[53]

Moreover, the three limitations in relation to the amendment procedure have been mentioned above: it is not possible to start or complete a procedure of revision when the integrity of the French territory is in jeopardy (e.g. during an invasion) or when the office of President of the Republic is vacant;[54] also, the republican nature of the regime cannot be changed. One might wonder whether the *Conseil constitutionnel* would intervene if a revision did not respect these condition. Although it is difficult to make any prediction of this kind, one might well ask whether a decision of the *Conseil constitutionnel* would have made any difference in 1940 and whether the *Conseil* would even have been heard considering the political (and military) circumstances.

### 2. The need for a revision

Although the *Conseil constitutionnel* does not have any jurisdiction to give an opinion, in 1976 it made a declaration regarding the organisation of the campaign leading to the election of the President of the Republic.[55] A loophole needed to be

---

[52] See C.Cons. 62-20, 6 November 1962, Rec. 27 and C.Cons. 92-313 23 September 1992, Rec. 94.
[53] That is to say the revisions requiring the intervention of the *Congrès*.
[54] This is a reference to what happened in July 1940 when the *Assemblée Nationale* handed to Pétain all the powers of the Republic.
[55] Opinion of 24 May 1974, Rec. 57.

filled: if a candidate were to die during the campaign, no provision was made for a party to present a new candidate. A revision of the Constitution was therefore adopted in order to deal with this eventuality

Article 54 of the Constitution gives jurisdiction to the *Conseil constitutionnel* to check international agreements and treaties against the Constitution; if the *Conseil* decides that a given treaty is not compatible with the Constitution, the Constitutionneeds to be amended before the treaty can be ratified. To this day only three such revisions have been necessary, to allow the ratification of the Maastricht Treaty, the Amsterdam Treaty and the Treaty on the International Criminal Court.

According to Article 61, the compatibility of ordinary statutes with the Constitution can be checked by the *Conseil*. In August 1993, the *Conseil constitutionnel* decided that a statute on immigration was unconstitutional: one of the provisions struck down simply implemented the system created by the Schengen Agreements to deal with political asylum seekers.[56] A concise revision of the Constitution intervened in November 1993 in an atmosphere highly charged with political controversies.[57]

*3. Avoiding a revision*

It is quite difficult to assess the role of the *Conseil constitutionnel* in avoiding the need for formal revision of the Constitution. Often the *Conseil* specifies the interpretation of the legislation which needs to be adopted in order to be compatible with the Constitution. The result is different for ordinary statutes and international treaties: as far as ordinary statutes are concerned, it simply means that more legislative provisions will be declared compatible with the Constitution, while as far as international treaties are concerned it means that a revision which would otherwise be necessary is avoided. This could be argued for the decision of 29-30 December 1976[58] about direct elections to the European Parliament: it is only because the *Conseil constitutionnel* denied some fundamental features of the European Communities that the Single European Act was found compatible with the Constitution.

Lastly, having redefined the texts which are included in the 1958 Constitution, the *Conseil* in fact revised it informally. Moreover, by integrating both the famous Declaration of Rights of 1789 and the Preamble of the 1946 Constitution

---

[56] Only one Contracting State is responsible for the application. If the demand for asylum is made in another State, it simply passes it on to the relevant Contracting State.

[57] The 1946 Preamble specifies that: 'Any person persecuted for his activities on behalf of freedom has the right of asylum in the territories of the Republic'. The *Conseil constitutionnel* had therefore argued that a provision implementing the Schengen Agreements which simply passed a demand of asylum to the responsible contracting party was not compatible with the principle quoted above. French authorities should always be able to decide on the right of asylum if the applicant is persecuted for his action in favour of freedom.

[58] C.Cons. 71-76 DC, Rec. 15.

into the formal Constitution, the *Conseil constitutionnel* has avoided the need for a formal declaration of rights along the lines of most modern constitutions.[59]

D. The Procedure of Revision: Some More Questions

There are still a number of grey areas as regards the working of Article 89:

1. How can MPs let it be known that they want to use their right of initiative when planning a revision of the Constitution?

The revision of 1963 is indicative of what needs to be done. In order to modify the spring parliamentary session, the *Assemblée Nationale* adopted a private Member's bill introduced by its legal committee. The proposal was clearly supported by the Government of the time, but it would be a real problem if the proposed revision was not supported by either the Prime Minister or the President of the Republic.

2. Has the President of the Republic a right not to proceed with a constitutional reform once it has been adopted by both chambers?

In 1973, Pompidou started a procedure of revision reducing the length of the mandate of the President of the Republic from seven to five years.[60] Although the proposal was adopted by both chambers separately, it was clear that the required majority of three-fifths would not be found if the *Congrès* were convened. Consequently, Pompidou decided to postpone this vote. He died a year later and the procedure was never completed. More recently, two revisions of tghe Constitution regarding the *Conseil Supérieur de la Magistrature* and the status of New Caledonia were similarly abandoned in January 2000. This time the decree, which had already fixed the date for the sitting of the *Congrés,* was repealed later. The political conditions for the revisions had not been met.[61]

Two questions arise from this: first, one might wonder whether the President has the discretion to stop, even temporarily, a procedure of revision and choose the time of the final vote; and secondly, since the procedure has been interrupted, could it be revived and finished without starting again from the beginning.

3. Would it be possible to submit to a referendum a revision which hasalready been rejected by the *Congrès*?

If a revision was rejected by the *Congrès*, it has been argued that the President might be able to resubmit the same text to a referendum. It is doubtful

---

[59] A revision which might have been difficult to undertake and for which a consensus might have been difficult to find.
[60] It would have the advantage of matching the length of the mandate of the lower chamber to that of the President.
[61] The reform of the *Conseil Supérieur de la Magistrature* was part of a package which had not yet been approved.

whether such a solution would be consistent with Article 89. However, it is clear that a decision of the electorate would to some extent clear the irregularities of such a procedure. It would be difficult to oppose a revision adopted by popular sovereignty.

4. What are the respective roles of the Prime Minister and the President of the Republic as regards a procedure of revision?

During a 'cohabitation' period, the President of the Republic is not supported by a majority in the *Assemblée Nationale* and has little legitimacy as a result. The situation arose in 1993 when it became necessary to amend the Constitution in order to fit in with the requirements of the *Conseil constitutionnel* concerning the right to asylum. The Interior Minister, Mr Pasqua, announced that if the President refused to support the procedure of revision and convene the *Congrès*, as it was possible for him to do under Article 89, a referendum would be called. Although Mr Mitterand declared that a referendum could not be called without his assent, he convened the *Congrès* as requested. However, this political episode shows that the respective roles of President and Prime Minister are not altogether clear and this could have serious implications as regards the proper working of the procedure.

## III. THE REGIME: EVOLUTION OR REVOLUTION?

Although the 1958 Constitution might appear to be a rather straightforward constitution, it hides a number of potential interpretations; and some have been resorted to in turn.

Moreover, certain revisions of the Constitution have had a different impact on the interpretation of the Constitution itself. Amendments have already been classified above, but it is important to study the way that they have been adopted in order to establish what the authors intended and the impact that they have had.

A. Various Strategies for Amending

Generally, the authors of constitutional revisions tend to draft the revisions so as to change the text only to the extent that is strictly necessary. Also, there has been a long standing constitutional movement which contests the all too presidential working of the regime. A number of reforms can be explained by this movement.

*1. A drafting policy: changing the strictly necessary*

An analysis of the revisions achieved so far reveals that amendments have been circumscribed as much as possible: in 1960, a number of paragraphs were added to the relevant articles: Articles 85 and 86; in 1962, Articles 6 and 7 were the only provisions redrafted; in 1963, one paragraph of Article 28 was changed; in 1974, two paragraphs were added to Article 61, and it was claimed at the time that the authors had been so economical with the change that in fact they had overlooked Article 54 and had forgotten to extend to international treaties the new right of MPs to refer texts to the *Conseil constitutionnel*.[62] In 1976, a number of paragraphs were added to Article 7 in order to deal with the loophole.

Again the later revisions of 1992, July and November 1993, 1995, 1996, 1998, January and July 1999 follow the same principle: for instance, in November 1993 an extra Article 53-1 was added to the Constitution, while in 1996, if two Articles had to be amended and an Article 47-1 inserted, it was simply because the revision created a new area of jurisdiction for the Parliament as well as a new legislative procedure.

Therefore as far as drafting techniques are concerned, the Constitution is usually tinkered with but no major redrafting has ever taken place. Even though some of the revisions have led to important constitutional change, there is no correlation with formal constitutional change. Obviously most of the change has happened at the level of practices, conventions and traditions.

## 2. *Readjusting the regime: an ever present consideration*

The regime, which took from the beginning a presidential turn, was accused of being too successful: Parliament, all powerful during the fourth Republic, was under such limitations that it could not play its democratic role any more.

In the 1970s, the revision which gave MPs the right to refer bills for reviewl to the *Conseil constitutionnel* proceeded from the idea that the status of parliamentarians should be raised and their powers increased.

During the revision necessary to ratify the Maastricht Treaty, both chambers entered into a battle with the government and bargained for more powers: a number of concessions were made and some extra provisions were added to the original draft of the constitutional statute. Moreover, in order to complete the revision, the government committed itself to proposing a more in-depth constitutional reform. The process started in November 1992. A constitutional committee for the revision of the Constitution was created; it submitted its proposals in February 1993. Unfortunately, parliamentary elections brought a new majority to power and most of the reform was abandoned: two constitutional bills had been submitted to the *Sénat* just before the elections; while the first one dealt with various provisions concerning the organisation of the judicial system,[63] the second envisaged the creation of a more democratic balance between the executive

---

[62] This was rectified in 1992, during the revision concerning the Maastricht Treaty.
[63] Three institutions were amended: ordinary courts could refer a statute to the *Conseil constitutionnel*, members of the government could be tried by the Haute Court de Justice and the body responsible for appointmens and disciplineof the judiciary, the *Conseil Supérieur de la Magistrature*, was made more independent.

and the legislature. The new majority processed the first bill[64] but dropped the second.

This might be the reason why, in 1995, another revision was resorted to: Chirac had promised during the electoral campaign to give more powers to Parliament. The 1995 revision created an annual parliamentary session and gave more powers to each chamber over the control of its agenda. It was but a pale copy of the second bill put forward by Mitterand in 1993 according to which, for instance, both chambers were given many more powers with regard to committees of inquiry[65] and the legislative procedure[66].

## 3. Institutionalising a practice

The formal revision process has twice been used to 'constitutionalise' a practice that was not really foreseeable when the Constitution was drafted in 1958.

As mentioned above, the role that was assumed by de Gaulle as President of the Republic was not really warranted by the text of the Constitution. De Gaulle's charismatic personality and historical legitimacy allowed him to transform the office of Head of State into the leading figure of the executive. However, it was difficult to believe that the next incumbent would enjoy the same authority; indirect elections do not bestow much legitimacy. The revision of 1962 was therefore absolutely necessary if the reading of the Constitution adopted by de Gaulle was to continue.

Similarly, the 1974 revision which led to the *Conseil constitutionnel* playing a totally different role to the one created by the Constitution in reality strengthened a choice made earlier by the *Conseil constitutionnel*. The turning point was, in fact, a decision of 1971 where the *Conseil* clearly established itself as guardian of rights and civil liberties. The revision of 1974 allowed this interpretation to grow and the role of the *Conseil* to be clearly established but it did not initiate the change. However, most bills are in fact referred to the *Conseil constitutionnel* by MPs. As a result, the Conseil has been able to build up a sophisticated body of case law in the area of human rights. This would have been impossible had the *Conseil* had to rely on references made exclusively by the President, the Prime Minister or the President of each chamber as was provided for originally. There would not have been enough cases to create a new role for the *Conseil constitutionnel*.

---

[64] The right of ordinary courts to refer a matter to the *Conseil constitutionnel* was also taken out of the bill.
[65] The bill not only increased the number of enabled legislative committees from six to eight, but it also permitted a minority of MPs to call for a committee of inquiry.
[66] A decision of both presidents of chamber could call a meeting of the *commission mixte paritaire*, made up of seven members of each chamber, to find a compromise on legislation which is under discussion.

*4. Looking for legitimacy*

Lastly, one revision of the Constitution was designed to provide the government with an enhanced legitimacy in order to implement a difficult and controversial political agenda. The revision of 1996 which extended the powers of the Parliament in the area of social security financing was not strictly necessary.[67] However, social unrest was such that the government wanted to show that the reform had strong support in parliament, hoping that it would give the government enough authority to adopt and apply all these rather unpopular measures. Considering later political developments, it is doubtful whether this trick worked. If the government had really wanted to be endowed with more legitimacy, electoral legitimacy and recourse to a referendum was a better way to achieve it.[68]

B. Amending the Constitution by Practice

The most striking phenomenon of the 1958 Constitution lies in the fact that the regime, its interpretation and its practices swing back and forth from a parliamentary system to a more presidential one. Moreover, as a result, one institution has also seen its role completely changed from what the Constitution had envisaged.

*1. From a parliamentary to a presidential regime and back*

The text of the Constitution clearly organised a parliamentary regime: the government appointed by the President of the Republic was to be supported by the confidence of the lower chamber. However, as already mentioned, the regime was interpreted from the beginning in a rather different manner by de Gaulle himself. The most important figure of the executive was soon to be the President of the Republic and not the Prime Minister (unlike what happened in the previous republics). The Prime Minister was appointed by the President and stayed in office at the discretion of the President. Moreover, the President defined the policy orientations to be followed by the government. He was *de lege* a head of State and *de facto* a head of government. The parliamentary regime was changed for a presidential one. This interpretation of the Constitution was consecrated by the revision of the Constitution of 1962. By allowing the President of the Republic to be elected directly, the legitimacy and role of the President was institutionalised.

---

[67] The jurisdiction of Parliament is included at Article 34, but Article 34 provides that the list can be revised by a simple organic law.
[68] The government chose to use the parliamentary procedure of revision, where both chambers meet in the *Congrès*, rather than call a referendum.

However, since the mandates of both the President of the Republic[69] and of the *députés*[70] of the *Assemblée Nationale* do not coincide, the French regime lapses on a regular basis into a parliamentary regime: the President of the Republic is elected for seven years while the *Assemblée Nationale* is elected for five; if after five years, the new legislature does not bring a majority supporting the presidential party, the President appoints the leader of the former opposition as Prime Minister.[71] The President of the Republic becomes a traditional Head of State and leaves to the Prime Minister the task of governing the country. Moreover, not only is the interpretation of the Constitution radically different but all conventions attached to one or the other interpretation change accordingly. This ability to change from a semi-presidential regime to a parliamentary one without any formal revision of the Constitution is a specific trait of the French constitutional regime.

## 2. Reaching for understanding

In order to better understand constitutional change at present in France, it might be useful to establish a list of the various elements that shape constitutional change and make it possible. So as to comprehend fully the phenomenon of constitutional change, it might also be helpful to evaluate the relative importance of each element and the pattern of relationships which emerges. However, for reasons of space it will not be possible go beyond the first stage.

### a. A web of practices, conventions and formal provisions

It has been pointed out that the important evolutions of the regime were reinforced and perpetuated by formal revisions of the Constitution. For instance, de Gaulle had enough personal and historical legitimacy in order to create an important role for the President of the Republic; however, for anybody else it would have been impossible to maintain such an prominent role. The same observation was also made about the changing role of the *Conseil constitutionnel*. Furthermore, the regime changes from being parliamentarian to presidential and vice versa, at regular intervals, because the two readings can now be found in the 1958 Constitution: there is a sort of competition between both interpretations. The institution of the President apart, the Constitution is still strongly parliamentarian in its structure.

Practices, conventions and formal amendments are literally entwined in French constitutional change. For instance, a web of formal provisions, conventions and practices has been created for any one of the two interpretations

---

[69] The President of the Republic is elected for seven years.
[70] The *députés* are elected for five years.
[71] This may happen sooner if the *Assemblée Nationale* elections are called earlier (as is the case at the time of writing with Jospin and Chirac).

of the regime. Furthermore, each element seems to feed on the other: practices and conventions have led to formal revision, which in turn has led to the creation of further practices and conventions, and the abolition of others. For instance, de Gaulle had little electoral legitimacy but attempted to acquire some by linking his fate to the result of every referendum that he organised. Later this practice was abandoned: today no President would be expected to resign after a negative referendum, but they all have the electoral legitimacy that direct elections bestow. A change in the formal constitution has led to a readjustment in some of the practices.

Here, constitutional change clearly appears to be a dynamic and permanent exercise. Constitutional change does not happen once and for all; the system of government, the regime evolves all the time.

### b. Emergence of 'new traditions'

It has been mentioned briefly above that there are (and this is true in most systems of government) traditions which will influence and sometimes even dictate constitutional change.

It might seem paradoxical to speak of a 'new tradition' but it reflects quite well the way fundamental values change and evolve, at least in the French system.

At first sight, it is easy to be struck by the novelty of the fundamental values which constitutional change embodies and reflects, but a closer look often reveals that these new values have a solid traditional basis.

The need to have a strong executive has been a recurring theme, a tradition, in French constitutional history; and there has been a great number of (more or less dictatorial) leaders, heads of State or 'republican monarchs'. However, there is also a clear break from the past, the appearance of a 'new tradition': for the first time, the 'republican monarch' is endowed with a strong popular legitimacy. There had been attempts in the past at supporting a strong executive by popular legitimacy but it had never worked before.[72]

Again, the acceptance of a strong control of constitutionality can be regarded as a complete break from the past and from the ideal of *la souveraineté de la loi*.[73] This was one reason why the *Conseil constitutionnel* was not made into a full constitutional court in 1958. It was not meant to check the substantive choices of any legislation, but its procedural validity only. By adopting the role of guardian of rights and civil liberties, the *Conseil constitutionnel* appears to have broken totally from the past, to have stood against history. Again, a 'new tradition' seems to have appeared. However, if one considers that the *Conseil d'Etat* through its case law had already created a long standing tradition of protection of rights and

---

[72] The bonapartist movement tried to achieve this, but in reality never managed it during either the first or second empire.
[73] The French equivalent of Parliamentary sovereignty.

civil liberties by the courts, it attenuates this idea of a complete break from the past.

### c. *Constitutional change and the political system*

Sometimes constitutional change has led to and facilitated deep changes in the political system and its functioning. The constitutional change is so important that it has a major effect on the political system itself.

The revision of the Constitution which led to the President of the Republic being recognised as so fundamental not only led to in-depth changes in the French political system, but, in turn, the success of the constitutional change was to a great extent due to an emerging and unexpected new political phenomenon: the 'parliamentary majority'. Before 1962, governments were invariably supported in Parliament by a coalition of numerous political parties at the centre of the political spectrum. For the first time in 1962, parliamentary elections saw the election of a party with a clear majority: from then on, the French political system came to know the 'majority phenomenon'; a party or a coalition of parties has a majority of seats in the *Assemblée Nationale* and supports the President (or the Prime Minister in a cohabitation period). This new phenomenon in 1962 has had a deep seated effect on French political life: for instance, political parties were completely reorganised around that period, a new political class emerged, a right-left polarisation appeared. The 1962 phenomenon was unexpected and if not accidental had certainly not been engineered by the adoption of a new constitutional instrument. However, without this upheaval of the political system, it is doubtful whether the 1958 Constitution would have been so successful at providing political and constitutional stability. It is certainly regarded today, as a, if not THE, fundamental element of the French political and constitutional system.

## IV. CONCLUSION: A CERTAIN IDEA OF CONSTITUTIONALISM?

Constitutionalism is often presented in the literature as a well defined and generally well charted concept. However, from what has been described above, it seems that France has a very specific idea of constitutionalism which is strongly influenced by its traditions of constitutional change and creation. In fact, it could be argued that there might be as many definitions of constitutionalism as there are different ways of achieving constitutional change.

From these observations, it is obvious that each constitutional system has developed its own understanding of constitutionalism. This needs to be taken into account if and when comparing constitutions: it is fundamental to research first what idea or tradition of constitutionalism is favoured in each system. Assuming the pre-existence of a unique definition of constitutionalism might seriously compromise the whole comparative enterprise.

Chapter Seven

# CONSTITUTIONAL CHANGE IN THE FEDERAL REPUBLIC OF GERMANY AND THE EFFECTS OF GERMANY'S EU-MEMBERSHIP ON THE GERMAN BASIC LAW

Dr. iur. Sven Reckewerth[*]

## I. INTRODUCTION

The Basic Law of 23 May 1949[1], Germany's Constitution, is the supreme law of the Federal Republic of Germany. It contains fundamental legal provisions which form the basis of the institutional organisation of the State. The Basic Law provisions can be broadly distinguished into basic human rights provisions and rules which govern the organisation of the State. The Basic Law is Germany's formal constitution and is therefore designed to provide a long-term system of rules governing the country's fundamental legal structure, although it is regarded as being open for constitutional change. However, on account of the Basic Law's intention to provide for stability, its provisions are protected from overhasty changes by a requirement for qualified majorities in the legislative bodies. The first part of this article looks at how constitutional change can be brought about and addresses the issue of whether several ways exist to amend the Basic Law.

The second part of this article investigates the effects of Germany's membership of the EU on its Constitution. It will look at those areas of German constitutional law in which there have been changes as a consequence of developments in Community law.

However, before the issue of constitutional amendment can be addressed, it should briefly be pointed out what German lawyers mean when they use the term 'constitutional amendment' (*Verfassungsänderung*). As the term 'constitution' has more than one meaning, the way in which this term is used throughout this article must be made clear. German constitutional lawyers draw a distinction between a

---

[*] Fellow in German Law, The British Institute of International and Comparative Law: Lecturer in Law, University College, London.
[1] The German Basic Law (*Grundgesetz der Bundesrepublik Deutschland*) of 23.5.49, English translation in: Federal Republic of Germany, Documents on Democracy in the Federal Republic of Germany, FRG Press and Information Office, Foreign Affairs Division, 2nd ed. 1994.

'constitution in a formal sense' and a 'constitution in a substantive sense'. The former term refers to the written legal document including all its provisions, which are designed to set up the fundamental legal structure of a society; these provisions are accordingly superior to any other law applicable in the territory, more deeply entrenched and enacted by way of a different procedure. The latter term refers to the factual structure of a State under its laws including all the legal provisions which govern the organisation of public life, but which are not enacted in a different way, which do not override any other law and which are not more deeply entrenched. The term 'constitutional amendment' refers only to changes to the 'constitution in the formal sense' and hence denotes the re-drafting of the provisions of the Basic Law.

As a consequence, 'constitutional amendment' does not refer to changes to the constitution in the substantive sense. Accordingly, an amendment to a statutory provision of electoral law, for example, would not be protected by the safeguard provisions designed to make constitutional change more difficult to achieve. Although such an amendment could have serious ramifications for the process of electing the Members of Parliament and hence for the composition of the government, the constitutional requirements for amendment do not apply.[2] The reason for this set-up can be seen in the fact that not all legal provisions are regarded as being equally fundamental to society. If every provision of substantive constitutional law were subject to the amendment requirements of Article 79 BL, necessary changes would be hindered because qualified majorities in the legislature would be required for such amendments. This would conflict with the function of the legislature which is generally designed to make and un-make statutory law as it pleases. Hence, constitutional amendment pertains only to changes to the constitution in the formal sense.

## II. SEVERAL WAYS TO AMEND THE BASIC LAW?

At a first glance, it appears conceivable that the Basic Law could be amended in three different ways. First, there is the procedure prescribed by Article 79 BL which is characterised by the enactment of a statute that expressly amends the Basic Law. Secondly, there is a possibility of the conclusion of an international treaty which entails subsequent constitutional amendments. Thirdly, the question arises of whether or not the Basic Law can be amended by a referendum.

A. The Amendment Procedure under Article 79 Basic Law

Article 79 BL lays down a number of constitutional requirements for amendments to the Basic Law. Article 79 (1) sentence 1 BL states that any provision of the Basic Law may be amended only by a law which expressly modifies or supplements its wording. Art 79 (2) BL requires such a law to be carried by a majority of two-thirds

---

[2] Bryde, in *v. Münch, Grundgesetz-Kommentar* (C.H.Beck Verlag, München, Germany, 1983), Art. 79, no. 2.

of the votes in both the Federal Parliament (*Bundestag*) and the Federal Council (*Bundesrat*). Article 79 (3) BL enumerates a number of elements which must not be affected by any constitutional amendment.

*1. Article 79 (1) Basic Law*

Article 79 (1) BL provides that any constitutional amendment requires the enactment by the federal legislature (*Bundestag* and *Bundesrat*) of a statute. The procedure by which such a law is passed is identical to that for ordinary legislation. The requirement for an express difference in the wording of the new version of an amended provision is accounted for by the demands of the principle of legal certainty (*Bestimmtheitsgrundsatz*). What this requirement is meant to avoid is that a statutory provision is enacted which amends the substance of the Basic Law without explicitly amending its wording. Accordingly, the Federal Constitutional Court held that a constitutional amendment must be clearly discernible;[3] hence, even if the required majorities were reached, it would not be possible for the legislature to adopt a law that substantively deviates from the Basic Law if it did not expressly change its wording.

*2. Article 79 (2) Basic Law*

Article 79 (2) BL provides for the requirement of a majority of two-thirds of the Members of the Federal Parliament (*Bundestag*) and two-thirds of the votes of the Federal Council (*Bundesrat*) for the enactment of a law that amends the Basic Law. As noted above, the reason why such a substantial impediment to constitutional amendments was introduced into the Basic Law lies in the fact that constitutional provisions affect the fundamental organisation of society and are clearly aimed at ensuring stability. Hence, it is presumed that an amendment to such a provision should require a higher degree of legitimacy derived from broader support in the democratically elected parliament and the body representing the *Länder*.

*3. Article 79 (3) Basic Law*

Article 79 (3) BL prohibits amendments to the Basic Law which concern the division of the Federation into *Länder*, their participation in the legislative process, or the principles laid down in Arts. 1 and 20 BL. The purpose of this immutability clause or, as we say, 'eternity clause' (*Ewigkeitsklausel*) is to perpetuate certain structural elements of the organisation of German society under the Basic Law. It could perhaps be argued that such a provision is undemocratic, as it prevents the people from making decisions with regard to these fundamental elements. However, when the Basic Law was enacted in 1949 the introduction of Article 79 (3) BL was

---

[3]  BVerfGE 9, 334, 336

regarded as providing the Basic Law with a necessary element of stability which in the light of the most recent German history was felt to have been lacking in the Weimar Constitution of 1919. Article 79 (3) BL intends to prevent a development identical with or similar to what happened in 1933 when Hitler rose to power in an apparently legal manner. The provision aims to render illegal all acts by which certain fundamental elements of the constitution would be repealed.[4]

Another argument for Article 79 (3) BL is that for the first time the Basic Law has striven to entrench a number of democratic values in constitutional law. The Basic Law is thus not value-neutral; rather, it obliges the public bodies to discard an overly positivist approach to the law which finds its sole legitimacy in the concept of majority decisions. Finally, the rejected concept of a value-neutral form of democracy paved the way for the view that the Basic Law created a democratic system which is prepared to take defensive action against whoever tries to undermine its core values (*Konzept der abwehrbereiten Demokratie*).[5]

In practice, the immutability clause creates a hierarchy of provisions (*Normenhierarchie*) within the Basic Law, as the elements to be perpetuated by Article 79 (3) BL are effectively given precedence over the remainder of the Basic Law provisions. Hence, Article 79 (3) BL provides a standard against which newly adopted or amended constitutional provisions can be tested in court.

B. Amendment by international treaty

In the process of the reunification of the two Germanies in 1990, several provisions of the Basic Law were directly amended by Article 4 of the Unification Treaty.[6] The question arises whether or not this form of constitutional amendment was valid, as the only amendment formula contained in the Basic Law is that of Article 79 BL. As regards amendment by international treaty, the Basic Law is silent. However, what at first sight appears to present a problem can be easily explained. Under German law, the rights and obligations of an international treaty can take effect only when the treaty is incorporated into domestic law.[7] The Unification Treaty was implemented by a statute enacted by the legislature (*Bundestag* and *Bundesrat*) on 23.9.1990,[8] and the requirement of Article 79 (2) BL for a constitutional amendment of a two-thirds majority in both the Federal Parliament and the Federal

---

[4] Maunz/Dürig, *Grundgesetz-Kommentar*, (C.H. Beck Verlag, München, Germany, 1994), Art. 79, no. 28.

[5] Maunz/Dürig, *Grundgesetz-Kommentar*, (C.H. Beck Verlag, München, Germany, 1994), Art. 79, no. 29.

[6] Treaty between the Federal Republic of Germany and the German Democratic Republic on the Establishment of German Unity - Unification Treaty of 31.8.90, Federal Gazette, part II, pp. 889 et seq. (*Vertrag zwischen der Bundesrepublik Deutschland und der Deutschen Demokratischen Republik über die Herstellung der Einheit Deutschlands - Einigungsvertrag*).

[7] Art. 59 (2) BL: 'Treaties which regulate the political relations of the Federation or relate to matters of federal legislation shall require the approval or participation of the appropriate legislative body in the form of a federal law'.

[8] Federal Gazette, part II, pp. 885 *et seq.*

Council was complied with. Hence, the amendments to the Basic Law as contained in the Unification Treaty were made in the only manner prescribed by the Basic Law which is by statute enacted by the legislature under the procedure governed by Article 79 BL. As a result, the amendments contained in Article 4 of the Unification Treaty were procedurally constitutional.

C. Amendment by popular vote

The question could be raised whether or not the Basic Law could be amended by way of a referendum. Article 146 BL, in its revised version, states that:

The Basic Law, which is valid for the entire German nation following the achievement of the unity and freedom of Germany, shall cease to have effect on the day on which a constitution adopted by a free decision of the German people enters into force.

This might be interpreted in such a way that the Basic Law could be amended or repealed *in toto* and subsequently re-enacted, including amendments, when the German people say so in a referendum.

The problem has already arisen within the context of reunification. The question was whether or not the reunification of the two Germanies should be brought about either by way of the German Democratic Republic (GDR) acceding to the Federal Republic of Germany under Article 23 (2) BL or by way of enacting a completely new German constitution under Article 146 BL including a popular vote.[9] Article 23 (2) BL, read in conjunction with the Preamble of the Basic Law, stated that in the event that other parts of the original Germany should accede to the existing Federal Republic, the Basic Law would automatically take effect in the newly acquired territories. Effectively, this provided for the incorporation of parts of Germany as it was defined by the borders of 31 December 1937 into the Federal Republic, which would retain its identity while the old German Democratic Republic would cease to exist. Article 146 BL stated more broadly that the German people remained called upon to complete the union and freedom of Germany in free self-determination and stipulated that the Basic Law would lose its validity on the day on which a new constitution would come into force which has been decided freely by the German people. This provision suggested that the Basic Law was originally envisaged as only a provisional arrangement, to be replaced by a new constitution in the event of reunification which would have created a new State originating from the fusion of the two German States, subsequent to which both of the old Germanies would have ceased to exist and a new entity under international law would have arisen. As the Parliament of the German Democratic Republic, in a 1990 vote, decided that the GDR should join the Federal Republic under Article 23 (2) BL, the option of recreating Germany and enacting a new constitution under

---

[9] Maunz/Dürig-Scholz, *Grundgesetz-Kommentar*, (C.H. Beck Verlag, München, Germany, 1994), Art. 146, no. 4,5.

Article 146 BL was effectively rejected.

It was argued that these two options could be employed cumulatively, as it was hoped that more popular input into the reunification process was necessary to provide greater legitimacy to the new German Constitution. However, the prevailing view was that the two options had to be understood as being alternatives because each of them entailed different consequences for the Basic Law. If the reunification was achieved under Article 23 (2) BL, the Basic Law would 'survive' and be turned at the same time into the definite all-German Constitution, whereas employing Article 146 BL would have resulted in a new constitution, and the Basic Law would have lost effect.

Another question was whether or not these two options could have been combined in such a manner that a referendum under Article 146 BL would have been held subsequent to the accession of the GDR to the Federal Republic. Thus, the Basic Law would have been put into effect for the whole of Germany, but it would have been subjected to the approval of the German people in a popular vote.[10] However, those who proposed to proceed in this manner overlooked the fact that both options for achieving German unity were clear alternatives, each resulting in different consequences for the Basic Law. In addition, it must be stressed that the sovereign German people have, at any time before or after the accession of the GDR, the right to repeal the Basic Law and to enact a new constitution. But the Basic Law cannot prejudice this, and in particular it cannot prescribe a specific procedure, i.e. a referendum. Hence, if the Basic Law could be construed as requiring a referendum to be held subsequent to the accession of the GDR, the Basic Law would constitute an encroachment on the sovereign power of the German people.[11]

Consequently, after the reunification, Article 146 BL was amended to take account of the new situation. The question which was asked at the beginning of this section, whether Article 146 BL, in its new version, provides another way of amending the Basic Law, can now be addressed after having established the significance for amending the Basic Law in the process of reunification. The provision now has only a declaratory function, as it acknowledges the people's sovereign power to repeal any existing constitution at any time and to create a new constitution. Consequently, Article 146 BL does not provide for a procedure for constitutional amendment; all it does is to guarantee that the maker of the constitution, the people, is not bound by any of the Basic Law's provisions. Conversely, it follows that the organs entitled to amend the Basic Law, i.e. the legislature, must abide by the procedure as provided for by Article 79 BL.

The foregoing reflects a basic distinction between constitutional amendment (*Verfassungsänderung*) and constitutional creation (*Verfassungsgebung*). As regards the former, the Basic Law provides only one way of enacting amendments

---

[10] Maunz/Dürig-Scholz, *Grundgesetz-Kommentar*, (C.H. Beck Verlag, München, Germany, 1994), Art. 146, no. 6.
[11] Maunz/Dürig-Scholz, *Grundgesetz-Kommentar*, (C.H. Beck Verlag, München, Germany, 1994), Art. 146, no. 7.

which is the procedure governed by Article 79 BL. This is regarded as a secondary power which is inner-constitutional and requires the legislative bodies to become active and, if they do so, to keep within the ambit set by Article 79 BL.

By contrast, constitutional creation is an entirely different process. It is the expression of a pristine, or primary, power of the people as the constitutional sovereign. It encompasses the abolition of an existing constitution and the creation of a new one. Hence, the Basic Law cannot predetermine whether or not the German people should decide to abolish the current constitution and, possibly, the way in which it may be replaced with a new one, as its provisions only bind the legislature amending the Basic Law. More specifically, Article 146 BL does not demand that a referendum be held in this situation.

This neutral position is a consequence of the underlying assumption that the Basic Law draws largely upon disastrous historical experience, as a result of which it intends to curtail the powers of the government, in particular those of the legislature, but not, however, those of the people who are, in their entirety, always free to replace the current constitution if they are dissatisfied with it. The function of Art 146 BL is merely to acknowledge this.

The only way of holding a referendum on a constitutional amendment, therefore, would involve Article 79 (2) BL, the provision which requires a two-thirds majority in both the *Bundestag* and *Bundesrat* for constitutional amendment, to be amended itself which, in turn, would require the said procedure to be followed. As a result, only after amending Article 79 (2) BL could a referendum in these matters be held.

Any attempt to amend the Basic Law by holding a referendum under Article 146 BL, without first amending Article 79 (2) BL, would amount to a circumvention of the safeguard provision of Article 79 (2) BL, which sets up a requirement of two-thirds majorities in the federal legislatures for amendment. The provision of Article 79 (3) BL, which bars amendments altering the basic federal structure of Germany and some basic rights guarantees altogether might be circumvented in the same manner. As a result these provisions, the function of which it is to protect the continuity, identity and priority of the Basic Law by making it more difficult to amend, could be rendered largely ineffective. The same interpretation might also mean that 'small' constitutional reforms, as amendments, would be subject to the strict requirements of Article 79 BL, while 'grand' reforms amounting to a replacement of the entire constitution, would be set a lower standard, that of a simple legislative majority and a referendum. Under such an interpretation, it would be within the powers of whoever currently held a simple political majority to repeal the Basic Law.

D. Exclusivity of the procedure under Article 79 BL and its justification

The above analysis has shown that the only way to amend the Basic Law is by applying the procedure as set out in Article 79 BL. Amendment by international treaty is really amendment by statute, i.e. by enacting the statute by which the international treaty is incorporated into the Basic Law, and it requires the necessary majorities to be observed as prescribed by Article 79 BL. Amendment by referendum is not possible, unless Article 79 (2) BL is itself amended. In particular, Article 146 does not open the way for amendment by referendum.

The reason for the exclusivity of Article 79 BL as the amendment procedure is primarily historical. The constitution which preceded the Basic Law, the Constitution of Weimar of 1919, never, *de iure*, lost effect. However, after the Enabling Law (*Ermächtigungsgesetz*) of 1933, by which Hitler effectively transferred the law-making powers from the legislature - the Reichstag - to the executive - the Reichs Government - and subsequent to the Reichstags Fire Decree (*Reichstagsbrandverordnung*) of 1933, which was enacted to suspend all the fundamental rights, the Constitution of Weimar, though never formally suspended or declared to have lost effect, was basically nothing more than an empty shell which had lost all legal significance. In particular, its amendment formula (Article 76 WRV) was virtually useless.

Consequently, the Basic Law tried to avoid the mistakes or inadequacies of the Weimar Constitution, in particular with regard to the amendment procedure. Article 79 (1) BL now tries to avoid a discrepancy between the text of a constitutional provision and its meaning, by stipulating that any amendment to the Basic Law must be recognisable when it is compared with the provision previously in effect. Article 79 (3) BL seeks to ensure that certain key elements of the Basic Law, i.e. the existence of a federal structure of Germany, the participation of the *Länder* in the process of enacting federal law, effective basic rights protection, the rule of law, the principles of the social State and democracy, are more deeply entrenched than others.

With regard to the issue of holding referenda in order to amend the Basic Law, there was considerable resistance to more plebiscitarian elements when the Basic Law was enacted. A particular anxiety was that the people had proved themselves to be too easily influenced by demagogues. The basic decision at the time was thus made in favour of more representative and less plebiscitarian democracy. Consequently, the Basic Law can only be amended by a referendum subsequent to an amendment to Article 79 (2) BL, the provision which requires two-thirds majorities in both the Federal Parliament (*Bundestag*) and the Federal Council (*Bundesrat*) and is thus interpreted as excluding referenda.

E. Judicial review

The German Federal Constitutional Court possesses the power to strike down any constitutional amendment if it finds it unconstitutional. As noted, a distinction is drawn between formal and substantive constitutionality. The former encompasses the aspects of competence, form, and procedure. Thus, first, a statute which amends the Constitution must have been enacted by the competent bodies, i.e. the Federal Parliament (*Bundestag)* and Federal Council (*Bundesrat*). Secondly, all the formal requirements must have been observed, the most important of which being the one demanding that the amended version of a provision be expressly different from the original version. Thirdly, the procedural requirements, i.e. essentially the two-thirds majorities in both *Bundestag* and *Bundesrat*, must have been complied with. Substantive constitutionality denotes the absence of a violation by the amendment of one or several other, necessarily higher-ranking, provisions of the Basic Law.

How can a new or an amended constitutional provision be unconstitutional? Generally speaking, a constitution contains legal provisions which are superior to statutory and customary law. It is therefore difficult to see how an amended provision of a constitution can violate other existing provisions of the same constitution, as all of them are apparently equal in rank. However, the Basic Law, in Article 79 (3), has designated to be immutable the division of the Federation into *Länder* (States), their participation in the legislative process, and the principles laid down in Arts. 1 and 20 (which include the principle of the social state and the rule of law). Consequently, if an amendment to the Basic Law were to conflict with one of the elements mentioned in Article 79 (3) BL, it would have to be struck down by the Constitutional Court. Hence, the Basic Law in effect contains provisions which are internally superior to those remaining and which provide a standard against which amendments may be tested.

To give an example, the Federal Constitutional Court ruled that the amended Basic Law provisions on the law of asylum (Article 16 a BL) were constitutional as they did not violate human dignity (Article 1 BL), which is one of the elements included in the protection under Article 79 (3) BL.[12] As a result, it becomes clear that the existence of so-called 'unconstitutional' constitutional law, i.e. a provision of the Basic Law which conflicts with one of the elements made immutable by Article 79(3) BL, is a practical possibility. Such a provision would have to be struck down by the Federal Constitutional Court. As yet, however, no provision of constitutional law has been held to be invalid.

As regards the procedure of the Constitutional Court, there are several ways of bringing a case before it. First, there are abstract proceedings of judicial review (*abstrakte Normenkontrolle*). These can be initiated by the Federal Government (*Bundesregierung*), a *Länder* government (*Landesregierung*) or one third of the Members of the *Bundestag*. The claimants have to show that the amended provision of the Basic Law conflicts with one of the elements enumerated by Article 79 (3) BL. If the Court so finds, it strikes down the particular provision.

Secondly, any German court of law can make a reference to the Federal Constitutional Court where it considers that a statutory or constitutional provision violates the Basic Law, in order to have this provision reviewed. This is the so-called 'concrete' review of legislation (*konkrete Normenkontrolle*). It requires the judge who has to decide a particular case to have doubts as to the constitutionality of the particular provision on which the decision in the case must be based. He would then have to suspend the proceedings to wait for the Federal Constitutional

---

[12] Federal Constitutional Court, judgments of 14.5.96, 2 BvR 1938/93, 2 BvR 2315/93, 2 BvR 1507/93, and 2 BvR 1508/93, 2 BvR 1516/93.

Court to make a ruling on the basis of which he would be obliged to proceed.

Thirdly, a case may be brought before the Constitutional Court by an individual. A so-called 'constitutional complaint' (*Verfassungsbeschwerde*) may be filed when a person feels his or her fundamental rights have been violated by the amended provision. However, in the case of a legal provision, such a complaint is admissible only in exceptional circumstances, namely when the provision in question currently and directly concerns the individual. The most likely case, however, will be when a provision needs to be implemented before it affects the individual. In this situation he or she can only bring a complaint against a final judicial decision in the particular matter.[13]

F. Constitutional realism: how difficult is it to amend the Basic Law?

Since the enactment of the Basic Law in 1949, there have been forty-three statutes which amended one or several of its provisions. In the light of the existence of Art. 79 BL, the provision which effectively makes the Basic Law more difficult, if not impossible, to amend, this appears to be an extensive number of constitutional amendments. The sheer length of the list of amendments indicates that constitutional law in Germany is by no means a static area of the law; in particular, in times of fundamental political changes, the constitution generally reflects some or most of the developments.

A good example of such almost revolutionary political changes is, of course, the reunification of the two Germanies in 1990. As a result of the former GDR dividing into five *Länder* (Mecklenburg-Vorpommern, Saxony-Anhalt, Brandenburg, Thuringia, and Saxony) and acceding to the Federal Republic, the composition of Germany's federal structure was clearly affected. To take account of this development, one amendment was made to raise from five to six the number of votes which each State with more than seven million inhabitants has in the Federal Council (*Bundesrat*), thus preventing the bigger *Länder* being under-represented. Another amendment, for example, concerned the redistribution of legislative powers between the federal government and the *Länder* and the rules for deciding whether or not the federal government is entitled to assume a right to legislate in the area of concurrent legislative powers.

But these were not the only amendments. The event of the reunification was welcomed as a good opportunity to give the Basic Law a relatively comprehensive overhaul, even though many proposals were ultimately rejected.[14] Amendments included the provisions on political asylum (Article 16 a BL), Germany's

---

[13] In the asylum-case, the individual brought the constitutional complaint against an injunction of the administrative court; this decision qualified as a final decision because it was capable of bringing about an irreconcilable disadvantage for the complainant. See in more detail: Benda, Ernst/Klein, Eckart: *Lehrbuch des Verfassungsprozeßrechts*, (C.F.Müller Juristischer Verlag, Heidelberg, Germany, 1991), pp. 186-6, no. 444.

[14] See in more detail: Gornig/Reckewerth: 'The Revision of the German Basic Law - Current Perspectives and Problems in German Constitutional Law', in *Public Law*, Spring 1997, pp. 137-158.

integration into the European Union (Article 23 BL), the right to vote in local elections (Article 28 (1) BL), the division of the German territory into *Länder* (Article 29 BL), the privatisation of railways (Article 87 e BL), postal services (Article 87 f BL), and air traffic institutions (Article 87 d BL), environmental protection (Article 20 a BL), and promotion of gender equality (Article 3 (2) BL).

Rejected amendment proposals included provisions regarding the external employment of the armed forces, the entrenchment of nationality provisions, a right of self-dissolution for the *Bundestag,* MPs' salaries, the introduction of further referenda, the enactment of social fundamental rights (e.g. a right to work, a right to full employment, to housing, etc.), an express right to confidentiality of personal data, a complete legalisation of abortion, a protection of forms of extra-marital cohabitation, a prohibition for employers to lock out employees during industrial action, minority protection, or general statements regarding humanity and sense of community.

## III. THE EFFECTS OF GERMANY'S MEMBERSHIP OF THE EU ON THE BASIC LAW

Ever since the conclusion of the Paris and Rome treaties in the 1950s by which the European Communities were created, Germany, as one of the founding Member States, has been playing an active role in promoting the process of European integration. This is particularly true in the light of Germany's significance after the unification in 1990, as a result of which the territorial scope of the treaties extended to all of Germany. German legal thinking has most likely influenced the development of Community law. Yet this effect of influencing legal processes has not been unilateral. In some ways the development of Community law has had implications for the development of German constitutional law, although, in my view, the constitutional changes directly necessitated by Germany's membership in the Community have not been overwhelming. This part of the article looks briefly at some areas of German constitutional law in which there have been changes as a result of developments of Community law. First, it is interesting to assess the level of fundamental rights protection under the Basic Law and how it has been affected by developments in Community law. Secondly, some light should be shed on the complex issue of Germany's accession to the EU, i.e. the constitutionality of the Act of the *Bundestag* by which Germany implemented the Treaty of Maastricht establishing the EU. This issue deserves attention because the Act in question was adopted on the basis of the new Article 23 of the Basic Law, the provision which was enacted in order to give Germany's further participation in the Community a clearer legal basis. Thirdly, the right of EU foreigners to vote in elections will be looked at briefly.

A. Fundamental rights protection

Fundamental rights are guaranteed by the Basic Law and protected by the Federal

Constitutional Court. As a result of the doctrine of supremacy of Community law over national law, the issue arose whether or not the Constitutional Court was entitled to exercise jurisdiction over disputes in which the applicants claimed that a secondary Community measure was invalid because it conflicted with fundamental rights enjoyed by the applicants under the German Basic Law. In 1974, the Federal Constitutional Court ruled that until such time as Community protection for fundamental rights measured up to that in the German Basic Law, Community measures would be subject to the fundamental rights provisions of the German Constitution.[15] Twelve years later, the same Court held in a similar case,[16] that the protection of fundamental rights in the Community had evolved sufficiently to meet the requirements of the German Basic Law. As a result, the Court acknowledged that the protection of fundamental rights in the Community had developed in such a way that it could be regarded as essentially equal to the protection under the German Basic Law. The Court therefore effectively refrained from exercising jurisdiction in matters of fundamental rights conflicting with secondary Community law.

These developments show that the effects of Community law on German constitutional law are frequently indirect rather than direct. In the area of fundamental rights these effects rarely result in amendments to the provisions themselves: rather the changes in the protection afforded by the Federal Constitutional Court are a reflection of developments in Community law. Hence, in a case of conflict between Community law and German fundamental rights, the individual must rely on the European Court for an assessment whether or not a particular Community measure violates the basic rights of the individual. The Federal Constitutional Court would most likely not regard this consequence as a deterioration of the individual's position as regards basic rights protection, as it stated that the degree of protection offered by Community law essentially equals that under German constitutional law.

B. The right to asylum

A specific field of basic rights protection in which Community law may have influenced German constitutional law is the area of asylum law. Prior to the amendments, the Basic Law provision on the basis of which asylum could be granted to persons who were politically persecuted was applied in a very generous way. Hundreds of thousands of mostly non-political refugees had entered Germany seeking asylum based on claims that they were politically persecuted in their home countries. A major cause of the increased numbers of asylum seekers during this period was believed to be the former Basic Law provision which created a temporary right to remain in Germany just by claiming persecution, regardless of

---

[15] *Internationale Handelsgesellschaft v. EVGF*, BVerfGE 37, 271 *et seq*; translated in [1974] 2 *CMLR* 540 (Solange I).
[16] *Wünsche Handelsgesellschaft*, BVerfGE 73, 339 *et seq.*, translated in [1987] 3 *CMLR* 225, (Solange II).

whether there was any evidence that it actually existed. It was sufficient for asylum seekers to spell out the word '*Asyl*' before a German border official to make it possible for them to stay in the Federal Republic for several years.

In order to counter further abuse of this very liberal provision, new asylum rules were incorporated into the Basic Law. One essential change was the replacement of the old provision with a new Article 16 (a), which continued to grant the right to asylum to persons facing political persecution in their home countries, but added relatively extensive powers which could limit the scope of the basic right by allowing the legislature to justify restrictions of it. One of the most evident restrictions is contained in one of the new provisions which states that asylum does not have to be granted to persons who entered the territory of the Federal Republic from a Member State of the EU. This is a rather far-reaching restriction, as it results in Germany being entitled to deny to asylum-seekers who have landed in another EU country the right to process their asylum applications. As Germany is more or less surrounded by other EU Member States, she has pretty much sheltered herself from an influx of asylum-seekers who arrived in those countries and who were formerly entitled to gain access to Germany from her neighbouring States.

It might be thought that this change of German asylum law was the result of policy requirements being imposed on Germany by the EU in the light of efforts to take a common approach towards asylum issues in an integrated Europe. However, this change of German asylum law cannot merely be accounted for by the demands of the EU. Evidence for this view can be found in the provision according to which the right to asylum can also be denied to asylum seekers coming from 'another State in which the Geneva Refugee Convention and the European Convention on Human Rights are in effect'. This provision is indicative of the fact that the Basic Law in any event would have been amended in order to restrict the previously over-generous asylum provisions. The 'Europeanisation' of the German asylum provisions would have likely proceeded in a more general European context, i.e. within the framework of the Council of Europe, regardless of the developments in Community law. It was the problems connected with exceedingly high numbers of asylum seekers which triggered the changes, rather than the pressures emanating from the Community.

C. The Amendment of Article 23 Basic Law and the Accession to the European Union

Germany's participation in the European Community was originally based on Article 24 (1) of the Basic Law which stated:

The Federation may by legislation transfer sovereign powers to international organisations.

However, this provision was felt to have been insufficient, as it did not clearly enough spell out, for example, whether or not, and if so to what extent, the measures adopted by international organisations, and hence the Community, would prevail over national legislation. Another unresolved issue was whether or not amendments to the Treaties would be subject to the terms of Article 79 (3) BL, the provision of the Basic Law which renders certain fundamental constitutional principles immutable. As a result of these uncertainties, some doubt arose as to whether Article 24 (1) BL could provide a sufficient legal foundation for the creation of a European Union, which was intended to go well beyond the status of a mere international organisation. Consequently, a new, rather lengthy, Article 23 BL was introduced, determining in great detail the relationship between Germany and the EU and replacing the pre-1990 Article 23 under which the former GDR had acceded to the Federal Republic and which was repealed after the German reunification. The first sentence of Article 23 (1) BL makes German participation in the EU conditional upon the existence of a

... European Union which is bound to democratic, law-governed, social and federal principles, and to the principle of subsidiarity, and which guarantees the protection of basic rights essentially comparable to those of this Basic Law.

The same provision also ensures that the Basic Law cannot be used as an alternative amending procedure. It expressly states that any Basic Law amendment necessary for the creation of the EU or for any changes to its contractual basis must still satisfy the procedural requirements of Article 79 (2) and (3) BL. Thus, two-thirds majorities of the *Bundestag* and *Bundesrat* must still be obtained, and changes which would affect the enforcement of certain rights guaranteed by the Basic Law or which would alter the German federal-state relationship cannot be made at all. Further, the new Article 23 deals extensively with the participation of German national and State bodies in the affairs of the EU, thus strengthening the position of the German *Länder* by making German participation in European unification contingent upon the principles of federalism and subsidiarity and compensating them for the loss of *Länder* powers in other areas.

As a consequence, the existence of Community law and its development triggered an amendment to the Basic Law, which, however, had the function of clarifying the law rather than changing its contents dramatically.

Both Article 23 and the Act by which Germany acceded to the EU were, immediately after their respective adoptions, subjected to judicial review in a constitutional complaint before the Federal Constitutional Court.[17] Dispute had arisen as to whether the Maastricht Treaty was going too far in its objectives. In particular, it was maintained that the democratic principle as enshrined in Article 38 BL was violated in the light of the fact that Germany had to transfer national powers to European institutions to a large extent. Article 38 BL is the provision which guarantees the right of the people to participate in the legitimation of public power and to acquire influence on its exercise through the electoral process. This principle of democracy has been declared, by Article 79 BL, to be unassailable. It

---

[17] *M. Brunner and others v. The European Union Treaty*, BVerfGE 89, 155, translated in 1 [1994] *CMLR* 57.

is considered to be fundamental, since the right to exercise public power and hence to carry out public functions is derived from the people and the persons exercising that power are fundamentally answerable to the people. It is crucial that a sufficient degree of democratic legitimation should be achieved.

Yet the Federal Constitutional Court did not accept the plaintiff's view and dismissed the complaint. It held that the functions of the European Union and the powers granted for their implementation were regulated in a sufficiently foreseeable manner, because the principle of limited individual powers was adhered to (*Prinzip der begrenzten Einzelermächtigung*), no power to extend its powers was conferred on the European Union (*'Kompetenz-Kompetenz'*), and the claiming of further functions and powers by the European Union and the communities was made dependent on supplementation and amendment of the Treaty and was and still is, therefore, subject to the affirmative decision of the national parliaments. According to the Court, the scope of the functions and powers granted to the European Union and to the institutions of the European Communities and the decision-making mechanisms laid down by the Treaty did not have the effect of reducing the content of the decision-making and supervisory powers of the *Bundestag* to an extent which infringed the democratic principle in so far as it was declared by Article 79(3) of the Basic Law to be unassailable.

With regard to Economic and Monetary Union, the Court held that the Act of Accession was constitutional since by ratifying the Maastricht Treaty; the Federal Republic of Germany was not subjected to an automatic progress to monetary union, which was unsupervisable and the momentum of which put it beyond control. Rather, the Maastricht Treaty opened the way to further integration of the European legal Community by stages, which at every step was subject to conditions which were already foreseeable so far as the legislature was concerned or to further assent from the Federal Government which may be influenced by parliamentary means.

As a result, Germany's role as a Member State of the European Union, committed to promoting the process of integration, was accepted by the Federal Constitutional Court as being within the scope of the Basic Law. The German Act, by which the Federal Republic acceded to the European Union in ratifying the Maastricht Treaty, was held to fulfil the requirements set up by the principle of democracy as entrenched in Article 38 BL.

The question arose as to what would happen if the Council of the European Union decided to go ahead with EMU even if not all of the Member States met the convergence criteria. As any alteration or even relaxation of those criteria would require a unanimous decision by the Council,[18] it was presumed that such a development would not have been opposed by Germany. It therefore appears to be very clear that the Federal Constitutional Court placed great emphasis on the strict adherence to the convergence criteria. The former president of the German central bank (*Bundesbank*) had already announced that he would bring an action before the

---

[18] Art. 6 of the Protocol of the Convergence Criteria Pursuant to Art. 109 j of the EC-Treaty.

Constitutional Court, if EMU were proceeded with in the absence of the convergence criteria being strictly satisfied. It would have been interesting to see how the Court would have reacted in this situation. From some of the remarks made in the Maastricht judgment, one might infer that the third stage of economic and monetary union had to be understood as a target rather than as a legally enforceable date, and the purpose of setting target dates according to established Community tradition tends to be to encourage and accelerate the integration process rather than to realise it within the time limit under all circumstances. However, other statements made by the Court seemed to indicate a different direction: for example, the Court held that the convergence criteria could not be amended by single Member States, which provided a sufficient guarantee that without German agreement, the convergence criteria could not be relaxed. Further, the Court stressed the fact that monetary union was conceived as a community based on stability.

The question arose whether the Court would hold that going ahead with EMU would be unconstitutional because too much sovereignty would be transferred onto the EU, resulting in a situation where a constitutional amendment would be required. Yet this would probably not have caused a major problem because amendments to Article 38 BL are not barred by the immutability clause of Article 79 (3) BL, so long as the principle of democracy, as stated in Article 20 (1) BL, is not interfered with. In my view, however, such a finding by the Federal Constitutional Court would have been rather unlikely because any change of the convergence criteria requires a unanimous decision in the Council and therefore, the influence of the German Parliament would be secured. As a consequence, the Court would have likely held that Article 38 BL, the provision which is based on the principle of democracy, was not violated. But if the Court had held that the introduction of EMU without strict adherence to the convergence criteria went beyond that permitted by Article 38 BL, a constitutional amendment would have been necessary.

The result of the Maastricht judgment of the Federal Constitutional Court was that neither Germany's accession to the European Union nor its membership of EMU has had a huge effect on the German Basic Law. The Court took the view that as long as the Member States remained the 'masters of the treaties' (*Herren der Verträge*), a transfer (or delegation) of powers to the EU was constitutional. What can be inferred from this, by way of inverse reasoning, is that only if the EU achieved the quality of a single State, would the constitutions of the Member States have to reflect that. But unless and until this has been achieved, the effects of membership of the EU on the German constitution have been only minor.

D. Amendment of Article 88 BL

A provision of the Basic Law which was amended as a direct result of European integration is Article 88 BL, the provision which deals with the German central bank (*Bundesbank*). This article was amended by adding a second clause allowing the transfer to the European Central Bank of some of the functions and powers of the *Bundesbank* in relation to the European Union framework, which, according to the new wording, is independent and bound to the primary aim of ensuring price stability under Article 107 of the EC Treaty.

E. The right of EU foreigners to vote in local elections

The right of EU foreigners to vote in local elections, which had been a matter of discussion in the Federal Republic for decades, conflicted with Article 20 (2) and Article 28 (1) BL because foreigners did not fall within the meaning of 'the German people', from whom all political power in the Federal Republic emanates. This right to vote in local elections has become topical because of Article 8 of the Maastricht Treaty which provides for the creation of European citizenship. The Federal Constitutional Court held that the introduction of a non-citizen right to vote in local elections required a constitutional amendment.[19] Accordingly, a third sentence was added to Article 28 (1) BL, allowing local residents to vote or run for office if they are nationals of any EU Member State, subject to related provisions of EU law.

F. Integration of the Federal Republic into a single European State?

The new Article 23 BL cannot be construed as providing a legal basis for the integration of the Federal Republic of Germany into a single European State. The aim of European integration is a 'European Union', not necessarily a single European State. In addition, the reference in Article 23 (1) BL to Article 79 BL must be understood as militating against an integration of Germany into a European State, as Article 79 BL makes it impossible for the legislature to substantially alter the quality of the Federal Republic as a sovereign State insofar as a revocation of its authority to extend its powers (*Kompetenz-Kompetenz*) or its participatory sovereignty over the Treaties as one of their 'Masters' is concerned.

An integration of the Federal Republic into a single European State could only be achieved, moreover, by an act of the people as the constitutional sovereign, the 'pouvoir constituant', not by acts of the legislature or other public bodies, the 'pouvoirs constitués", which are barred from doing so by Article 79 (3) BL. Accordingly, Article 23 BL does not hinder the Federal Republic from becoming part of a single European State, as this provision is generally open to European integration. Yet it prevents the legislature and other bodies from taking this course but does not stop the German people from doing so if they decide that this would be the right thing for them to do. But how this would have to be carried out, for instance whether a referendum would be required, is not provided for by the Basic Law.

---

[19] BVerfGE 83, pp. 37 *et seq.*

Chapter Eight

# THE POLITICS OF CONSTITUTIONAL AMENDMENT: HUNGARY'S LASTING TRANSITORY CONSTITUTION

György Szoboszlai[*]

## I. INTRODUCTION
## THE IMPORTANCE OF INITIAL CHOICE:
## CONSTITUTIONAL IMPRINTING

Following British traditions, Hungary had developed her modern Statehood without a written constitution. Here the historical reasons were basically different: most importantly the belatedness of capitalist development, the lack of full national-political independence and, in conjunction with the first mentioned cause, the strong legal and economic position of historical classes. The trauma of the Second World War swept away the old basis of traditional rule, based on customs, and the so-called historical constitution.

The first Hungarian written constitution was enacted in 1949, and its original structure was valid until 1989. This constitution created a peoples' republic built on the unity of State power and it reflected the values of a formal – although empty – Parliamentarianism. The political transformation to a pluralistic political system in 1988-1989 made inevitable the rebuilding of Statehood as well. In September 1989 a political document was accepted as a result of round-table talks among the ruling State-socialist party, the united opposition forces, and the so-called 'third side' representing civic organisations, and based on this compromise Parliament thoroughly modified the existing 1949 Constitution. This fundamental modification affected the most important pillars of the constitutional structure, and thus enacted a genuinely new, albeit formally interim constitution in October 1989.

The pact-making parties regarded this document as a set of constitutional rules which eased the completion of social transformation to a fully fledged market economy.[1] The text of the materially new, republican constitution (the reference to the people in the title has been omitted, and the text (Article 1) plainly states 'Hungary shall be a republic') was built on the old formal structure: this fact was expressed by maintaining the order of main parts, the old numbering and the date

---

[*] Senior research fellow, Institute of Political Sciences of the Hungarian Academy of Sciences, Ph.D. in political science, lawyer.
[1] For the role of codification in the course of transition, see András Sajó, *States of Post-Communism* (East European Reporter, May-June 1992).

of the original basic law (Act XX of 1949). In the legal sense this means that the 1989 reformulating was an overall modification of the existing one accepted by a two-thirds majority of Parliament. The transitory nature of the revised law was voiced in its first, introductory sentence: 'In order to promote a peaceful transition to a State, based on the principle of rule of law, having a multiparty system, Parliamentary democracy and social market economy, the National Assembly, for the period before the enactment of the new constitution of the country, determines the text of the constitution as follows'.[2] Whether the revised 1989 Constitution is old or new has been the subject of constant political debates ever since. Among professionals this is not a real question. In the legal-formal sense the constitution is still the original one with drastic changes, but regarding its social-political content it is a genuinely new document.

Just after the first pluralistic, multiparty elections in spring 1990, the leading government and the biggest opposition party (Hungarian Democratic Forum and the Alliance of Free Democrats), having a comfortable enough majority to amend the constitution, promptly decided on an important structural change to the freshly revised basic law – as they claimed – for the sake of governability. The most important piece of modification was the replacement of the collective government elected to Parliament by a more independent prime ministerial form in which only the prime minister is elected, the ministers are nominated by and dependent on the head of government and they are both appointed by the president of the republic (the President). At the same time stabilisation of the executive has been achieved by the introduction of a constructive veto of no-confidence. This originally German invention has been incorporated into the government structure to enhance the independence of the government *vis-á-vis* Parliament so that easy overturning of the governing coalition based on short-sighted party interests may be resisted. Another important issue was the elimination of all elements of compromise from the text which had been incorporated into the 1989 reform constitution under the pressure of the former reform-socialist elite. By this second important reform of the 'old constitution' the actors – especially the liberal thinkers and some conservative political scientists – regarded the basic law complete and coherent enough to serve as the framework for dismantling State-socialist ownership in the economy and legalising the painful and conflict-ridden process of privatisation of State assets, regarded by many as the means by which the new elite could make an accumulation of capital.

The Constitution of 1949, modelled after the Soviet Constitution of 1936, contained a host of individual rights and freedoms without any significance or proper legal-political guarantees. The social order was based on the preponderance of State ownership, and collective forms of ownership dominated over personal or individual property rights. In the spirit of a non-market, planned economy the role of the State was overwhelming in every respect of public – and to some extent

---

[2] The text of the constitution appears in the author's translation in this paper. See also *The Rebirth of Democracy. 12 Constitutions of Central and Eastern Europe.* 2nd edition, Council of Europe Publishing, 1996.

private – life. Different economic models could be realised in the general constitutional framework, the rigid plan-directive based economy of the 1950s, a semi-decentralised planned economy using market elements in the late 1960s and 1970s, and a more decentralised, liberalised State-controlled economic system in the 1980s heading to the full transformation of the whole political system. Indeed, the process of decentralisation and economic liberalisation helped political fragmentation, informal pluralisation and – with the help of the emerging civil society organisations – the overt political pluralisation of the regime. The result is well-known: at the end of the 1980s the political transformation was coded into the legal system and, formally, it affected the constitution itself.

Formally there has always been only one constitution, the Act XX of 1949, which has been amended several times during the last five decades, partly because of structural causes, partly for legal-political reasons. As a result of the overall economic reform of 1968 (introduction of market elements into the world of public enterprises and collective agricultural co-operatives) the constitution was generally revised in 1972, without altering the main structural elements. These were: the formal primacy of the highest representative body, the national assembly (Parliament) as the legal source of national sovereignty; the general substitution position of the so-called Presidential Council (the collective head of state) which made it possible to enact regulations having the legal force and functions of laws (law-decrees issued by the Presidential Council of the Peoples' Republic); the lack of constitutional power-sharing among the different branches of constitutional institutions; the guiding role of the ruling State-socialist party explicitly expressed in the constitution (which was, as such, introduced in 1972: the original text referred only to the guiding role of the working class was mentioned); the lack of workable guarantees of basic human and civic rights etc.[3]

The late 1980s brought about a political situation of accelerated change as a result of the liberalisation of the economy and the widespread democratic spirit that was first of all nurtured by the mass media and by the higher bureaucratic and intellectual elite. Even the majority of the ruling single party elite proved to be in favour of a smooth democratic transition after the fall of the old leadership in 1987. In that year the political and legal role of the symbolic Presidential Council was confined to the role of collective head of state, stripping from it its powerful regulatory functions. Formal Parliamentarism began to be vitalised. The watershed year of important transitory events was 1988. By this time the legal structure of a market economy was accepted by Parliament: a bill on modem business association

---

[3] Art. 3 of the act stipulated: 'The leading force of society is the Marxist-Leninist party of the working class.' Given that there existed only one political party, the Hungarian Socialist Workers' Party, there was no ambiguity in this wording. The term 'communism' was not mentioned in State documents, because, of course, the social system had nothing in common with the theory of communism. The constitution did not forbid the foundation of independent political parties. In 1988, when the first new party, the Federation of Y Young Democrats, was organised, its founders could rightly refer to art. 65 of the constitution that guaranteed freedom of association. When direct political control was eliminated, the new parties could have been registered as associations. See the author: 'Parliamentarism in the Making: Crisis and Political Transformation in Hungary' (in Arend Lijphart and Carlos H. Waisman: *Institutional Design in New Democracies. Eastern Europe and Latin America,* 1996) pp.117-136.

was passed without any political obstacles (Act VI. On Business Association.) This proved to be a milestone event in subsequent economic development. On the political scene new independent political organisations appeared, partly in the form of mass movements, partly as revitalisation of historical parties which were silenced in the early 1950s by Stalinist rule. These new developments were legalised by the acceptance of a liberal-spirited law on associations which opened the path for legalisation of political parties.[4] Full political pluralisation became not only inevitable, but the primary goal of the opposition elite.

## II. THE PROCESS LEADING TO THE BIRTH OF THE PRESENT CONSTITUTION

The existing constitutional arrangement was prepared by the Ministry of Justice in the second half of 1989, parallel with roundtable talks on the political rules of the game of transition. The amendment process required a simple two-thirds majority of the 352 members of Parliament. This meant the support of at least 235 MPs was needed. Every MP could initiate any modification of the proposal, and in theory even a completely new text could have been submitted by an individual MP. Of course, the government was the master of the process but the text was written by politicians participating in the bargaining game. The then existing Parliament was elected in 1985 based on semi-competitive and liberal election rules, and MPs realised that their historical role was to help the peaceful transformation. We have to note that the enactment of the materially new constitution was preceded by the introduction of a series of very important laws of constitutional relevance. This meant that by the time of formulating the constitutional text itself, its imprints were already very strictly defined. What was important was the fact that constitutional reform stabilised those laws of special importance, which required a simple two-thirds majority for amendment.

Once the political agreement was secured the acceptance could not be questioned, because of the one-party nature of the then existing assembly. Although there were some dozens of opposition MPs, they did not represent any particular party as a rule, and, what is more important, they were in favour of transformation. In these circumstances the process was smooth, and the meeting of the two-thirds requirement in Parliament was not threatened even for a moment.

---

[4] The original state socialist constitution prescribed that freedom of association had to be regulated in the legal form of act (Act of Parliament). It is not surprising that this act was never accepted or even formulated. Instead the particularities of association were stipulated in a law-decree of the Presidential Council. If there had existed a Constitutional Court, it would have declared this arrangement plainly unconstitutional. The lack of the rule of law principle can be traced by the legal fate of freedom of association.

## III. AMENDMENT RULES IN THE CONSTITUTION: THE CONTINUANCE OF ELEMENTS OF THE LEGA.L ORDER BEFORE AND AFTER THE POLITICAL TRANSFORMATION

There is no sharp division between the systems just before and after the transition as a result of the gradual nature of the constitutional development, the piecemeal way of amendment. That is why there are no special provisions regarding the continuance of elements of the legal order. The concept of continuity was not questioned at all. According to the Hungarian legal culture the outdated regulations are from time to time selected and made void (deregulation). One of the closing stipulations of the amended constitution simply states that: 'The Government shall submit the bills necessary for the enforcement of the Constitution to the National Assembly' (Article 78/2). This article does not specify the tasks of the government; it can refer to those regulations affected by the new constitutional rules. Much depends on the nature of conflict caused by the modifications. If a complete law becomes questionable, it is the task of the government to take the matter before Parliament for re-regulation or annulling. In this case the old law is invalidated as a whole or in part. If special regulatory elements are affected by the constitutional amendment, the government must submit the bill for modification or repeal the parts in question.

But the dilemma of constitutionality is not a simple one to be seen as black and white. In most cases the government is not even able to realise, or is not willing to accept, that a valid law or other regulation is not in harmony with the new constitutional order or becomes contradictory in the new context. In this situation the only solution can be the extra-Parliamentary control, the functioning of the Constitutional Court. The Court can examine the constitutionality of laws and statutes without time limit. The proposal to examine a law in effect can be submitted to the Court by anybody without any restrictions. The law on the Constitutional Court specifies the special rules when the initiation comes from Parliament, its standing committee, the president of the republic, the government or its members, the president of the State Audit Office, the president of the Supreme Court, and the Chief Prosecutor. Any of these persons can turn to the Court and can ask for scrutiny of the accepted laws.

The judiciary is not entitled to constitutional review of a law or piece of regulation. If the question of an applicable law or other regulation emerges during a civil or criminal procedure, the parties can initiate the constitutional examination of the applicable regulation and the judge decides on submission of the case to the Constitutional Court.

In the period between 1990-2000 the Court examined the constitutionality of hundreds of regulations at different levels, laws, government and ministerial decrees, and even local government regulations. Among them only a minority represented those regulations enacted before the acceptance of the 1989-1990 constitutional reforms.

## IV. PROCEDURES IN PLACE FOR AMENDING THE CONSTITUTION

As indicated above, the present Hungarian Constitution is easily modified or amended: only the two-thirds voting requirement applies, at least in a legal sense. Due to the lack of a second chamber, there is no special representative body to supervise the decisions of Parliament. The amending rule is a much debated issue in the present procedure of replacing the interim, transitory constitution with a completely new one which would end the political transformation. It is a widely accepted view that it is necessary to make the amendment more difficult.

The present amendment rule was originally introduced in 1949 when the first written constitution of the country was created. In those circumstances the relative flexibility of the amendment rules was an important issue, because the political controllers did not wish to tie their own hands. The constitution was not regarded as a sacred text, difficult to alter. The holder of sovereignty was the national assembly and the procedural rules were not conceived as guarantees in themselves. This view can be associated with historical traditions: each regime was entitled to its own legality and the legality of the past regime was not respected. Too many regime and system changes taught politicians and people that even regulations of constitutional importance may change with the drying up of morning dew. In the circumstances of State-socialism the significance of the basic law was inferior to the real world of power politics. The ultimate guarantee of the regime came from formal parliamentary democracy: mass organisations and the political party of the 'working class' were regarded the real safeguards of 'socialist democracy'. In the dictatorial period, before the 1956 uprising, the constitution was a paper document: in the lack of formal and informal plurality it could be changed at the wish of the political bureau at any time. The voting machine of the general assembly worked without any dissent. The situation did not change too much when the system gained informal legitimacy by introducing, from the late 1960s on, informal interest representation channels.

The real question is why this amendment rule was upheld in the two waves of deep constitutional reforms in 1989-1990. The explanation is again political and not legal, and seems not to be too complicated. The constitution reform drafters intentionally kept open the gates to relatively easy amendment procedures, because of the very nature of the systemic transformation. Too strict amendment rules would have resulted in early freezing in of the constitutional model regarded as transitory and incomplete.

The gradual transformation between 1987-1990, and even further, was the achievement of the upper level political elite, and therefore was not legitimised by the wider population, the people, the ultimate source of legitimacy and sovereignty.[5] The constitutional rebuilding took place without the participation of the active population and it was not legitimised by referendum. In the whole post-socialist period there were only two valid referenda: the first in 1989 on political issues and

---

[5] According to the present constitution: 'In the Republic of Hungary all power belongs to the people which exercises its sovereignty through its elected representatives and in a direct way'. (Art. 2/2)

the presidential election, the second in 1997 on the NATO membership of the country.[6]

The means of direct democracy was successfully used in the early transformation process, in 1989, but not in an active way: on the contrary, it was a political manoeuvre in the political struggle of elite groups. In this exceptional case two political parties succeeded in mobilising the population in order to decide on the timing of the election of the first democratically elected president of the republic. The direct or indirect election of the president was at stake. According to the regulations in effect at the time of the plebiscite, the first president was to be elected by the people if elected prior to the first multi-party general elections. The plebiscite proved to be successful: even with a very narrow margin, the public decided to hold the election of the president after the parliamentary elections. The reply of the incumbent reform-socialist government was to amend the constitution in order to elect the president directly. There was no obstacle to this step, because the consensus among socialist MPs was rather stable on this question, and they had constituent power in Parliament. The new constitutional rule proved to be short-lived. It was not a surprise that the very first move of the newly elected Parliament in April 1990 was to amend the constitution: the old opposition gaining political control agreed to have a pure parliamentarian model in which the president has a more or less decorative role and does not interfere in the legislative and executive processes. The amendment ordered the indirect election of the president, that is, he or she is elected by Parliament, in the end with a simple majority.[7]

The above shows that in underdeveloped extreme parliamentarism the upper party elite makes decisions without seeking – a broader source of legitimacy. Legitimising constitutional changes is not conceived as an active, politically defined and procedurally conceptualised process. On the contrary, constitution-making is regarded as the privilege of the legislature, supported by a sufficient majority in the House. Because of the characteristics of the electoral system, namely its inclination to a high level of disproportionality, parliamentary elections tend to produce a winner who has a disproportionate rate of mandates compared to the preference vote. At least this is the result of the three general elections so far.[8]

There was only one instance that referred to a wider legitimacy beyond Parliament in the constitutional amendment or constitution making process. Even

---

[6] This second referendum was held under the terms of the new law on direct democracy (Act III of 1997 on national referendum and plebiscite). Just before the procedure Parliament modified the Constitution in order to ease the validity rules. The majority participation requirement (more than 50% of the eligible voters) was annulled; the new limit was that more than 25% of the eligible voters and more than 50% of the active voters be in favour of the proposal no matter how many people participate. This cautiousness proved to be justified, because less than 50% of the voters showed up.

[7] To change this new arrangement the Hungarian Socialist Party (HSP) initiated a referendum in summer 1990. The initiation was successful, but the governing elite summoned for a boycott of the referendum and the timing was also very unfavourable. These circumstances explain that the move resulted in complete failure and the referendum had to be declared legally invalid.

[8] The level of disproportionality is around 20 per cent measured by the Loosemore-Hanby index. The winning party tends to be over-represented and it is very probable that the two strongest parties obtain constitution-amending capacity. This was the case in 1990, 1994 and 1998 alike.

before the acceptance of the 1989 reform Constitution, the law on referendum and popular initiative ordered that the acceptance (confirmation) of the constitution should be decided through referendum.[9] The same law stipulates that if the result of the referendum was negative, a second referendum has to be held within a year. This rule was not incorporated into the constitution and many lawyers questioned the constitutional validity of this regulation on the ground that the law on referendum was accepted before the acceptance of the 1989 constitutional reform. The new regulation (1997) on referendum does not contain this requirement, but the majority of experts do not question the rationality of the arrangement, the need of a popular vote on the new constitution.

Evidently these legal prescriptions refer exclusively to the enhanced legitimacy requirement of a completely new constitution. A partial modification, irrelevant of its political or constitutional importance, does not necessarily require popular control. Nevertheless, many regard this mode of regulation as imperfect and unsatisfactory. And indeed, in the course of formulating the concept of the new constitution, there is a general agreement that the amendment formula must be changed to a stricter and more sophisticated procedure.[10]

## V. THE PRACTICE OF AMENDING THE CONSTITUTION

According to the revised Constitution of 1989-1990 Parliament is the constituent power. In this respect the original 1949 constitutional model was not affected. The principle of separation of state powers is not explicitly incorporated into the constitution, even if this principle is widely acknowledged, and 'is respected in the rulings of the Constitutional Court. The lack of an explicit reference to the separation of powers is the characteristic of parliamentary systems: the supreme organ is the Parliament and its powers are restricted only by the human and civic rights expressed in the most important international agreements and conventions. In this spirit the role of Parliament is not confirmed to the exercise of legislative powers; the constitutional text states that Parliament is the supreme organ of state power and popular representation.

In a parallel opinion, a Constitutional Court member interpreted the missing, overtly un-institutionalised principle of separation of powers. The ruling noted that this basic notion is mentioned neither in the preamble nor in other regulations of the constitution, but it cannot be in doubt that this principle is realised in its numerous rules.[111] In another ruling the Court explicitly declared – interpreting the constitution – that no other power branch outside legislation is ordered under the

---

[9] Act XVII of 1989 on the referendum and popular initiatives (Art. 7).

[10] For discussion of the politics of amendment after the transition, see Stephen Holmes and Cass R. Sunstein: 'The Politics of Constitutional Revision in Eastern Europe' In *Responding to Imperfection. 77Ie 77Ieory and Practice of Constitutional Amendment* (ed. Sanford Levinson, 1995).

[11] The judge found this indirect realisation natural and explained it by the fact that the recognition of the principle was general and an inalienable part of democratic constitutionalism. The ruling refers to the 1798 Declaration of the Rights of Man and Citizen. The parallel opinion quotes the 16th article of the Declaration: ' A society in which rights are not guaranteed by institutions and powers are not divided has no constitution' (Ruling No. 38 of 1993).

authority of Parliament as a result of the constitutional principle of separation of powers built into the general structure of the constitution.[12]

Nevertheless, the lack of explicit formulation of the requirement is telling, and many experts hold the view that it is not by chance that during the revision of the constitution the need for explicit separation of state powers was not accentuated. The prevailing idea and the most widely accepted common value was a constitutional model in which Parliament would play the most important political role. In this Westminster type of state model the National Assembly exercises the rights originating from popular sovereignty.[13]

Taking into account the hidden logic of this accentuated parliamentary model it is not surprising that there are no special rules for the amendment of the constitution. The text plainly states that to amend the constitution and to decide on certain issues determined by the constitution, a two-thirds vote of assembly representatives is needed (Article 24/3). The legal form of the constitution is the Act (the officially published law), therefore those who can initiate amendment of the constitution are those who can submit proposals for the passing of or modification of a law. The constitution itself determines the right to submit a piece of legislation or draft bills: legislation may be initiated by the president of the republic, the government, any committee of the House and any national assembly representative.

Evidently, in practice, the amendment of the constitution is a question of prime political importance, and therefore the initiation always originates from the government. The preparation of any modification of the basic law is a genuinely political process. After the birth of such a political decision, the legal preparation of the text is undertaken by the Ministry of Justice: each government ministry takes part in the formulation of the text.

Before the democratic transformation the amendment of the constitution was a relatively frequent means of legislative power, although one could claim that its necessity was questionable in a number of cases. Only essential social development would have been an excuse for frequent modifications. After the transition the constitutional amendment proved to be exceptional.[14]

---

[12] Ruling 41/1993.

[13] In this framework the constitution declares that Parliament 'Guarantees the constitutional order of society, determines the structure, orientation and conditions of government' (Article 19/2). The constitution goes even further when it explicitly states: 'In this capacity the National Assembly enacts the Constitution of the Republic of Hungary' (Article 19/3/a).

[14] Since the essential reform (Act XXXI of 1989) there were thirteen modifications. Taking into account the necessity for social transformation, this cannot be regarded as destabilising practice. Act XVI on the direct election of the president and was decided by the old regime before the first multi-party election. This was reversed by the main amendment Act XL of 1990 on the constitutional reform after the election of a new Parliament which completed the legal-democratic transition. Most of the modifications were made in 1990, following the requirements of the systemic change. The consecutive amendments are: Act XXIX of 1990, Act XLIV of 1990, Act LIV of 1990, Act LXIII of 1990, Act CVII of 1993, Act LXI of 1994, Act LXXIII of 1994, Act LXXIV of 1994, Act XLIV of 1995, Act LIX of 1997 and Act XCVIII of 1997. Act XLIV of 1995 refers to the procedural rules for creating and preparing the text of a new constitution and was valid only until the end of the mandate of the national assembly elected in 1994.

In an indirect way, the Constitutional Court can exert influence on Parliament, in order to promote the idea of amending the basic law. In its jurisdiction the Court often faces the reality of missing constitutional regulations. In this case, the Court can summon Parliament to amend the constitution, but there is no legal consequence of the passivity of the House. The Court is not entitled to directly revise the constitutionality of a passed amendment, because its activity can be carried out within the existing framework of the basic law. The opposite may happen, albeit rarely. It has happened that the Court declared a special regulation of a law unconstitutional, and the reaction of the majority of Parliament was to incorporate the annulled text into the constitution. One example is the voting right of those holding Hungarian citizenship who stay abroad on the day of election. Originally the electoral law (Act XXXIV of 1989) excluded Hungarians living abroad from exercising their voting right, stipulating that those absent from the country on the day of elections are prevented from voting. Just before the 1990 spring general elections a claim was filed at the Constitutional Court against the actual regulation of the electoral law by a Hungarian citizen living in Algeria. The Court has found the regulation unconstitutional on the grounds that the constitution guaranteed the right to vote to those citizens having permanent residence in the country. The Court argued that Parliament violated this constitutional right by instituting the regulation instead of making it possible for citizens living abroad to vote. The Court did not examine the merits of the constitutional stipulation which has guaranteed the voting right only for those Hungarians having permanent or provisional residence in the country, accepting the reason offered in the official explanation of the electoral law: those not having ties to the country are prevented from voting. In turn, the Court argued that in given modem communications, those who have the constitutional right to vote must not be blocked from voting if they are not actually in the homeland. As a result of the ruling the affected piece of regulation has been declared void. Parliament did not accept the essence of what the Court really claimed, that is did not grant voting rights to Hungarians living abroad. This was a political issue, because the Hungarian citizenship regulation is extremely liberal and therefore the number of those who can be affected by a liberal electoral codification can go beyond controllable limits. There were also speculations on the political orientation of potential voters and this aspect could influence the outcome of the debate. Parliament chose the simplest solution by promptly incorporating the unconstitutional regulation into the text of the constitution, giving it full constitutional force incontestable by the Court. The amended text says that every Hungarian citizen of voting age, if he or she has a permanent residence in Hungary, has the right to be elected as a member of the national assembly, local government or minority local government, and has the right to participate in such elections as well as in national, local referendums and plebiscites, on the condition that he or she is within the territory of the country on the day of elections (Art. 70/1). This new regulation in the basic law is still valid, albeit widely debated by the conservative parties who are longing to broaden their electorate from outside the country. The example clearly shows the nature of the legislative power by which Parliament is a constituent power.

The relative ease of amendment on the one hand, and the nature of social development and belated modernisation on the other hand, explains the fact that the constitution in Hungary has rather frequently been amended during the decades between 1956-1989. This process has seemed to slow down during recent years, a fact which can be explained by the stabilisation of society and the changing nature of the transformation itself. Before the 1989-1990 democratic (and at the same time capitalist) transformation, the amendments were in connection with organisational changes (except for the overall reform in 1972 that reflected the democratisation within the framework of the State-socialist, etatist model). In the reform era, between the early 1970s and the late 1980s, the constitutional amendments were again of a technical nature with some minor exceptions. As indicated above, the constitutional reforms in 1989 and 1990 resulted in a completely new constitution under the old label. Before the transformation, the constitutional modifications were triggered by the decisions of the ruling single party and the assembly acted as a formal legitimising body. In the process of the system re-building the amendments were the means of system creation and the reform government played a crucial role in initiating and directing the whole process. In this short period the higher level state bureaucracy was extremely active. Direct political control was missing and in the ensuing political vacuum the legal achievements were exemplary. After the transformation the election results influenced the fate of the constitution. As a consequence of a rather disproportionate electoral system which favours the winning party and rewards the most successful one by giving it extra seats compared to the popular vote, at least two parties are needed for a constitutional change. In the 1990-1994 parliamentary cycle the governing coalition was not strong enough to amend the basic law, and therefore the co-operation of the biggest opposition party was needed if changes were to be made. This fact explains that in the first parliamentary period there were a mere two amendments, including the major spring 1990 reform package. The second amending bill was passed in 1993. In the second Parliamentary cycle the government coalition obtained a parliamentary share of more than 72 per cent which enabled the two governing parties to amend the constitution without the consent or co-operation of the shrunken opposition. The new government proved to be equally cautious and deliberately did not use its legally secured super majority too often: in the first year of office there were three changes, and in 1995 only one change. The latter restricted the capacity of amendment itself.

After the second pluralistic elections a new situation emerged, not only in a political sense but also with respect to constitutionalism. During the campaign all major parties accentuated the need of a new constitution which would put an end to the then existing interim, explicitly transitory constitutional situation. The parties offered the public their own version of a new basic law. The new government has given high priority to the cause of constitution-making, but the preparations were delayed due to the uncertainty of co-operation between the overwhelming parliamentary majority and the much smaller opposition. The form of participation of the government in the process was also unclear. The only certain element was in order to promote the idea of amending the basic law. In its jurisdiction the Court often faces the reality of missing constitutional regulations. In this case, the Court can summon Parliament to amend the constitution, but there is no legal consequence of the passivity of the House. The Court is not entitled to directly revise the constitutionality of a passed amendment, because its activity can be carried out within the existing framework of the basic law. The opposite may happen, albeit rarely. It has happened that the Court declared a special regulation of a law unconstitutional, and the reaction of the majority of Parliament was to incorporate the annulled text into the constitution. One example is the voting right of those holding Hungarian citizenship who stay abroad on the day of election. Originally the electoral law (Act XXXIV of 1989) excluded Hungarians living abroad from exercising their voting right, stipulating that those absent from the country on the day of elections are prevented from voting. Just before the 1990 spring general elections a claim was filed at the Constitutional Court against the actual regulation of the electoral law by a Hungarian citizen living in Algeria. The Court has found the regulation unconstitutional on the grounds that the constitution guaranteed the right to vote to those citizens having permanent residence in the country. The Court argued that Parliament violated this constitutional right by instituting the regulation instead of making it possible for citizens living abroad to vote. The Court did not examine the merits of the constitutional stipulation which has guaranteed the voting right only for those Hungarians having permanent or provisional residence in the country, accepting the reason offered in the official explanation of the electoral law: those not having ties to the country are prevented from voting. In turn, the Court argued that in given modem communications, those who have the constitutional right to vote must not be blocked from voting if they are not actually in the homeland. As a result of the ruling the affected piece of regulation has been declared void. Parliament did not accept the essence of what the Court really claimed, that is did not grant voting rights to Hungarians living abroad. This was a political issue, because the Hungarian citizenship regulation is extremely liberal and therefore the number of those who can be affected by a liberal electoral codification can go beyond controllable limits. There were also speculations on the political orientation of potential voters and this aspect could influence the outcome of the debate. Parliament chose the simplest solution by promptly incorporating the unconstitutional regulation into the text of the constitution, giving it full constitutional force incontestable by the Court. The amended text says that every Hungarian citizen of voting age, if he or she has a permanent residence in Hungary, has the right to be elected as a member of the national assembly, local government or minority local government, and has the right to participate in such elections as well as in national, local referendums and plebiscites, on the condition that he or she is within the territory of the country on the day of elections (Art. 70/1). This new regulation in the basic law is still valid, albeit widely debated by the conservative parties who are longing to broaden their electorate from outside the country. The example clearly shows the nature of the legislative power by which Parliament is a constituent power.

The relative ease of amendment on the one hand, and the nature of social development and belated modernisation on the other hand, explains the fact that the constitution in Hungary has rather frequently been amended during the decades between 1956-1989. This process has seemed to slow down during recent years, a fact which can be explained by the stabilisation of society and the changing nature of the transformation itself. Before the 1989-1990 democratic (and at the same time capitalist) transformation, the amendments were in connection with organisational changes (except for the overall reform in 1972 that reflected the democratisation within the framework of the State-socialist, etatist model). In the reform era, between the early 1970s and the late 1980s, the constitutional amendments were again of a technical nature with some minor exceptions. As indicated above, the constitutional reforms in 1989 and 1990 resulted in a completely new constitution under the old label. Before the transformation, the constitutional modifications were triggered by the decisions of the ruling single party and the assembly acted as a formal legitimising body. In the process of the system re-building the amendments were the means of system creation and the reform government played a crucial role in initiating and directing the whole process. In this short period the higher level state bureaucracy was extremely active. Direct political control was missing and in the ensuing political vacuum the legal achievements were exemplary. After the transformation the election results influenced the fate of the constitution. As a consequence of a rather disproportionate electoral system which favours the winning party and rewards the most successful one by giving it extra seats compared to the popular vote, at least two parties are needed for a constitutional change. In the 1990-1994 parliamentary cycle the governing coalition was not strong enough to amend the basic law, and therefore the co-operation of the biggest opposition party was needed if changes were to be made. This fact explains that in the first parliamentary period there were a mere two amendments, including the major spring 1990 reform package. The second amending bill was passed in 1993. In the second Parliamentary cycle the government coalition obtained a parliamentary share of more than 72 per cent which enabled the two governing parties to amend the constitution without the consent or co-operation of the shrunken opposition. The new government proved to be equally cautious and deliberately did not use its legally secured super majority too often: in the first year of office there were three changes, and in 1995 only one change. The latter restricted the capacity of amendment itself. After the second pluralistic elections a new situation emerged, not only in a political sense but also with respect to constitutionalism. During the campaign all major parties accentuated the need of a new constitution which would put an end to the then existing interim, explicitly transitory constitutional situation. The parties offered the public their own version of a new basic law. The new government has given high priority to the cause of constitution-making, but the preparations were delayed due to the uncertainty of co-operation between the overwhelming parliamentary majority and the much smaller opposition. The form of participation of the government in the process was also unclear. The only certain element was that the two governing parties wanted a draft based on consensus and required the support of at least one opposition party. But it shortly turned out that this requirement was not enough: the opposition parties wanted more, with the exception of a right-wing party, the Independent Smallholders' Party (ISP). The ISP claimed that they should have an equal role irrespective of the parliamentary party proportions.

Meanwhile, in early 1995 the Ministry of Justice prepared – with the participation of an expert group independent of the Ministry – a viable concept of regulation of the new constitution and this document was offered for wide and open domestic and international debate. The document speeded up the process and the parliamentary parties agreed on the procedural questions of the preparation. In summer 1995 a special parliamentary committee was set up – the Committee for the Preparation of the Constitution of the National Assembly – and the representatives started to work first on the concept of regulation. The document of the Ministry of Justice has now been put aside, but in an informal way it greatly influenced the committee concept formation. The standing of this special body meant that the government had given up its formal legal power to define the new constitution because, implying a good deal of self-restraint, they realised that a wider social consensus was necessary going beyond immediate party interests. The new situation also meant a practical moratorium on any possible amendment of the existing constitution. The House rules were also modified with respect to the constitutional preparations and Act XLIV of 1995 amending the constitution introduced a temporary regulation of the quorum requirement.[15] Later during this second government cycle it turned out that there were basic clashes of philosophy among the political parties represented in Parliament in the questions of constitution making process. Although the preparatory committee finally accepted a coherent version of a new constitution, among the parliamentary parties there was no basic agreement on its viability and, more importantly, its necessity. Seeing the impasse of this high level of consensus the governing coalition regarded the process as a weapon of the opposition to block the coalition government to amend the basic law. By realising this trap the government has given up its wish to have a new constitution, and has decided to amend the constitution in 1997 (Act LIX on the amendment of the Constitution, enacting the new basic regulations of referendum and plebiscite into the basic law). This was the very moment of freezing in of the transitory constitution. The government has realised that there is no essential political and legal need for a new document in the lack of basic consensus of political forces. A piecemeal way of constitutional development was accepted instead, in which the actual parliamentary distributions are decisive. The campaign before the 1998 general elections did nit touch the constitutional problematique: the model was regarded basically successful in the real practice and the political shortcomings could not been explained by constitutional inadequacies. There remained only one evergreen constitutional issue, the form of election of the president, but even this question is only exciting for the politicians and the active, but smaller minority, the wider public is not committed too much. It is not a surprise that after the 1998 election the government did not put the constitution-making on its agenda. The coalition did not have the 2/3 majority and opting for a conflictual governing style the lines between the two side have stiffened. That is why the incumbent government, having realised the deep cleavages among the different political ideologies concerning the constitution-making process, have

---

[15] Art. *24/5* stipulates that 'For accepting the parliamentary decision on the detailed regulations of the preparation of the new constitution, a four-fifths vote of National Assembly representatives shall be required'.

decided to seek only partial compromises with a strong opposition having veto power.

## VI. PARTICULARITIES OF THE PROCEDURES FOR CONSTITUTIONAL AMENDMENT

By its own inner nature, constitutional amendment is more a political than a legal procedure.[16] To be sure, the legal aspects are also very important, but they do not cause serious problems in general. In contrast, the political elements are much more unpredictable and they are difficult to handle. Once the political consensus is reached, the amendment procedure is smooth and rapid, especially in the case of a partial modification of the text.

The overall reform, and especially the drafting of a new constitution, is a much more complicated matter. While an ordinary amendment, touching only a certain part of the basic law, does not involve legitimacy problems and clashes of identification, the general modification or drafting of a completely new text poses a lot of controversial issues.

The main problem of the present drafting process is, who is the subject of constitution-making? On a normative basis the question is not really complicated: the government is responsible for due preparation and Parliament takes the decision for which a two-thirds majority is needed. The procedural aspects of the preparation are that of a normal bill, and are defined by the House Regulations. Governmental bureaucracy is active in the preparation and this guarantees the necessary expertise, minimising the inadequacy or harmonisation pitfalls.

A lot of criticism is voiced, mainly by extra-parliamentary forces, that Parliament monopolises the preparation process and social organisations, interest-representing groups, are not allowed to participate in it. This complaint can be relevant to some extent, because the drafting procedure is not public and the parliamentary parties exclude other potential actors thus insuring the preponderance of short-run party political interests. It is widely accepted among elite political formations that the present interim constitution represents a balanced parliamentary system in which popular control is sufficiently counterbalanced by the accentuated role of Parliament within the system of separate powers. Although there is no explicit parliamentary supremacy over the other branches, especially the judiciary and the Constitutional Court, the existing form of parliamentarianism effectively combines the legislative and executive powers.

This model creates stable government, but the control over state bureaucracy is rather ineffective. The governing party or party coalition, through its parliamentary majority, controls the legislative process, the government, elects the president and other important state officials. If the government disposes of a two-thirds majority, it can modify the basic laws of constitutional importance (local

---

[16] For the political and legal aspects of the transition see Jon Elster, 'Constitutionalism in Eastern Europe: An Introduction' *(University of Chicago Law Review* 58, 1991).

governments, the electoral and judicial system etc.) and the constitution itself without effective opposition or other control. This model is not accepted by each party in Parliament. The most often debated issues are the powers and election formula of the President of the Republic (by Parliament or by popular vote), the institutionalisation of a second chamber, the voting rights of Hungarians living outside the country, the role and powers of the Constitutional Court, the interpretation of popular sovereignty (the role of referenda), the role of social and economic rights and the interpretation of the so-called social state.

There is no consensus within the drafting committee on these questions, and the majority rejected the proposal of experts and opposition parties that a preliminary referendum should be held on the most important alternatives.[17] Instead the six-party agreement on the preparation of the new constitution handles the situation of the lack of consensus in such a way that the constitutional regulation in effect survives. This agreement in itself means that there is a chance for a freezing in of the present constitution; this would be very counterproductive because it excludes the changing of evidently unsatisfactory regulations. I have to mention as an example the nomination and the election of the Constitutional Court judges. In the present system Parliament exclusively controls this process and the selection of justices is over-politicised. The parliamentary nomination committee is based on party parity, each party having one vote irrespective of its real power. This set-up can effectively block successful nominations. A multi-channel nomination would be evidently more democratic and less politicised, but party elites strive to preserve their acquired power in this respect and in other domains as well.

## VII. BALANCE BETWEEN THE NEED FOR STABILITY AND CERTAINTY IN THE CONSTITUTION AND THE NEED FOR THE CONSTITUTION TO CHANGE IN RESPONSE TO THE CHANGING NEEDS OF SOCIETY

As I have already mentioned, the two basic reform waves resulted in a new, stable Constitution regardless of the fact that there are parts in it which are outdated and do not reflect real legal and social developments.[18] The novelty of a new constitution would be doubtful, because the basic structure of parliamentarianism would not be changed, and the relationships among the most important actors – the legislative, the executive, the president and the Constitutional Court – would not be rebuilt or reinterpreted. This is why there are experts who hold the view that there is no need for a new constitution, instead a developmental concept should be implied. According to this view what is needed most is the broadening of the legitimisation of the basic law and the modification of the amendment process. The first step was taken by the 1995 amendment, when parties represented in Parliament

---

[17] Kálmán Kulcsár, sociologist of law, Minister of Justice during the crucial transformation period, 1988-90, first proposed publicly the use of referendums to gain popular support before deciding the most important questions in Parliament.

[18] For example, the right to work is still a fundamental right having no legal guarantee at all, and the unemployment rate is around 10 per cent.

agreed on the preparation of the new constitution. As a result of this pact the constitution was amended and the amendment formula was supplemented with stipulations on the preparation of the new constitution. The four-fifths quorum requirement referred to the preparation rules and did not affect the amendment voting rules, the two-thirds majority rule. It was also widely accepted that the new constitution had to be put to referendum and, as a consequence, future amendments should have the same combined acceptance regulations, that is the two-thirds voting in Parliament and a subsequent referendum. As I mentioned earlier, the preparation of a new constitution was not successful and the temporary agreement on the new quorum requirement has become void at the end of the second parliamentary cycle.

The flexible amendment rule has served the transformation in a positive way so far. It is now realised that a constitutional-legal possibility to amend the basic law is not automatically a real political possibility, because society is very sensitive if fundamental changes are made on a partisan basis. There is a strong and widespread feeling that there must be broad consensus of parliamentary forces when deciding on important national matters. This situation may change, and I can foresee special circumstances which may legitimise determined, charismatic political behaviour, especially in a crisis situation or if the political system is not able to integrate a society deeply divided by antagonistic economic conflicts. For the time being the simplified amending rule can be regarded as functional in the rapid transformation and democratisation of the new, pluralistic regime.

## VIII. THE PROBLEM OF THE CONSTITUTIONALITY OF AN AMENDMENT OR ITS CONSISTENCY WITH THE REST OF THE CONSTITUTION, AND THE ROLE OF THE COURTS

In the absence of a second chamber there is no built-in process for control of the constitutionality of an amendment, and the Constitutional Court is also prevented from such an activity because the Court cannot effectively act on the constitutionality of the basic law itself. The Court can criticise the amendment but is not able to introduce any legal means against it. In theory there is only one special way of control: the preliminary constitutional control of the bill. The law on the Constitutional Court (Act XXXII of 1989) made it possible to investigate the constitutionality of a bill. In a famous ruling the Court interpreted its own responsibility for preliminary control and set up requirements for preliminary constitutional scrutiny. The justices reasoned that this check can be rational on the condition that the bill cannot be modified further in parliamentary debate. This means that the condition is twofold: the bill is not yet voted on, and the general assembly debate is already closed. According to the law Parliament, any parliamentary committee and fifty members of Parliament, can initiate preliminary control of a bill. This regulation can be applied to an amending bill that is going to be part of the constitution, because before the formal acceptance it does not have the legal status of a constitutional text. I have to admit that the issue is nowadays very controversial.[19]

Only the Constitutional Court is entitled to review the constitutionality of laws. If in a normal court procedure the judge identifies a regulation contrary to the constitution, he or she may suspend the procedure and submit the matter for decision by the Constitutional Court. The parties in the procedure are also entitled to initiate that the judge takes such a move.

This constitutional arrangement means that in the circumstances pertaining to Hungary, judicial interpretation does not involve an autonomous decision on the constitutionality of norms within the normal court system; therefore this indirect judicial control, realisable only through the Constitutional Court, is very weak. Thus the courts can investigate the constitutionality of a regulation which involves sovereign interpretation without immediate consequences. Practical experience shows that the judges are frequently not using their right to interpret constitutionality and they are inclined to perform this role in a moderate, self-restraining way. This moderate judicial behaviour can be explained by tradition. The judiciary in the normal civil and criminal court system is accustomed to implementation of the existing legal norms and the possible clashes of interpretations are still solved based on the guiding role of the Supreme Court. The justices have to be accustomed to the new legal culture in which the constitution is not merely a set of elegant principles high above the real legal practice, but is a real, applicable legal norm that legitimises not only judicial function but is superior to law making activity as well, and, as a consequence, they have to learn that laws and regulations are not evidently in accordance with the basic law.

So far judicial interpretation of the constitution has not resulted in constitutional amendment, apart from the one exception already mentioned. It is more characteristic that the interpretation of special constitutional norms obviates the need for formal amendment or at least postpones it. The Constitutional Court is entitled to the so-called abstract interpretation of the constitution. This function of the Court does not lead to any modification of the constitution or other norms, because its aim is to ascertain the real message or intention of the specific constitutional norm. The most well known case is the interpretation of the role of the President of the Republic in 1992, namely the realisation of his appointment rights, its constitutional framework and legal conditions.[20] This and other

---

[19] Quite recently the House Committee ordered the immediate final vote on a bill after the closing of the debate. In this concrete matter there were 54 representatives of the main governing party. The HSP initiated a Constitutional Court procedure on a bill submitted by the government (the incompatibility of certain economic functions with the status of a member of Parliament) before its final vote. The vote on the bill was ordered by the President of the House based on the decision of the House Committee, and it was actually voted positively. The legal reasoning has blocked the prevalence of a basic right of MPs, a right guaranteed by law .The move was taken before the Constitutional Court and the Court declared it plainly unconstitutional. In response, the government prepared a bill to eliminate the right of representatives to initiate preliminary control.

[20] The debate was triggered by a decision of the president, by which he refused the nomination of the presidents of public radio and television submitted by the government. The thorough interpretation of the Court has defined the limits of the nomination right and made clear that refusal is an exceptional means only to apply when a government proposal threatens the democratic functioning of the State organisation (Ruling 36/1992). The controversial nature of the matter was demonstrated by the fact that

interpretations of the Court were widely criticised by experts on the ground that the interpretation is limitless and goes beyond the wording of the constitution. Some critics quoted from an interview given by the Court president in which he interpreted the role of the Court in a very broad sense as comprising the realisation of the so-called 'invisible constitution' behind the existing one. Although the activist behaviour was an openly expressed value of the Court, even some judges warned about the dangers of the non-restricted use of interpretation and proposed more caution and more self-restraint.

The most controversial issue of constitutional amendment is the role of direct democracy, namely the question whether referendum can be used to oblige Parliament to change the basic law. The Constitutional Court has decided in 1993 that even an indirect modification as a result of mandatory referendum initiated by the citizens is against the constitution. The Court reasoned that the primary form of sovereignty in the existing parliamentarian system is the representative function of Parliament, and the direct democracy has only a supplementary function. This highly debated decision was based on the structure of the Constitution and the theory of parliamentarism. At the same time the Court ruled that a new regulation should have been made because the then existing law on referendum had been accepted prior to the basic constitutional reform in 1989. This decision obliged the general assembly to accept the new law no later than the end of 1993. Parliament did not fulfil the court's decision, and in the absence of any sanction this happens very frequently. Only in 1997 was accepted the modification of the Constitution incorporating the basic stipulations into the basic law. The law on referendum was enacted in the following year. The new regulation seemed to create a completely different situation by giving a special force to the mandatory referendum initiated by the citizens. The law precisely listed the cases in which mandatory referendum could not be proposed.

Based on this new constitutional regulation the Constitutional Court ruled (Ruling 52/1997) that 'direct exercise of political power is an exceptional form of popular sovereignty, but if it is exceptionally exercised it is above the representative power'. The Court also ruled that mandatory referendum initiated by the people precedes the facultative referendum that can be initiated by Parliament. In this decision the Court sharply criticised Parliament because it did not created the new law on referendum, and to put some emphasis to its commitment the Court annulled the whole act by the end of 1997. Since Parliament did not accept the new law until February 1998, there was a time during which a basic right of the citizens has been suspended.

This decision did not touch the problem of constitutional modification, and many thought that the Court has reinterpreted its earlier, very restrictive

---

there were three dissenting opinions. In another decision, the Court interpreted the role of the President in relation to the armed forces, and the real content of his role as the commander-in-chief of the Hungarian Defence Forces.

interpretation. Two years later it turned out that this was not the case. In a decision taken in July 1999 the Constitutional Court declared that 'the modification of the Constitution can be made only in the procedural form stipulated in the basic law; a referendum initiated by the citizens in order to modify the Constitution is not viable.' According to the interpretation of the Court the presently valid Constitution does not explicitly allow the change of the basic law directly by the public, and therefore mandatory national referendum initiated by the citizens as a legal means cannot be used to attain this political aim. The Court interpreted the basic law in a very narrow conservative way and stated that only the modification of the basic law by Parliament could be tested through a mandatory national referendum. This court decision was regarded controversial by many, and some prominent experts – for example a former court member – voiced their differing opinion which classified the decision as totally mistaken.

The court decision was made in a concrete matter: a group of citizens initiated a referendum on the form of election of the president of republic. The formulation of the question was necessarily tested by the National Election Committee before the collection of signatures based on the stipulations of the Act C of 1997 on Electoral Procedure. The Committee have taken into consideration the fact that the Constitution was amended in 1997 (Act XCVIII of 1997 on the modification of the Constitution of the Republic of Hungary) in order to create the guaranties of the referendum as a basic element of popular sovereignty.

This new regulation did not mention the possibility of amendment of the basic law through a referendum, but had given a definite list on the subjects in which mandatory referendum initiated by 200.000 citizens were explicitly excluded. The list has contained ten items: 1) content of acts regulating the budget, the execution of the budget, national tax items and duties, custom duties; 2) obligations originating from valid international agreements and the content of acts regulating these obligations; 3) the regulations on the referendum and plebiscite of the Constitution; 4) national conditions of local taxes; 5) personal and organisational questions in the competence of the national assembly; 6) the dissolution of Parliament; 7) the programme of the government; 8) declaration on state of war, emergency or extraordinary situation; 9) dissolution of representative body of local government; 10) general amnesty.

The Committee referred to the item 3) and reasoned that the basic law itself excluded the possibility of constitutional amendment with regard to a special constitutional matter and 'a contrario' all other constitutional norms not falling under other specially defined prohibitive regulations can be questioned in a referendum. The Court did not accept this formal logic and referred to its earlier decision of 1993, in which the Court ruled that 'Exercise of rights originating in the popular sovereignty by the national assembly or via referendum can only be realised according to the regulations of the Constitution. Question put to referendum cannot contain indirect modification of the Constitution'. The Court reasoned that the legislation is defined as the function of the national assembly and the modification of the constitution is also defined as a exclusive parliamentarian right in the Constitution. Since Hungary has a parliamentarian constitutional system, referendum can only be a supplementary means with regard to the parliamentarian representation, as explicitly stated in the 1993 Court decision.

The decision of the Court is debated ever since, but the decision is mandatory to everybody and therefore has a far-reaching effect on the importance of the referendum in Hungary: it cannot be used as a grass roots correctional form or political means in order to change the constitution via public action. This situation can only be changed by modifying the Constitution explicitly opening the way before a special form of referendum that can result in the modification of the existing Constitution.

The impact of the Court's interpretation of the political system cannot be precisely estimated so far. Nevertheless we can acknowledge the fact that the activity of the Court as a whole is the most important development in our modern constitutional history. It has a very powerful impact on the functioning of the executive branch, especially the government, and on the legislature as well. In the longer run constitutional control would be a powerful counter-balance to the combined, party-dominated centre of power, the Parliament-government angle. Without such a control political elite power would not be effectively limited and only subsequent 'punishment voting' would establish political responsibility. In unstable democracies in which the informal rules are weak this solution does not seem to fulfil the requirements and expectations.

## XI. CONCLUSIONS

At present there is no political agreement on the new constitution, although the previous government accepted the codification guidelines of the text. Without the support of opposition parties there is no chance for the acceptance of the basic law, even if the experts can agree on the formal version. This situation demonstrates that the initial structure tends to freeze in and constitution-making needs a high level of political consensus. Without the pressure of historic events and deep social transformations the constitutional structure represents a high level of stability. In addition, the legal amendment requirement does not mean a free pass for change on the side of a government having a comfortable majority. In the new democracies the intellectual elite and the wider politicised society are extremely sensitive to unbalanced changes in the basic legal and constitutional structure – constructed as a result of negotiations and political compromise. At the same time legal development is not yet completed: the economic transformation and the European integration require further modifications of the initial model. The hidden contradictions can be and should be solved from time to time. Instead of a completely new constitution the developmental modification process is much more viable and it is in harmony with the real post-transition social circumstances.

Chapter Nine

# JUDICIAL ROLE IN CONSTITUTIONAL AMENDMENT IN INDIA: THE BASIC STRUCTURE DOCTRINE

Dr Mathew Abraham[*]

## I. INTRODUCTION

This chapter looks into the power of Parliament and the procedure to amend the Constitution in India. It focuses on the active role of the Indian judiciary in evolving a novel constitutional law doctrine to test the validity of constitutional amendments. The basic structure doctrine, which was initially seen as an unsafe field of constitutional quicksand,[1] has within the last two decades gained ground to become a bedrock to check the power of Parliament to amend the Constitution.[2]

## II. THE NATURE OF THE INDIAN CONSTITUTION

The Constitution of India 1950, as a legal document, marked the birth of "modern India".[3] The constitution conveys the spirit of independence and envisages a process of indigenous reconstruction.[4] The aims and ideals envisaged by the constitution

---

[*] LL.M., Ph.D (SOAS, London 1995); of Lincoln's Inn, Barrister of England and Wales; Advocate of the High Court of Kerala, India.
[1] Baxi, Upendra, "The constitutional quicksands of Kesavananda Bharati and the twenty-fifth amendment", (1974) 1 SCC Journal 45-67 (SCC = Supreme Court Cases).
[2] See, Wade, Prof. William, "Constitutions - Bedrock or Quicksand?" in *Public Law in Britain and India*, 1992, Bombay, Tripathi, 1-27 at 12-13.
[3] The standard works on Indian constitutional law which I have referred to are: Austin, Granville, *The Indian constitution: cornerstone of a nation*, 1966, Oxford, Clarendon Press; Pylee, M.V., *Constitutional Government in India*, (3rd rev. edn.), 1977, Bombay, Asia Publishing House; Seervai, H.M., *Constitutional Law of India*, (3rd edn.), vols.1-2 and supp.1, 1983, 1984, 1988, Bombay, Tripathi; Jain, M.P., *Indian Constitutional Law*, (4th edn.), 1987, Bombay, Tripathi; Pandey, J.N., *Constitutional Law of India*, (20th edn.), 1989, Allahabad, Central Law Agency; Basu, Durga Das, *Constitutional Law of India*, (6th edn.), 1991, New Delhi, Prentice-Hall of India.
[4] For a critical insight into the early decades of independent India's political and economic development see Rudolph, Lloyd I. and Susanne H. Rudolph, *The modernity of tradition: political development in India*, 1967, Chicago, Chicago University Press; Frankel, Francine R., *India's political economy 1947-1977: the gradual revolution*, 1978, Princeton, Princeton University Press; Nayar, Baldev Raj, *India's mixed economy: the role of ideology and interest in its development*, 1989,

also call for the creation of a new legal order. The framework of the constitution was apparently built upon the British constitutional law tradition.[6] Although the parliamentary system and the cabinet form of government broadly follows the British model, it is well-known that one can discern in the constitution the influence of several modern constitutions. Federalism in India relies on principles from the American, Canadian and Australian constitutions.[7] The American Bill of Rights had a great impact on the formulation of the Fundamental Rights and the inspiration for the Directive Principles of State Policy had come from the Irish Constitution.[8]

At the time of drafting the constitution itself, it was observed by Dr Ambedkar, the chairman of the drafting committee of the Constituent Assembly, that:

The only new things, if there can be any, in a constitution framed so late in the day are the variations made to remove the faults and to accommodate it to the needs of the country.[9]

## III. A BRIEF HISTORY OF THE INDIAN LEGAL SYSTEM

The present system of law in India, for all practical purposes, has its basis in the legal system developed for India by the British. The foundation of the Indian legal system can be said to have its origin in the Judicial Plan of 1772 adopted by Warren Hastings to establish a legal system to maintain law and order and to secure property rights.[10] With the expansion of British rule, the gradual establishment of an English system brought to an end the system of law developed by the Moghul administration which in turn had displaced numerous systems which had flourished under various Hindu Kingdoms of the past.

The characteristic features of the early legal system developed by the English lay in the administration of justice in accordance with the principles of equity and good conscience and in the importance accorded to the rule of law.[11] By the second half of the 19th century, the legal system was virtually revolutionised, with a spate of legislation which was influenced by a desire to introduce English law and to shape the system from an English lawyer's view point.[12] The desire to build an

---

Bombay, Popular Prakashan.

[6] Two earlier documents enacted by British Parliament for the governance of India, Government of India Act 1919 and the Government of India Act 1935, provided a rough basic framework for the creation of the constitution.

[7] For authoritative early analysis of Indian federalism see Jain, M.P., "Federalism in India", (1965) 6 *Journal of the Indian Law Institute*, 355-379; Jacob, Alice, "Centre-state governmental relations in the Indian federal system", (1968) 10 *Journal of the Indian Law Institute*, 583-636.

[8] Seervai, *Constitutional Law of India*, vol.2, at 1577. Bhagwati J. has distinguished the Indian modifications of the Irish provisions, which made them more effective, in *Minerva Mills Limited v. Union of India*, AIR 1980 SC 1789 at 1847-1850.

[9] See Jain, M.P., *Indian constitutional law*, at p.6 referring to the *Constituent Assembly Debates*, vol.7, pp.35-56.

[10] Jain, M.P., *Outlines of India's Legal History* (3rd edn.) 1972, Bombay, Tripathi, at p.77.

[11] Derrett, J.D.M., "Justice, equity and good conscience in India", in J.N.D. Anderson (ed.), *Changing law in developing countries* 1963, London, Allen & Unwin, pp.114-153.

[12] Banerjee, A.C., *English Law in India* (1984), p.189.

Empire gave rise to resentment against British rule and led to independence. Although a great human tragedy ensued in creating Pakistan by partitioning India, the transition from British rule did not bring about any significant change to the established legal system.[13]

In fact, even a decade after independence, the then Attorney-General of India, at the Hamlyn Law Lecture, depicted the Indian legal system as one well within the mainstream of the English common law systems and enriched with the common law tradition.[14] According to him, the structure and powers of the court, the roles of judges and lawyers, the adversarial system of trial, the reliance on judicial precedent and the shared funds of concepts and techniques, bring the Indian legal system into the mainstream of English common law systems.[15]

The common law in India in the wide meaning of the expression would include not only what in England is known strictly as the common law, but also its traditions, some of the principles underlying the English statute law, the equitable principles developed in England in order to mitigate the rigours of the common law, and even the attitude and methods pervading the British system of administration of justice.[16]

A. The Making of a Flexible Constitution

Immediately after independence in 1947, the struggle to live as an independent nation centred upon the framing of the constitution itself.[17] The making of the Constitution of India was a task of titanic proportions. The initial aim of constitution-making was to establish a democracy based on the ideals of justice, liberty, equality and fraternity. The need for a new constitution forming the basic law of the land for the realisation of these ideas was paramount at that time.[18] Dr Ambedkar made the following observations on the principles adopted by the committee:

The Constitution is a fundamental document. It is a document which defines the position and power of the three organs of the State - the executive, the judiciary and the legislature. It also defines the powers of the executive and the powers of the legislature as against the citizens, as we have done in our chapter dealing with Fundamental Rights. In fact, the purpose of a

---

[13] By Art. 372 of the Constitution, all the laws in force immediately before the commencement of the constitution shall continue in force until altered or repealed or amended by a competent legislature or other competent authority.
[14] Setalvad, M.C., *Common law in India*, 1960, London, Stevens & Sons Ltd.
[15] *Ibid*, at 3.
[16] *Id*.
[17] For details on the process of constitution-making see Rau, B.N., *India's constitution in the making*, 1960, Delhi, Orient Longmans; Rao, B. Shiva *et al.*, *The framing of India's constitution*, vols.1-5, 1966-1968, New Delhi, The Indian Institute of Public Administration. See also, Anand, C.L., *Constitutional law and history of government of India*, (6th edn.), 1990, Allahabad, The University Book Agency, 305-930. For historical details see Seervai, *Constitutional law of India*, vol.1, ch.1; Rao et al., *Framing of the Indian constitution: a study*, vol.5, 1-92.
[18] Pylee, *Constitutional Government in India*, at p.24.

constitution is not merely to create the organs of the State but to limit their authority, because, if no limitation was imposed upon the authority of the organs, there will be complete tyranny and complete oppression. The legislature may be free to frame any law; the executive may be free to take any decision; and the Supreme Court may be free to give any interpretation of the law. It would result in utter chaos.[19]

How exactly the aims and ideals envisioned by the members of the Constituent Assembly ought to be achieved might not have been clear at that time. Having regard to the fact that there are various ways by which economic democracy may be brought about, it was then felt that there would be no purpose in giving a rigid form to something which is not rigid, which is fundamentally changing and must keep on changing.

B. Constitutional Provisions for Amendment

The framers of the constitution therefore provided a fairly reasonable procedure for amendment which was considered as neither rigid nor flexible at that time. In the last four and a half decades there have been over seventy-six amendments which show that the constitution is more flexible than rigid.

The constitution provides for three categories of amendments: first, those that can be effected by Parliament by a simple majority;[20] secondly, those that require a special majority and thirdly, those that require, in addition to a special majority, ratification by at least one half of the state legislatures. The main provisions specifically dealing with the last two categories are contained in Article 368 of the Constitution.

Article 368, which provides for the general amending power and prescribes the procedure for amendment, was itself amended several times, particularly by the Twenty-fourth Amendment Act 1971 and the Forty-second Amendment Act 1976.[21]

---

[19] See, Rao, Shiva, et al, *The Framing of India's Constitution: A Study*, 1968, The Indian Institute of Public Administration, New Delhi at 832.

[20] There are four areas under this category where Parliament may by a simple majority make laws which would amend the constitution. No such law shall be deemed to be an amendment for the purpose of Art 368. They are: (i) Art. 4(2) read with Arts. 2 and 3 authorise Parliament to establish or admit new states and alter the areas, boundaries or names of states contained in the First and Fourth Schedules of the Constitution; (ii) Art. 169(3) authorises Parliament to provide for the abolition or creation of the legislative Council in a state and amend the constitution for that purpose; (iii) Paragraph 7 of the Fifth Schedule authorises Parliament to amend that Schedule which contains provisions as to the administration and control of Scheduled Areas and Scheduled Tribes; (iv) Paragraph 21 of the Sixth Schedule authorises Parliament to amend that Schedule which contains special provisions for the administration of Tribal Areas.

[21] The provisions under this Article before the amendments were as follows:
Art. 368: Procedure for amendment of the Constitution:-
An amendment of the Constitution may be initiated only by the introduction of a Bill for the purpose in either House of Parliament and when the Bill is passed in each House by a majority of the total membership of that House and by a majority of not less than two-thirds of the members of the House present and voting and it shall be presented to the President for his assent and upon such assent being given to the Bill the Constitution shall stand amended in accordance with the Bill:

After the 24th and 42nd Amendments, made pursuant to Supreme Court rulings curtailing Parliament's power, Article 368 now reads as follows:

Art. 368: Power of Parliament to amend the Constitution and Procedure therefor:-

(1) Notwithstanding anything in this Constitution, Parliament may in exercise of its constituent power amend by way of addition, variation or repeal any provision of this Constitution in accordance with the procedure laid down in this article.

(2) An amendment of this Constitution may be initiated only by the introduction of a Bill for the purpose in either House of Parliament, and when the Bill is passed in each House by a majority of the total membership of that House and by a majority of not less than two-thirds of the members of that House present and voting, it shall be presented to the President who shall give his assent to the Bill and thereupon the Constitution shall stand amended in accordance with the terms of the Bill:

Provided that if such amendment seeks to make any change in:

(a) article 54, article 55, article 73, article 162 or article 241, or
(b) Chapter IV of Part V, Chapter V of Part VI, or Chapter I of Part XI, or
(c) any of the lists in the Seventh Schedule, or
(d) the representation of States in Parliament, or
(e) the provision of this article, the amendment shall also require to be ratified by the Legislatures of not less than one-half of the States by resolutions to that effect passed by those Legislatures before the Bill making provision for such amendment is presented to the President for assent.

(3) Nothing in article 13 shall apply to any amendment made under this article.

(4) No amendment of this Constitution (including the provisions of Part III) made or purporting to have been made under this article [whether before or after the commencement of section 55 of the Constitution (Forty-second Amendment) Act, 1976] shall be called in question in any court on any ground.

(5) For the removal of doubts, it is hereby declared that there shall be no limitation whatever on the constituent power of Parliament to amend by way of addition, variation or repeal the provisions of this Constitution under this article.

The amendments made to Article 368 particularly by the 24th and the 42nd

---

Provided that if such amendment seeks to make any change in:
(a) article 54, article 55, article 73, article 162 or article 241 or
(b) Chapter IV of Part V, Chapter V of Part VI or Chapter I of Part XI, or
(c) any of the lists in the Seventh Schedule, or
(d) the representation of States in Parliament, or
(e) the provision of the article,
the amendment shall also require to be ratified by the Legislature of not less than one-half of the States by resolutions to that effect passed by those Legislatures before the Bill making provision for such amendment is presented to the President for assent.

amendments have effected the following changes to the original meanings:

(i) Originally it was not obligatory for the President to give his assent to a bill for the amendment of the constitution. Now it is obligatory under Article 368 Clause 2.
(ii) Under the original provision the word "amendment" was left unexplained. Now by Clause 1 "amendment" would include "addition, variation or repeal of any provision of this Constitution".
(iii) Clause 3 in Article 368 and Clause 4 in Article 13 inserted by the 24th Amendment sought to create unlimited power of Parliament to amend the Constitution by exempting constitutional amendments from the prohibitions of Article 13.
(iv) Clauses 4 and 5 inserted by the 42nd Amendment sought to establish that there are no limitations whatsoever to the power of Parliament and also that constitutional amendments shall be immune from judicial review. However these two clauses have been annulled by the Supreme Court. I shall deal further with them below.

C. The Role of the Indian Judiciary

In order to understand the judicial role in constitutional amendment in India it is important to know the role of the Indian judiciary in general. Under the original framework of the constitution the judiciary has been given an extraordinary role as the protector of fundamental rights. Article 13 of the constitution forbids the State to make any law which takes away or abridges the fundamental rights and any law made in contravention shall be void. Article 13 has placed the judiciary as a sentinel on the *qui vive*.

In addition to the power conferred by Article 13, two main remedial provisions in the constitution, which are relevant for this study, confer extraordinary jurisdiction of the Supreme Court and the High Courts. These are the powers of the Supreme Court under Article 32 and of the High Courts under Article 226. These provisions empower the superior courts to issue directions, orders or writs or any appropriate remedy for the enforcement of a fundamental right. Under Article 32 the right to move the Supreme Court for the enforcement of the fundamental rights is also guaranteed.

The extraordinary constitutional powers conferred upon the higher judiciary and the enforcement of fundamental rights through the extraordinary constitutional remedies is an important facet of the entire operational gamut of Indian constitutional law.[22] The power of judicial review, enabling the courts to set limits

---

[22] For details see Markose, A.T., *Judicial control of administrative action in India*, 1956, Madras, Madras Law Journal Office, 308-315; Jain, M.P. and S.N. Jain, *Principles of administrative law*, (3rd edn.), 1979, Bombay, Tripathi, 376-472; Sathe, S.P., *Administrative law*, (4th edn.), 1984, Bombay, Tripathi, 304-390; Ramachandran, V.G., *Administrative law*, (2nd edn.), 1984, Lucknow, Eastern Book Co., 445-458; Massey, P., *Administrative law*, (3rd edn.), 1990, Delhi, Eastern Book Co., 203-240.

not only on executive actions but also on legislative power, both in theory and in practice, makes the Indian Supreme Court wield a form of political power unknown elsewhere.[23] Several important socio-legal studies focused on the Indian Supreme Court have shown the unique role of the Indian judges and the use of their judicial power.[24]

The extensive jurisdiction conferred upon the superior courts by the constitution was also gradually expanded by the judiciary itself.[25] The courts' decision in some cases appear to be typically legislative in nature. The central role played by the court in numerous public interest litigations has been explained as an exercise of usurping rule-making power by the court.[26]

Thus, judicial review in India is an explicitly and politically assigned role, as the provisions for judicial review sanction the courts' involvement in the ongoing political process. Court decisions have resolved several controversial and sensitive policy issues where even legislative attempts had failed earlier. Not surprisingly, it has been criticised that the role of the higher judiciary in India has gradually become more overtly political.[27] However, the role of the Indian judiciary, particularly in evolving the basic structure doctrine, is one of the many areas which has been acknowledged as unique and novel.[28]

C. The Evolution of *the Basic Structure Doctrine*

Since 1951, the scope of the amending power contained in Article 368 has been questioned before the Supreme Court of India. The question mainly centred on whether the fundamental rights were amendable. The worst and often affected right was the right to property. *Shankari Prasad Singh Deo v. The Union of India*[29] was the first case where the validity of the first amendment to the constitution which curtailed the right to property was challenged. The Supreme Court did not accept the argument that the fundamental rights were beyond reach of the process of constitutional amendment merely because Article 13 forbade the State from making any laws which took away or abridged fundamental rights.

A similar matter came before the Supreme Court in 1965 in *Sajjan Singh v.*

---

[23] Gadbois, "The Supreme Court of India as a political institution", in Dhavan *et al.*, *Judges and the judicial power*, at 250-251. For further details see Bhatia, K.L., *Judicial activism and social change*, 1990, New Delhi, Deep & Deep; Bhagwati, P.N., "Judicial activism and public interest litigation", (1985) 23 *Columbia Journal of Transnational Law*, 561-567.

[24] See generally, Gadbois, George H., "The Supreme Court of India as a political institution", in Dhavan *et al.*, *Judges and the judicial power*, 250-267; Singh, Bakshish, *Supreme Court of India as an instrument of social justice*; Dube, *Role of Supreme Court in Indian constitution*, and Baxi, Upendra, *Courage, craft and contention: the Indian Supreme Court in the eighties*, 1985, Bombay, Tripathi.

[25] For details see Das, Gobind, *Supreme Court in quest of identity*, 1987, Lucknow, Eastern Book Company.

[26] Cunningham, "Public interest litigation in Indian Supreme Court', at 513-515.

[27] Das, *Supreme Court in quest of identity*, at 246-257.

[28] Wade, Prof. William, *Public Law in Britain and India*, 1992, at p.12.

[29] AIR 1951 SC 458. (AIR = All India Reporter; SC = Supreme Court).

*State of Rajasthan*[30] where the validity of the 17th amendment to the constitution was challenged. The majority refused to accept the argument that fundamental rights were inviolable and beyond the reach of a constitutional amendment. Two judges dissented from the majority view and their dissenting view led to a further challenge of the 17th amendment by a large bench of eleven judges in 1967 in the case of *I C Golak Nath v. State of Punjab*[31].

In *Golak Nath* an important argument was whether the word "amendment" could be used to abrogate or rewrite the whole of the constitution or drastically change its basic tenets such as the parliamentary form of government, federalism, or the democratic process. No categorical answer was given to the argument as to whether a power could be read into Article 368 to abrogate the constitution and substitute it with a new one. However, in a thinly divided Court of 6:5, the majority held that fundamental rights were not amendable by a constitutional amendment and overruled the earlier decisions.

*Golak Nath* created a great political controversy in the country since the Court's decision virtually prevented any further amendments. There was pressing political need for economic and social reforms and such reforms would inevitably involve an infringement of the fundamental rights. As a result of the judgment in *Golak Nath*, in 1971 Parliament passed the 24th Amendment which expressly provided that Parliament has power to amend any part of the constitution including the fundamental rights. This was done by not only amending Article 368 but also amending Article 13.

The 24th Amendment was then challenged before the Supreme Court questioning mainly the extent of the amending power conferred by Article 268. A constitutional law crisis arose with the judiciary and Parliament apparently in conflict. The controversy created by the decision in *Golak Nath* was resolved by the judiciary in 1973 by the epoch-making case of *His Holiness Kesavanada Bharati Sripadagalvaru v. State of Kerala*[32] (also known as the *Fundamental Rights* case).

In *Kesavananda*, a Supreme Court bench of thirteen judges was divided severally with differing views and separate judgments. However, the Court by majority overruled *Golak Nath* and held that it was wrongly decided. *Kesavananda* held that Parliament can amend any part of the Constitution, including the fundamental rights, provided it does not alter the "basic structure and framework" of the Constitution. Therefore, amendments would only be valid if they fitted harmoniously into the basic constitutional structure which must be preserved at all time. Thus in *Kesavananda* a new constitutional doctrine was evolved by the Indian Supreme Court.

In *Kesavananda* the Court did not define precisely the essential features of the basic structure of the constitution. What constituted the basic structure cannot be formulated but must be developed on a case-by-case basis. However the judges

---

[30] AIR 1965 SC 845.
[31] AIR 1967 SC 1643.
[32] AIR 1973 SC 1461.

gave some illustrations for guidance, which are:

a) supremacy of the constitution;
b) democratic forms of government;
c) federal character of the constitution;
d) separation of powers between the legislature, the executive and the judiciary;
e) secular character of the constitution.

The *Kesavananda* decision initially created confusion in Indian legal circles and was seen as a constitutional quicksand.[33] The features of the basic structure which remained hidden in the breasts of the judges soon gained ground in 1975 in *Indira Nehru Gandhi v. Raj Narain*[34]. In this case the Supreme Court invalidated the constitutional amendment made specifically to remedy the defects of the then prime minister's election. The *Kesavananda* decision was confirmed unanimously by all five judges and they also strengthened the doctrine by adding that rule of law and democratic principles for free and fair elections were essential features of the basic structure of the constitution.

Consequent to the decisions in *Kesavananda* and *Indira Nehru Gandhi*, the 42nd Amendment was passed by Parliament in 1976 adding new clauses to Article 368. Clauses 4 and 5 sought to exclude the jurisdiction of the courts and declared that there shall be no limitation on the constituent power of Parliament to amend the Constitution. In spite of the express words added by Parliament to put an end to judicial intervention, the 42nd Amendment was nevertheless challenged in *Minerva Mills Ltd. v. Union of India*[35] on the ground that they destroyed the basic structure of the constitution.

In 1980 the Supreme Court in *Minerva Mills* struck down Clauses 4 and 5 of Article 368 inserted by the 42nd Amendment, as they destroyed the basic structure of the constitution. The Court made it clear that the constitution, and not the Parliament, is supreme in India. The Court held that:

Since the Constitution had conferred a limited amending power on Parliament, Parliament cannot under the exercise of that limited power enlarge that very power into an absolute power. Indeed, a limited amending power is one of the basic features of our Constitution and, therefore, the limitations on that power cannot be destroyed. In other words, Parliament cannot, under Article 368, expand its amending power so as to acquire for itself the right to repeal or abrogate the Constitution or to destroy its basic and essential features. The donee of a limited power cannot by the exercise of that power convert the limited power into an unlimited one.[36]

Therefore, with *Minerva Mills* the long-drawn conflict between Parliament and the

---

[33] Baxi, Upendra, "The constitutional quicksands of Kesavananda Bharati and the twenty-fifth amendment", (1974) 1 SCC Journal 45-67.
[34] AIR 1975 SC 2999.
[35] AIR 1980 SC 1789.
[36] AIR 1980 SC 1789 at 1798 para 22.

judiciary has been conclusively resolved and the constitutional quicksand in a vague and uncertain doctrine has established itself as a bedrock doctrine.

Thereafter the basic structure doctrine was approved and applied in many cases by the Court - in 1981 in *Waman Rao v. Union of India*[37] and *S.P. Gupta v. Union of India*[38], in 1987 in *S.P. Sampath Kumar v. Union of India*[39] and *P. Sambamurthy v. State of Andhra Pradesh*[40] and in 1994 in *Attorney General for India v. Amrit Lal Prajivandas.*[41]

In the last case the doctrine of basic structure was considered and approved by a bench of nine judges while upholding the validity of various laws to control foreign exchange and smuggling activities.

Very recently, the basic structure doctrine was again considered and applied by the Supreme Court in *L Chandra Kumar v. Union of India*[42] in deciding the validity of certain constitutional provisions and laws made for establishing administrative tribunals[43]. The Supreme Court reiterated that the power of judicial review is an essential feature of the basic structure of the constitution and declared unconstitutional the provisions that sought to exclude the jurisdiction of the High Courts and Supreme Court.

## IV. CONCLUSION

The Constitution of India, as it reads today, confers uncontrolled power for Parliament to amend the constitution. However, the last word remains with the judiciary with its power of judicial review to test the validity of the amendment by invoking the basic structure doctrine. The doctrine confers wide discretion to the judges to say what they consider to be the basic or unalterable law of the land. This in effect gives flexibility which helps to counteract the excessive flexibility of the constitution itself.

---

[37] AIR 1981 SC 271.
[38] (1981) Supp SCC 87.
[39] AIR 1987 SC 386.
[40] AIR 1987 SC 663.
[41] (1994) 5 SCC 54 at p 71.
[42] (1997) 3 SCC 261.
[43] The impugned constitutional provisions were clause 2(d) of Art. 323A and clause 3(d) of Art. 323B. Articles 323A and 323B were added by the 42nd Amendment in 1976.

Chapter Ten

# THE CREATION AND AMENDMENT OF CONSTITUTIONAL NORMS IN IRELAND

Padraic Taylor[*]

## I. INTRODUCTION

The present Constitution of Ireland came into being in 1937. The Constitution was the brainchild of Eamon de Valera who sought, through its adoption, to establish a new constitutional framework free from any signs of subservience to Britain. With this main purpose in mind he also took the opportunity to enshrine within the Constitution the particularly conservative, Roman Catholic and nationalist values which he and many Irish Catholics of his time strove to uphold. A glimpse of de Valera's vision for Ireland can be seen in his speech broadcast to the nation on St. Patrick's Day 1943:

The Ireland which we have dreamed of would be the home of a people who valued material wealth only as a basis for right living, of a people who were satisfied with frugal comfort and devoted their leisure to things of the spirit, a land whose countryside would be bright with cosy homesteads, whose fields and villages would be joyous with the sounds of industry, with the romping of sturdy children, the contests of athletic youths, the laughter of comely maidens; whose firesides would be forums for the wisdom of serene old age. It would, in a word, be the home of a people living the life that God desires that men should live.[1]

The Ireland of today is far removed from de Valera's dream. Far from enjoying the spiritual rewards of frugal living, the people of Ireland are busy reaping the financial rewards of the fastest growing economy in Europe. The sounds of industry are more likely to come from the computer keyboards of a Dublin 'dot.com' than the fields and villages of rural Ireland. De Valera would probably be shocked by the lack of spiritual matters which today's 'comely maidens' contemplate in their leisure time and God, or at least the Catholic Church, does not play so nearly large a part in people's lives as was the case in 1937.

Yet this modern, prosperous society which is still organised and governed by

---

[*] Trainee solicitor at Simmons and Simmons; former Research Officer at the British Institute.
[1] Moynihan, M., *Speeches and Statements by Eamon de Valera 1917-1973* (Dublin and New York 1980).

the 1937 Constitution. It is not surprising therefore that constitutional change has been a live issue in Ireland for the past two decades. The voice of liberal secularism has become increasingly louder during that period, demanding changes to the constitution to meet the needs of modern Irish society. In response, the forces of conservatism have argued for the preservation of the particularly Catholic aspects of the constitution, such as the prohibition on divorce, and indeed for their reinforcement, for example with the addition of a constitutional ban on abortion. Much of the debate on constitutional change has centred on moral issues and the related matter of church influence on matters of state. However membership of the European Communities, now the European Union, has also contributed to the debate on constitutional change. So far membership of the EU has necessitated four constitutional amendments.

It is these events which provide the backdrop to the issues discussed in this chapter. The chapter begins with a brief account of the constitution's history followed by a summary of its contents. Most of the chapter is devoted to an examination of the role of the courts in the area of constitutional amendment. The initial historical and descriptive narrative aims to put this examination into context and also gives some insight into the ideological basis of the constitution which underpins the principles applied by the courts when dealing with the issue of constitutional amendment. An attempt is then made to identify these principles and to explore their operation.

## II. HISTORY OF THE CONSTITUTION

The present constitution of Ireland was enacted by the people through plebiscite in 1937, replacing the previous constitution of the Irish Free State of 1922. The 1937 Constitution was adopted with the primary intention of removing all marks of subservience to the British Crown. The constitution is republican in character although Ireland did not formally become a republic until the Republic of Ireland Act 1948 was passed following withdrawal from the Commonwealth.

A. The 1922 Constitution

The southern twenty-six of Ireland's thirty-two counties achieved independence from Britain in 1921 under a treaty which created the Irish Free State (*Saorstát Éireann*), a dominion within the British Commonwealth with similar status to that of Canada. The constitution of the Irish Free State was enacted by the Parliament of Ireland, *Dáil Éireann*, in 1922 and was that of a British dominion recognising as it did the British monarch as the head of state.

The 1922 Constitution was drafted within the confines set by the Anglo-Irish Treaty of 1921. The Treaty was negotiated between Lloyd George and other members of the British cabinet and a delegation, led by Michael Collins, representing the self-proclaimed government of the Irish Republic. This government was made up of members of Sinn Féin, a republican political party committed to the attainment of Irish independence.[2] The General Election of 1918 gave Sinn Féin seventy-three of the 105 seats in Ireland, but the Sinn Féin MPs refused to sit in the Westminster Parliament, establishing instead Dáil Éireann, and electing an Irish government headed by Eamon de Valera.

The Anglo-Irish Treaty caused a bitter split within Sinn Féin and a large minority within the party, led by de Valera himself, refused to support it.[3] Civil war between pro-Treaty and anti-Treaty forces ensued, which lasted from June 1922 to April 1923, ending when the anti-Treaty forces called a cease-fire.

In the absence of the anti-Treaty deputies, the Dáil proceeded to adopt a constitution for the new state which was in the form of a schedule to the Irish Free State Act 1922 (hereinafter referred to as the Constituent Act).

The Preamble of the Constituent Act declared that the all lawful authority came 'from God to the people' and Article 2 of the constitution declared that all powers of government came from the people. This marked a revolutionary departure from the British model, and commonwealth traditions at the time, whereby sovereignty was vested in the monarch.

Article 1 of the constitution provided that the Irish Free State was a member of the British Commonwealth of Nations. A legislature, called the *Oireachtas*, was established which consisted of two Houses of Parliament and the King.[4] The Houses of Parliament consisted of a Chamber of Deputies called Dáil Éireann (similar to the British House of Commons) and a Senate, known as *Seanad Éireann*. The constitution made provision for an executive council to 'advise in the government' of the state but executive power was vested in the King.[5] The executive council, which was responsible to the Dáil, was headed by a president of the executive council, appointed by the Dáil, and consisted of between five and seven other ministers appointed by the President. According to Article 51 the King's power was to be exercised 'in accordance with the law, practice, and constitutional usage governing the exercise of the Executive Authority in the case of the Dominion of Canada by a Representative of the Crown [the Governor General]'.[6] Article 51 thereby incorporated into the constitution the convention whereby the King and the Governor-General would exercise power only on the advice of the cabinet, so in reality executive power was exercised by the executive council.

Articles 64-72 of the constitution established a system of courts consisting of a supreme court, a high court and 'courts of local jurisdiction'. Membership of the

---

[2] Sinn Féin (We Ourselves) was founded in 1905. The Sinn Féin party known to most people today is that led by Gerry Adams, the smallest of the contemporary Irish political parties which can trace their roots to the party founded in 1905, the largest two being Fianna Fáil and Fine Gael.

[3] The Treaty was accepted by sixty four votes to fifty seven in the Dáil. The most repugnant aspect of the Treaty for those who opposed it was the maintenance of the King as head of state and the requirement of members of the Parliament of the Irish Free State to swear an oath of allegiance to the King.

[4] Article 12.

[5] Article 51.

[6] Article 60 established the office of Governor-General.

Commonwealth impinged on the judicial system to the extent that the constitution provided for a right of appeal to the Judicial Committee of the Privy Council.[7]

The constitution conferred on the courts a power to review the validity of legislation.[8] Judicial review of legislation was a necessary consequence of the restrictions which were placed upon the powers of the Oireachtas by the Constituent Act. These restrictions included a prohibition on legislation which conflicted with the terms of the Treaty, or which infringed the basic rights guarantees contained for the most part in Articles 6-9.

Amendment of the constitution was dealt with in Article 50. The procedure provided for in Article 50 envisaged that a Bill to amend the constitution would firstly be passed by both Houses of the Oireachtas and then approved through referendum by a majority of those registered to vote or, if less than fifty-one per cent of the electorate voted, by two-thirds of votes cast. Article 50 also provided, however, for a transition period of eight years from the time of its enactment during which the constitution could be amended by ordinary Acts of Parliament. This meant that amendment could be effected through ordinary legislation until 6 December 1930. The constitution was amended by an Act of the Oireachtas in 1929 to extend this period for another eight years.[9] As the constitution was repealed and replaced by the present constitution in 1937, the procedure for amendment provided for in Article 50 was therefore never used.

One unsatisfactory consequence of the maintenance by the Oireachtas of its power to amend the constitution without referendum was that it deprived the courts of their power to review legislation. Many amendments were effected by ordinary legislation but not all amendments were achieved through legislation specifically declared to be for the purpose of amending the constitution. A practice developed whereby a clause was included in legislation stating that the provisions of the legislation were to prevail where they conflicted with the constitution. Where such legislation was inconsistent with the constitution, then, it was deemed to have amended the constitution so as to eliminate the inconsistency. While the courts criticised these clauses they nonetheless felt obliged to uphold them and were consequently deprived of their power of judicial review of legislation throughout the life of the 1922 Constitution.

B. From Dominion to 'External Association'

Unlike many of his compatriots in the anti-Treaty faction, de Valera had not seen the attainment of a republic as a realistic objective at the Treaty negotiations. However, not willing to settle for dominion status, he hoped for the achievement of a compromise which he termed 'external association'. This concept gave Ireland full internal sovereignty, depriving the King of even a symbolic role, while at the

---

[7] Article 66.
[8] Article 65.
[9] Constitution (Amendment No. 16) Act 1929.

same time keeping Ireland within the Commonwealth and maintaining the King as the representative of Ireland for certain external purposes. External association essentially involved Ireland adopting a republican constitution while remaining within the Commonwealth, and recognising the British monarch as Head of the Commonwealth. It was the failure of the negotiators to obtain this within the terms of the Treaty which prompted de Valera to condemn the Treaty, thus plunging the country into civil war in 1922.

Following the civil war and the general election of 1923, the Treaty requirement for deputies in the Free State Dáil to take an oath of allegiance to the King prevented de Valera and his followers from taking their seats there until 1927 when, as members of the newly formed Fianna Fáil party, they decided to compromise on the oath issue by signing the requisite declaration but refusing to read it aloud.

Fianna Fáil won the 1932 general election and de Valera's main objective in government was to change the constitutional status of the Irish Free State from that of dominion to that of external association. In 1931 the Imperial Parliament passed the Statute of Westminster to implement the declaration made at the Imperial Conference in 1926 to the effect that Britain and the Dominions were equal in status in all matters. The Statute of Westminster granted to the Irish government the power to amend the Treaty settlement without obtaining the approval of the Imperial Parliament in Westminster. De Valera grasped this opportunity to embark on a programme of legislation designed to undermine the position of the crown with regard to Ireland's internal constitutional arrangements. Such moves were treated with disapproval by the British Government but there was little they could do to prevent it.

De Valera's legislative programme gradually eroded the position of the King in the constitution,[10] culminating in the Constitution (Amendment No. 27) Act 1936 and Executive Authority (External Relations) Act 1936 which had the combined effect of removing nearly all references to the King in the constitution and providing that the constitution recognised the King only as head of the Commonwealth. External association was thus achieved.

Although de Valera had achieved what he had set out to do, he nonetheless wanted to replace the 1922 Constitution with an entirely new constitution. The adoption of a new constitution would mark a new departure from the old order, free from any connection with the Treaty.

The final draft of this new constitution was approved by the Dáil on 14 June 1937 and adopted by the people in a plebiscite on 29 December 1937.

The 1937 Constitution contained no reference to the King, even as Head of the Commonwealth, and created the office of President whose functions as described in the constitution were clearly those of a head of state. The President was head of state for internal purposes, but the External Relations Act continued in force so Ireland remained within the Commonwealth. Ireland's status, therefore, remained

---

[10] The first major change effected by the new Fianna Fáil government was to remove the oath of allegiance to the King through the Constitution (Amendment No. 22) Act 1933.

one of external association. In 1948 the External Relations Act was repealed by the Republic of Ireland Act which transferred all external executive functions to the President and thereby broke the last constitutional link with the United Kingdom.

## III. THE 1937 CONSTITUTION[11]

The structure of the state as prescribed by the 1937 Constitution is very similar to the 1922 model. The main difference between the two constitutions is that the 1937 Constitution is republican in nature whereas the previous constitution was designed to cater for the needs of a British Dominion.

The opening paragraphs of the constitution signify a new departure in Irish constitutional law. The 1937 Constitution begins, in the Preamble, by invoking the 'Most Holy Trinity, from Whom is all authority and to Whom, as our final end, all actions both of men and States must be referred'. This is followed by a declaration whereby 'the people of Éire... adopt, enact and give [themselves] this Constitution'. There is no doubt but that the enacting authority is the people themselves. The constitution's legitimacy is based on its enactment by the people, not on the Treaty or any acts of the Dáil established pursuant to that Treaty. The Dáil's role was simply to approve a draft text. De Valera wanted a clean break with the old regime and enactment by the people of a new constitution guaranteed the legitimate establishment of a new order, untainted by any connection with the Treaty.

The paramount role of the people is also expressed in Article 6 of the constitution which states that '[all powers of government, legislative, executive, and judicial derive, under God, from the people' who are declared to have the right 'in final appeal, to decide all questions of national policy, according to the requirements of the common good'.

The emphasis placed on the role of the people is central to the ideological basis of the constitution. The right of the people, as the creators of the constitution, to decide all matters with regard to the constitution is supreme. This is a fundamental principle which, as will be seen later, has been central to the reasoning of the Irish courts in their consideration of constitutional amendment.

The reference in Article 6 to 'legislative, executive and judicial' powers of government incorporates the separation of powers doctrine. Article 6 does not expressly prescribe a 'separation of powers' but later provisions make the separation of powers a real limitation.

The legislature is governed by Article 15.2.1° which vests the law-making power exclusively in the National Parliament, again called the Oireachtas. The Oireachtas consists of two houses - a lower house, again called Dáil Éireann, and an upper house called Seanad Éireann or the Senate. All Acts of the Oireachtas must be made by way of a procedure in the two Houses through which a Bill is

---

[11] On the 1937 Constitution generally, see Casey, *Constitutional Law in Ireland*, 2nd ed. (London 1994); Forde, *Constitutional Law of Ireland*, (Cork and Dublin 1987); Kelly, *The Irish Constitution*, 3rd ed. (Dublin 1994); Morgan, *Constitutional Law of Ireland*, 2nd ed. (Dublin 1990).

deemed to have been passed by both Houses followed by the signature of the Bill by the President. On signature a Bill becomes an Act of the Oireachtas.

Unlike the British model, the Irish constitution does not give Parliament supremacy and all Acts of the Oireachtas must be consistent with the constitution. Any Act which is in any respect repugnant to the constitution is invalid to the extent of such repugnancy. Acts of the Oireachtas must not infringe any of the basic rights guaranteed to the individual in Articles 40-44. Many rights are specifically guaranteed in the text of the constitution whereas the existence of other unspecified rights has been implied by the courts from the broad requirement in Article 40.3.1° that the state guarantees 'to defend and vindicate the personal rights of the citizen'. The High Court and Supreme Court are empowered to test Acts of the Oireachtas for constitutionality in ordinary proceedings.

Executive power is lodged in the government which consists of a Prime Minister, called the Taoiseach, and fourteen other members.[12] The government is drawn from the Oireachtas and answerable to, and may be removed by, the Dáil, but is not responsible to the Senate.

The judicial power is dealt with by Articles 34 to 37 which provide for a system of four principal courts with the High Court and Supreme Court having jurisdiction to review the constitutionality of laws, whether pre-independence laws, enactments of the Oireachtas of the Irish Free State, enactments of the present Oireachtas, or rules of common law.

The Supreme Court is the final court of appeal and is the only court which can review the constitutionality of Bills, as opposed to enacted statutes. The constitutionality of a Bill may only be considered by the Supreme Court where it is requested to do so by the President who is empowered under Article 26 of the constitution to make such a request before signing.

The constitution provides in Article 11 that 'there shall be a President'. Since Ireland became a Republic in 1948 the President has been the head of state for all purposes, both internal and external.

Article 50 of the constitution carries across the laws in force in Saorstát Éireann so as to continue in force under the new constitution to the extent that they are consistent with that constitution. This corresponds with Article 73 of the old constitution which rendered all pre-independence Irish law applicable in the new state except to the extent that it conflicted with the constitution. The effect, then, of Article 50 of the 1937 Constitution is to continue in force, to the extent that they are consistent with the constitution, pre-independence laws of the old Irish Parliament,[13] Acts of the Parliament of the United Kingdom prior to independence, Acts of the Oireachtas under the 1922 Constitution, and rules of common law.

---

[12] Articles 28 and 29.
[13] Ireland had its own Parliament, with restricted powers, from medieval times until the Act of Union 1800, albeit under the control of the English Crown, and subsequently the British Crown.

## IV. THE AMENDMENT PROCEDURE

The 1937 Constitution is a rigid constitution in the sense that it cannot be amended by an ordinary Act of the Oireachtas. The amendment procedure is laid down by Articles 46 and 47 of the constitution. The constitution can only be amended following a decision of the people by way of referendum.

Article 46 requires every proposal for amendment to be initiated in the Dáil as a Bill which on being passed or deemed to be passed by both Houses of the Oireachtas must be submitted by referendum to the decision of the people. During the first three years of the life of the constitution amendment by ordinary legislation was allowed, but Article 46 made it clear that this period could not be extended.[14] Two amendments were made during this transitory period.

Article 47 governs referendums,[15] providing that a proposal to amend the constitution is deemed to have been approved by the people if the majority of votes cast are in favour of the proposal.

Following a referendum the President must sign the Bill containing the proposal for amendment upon being satisfied that the requirements of Article 46 have been complied with and that the proposal has been duly approved by the people in accordance with the provisions of Article 47.[16]

There have been nineteen amendments to date.[17] The greatest number of changes were effected by the First and Second Amendments during the transitory period. The First Amendment (1939) extended the emergency provisions in Article 28 in response to the outbreak of the second world war. The Second Amendment (1941) effected over twenty changes to the constitution. Most of these changes were technical and linguistic, however the emergency powers were extended yet again

---

[14] Article 51 of the Constitution provided for the amendment of the Constitution by ordinary legislation for a three year transitory period but clearly stated that it should cease to have effect after the expiration of the three year period. Article 51 was drafted so as to avoid the situation which arose under the 1922 Constitution whereby the transitory period itself was extended by ordinary legislation. Articles 51 to 63 were transitory articles dealing with various aspects of transition to the new constitutional order. These articles all expired after the three year transitionary period since when they have been omitted from the official text.

[15] The Constitution not only provides for referendums to amend the Constitution, but also, in Article 27, for the reference of other Bills to people. This procedure has never been used but its inclusion in the Constitution again demonstrates the fundamental importance attached to the role of the people and their right to make the final decision on all matters of policy, referred to in Article 6.

[16] A *Constitutional Review Group* was established by the Government in April 1995 to review the Constitution and to establish areas where constitutional change may be necessary. The Group produced a Report in May 1996 which examined every Article of the Constitution. With respect to Article 46 the Group looked at the possibility of permitting amendments of a purely stylistic and technical nature to be effected through ordinary legislation. The Group rejected this proposal because of the difficulties which could arise in defining what was purely stylistic or technical (p. 399 of the Report). The Group also considered and rejected the idea of amendment initiated by popular initiative (p. 401).

[17] For details on these amendments see: Foley and Lalor (eds.), *Gill and Macmillan Annotated Constitution of Ireland*, (Dublin 1995); Department of the Environment and Local Government website at *www.environ.ie/elections/refers3.html*

and Articles 26 and 34 were amended to provide that the Supreme Court must deliver only one opinion when deciding on the constitutional validity of a Bill under Article 26, or of an Act under Article 34.[18]

Since the expiry of the transitory period amendments have been effected by referendum only. Amendments have covered a wide range of issues from those which could be considered technical legal matters[19] to more controversial matters of policy. Membership of the EU has necessitated four amendments, starting of course with an amendment to allow accession to the EEC in 1972[20] and continuing more recently with ratification of the Amsterdam Treaty.[21] Controversial moral issues have featured with, for example, the addition of Article 40.3.3°[22] which guarantees the right to life of the unborn, and the removal of the constitutional ban on divorce.[23] Most recently, attempts to broker a political solution in Northern Ireland have brought about the removal of the constitutional claim to the territory of Northern Ireland.[24]

## V. ROLE OF THE COURTS

From a legal point of view the most interesting dimension to constitutional amendment in Ireland has been the role of the courts. There are many aspects to this role which has in certain cases had a direct and immediately identifiable impact on particular amendments, but has also had a more subtle and indirect impact on the whole question of constitutional change and its necessity. In order to give all these aspects a full treatment, the role of the courts is best looked at under the following headings.

1. The role of the courts in the amendment process
2. Judicial activism and the need for constitutional amendment
3. Natural law and the lawfulness of an amendment

*1. The role of the courts in the amendment process*

The central issue involved in all the litigation surrounding the constitutional amendment process has been that of the separation of powers and the question of

---

[18] The Supreme Court has held that the rule on single opinions on the constitutionality of Acts does not apply to pre-1937 Acts; does not apply to questions simultaneously in issue along with the constitutional validity of a law; and does not apply to ancillary rulings. See Kelly, op cit., pp. 527-530.
[19] For example: lowering the voting age from 21 years to 18 (Fourth Amendment, 1972); refusal of bail by a court where such refusal is considered necessary to prevent the likely commission of a serious offence (Sixteenth Amendment, 1996); regulation of the circumstances in which Cabinet discussions may be disclosed (Seventeenth Amendment, 1997).
[20] Third Amendment, 1972.
[21] Eleventh Amendment, 1992.
[22] Eighth Amendment, 1983.
[23] Fifteenth Amendment, 1996.
[24] Nineteenth Amendment, 1998.

whether this doctrine prohibits interference by the courts in the amendment process.[25] There are three situations in which the courts have had to consider their role with regard to constitutional amendment and referendums to amend the constitution. First, the courts have been asked to restrain the holding of a referendum.[26] Secondly, the courts have had to consider a case designed to secure the holding of a referendum to amend the constitution. Thirdly, the courts have been asked to consider the manner in which the government has conducted referendums to amend the constitution. The first category involved the question of judicial intervention in the legislative process. The last two categories involved the question of whether the courts were prohibited from interfering with acts of the executive. The second category does not, of course, entail interference with the amendment process itself but the separation of powers issue is directly involved, and the decision directly secured the holding of a referendum.

*a. judicial interference with the legislative process*

As was mentioned earlier, the Eighth Amendment to the constitution effected an express constitutional prohibition on the provision of abortion in Ireland, through the addition of Article 40.3.3°. This has undoubtedly been the most controversial amendment to the constitution and it is no surprise that litigation concerning constitutional amendment first arose out of the Eighth Amendment.[27]

Abortion was already a criminal offence under section 58 of the Offences Against the Person Act 1861 but a belief existed in some quarters that it was necessary to give the unborn the higher protection of a constitutional right to life.[28] This belief was undoubtedly reinforced by the decision of the US Supreme Court in *Roe v. Wade*[29] to read into the constitutional right to privacy a right for a woman to terminate a pregnancy. The examination, later in this chapter, of the fundamental rights guaranteed in the constitution will show there was no possibility of the Irish courts making a similar decision.

The amendment proposed and adopted stated:

---

[25] On the separation of powers generally, see Morgan, *The Separation of Powers in the Irish Constitution*, Dublin 1997.
[26] In her article, *Constitutional Change, Referenda and the Courts in Ireland* [1997] PL 125, Ann Sherlock classifies the litigation concerning constitutional amendment under four headings: litigation to review an accepted amendment; litigation to stop the holding of referendums; litigation to secure the holding of a referendum; and litigation concerning the conduct of referendum campaigns. The first category identified by Sherlock will be dealt with later in this chapter when discussing the issue of the lawfulness of an amendment. The other cases discussed by Sherlock will be examined with reference to the two central issues identified below.
[27] For a detailed account of the law relating to abortion law in Ireland see Kingston and Whelan, *Abortion and the Law* (Dublin 1997).
[28] For an account of the background to the referendum, see *ibid*, p. 4 and J.J. Lee, *Ireland 1912-1985 Politics and Society* (Cambridge 1989) pp. 653-657
[29] 410 US 113 (1973).

The state acknowledges the right to life of the unborn and, with due regard to the equal right to life of the mother, guarantees in its laws to respect, and as far as practicable, by its laws defend and vindicate that right.

The first attempt to halt the referendum was made in the case of *Roche v. Ireland*[30] in which the plaintiff claimed that the proposed amendment was too vaguely worded as a result of which he could not know how he should vote and would have to abstain. Thus, he claimed, he was deprived of his constitutional right to vote. He sought an injunction restraining the holding of the referendum.

Miss Justice Carroll in the High Court, stated that a constitutional amendment involved 'a particularly solemn legislative process; not only the Oireachtas but the people also took part. She held that the courts had no jurisdiction to interfere in this process, stating that the separation of powers under the constitution precluded such interference. She referred to the case of *Wireless Dealers Association v. Fair Trade Commission*[31] in which it was clearly established that the only jurisdiction which a court had to consider the constitutionality of a Bill, as opposed to an Act, was when the President referred a Bill to the Supreme Court under Article 26 requesting a decision as to its constitutionality. It was clearly established that the courts could not interfere in the ordinary legislative process - *a fortiori* they could not interfere in the more solemn legislative process of a constitutional amendment.

The second case arising out of the Eighth Amendment was *Finn v. Attorney General*.[32] The plaintiff here tried to argue that the substance of the proposal was superfluous and not permitted by the constitution because the right to life of the unborn child was already protected by the constitution. Again an injunction restraining the holding of the referendum was sought. Barrington J in the High Court followed the reasoning of Carroll J in *Roche*, stating however that in his view what was involved was not a straightforward question of separation of powers but a question of the courts not interfering with a power of the people which they, the people, had reserved to themselves when adopting the constitution:

Much time was spent at the hearing in debating the separation of powers contemplated by Articles 15, 28, and 34 of the Constitution, and [counsel] stressed the independence and powers of the judiciary. But it appears to me that this case is concerned not with those issues but with the exercise by the people of the power which they have reserved to themselves to amend the Constitution when invited to do so by the two Houses of the Oireachtas. I agree with what Miss Justice Carroll said on this subject in her recent decision in *Roche v. Ireland* when she referred to a referendum as a 'solemn process of legislation and where she drew the analogy with the decision of the Supreme Court in *Wireless Dealers association v. Fair Trade Commission*. Article 6 of the Constitution contemplates the establishment of certain organs of government - legislative, executive and judicial; but it also refers to the residual powers which the people reserve to themselves 'in final appeal, to decide all questions of

---

[30] High Court, unreported, 17 June 1983.
[31] Supreme Court, unreported, 14 March 1956.
[32] [1983] IR 154.

national policy according to the common good.'[33]

Barrington J. does not see the issue merely as one of separation of powers between the organs of state but rather as a question of the ultimate right of the people to make the final judgment on any matter without interference from any organ of state. This line of reasoning was echoed by Walsh J in the later case of *Crotty v. An Taoiseach*,[34] discussed below, in which he stated: 'In the last analysis it is the people themselves who are the guardians of the Constitution'.[35] The importance which the courts attach to this fundamental principle is further demonstrated in cases such as *McKenna v. An Taoiseach (No. 2)*[36] and the *Regulation of Information Bill Case*[37] which are also discussed below.

The Eleventh Amendment prompted further litigation along the lines of *Roche* and *Finn*, with the same result for the plaintiffs. This amendment was adopted to pave the way for ratification of the Maastricht Treaty. In *Slattery v. An Taoiseach*[38] the plaintiffs argued that the government had failed to provide the citizens of the state with sufficient information on the Maastricht Treaty to enable them to vote in the referendum in an informed manner. They sought an injunction to restrain the holding of the referendum. The plaintiff lost in the High Court where Costello J held the matter to be non-justiciable. This aspect of the case will be discussed in the next section which deals with judicial interference with acts of the executive. On appeal to the Supreme Court it was held that to grant the plaintiffs the relief sought would be a wholly unwarranted intrusion by the courts into the legislative domain provided for under the constitution.

Hederman J stated that in his opinion '[the real point of this case is to ask this Court to prevent the operation of legislative and constitutional procedures which are in train. This is something the court has no jurisdiction to do'.[39]

While the plaintiffs here were not asking the court to review a Bill to amend the constitution, as was the case in *Roche* and *Finn*, but rather to review the behaviour of the government in the conduct of the campaign, the relief sought amounted to a request to interfere in the legislative domain. Such interference was not possible under the separation of powers provided for in the constitution.

It is clear that the courts will not grant an injunction to restrain a constitutional referendum under any circumstances. The immediate reason for this is that the procedure to amend the constitution is a special legislative process, but a legislative process nonetheless, which is set in train with the introduction of a Bill to amend the constitution in the Oireachtas and is completed with the signing of that Bill by the President, following a referendum adopting the amendment. To interfere with

---

[33] Ibid at 162.
[34] [1987] IR 713.
[35] Ibid at 782.
[36] [1966] 1 ILRM 81.
[37] [1995] 2 ILRM 81.
[38] [1993] 1 IR 286.
[39] Ibid at 299.

this process would be contrary to the separation of powers as an unwarranted interference with the legislative process. The unconstitutionality of such interference is emphasised by the fact that the constitution provides no procedure for review of a Bill other than that under Article 26 which empowers the President to refer a Bill to the Supreme Court for a ruling as to its constitutionality. In the case of a Bill to amend the constitution the President would be offered the opportunity to use the Article 26 procedure only upon submission of the Bill to him or her for signature, which would of course be after a referendum endorsing the amendment. Separation of powers prohibits interference with the ordinary legislative process so *a fortiori* must prohibit interference with the amendment legislative process. With regard to the amendment process, however, a fundamental principle is at issue which underlies the immediate reason given and that is that the people have the right freely and without interference from any organ of State to make the final decision on all matters of policy. This right is the central feature of the democratic character of the state and can never be interfered with. This was recognised by Barrington J in *Finn* and its importance is highlighted in *McKenna (No. 2)*[40] and the *Regulation of Information Bill Case*,[41] considered below.

*b. judicial interference with acts of the executive*

There is only one instance in which proceedings were commenced with the intention of securing the holding of a constitutional referendum, and this was the case of *Crotty v. An Taoiseach*.[42] That case is significant in the area of constitutional amendment not only because it directly precipitated the holding of a referendum but also because the dicta in that case on the issue of the separation of powers between the executive and judicial branches of government have since been relied upon by courts to establish their right to interfere with the manner in which the government conducts constitutional referendums.

The plaintiff in *Crotty v. An Taoiseach* sought an injunction restraining the government from ratifying the Single European Act, a treaty amending various aspects of the Treaties of the European Communities. The plaintiff claimed that the ratification of this Treaty involved a surrender of sovereignty which it was beyond the constitutional powers of the government to effect without an amendment to the constitution approving of such a surrender of sovereignty. While the plaintiff lost in the High Court he was successful on appeal to the Supreme Court which held that the purported ratification of Title III of the Single European Act, whereby Ireland would agree to adopt its foreign policy positions only following consultation with other members of the European Communities, involved the surrender of part of the sovereignty of Ireland in the conduct of its foreign relations. In purporting to alienate any of the powers vested in it by the constitution in the area of foreign

---

[40]   [1996] 1 ILRM 81.
[41]   [1995] 2 ILRM 81.
[42]   [1987] IR 713.

relations, or in trying to fetter the sovereignty of the state or the people, the government had acted beyond the powers entrusted to it by the constitution. Alienation of any powers of government or any surrender of sovereignty could not be done without recourse to the people through referendum to amend the constitution. The courts as sole arbiters upon breaches of the constitution were, it was argued, obliged to restrain the government.

The case hinged on the question of whether the courts had the right to interfere with the exercise by the government of its powers with regard to external relations in light of the provisions of Article 29.4.1° of the constitution which states:

The executive power of the State in or in connection with its external relations shall in accordance with article 28 of this Constitution be exercised by or on the authority of the Government.

In the Supreme Court, Finlay CJ acknowledged that the separation of powers between the legislature, the executive and the judiciary, set out in Article 6 of the constitution, is fundamental to all its provisions.

With regard to judicial interference with the executive he went on to say that there was nothing in Articles 28 or 29 from which a general right of the courts to interfere with the exercise of the executive power could be implied in the area of external relations. He continued however:

This does not mean that the executive is or can be without control by the Courts in relation to carrying out executive powers even in the field of external relations. In any instance where the exercise of that function constituted an actual or threatened invasion of the constitutional rights of an individual, the Courts would have a right and duty to intervene.[43]

He found support for his view in the Supreme Court decision in *Boland v. An Taoiseach*,[44] quoting the following passage from Fitzgerald CJ's judgment in that case:

Consequently in my opinion, the courts have no power either express or implied, to supervise or interfere with the exercise by the Government of its executive functions, unless the circumstances are such to amount to a clear disregard by the Government of the powers and duties conferred on it by the Constitution.[45]

Finlay CJ did not consider that it had been established that adherence by the state to the terms of Title III of the SEA amounted to 'a clear disregard by the Government of the powers and duties conferred on it by the constitution' however the majority, although in agreement with his reasoning, concluded differently and an injunction restraining ratification of the Treaty was granted.

The constitution was subsequently amended to allow the ratification of the

---

[43] Ibid at 774.
[44] [1974] IR 338.
[45] Ibid at 362.

Single European Act. As mentioned above the *Crotty* decision has since formed an important base from which to challenge the manner in which a referendum is being conducted and the case law dealing with such challenges will now be considered.

The first case in which a plaintiff claimed that a referendum campaign was being conducted in a manner which infringed her constitutional rights arose out of the referendum on the Eleventh Amendment which provided for the ratification of the Maastricht Treaty. The case was *McKenna v. An Taoiseach (No. 1)*[46] in which the plaintiff argued that the government was acting in breach of the constitution by using public funds to campaign for the adoption of the proposed referendum. The plaintiff claimed that this amounted to an infringement of her constitutional rights *inter alia* to express freely her convictions and opinions. She sought injunctive relief alternatively (a) restraining the government from spending public funds on the vote 'yes' campaign or (b) requiring the government to allocate funds to groups opposing ratification. Costello J in the High Court displayed some sympathy for the plaintiff's grievance but held that it was in the political and non-justiciable sphere and that the judiciary was not empowered by the constitution to remedy such a grievance.

Costello J. stated in his judgment that:

The extent of the role the Government feels called upon to play to ensure ratification is a matter of concern for the executive arm of government, not the judicial. The Dáil decides what monies are to be voted for expenditure by the Government on information services (which would include an advertising campaign in support of an affirmative vote in a referendum). Should the Government decide that the national interest required that an advertising campaign be mounted which was confined to extolling forcibly the benefits of an affirmative vote, it would be improper for the courts to express any view on such a decision.

The rationale behind the decision is based on separation of powers. This was a matter entirely within the executive sphere and the separation of powers demanded that the courts do not interfere. Costello J went on to say:

...not every grievance can be remedied by the courts. And judges must not allow themselves to be led, or indeed wander, into areas calling for adjudication on political and non-justiciable issues. They are charged by the Constitution with exercising the judicial power of government and it would both weaken their important constitutional role as well as amount to an unconstitutional act for judges to adjudicate.

While not explicitly adopting a 'political question' doctrine with regard to justiciability, such as that applied by the US courts,[47] this is in practice what he appears to have done. However, unlike the US Supreme Court in *Baker v. Carr*, Costello J does not attempt to lay down a test for non-justiciability defining what

---

[46] High Court, unreported, 8 June 1992.
[47] See *Baker v. Carr* (1962) 369 US 186; *Powell v. McCormack* (1969) 395 US 486; *Goldwater v. Carter* (1979) 444 US 996.

are 'political and non-justiciable issues'.[48] The most likely interpretation of Costello J's decision is that he could not find any legal right to be at issue and consequently deemed the plaintiff's grievance to be purely political and therefore non-justiciable. In light of the decision in *Crotty* it is inconceivable that Costello J intended to mark all executive acts off-limits to judicial review. He was instead pointing out that any claim against the executive by a plaintiff who could not establish any judicially enforceable right was of a purely political nature. The separation of powers demanded that the courts decline consideration of such matters.

On the same day as he decided *McKenna (No. 1)* Costello J decided the case of *Slattery v. An Taoiseach*[49] which is dealt with above. Costello J applied the same reasoning to *Slattery*, concluding that his complaint about the conduct of the referendum campaign was not a matter for the courts to consider. The Supreme Court however concentrated on the fact that the plaintiff was seeking an injunction to restrain the holding of the referendum, the granting of which the court considered to be an unwarranted interference with the legislative process.

A further case arising from the Eleventh Amendment was *McCann v. An Taoiseach*[50] in which the plaintiff sought an injunction to restrain a television broadcast by the Taoiseach advocating the ratification of the Maastricht Treaty and the adoption of the requisite amendment. The High Court held that the relevant legislation permitted broadcasts by a minister in favour of a particular outcome in a referendum and gave no right to reply to those opposed to the proposed amendment. No constitutional right with regard to these broadcasts was held to exist.

The courts in these cases clearly ruled out any interference with the manner in which the government conducted a referendum campaign which they considered to be in the political domain. The separation of powers in the constitution rendered these matters to be non-justiciable.

Review of the Government's conduct of a referendum seemed for the most part to be outside the purview of the courts.

Notwithstanding the lack of success of her first case, or indeed of any similar cases, Ms McKenna again pursued the issue of public funding for a partisan referendum campaign in *McKenna v. An Taoiseach (No. 2)*.[51] This case was brought during the 1995 referendum campaign resulting in the Fifteenth Amendment which removed the constitutional prohibition on the granting of a divorce. The government allocated IR£500,000 of public money to the campaign for the removal of the constitutional ban on divorce which Ms. McKenna again claimed consisted of a breach of her constitutional rights. She was again unsuccessful in the High Court where Keane J held that this was not a justiciable matter but rather one to be dealt with by the executive and legislative branches of

---

[48] In *Baker v. Carr* (1962) 369 US 186, at 217, Brennan J. laid down six criteria to indicate the kinds of questions not subject to judicial resolution.
[49] [1993] IR 286.
[50] [1994] 2 IR 1.
[51] [1996] 1 ILRM 81.

government.

On appeal, however, a majority in the Supreme Court found in favour of the plaintiff. Using public money to fund a campaign in favour of adoption of the proposed amendment was an interference with the democratic process which infringed the concept of equality 'fundamental to the democratic nature of the state'.

Hamilton CJ reaffirmed the principles laid down in the two previous Supreme Court decisions in *Crotty v. An Taoiseach*[52] and *Boland v. An Taoiseach*[53] and summarised them as follows:

(1) The Courts have no power, either express of implied, to supervise or interfere with the exercise by the Government of its executive functions provided that it acts within the restraints imposed by the Constitution on the exercise of such powers.
(2) If, however, the Government acts otherwise than in accordance with the provisions of the Constitution and in clear disregard thereof, the courts are not only entitled but obliged to intervene.
(3) The courts are only obliged to intervene if the circumstances are such as to amount to a clear disregard by the Government of the powers and duties conferred on it by the Constitution.[54]

The Chief Justice went on to hold that in the instant case the action of the government in publishing information with regard to the referendum and in expressing its views as to how people ought to vote was not in fact an action in the exercise of the executive power of the state. This conclusion was based on the fact that neither the constitution nor legislation gave any role whatsoever to the government with regard to providing information during a referendum. This did not of course inevitably mean that the action was not permissible as many of the legitimate functions of the government are not part of its executive power of government. The action complained of did however constitute an interference with the democratic process for the amendment of the constitution and infringed the concept of equality which is fundamental to the democratic nature of the state. Not only was compliance with Articles 46 and 47 required but the constitutional rights of citizens must also be respected.

Despite the fact that the separation of powers was not relevant to the particular circumstances of the *McKenna (No. 2)* case, the Supreme Court made it perfectly clear that even where executive acts were at issue the constitution must be respected and the courts will intervene where it is not.

The difference between the approach of Costello J in *McKenna (No. 1)* and that of the Supreme Court in *McKenna (No. 2)* would appear to hinge on the fact that Costello J did not identify any constitutional or legal issues to be involved whereas the Supreme Court did. Costello J saw the plaintiff's grievance to be purely political, whereas the Supreme Court saw a serious constitutional question to be at

---

[52] [1987] IR 713.
[53] [1974] IR 713.
[54] [1996] 1 ILRM 81, at 94.

issue. The Supreme Court held the government's actions to constitute an interference with the democratic process. Again the fundamental importance which the courts attach to the role of the people comes to the fore. The people's right to decide whether or not to adopt a constitutional amendment is supreme and no interference with the exercise of this right is permissible.

Following the divorce referendum, in which the amendment removing the prohibition on divorce was narrowly accepted, a declaration invalidating the result was sought by the plaintiff in *Hanafin v. Minister for the Environment*.[55] The plaintiff's claim was that the Government's 'vote yes' campaign, held to be unconstitutional in *McKenna (No. 2)*, had materially affected the voting and that the result was consequently null and void. The High Court held that on the facts it had not been shown that the Government's publicly funded campaign had materially affected the result. The Supreme Court upheld the decision of the High Court, holding that the court could not enquire into the motives which caused the people to vote in the way they did. The people are presumed to know what they want and to have understood the proposed referendum and all of its implications. The courts again emphasised the deference with which the organs of state must treat the will of the people. The courts must respect the will of the people and unless it can be shown that their decision was materially affected by unwarranted interference by the government the courts could not invalidate the result of the referendum.

## 2. Judicial activism and the need for amendment

The most dramatic changes in Irish constitutional law since 1937 have undoubtedly occurred in the area of fundamental rights protection. These changes cannot be attributed to any formal amendments to the constitution, however, but rather to judicial creativity. Such judicial activism has significantly expanded the extent of the protection afforded by the constitution. This has rendered it unnecessary to amend the constitution in order to add specific fundamental rights guarantees as and when inadequacies in the text were perceived.

As mentioned earlier, Articles 40 to 44 of the constitution of Ireland guarantee fundamental rights. Article 40.1 guarantees the right to equality before the law. Article 40.4 states that '[n]o citizen shall be deprived of his personal liberty save in accordance with the law' and enshrines the right of habeas corpus in the constitution. The inviolability of the home is protected by Article 40.5 and Article 40.6 guarantees freedom of expression, freedom of assembly and freedom of association. The family receives constitutional recognition and protection in Article 41 and the right to free primary education is guaranteed in Article 42. Article 43 incorporates a right to private property and freedom of conscience and religion are protected by Article 44.

These however are not the only fundamental rights guaranteed by the constitution. Article 40.3 imposes a broad obligation on the state upon which the

---

[55] [1996] 2 ILRM 161.

courts have relied to imply the existence of a significant body of unspecified personal rights entitled to protection. Had the courts recoiled from such activism the only way in which these rights would have received the constitutional protection which they currently enjoy would have been through extensive, and possibly repeated, amendment of the constitution.

Article 40.3 states:

1° The State guarantees in its laws to respect, and, as far as practicable, by its laws to defend and vindicate the personal rights of the citizen.

2° The State shall in particular by its laws protect as best it may from unjust attack and, in the case of injustice done, vindicate the life, person, good name, and property rights of every citizen.

Although the courts have used Article 40.3.1° to imply the existence of many fundamental rights over the past 40 years, their initial treatment of this section was diffident and rendered it quite ineffective in its early life as a means of bestowing any substantial benefits on the citizen.

For example *In Re Article 26 and the Offences Against the State (Amendment) Bill 1940*[56] involved consideration by the Supreme Court, following a reference by the President under Article 26, of a Bill designed to provide for internment without trial. In considering this issue the Court looked in passing at Article 40.3 and saw no serious criterion for judicial review in this sub-section. One of the many questions which the courts could have analysed when given the opportunity was that of whether the 'personal rights' referred to in Article 40.3.1° were confined to those listed in Article 40.3.2°, and if not, what they did cover. The courts did not however attempt any meaningful analysis of Article 40.3.1° until the 1960s.

It has to be said that this reluctance to grapple with the meaning of Article 40.3 fits in with the general approach to constitutional interpretation and judicial review in the 1940s and 1950s. Basil Chubb has described the courts' approach during this period as 'cautious' and 'inhibited'.[57] The reason for this cautious approach to constitutional interpretation can probably be at least partly attributed to the fact that many of those on the bench at the time were trained in the British tradition with its emphasis on common law, judicial precedent and parliamentary sovereignty which does not encourage the judiciary to adopt a creative approach. Loren P. Beth has said in this regard that the Irish judiciary of this period 'tended to tiptoe gingerly around judicial review because their English common law backgrounds led them to distrust the discretionary power involved in it'.[58] Their experience of operating under the 1922 Constitution would have induced little change in attitude because, although it was intended that statutes found to be in conflict with the constitution would be held void, what in fact happened was that conflicting legislation was

---

[56] [1940] IR 136.
[57] Chubb, *The Constitution and Constitutional Change in Ireland* (Dublin 1978), p. 73.
[58] *The Development of Judicial Review in Ireland, 1937-1966* (Dublin, 1967) p. 3.

interpreted as having implicitly amended the constitution. It was only from the late 1950s onwards, when younger judges familiar with the idea of a written constitution and comfortable with the concept of entrenched fundamental rights began to make their mark, that a bolder approach was taken.

This new approach started to make an impact in the late 1950s and early 1960s when courts began to imply the existence of unspecified or 'unenumerated' rights from a reading of other specific guarantees in the constitution . A pioneering judgment in this regard was that of Budd J in *Tierney v. Amalgamated Society of Woodworkers*[59] in which a guarantee to a right to work and earn a livelihood was read into Article 40.3.1°. This was seen as an obvious extension of the right to property expressly guaranteed in Article 40.3.2°. In *Educational Co. Ltd. v. Fitzpatrick (No. 2)*[60] the right to refuse to join a trade union was implied from the guarantee to freedom of association contained in Article 40.6.1°iii.

The landmark decision in this context was however *Ryan v. Attorney General*[61] in which the Supreme Court declared that Article 40.3 contained 'unspecified personal rights'. This case involved a claim that the Health (Fluoridation of Water Supplies) Act 1960, which provided for the fluoridation of the public water supply, was unconstitutional in that it obliged the plaintiff and her family to drink water containing fluoride, which she claimed was dangerous to health, and therefore amounted to a breach of a 'right of bodily integrity' which was guaranteed by Article 40.3.1°. In the High Court Kenny J held against the plaintiff on the ground that fluoride was not shown to be dangerous; however he acknowledged that there did exist a right to bodily integrity. He expressly stated that 'the personal rights which may be invoked to invalidate legislation are not confined to those specified in Article 40 but include all those rights which result from the Christian and democratic nature of the state'.[62]

The Supreme Court agreed with Kenny J on the existence of unspecified rights:

> The Court agrees with Mr. Justice Kenny that the 'personal rights' mentioned in s 3.1 are not exhausted by the enumeration of 'life, person, good name and property rights' in s 3.2 as is shown by the use of the words 'in particular'; nor by the more detached treatment of specific rights in the subsequent sections of the article. To attempt to make a list of all the rights which may properly fall within the category of 'personal rights' would be difficult and, fortunately, is unnecessary in this present case.[63]

It was clear then that the 'personal rights' guaranteed by Article 40.3.1° were not just those listed in Article 40.3.2° and covered a broad range of rights. In *Ryan* Kenny J saw the 'Christian and democratic nature of the State' as the source of unenumerated rights. He based his conclusion as to the Christian nature of the state

---

[59] [1959] IR 254.
[60] [1961] IR 345.
[61] [1965] IR 294.
[62] Ibid at 312.
[63] Ó Dálaigh CJ, ibid, at 345.

on a reading of the preamble along with Article 6 of the constitution. The Preamble states that the people of Éire adopt the constitution '[i]n the Name of the Most Holy Trinity' and 'acknowledging all [their] obligations to our Divine Lord Jesus Christ'. Article 6.1 provides that '[all powers of government, legislative, executive and judicial, derive, *under God*, from the people...' [emphasis added]. The democratic nature of the state is apparent from Article 5 which states simply 'Ireland is a sovereign, independent, democratic state.'

The right to bodily integrity has since been broadened to cover a right not to have health endangered by the state[64] and a right to freedom from torture and inhuman and degrading treatment.[65]

Since *Ryan* the courts have implied the existence of a substantial body of rights protected by Article 40.3.1° drawing upon various sources to determine which rights are protected, including other specific constitutional provisions, a general reading of the constitution and rights at common law. The courts have however recognised natural law as the ultimate source of these rights. There is no express mention of natural law in the judgment of Kenny J in *Ryan*, but the decision is very much based upon a recognition of the existence of higher law. Kenny J invoked 'the Christian and democratic nature of the state' as the source of unenumerated rights.

An express reliance on natural law can be found in *McGee v. Attorney General*[66] where the Supreme Court implied a right to marital privacy under the constitution. The plaintiffs in this case, a married couple, successfully challenged the constitutionality of a law prohibiting contraceptives. The recognition of a natural law which precedes all positive law, including even the constitution itself, is clear from the following passage of Walsh J:

Articles 41, 42 and 43 emphatically reject the theory that there are no rights without laws, no rights contrary to the law and no rights anterior to the law. They indicate that justice is placed above the law and acknowledge that natural rights, or human rights, are not created by law but that the Constitution confirms their existence and gives them protection...

Walsh J clearly views certain 'natural rights' to be 'above the law'. They are not granted by the constitution but merely recognised by it. They are superior to the constitution itself.

This passage was referred to by Gannon J in *The State (Healy) v. Donaghue*[67] which involved consideration of the requirement in Article 38 that no person shall be tried on any criminal charge save in due course of law. Gannon J looked at the issue of the rights of an accused person and said:

---

[64] *The State (C.) v. Frawley* [1976] 365; *State (Richardson) v. The Governor of Mountjoy Prison* [1980] ILRM 82.
[65] *State (C.) v. Frawley*.
[66] [1974] IR 284.
[67] [1976] IR 325.

The sense of justice is fundamental in human nature and from it derive essential rights which do not require any positive law for their enunciation ... In my view they are rights which are anterior to and do not merely derive from the constitution.[68]

Along with a right to bodily integrity and a right to marital privacy the courts have also relied upon Article 40.3.1° to imply a right to individual privacy,[69] the right to work and earn a living without discrimination based on sex,[70] a right of access to the courts,[71] the right to communicate,[72] the right to travel,[73] and the right to justice and fair procedures in decision making.[74]

A number of rights relating to the family have also been held to be implicitly guaranteed by Article 40.3.1°. Article 41 of the constitution deals specifically with family rights but some not mentioned in that article have been held to be implicitly guaranteed by Article 40.3.1°. In *Ryan v. Attorney General* Kenny J referred to the right to marry as one of the unspecified rights guaranteed by the constitution. In *Murray v.Ireland*[75] the right to procreate was held to be a personal right guaranteed by Article 40.3.1°. An unmarried mother who cannot establish any rights to custody of her children based on Article 41, which has been held to deal only with the family based on marriage, can rely on Article 40.3.1° to assert a personal right to custody and care of her children.[76]

The question must be asked, however, as to what actually is this 'natural law' upon which the courts have so freely relied to extend fundamental rights protection. If we look at the origins of the unenumerated rights doctrine in *Ryan* we see that its source was found in the 'Christian and democratic nature of the State'. In *McGee* the following passage in the judgment of Walsh J provides further enlightenment:

Both in its Preamble and in Article 6, the Constitution acknowledges God as the ultimate source of all authority ...[n]atural or human rights ... are part of what is generally called the natural law. There are many who argue that natural law may be regarded only as an ethical concept and as such is a reaffirmation of the ethical content of law in its ideal of justice. The natural law as a theological concept is the law of God promulgated by reason and is the ultimate governor of all the laws of men. In view of the acknowledgment of Christianity in the Preamble and in view of the reference to God in Article 6 of the Constitution, it must be accepted that the Constitution intended the natural human rights I have mentioned as being in the latter category rather than simply an acknowledgment of the ethical content of law in its ideal of justice.[77]

---

[68] Ibid, at 335 and 336.
[69] *Norris v. Att. Gen.* [1982] IR 284; *Kennedy v. Ireland* [1987] IR 587, [1988] ILRM 472.
[70] *Murtagh Properties v. Cleary* [1972] IR 330.
[71] *Macauley v. Minister for Posts and Telegraphs* [1966] IR 345.
[72] *Att. Gen. and Minister for Posts and Telegraphs v. Paperlink Ltd.* [1984] ILRM 373; *Kearney v. Minister for Justice, Ireland and Att. Gen.* [1987] 47.
[73] *Ryan v. Attorney General* [1965] IR 294; *The State (M.) v. Att. Gen.* [1979] IR 73.
[74] *Garvey v. Ireland* [1980] IR 75.
[75] [1985] IR 532; [1985] ILRM 542.
[76] *The State (Nicolaou) v,. An Bord Uchtala* [1966] IR 567.
[77] [1974] IR 284, 317-318.

This leaves us in no doubt but that the natural law theory upon which the unenumerated rights doctrine is based is a theocratic one, the anchor for which is the Preamble and the reference to God in Article 6.

Furthermore, it would appear that this theory is very much based on the teachings of St. Thomas Aquinas according to which the law of God is revealed to men through the use of human reason. This is evidence in the reference by Walsh J above to 'the law of God promulgated by reason'. Mr Justice Walsh and Mr. Justice Costello have also endorsed a Thomistic approach to natural law in extra-judicial writings.[78]

While we can therefore establish to some degree the nature of this natural law theory, this does not leave it without its difficulties. Gerry Whyte has pointed out three problems with natural law theory as espoused by the Irish courts.[79] First, a Thomistic approach is problematic because of its close association with one particular religious denomination, the Roman Catholic Church. Whyte concedes, however, that the reliance on natural law has not resulted in the endorsement of any specifically Roman Catholic teaching. Indeed, in *McGee* natural law was used to uphold the right of married couples to use artificial contraception, a practice which clearly contradicts Catholic teaching. Secondly, because of its imprecise nature it is difficult to know what natural law requires in a given situation. Thirdly, this uncertainty as to what natural law requires can give rise to a fear that it may be used as a cloak for wide-ranging judicial law-making.

The last problem outlined by Whyte is of particular relevance in the context of constitutional amendment and is discussed further in the next section.

It is apparent that the protection of human rights afforded by the Constitution of Ireland has been greatly enhanced by the activism of the Irish courts. The courts have supplemented the fundamental rights provisions of the constitution through creative use of Article 40.3 to grant individuals a degree of protection hardly envisaged by its drafters. Had the courts maintained the conservative and timid approach demonstrated during the early life of the constitution the degree of fundamental rights protection now provided by the constitution could only have been achieved through extensive amendments to specifically include in the text of the constitution guarantees to the rights now protected through Article 40.3.1°.[80]

---

[78] Mr Justice Walsh, 'The Constitution and Constitutional Rights' in Litton, ed., *The Constitution of Ireland 1937-1987* (Dublin, 1988); Mr Justice Costello, 'Natural Law, the Constitution and the Courts' in *Essays in Memory of Alexis Fitzgerald* (Dublin, 1987).

[79] Whyte, 'Natural Law and the Constitution' (1996) 15 ILT 8.

For further discussion of natural law theory see: Hogan, 'Constitutional Interpretations' in Litton, ed., *The Constitution of Ireland 1937-1987* (Dublin, 1988); Hogan, 'Unenumerated Personal Rights: Ryan's Case Re-evaluation', (1990-1992) 25-27 Ir.Jur. 95; Humphries, 'Interpreting Natural Rights', (1993-1995) 28-30 Ir.Jur. 221; Twomey, 'The Death of Natural Law?', (1995) 14 ILT 270.

[80] The *Constitution Review Group* recommended amendment of Articles 40-41 of the Constitution to ensure that the standards set by the European Convention on Human Rights and other international human rights instruments were met. The Group recommended amending Article 40.3.1° to provide a comprehensive list of rights to be protected, including those already recognised by the courts, and drawing upon the European Convention and the International Covenant on Civil and Political Rights.

The unenumerated rights doctrine could also be viewed as an interference with the democratic process and as an usurpation by the courts of the power to amend the constitution which the people have reserved to themselves. The wording of Article 40.3.1° does however indicate that rights other than those specified in the text of the constitution are to be protected and can be interpreted as a mandate given to the courts to infer the existence of other rights. Nonetheless, where the courts rely on ideas of natural law as the source of rights there exists a real danger that they will stray too far from the confines of the constitution and exceed the powers conferred on them by the constitution. This could pose a serious threat to the democratic nature of the state and a direct attack on the exclusive right of the people to amend the constitution. It is this problem which will be examined next.

*3. Natural law and the lawfulness of an amendment*

There is no immutability clause in the constitution of Ireland to the effect that the protection of certain rights guaranteed by the constitution may not be removed by amendment, such as is contained in Article 79(3) of the German Basic Law.[81] However, as mentioned above, many of the fundamental rights guaranteed by the constitution are not dependent upon the text of the constitution but exist in natural law, which is seen as antecedent to and superior to the constitution. The constitution therefore recognises these rights, it does not grant them.

This emphasis placed on natural law by the courts begs the question of whether it is possible for the courts to declare invalid any amendment to the constitution which they deem to be inconsistent with natural law. A former High Court judge, Mr. Justice O'Hanlon, has in fact argued that the courts can do precisely this and has claimed that the Thirteenth and Fourteenth Amendments were unlawful. These Amendments qualified the prohibition on abortion so that it could not be relied upon to restrict travel or receipt of information on abortion services lawfully available abroad.[82] He sustained this argument with reference to a number of judgments which support the view that the unborn have a natural and inherent right to life. One such judgment was that of Walsh J in the Supreme Court in *G. v. An Bord Uchtála*,[83] where he made the following statement on the natural rights of the child:

The child's natural rights spring primarily from the natural right of every individual to life, to be reared and educated, to liberty, to work, to rest and recreation, to the practice of religion, and to follow his or her conscience. The right to life necessarily implies the right

---

The recommendation with regard to Article 40.3.1° was partly prompted by a recognition of the problems which could arise in relation to the unenumerated rights doctrine, which have already been mentioned but are discussed at greater length in the next section.

[81]   The Constitution Review Group rejected the idea of adding such a clause (p. 397, *Report of the Constitution Review Group*, 1996).

[82]   O'Hanlon, *Natural Rights and the Irish Constitution* (1993) 12 ILT 8.

[83]   [1980] IR 32.

to be born.... It lies not however in the power of the parent to terminate its existence.... The child's natural right to life and all that flows from that right are independent of any right of the parent as such.[84]

O'Hanlon J also referred to the judgment of McCarthy J in *Norris v. the Attorney General*[85] where he said that 'the provisions of the preamble [to the Constitution] which I have quoted earlier in this judgment would appear to lean heavily against any view other than that the right to life of the unborn child is a sacred trust to which all organs of government must lend their support'.

These pronouncements lead O'Hanlon J to the conclusion that 'the protection of fundamental rights in the Irish Constitution (and in particular the right to life of the unborn) is firmly grounded on what is called Natural Law'. According to O'Hanlon J, the Preamble and Article 6 identify 'the Most Holy Trinity' as the source of this natural law. He reaffirms a theocratic theory of natural law concluding that 'no law could be adopted and no judicial decision could lawfully be given, which conflicted with the Natural Law (which we recognise as being of divine origin).'

O'Hanlon J's assertions have been challenged on a number of grounds, not least that an assumption by the courts of a power to invalidate an amendment properly effected by the people on the basis of some vague notion of divine law would seriously threaten the democratic nature of the state. In his answer to O'Hanlon J's arguments Tim Murphy points out that Kenny J referred not only to the 'Christian' nature of the state but also to its 'democratic' nature, and that this was ignored by O' Hanlon J[86].

On the whole natural law issue Murphy points out there are two basic kinds of natural law theory, one based solely on human reason and another based on faith in the existence of a deity. Even if one confines oneself to natural law based on Christian beliefs one still encounters conflict between Catholic and Protestant theories on divine law with regard to many sensitive issues such as contraception, sterilisation and abortion. Any legislative enactment or indeed constitutional amendment dealing with these areas will inevitably be in conflict with some interpretation of natural law. For the judiciary to have the power to strike down laws on the basis of inconsistency with whatever natural law theory the court of the day feels inclined to follow would be an unacceptable interference with the democratic process.

Murphy goes on to argue that O'Hanlon J's choice of judicial pronouncements were selective and that further reference to the cases relied upon by him casts his conclusions into doubt. In *McGee* Walsh J stated that it was impossible to define exactly what is natural law and that in a pluralist society the courts cannot be asked to choose between the differing views of theologians. As already mentioned, Murphy stresses the importance which Kenny J attached to the democratic nature

---

[84]  70 ibid, at 69.
[85]  [1982] IR 284.
[86]  Murphy, *Democracy, Natural Law and the Irish Constitution* (1993) 12 ILT 81.

of the state in *Ryan*. Kenny J's reference to a Papal Encyclical which was emphasised by O'Hanlon J is contrasted with the decision in *McGee* to imply a right of married couples to use contraceptives (which is against Catholic teaching). He also points out that in referring to McCarthy J's judgment in the *Norris* case O'Hanlon J declines to mention that this was a dissenting judgment which supported the right of homosexuals to engage in sexual activity, which is also contrary to Catholic teaching.

Murphy's unease at a judicial power to invalidate laws deemed inconsistent with natural law is understandable. However his arguments against the claim that the courts have relied on a natural law theory based on Christian belief are not. He points to Walsh J's statement to the effect that the courts are not in the business of choosing between the views of theologians and to situations where, despite recognising the constitutional significance of natural law, judges upheld rights contrary to Catholic teaching. All this shows is that the courts did not adhere to purely Roman Catholic doctrine in deciding what was required by natural law in a given situation. They did, however, take a Thomistic approach which is of course Christian in nature.

So I return to the question of whether the courts could declare a properly adopted constitutional amendment unlawful as being contrary to natural law. It is clear from the passages relied upon by O'Hanlon J that prior to the Eighth Amendment the courts recognised an unenumerated constitutional right to life of the unborn which now exists side by side with the express guarantee in Article 40.3.3°. If this unenumerated right is a natural law right superior to all positive law, would it therefore be unlawful to effect an amendment to guarantee to women the right to terminate a pregnancy? The assumption by the courts of a power to strike down a constitutional amendment on the basis of its conflict with a divine law, which they themselves reserve the right to interpret and apply, is a frightening prospect for a democratic secular state. However, as O'Hanlon J's thesis shows, it would not be impossible for the courts to find authority upon which to base a claim to such power.

If the judiciary did assume such a power the question would arise as to whether there is any way in which it could be taken from them. The starting point for the courts in establishing the supremacy of natural law would appear to be the references to God in the Preamble and Article 6. One apparent method of getting to the root of the problem would be to amend the constitution to remove references to God. Presumably, however, if natural law places a limitation on the people as to what rights they can add to or remove from the constitution by virtue of their obligations towards God, removal of the references to God would not make any difference. The constitution does not create natural law and it certainly does not create God - it acknowledges the obligations of the people to God and the limitations which these obligations place upon the people. Removal of the references to God would not be contrary to natural law but would not oblige the courts to change their position on the subjection of all organs of government and the people themselves to the rules of natural law.

Mr. Justice O'Hanlon's thesis was in fact put to the test by the Supreme Court in 1995 in *The Regulation of Information Bill Case*,[87] a reference by the President to the Supreme Court under Article 26 of a Bill permitting the publication and procurement of information relating to abortion services abroad. The Bill was intended to regulate the provision of such information previously held unlawful by the courts as contrary to Article 40.3.3°[88] but now permitted, following the Fourteenth Amendment. In that case the court took the unusual step of appointing counsel to represent the arguments on the right to life of the unborn and counsel to represent the arguments on the right to life of the mother. It was argued by counsel representing the unborn that the Fourteenth Amendment was contrary to the natural law right to life of the unborn which is acknowledged by the Eighth Amendment. Natural law, it was argued, is the foundation upon which the constitution was built and ranks superior to the constitution. Therefore, no provision of the constitution which is contrary to natural law can be enforced by the courts.

Delivering the judgment of the Court, Hamilton CJ rejected this argument. He referred to the judgment of Budd J in *Byrne v. Ireland*[89] in which it was stated that '...it is the people who are paramount...'. He went on to emphasise that the constitution confines and restricts the powers of the state and the organs of the state. He then looked at the question of unenumerated rights, referring to the *Ryan* case and the *McGee* case stressing the emphasis placed by Walsh J in the *McGee* case on the desire expressed by the people in the Preamble to promote the common good with due observance to 'prudence, justice and charity'. According to Walsh J, the judges must therefore interpret the rights protected by the constitution in accordance with their ideas of prudence, justice and charity:

In the performance of this difficult duty there are certain guidelines laid down in the Constitution for the judge. The very structure and content of the articles dealing with fundamental rights clearly indicate that justice is not subordinate to the law. In particular, the terms of Article 40.3 expressly subordinate the law to justice. Both Aristotle and the Christian philosophers have regarded justice as the highest human virtue. The virtue of prudence was also esteemed by Aristotle as by the philosophers of the Christian world. But the great additional virtue introduced by Christianity was that of charity. ... According to the Preamble, the people gave themselves the Constitution to promote the common good with due observance of prudence, justice and charity so that the dignity and freedom of the individual might be assured. The judges must, therefore, as best they can from their training and their experience, interpret these rights in accordance with their ideas of prudence, justice and charity. It is but natural that from time to time the prevailing ideas of these virtues may be conditioned by the passage of time; no interpretation of the Constitution is intended to be final for all time. It is given in the light of prevailing ideas and concepts.[90]

---

[87] In Re Article 26 of the Constitution and the Regulation of Information (Services Outside the State for Termination of Pregnancies) Bill 1995 [1995] 2 ILRM 81. See Kingston and Whelan, *op. cit.*, 21, p. 205; Twomey, *The Death of Natural Law* (1995) 13 ILT 370.

[88] *Att.Gen.(Society for the Protection of the Unborn Children (Ireland) Ltd.) v. Open Door Counselling Ltd.* [1988] IR 593; [1989] ILRM 19.

[89] [1972] IR 241.

[90] [1974] IR 284, at 318.

From this, the Supreme Court came to the astonishing conclusion that the courts at all stages recognised the constitution as the fundamental law of the state and at no stage recognised the provisions of natural law as superior to the constitution. The courts, it was held, have identified unenumerated personal rights where these could be reasonably implied from the provisions of the constitution. In determining, where necessary, the rights which are superior or antecedent to positive law or which are imprescriptible or inalienable, the courts must act in accordance with the guidelines laid down in the constitution and must interpret them in accordance with their ideas of prudence, justice and charity. The Court stated its position as follows:

From a consideration of all the cases which recognised the existence of a personal right which was not specifically enumerated in the Constitution, it is manifest that the Court in each case had satisfied itself that such personal right was one which could be reasonably implied from and was guaranteed by the provisions of the Constitution, interpreted in accordance with its ideas of prudence, justice and charity.

The Courts as they were and are bound to, recognised the Constitution as the fundamental law of the State to which the organs of the State were subject an at no stage recognised the provisions of the natural law as superior to the Constitution.[91]

Any amendment carried out in accordance with the requirements of Article 46 forms part of the supreme and fundamental law of the state expressing as it does the will of the people, and no provision of natural law is superior to the fundamental law of the state.

For the Supreme Court to do anything other than uphold a properly enacted amendment would have been unacceptable in a democratic state. However, the reasoning of the Court in reaching its decision is problematic. For the Court to deny that natural law has in the past been recognised as superior to the Constitution is truly remarkable given the decisions, referred to above, in which this principle was clearly enunciated. For the Court to cite the judgment of Walsh J in *McGee* in support of this denial is even more remarkable, given that this was the decision in which natural law theory was firmly established in Irish Constitutional law. While Walsh J stated that constitutional rights should be interpreted in the light of prevailing ideas of prudence, justice and charity, the overriding emphasis in his judgment was on the existence of 'natural rights' which 'are not created by law but that the Constitution confirms their existence'. I would suggest that when Walsh J referred to prevailing ideas of justice and the other virtues, he was referred to the process by which natural law was to be discovered through the use of reason. These prevailing ideas did not in themselves constitute natural law but were to be engaged in the reasoning process. In the passage cited by the Supreme Court, Walsh J clearly discusses the concepts of prudence, justice and charity in the context of Christian Aristotelianism. The Supreme Court grabs at these references to prudence, justice

---

[91] [1995] 2 ILRM 81, at 107.

and charity, tears them from their Thomistic context and uses them to establish 'prevailing ideas and concepts' as the source of unenumerated rights.

Despite the satisfactory result in the *Information Bill Case* it is disappointing that the Supreme Court could not bring it about through some means more subtle than a blatant denial of a well-established doctrine. A more reasoned decision should have been forthcoming in such an important case.

While the conclusion of the Court in this case is to be welcomed, the reasoning is problematic with regard to inalienable and imprescriptible rights. It was the specific recognition of such rights by the constitution which led Walsh J in *McGee* to conclude that certain rights exist which are superior to positive law. He saw natural law as the source of these rights. The Supreme Court has now rejected arguments that natural law is superior to the constitution and has established ideas of prudence, justice and charity as the source of fundamental rights. The protection afforded by the constitution can therefore change along with prevailing ideas of prudence, justice and charity. The Court acknowledged that certain rights are inalienable and imprescriptible and states that these rights are also to be determined with reference to prudence, justice and charity. It is difficult to see how rights can be inalienable and imprescriptible while at the same time being open to change or even abolition when prevailing ideas demand it. It would appear therefore that so called inalienable and imprescriptible rights are no more superior to the law that any other rights and can be changed just as easily if the people so direct.

One alternative put forward by Gerry Whyte was for the Court to acknowledge that it had previously endorsed Thomistic natural law theory but to point out that to the extent we can all use our reason we can have equally valid views on what Thomistic natural law demands. Therefore thee should be a strong presumption that legislators act in a manner which is consistent with natural law. This presumption should even be stronger where the people vote in a referendum to amend the Constitution.[92] I would suggest that one area where the presumption could be refuted would be in the case of an attempt to remove the protection afforded to the inalienable and unprescriptable rights specified in the Constitution.

## VI. CONCLUSION

In choosing plebiscite as the means of enacting the constitution in 1937 de Valera was motivated primarily by a desire to establish a new order, the validity of which was in no way dependent upon the Treaty. Enactment by plebiscite gave the new constitution an unquestionable legitimacy and deprived any treaty-based organ of any function in its creation. The people gave themselves the constitution and its legitimacy was dependent entirely on their act of adoption. The continued legitimacy of the constitution relied upon the continued right of the people to make the final decision on any matter of policy and their exclusive right to amend the constitution. Any attempt to interfere with the right of the people to amend the

---

[92] Whyte, *op. cit.*, p.11.

constitution constitutes an attack on the ideological basis of the constitution.

It is for this reason that the courts have taken the defence of the people's ultimate right to decide on constitutional change as their supreme consideration when dealing with constitutional amendment. In *Crotty* they checked an attempt by the government to surrender sovereignty, which only the people were empowered to surrender. In *Roche, Finn* and *Slattery* the Courts refused to intervene with the 'solemn legislative process' of amendment. In *McKenna (No. 2)* the Supreme Court defended the right of the people to decide in a referendum without unwarranted interference by the government.

The unenumerated rights doctrine has proved a valuable source of human rights protection in Ireland but inherent in the previously declared source of that doctrine was a latent threat to the supreme right of the people to amend the constitution, a threat which eventually manifested itself in the *Regulation of Information Bill Case*. In that case the Supreme Court again felt duty bound to defend the right of the people to amend the constitution. It is, however, unfortunate that the Court in that case put so little effort into its reasoning in order to reach what was, undoubtedly, the only acceptable result.

The principle underlying all the decisions on constitutional amendment is that the role of the people is paramount. The exclusive right of the people to amend the constitution is an aspect of sovereignty as vested in the people. Any attempt to undermine this right is an attack on the sovereignty of the State and will not be permitted by the courts.

Chapter Eleven

# CONSTITUTIONAL REVISIONS AND REFORMS: THE ITALIAN EXPERIENCE

Paolo Galizzi[*]

## I. INTRODUCTION

The debate on constitutional reforms is a constant feature in Italian politics. The instability of governments for which Italy is well known has often been linked to the constitutional arrangements which emerged after the end of World War II.[1] The pressure to modernise and to strengthen the Italian constitutional system has increased in the past few years. Political scandals, the emergence of a federalist/secessionist movement in the North of the country and the process of European integration and monetary union have further highlighted the inadequacy of the current constitutional arrangements.

Various proposals to address the instability of Italian governments and to revise the current Constitution have been put forward, so far with no success. The latest comprehensive proposal to reform the Constitution was drafted by a Bicameral Commission (*Commissione D'Alema*). All the main political parties initially supported this latest proposal. However, subsequent disagreements among the leading parties emerged during the parliamentary scrutiny of the Commission's proposal and the reforms were never adopted.

Due to the volatile nature of the Italian political system, it is almost impossible to predict whether a comprehensive reform of the Constitution will occur in the near future, but one can say with some confidence that it is highly unlikely that any significant change will take place before the next general elections.[2]

The Italian experience of constitutional revision and reform merits attention for at least two reasons: first, Italy has experienced the use of several techniques and methods to revise its Constitution; secondly, most constitutional systems have been

---

[*] Lecturer in Law, University of Nottingham. This chapter was originally written in 1997 and has been subsequently updated to take into account developments which occurred up to July 2000. I would like to thank my mentor, Professor Erika Szyszczak, for her invaluable guidance at this stage of my career and more specifically for her comments on a draft of this chapter. The usual disclaimer applies.

[1] The current Prime Minister, Giuliano Amato, was appointed on 25 April 2000. Mr Amato is presiding over the 53rd government since the introduction of the 1948 Constitution. For more detailed information on the republican governments since 8 May 1948 see *www.camera.it* .

[2] Parliamentary elections are due, at the latest, by April 2001. Some political commentators are predicting earlier consultations.

analysed in great detail and suggested as models to solve Italy's institutional problems.

This chapter will summarise the most significant attempts to reform the Italian Constitution and will try to outline lessons that can be learned from such experience.

## II. HISTORICAL BACKGROUND OF THE ITALIAN CONSTITUTION

In order to understand the current constitutional arrangements, it is necessary to outline briefly the origin of the Italian State. The following summary is by no means a comprehensive analysis of Italian constitutional history, but it will provide a general framework to understand the debate on constitutional reforms in Italy.[4]

Three key periods can be identified for our purposes: the creation of Italy in 1861; the fascist experience under Mussolini's regime; and the adoption of the Republican Constitution at the end of World War II.

A. The Kingdom of Italy

The Kingdom of Italy (*Regno d'Italia*) was proclaimed in 1861, after a process of national unification led by the Kingdom of Piedmont-Sardinia.[5]

The Kingdom of Piedmont-Sardinia was a constitutional monarchy. Its basic constitutional legal instrument, the *Statuto Albertino,* was "granted" by the King to its citizens on 4 March 1848. With the completion of the process of national unification, the application of the *Statuto Albertino* was extended to the entire national territory and it became the first constitution for all Italian subjects.[6]

The Kingdom of Italy was therefore created as a constitutional monarchy.

Subsequent modifications of the Italian constitutional order were later adopted under the influence of liberal ideas of democracy and freedom, which were gaining strength in Europe.[7]

Those changes were, however, destined to be short-lived.

---

[4] For a more detailed analysis of the constitutional history and for further references see, *inter alia*, P. Biscaretti di Ruffia, *Diritto costituzionale: istituzioni di diritto pubblico*, XV ed., Napoli, 1989; V. Italia and C.E. Traverso, *Elementi di diritto pubblico*, Milano, 1992; L. Paladin, *Lezioni di diritto costituzionale*, Padova, 1989; G. Amato and A. Barbera, *Manuale di diritto pubblico*, IV ed., Bologna, 1994; G.U. Rescigno, *Corso di diritto pubblico*, Bologna, 1994/1995; G. Rolla, *Manuale di diritto pubblico*, Torino, 1994; G. Vignocchi and G. Ghetti, *Corso di diritto pubblico*, Milano, 1994; T. Martines, *Diritto costituzionale*, IX ed., Milano, 1997.

[5] The Kingdom of Italy (*Regno d'Italia*) was proclaimed with the Law of 17 March 1861, n. 4671 at the end of the process of national unification.

[6] The *Statuto Albertino* was granted to his subjects by the King, Carlo Alberto, under popular pressure for liberal political reforms. The *Statuto Albertino* was prepared by a Committee presided over by the King and was a concession from the King, who voluntarily agreed to limit his absolute powers in favour of a more democratic system. It was therefore a so-called Constitution *octroyée*. The *Statuto Albertino* was a flexible constitution and did not provide a specific procedure for its revision: modifications could therefore be adopted according to the ordinary legislative procedure.

[7] For example, in 1919 the right to vote was extended to all males over the age of 21.

B. The fascist regime

After the First World War, Italy was to embark on a period of dictatorship.

Between 1919 and 1922, the political system went through great instability. Italy, like many other European countries, was faced with severe institutional and economic problems left over by the war: five different governments were in office during this period, but they were all unable to tackle these issues, paving the way for the emergence of the fascist regime.

Taking advantage of the deteriorating political and economic situation, on 28 October 1922 Benito Mussolini, the leader of the Fascist Party, organised the so called *'Marcia su Roma'* (march on Rome), often considered to mark the beginning of the fascist regime in Italy. The 'march on Rome' was intended to put pressure on the King to nominate Mussolini head of the government. The King bowed to such pressure and designated Mussolini as the new Italian Prime Minister. This move would later be one of the reasons for the fall of the monarchy in Italy.

The government, presided over by Mussolini, obtained a vote of confidence in Parliament in a climate of fear and intimidation. However, from a purely formal point of view, constitutional legality was maintained.[8] The autocratic and dictatorial character of the new regime was quickly to become apparent: restrictions on political and civil liberties were soon introduced.[9]

The fascist regime began to unfold during World War II. Italy, because of her alliance with Germany, became involved in the war. This cost her heavy defeats by the Allied Powers, particularly in the southern part of the country. The increasing difficulties and popular discontent resulted in the isolation of Mussolini within his own ranks and allowed the King to dismiss him as Prime Minister (following a motion of no confidence by the *Gran Consiglio del Fascismo*[10] on 24-25 July 1943).[11]

The King nominated a new Government and designated Badoglio as the new Prime Minister. The new government was composed of non-politicians and was under the guidance of the King. The Badoglio government restored the constitutional order provided by the *Statuto Albertino* and abolished some of the instruments introduced by the fascist legal system.

One of the most important acts of the Badoglio government was the signature of an armistice with the Allied Powers on 8 September 1943. With this action, Italy

---

[8] Opinions are divided on the continuity of the constitutional legality after the emergence of the fascist regime. For a further analysis of the different opinions, see the authors cit. *supra* n.1.

[9] Just to give a few examples of the degeneration of the constitutional legal order, which was favoured by the weakness of the Statuto Albertino and of the constitutional system as a whole, one can recall that the law of 24 December 1925 provided that the government was no longer responsible before Parliament. Later the regime approved legislation allowing only the existence of one party, the Fascist Party, whose organs increasingly became organs of the State apparatus. The regime passed legislation controlling personal freedom and every dissident voice was firmly repressed.

[10] The *Gran Consiglio del Fascismo* was from 1922 an organ of the Fascist Party, which was later transformed into a constitutional organ in 1928/1929 with the task, *inter alia*, of giving opinions on all matters of a constitutional character.

[11] From a constitutional point of view, the King sacked Mussolini (*il Duce* as he was then known) using his royal prerogative to dismiss 'his' Ministers under Article 65 of the *Statuto Albertino*, a power very rarely used before.

broke her alliance with Germany, which in retaliation occupied the north of the country. Italy was at that point divided in two parts, ruled by conflicting governments: the King's government ruling the south and a government led by Mussolini in the north, where a so-called Italian Social Republic was established with German support (*Repubblica Sociale Italiana*).

In the meantime, Italian political forces organised themselves under a Committee for National Liberation (*Comitato di Liberazione Nazionale - CLN*), which played a fundamental role in the liberation of Italy and in the post-war constitutional arrangements. For our purposes, it is important to highlight that, during this period, a fundamental disagreement between the Crown and the political parties of the Committee for National Liberation emerged: the core of the disagreement concerned the future of the monarchy and of the King himself. The monarchy was considered too compromised by its mistakes during the fascist regime and therefore the Committee for National Liberation supported its abolition in favour of a republic.

The conflict between the King and the Committee was temporarily resolved with an 'institutional truce' (so called *'svolta di Salerno'*): the two sides agreed to postpone the solution of the 'institutional question' on the future of the monarchy at the end of the military hostilities. As part of the deal, the King agreed to abdicate in favour of his son after the liberation of Rome and accepted that the future of the monarchy would be decided in a referendum to be called soon after the end of the war.

On 5 June 1944, after the liberation of Rome, the King, Vittorio Emanuele III, nominated his son, Prince Umberto, as Lieutenant General. With this designation, the King had in effect transferred all the royal powers to his son. The King finally abdicated on 9 May 1946 and Prince Umberto was crowned as the new King of Italy, a position that he was destined to hold for only a month.

C. The Republican Constitution

On 25 June 1944, the Lieutenant General, Prince Umberto, issued a royal decree calling for the election of a Constituent Assembly soon after the liberation of the national territory. The Constituent Assembly would be entrusted with the task of choosing the form of State (monarchy or republic) and of preparing a new Constitution.[12] Later, it was decided that the choice between monarchy and republic was to be made directly by the Italian people, in a referendum to be held on the same day as the election of the delegates for the Constituent Assembly.[13]

The election of the members of the Constituent Assembly and the referendum on the form of State took place on 2 June 1946. The majority was in favour of a republic.[14] The King, Umberto II, who had reigned for only a month, was forced to leave Italy in exile and the Prime Minister temporarily assumed the functions of Head of State.

---

[12]  Decreto legge 25 giugno 1944, n. 151.
[13]  Decreto Legislativo Luogotenenziale 16 marzo 1946, n.98.
[14]  12,717,923 votes were in favour of the republic and 10,719,284 votes were expressed for the monarchy.

The newly elected Constituent Assembly met for the first time on 25 June 1946 and elected a provisional Head of State, Enrico De Nicola, on 28 June.

To concentrate on the preparation of the text of the new Constitution, the Constituent Assembly decided to delegate the legislative function to the government, under its control and supervision.

The preparation of a draft text of the new Constitution was assigned to a special Commission, composed of 75 members of the Constituent Assembly (*Commissione dei 75*). The *Commission dei 75* was further divided into three sub-commissions with specific competence on civil rights, organisation of the State and economic and social relationships. These sub-commissions were further divided in several working groups to deal with more specific issues (for example on the structure of the regional system, etc.).

The Commission of 75 presented its final proposal to the Constituent Assembly on 31 January 1947 and, after a long debate, the final text of the Constitution was adopted on 22 December 1947. The new republican Constitution entered into force on 1 January 1948.

The new constitutional order was completed with political elections that took place on 18 April 1948. This event marked the end of a constitutional era that led to the creation of the Italian republic and the beginning of a new republican era. It was now time to implement the provisions and aspiration of the new Constitution.[15]

In short, the 1948 Constitution is composed of 139 articles. The first 12 articles provide the fundamental principles on which the republican legal system is based. The Constitution is then divided in two further parts: Part I deals with rights and duties of citizens (*Dei diritti e dei doveri dei cittadini*), whilst Part II deals with the structure and organisation of the political and legal system (*Ordinamento della Repubblica*).[16]

The Constitution strongly guarantees and protects individual freedoms and has according to many authors created weak institutions with strong checks and balances. To understand the republican Constitution and the choices made by the

---

[15] It has to be said that for a long time several provisions of the new Constitution were not implemented. For example, the Constitutional Court was created only in 1956 and the regional reform of the State was completed only in 1970.

[16] To sum up, Parliament is the central institution in the constitutional order. It is composed of a Chamber of Deputies (*Camera dei deputati*) and a Senate of the Republic (*Senato della Repubblica*), which have almost identical powers. The Government is headed by a Prime Minister *(Presidente del Consiglio)* nominated by the Head of State. The judicial system is independent and is governed by an autonomous body to preserve such independence. The Constitution provides for a decentralisation of power, thus creating regional, provincial and local entities. To guarantee the constitutional order, a Constitutional Court has been created. The Constitutional Court has the power to check the conformity of legislation with the provisions of the Constitution and acts as referee in case of conflicts between the different organs of the State. The Head of State is known as President of the Republic and is elected by Parliament. He/she has a merely symbolic status. Provisions of the written Constitution, the 'formal' Constitution, have often been replaced by provisions of the 'material Constitution', that is to say by a constitution that is the result of the evolution and interaction between several factors like customs, politics, social events and so on. For example, the President of the Republic according to the Constitution has a merely representative role. However, on many occasions, and in particular in the last decade, the President of the Republic has exercised increasing influence in the Italian political life, depending on the personality of the holder of the office and on the particular political situation. See authors cit. *supra* n. 1.

Constituent Fathers, it is fundamental to bear in mind that this instrument was drafted after the experiences of the fascist regime and of World War II. Furthermore, it is essential to remember that the Italian Constitution is the result of compromises between (at least) three different ideological stances well represented in the Constituent Assembly: the Catholic, liberal and socialist traditions.

The criticisms and debates on the revision of the 1948 Constitution, as mentioned, centre particularly on the need to reform its institutional arrangements, which are often blamed for the weakness and instability of governments.

## III. THE PROCEDURE FOR THE REVISION OF THE CONSTITUTION[17]

An analysis of constitutional revisions in a given country must necessarily start from the examination of the provisions in a given Constitution of the procedures for its modification.

Before doing that, it is important to stress that the 1948 Italian Constitution is a rigid constitution. Its drafters were well aware of the weakness of the *Statuto Albertino*, whose provisions could be easily modified by a particular political faction having a simple parliamentary majority. The Constituent Fathers therefore adopted a procedure for the revision of the Constitution requiring a high degree of consensus for any modification to be put in place.

The procedure for the revision of the Constitution is governed by Article 138[18] of the Constitution.[19]

Proposals for the revision of the Constitution may be made by the Government, each Member of Parliament, Regional Assemblies and ordinary voters (through a proposal signed by at least 50,000 voters).[20]

---

[17] On this matter, see *supra* n.1. More specifically and for further references see also A. Pizzorusso, 'Revisione della Costituzione e leggi costituzionali', in *Commentario della Costituzione* (Articoli 134-139), Bologna, 1981, p. 703 ff.; S.M. Cicconetti, 'Revisione costituzionale', in *Enciclopedia del diritto*, vol. XL, Milano, 1989, p. 134 ff.

[18] Article 138 reads as follows:

'Le leggi di revisione della Costituzione e le altre leggi costituzionali sono adottate da ciascuna Camera con due successive deliberazioni ad intervallo non minore di tre mesi, e sono approvate a maggioranza assoluta dei componenti di ciascuna Camera nella seconda votazione.

Le leggi stesse sono sottoposte a referendum popolare quando, entro tre mesi dalla loro pubblicazione, ne facciano domanda un quinto dei membri di una Camera o cinquecentomila elettori o cinque Consigli regionali. La legge sottoposta a referendum non è promulgata, se non è approvata dalla maggioranza dei voti validi.

Non si fa luogo a referendum se la legge è stata approvata nella seconda votazione da ciascuna delle Camere a maggioranza dei due terzi dei suoi componenti'.

[19] A particular procedure is provided by Article 132 of the Constitution for the modification and creation of Regions.

[20] The right to propose ordinary legislation is regulated by Article 71 of the Constitution. Constitutional experts unanimously agree that the same applies to the right to propose constitutional laws. The right of regional assemblies to propose legislation is provided by Article 121 of the Constitution. Article 99 of the Constitution also guarantees the right to propose legislation to the *Consiglio Nazionale dell'economia e del lavoro* (National Council for Economy and Employment), but with the law of 5 January 1955, n. 3, it is specifically prescribed that the Council does not have the right to propose constitutional laws. On these questions, see S.M. Cicconetti, *op. cit.*, in particular footnote n.12.

Constitutional revisions and constitutional laws are adopted by two consecutive deliberations by both Houses of Parliament (*Camera* and *Senato*). In particular, the second deliberation must take place 'not less than three months from the first vote and the proposal must be approved by an absolute majority of the members of each Chamber to become effective'. The lapse of time between the first and the second reading of a proposal for constitutional revision is aimed at giving a period to further ponder the consequences of such proposal. If a constitutional amendment is not approved by a two-thirds majority of the members of each Chamber, a popular referendum may be held within three months from the publication of the proposal approved by Parliament in the *Official Journal*. Such constitutional referendum may alternatively be requested by a fifth of the members of each Chamber, by 500,000 voters, or by five Regional Assemblies.

The constitutional referendum allows the electorate to approve or reject the constitutional modification in question.

There is only one explicit limit on constitutional revision: Article 139[21] provides that the republican form of the State cannot be the object of constitutional revision. Doctrine is divided on the meaning of this provision: according to the prevailing opinion, this limit is absolute and therefore the Republican form of State could not be modified under any circumstance. Others believe that this limit should not be considered as an absolute one.[22]

Apart from the explicit limit mentioned above, some authors argue that there are also implicit limits on possible constitutional revisions: those limits consist in the prohibition of constitutional modifications that may conflict with general and fundamental principles of the Constitution. The Constitutional Court will monitor and control constitutional revisions, to make sure that modifications do not undermine those basic and fundamental principles.

The procedure prescribed by Article 138 has been used several times, but exclusively for revisions of specific provisions of the Constitution or for the adoption of constitutional laws (the latter principally to implement provisions of the Constitution).[23] However, the debate on constitutional reforms in Italy has focused on a much more ambitious project: a comprehensive modification of the institutional arrangements and key features of the republican legal order. Article 138 could also, in theory, be used for such comprehensive revisions. Other instruments and techniques, however, have been preferred and adopted for the various attempts to modify the institutional provisions of the republican

---

[21] Article 139 reads as follows: 'La forma repubblicana non può essere oggetto di revisione costituzionale'.

[22] For example, the first opinion is expressed by Martines, *op. cit.*, p. 360; Paladin, *op. cit.*, p. 159; the opposite view is expressed by Biscaretti di Ruffia, op. cit. According to this author, there are also no absolute implicit limits to constitutional revision.

[23] The three most recent constitutional reforms adopted by the Italian Parliament concern the direct election of regional presidents (Legge costituzionale 22 novembre 1999, n. 1), the modification of Article 111 of the Constitution to include detailed provisions on the right to a fair trial (Legge costituzionale 23 novembre 1999, n.2) and finally a modification of Article 48 of the Constitution to allow Italian citizens resident abroad to exercise the right to vote in their country of residence (Legge costituzionale 17 gennaio 2000, n. 1). For further details, see the website of the Italian parliament: www.camera.it or www.senato.it.

Constitution.

## IV. CONSTITUTIONAL REFORMS IN ITALY: A NEVER-ENDING STORY?[24]

We have already mentioned that proposals for comprehensive constitutional reforms have been a constant feature of Italian politics in the past 30 years. Short-lived governments in particular have focused politicians' mind on the compelling need to adopt reforms to guarantee a better system of government in Italy.

Various reasons have been put forward by political analysts to explain the reasons for such instability. Governments' instability has often been inherently linked to the 1948 constitutional arrangements. It is useful to stress again that the 1948 Constitution was influenced by the experience of the previous fascist dictatorship and that the Constituent Fathers drafted the new text with the aim of avoiding a possible repetition of such an event.

With this aim in mind, the 1948 Constitution avoided the concentration of political power in one main organ, preferring instead a system in which political power was shared and exercised by different constitutional organs, on a level of equality, creating a system of strong checks and balances. A strong Parliament is at the centre of such system, with two Chambers, *Camera* and *Senato*, with almost identical powers and functions (a system known as 'perfect bicameralism' – *bicameralismo perfetto*).

As mentioned, these institutional arrangements were aimed at avoiding the possibility for one organ to prevail over another. This aim was certainly a laudable one, but it may have led to the underestimation of the risk of having a system paralysed by institutional conflicts. Furthermore, critics have argued that the system created by the Constitution has resulted in an inefficient decision-making system, with serious problems in identifying and allocating responsibility.

The weakness of governments has also been increased by the electoral system, although not regulated by the Constitution but by ordinary legislation. Parliamentary elections have been conducted under a pure proportional system (changes to the electoral system have only been recently introduced, as we will see). One of the negative consequences of such a system (or some may argue one of the positive aspects of proportional representation) is the fragmentation of the political forces represented in Parliament and the consequent need of having coalition governments. Italian governments have been composed of broad coalitions representing between two and 12 different political parties. Governments' action has suffered from such composition and has been often paralysed by conflicting interests. Furthermore, such conflicts have in many cases caused the premature end of several governments.

Blaming constitutional arrangements for the instability of the Italian political system is an easy option for political forces to justify their actions (or inaction). However, it is highly questionable whether the blame levelled at the current Constitution is entirely justified. One could argue that the instability of Italian

---

[24] For a complete and detailed analysis of the debates and attempts of constitutional reforms in Italy (and for further references) see F. Teresi, *La strategia delle riforme. Le riforme istituzionali in Italia tra governabilità e trasparenza*, IV ed., Torino, 1995.

governments may have a lot to do with the political culture of the country rather then with the particular constitutional arrangements in force (in fact similar constitutional arrangements have been rather successful in other countries). Constitutional reforms may improve the situation, but alone will not be a panacea to the illness of the Italian political system as many predict.

To sum up, having identified the current constitutional arrangements as the main reason for the institutional instability of Italian governments, several proposals aimed at giving greater stability to governments[25] and to the republican institutions have been discussed and analysed by committees, academic studies, parliamentary debates, presidential messages and commissions.[26]

The most significant attempts of constitutional revisions in Italy occurred through the creation of Bicameral Commissions charged with the specific and only task of drafting proposals for the modification of the Constitution. New impetus to the movement for constitutional reforms was given by referenda held in 1991 and 1993 and by the deep changes in the Italian political landscape produced by judicial investigations and the emergence of new political parties at the end of the eighties. The various Commissions have so far failed and they have not yet been able to produce comprehensive constitutional reforms in Italy.

We will now proceed to a brief analysis of the activities of the three Commissions set up to draft constitutional reforms and of their proposals.

## A. The *Commissione Bozzi*

The first main attempt to revise the Italian Constitution occurred through the creation of a parliamentary commission, known as *Commissione Bozzi* from the name of its President, created with the aim of drafting an organic text for the revision of the Constitution. The *Commissione Bozzi* was constituted following a motion approved by both Houses of Parliament on 14 April 1983 and started its activities on 30 November 1983.

The Commission was composed of 20 senators and 20 deputies, nominated by the Presidents of the two Chambers of Parliament. Its task was to 'formulate proposals for constitutional and legislative reforms, to reinforce the republican democracy, to give stability and reinforce its efficiency, giving it modern technical instruments, also enabling it to govern the democratic economy'.

The motion establishing the Commission identified the key issues and problems that had to be addressed:

1) The electoral system for parliamentary elections; 2) the structure of Parliament and possible options for a unicameral or bicameral system; 3) problems relating to the legislative procedures; 4) problems relating to the political and constitutional structure of the Government; 5) the relationships within the Government (between the Prime Minister and Ministers and so on); 6) the President of the Republic; 7) problems concerning public administration; 8) the judicial system and justice; 9) problems concerning administrative controls; 10) the

---

[25] On average Italian governments lasted less than 11 months.
[26] A detailed analysis of the various initiatives undertaken in the Italian Parliament can be found on the following website: *www.senato.it/parlam/bicam/rifcost/dossier* .

autonomy of local governments and regions; 11) forms of direct democracy (referenda); 12) the relationship between public authorities and citizens; 13) the relationship between State and social associations; 14) problems concerning democracy and trade unionism; 15) the status of parliamentarians; 16) a different and wider access to constitutional justice.

The Commission concluded its work on 29 January 1985 and approved a final report (with only 16 votes in favour and two abstentions out of a total of 40 members). The other members of the Commission adopted six minority reports.[27]

The Commission's main report suggested that there was no need to radically alter the fundamental values and structure of the 1948 Constitution. The Commission, for example, suggested the modification of some provisions relating to fundamental rights (for example the specific introduction of a right to a clean environment was suggested). It also believed that a differentiation in the work of the two Houses of Parliament was necessary. Minor modifications to the structure of the Government were also envisaged.

The Commission's report was never discussed by Parliament, although it was the subject of many debates in the academic and political arena. The Commission's proposal had been very disappointing, having failed to live up to expectations for radical and fundamental reforms.

The Commission's timid proposals were due to its failure to reach a consensus among its members and to make clear decisions on many issues. The Commission often limited itself to merely registering the position of the different parties on a specific topic. For example, on electoral reforms, the Commission simply recorded the opinions of its members, without trying to mediate and formulate its own proposal.

The outcome of the Commission's work reflected the deep divisions between the political parties on constitutional reforms. Some political parties wanted only cosmetic or minor changes, others wanted significant reforms and finally a few wanted a major radical revision of the Constitution. The work of the Commission obtained at least one important result: it recorded the position of the various political forces on constitutional reforms and could be used as a starting point for the future. The Commission's work was in fact often recalled by successive Governments and in parliamentary debates on the matter.[28] The question of constitutional reforms could no longer be avoided after the Commisione Bozzi and it has in fact been a major concern for all Italian Governments.[29]

---

[27] The final report was approved with the votes of the Christian Democrats Party (*Democrazia Cristiana*), the Socialist Party (*Partito Socialista Italiano*), the Republican Party (*Partito Repubblicano Italiano*) and the Liberal Party (*Partito Liberale Italiano*); the Communist Party (*Partito Comunista Italiano*) and the Social Democratic Party (*Partito Social Democratico Italiano*) abstained; the Italian Social Movement - National Right (*Movimento Sociale Italiano - Destra Nazionale*), the Independent Left (*Sinistra Indipendente*), the Union Valdotaine and Proletary Democracy (*Democrazia Proletaria*) voted against.

[28] Teresi, *op. cit.*, p. 56.

[29] For example, the second government presided by Mr Craxi (1986) was presented as a government with the aim of providing a significant and wide-ranging project of institutional reforms; the Government presided by Mr Goria (1987) had similar objectives; the Government presided by Mr De Mita (1988) was defined as a 'constituent government' for its ambition in this area. On a more detailed

B. The Italian 'Revolution'

As mentioned above, the movement for constitutional reform received an enormous boost by the evolution (or revolution) of the Italian political landscape at the end of the eighties. Such evolution was triggered by several factors, mainly the process of European integration, the emergence in Northern Italy of a federalist movement, the Northern League,[30] and the actions of the judiciary.[31]

These events led to increasing calls for significant constitutional reforms to modernise the political system, to make it more efficient and transparent. Public opinion had the opportunity to make its views clearly heard in a referendum held on 9 June 1991.[32] In this referendum, the electorate was called to vote for the abolition of a legislative provision on the election of the Chamber of Deputies. The promoters of the referendum wanted to abolish the possibility for voters to express several preferences for candidates included in the list of the party of their choice and allow instead only one preference to be given to one candidate in the chosen list.

The question *per se* was not of particular significance. However, the referendum assumed a fundamental political importance. The main political forces opposed the referendum and invited the electorate to abstain, trying to invalidate the outcome of the referendum.[33] The referendum was therefore perceived as a choice between reforms and keeping the existing system.

The abolition of the specific provision in question was approved by 95.6% of the voters (62.5% of the electorate took part in the referendum).

The outcome of the referendum sent a clear message of a desire for change to the political establishment.

The following years were marked by more turbulence in the political landscape. For our purposes, two main events need to be recalled.

The first is the creation of a new Bicameral Commission for the revision of the Constitution in July 1992, which we will analyse below.

The second is the holding of new referenda on 18 April 1993: 77% of the electorate voted on proposals for the abrogation of several pieces of legislation. In particular, one question concerned the abolition of public funding for political parties (over 90% of voters supported the abrogation). Another question concerned

---

reconstruction of the various proposals of the different governments, see Teresi, *op. cit.*, p. 57.

[30] The Northern League's aim is to fundamentally reform the structure of the Italian State in a federal direction (sometimes this movement has also advocated the creation of a new separate state in northern Italy).

[31] Several criminal investigations on corruption and illegal financing of political parties have involved some of the main figures in the political establishment (the so called Clean Hands – *Mani Pulite* - operation). In particular, as a result of such investigations and prosecutions, some of the main political figures and parties that dominated Italian politics since the creation of the 1948 Constitution have disappeared or were forced to reorganise themselves.

[32] According to Article 75 of the Constitution it is possible to call a referendum for the total of partial abrogation of legislation if 500,000 voters or five Regional Assembly so request. The Constitution provides some limits on the matters that can be subject to referendum and the final decision on the admissibility of a request rests with the Constitutional Court.

[33] According to Article 75 of the Constitution, a referendum is valid only if the majority of the electorate expresses its vote.

the modification of the electoral system for the Senate which resulted in the introduction of a mechanisms similar to the first past the post system (almost 82% of voters supported this measure).[34]

These results confirmed further the strength and the desire for constitutional reforms in the country.

C. The *Commissione De Mita-Iotti*

The second Bicameral Commission to deal with constitutional reforms, known as *Commissione De Mita-Iotti* from the name of the two political leaders called to preside it, was created on 23 July 1992 and was composed of 30 deputies and 30 senators.

The Commission was again given the task of drafting an organic project for the revision of Part II of the Constitution, the part dealing with the institutional structures of the Republic. In particular, the Commission was to look at options for reform of Parliament, President of the Republic, Government, Judiciary, regional system and electoral legislation (the latter not being a matter governed by the constitution, as already mentioned).

The Commission organised its activities in four Committees on the Form of State, the Form of Government, Electoral Law and Constitutional Guarantees.

The Commission was given, with a constitutional law, the power to submit its report to Parliament.[35] A proposal was presented to the two Houses of Parliament on 11 January 1994, but it was never examined because of the early dissolution of Parliament on 16 January 1994.

The *De Mita-Iotti Commission*'s proposal provided for wide ranging reforms. In particular, it proposed the conferment to central Government of competence in specified matters, giving residual competence in all other matters to the Regions. The Prime Minister was to be directly elected by Parliament and he/she would have had exclusive responsibility in the choice of the members of his/her government. The Commission proposed the introduction of new legislation concerning budgetary arrangements, the legislative power of the Government and the organisation of public administration. Finally, the Commission proposed the reduction of the term of the legislature to four years and wider investigative powers for the Houses of Parliament.

The Commission was, however, unable to reach an agreement on several key issues, including the composition and the function of the two Chambers and the organisation of the judicial system and of the Constitutional Court.

As mentioned above, however, these proposals were never discussed by Parliament. For the second time a parliamentary Commission specifically charged with the task of agreeing constitutional reforms had failed to achieve its objective.

---

[34] According to Article 75 of the Constitution, referenda can only be called for the abrogation of legislation. However, by abrogating only parts of legislation, it was in fact possible to 'create' a new electoral system for the Senate.

[35] Legge costituzionale 6 Agosto 1993 n. 1.

## V. THE BICAMERAL COMMISSION FOR CONSTITUTIONAL REFORMS

Following the dissolution of Parliament, a new election held in 1994 saw the victory of a centre right coalition, led by Mr Berlusconi, who became the new Prime Minister. During the premiership of Mr Berlusconi[36] the debate on constitutional reforms continued. However, a political crisis in the centre-right coalition led to the establishment of a caretaker government until new elections were held in 1996.[37] These elections were won by a centre-left coalition under the premiership of Mr Prodi.[38]

Constitutional reforms were one of the key electoral pledges of the centre-left coalition and indeed of all political parties. The main political parties agreed to the establishment of a new Bicameral Commission for Constitutional Reforms, this time created by a constitutional law.[39]

The Commission was composed of 70 members, 35 deputies and 35 senators, and started its work on 8 February 1997. The Commission elected as its President Mr D'Alema, the then leader of the Left Democratic Party, the main party in the government coalition.

The Commission completed its work in November 1997 and adopted a proposal for the comprehensive revision of the second part of the Constitution.

The Commission's text was adopted with the approval of the main political forces and this led to optimism about the possibility of its parliamentary approval. However, the consensus reached within the Bicameral Commission collapsed in Parliament. In June 1998 Parliament took notice of this failure and, yet again, an attempt at constitutional revision failed to produce the hoped outcome.[40]

The text approved by the Bicameral Commission would have represented a significant and radical change of the existing constitutional model.

The proposal suggested a move towards a federal State, in which all residual powers were to be conferred to local, provincial and regional authorities.[41]

---

[36] Mr Berlusconi's government was nominated on 10 May 1994 and resigned on 22 December 1994.
[37] The government was presided by Mr Dini (nominated on 17 January 1995 and resigned on 11 January 1996).
[38] Mr Prodi presided the government from 17 May 1996 until his resignation on 9 October 1998. The premiership was then taken over by Mr D'Alema on 21 October 1998. Mr D'Alema resigned on 18 December 1999, but was reinstated on the following 22 December. He finally resigned on 19 April 2000 and was substituted by the current Prime Minister Mr Amato on 25 April 2000. Parliamentary elections, as mentioned, are due at the latest by April 2001.
[39] Legge costituzionale 24 Gennaio 1997 n. 1.
[40] *The Economist* on 6 June 1998 recorded this outcome in an article entitled 'Italy's constitution. Funeral march?' In particular, the article observed: 'Italy's constitution on June 2nd, which happened to be the 52nd birthday of the Italian republic, a bold attempt to rectify the worst failings of its political system was pronounced dead – or at any rate in a deep coma. This gloomy diagnosis followed the failure of an attempt at constitutional reform known as the bicamerale, after the parliamentary committee that struggled hard to reach agreement on some desirable changes. The collapse sends a lamentable message: none of the institutions or individuals involved in Italian politics seems prepared to sacrifice short-term interests for the country's political health'.
[41] Articles 55–63 of the Commission's text.

A fundamental change was proposed for the President of the Republic, who was to be elected directly by the electorate (at present he/she is elected by both Houses of Parliament with the addition of few regional representatives). This issue proved to be one of the most controversial and was one of the main reasons for the collapse of the political agreement on constitutional reforms.

Other measures were aimed at limiting the number of Members of Parliament and at differentiating the role of the two Houses of Parliament. The Government was to be headed by a Prime Minister, nominated by the President of the Republic and accountable to the Chamber of Deputies.

Two interesting new provisions merit mention. First, if the proposal had been approved, a new Article 110 would have guaranteed constitutionally the independence and autonomy of the Bank of Italy. Secondly, two new provisions would have regulated the Italian participation in the European Union. Article 114 confirmed Italy's participation in the process of European unification, on equal conditions with the other Member States and in conformity with its fundamental constitutional values and fundamental human rights. Article 115 provided a more significant involvement of Parliament in the definition of European policies.

Significant changes would have been introduced to the organisation of the judicial system and of the Constitutional Court.

The proposal of the Bicameral Commission was criticised for being a dangerous mix of various constitutional regimes rather then a clear choice in favour of one system or another.[42]

After the failure of the Bicameral Commission in June 1998, the debate on constitutional reforms has continued. No real progress has been made on a comprehensive revision of the Constitution. Disagreement between the main political forces seems to have increased in the past two years. Different views are expressed now on the most appropriate instrument to be adopted for constitutional reforms. Some favour constitutional modification adopted under Article 138 of the Constitution. Others believe that another Bicameral Commission may be able to achieve what three predecessors could not. Finally, some believe that a Constituent Assembly may be the only solution to the long-awaited reforms.

## VI. CONCLUSION

It may be easy to explain how a Constitution was created and the procedures provided for its revision. It is more difficult to try to explain the reasons behind the

---

[42] 'The politicians have spent six of the past 12 months arguing over how to approach constitutional reform and the remainder haggling over proposals. For a government with so manifestly little sense of State, it is not surprising that the blueprint for change - agreed at the end of June by the constitutional reform commission - should be a disappointing hybrid'. *Financial Times Survey*, Italy, 21 July 1997, p. 5. *The Economist*, 5 July 1997, argued: 'Maybe it was too much to ask. Rare is the political establishment that puts itself voluntarily under a constitutional knife. This week, Italy's body politic shrank from the sort of wholesale operation that might have given it pain – and a genuinely new lease of life. Instead, it offered to submit itself to a little local surgery. After six months of argument, the special parliamentary commission, known as the bicamerale, which was supposed to present a long-term cure for Italy's debilitating system of government, came up with a muddled bunch of palliatives which might even, in the end, make matters worse'.

need for constitutional reforms. In addition, the difficulty is further complicated when one is trying to analyse a continuing situation.

To sum up, almost all the possible instruments for the creation of constitutional norms and for constitutional revision have been applied in the Italian experience. This article has attempted to give a general overview of the most significant ones.

The first Italian Constitution, the *Statuto Albertino*, was a concession of the sovereign. Constitutional changes were later introduced by the fascist regime, which did not find any legal obstacles in its way. This has been blamed on the weakness of procedures for the revision of the Statuto Albertino (although, it is questionable whether a different and stronger Constitution would have realistically been an obstacle to the development of the fascist regime).

The present Constitution was adopted at the end of World War II by a Constituent Assembly entrusted solely and specifically with this task.

Attempts to modify the current Constitution have taken several forms, but the most significant, and so far unsuccessful ones, were proposals to rewrite the second part of the Constitution made by Parliamentary Commissions.

Looking at the Italian experience, the best tool to achieve a comprehensive revision of constitutional arrangements seems to be represented by the establishment of a Constituent Assembly, with the specific power to adopt a text at the end of a given period. In our opinion, such text should then be subject to confirmation by popular referendum.

The Italian experiment with constitutional reforms is still ongoing and it is hard to predict whether this process will eventually lead to successful reforms. It is doubtful whether the stability that Italy needs may be found through constitutional changes alone. Certainly, constitutional reforms aimed at reinforcing institutions and at providing more defined rules on accountability can at least influence the changes necessary in the political system as a whole to create an efficient and stable modern democratic environment. The legal instruments to adopt such reforms can only function if there is the political will to achieve concrete results. This political will seems to have been the missing element in the Italian experience with constitutional reforms and in our opinion is the key to understanding the failure so far of all the attempts of comprehensive institutional modifications.

Chapter Twelve

## THE CONSTITUTIONAL AMENDMENT PROCESS IN MALAYSIA

Andrew Harding[*]

I. INTRODUCTION

The Malaysian Constitution is a unique expression of the country's varied culture and history. It is an amalgam of diverse elements, some having their origin in traditional Malay constitutional ideas, some in British, some in Indian, and some again which derive from a modern Malaysian context determined by the political realities of its multi-cultural social and political life. For those who are totally unfamiliar with the modern Malaysian Constitution, a brief outline of its main features may be helpful.[1]

In general terms the Malaysian Constitution owes much to the Indian Constitution, which came into force only seven years before it (in 1950), in that it embodies British principles of government and constitutional conventions, but also embodies constitutional rather than parliamentary supremacy; and indeed many provisions of the Malaysian Constitution are based on their Indian equivalents. One of the paradoxes of the Malaysian Constitution is that, although much of it is based on English law, British constitutional law itself proceeds from an entirely different premise, that of parliamentary supremacy. In Malaysia, therefore, the constitution is the fundamental law from which the validity of all other laws derives, and is superior to all other forms of law; thus the judiciary has the power to strike down a law as being contrary to the constitution. In Britain, on the other hand, all laws made by Parliament are of equal legal force, and none is set higher than another:

---

[*] Professor of Law, Department of Law, School of Oriental and African Studies, London University.
[1] For further discussion of constitutional law in Malaysia, see Harding, A.J., *Law, Government and the Constitution in Malaysia* (The Hague, Kluwer, and Kuala Lumpur, Malayan Law Journal, 1996); Sheridan, L.A. & Groves, H.E., *The Constitution of Malaysia* (4th ed, Singapore, Malayan Law Journal, 1987); Tun Mohamed Suffian Hashim, *An Introduction to the Constitution of Malaysia*, (2nd ed, Kuala Lumpur, Government Printer, 1976); Tun Mohamed Suffian Hashim, Lee, H.P. & Trindade, F.A. (eds), *The Constitution of Malaysia: Its Development, 1957-1977* (Kuala Lumpur, OUP, 1978); Trindade, F.A. & Lee, H.P.(eds), *The Constitution of Malaysia: Further Perspectives and Developments* (Kuala Lumpur, OUP, 1986).

there is no legal standard or criterion of constitutional validity.

On the face of it, the distinction between constitutional supremacy and parliamentary supremacy is evident in the constitution, which at Art.4(1) declares that '[t]his Constitution is the supreme law of the Federation and any law passed after Merdeka Day [Independence Day: 31 August 1957] which is inconsistent with this Constitution shall, to the extent of the inconsistency, be void'. The theoretical supremacy of the constitution must be considered, however, against the enormous breadth of parliamentary and executive power, and the relative weakness of judicial review as a counter-balance to the other branches of the State. Nonetheless, the requirement of a two-thirds parliamentary majority for most constitutional amendments, and the fact that the judiciary has on occasion struck down legislative acts, establishes the legal supremacy of the constitution as the most basic rule known to Malaysian law.

An independent judiciary headed by a Federal Court is responsible for interpreting the constitution and exercising judicial powers.

The constitution reserves legislative and executive powers to the States and provides for mandatory revenues to be paid to the States by the federation. It also gives the judiciary power to police the border between State and federal powers. However, the powers of the federal legislature and executive are much greater than is consistent with true federation. Malaysia can at best be called a quasi-federation, in which the States have some autonomy, but the federation is conspicuously more powerful. Special legislative and executive powers are reserved to the States of Sabah and Sarawak, each of whose Governments is empowered to prevent certain constitutional amendments affecting that State. Each State has its own elected Legislative Assembly, Head of State, and Executive Council (Cabinet), headed by a *Menteri Besar* or Chief Minister.

The federal Head of State is the *Yang di-Pertuan Agong* (Supreme Head), who is elected by the Rulers (Sultans) of the nine Malay States from their own number in such a way that the office rotates among them, changing hands once every five years. He is a constitutional head, who acts on government advice like the British sovereign. The nine Rulers meet in a unique body known as the Conference of Rulers, which enjoys certain constitutional powers. The Rulers are Heads of Islam in their States, but are required to act on the advice of the State Government. The four States which are not Malay States (Penang, Melaka, Sabah and Sarawak) each have as Head of State a Governor with similar constitutional powers to the Rulers.

Malaysia is a Westminster-model democracy in which the Prime Minister, appointed by the *Yang di-Pertuan Agong*, is the member of the *Dewan Rakyat* (lower house) who in the judgment of the *Yang di-Pertuan Agong* is likely to command the confidence of the majority of its members. In practice the Prime Minister has always been the President of UMNO (United Malay National Organisation), which has always taken other (usually communally defined) parties into a coalition government, presently called the *Barisan Nasional*.

The federal legislature is Parliament, which consists of

(i) the *Dewan Rakyat* (the lower house), elected on a universal franchise;
(ii) the *Dewan Negara* (the upper house), appointed by the Federal Government and the Legislative Assemblies; and
(iii) the *Yang di-Pertuan Agong*.

The consent of all three is required for a Bill to become law.

The executive is organised along Westminster lines, being headed by the Prime Minister and a Cabinet, which is collectively responsible to Parliament.

The constitution includes a Bill of Rights, which is intended to override legislation, and which includes the rights of liberty of the person, civil liberties, and freedom of religion. However, the executive is empowered to proclaim an emergency, during which the executive, or Parliament when it sits, may pass legislation which is contrary to the constitution. Even under ordinary circumstances, Parliament has special powers to enact legislation against subversion in a manner contrary to certain constitutional rights. The right to equal protection of the law is circumscribed by provision under the constitution for certain 'special privileges' for Malays and other native peoples of Malaysia (known as '*bumiputera*').

Most constitutional amendments require a two-thirds' majority in each of the two Houses of Parliament to become law. Some require the consent also of the Conference of Rulers, and some others require the consent of the Government of Sabah or Sarawak. So far the Government of the day has almost always commanded a two-thirds' majority, and no Bill to amend the constitution has been defeated; twenty-three such Bills have been passed, some of them very controversial.

## II. CONSTITUTIONAL AMENDMENTS

Amendments to the constitution are governed by Article 159, which provides four different methods of amendment,[3] according to the provision which is sought to be amended.

A. Amendments Requiring Special Majorities

Ordinarily the constitution can be amended simply by a Bill for that purpose which receives the support of the votes of not less than two-thirds of the total number of

---

[3] The four methods discussed below were recognised by Raja Azlan Shah FJ in the Federal Court in *Loh Kooi Choon v. Government of Malaysia* [1977] 2 *MLJ* 187, 189. See, further, Lee H.P., 'The Amendment Process under the Malaysian Constitution' (1974) *JMCL* 185; Lee, H.P., 'Constitutional Amendments in Malaysia: a Quick Conspectus' (1976) 18 *Mal LR* 59; Mohamed Salleh Abas, 'Amendment of the Malaysian Constitution' [1977] 2 *MLJ* xxxiv; Hickling, R.H., 'An Overview of Constitutional Changes in Malaysia: 1957-1977', Ch.1 of Tun Mohamed Suffian, Lee, H.P., & Trindade, F.A., *The Constitution of Malaysia: Its Development 1957-1977* (Kuala Lumpur, OUP, 1978); Lee, H.P., 'The Process of Constitutional Change', *ibid.*, Ch.15.

Members of each House of Parliament on its second and third readings.[4] This requirement attaches to Bills to amend most of the provisions of the constitution.[5] This can be called the ordinary method of amendment.

B. Amendments Not Requiring Special Majorities

Certain constitutional provisions can be amended by an ordinary law which does not require the special majorities specified by Article 159(3). These include some matters which are of considerable importance. For example, Parliament may, by an ordinary law,

(i) admit a State to the Federation, alter the boundaries of States, or change the federal capital;[6]
(ii) restrict freedom of movement within the Federation, and also freedom of speech, assembly and association;[7]
(iii) alter the composition of the *Dewan Negara* and the rules for appointment and election of its members;[8]
(iv) pass laws to correct disregard of the constitution or the State Constitution by a state;[9]
(v) alter the States' capitation grants;[10]
(vi) create inferior courts and regulate appeals from the High Court to the Federal Court;[11] and
(vii) legislate against subversion and pass emergency laws so as to override constitutional provisions.[12]

Any constitutional amendments which are incidental to, or consequential on the exercise of any of these powers, are also excepted from the special-majority requirements.[13]

There appears to be no obvious principle by which these provisions are distinguished from the other provisions of the constitution with regard to the method of their amendment.

---

[4] Art.159(3).
[5] i.e. all except those for which a special method is prescribed: see below. This applies also to Bills to amend legislation passed pursuant to Art. 10(4), which allows Parliament to make laws prohibiting the questioning of the so-called 'sensitive issues', for which see below.
[6] Arts. 2, 154, 158(4)(b).
[7] Art. 9(2),(3); Art. 10(2),(3).
[8] Art. 45(4); Sch.7.
[9] Art. 71(3).
[10] Art. 109(2),(4).
[11] Art. 121(1); Art. 128(3).
[12] Art. 149(1); Art. 150(5).
[13] Art. 158(4).

## C. Amendments Requiring the Consent of the Conference of Rulers

A number of constitutional provisions and ordinary laws cannot be amended without (in addition to any other requirements such as the special majorities) the consent of the Conference of Rulers. These provisions comprise the so-called 'sensitive issues';[14] in particular Article 37(4) provides that no law directly affecting the privileges, position, honours or dignities of the Rulers may be enacted without the consent of the Conference.

## D. Amendments Requiring the Consent of the Government of Sabah or Sarawak

Constitutional amendments affecting Sabah or Sarawak with regard to certain matters may not be made without the consent of the *Yang di-Pertua Negeri* (i.e. the Governor of the State, acting on advice). These matters include the equal treatment as regards their citizenship of persons born or resident in these States; the constitution and jurisdiction of the High Court of Sabah and Sarawak, and the appointment, removal and suspension of its judges; federal and state legislative powers and financial arrangements; religion, the national language, and the special treatment of natives of the State; and the rights and powers of the Government of the State regarding entry into and residence in the State.[15]

## III. IMPLIED AMENDMENT

Although it is not stipulated in the constitution, it would appear that a Bill which is inconsistent with the constitution, but which nonetheless receives the support of two-thirds of the members of the two Houses of Parliament on second and third readings, does not thereby amend the constitution. In other words, there is no doctrine of 'implied amendment'.[16] Article 159(3) refers to 'a Bill *for making any*

---

[14] Art. 158(5). These are the special privileges of *bumiputera* (i.e. Malays and natives of Sabah and Sarawak); citizenship; the monarchy; and the national language, which is *Bahasa Malaysia* or *Bahasa Melayu* (Malay).

[15] Art. 161E(2),(3). In addition constitutional amendments made in connection with the admission of Sabah and Sarawak to the Federation are not excepted from the special-majority requirements of Art. 158(3).

[16] Cf. *Kariapper v. Wijesinha* [1968] AC 917, PC. It is suggested that the doctrine of implied amendment has no application to Malaysia because of the different requirements in that case, which concerned the Constitution of Ceylon, for a constitutional amendment, and also because the wording of the amendment provision is different. However, the point is contended, but also disputed, in relation to the Singapore Constitution: Jayakumar, S., 'Legislation Comment: the Constitution (Amendment) Act 1979 (No 10)' (1979) 21 *Mal LR* 111; Andrew Phang Boon Leong, 'The Theory of Implied Amendment in Singapore - A Reappraisal' (1980) *Law Times* 26; Penna, L.R., 'Diceyan Perspective of Supremacy and the Constitution in Singapore' (1990) 32 *Mal LR* 207. The doctrine of implied amendment has not been litigated in Malaysia or Singapore. For discussion of parliamentary and constitutional supremacy in Singapore, see, further, Harding, A.J., 'Parliament and the Grundnorm in Singapore' (1983) 25 *Mal LR* 351.

*amendment* to the Constitution';[17] it would seem that a Bill enacted in the manner indicated above could not properly be regarded as a Bill for making an amendment. If so, a constitutional amendment Bill must show on its face an express intention to amend the constitution. If this were not so, the constitution could not properly be regarded as supreme law, and the effect of its provisions and of any legislation would be uncertain.

## IV. THE BASIC-STRUCTURE DOCTRINE

Another question, and one of great importance, is whether a constitutional amendment can be declared by the courts to be invalid on the grounds that it destroys the basic structure of the constitution. It could be argued that there are implied restrictions on the power of constitutional amendment. This proposition was upheld by the Supreme Court of India in the Fundamental Rights Case, *Kesavananda Bharati v. State of Kerala*, in 1972.[18] The same argument has been advanced in litigation in Malaysia, but so far has been frowned upon by the courts. The matter has an interesting history.

First, in *Government of the State of Kelantan v. Government of the Federation of Malaya & Tunku Abdul Rahman Putra Al-Haj* in 1963, in which the constitutionality of the Malaysia Act 1963, which created a new Federation, was challenged on the ground that the states of the Federation of Malaya had not been consulted, Thomson CJ left open in *obiter dicta* the possibility of Parliament doing something 'so fundamentally revolutionary as to require fulfilment of a condition which the constitution itself does not prescribe'.[19] In effect he was countenancing the possibility, without deciding, that there might be *implied* limitations on the power of constitutional amendment, and that these limitations might be procedural, resting on the mutual obligations of federated States.

Second, it was held in *Loh Kooi Choon v. Government of Malaysia*[20] that a constitutional amendment cannot be invalidated under Article 4(1) merely because it is inconsistent with the constitution, since the constitution, as the supreme law, cannot be inconsistent with itself: an amendment which complies with Article 159(3) becomes part of the constitution. In the course of this decision Raja Azlan Shah and Wan Suleiman FJJ doubted whether the doctrine of implied limitations on the amending power had any application to the Malaysian Constitution:

A short answer to the fallacy of this doctrine is that it concedes to the court a more potent power of constitutional amendment through judicial legislation than the organ formally and

---

[17] Emphasis added.
[18] [1973] SCR Supp.1; AIR 1973 SC 1461. This case and other Indian cases, together with the Malaysian and Singaporean cases, have been conveniently extracted and commented on in Kevin Tan Yew Lee and Thio Li-ann, *Constitutional Law and Malaysia & Singapore* (2nd ed., Singapore, Malayan Law Journal, 1997), 122-58.
[19] [1963] *MLJ* 355.
[20] [1977] 2 *MLJ* 187.

clearly chosen by the constitution for the exercise of the amending power.

In *Phang Chin Hock v. Public Prosecutor*[21] the Federal Court confronted the issue once more, holding, again *obiter*, that the doctrine of implied limitations had no application to Malaysia, but that the impugned provisions of the Emergency (Essential Powers) Act 1979 were not in any event contrary to the basic structure of the constitution. The reasoning advanced by Suffian LP rested on the following differences between the Malaysian and the Indian Constitutions:

(i) The Indian Constitution was drafted by a Constituent Assembly established for the purpose, whereas the Malaysian Constitution was the fruit of Anglo-Malayan efforts in which the Malayan Parliament played no part.
(ii) The Indian Constitution contains two elements, a Preamble and Directive Principles, which are not present in the Malaysian Constitution. These elements were heavily relied upon by the Supreme Court of India.

Since then the basic-structure doctrine has been rejected in two Singapore cases.[22]

Although it is possible to doubt the correctness of the view taken by the Malaysian and Singaporean courts on this matter, it seems unlikely that they will reverse their position. Nonetheless, it is interesting that the Malaysian courts have seen fit not to express their views in terms of *ratio decidendi*: if they did, in relation to a particular constitutional amendment, feel inclined to reverse their position, it would not be necessary for them to overrule any previous decision; and they have been keen to draw attention to the lack of application of the doctrine to the particular amendments in question in the cases. It could be that this question has been deliberately left open as a kind of insurance policy against extreme use of the amending power.

There are many arguments concerning the basic-structure doctrine, which reflect different views of constitutional law, and may indeed be more persuasive in one setting than in another. Tun Suffian's points concerning the application of the doctrine to Malaysia are not entirely convincing.[23] Surely after forty years of independence and numerous amendments, Malaysian citizens cannot regard the constitution as a foreign imposition? It has been expressly and impliedly accepted

---

[21] [1980] 1 *MLJ* 70. To similar effect is the decision in *Mark Koding v. Public Prosecutor* [1982] 2 *MLJ* 120, in which a Federal Court bench of five judges again deemed it unnecessary to consider whether Parliament had the power to amend the Constitution in such a way as to destroy the basic structure of the Constitution, the amendment concerned being the restriction on freedom of speech in Parliament under Art. 63.

[22] *Teo Soh Lung v. Minister of Home Affairs* [1989] 2 *MLJ* 449; *Vincent Cheng v. Minister for Home Affairs* [1990] 1 *MLJ* 449. Again it was held that the amendments in question, restricting the scope of judicial review of preventive-detention orders, did not in any event destroy the basic structure of the constitution.

[23] See Harding, A.J., 'The Death of a Doctrine? *Phang Chin Hock v. Public Prosecutor*' (1979) 21 *Mal LR* 365.

by the populace as well as by politicians, lawyers and judges, and was accepted even in 1957 by every legislative forum and all the traditional Rulers on behalf of their States.

A more general objection to the basic-structure doctrine is that it is impossible to decide which features of the constitution are basic. However, that task has already been performed in relation to the Malaysian Constitution by Raja Azlan Shah FJ, rejecting the doctrine, in *Loh Kooi Choon*, when he said:

> The constitution is not a mere collection of platitudes. It is the supreme law of the land embodying three basic concepts. One of them is that the individual has certain fundamental rights upon which not even the power of the State may encroach. The second is the distribution of sovereign power between the States and the Federation, that the thirteen States shall exercise sovereign power in local matters and the nation in matters affecting the country at large. The third is that no single man or body shall exercise complete sovereign power, but that it shall be distributed among the Executive, Legislative and Judicial branches of government, compendiously expressed in modern terms that we are a government of laws not of men.[23]

Moreover, principles apart, there is utility in preserving the most fundamental features of the constitution from amendment when amendment has become such a frequent occurrence, and there is in fact a real danger that the basic structure of the constitution may be amended out of existence. Indeed it might be argued persuasively that this has already occurred, and precisely because there is no restriction on the power of constitutional amendment. The basic-structure doctrine need not prevent desirable amendments (indeed a complex document like the Malaysian Constitution could not stand for ever written in stone), but would subject amendments to some form of scrutiny, and preserve the essence of constitutional government. This may occasionally hinder some of the kind of legislation which the Government considers convenient, but would reassure the citizenry, not to mention State governments, that some important things will not change. This is more persuasive as successive amendments appear to interfere with ever more basic features of the constitution, such as the separation of powers, fundamental rights, and states' rights.

The main objections to the doctrine are that it is not explicit in the constitution, and that it would involve the judiciary in political controversy. The former point applies to many of the most important constitutional doctrines which have been developed. The latter point is probably true, but it is worth noting that the judiciary has not in fact avoided political controversy in rejecting the doctrine, or indeed at all: constitutional decisions are always in some sense politically controversial.

---

[23] [1977] 2 *MLJ* 188.

## V. CONSTITUTIONAL SUPREMACY AND THE CONTROLLED CONSTITUTION

Whatever the position with regard to the basic-structure doctrine, in view of the fact that constitutional amendments generally have different requirements from those which apply to ordinary laws, the Malaysian Constitution can be called 'controlled' as opposed to 'uncontrolled'. In terms of the Privy Council's decision in *McCawley v. The King*,[24] this means that the constitution cannot be amended by legislation which is merely inconsistent with it, because the constitution is a higher form of law than ordinary statutes which can be amended in such fashion: the constitution-makers 'have created obstacles ... in the path of those who would lay rash hands upon the ark of the Constitution.'[25]

It is sometimes argued that this apparently fundamental distinction is of little relevance in Malaysia because the powers of Parliament, though theoretically limited by the constitution, are in practice virtually unlimited. This is due to two causes.

First, the Alliance/Barisan Nasional Government, in power ever since *Merdeka*, has retained its two-thirds' parliamentary majority virtually throughout its tenure, and has therefore been able to secure amendments to the constitution at will. Since most fundamental or controversial legislation has required constitutional amendment, the constitution has not proved to be a significant restriction on the exercise of legislative power.

Second, the constitution provides for emergency powers to be exercised by the Government pursuant to an emergency proclamation, and in fact Malaysia has been technically under emergency law ever since 1964.[26] This has the consequence that whatever cannot be achieved through the exercise of ordinary legislative and executive powers can usually be achieved through the exercise of emergency powers. In practice the emergency powers which have been assumed by the executive and the legislature have been extremely wide. The result, again, is that the constitution scarcely imposes any limits on the executive or the legislature.

While these facts are both true and indeed destructive of the restraints which the constitution was supposed to place on the executive and the legislature, the distinction between constitutional supremacy and parliamentary supremacy is still a valid and important one, and has a number of consequences.

First, it should be noted that the facts outlined above are purely contingent ones, albeit matters of long practice. Were the Barisan Nasional to lose its parliamentary two-thirds' majority, the significance of the distinction between

---

[24] [1920] AC 691; the distinction was applied, but *McCawley* distinguished, in *Bribery Commissioner v. Ranasinghe* [1965] AC 172, 196.
[25] Ibid, per Lord Birkenhead at 703. The distinction does not depend on whether the constitution is written or unwritten, as a written constitution can still be controlled.
[26] See Harding, above n.1, Ch.9.

constitutional and parliamentary supremacy would immediately become much greater than it is at present. If the emergency proclamation were revoked, which would repeal all emergency legislation at a stroke, then the distinction would become even more significant.

Second, to have a written constitution which is the supreme law of the land has important effects on the nature of political discourse. Since many controversial matters have a specifically constitutional, as opposed to merely a political, dimension, the constitution is constantly being brought before the public mind, and politicians must constantly couch their arguments in terms of notions such as constitutionality, fundamental liberties, states' rights, the rule of law, and the separation of powers. To amend the constitution is simply not the same thing, *legally or politically*, as enacting ordinary legislation. The result in terms of education of the public in constitutional matters has been considerable; but it is doubtful if this would have been so if the constitution merely embodied parliamentary supremacy.

Third, it would be wrong to ignore the practical and legal effects of constitutional supremacy. Some statutes have in fact been declared unconstitutional. Even cases where legislation has been upheld will have had an effect in terms of alerting the relevant authorities to the possibility of legislation being unconstitutional. There have undoubtedly been legislative proposals which have never been translated into bills or not introduced in Parliament because they would be met with constitutional litigation if they were. Attorneys-general and state legal advisers throughout the Federation must and do have regard to fundamental rights and the division of legislative powers between the States and the Federation when they draft statutes. In addition, constitutional supremacy probably has the effect, as explained above, of requiring a constitutional amendment Bill to show an express intention of amending the constitution.

Fourth, as a matter of logic, legal supremacy or sovereignty must not be confused with political supremacy or sovereignty. It is perfectly possible for political sovereignty and legal sovereignty to lie in different hands.

Constitutional supremacy does have some practical effects, direct as well as indirect. The constitution clearly does embody constitutional rather than parliamentary supremacy, but it must be conceded that the practical as opposed to jurisprudential significance of this distinction is of limited importance in the Malaysian polity at the present time.

## VI. EXTENT OF USE OF THE AMENDING POWER

The power to amend the constitution has been extensively used since the Federal Constitution came into force in 1957. Since then there have been to date twenty-three Constitution (Amendment) Acts, a strike-rate of more than one every two years, effecting more separate constitutional amendments than there are provisions of the constitution, which contains 225 Articles, forty-two of which were enacted by constitutional amendment.[27]

The amendments have been extensive not only in number, but in their effects. They have affected almoast every aspect of government. To take a few examples, constitutional amendments have affected the following:

(i) The structure of the Federation itself, via the admission of Sabah, Sarawak and Singapore in 1963; the expulsion of Singapore in 1965; federal finance; and dismissal of the Chief Minister of a state.
(ii) The monarchy, via removal of the immunity from suit of Rulers; the royal assent; acting on advice; and the powers of the Conference of Rulers.
(iii) Controls over exercise of emergency powers.[28]
(iv) Fundamental rights, in particular liberty of the person, freedom of speech, assembly and association, and equality before the law.
(vi) The exercise of legislative powers, elections, and the constitution and privileges of Parliament.
(vii) The judicial power and the jurisdiction of the superior courts, and reversal of the effect of judicial decisions.
(viii) The constitutional amendment process itself.

The most notable series of amendments (known as the '*rukunegara*' (national ideology) amendments) occurred in 1971, when Article 153, which dealt with the special privileges of Malays, was extended from Malays to natives of Sabah and Sarawak, and the principle of special privilege was applied to admission to tertiary educational institutions.[29] Also under the *rukunegara* amendments, these provisions, and others concerning the national language, citizenship and the monarchy (the so-called 'sensitive issues'), were given special entrenchment, requiring the consent of the Conference of Rulers, as well as the required two-thirds' parliamentary majority, before they could be amended or repealed.[30] Questioning of special privileges and other sensitive issues came to constitute the offence of sedition, and Parliament was given power to restrict freedom of speech accordingly. It became an offence to question policy on these issues (as opposed to implementation thereof) even on the floor of Parliament or a State Legislative Assembly.

Many amendments have been passed with great rapidity; an extreme case was the Constitution and Malaysia (Singapore Amendment) Act 1965, by which Singapore was expelled from the Federation. This important constitutional amendment was passed by both Houses in the alarmingly short period of three hours, MPs having sighted the Bill only the same day. MPs from Sabah and

---

[27] I have not been able to count the precise number of separate amendments, which I believe to be nearly three hundred.
[28] See below.
[29] Constitution (Amendment) Act 1971 (A30); Art. 153(8A).
[30] Art. 39.

Sarawak, and even the Governments of those States, were not consulted in spite of their special interest in the matter, and even the Cabinet did not discuss it. Similarly, the Constitution of Sarawak was *amended temporarily* by an Emergency Act in 1966, Sarawak MPs having been given virtually no notice of the Bill, which had the effect of creating a power for the Governor to dismiss the Chief Minister.

That the constitution could be amended so quickly and with so little notice to MPs gave rise to concern, and in 1966 an opposition MP introduced a private member's Bill to amend the constitution so as to require a lapse of at least one month between the First and Second Readings of a Bill to amend the constitution. In view of the Government's apparently permanent two-thirds majority, it is most unfortunate that the Bill failed, as it would have provided the minimal protection which the constitution surely deserves.

As an indication of the dominance of the executive in matters of constitutional amendment, it is interesting to note that, following a political crisis in UMNO in 1988/9, the Government was able to secure, within a period of only six and a half months, identical constitutional amendments in nine of the thirteen states, prohibiting resigning Assemblymen from standing again for election for five years from the date of resignation. The purpose of these amendments, which were similar to an amendment to the Federal Constitution itself in 1990,[31] was to prevent floor-crossing MPs from provoking by-elections by resigning their seats.

## VII. EMERGENCY POWERS

The effect of constitutional amendments on emergency powers is disturbing. Article 150(1) confers on the Government broad powers to introduce emergency rule:

If the *Yang di-Pertuan Agong* is satisfied that a grave emergency exists whereby the security, or the economic life, or public order in the Federation or any part thereof is threatened, he may issue a Proclamation of Emergency making therein a declaration to that effect.

Under Article 150(2), as amended in 1981, an emergency proclamation may be issued before the actual occurrence of threatened events, by way of preventive action, if the *Yang di-Pertuan Agong* is satisfied that there is imminent danger of its occurrence.[32] Article 150(2A), also introduced in 1981, allows the issuing of proclamations on different grounds or in different circumstances, regardless of the existence of other proclamations; thus two or more emergency proclamations may validly overlap, chronologically or even geographically, and the latter does not

---

[31] Art. 48(6), inserted by the Constitution (Amendment) Act 1990 (A767).
[32] Presumably this would occur when the Government had credible intelligence reports indicating some impending security threat.

impliedly revoke the earlier.[33]

In *Stephen Kalong Ningkan v. Government of Malaysia* the Privy Council, considering the meaning of 'emergency' in Article 150(1), stressed the breadth of the concept:

> It is not confined to unlawful use or threat of force in any of its manifestations ... the natural meaning of the word itself is capable of covering a very wide range of situations and occurrences, including such diverse elements as wars, famines, earthquakes, floods, epidemics and the collapse of civil government.[34]

However, it must be grave and 'such as to threaten the security or economic life of the Federation or any part of it'.[35]

Thus by constitutional amendment and by judicial interpretation the power to proclaim an emergency has been made breathtakingly wide, even though the original intention of the provisions was to limit and define the circumstances in which emergency powers could be invoked.

In addition, there is not even any obligation on the executive to summon Parliament following an emergency proclamation; before the 1981 amendments Parliament had to be called as soon as was practicable, although this requirement did not prevent executive rule without Parliament for a period of twenty-two months in 1969-71. As the constitution now stands, even this is not a requirement: in other words the executive can suspend the operation of Parliament indefinitely. This is not a mere theoretical possibility when one considers the reluctance on the part of the executive to revoke emergency proclamations, and the fact that elections stir up emotions which could well be used as a justification for proclaiming an emergency.

## VIII. CONCLUSIONS

The period since 1957 has seen the gradual erosion of the original constitutional principles by the enactment of frequent constitutional amendments, each of which has moved Malaysia a step away from the original ideal. This can be seen, and is often presented, as a cost paid for Malaysia's social and economic achievements. Whether this is so is debatable but hardly to the point. The changes in question have been very far-reaching and required careful consideration. This has sometimes

---

[33] Indeed a 1966 emergency relating to Sarawak overlapped with a 1964 federal emergency; and a 1977 emergency relating to Kelantan overlapped with the 1969 federal emergency. For discussion of the effect of a later proclamation on an earlier, see Sheridan, L.A. & Groves, H.E., *The Constitution of Malaysia* (4th ed, Singapore, Malayan Law Journal, 1987), 387-91. In *Johnson Tan Heng Seng v. Public Prosecutor* [1977] 2 *MLJ* 66, it had been held that a proclamation of emergency could not lapse by effluxion of time; see also *Mark Koding v. Public Prosecutor* [1982] 2 *MLJ* 120, and contrast *Teh Cheng Poh v. Public Prosecutor* [1980] AC 45, [1979] 2 WLR 623, [1979] 1 *MLJ* 50, PC.
[34] [1968] 2 MLJ 238.
[35] Art. 150(1).

been achieved through the political bargaining process between the ruling parties, but the constitution itself has not succeeded in ensuring that care has been taken, principally because the amendment process, designed to ensure broad consensus before important constitutional changes took place, has been entirely taken over by the executive. It is no justification for this that the electorate has returned the same coalition to power with a large majority, because the electoral process itself has, by progressive constitutional amendments, ensured that the Government's majority far exceeds the proportion of votes it has won, principally by weighting the system in favour of rural areas.[36]

It is hard to imagine how the situation could be rectified short of a complete constitutional rethink, which presently is demanded only by the opposition parties, which have lost ground with each amendment. Even were they to increase their representation or take over the reins of government, it is unlikely they would have much interest in making the constitutional amendment process more difficult for themselves: it is often forgotten that the amendment process can be used to bolster constitutional government, not just to destroy it.

No, the fault lies with the fathers of the constitution, who did not think through the consequences of the amendment process. More attention should have been given to the procedure and the majorities required. The Reid Commission were well aware that the incumbent parties had an overwhelming majority which was likely to continue. They could not have assumed that the parliamentary process would work roughly as in India, Britain or Australia. There was no sense in their Report[37] that even an executive enjoying a huge majority should have restrictions on its power of constitutional amendment. And it is quite clear from the Malaysian experience that the nature of amendment procedure *does matter in practice*: the failure to place any restriction (not even the requirement of reasonableness, as in India) on the amendment of Article 10, which deals with freedom of speech, assembly and association, and the failure to place any real restriction on amendment of the liberty of the person, have both resulted in an exceptional degree of erosion of those rights compared with other rights, principles and institutions which were better protected.

What would have worked? What would work now given a change in the constitutional environment?

I would suggest that the amendment process is so fundamental that it should be regarded as the most important aspect of the constitution, and that it should elaborate with care different methods of amendment for different provisions. Some provisions (for example judicial independence) are so fundamentally part of the basic structure that they should be beyond change without invoking the very process which drafted the constitution itself; accordingly the judiciary should have jurisdiction to pronounce on whether the basic structure has been interfered with;

---

[36] Sch.12, para.2.
[37] *Federation of Malaya Constitutional Commission, 1956-7 Report* (Kuala Lumpur, Government Printer, 1957).

if it has, the amendment should only be effected by convening a broad-based constituent assembly. Other provisions should require a referendum. Others should require special majorities which are onerous enough to require a broad consensus between, rather than within, political parties. Other less controversial provisions should be capable of being amended by an ordinary law.

It is another question how one would reach such a position. It would, quite clearly, have to form part of a broader constitutional resettlement. In the meantime the Malaysian experience is a salutary reminder for those who seek constitutional stability in the principle of special majorities.

Chapter Thirteen

# WHY THE JUDICIAL ANNULMENT OF THE CONSTITUTION OF 1999 IS IMPERATIVE FOR THE SURVIVAL OF NIGERIA'S DEMOCRACY

Tunde I. Ogowewo [*]

*To uphold the 1999 document as our constitution and thereby accept the disappearance of the 1979 Constitution is to expose the 1999 Constitution to the same fate that has befallen the 1979 Constitution; but to uphold the 1979 Constitution is to announce to all future coup plotters that it is not within their power to erase their crime against the people of Nigeria by white-washing it with a document that they have written and imposed on us.*[1]

## I. INTRODUCTION

That the Federal Republic of Nigeria is today being governed in accordance with a constitution[2] that is illegitimate is a fact that admits of very little doubt.[3] Many have recognised the constitution's lack of moral authority.[4] Yet two things have

---

[*] Lecturer, School of Law, King's College London, University of London. I wish to record my gratitude to Professor Nelson Enonchong, Dr Fidelis Oditah, John Ofutu and Dr Peter Oliver for the very helpful discussions I had with them in the course of preparing this chapter. I, however, bear all responsibility for whatever errors are contained in the chapter. An earlier version of this chapter was published in the Journal of African Law, Volume 44, Number 2, 2000. The editor is grateful to Oxford University Press for permission to republish this chapter.
[1] T.I. Ogowewo, 'Back to the 1979 Constitution', *The Guardian*, 23 December 1999.
[2] The Constitution of the Federal Republic of Nigeria, 1999. It came into force with effect from 29 May 1999. For a short commentary on its provisions, see 'A New Constitution for Nigeria' (2000) 44 J.A.L. 129.
[3] According to Professor Nwabueze, '[t]he legitimacy of a constitution is concerned with how to make it command the loyalty, obedience and confidence of the people.' See B.O. Nwabueze, *The Presidential Constitution of Nigeria* (1982) 4.
[4] See S.A. Benjamin, '1999 Constitution: Implications for Political Structure' in *Issues in the Review of the 1999 Constitution of the Federal Republic of Nigeria* (Ed. O. Ajakaiye and S.A. Benjamin) (Nigerian Institute of Social and Economic Research (NISER) 1999), p.23. A non-governmental organisation (the Campaign for Democracy) in a statement signed by its chairman, Dr. Beko Ransome-Kuti, said: 'We wish to point out that it is a fraudulent document. At no time did we, the peoples of different nationalities in the geographical space called Nigeria, freely meet to discuss the formation of Nigeria and the conditions under which the people of different nationalities will associate.' See S. Bakoji, 'Whither the 1999 Constitution?', *PostExpress*, 23 May 1999.

escaped notice. First, that in the conception and promulgation of the 1999 Constitution a great deceit was practised on the Nigerian people by the departing provisional ruling council (PRC) of the military government. Second, that the 1999 Constitution is, in fact, void. The first point has never been recognised and many may instinctively confuse it with the separate issue of the constitution's lack of legitimacy. Though the two issues are no doubt closely related they are different. One aim of this chapter is to expose this deceit. The second point that has escaped notice will occasion great surprise because even those that attest to the constitution's illegitimacy readily concede its legality. This chapter aims to show that this is a concession too far. It provides a novel legal theory to establish conclusively that this constitution is a nullity. It shifts the focus from the constitution's obvious lack of moral authority (the legitimacy question) to the question of the constitution's legal validity. In so doing, the chapter provides the courts with the legal grounds for the annulment of this constitution. It also formulates two rules for dealing with the consequential issues that would ensue following the constitution's annulment.

The call for the judicial rejection of this constitution is not academic, as many may immediately assume. It is a matter that goes to the very survival of Nigeria's democracy. This is because the annulment will pave the way for the prosecution of those that subverted Nigeria's democracy on 31 December 1983. Prosecuting retired coup plotters, rather than rewarding them, as is presently the case, will have the effect of altering the risk-benefit calculus of a future coup plotter. Presently, would-be coup plotters know that they face only one risk when planning a coup: the risk of failure. Where this risk is low[5] and the gains of success are high, such persons can be expected to attempt a coup. If history is a guide, the usurpers can expect to remain in power for a long time and retire with stupendous ill-gotten wealth.[6] Nigerian law, in fact, now rewards usurpers. This is because a few days before the military relinquished power to the civilians on 29 May 1999, a decree was promulgated that goes to underscore the magnitude of the unabashed greed and vanity of the military class that have ruled Nigeria for 30 years. The Remuneration of Former Presidents and Heads of State (and other Ancillary Matters) Decree[7] lavishes all manner of benefits on former Heads of State,[8] Vice Presidents, Chiefs of General Staff and their respective families. For instance, the decree provides that

---

[5] A study of coup plotting in Nigeria would indicate that the risk of failure is very low or even non-existent where the coup against the civilian government is planned by the top brass of the military and at a time when there is public disaffection for the government in power.

[6] Recent press reports indicate that General Abacha and his family looted up to US$8 billion from Nigeria. See 'Another $1.25b Abacha loot frozen in Luxembourg' in www.NigeriaNews.net, 10 May 2000.

[7] Decree No. 32 of 1999. This decree was signed 19 days before the military handed over the government to the civilians.

[8] The term is defined in s. 1(a) as 'Presidents' and 'Heads of State'. The latter is the term by which non-democratic leaders are referred to, although one such military leader (General Babangida) styled himself 'President'. A reading of the decree leaves one in no doubt that the decree contemplates civilian Presidents and military Heads of State (and their deputies, such as Vice Presidents (civilian) and Chiefs of General Staff (military): see s 1(b)).

a retired military leader shall be entitled to the sum of 350,000 naira per month,[9] the services of a personal officer, not below the rank of a chief administrative officer,[10] a personal secretary,[11] three vehicles that are liable to be replaced every four years,[12] the services of chauffeurs,[13] free medical treatment within and outside Nigeria for himself and members of his family,[14] 30 days annual State funded vacation within and outside Nigeria,[15] a well furnished and equipped office, and a well furnished five bedroomed house, both in any location of choice in Nigeria.[16] The munificence of the State continues even after the Head of State expires. When deceased, the spouse and children shall be entitled to the payment of 1 million naira per annum – however, if *she* (the decree assumes that the spouse will always be female) remarries then this entitlement is lost![17] Furthermore, the national flag is to fly at half-mast for a period of three days as a sign of national mourning at all buildings, ground and naval vessels of the Federal Government and at all Nigerian embassies abroad.[18]

Clearly, successful coup plotting pays handsomely in Nigeria.[19] The message now being sent to those in the military establishment is that future coup plotters can violate the supremacy clause[20] of the constitution, rule by decree, and after having looted the treasury and violated the human rights of the citizenry, they may choose to relinquish power when they want and on their own terms – writing a new constitution for the country again – without the fear of punishment. If the cycle of coups is not to be endless the vanguards of Nigerian civil society must address this issue proactively. The time to act is not when the horse has bolted from the stable. To be sure, the prospect of international condemnation will not deter coups, as the

---

[9] S. 1(a)(i). Pursuant to s. 3 this amount shall be subject to review whenever there is an increase in the salary of the serving Head of State.
[10] S.1(1), Part 1 of the Schedule to the Decree.
[11] S.1(2), *ibid.*
[12] S. 3(1), *ibid.*
[13] S. 3(2), *ibid.*
[14] S. 5(1-2), *ibid.*
[15] S.5(3), *ibid.*
[16] Ss. 6 - 7, *ibid.*
[17] S. 2(1)(a) and s.2(3).
[18] S. 10, *ibid.* The decree goes into great detail in outlining the benefits of an ex-military leader. For instance, he is to have free postal privileges within and outside Nigeria (s. 8) and one direct telephone line at the Federal Government's expense (s. 9). He is (with his spouse) to take third position in the order of precedence after the serving President and Vice President at public functions and is entitled to a diplomatic passport for life and to protocol within and outside Nigeria. See s.4, Part 1 of the Schedule to the Decree.
[19] There is no reason to think that Generals Buhari, Babangida, the Abacha family and General Abubakar are not already claiming these entitlements.
[20] The supremacy clause (s.1) of the Constitution of 1999, replicates the wording of the supremacy clause (s.1) of the Constitution of 1979. S.1(1) provides: 'This Constitution is supreme and its provisions shall have binding force on all authorities and persons throughout the Federal Republic of Nigeria'. S.1(2) provides: 'The Federal Republic of Nigeria shall not be governed, nor shall any person or group of persons take control of the government of Nigeria or any part thereof, except in accordance with the provisions of this Constitution'. S.1(3) provides: 'If any other law is inconsistent with the provisions of this Constitution, this Constitution shall prevail, and that other law shall to the extent of the inconsistency be void'.

recent coups in Pakistan, Côte d'Ivoire and Fiji have demonstrated.[21] Furthermore, it would not be in alignment with the interests of foreign governments to impose an embargo on the purchase of Nigeria's oil. Other sanctions – such as the withdrawal of aid – have no real deterrent value. Nigeria's cash flows from its oil exports insulate it from such pressures.

This chapter accordingly argues that it is now within the power of any democratic government in Nigeria and the vanguards of civil society to alter the risk-benefit calculus of coup plotters by introducing – what should always be in the calculus – the risk that even when the successful coup plotters depart the scene, they will be called to account for their crimes. Since such a prosecution can only succeed if the present constitution, which contains an immunity clause,[22] is annulled, this chapter adduces the legal basis for its judicial annulment.[23] For a proper understanding of the thesis presented in this chapter, it is necessary briefly to rehearse Nigeria's constitutional history[24] and to highlight certain features of constitution-making in Nigeria that have served to undermine all of Nigeria's post-independence constitutions. The aim is not to conduct an analysis of the relative merits of each constitution's contents,[25] rather it is to consider the logically prior issue of how each constitution was made and the flaws that characterised the process. Rarely is this issue considered, but a moment's reflection will show that it is this issue that is, in fact, determinative of a host of other issues, such as the constitution's contents.[26]

---

[21] Another dimension of these coups is that they serve to encourage coups elsewhere. When would-be military usurpers observe that the international community has failed to take concrete steps to reverse a coup elsewhere, they are encouraged to proceed with their usurpation.

[22] S. 6(6)(d) of the Constitution of 1999 excludes the exercise of judicial powers 'from any action or proceedings relating to any existing law made on or after 15th January, 1966 for determining any issue or question as to the competence of any authority or person to make any such law'. By excluding the judicial powers of the courts from such questions, the military aimed to confer immunity on all usurpers from 15 January 1966 (the date of the first coup) to when the constitution came into force.

[23] An inter-party constitutional reform group has been constituted to identify areas where constitutional amendments are necessary. This is not, however, the appropriate solution, since a void constitution cannot be amended. Besides, it is doubtful that this would result in the repeal of the immunity clause in s.6(6)(d). Indeed, it has been announced by the chairman of the National Assembly Committee on the Review of the 1999 Constitution that ex-military leaders will be involved in the fashioning of a new constitution. See, 'Ex-Leaders to be part of Constitution Review', *The Guardian*, 31 May 2000.

[24] See, O. I. Odumosu, *The Nigerian Constitution: History and Development* (1963), T.O. Elias, *Nigeria: The Development of its Laws and Constitution* (1967), J.O. Akande, *The Constitution of the Federal Republic of Nigeria 1979 – with annotations* (1982), B.O. Nwabueze, *The Presidential Constitution of Nigeria* (1982), B.O. Nwabueze, *A Constitutional History of Nigeria* (1982), H. Chand, *Nigerian constitutional law* (1982), B.O. Nwabueze, *Federalism in Nigeria Under the Presidential Constitution* (1983), D.O. Aihie, *Selected Essays on Nigerian Constitutional Laws* (1985), B.O. Nwabueze, *Nigeria's Presidential Constitution: The Second Experiment in Constitutional Democracy* (1985), and U. Udoma, *History and the Law of the Constitution of Nigeria* (1994).

[25] Such as the division of powers between the federal and State governments and the question of revenue allocation.

[26] See, V.R. Mottoh-Migan, *Constitution Making in Post-Independence Nigeria: A Critique* (1994) and T. Mamman, *The Law and Politics of Constitution-Making in Nigeria, 1862 – 1989: Issues, Interests and Compromises* (1998).

## II. A TRADITION OF CONSTITUTIONAL ILLEGITIMACY

On 29 July 1960 the Parliament of the United Kingdom passed the Nigeria Independence Act pursuant to which Nigeria gained fully responsible status within the Commonwealth with effect from 1 October 1960.[27] This was the culmination of the various constitutional conferences which had been held and the resolution passed by the Nigerian Parliament on 16 January 1960 demanding independence for the whole country.[28] The Constitution of 1960, bequeathed by the imperial government, like the pre-independence constitutions,[29] could not, however, be described as an act of the people, in the sense of being made by them either directly in a referendum or through a constituent assembly of elected representatives.[30] The imperial government had continued with the tradition of constitutional illegitimacy which it had cultivated in Nigeria ever since it introduced the Lugard Constitution of 1914.[31] Professor Nwabueze has pointed out that '[t]he independence constitution was the product of a final exercise of the [suzerain] power by the departing colonial

---

[27] Nigeria Independence Act, 1960, (8 & 9 Eliz. 2, c. 55).
[28] The last one was the May 1960 constitutional conference.
[29] The Lugard Constitution (1914–1922), The Clifford Constitution (1922 – 1946), the Richards Constitution (1946-1950), the Macpherson Constitution (1951-1954), and the Lyttleton Constitution (1954-1960). The Clifford Constitution replaced the Legislative Council for the Colony and the Nigerian Council. The new Legislative Council was adjudged a success because it introduced the elective principle. See T.O. Elias, *Nigeria: The Development of its Laws and Constitution* (1967) 26-27. The Clifford Constitution, however, ran into problems because it excluded Nigerians from membership of the Executive Council and it had a system of nominated members (a feature still prevalent in modern constitution making in Nigeria). To correct these problems, the Richards Constitution was introduced. According to Professor Elias (at p.37): '[I]t did not, however, go far enough, at least in Nigerian eyes. In any case, it had been conceived by Governor Bourdillon and designed by Governor Richards without full consultation with the people, and it was not generally well received on that score'. The Macpherson Constitution was the result of more consultation with the people and in this sense it was an advance on the previous constitutions. Its provisions reflected this. For instance, if a Regional law was inconsistent with a federal law with respect to the same subject matter, the Regional law prevailed over the federal law if the latter was enacted before the former. This contrasts very much with the position under recent constitutions in which the federal government has enormous powers to such an extent that it derogates from the principle of federalism. The point being made is that the process by which a constitution is fashioned is determinative of the contents of the constitution. Unfortunately, in 1954 when a new constitution was fashioned, the Imperial government abandoned the practice (seen in 1951) of consulting at grass roots level. It is, therefore, hardly surprising that in the fashioning of Nigeria's subsequent constitutions, the appropriate process by which the constitution ought to have been fashioned has not been followed. There is thus a tradition of constitutional illegitimacy.
[30] See B.O. Nwabueze, *The Presidential Constitution of Nigeria* (1982), 6. The last constitutional conference was described by Professor Odumosu thus: 'In May 1960 there was a small Conference in London which was concerned with outstanding matters in connection with Nigeria's approaching independence. *Only governments* (italics supplied) were represented at the Conference which had before it a draft of the Independence Constitution for Nigeria.' See, O.I. Odumosu, *The Nigerian Constitution: History and Development* (1963) 132.
[31] This can be contrasted with the case of India, where the colonial government's plans on constitutional reform were rejected because it did not express the will of the people of India. Instead, a constituent assembly, which derived its power and authority from the Indian people, was what provided the country with an 'Indian-made' Constitution. See G. Austin, *The Indian Constitution: Cornerstones of a Nation* (1966) pp. 1-8.

authority".[32] This certainly placed a question mark on its legitimacy. Nor was the republican Constitution of 1963 free of this defect, either. Again, according to Professor Nwabueze:[33]

> The adoption of a republican Constitution in 1963 was decided upon entirely by the prime minister and the regional premiers who, meeting for just one day, agreed among themselves that a republican constitution should reproduce the 1960 imperial Constitution with such amendments as would conform it to a republican status.

This legitimacy problem undermined the republican constitution in at least three ways. First, politicians had no great inhibition in disregarding its terms.[34] As has been stated elsewhere, 'a legislative assembly which enacted a constitution is not likely to treat its own creation as being above it'.[35] Second, the idea that the constitution could be violated with little or no consequence was easily planted in the psyche of the people, since 'the idea of a constituion enacted by the legislative assembly being supreme over its creator is hardly intelligible [to the people]'.[36] Finally, it removed any inhibition usurpers may have had in seizing control of the State.[37] For on 15 January 1966, there was a military coup.[38] A decree that purportedly suspended parts of this constitution was accordingly promulgated.[39] Nigeria was not to have a democratic government until 13 years later.

When departing on 1 October 1, 1979 the military relinquished power to the civilians and promulgated a new constitution.[40] Unlike the 1960 and 1963 Constitutions, the Constitution of 1979 was the product of a constituent assembly of elected citizens acting as representatives of the people. A draft constitution bill

---

[32] *Ibid*, 6. This point is recognised by other commentators. See V.R. Mottoh-Migan, *Constitution Making in Post-Independence Nigeria: A Critique* (1994) 65.
[33] *Ibid*.
[34] One way in which the constitution was undermined and which partly led to the coup of 1966 was the unprecedented rigging in the Western Region in October 1965.
[35] B.O. Nwabueze, *The Presidential Constitution of Nigeria* (1982), 6.
[36] *Ibid*.
[37] Commentators have recognised that the failure of the first republic was partly attributable to the constitution. See D.I.O. Eweluka, 'Constitutional Aspects of the Military Take-over in Nigeria' (1967) 2 *Nigerian Law Journal* (No.1) 1, 2. This point has greater relevance presently because the Constitution of 1999 lacks legitimacy, having been introduced by the previous military government. The military now face no serious inhibition in violating it.
[38] For a graphic account, see O. Achike, *Military Law and Military Rule in Nigeria* (1978), 99-100.
[39] The Constitution (Suspension and Modification) Decree No.1 of 1966. For commentary on the legal changes that resulted from the coup, see E.A. Keay, 'Legal and Constitutional Changes in Nigeria Under the Military Government [1966] 10 J.A.L. 92 and F.R.A. Williams, 'Legal Development in Nigeria, 1957-67: A Practising Lawyer's View' [1967] 11 J.A.L. 77. Interestingly, in March 1966 General Ironsi (the Head of State after the coup) set up a Constitutional Review Study group to 'identify ... the constitutional problems in the context of one Nigeria'. When inaugurating the committee, he stated that the form of government to be set up would only be established after consultation with the people to be followed by a referendum. See U. Udoma, *History and the Law of the Constitution of Nigeria*, (1994) 232-233. The idea of promulgating a constitution after a referendum, so as to give the constitution legitimacy, has never been pursued.
[40] Constitution of the Federal Republic of Nigeria (Enactment) Decree 1979, Cap 62, Laws of the Federation of Nigeria, 1990.

had been presented to this assembly by the constitution drafting committee, a committee of 49 independent people chosen for their specialist knowledge or background. In fashioning the draft constitution, the committee had considered memoranda from the general public in response to its invitation.[41] It was this bill which later became the constitution. The constituent assembly was not a mere deliberative body, since it had the power to take decisions on the form and content of the constitution.[42] It was composed of 230 members, of whom 20 were appointed by the government and seven were the chairman of the constitution drafting committee and the chairpersons of its sub-committees. The remaining 203 members were elected by the local councils acting as electoral colleges. Viewed from this perspective, the Constitution of 1979 can be described as Nigeria's first (and only) constitution that was an act of the people.[43] This is not to suggest, however, that the making of the constitution was beyond reproach.[44] First, as noted above, the military government appointed some members of the constituent assembly. This imperfection should not, however, be overstated, since the appointees were a tiny minority. Such a minority could in no way have overridden the views of the elected members. The second defect was that the military government made a number of substantive amendments to the draft constitution before promulgating it.[45] This obviously placed a question mark on the legitimacy of the provisions that the

---

[41] Approximately 400 memoranda were received. See *Report of the Constitution Drafting Committee*, (1976) ii.

[42] B.O. Nwabueze, *The Presidential Constitution of Nigeria* (1982), 2-3.

[43] This is seldom recognised. One exception is the incisive comment of Adeniyi Ojebisi in 'Behold the Long-awaited Constitution' *PostExpress*, 7 May 1999. He said: 'The nation's first autochthonous home-made constitution was promulgated in 1979 following many months of debate by the elected representatives of the people of Nigeria.' An autochthonous constitution is one that involves a breach of continuity with a former constitution. Military rule led to a breach of legal continuity and, therefore, the new constitution was autochthonous, since it could not derive its authority from the earlier Constitution.

[44] On this, see J.S. Read, 'The New Constitution of Nigeria 1979: The Washington Model?' [1979] 23 J.A.L. 131, 134-135. One is not referring here to the defects of the constitution – such as the over-concentration of powers in the federal government. The defects being alluded to are those that are anterior to the terms of the Constitution. They centre on the control of the constitution-making process by the military administration.

[45] The preamble to the enactment decree stated as follows:
'Whereas the Constituent Assembly established by the Constituent Assembly Act 1977 and as empowered by that Act has deliberated upon the draft Constitution drawn up by the Constitution Drafting Committee and presented the result of its deliberations to the Supreme Military Council AND *the Supreme Military Council has approved the same subject to such changes as it has deemed necessary in the public interest and for purposes of fostering the promotion of the welfare of the people of Nigeria*' (emphasis added).
See Constitution of the Federal Republic of Nigeria (Enactment) Decree 1979, Cap 62, Laws of the Federation of Nigeria 1990. The military government, for instance, added s. 274(5) and (6), which had the effect of entrenching certain military decrees (such as the Nigerian Security Organisation Decree 1976 and the Land Use Decree 1978) in the constitution. It was this that led Dr T.A. Aguda to state that: 'From this point of view and from a purely legal point of view, the Obasanjo government [1976-1979] made the Constitution tell a big lie about itself by saying in the preamble that 'We the people of the Federal Republic of Nigeria do hereby make and enact and give ourselves the following Constitution.' See T.A. Aguda, *The Judiciary in the Government of Nigeria* (1983), 114. In this chapter, two rules have been devised for severing such provisions from the Constitution of 1979.

military government inserted. That those provisions are in a document that represents the will of the people does not mean they thereby become sanctified and acquire legitimacy. This particular impurity should not, however, be confused with the kind of defect that renders an *entire* constitution illegitimate. Besides, the blemish did nothing to erase the fact that the supremacy clause[46] of the constitution expressed the will of the Nigerian people to govern themselves democratically in accordance with the terms that *they* agreed upon. In any case, it will be seen below that two rules have been devised for severing these offending provisions from the Constitution of 1979. The most accurate description of this constitution (when compared with Nigeria's previous and subsequent constitutions) was by Bola Ige, who opined: 'the 1979 Constitution was the nearest to how a constitution can be properly and democratically produced in the eighty-one years of Nigeria's life'.[47]

After four years of democratic government under the Constitution of 1979 and at a time when public disaffection with the civilian government was high, the military, led by General Buhari, overthrew the civilian administration on 31 December 1983. A decree was consequently promulgated purporting to suspend the supremacy clause of the constitution.[48] The military justified its intervention on the ground that it was a corrective regime, which implicitly suggested that military rule would have a short duration. It is an acknowledged fact, however, that rather than being corrective, it proved damaging; rather than staying for a short duration, it held on to power for 16 years. It is pertinent to point out at this juncture that military regimes are inherently unstable. The new regime sooner or later itself becomes a target for counter-coups by competitors for power within the military class. Such counter-coups invariably lead to consequences not envisaged by the initial coup plotters.[49] It was, therefore, hardly surprising that Generals Babangida and Abacha, fellow coup plotters with General Buhari, capitalised on public disaffection with the high-handed nature of the government (of which they were a part) and toppled Buhari in a palace coup on August 27, 1985. It is worth observing that Nigerian commentators who argue that the panacea to coups against a democracy is good governance ignore this competition for power, which is now the chief reason for coups. Such commentators remain fixated on the reasons for Nigeria's first coup and the proffered (but not necessarily true) reasons for subsequent coups, whilst remaining oblivious to the change in the dynamics of coup plotting in Nigeria.

Babangida's administration instituted a transition to democracy programme which was notable for its flawed and interminable nature. Politicians were banned and unbanned by the government; it disbanded political parties and then proceeded

---

[46] See n.20 above.
[47] See, B. Ige, 'Constitutions and the Problem of Nigeria', *13th Annual Lecture Series of the Nigerian Institute of Advanced Legal Studies* (1995) 29.
[48] Constitution (Suspension and Modification) Decree No. 1 of 1984.
[49] For instance, Major Kaduna Nzeogwu's coup eventually plunged the country into a civil war and General Buhari's coup denied the country democratic rule for 16 years. During this period, Nigeria was subjected to the worst kind of rule it has ever experienced.

to create new ones and even wrote their manifestos.[50] In preparing for its departure from governance, the administration had introduced in an eclectic manner a new constitution, the Constitution of 1989.[51] This document, which clearly lacked legitimacy,[52] was introduced gradually as from 1 October 1992[53] because the military still clung to power, contrary to the promise to relinquish power on 1 October 1990. Complete power was to be handed over to a democratic government in 1993. However, the military administration aborted this by the annulment of the results of the 12 June 1993 presidential elections. The opposition to the annulment forced Babangida to resign on 27 August 1993. The military in a symbolic gesture then transferred power to a contraption it had devised and termed the Interim National Government. It would be a perversion of language to call this unelected body a democratic government. It lasted not more than three months, for on 17 November 1993 it was completely dismantled by its creators.

General Abacha, who was Chief of Defence Staff in Babangida's administration, now became Head of State. A new suspension decree was promulgated.[54] This decree restored the Constitution of 1979 with certain modifications. The Constitution of 1989 had been consigned to the ever-mounting rubbish heap of constitutions. As usual, the new suspension decree subordinated the restored constitution to military decrees by purporting to suspend its supremacy. The Abacha administration embarked on its own transition exercise and commenced fashioning yet another constitution for Nigeria.[55] It was assumed that the plan was for Abacha to be transformed into a civilian President under this constitution. This was not to be as he died on 8 June 1998.

General Abubakar, who had held the third most important position in the Abacha cabinet, assumed office on June 9. He returned Nigeria to democratic rule on May 29, 1999. That his transition process to democratic government lasted less than a year, while those of Babangida and Abacha cumulatively lasted 15 years, is a fact that has prevented the searchlight of enquiry from being turned on the deceit that characterised the process by which the unelected PRC fashioned and imposed an umpteenth constitution on Nigeria.[56] General Abubakar single-handedly repealed

---

[50] The military administration created two parties: the 'Social Democratic Party' – 'a little to the left' – and the 'National Republican Convention Party' – 'a little to the right'. These categorisations were by the military administration.
[51] Constitution of the Federal Republic of Nigeria (Promulgation) Decree 1989, Cap. 63, Laws of the Federation of Nigeria 1990.
[52] It was the result of a constituent assembly of 450 elected members and 111 nominated members. A section of the community termed 'radicals or extremists' was also excluded by the military. Even after this, the final report then had to be approved with amendments by the military administration. These two facts detracted from its legitimacy. See J.S. Read, 'Nigeria's New Constitution for 1992: The Third Republic' (1991) 35 J.A.L. 174. For a devastating critique, see I.O. Agbede, 'Conflict of Legitimacy: An examination of the Proposed Supervisory Role of the Military in the Transition to Civil Rule' in *Proceedings of the Eight Working Sessions of the National Conference on the Draft Constitution (28-30 June 1988)* (Nigerian Institute of Advanced Legal Studies, Lagos), 19-23.
[53] Constitution of the Federal Republic of Nigeria (Promulgation) Decree 1989, Cap 63, Laws of the Federation of Nigeria 1990.
[54] Constitution (Suspension and Modification) Decree No. 107 of 1993.
[55] See *Report of the Constitutional Conference Containing the Draft Constitution* (1995).
[56] The Constitution of the Federal Republic of Nigeria (Promulgation) Decree 1999.

the Constitution of 1979.[57] The constitution that was introduced in its stead returned Nigeria to the tradition of constitutional illegitimacy, begun by the imperial government and developed by the military, which the Constitution of 1979 had gone some way in reversing.[58] This is not a theoretical point. Professor Nwabueze has said that '[i]t cannot be disputed that a major cause of the collapse of constitutional government in many of the new States has been the general lack of respect for the constitution among the populace and even among the politicians themselves'.[59] He points out that a constitution cannot hope to command the loyalty, respect and confidence of the people if it is not an act of the people.[60]

## III. CONCEIVING AND PROMULGATING THE CONSTITUTION OF 1999 IN DECEIT

It should now be evident that the military came (and clung) to power through deceit. What is not common knowledge is that the military relinquished power in deceit. This becomes apparent if the question is asked, why did the military purport to abrogate the Constitution of 1979 (and enact a new constitution) when relinquishing power? After all, the use of the word 'suspend' in the suspension decree implies that what was put in abeyance would come back to life at some point in the future. Quite apart from the hubristic 'sheer desire of each military government to be associated with a new Nigerian constitution',[61] the reason for promulgating a new constitution was that the military were intent on erasing the crime that was committed when they infringed the supremacy clause of the Constitution of 1979.[62]

---

[57]  See the Constitution of the Federal Republic of Nigeria (Certain Consequential Repeals) Decree 1999. This decree, which purports to repeal the 1979 Constitution, came into force on 29 May 1999. Although the PRC was the ruling body under the last military government, the Head of State did not need to consult with other members of the PRC before promulgating decrees. This is because s. 3(1) of Decree No. 107 of 1993, which deals with the procedure for promulgating decrees, states that '[t]he power of the Federal Military Government to make laws shall be exercised by means of Decrees signed by the Head of State'. In *A.G., Federation v. Guardian Newspapers Ltd* [1999] 9 N.W.L.R. 187, Karibi-Whyte J.S.C. said at 239 that:

'This provision is short, terse and seems to me complete and self-explanatory. It has not prescribed any procedure. It merely says how the making of laws shall be exercised. Whatever procedure was adopted by the Federal Military Government in the exercise of its law making powers it appears would satisfy the constitutional requirement. It may prescribe no procedure as in the instant case. ...I find nothing in the provisions of the Constitution of 1979 as amended [by the suspension decree] or in any other decree in support of the contention that the participation of members of the Provisional Ruling Council is a necessary pre-condition in the procedure in the promulgation of a Decree.'

[58]  Mr Justice Nwokedi, the Chairman of the Human Rights Commission, in an interview with the press said: 'We have been 30 years under the army without respect for anything called a constitution, and by now, we have lost a sense of constitutionalism.' Quoted in S. Bakoji, 'Whither the 1999 Constitution?' *PostExpress*, 23 May 1999.

[59]  B.O. Nwabueze, *The Presidential Constitution of Nigeria* (1982), 4-5.

[60]  *Ibid.*

[61]  V.R. Mottoh-Migan, *Constitution Making in Post-Independence Nigeria: A Critique* (1994) 80. The author points out that this is similar to Nigeria's colonial experience when the respective constitutions were identified with the names of the Governors that initiated them.

[62]  See n.20 above.

The view was that if the constitution disappeared, it would be impossible to prosecute the coup plotters who flouted its supremacy clause and those who aided and abetted this offence by their endless transition programmes.[63] Furthermore, to guarantee their immunity from prosecution, they introduced a new constitution with an immunity clause.[64] Another reason for the abrogation is that a new constitution opens the door for a future intervention of the military class in the governance of Nigeria, since its promulgation removes a real deterrent to coups against a democracy. Future coup plotters, if successful, can claim to suspend the Constitution of 1999 and, when leaving, write a new constitution for Nigeria. In effect, the cycle of coups becomes an endless one. Without appreciating its significance, a commentator once remarked that '[t]he restoration of civilian administration on the exit of the military has always been followed by an exercise in constitution making'.[65] With each exercise the Nigerian elite have never failed to join in a debate about the contents of the proposed constitution.[66]

It seems that the PRC, in fact, had two objectives in view when introducing a new constitution - (a) to immunise former members of the military class from prosecution; and (b) to pave the way for current and future members of the military class to intervene in the governance of Nigeria when the conditions for a coup are in place. In this respect, the Nigerian military is best viewed as a class that seeks to protect and advance the interests of its members.[67] Further proof of this trait is evident from the reaction of the military government to the introduction of a clause into the draft Constitution of 1989, to the effect that any unconstitutional take-over

---

[63] This reasoning is dismissed below.
[64] See s. 6(6)(d) of the Constitution of 1999.
[65] D. Kanu, 'One More Constitution' *PostExpress*, 8 May 1999.
[66] The dynamics of the co-operation between the civilian elite and the military class in Nigeria is an interesting phenomenon. It has been pointed out that 'the civilian elite may often have clamoured for democratic change, but they have always been quick to co-operate with the army after it has overthrown a democratic government.' See A. Alao, 'Security Reform in Democratic Nigeria' at 10 (Working Paper No.2 of The Conflict, Security & Development Group at the Centre for Defence Studies, King's College London).
[67] The entry of the military into governance generates conflicts within the military class. Outside governance they are united in their desire to infiltrate governance. Whilst in governance, although they are united in their desire to remain in governance, there are conflicts that centre on the competition for power. Dr Alao has observed: 'the military institution was divided in many ways, but it seemed united in its determination to influence national politics. Furthermore, its membership wanted to remain in power at all costs, even in a civilian form after retirement.' See A. Alao, 'Security Reform in Democratic Nigeria' at 10 (Working Paper No.2, of The Conflict, Security & Development Group at the Centre for Defence Studies, King's College London). It is hardly surprising that retired military officers dominate the present civilian government of General Obasanjo. Nor is it any surprise that in the first budget presented to the National Assembly on 24 November 1999 the Ministry of Defence received the second highest budgetary allocation. (see *op. cit.*, Alao, 42). The military institution from its very origins, as Glover's Hausas' in 1862, which later became the West African Frontier Force in 1897, was always a rent-seeking force. Achike notes in *Military Law and Military Rule in Nigeria* (1978) at 22, that 'it is common knowledge that before the advent of military rule in Nigeria, soldiers were not popular. He quotes Sir Ahmadu Bello who said: 'When the British came to the North, they started recruiting their army of soldiers by getting slaves who had ran away from their masters, labourers from the markets and so on, and had them enlisted in the force. They had a bad start then.' *House of Representatives Debate*, 19 August 1952.

of government 'shall remain a punishable crime at all times under Nigerian law'.

The military government of the day rejected this proposed clause![68] A similar clause in the draft 1995 Constitution(s.1(3)) was also rejected by the PRC when fashioning the Constitution of 1999. To achieve these objectives without calling attention to them, the PRC resorted to an elaborate artifice. The deceit was practised in two stages. First, in December 1998 it inaugurated a 25-member Constitution Debate Committee. To give it a veneer of credibility, a Court of Appeal judge was appointed as its head. Invariably, the Nigerian elite, in search of relevance, have never failed to lend themselves to the schemes of the military, so it was hardly surprising that Justice Niki Tobi agreed to serve. In serving, he was only following in the footsteps of Justice Karibi-Whyte, a Supreme Court judge, who had headed a committee which wrote Abacha's draft Constitutionin 1995. Justice Tobi's unelected committee was given the responsibility of co-ordinating a debate over the constitution to be adopted. The deceit here lies in the fact that the PRC sought to give the constitution which they would ultimately impose on Nigeria a semblance of legitimacy by setting up the machinery for some kind of pseudo-public participation in the fashioning of the constitution. The 405 people who purportedly made written submissions to this committee were not representatives of the Nigerian people. Okonmah rightly reminds us that '[t]he sacredness of a Constitution is born out of the elaborate process through which it is born. [In the case of the Constitution of 1979], it entailed the election of representatives to a constituent assembly in 1978 at which representations from all segments of the Nigerian society were collated and considered'.[69] The PRC never really intended the people of Nigeria to fashion their own constitution. That this is so is evident from the fact that the PRC had the power to approve with amendments what their 25 appointees had produced. Receiving the report from Justice Tobi, General Abubakar declared that 'the report would assist the PRC in taking a final decision on the forthcoming constitution'.[70] Indeed, the Preamble to the Constitution of the Federal Republic of Nigeria (Promulgation) Decree 1999 states:

WHEREAS the Provisional Ruling Council has approved the report subject to such amendments as are deemed necessary in the public interest and for the purpose of promoting the security, welfare and good governance and fostering the unity and progress of the people of Nigeria with a view to achieving its objective of handing over an enduring Constitution to the people of Nigeria.

A few commentators have recognised this particular deceit. Beko Ransome-Kuti of the Campaign for Democracy has stated: 'the document was put together after various manipulations including the hand-picking of a constitutional co-ordinating committee and eventually approved by the unelected Provisional Ruling Council

---

[68] J.S. Read, 'Nigeria's New Constitution for 1992: The Third Republic' [1991] 35 J.A.L. 174, 175. As shall be demonstrated below, such a clause is not necessary to achieve this objective.

[69] Patrick D. Okonmah, 'Perspectives on Human Rights Violations in Nigeria' in Africa Legal Aid Quarterly (July – September 1998), 11.

[70] 'Constitutional Debate Committee Recommends Adoption of 1979 Constitution' *PostExpress*, 1 January 1999.

(PRC) that has made our lives miserable all these years'.[71]

The second stage of the deceit is what has completely eluded notice. Submitting the report to the last dictator, Justice Tobi stated that the Nigerians who had made submissions to his committee had been in favour of the retention of the Constitution of 1979. Hence, his committee recommended that this Constitution be adopted with some amendments in order to make it up to date.[72] Nigerians thought that this would take the form of an amendment to the Constitution of 1979 to reflect the increased number of States in the federation and such like. Unknown to them, what the committee and the PRC really intended was to introduce a new constitution with an immunity clause. The PRC then misled the people by announcing that it was the '1979 Constitution with amendments'.[73] After General Abubakar signed this document into law, this is what he said:[74]

[T]he new document takes largely after the 1979 Constitutionas it is clear that Nigerians prefer that old document, hence the Provisional Ruling Council (PRC) exhaustively deliberated upon and approved the same constitution – updated and amended in line with the report of the Justice Niki Tobi led Constitution Debate Co-ordinating Committee.

Indeed, the rather elaborate Preamble of the Constitution of the Federal Republic of Nigeria (Promulgation) Decree 1999 states *inter alia*:

WHEREAS the Constitutional Debate Co-ordinating Committee benefited from the receipt of large volumes of memoranda from Nigerians at home and abroad and oral presentations at the public hearings at the debate centres throughout the country and the conclusions arrived thereat and also at various seminars, workshops and conferences organised and was convinced that the general consensus of opinion of Nigerians is the desire to retain the provisions of the 1979 Constitution of the Federal Republic of Nigeria with some amendments.

Even though the people's wishes, as ascertained by this flawed consultation process, was that the Constitution of 1979 be restored, the PRC introduced a different document, but gave the false impression that it was the Constitution of 1979 with amendments which it introduced. Any observer of the statute books would have noticed that General Abubakar had, in fact, single-handedly repealed the Constitution of 1979.[75] It is not appreciated that there is a world of difference

---

[71] Statement released by the Campaign for Democracy quoted in 'Whither the 1999 Constitution?' by Sukuji Bakoji in *PostExpress* 23 May 1999.
[72] *Supra*, n.70.
[73] 'Abubakar signs Constitution into Law', *PostExpress*, 7 May 1999. The nation was misled into thinking that the amendments would be such as to update the Constitution, such as the introduction of provisions that take cognisance of the increased number of States in the federation and such like. However, the intention of the unelected PRC was to introduce other provisions. Such provisions, in the words of the Preamble of the Constitution of the Federal Republic of Nigeria (Promulgation) Decree 1999, are those that 'are deemed necessary in the public interest and for the purpose of promoting the security, welfare and good governance and fostering the unity and progress of the people of Nigeria'.
[74] *Supra* n.65.
[75] See the Constitution of the Federal Republic of Nigeria (Certain Consequential Repeals) Decree 1999.

between this constitution and the Constitution of 1999, even if the latter substantially reproduced the contents of the former. This is because they are two separate constitutions. The difference in dates is not a matter of form. Thus, while the existence of the Constitution of 1979 makes it possible to prosecute the coup plotters of 31 December 1983, the Constitution of 1999 – with its immunity clause – makes such a prosecution impossible. Unfortunately, this technical point was missed. Having accepted the constitutional framework provided by the PRC, the new civilian government began to operate within it. This meant that there was no mechanism for jettisoning it. The only way of changing any part of the constitution was by amending it. This is, as can be expected, quite difficult.[76] Nigerians had thus become prisoners of this illegitimate constitution. This has produced the rather startling consequence that laws passed by the elected legislature and signed into law by the elected President can be assailed on the ground that it conflicts with this constitution – a document written by a coterie of individuals and imposed on Nigeria without her consent. The will of the Nigerian people, as expressed by their representatives, is now dependent on this document. Nigerian legal experts have failed to point to this anomaly.

It may be argued that the constitution's lack of legitimacy was cured by ratification when Nigerians went to the polls in 1999. Even if it were possible for an election on the basis of a constitution to have a ratifying effect – a dubious proposition in itself – this argument can hardly be sustained in this context, since the constitution was published only after elections had been held. In what will go down in the annals of Nigeria's constitutional history as a complete farce, Nigerian politicians contested for offices which did not exist and whose powers were unknown and the people went to the polls at a time when the terms of this constitution were completely unknown![77]

## IV. THE LEGAL FEASIBILITY OF PROSECUTING THE 31 DECEMBER 1983 COUP PLOTTERS

The legal feasibility of prosecuting the individuals who subverted Nigeria's democracy is dependent on the extent to which the PRC has succeeded in achieving its first objective. It will be recalled that in imposing a new constitution on the country, there were two objectives in view. First, to secure an effective immunity for the coup plotters and their aiders and abettors. Second, to pave the way for current and future members of the military class to intervene in the governance of Nigeria at a propitious time in the future. Superficially, it would appear that the PRC has succeeded in achieving the first objective. Not only has the violated norm

---

[76] Ordinary constitutional amendments may be effected by both chambers of the National Assembly, with a two-third majority of all members in each House and the approval by resolution of the Houses of Assembly in at least two-thirds of the States. See s. 9 of the Constitution of 1999.

[77] Mr Justice Nwokedi, the Chairman of the Human Rights Commission, in an interview with the press was quoted as asking rhetorically: 'Have you ever heard about a country conducting an election without a Constitution'. Quoted in S. Bakoji, 'Whither the 1999 Constitution?' *PostExpress*, May 23, 1999.

been repealed, a new norm with an immunity clause has been introduced. If this were the true legal position, it would mean that where bandits take over the State and govern for 16 days but relinquish power after writing a new constitution for the country, the new government would be unable to prosecute the felons. The law is not this foolish. The recent prosecution of George Speight and his accomplices for treason after successfully executing a coup in Fiji on 19 May 2000 buttresses this point.

The correct legal position is that the purported suspension and abrogation of the Constitution of 1979 cannot erase the crime. It is often assumed that repealed laws do not exist, but they clearly do.[78] Joseph Raz has said in this respect: 'No termination of a norm legalizes offences committed while the norm was in force: offences committed while the norm existed can, of course, be punished later'.[79] It has, therefore, been held that where an offence is committed against an enactment, which is subsequently repealed, where proceedings were taken after the date of repeal in respect of that offence, the offence was against the repealed Act and it should be brought under that Act, even though repealed.[80] Besides, section 6(1) of the Interpretation Act[81] settles the matter beyond all doubt. Pursuant to that provision, the repeal of an enactment shall not 'affect any penalty, forfeiture or punishment incurred in respect of any offence committed under the enactment' [and a repeal is not to] 'affect any investigation, legal proceeding or remedy in respect of any such right, privilege, obligation, liability, penalty, forfeiture or punishment'. Finally, the criminal offence which was committed is that of treasonable felony under the Criminal Code Act.[82] This is the offence for which the coup plotters should be prosecuted. Section 41(a) and (b) of the Criminal Code Act, which prescribes the penalty of life imprisonment for a treasonable felony, provides that:

[A]ny person who forms an intention...to (a) remove during his term of office otherwise than by constitutional means the President as Head of State of the Federation and Commander-in-Chief of the armed forces thereof; or (b) to likewise remove during his term of office the Governor of a State...and manifests such intention by an overt act, is guilty of a felony and is liable to imprisonment for life.

One legal argument against such a prosecution may be that, according to the terms of section 43 of the Criminal Code Act, a person cannot be tried for this treasonable felony, unless the prosecution is commenced within two years 'after the offence is committed'. This argument is easily defeasible. The real question here is, when was the offence committed? Was it committed on 31 December 1983 or from 31 December 1983 until the military handed over power to a democratic government? Clearly, it must be the latter. A treasonable felony involving the unconstitutional dislodgement of the incumbent from office and a claim by the usurper to that office

---

[78] See J.M Finnis, 'Revolutions and Continuity of Law' in *Oxford Essays in Jurisprudence* (Ed A.W.B. Simpson) (2nd series) (1973), 44, 61-65.
[79] J. Raz, *Concept of a Legal System*, 58.
[80] *Taylor v. McGirr* (1986) 2 BCC 99,176.
[81] Cap 192, Laws of the Federation of Nigeria 1990.
[82] Cap 77, *ibid*.

is not a once-and-for-all act accomplished at some *punctum temporis*. The proposition that it becomes impossible to prosecute a person simply because he committed the relevant offence over a long period of time is not a very sensible one. As a matter of policy, it would seem that section 43 is directed at a situation where a treasonable felony is committed and the law enforcement agencies of the State are able to act but refuse to act for two years after the offence is committed. It was not meant to cover a situation where the law enforcement agencies are unable to act because the offence is continuing. It is submitted that time begins to run not from when the commission of the offence commenced but from when the continuing offence ended. Accordingly, the cut-off date is 29 May 2001. It is hoped that a prosecution will be brought before this date. But if this is not done, then there is no reason why the coup plotters should not be prosecuted under section 44 of the Criminal Code Act, which has no such cut-off date. This section deals with the offence of inciting to mutiny. Since a military coup involves a mutiny against the Commander in Chief of the Armed Forces, any person who incites any person serving in the armed forces to mutiny contrary to section 44 is liable to imprisonment for life.

From the foregoing analysis, it is clear that the purported suspension and abrogation of the constitution has done nothing to erase the crime of the coup plotters. Belgore J.S.C. recently pronounced in *Abacha* v. *Fawehinmi*[83] that a 'coup d'état is a treasonable offence but that is only when it fails'. It is, however, the view of this writer that there is no reason in principle why even when its execution is successful, it cannot be regarded by the courts as a treasonable offence to be punished in the future once the conditions for a prosecution are in place. It can be expected, however, that the coup plotters would argue, were they to be prosecuted, that section 6(6)(d) of the constitution promulgated by the PRC gives them immunity. In the section following the next, the legal basis for the annulment of this immunity-granting constitution shall be advanced. Once this constitution falls, the way will be clear for a prosecution.

In regard to the second objective, it may seem that by purporting to immunise successful past coup plotters from prosecution – a state of affairs that seems to have been generally acquiesced in by Nigerians – the PRC have succeeded in paving the way for current and future members of the military class to intervene in the governance of Nigeria when the conditions for a coup are in place. In this respect, it is obvious that there is a link between the two objectives. If the first objective is achieved (i.e. the immunisation of successful past coup plotters), it would then follow that the second objective (paving the way for a future coup because of the absence of a deterrent factor) will equally be achieved. Accordingly, the key to preventing the achievement of the second objective is to ensure that the coup plotters of 31 December 1983 and their accomplices are prosecuted. This makes the annulment of the Constitution of 1999 imperative. Before discussing the legal basis for its annulment, it is necessary to deal with a practical issue, to wit, how a plaintiff who wishes the judiciary to annul the constitution can obtain standing to

---

[83] [2000] 6 N.W.L.R. 228, 299E.

sue. This is because the problem of obtaining standing to sue may jeopardise this enterprise if it is not well handled.

## V. OVERCOMING THE PROBLEM OF *LOCUS STANDI*

A threshold issue to be considered before a court can entertain arguments for annulling the constitution is that of standing to sue. The plaintiff has to establish his *locus standi*. Since the plaintiff's standing can be questioned at any stage in the proceedings and even on appeal and can be raised *suo motu* by the court, it is important to ensure that the plaintiff has standing. If the argument is simply that a plaintiff who seeks to get the courts to declare the constitution void has standing (on the ground that he is subject to the constitution), then it seems certain that such an argument will fail under the existing standing rule. For this argument to have any chance of success the plaintiff will need to convince the courts that the present standing rule is wrong.[84] Since it is likely that the plaintiff would prefer to fight one battle rather than two,[85] the plaintiff would be well advised to construct a case that satisfies the present standing rule. Under this rule, the plaintiff will be accorded standing if he can show that his 'civil rights' have been threatened or infringed by the thing in respect of which his complaint relates.[86]

For this purpose, the term 'civil rights' has been construed to mean 'private legal rights'.[87] This is commonly regarded as the irreducible constitutional

---

[84] This author has attacked the prevailing standing rule elsewhere. See, T.I. Ogowewo, 'The Problem With Standing To Sue in Nigeria' (1995) 39 J.A.L. 1, and T.I. Ogowewo, 'Wrecking The Law: How Article III of The Constitution of the United States led to the Discovery of a Law of Standing to Sue in Nigeria' (2000) Brooklyn Journal of International Law (Forthcoming).

[85] The two battles are formidable ones. First, the plaintiff would have to demolish a standing rule that is assumed to be constitutional. Second, the plaintiff would have to demolish the constitution itself. The recent decision of the Supreme Court in *Owodunni v. Registered Trustees of Celestial Church of Christ and 3 ors*, (2000) 6 S.C. (Part III) 60, may have made the first battle unnecessary. The court in that case accepted this author's thesis, first advanced in 1995 (see *ibid.*) that standing to sue is not a constitutional issue. By breaking the link between standing and section 6(6)(b) of the constitution, this case (if understood by the courts and the profession) has solved the problem of standing to sue in Nigeria.

[86] The test for the application of this rule has been formulated by in the following terms: 'standing will only be accorded to a plaintiff who shows that his civil rights and obligations have been or are in danger of being violated or adversely affected by the act complained of.' See Bello J.S.C. in *Adesanya v. President of the Federal Republic of Nigeria and anor* [1981] 1 All N.L.R. (Part 1) 1 at 39.

[87] See Bello J.S.C. in *Adesanya's* case [1981] 1 All N.L.R. (Part 1) 1 at 39 and the judgement of the Court of Appeal [1981] 2 All NLR (Part 1), 1, 18 (which was affirmed by the Supreme Court); see also Bello J.S.C. in *Attorney General of Kaduna State v. Hassan*, [1985] 2 N.W.L.R. 483 at 508D and 509A-B, Oputa J.S.C. in *Thomas v. Olufosoye* [1986] 1 N.W.L.R. 669, 691E-F, and Belgore J.S.C. in *Odeneye v. Efunuga* [1990] 7 N.W.L.R. 618, 639E-F. See also *Alofoje v. F.H.A.* [1996] 6 N.W.L.R. 559, 567G, *Adegbite v. Raji* [1992] 4 N.W.L.R. 478, 488A-C and *Amodu v. Obayomi* [1992] 5 N.W.L.R. 503, 512F-513C. In *Ejiwunmi v. Costain (W.A.) Plc* [1998] 12 N.W.L.R. 149, Musdapher J.C.A. states (at 164H): 'The issue that now has to be decided is whether the statement of claim has disclosed any personal legal right for which the respondent is entitled to any remedy and if at all they have a right which has been violated.' Uwaifo J.C.A. said in *Olagbegi v. Ogunoye II* [1996] 5 N.W.L.R. 332, 352, that for there to be *locus standi* 'the statement of claim must disclose a cause of action vested in the plaintiffs regarding their rights or obligations which have been violated in the subject-matter'. See also *In Re Adetona* [1994] 3 N.W.L.R. 481, 488E-F where Tobi J.C.A. said: '*Locus standi* can only arise from a right cognisable and conferred on the plaintiff by law. Where there is no *such right*, the plaintiff cannot be said to have

minimum for standing. According to the Supreme Court in *Odeneye* v. *Efunuga*,[88] such legal rights can be conferred by the Constitution,[89] a statute,[90] the common law[91] or customary law.[92] Hence, where a public right has been breached (such as here where the claim is simply that the constitution is a nullity) the plaintiff will be denied standing. If the plaintiff cannot somehow point to his legal right which is threatened or has been infringed, the court would strike out the suit and save itself the trouble of dealing with this important issue.

However, an ingenious way of getting standing under the present standing rule will be for the litigant to identify a constitutional right of his that was infringed at a time when the Constitution of 1999 had purportedly come into force – such as a fundamental right guaranteed under Chapter IV – and then bring an action to protect this civil right under the Constitution of 1979. By pointing to an infringed civil right the standing hurdle would have been overcome, and by suing under the Constitution of 1979 the issue of whether the Constitution of 1979 still exists would have been raised for a judicial determination. The court will not be acting outside its remit if it makes such a determination, since the issue here is a question which only the judiciary can answer. It is not any different from the question of whether a President of a democratic government (or a usurper) can unilaterally abrogate a country's constitution. It can be expected that this issue will ultimately be decided by the Supreme Court. The task of the plaintiff will, therefore, be to convince at least four justices out of a total number of seven of the merits of his arguments.[93] It is to these arguments that we must now turn.

## VI. THE LEGAL BASIS FOR ANNULLING THE 1999 CONSTITUTION

Two independent grounds for annulling this constitution can be advanced. The first

---

a standing (sic) to commence or institute the action.' See also *Attorney General of Anambra State v. Eboh* [1992] 1 N.W.L.R. 491, 505F-G, 510B, *Busari v. Oseni,* [1992] 4 N.W.L.R. 557 at 587-589 and *Albion Const. Ltd v. Rao Investments Ltd* [1992] N.W.L.R. 583, 593D-H. The courts sometimes state this test as a sufficient interest test but use the term to denote the required quantum of interest – that quantum being a legal right. See e.g. *Kilfco Ltd v. Philipp Holzmann A.G.* [1996] 3 N.W.L.R. 276, 296G, *Ogbuehi v. Governor of Imo State* [1995] 9 N.W.L.R. 53, 87B, *Keepler v. Ofosia* [1995] 3 N.W.L.R. 415, 429G, *Adeyemi v. Olakunri* [1994] 2 N.W.L.R. 500, 507H-508B, *Bamidele v. Commissioner for Local Government* [1994] 2 N.W.L.R. 568, 583H-584A, and *Okafor v. Asoh* [1999] 3 N.W.L.R. 35, 55, where the court uses the term 'sufficient legal interest'.

[88] [1990] 7 N.W.L.R. 618, 639.
[89] Such as any of the constitutionally guaranteed rights in Chap. IV of the Constitution. They are the right to life, dignity of person, personal liberty, fair hearing, private and family life, freedom of thought, conscience and religion, freedom of expression and the press, peaceful assembly and association, freedom of movement, freedom from discrimination, the right to acquire and own immovable property anywhere in Nigeria and protection from compulsory acquisition of property.
[90] See e.g. *Egolum v. Obasanjo* [1999] 7 N.W.L.R. 355, *Adenekan v. Ajayi* [1998] 8 N.W.L.R. 473 and *Financial Merchant Bank Ltd v. Nigerian Deposit Insurance Corporation* [1995] 6 N.W.L.R. 226.
[91] Such as the right to sue on a contract.
[92] See e.g. *Oyediran v. Bolarinwa* [1998] 12 N.W.L.R. 559, 561.
[93] This is far easier to achieve than trying to convince the members of the National Assembly (the Senate and the House of Representatives) and the various State Houses of Assembly to amend the Constitution of 1999 pursuant to s. 9 of the constitution.

ground is that the constitution is founded on an illegality flowing from a breach of the supremacy clause of the Constitution of 1979. A Nigerian academic has, however, said: 'Whether the legality of any coup can be successfully challenged through this provision is... doubtful'.[94] Although the writer did not pursue the point, four conceivable objections against this ground can be advanced. First, it could be argued that the effect of the suspension of the supremacy clause was that there was no illegality. According to this argument, the suspension decree had the effect of putting in suspense the law that was infringed and the repealing decree had the effect of ending the existence of the suspended law. Since the infringed law no longer exists, there can be no question of illegality. The premise of this argument is that the existence of illegality is predicated on the continued existence of the law that has been infringed. The second objection will be that if the Constitution of 1999 is struck down on the ground that it is founded on an illegality, then this must entail the striking down of all the laws passed by the military after 31 December 1983, and if this were done, legal chaos would be unleashed in the country, since a significant number of Nigeria's laws have a military provenance. The third objection will be that if the constitution is struck down on the ground that it is founded on an illegality, then this should apply to the Constitution of 1979, since it was introduced by the military also. The fourth objection will be that if the constitution is annulled there will be a constitutional vacuum. No other objection apart from these four is envisaged.

It will be noticed that the first objection attempts to remove the foundation of the illegality argument. The basis of this objection goes to the very nature of law itself: it assumes that power is the basis of an enduring validity of a norm. If this is so, then it would mean that if bandits take over the government and promulgate laws which suspend the offence of theft, they can loot the country and, even after departing, their actions will still carry the stamp of legality. This analogy highlights a weakness of the first objection. Another weakness of this objection is that it assumes that once a law is no longer in force, it becomes impossible to identify an illegality that arose on account of the fact that the law was breached at a time when it was in force. It is trite that the law which applies to a cause of action is the law in force at the time when the cause of action arose.[95] Earlier it was demonstrated that repealed laws do exist in the sense that an infringement of the law at the time the law was in existence still carries legal consequences even if the law is subsequently repealed.

The second ground for annulling the constitution is different from, though not inconsistent with, the illegality ground. It is the ground that this chapter puts forward as its central thesis. The ground is based on the conceptual impossibility of suspending and abrogating the Constitution of 1979. As the ground does not rest on the contentious issue of illegality, it does not succumb to the first objection. After expounding this ground for annulment, a response to each of the remaining three objections shall be provided, since the objections apply to this ground as well.

---

[94] J.O. Akande, *The Constitution of the Federal Republic of Nigeria 1979* (1982) 2.
[95] *Adekunle v. Aremu* [1998] 1 N.W.L.R. 203.

## VII. THE CONCEPTUAL IMPOSSIBILITY OF SUSPENDING AND ABROGATING A CONSTITUTION

Can the provisions of a constitution in truth be suspended by fiat? Apparently, Nigerian jurists and judges assume that this is possible.[96] Even the famous *Lakanmi v. Attorney-General*[97] decision – a case where the Supreme Court seemed to be taking a firm stand against the military – recognised the then federal military government as 'the Supreme Legislative body', contrary to the provisions of the republican constitution.[98] Not comfortable with the limited degree of judicial review established by this decision, the military government reacted by promulgating a decree (The Federal Military Government (Supremacy and Enforcement of Powers) Decree 1970)[99] that laid down the rule that the validity of a decree could not be questioned on any ground. Implicitly, it also laid down the principle – a principle accepted even in *Lakanmi's* case – that the military can suspend provisions of a constitution. After this case, it also became the practice of every military government to introduce an ouster clause into their decrees.[100] This had the effect of preventing the courts from questioning the validity of the decree or anything done (or purported to be done) pursuant to the decree.[101] These developments explain why commentators and the courts have all accepted without question that a constitution can be suspended and abrogated.[102]

---

[96] D.I.O. Eweluka in 'Constitutional Aspects of the Military Take-over in Nigeria' (1967) 2 Nigerian Law Journal (No.1) 1, 5, states that: 'A coup d'etat cannot succeed in a country without destroying the country's existing constitution.'

[97] [1971] U. Ife. L.R. 201.

[98] What the case established was not that the military could not suspend a constitution – it was assumed that this was possible (in fact, before this case the Supreme Court had in *Issac Boro v. The Republic* (1966) SC 377/1966 given implicit approval of the military government) – but that it could not pass decrees that infringed the constitutional principle of separation of powers. The court held that a decree that constituted a legislative judgment offended Chapter III of the republican constitution (which had not been suspended) and, therefore, it could be invalidated on that ground.

[99] Decree No.28 of 1970.

[100] For a study and statistical analysis of the prevalence of ouster clauses in Nigeria, see G. Fawehinmi, 'Denial of Justice through Ouster of Court's Jurisdiction in Nigeria' in *Contemporary Issues in Nigerian Legal System* (sic) (edited by E.S. Olarinde, K. Adeigbe and O. Chukura), (1997), 67.

[101] See e.g. The Federal Military Government (Supremacy and Enforcement of Powers (Amendment No. 2) Decree No. 16 of the 1994.

[102] Hence in *A.G., Federation v. Guardian Newspapers Ltd* [1999] 9 N.W.L.R. 187, Karibi-Whyte J.S.C. stated at 240:

'By the promulgation of the Constitution (Supremacy and Enforcement of Powers) Decree No. 28 of 1970, courts of this country were brought under the absolute control of Military Decrees. Successive Military Governments, in 1984, and now Decree No. 107 of 1993, have adopted this same position. The resulting position in these decrees is that no court in Nigeria has jurisdiction to question the vires of the Military Government to promulgate a decree, or the validity of the decree, or to declare any decree null and void. The following decisions represent a consistent line of such judicial decisions of this court. *Hope Harriman v. Mobolaji Johnson* (1970) All NLR 503, *Adenrele Adejumo Nigerian Construction Co. Ltd. v. Col. Mobolaji Johnson* (1974) All NLR (2nd Edn. Vol. 1) 26 at 30, *Adejumo v. Military Governor of Lagos State* (1972) 1 All NLR (Pt.1) 159, *Uwaifo v. A-G, Bendel State* (1983) 4 NCLR 1; *A-G of the Federation v. Sode* (1990) 1 NWLR (Pt. 128) 500 at p. 518, *Obada v. Military Governor, Kwara State* (1990) 6 NWLR (Pt. 157) 482, *Labiyi v. Anretiola* (1992) 8 NWLR (Pt. 258) 139, *Osadebey v. A.G, Bendel State* (1991) 1 NWLR

It shall now be demonstrated that a suspension of any part (or the abrogation) of a constitution by a decree is conceptually impossible, and that it is something else which occurs when the military purport to suspend provisions of the constitution. Our starting point is that a constitution is the expression of the will of the people as to how they shall be governed.[103] The Canadian Supreme Court in the *Re Manitoba Language Rights* case[104] lucidly put it this way: '[t]he Constitution of a country is a statement of the will of the people to be governed in accordance with certain principles held as fundamental and certain prescriptions restrictive of the powers of the legislature and government'. Therefore, the written compact of the Nigerian people expressed their will to be governed democratically in accordance with the terms of their compact. Hence, Professor Ben Nwabueze refers to the constitution as the 'popular will'.[105] Patrick Okonmah recognised this trite point when he said:[106] 'Written constitutions or indeed any constitution for that matter, represent the collective will of the people expressed as the supreme rules to which all citizens are subject and habitually obey'. It is, therefore, a matter which does not call for argument that this will – which may be written or unwritten – is a fact that cannot be altered by fiat. Whilst it is certainly the case that the expression and enforcement of the will can be impaired, the will itself cannot be made to disappear by fiat. To put it differently, to suspend or abrogate this will is as impossible as attempting to change by fiat the opinion of a person. There are things that even decrees cannot do. Therefore, rather than actually suspend the will of the people, it is something else which occurs when a suspension decree is promulgated. It is that the decree operates to impair the expression and enforcement of the will of the people as to how they shall be governed.

This is an important insight. Notice how it calls attention to the fact, hitherto unnoticed, that the will of the Nigerian people never disappeared. All that happened was that its expression and enforcement were impaired. The position is similar to the case of a foreign invader who invades a country and rules it. The will of the invaded people does not disappear – it still remains – but the expression and enforcement of this will is impaired through superior force. Consider the constitutional history of Estonia.[107] The republic of Estonia was declared on 24 February 1918 and a constitution was adopted in 1938. It was invaded and occupied by the Soviet Union on 17 June 1940. The occupation and usurpation lasted over 50 years. However, on 20 August 1991, Estonia, in recognition of the fact that the will of its people as enshrined in its Constitution of 1938 did not disappear even after 51 years of occupation by usurpers, re-established its independence on the

---

533.'

[103] The Constitution Drafting Committee in its report that led to the Constitution of 1979 had stated: 'A Constitution is in reality the agreement of the entire nation as to how they wish to be governed.' See, *Report of the Constitution Drafting Committee* Vol. 1, (1976) iv.

[104] [1985] 1 R.C.S. 721, 745.

[105] B.O. Nwabueze, *Nigeria's Presidential Constitution: The Second Experiment in Constitutional Democracy* (1985), 1.

[106] Patrick D. Okonmah, 'Perspectives on Human Rights Violations in Nigeria' in Africa Legal Aid Quarterly (July – September 1998), 11 at 14.

[107] I thank Dr Mads Andenas for drawing my attention to this point.

basis of historical continuity of statehood and adopted a constitution on the basis of Article 1 of the Constitution of 1938. If 51 years of unconstitutional rule could not make Estonia's Constitution vanish, why should 16 years of unconstitutional rule make Nigeria's Constitution of 1979 disappear?

That during the period of impairment the courts obeisantly[108] and continuously pronounced the Federal Military Government as 'the Supreme Legislative body' (as was done in *Lakanmi's* case) or military decrees as supreme to the Constitution (as was done in the recent *Attorney General of the Federation v. Guardian Newspapers and ors* case)[109] does not alter this analysis. Indeed, it only goes to demonstrate that the superior force of the military impaired the enforcement of the people's will. Those cases had to be decided in that way because the courts were being called upon to pronounce on the validity of military decrees *during military rule*. The decrees produced a state of judicial duress. The courts had little choice but to uphold the laws of the junta.[110] They would have acted in the same way, even if the government had been taken over by *area boys*.[111] The decisions that have upheld usurpations elsewhere, such as *State v. Dosso*[112] (Pakistan), *Uganda v. Comm. of Prisons, ex parte Matovu*[113] (Uganda), *Madzimbamuto v. Lardner-Burke*[114] (Southern Rhodesia), *Bhutto v. Chief of Army Staff*[115] (Pakistan), *Valabhaji v. Controller of Taxes*[116] (Seychelles), *Mokotso v. King Moshoeshoe II*[117] (Lesotho), and *Matanzima v. President of Transkei*[118] (Transkei) can be explained on this ground. Commenting on the aftermath of *Lakanmi*, Tayyab Mahmud states:[119]

The aftermath of Lakanmi is very instructive for any study that aims at identifying suitable judicial responses to successful coups d'etat. It clearly demonstrated the practical limitations a court confronts when faced with the fait accompli of usurpation. The usurper's monopoly of coercive power allows them to ignore any adverse pronouncement by the judiciary or even to browbeat it into submission.

---

[108] A remarkable instance of this was when Ejiwunmi JSC referred to usurpers in the following terms: 'the succeeding Military Governments that have had the privilege of governing this country'. See *A.G., Federation v. Guardian Newspapers Ltd* [1999] 9 N.W.L.R. 187, 285D.
[109] [1999] 9 N.W.L.R. 187.
[110] Tayyab Mahmud in 'Jurisprudence of Successful Treason: Coup d'Etat & Common Law' (1994) 27 Cornell Int. Law Journal 49, has shown that a court has four options when confronted with the successful execution of coup, viz., (i) validate the usurpation of power; (ii) declare the usurpation unconstitutional and hence invalid; (iii) resign and thereby refuse to adjudicate the legality of the demise of the very constitution under which the court was established or (iv) declare the issue a non-justiciable political question. He argues (at 100ff) that the last option is the most appropriate option to take.
[111] A Nigerian colloquialism for street urchins.
[112] (1958) P.L.D.S.Ct. 533.
[113] (1966) E. Afr. L.R. 514.
[114] [1968] 2 S. Afr. L.R. 284 (Rhodesia App. Div).
[115] (1977) P.L.D. S.Ct. 657.
[116] Civil Appeal No. 11 of 1980, Seychelles Court of Appeals (7 Commonwealth L. Bulletin 1249 (1981).
[117] (1989) L.R.C. Const. 24.
[118] [1989] 4 S. Afr. L.R. 989.
[119] 'Jurisprudence of Successful Treason: Coup d'Etat & Common Law' (1994) 27 Cornell Int. Law Journal 49, 72-73.

However, when the source of the impairment disappears, the will – which never disappeared – reasserts itself. The will in the form of the Constitution which was purportedly abrogated can now be enforced. One aspect of this will is the duty of the courts under section 6 of the Constitution of 1979 to enforce all of the constitution's justiciable provisions. Since the Constitution could not be made to disappear by fiat, the courts have a duty under it to enforce its provisions. Therefore, to assert that Decree No. 63 of 1999[120] repealed the Constitution of 1979 is to accept that a decree can abrogate the will of the people. This proposition only needs to be stated to be rejected. Quite apart from the conceptual impossibility of so doing, it is difficult to see how this is possible when section 14(2)(a) of the Constitution of 1979 provides that 'sovereignty belongs to the people of Nigeria', a provision that even the military usurpers at no time purported to suspend. If sovereignty resides in the Nigerian people and the people have expressed their will in a constitution, then this constitution cannot be made to disappear by the fiat of one person. Therefore, once the state of judicial duress ceased, it became an absurd proposition to continue to recognise those precedents which validated military rule or the laws promulgated by the military, such as the decree repealing the Constitution of 1979 and the decree promulgating the Constitution of 1999.

The question has to be asked, however, why has this conceptual impossibility not hitherto been recognised? It seems that Nigerian jurists allowed themselves to become confused by a red herring. They engage in debates as to whether or not a successful coup is a revolution[121] and whether or not the resultant suspension decree is a grundnorm. In this respect, they all purport to subscribe to Hans Kelsen's theory of legal discontinuity.[122] As de Smith has said, the courts have 'swallowed Kelsen hook, line and sinker'.[123] More importantly, they have misunderstood Kelsen. Simply stated, the theory of legal discontinuity asserts that every illegal change in the constitution of a State is a revolution, and that a revolution destroys the entire legal order, replacing it with a new one. In his exposition of this theory, Kelsen included *coup d'etats* among the revolutions that effect the destruction and creation of legal systems.[124] Accordingly, in analysing the constitutionality of military rule, Nigerian jurists have reasoned in this wise:[125] the successful execution of a coup is a revolution[126] and the suspension decree promulgated by the usurpers

---

[120] The Constitution of the Federal Republic of Nigeria (Certain Consequential Repeals) Decree 1999.
[121] See e.g. D.O. Aihie and P.A. Oluyede, *Cases and Materials on Constitutional Law in Nigeria* (1979) 230-241.
[122] Hans Kelsen, *General Theory of Law and State* (1946). See also Hans Kelsen, *The Pure Theory of Law* (1967).
[123] Stanley A. de Smith, 'Constitutional Lawyers in Revolutionary Situations' (1968) 7 W. Ontario L. Rev. 93, 103.
[124] *General Theory*, 117; *Pure Theory*, 209.
[125] See e.g. O. Achike, *Military Law and Military Rule in Nigeria* (1978), p. 125.
[126] Uwaifo J.S.C. in *A.G., Federation v. Guardian Newspapers Ltd* [1999] 9 N.W.L.R. 187, 220 said: '[I]t must be acknowledged that when there is a successful abrupt change of government in a manner not contemplated by the Constitution, a revolution is deemed to have taken place. It follows that if such change was brought about by the military, it is a military revolution even if it was a peaceful change'.

thereby becomes the grundnorm.[127] *Ergo*, whatever the military do – such as promulgating a new constitution with an immunity clause and repealing the existing constitution – must be recognised not only during military rule *but also after military rule*, because the revolution has put an end to one legal system and has initiated a new one.

It is highly doubtful that Kelsen himself would have agreed with this conclusion. Kelsenian scholars have pointed out that the courts which have used Kelsen in this way have 'misrepresented Kelsen's positivist Pure Theory and its concept of Grundnorm in order to disguise from observers, and perhaps from themselves, the profoundly political nature of their actions'.[128] In his discussion of the temporal sphere of validity of a norm, Kelsen said: 'A legal norm can retroactively annul the validity of an earlier norm'.[129] This norm need not be a new enactment; according to Kelsen, it can be a judgment of a court.[130] So even Kelsen recognises that the courts can annul the Constitution of 1999. Nigerian jurists have misunderstood Kelsen's theory in another respect. By treating it as prescriptive, a theory (and a misunderstood one at that) has been elevated into a rule of decision. Like all theories that seek to explain phenomena, the theory of legal discontinuity is explanatory, not prescriptive. Even Kelsen has said: 'The science of law has to know the law – as it were from the outside – and to describe it. The legal organs, as legal authorities, have to create the law so that afterwards it may be known and

---

[127] A.G., *Federation v. Guardian Newspapers Ltd* [1999] 9 N.W.L.R. 187. See also, K. Eso, *Nigerian Grundnorm* (Idigbe Memorial Lecture 1985).

[128] T.C. Hopton, 'Grundnorm and Constitution: The Legitimacy of Politics' (1978) 24 McGill L.J. 72, 73. Hans Kelsen had said in his *General Theory*, 11: 'If the revolutionaries fail, if the order they have tried to establish remains inefficacious, ... their undertaking is interpreted, not as a legal, law-creating act, as the establishment of a constitution, but as an illegal act, as the crime of treason'. It is clear that Kelsen was not referring to success in executing the coup [the revolution] as a necessary condition for avoiding a prosecution for treason in the future. For there not to be a prosecution, not only the execution of the coup must be successful but also the new order must itself be efficacious. In such a case, the law-creating act is legal. This is because there has been a permanent usurpation. It is only when there has been a permanent usurpation that it obviously becomes impossible to prosecute the coup plotters, since there will be a new order. Kelsen clearly saw the failure of a coup not as failure in the execution of the coup – since in this case there is no coup but merely an attempted coup – but as a failure to establish a new order. If this were otherwise, it would then follow that where there is a coup which is successfully executed but which involves the coup plotters relinquishing power voluntarily or involuntarily 16 days after the coup and after having imposed a new constitution on the country, Kelsen would have thought that the people would, regardless of choice, be bound to obey the new constitution. This is not a view to which Kelsen would have subscribed. Indeed, he would have regarded the introduction of the constitution as an 'illegal law-creating act'. In fact, Kelsen's theory is more suited to revolutions (since the term implies a permanent change) than coup d'etats. Tayyab Mahmud in 'Jurisprudence of Successful Treason: Coup d'Etat & Common Law' (1994) 27 Cornell Int. Law Journal 49 at 102, has observed that a revolution 'envisages a complete metamorphosis that affects both civil society and the entire State; the transformation is so pervasive that legitimacy of the new order is completely autonomous of the processes and institutions of the old order. The content of the legal order and the structure of judicial institutions are typically changed'. It is the permanence of the new order that destroys the old order. Since most Western constitutions have their origins in revolutions that resulted in permanent change, it is obvious that this is what Kelsen had in mind.

[129] *Pure Theory*, 13.

[130] *Ibid*, 19.

described by the science of law'.[131]

It is true that Kelsen did assert that a revolution puts an end to one legal system and initiates a new one, but his theory was never meant to explain the effect of a usurpation which, although successfully executed, did not ultimately succeed, such as where the usurpers subsequently relinquished power – here only the execution of the coup is successful. A truly successful coup or revolution is a permanent usurpation. Where the coup leads to permanent military rule, for instance, there is an efficacious new order. If the question is then asked, why do the citizens obey the laws of this order?, a legal theorist of the Kelsenian School would answer that it is because the old order (democratic government) has been destroyed and a new order (military rule) has been created. It is only in this context that Kelsen's theory of discontinuity has explanatory force, since it explains why the rules in the new legal system are habitually obeyed. His theory did not seek to explain the situation which occurs where coup plotters succeed in usurping constitutional authority but later relinquish power after 16 days or 16 years. But if the theory purported to do so, then it becomes necessary to meet Kelsen head on[132] and to reject his theory on the ground that it has no explanatory force in this context, since rational people will not consider themselves bound by all the laws of the usurpers,[133] such as the laws granting the usurpers immunity.[134] It is for this reason that courts elsewhere have rejected this version of Kelsen when their adjudication occurs at a time when the usurpers have relinquished power. In the Ghanaian case of *Sallah v. Attorney-General*,[135] the court was able to reject this version of Kelsen since the soldiers had relinquished power. Apaloo J.A. said: [136]

I cannot believe that with the known pragmatism that informs judicial attitudes towards questions of legislative interpretation, the Attorney-General can have thought an argument such as this was likely to carry seasoned judicial minds. We should fail in our duty to effectuate the will of the Constituent Assembly if we interpreted the Constitution not in accordance with its letter and spirit but in accordance with some doctrinaire juristic theory.

Further on he said:[137] 'the experience of the world teaches one that there is often considerable divergence between theory and practice; between the process of authorship and judicial adjudication'. In the Pakistani case of *Jilani v. Government*

---

[131] *Ibid*, 72.
[132] It is important to note that Kelsen's theory has been questioned by many scholars. See J.M Finnis, 'Revolutions and Continuity of Law' in *Oxford Essays in Jurisprudence* (Ed A.W.B. Simpson) (2nd series) (1973), 44.
[133] In fact, Kelsen would have described such an exercise of legislative power by the usurpers as an 'illegal, law-creating act'. See T. Ogowewo, 'The Laws of the Maiguards' *Tell Newsmagazine*, 2 August 1999 where this author drew attention to the absurdity of automatically applying the laws of the usurpers.
[134] Indeed, the fact that the military inserted an immunity clause into the constitution suggests that they are aware that a crime was committed and their period in power is not enough to erase the crime.
[135] 20 April 1970, Unreported. Reprinted in 2 S.O. Gyandoh, Jr & J. Griffiths, *A Sourcebook of the Constitutional Law of Ghana* (Accra) (1972) 493.
[136] *Ibid*. 508-509.
[137] *Ibid*.

of *Punjab*[138] the Supreme Court overruled its earlier decision in *Dosso*, which has been described as a *carte blanche* for treasonable conduct,[139] and rejected a Kelsenite argument that would have validated all the laws of the usurpers who had since relinquished power. Hamoodur Rahman C.J. said:[140]

Kelsen's theory was, by no means, a universally accepted theory nor was it a theory which could claim to have become a basic doctrine of the science of modern jurisprudence...He was propounding a theory of law as a 'mere jurists' proposition about law. He was not attempting to lay down any legal norm or legal norms which are 'the daily concern of Judges, legal practitioners or administrators.

The court also pointed out that using Kelsen to validate the actions of usurpers is a misapplication of Kelsen. Hamoodur Rahman C.J. said:[141]

It was, by no means, [Kelsen's] purpose to lay down any rule of law to the effect that every person who was successful in grabbing power could claim to have become also a law-creating agency. His purpose was to recognise that such things as revolutions do also happen but even when they are successful they do not acquire any valid authority to rule or annul the previous grund-norm until they have themselves become a legal order by habitual obedience by the citizens of the country.

After coup plotters had successfully executed a coup in Cyprus on 15 July 1974 but later relinquished power on 23 July, the Cypriot court in the case of *Liasi v. Attorney-General*[142] agreed with the submission of both parties that 'the *sub judice* decision [a decision terminating the appointment of the plaintiff] is legally non-existent and illegal as emanating from ...the act of a public authority, which in itself was legally non-existent'. Finally, in the Bophuthatswana case of *State v. Banda*,[143] the successful coup plotters who were later subdued by the South African military were successfully tried for treason.

All these cases serve to demonstrate that once the usurpers relinquish power, the courts have been able to pronounce their acts as treason and to deny automatic recognition to their laws. Therefore, to apply *Dosso*[144] and its progeny even after

---

[138] (1972) P.L.D. S.Ct 139.
[139] F. Hasan, 'A Juridical Critique of Successful Treason: A Jurisprudential Analysis of the Constitutionality of a Coup d'etat in Common Law' (1984) 20 Stan. J. Int'l Law 191.
[140] (1972) P.L.D. S.Ct 139, 179.
[141] *Ibid*, 180.
[142] (1975) C.L.R. 558.
[143] [1989] 4 S. Afr. L. R. 519.
[144] The Chief Justice of Pakistan in *Dosso*, the author of the main opinion, had said: '[the coup] having been successful...satisfies the test of efficacy'. '[Therefore, the Laws (Continuance in Force) Order], however transitory or imperfect it may be, is a new legal order and it is in accordance with that Order that the validity of the laws and the correctnesses of judicial decisions has to be determined'. See (1958) P.L.D. S. Ct. 533 at 540. According to Tayyab Mahmud, the *Dosso* judgment 'provided the first express transformation of Kelsen's theories of constitution and revolution into a judicially pronounced common law doctrine of revolutionary legality'. See, Tayyab Mahmud, 'Jurisprudence of Successful Treason: Coup d'Etat & Common Law' (1994) 27 Cornell Int. Law Journal 49 at 56. Before then, Kelsen's theories were simply theories. It is interesting to note, as Mahmud points out, that this case was

# WHY ANNULMENT OF THE NIGERIAN 1999 CONSTITUTION IS IMPERATIVE 291

the usurpers have relinquished power is to be a slave to a misunderstood theory. Accordingly, in approaching the question of the constitutionality of military rule, an important distinction needs to be drawn between a challenge to the constitutionality of military rule during military rule and a challenge after military rule. The revolutionary validity analysis is the only legal response during military rule because of the state of judicial duress. Here, Kelsen's theory has considerable explanatory force.[145] It explains why the judges enforce the laws of the usurpers while the usurpation lasts. Likewise is the case where military rule (the new revolutionary order) is permanent. The theory explains why people habitually obey the laws of this new order.[146] However, the appropriate legal response to a challenge after military rule – which by definition means that the coup (as opposed to its execution) was not successful[147] – must be that the successful execution of the coup merely impaired for a time the expression and enforcement of the will of the people,[148] and that once the impairment ceased, the will of the people, which could never disappear, reasserts itself. Accordingly, after the military depart, the new constitution which they imposed on the country and their laws are not to be automatically recognised.

Unfortunately, because Nigerian courts fail to appreciate that the function of a theory is explanatory, and not prescriptive, a Nigerian judge confronted with the laws of the usurpers even after the usurpers have relinquished power will reason that he must (*mis*)apply Kelsen's theory to the facts. By elevating a misunderstood version of Kelsen's theory into a rule of decision, the laws of the coup plotters continue to be pronounced as valid even after relinquishing power.[149] Yet Kelsen

---

decided only 20 days after the coup and the regime that was thereby validated was itself overthrown within a day of the court's pronouncement. If its logic is to be followed, it then means that if soldiers successfully take over the government on one day and relinquish power on the next day, the transitory nature of their laws notwithstanding, such laws should be accorded recognition even when they have left. It is this view that currently holds sway in Nigeria. Apart from the flawed logic of *Dosso*, it is important to note, as Tayyab points out at 74, that 'the main author of Dosso was involved with drafting the very martial law order which was at issue in the case'. It was partly for this reason and the flawed logic of the opinion that *Dosso* was rejected when the Pakistani Supreme Court had occasion to pronounce on the validity of military rule – at a time when the usurpers had relinquished power – in *Jilani v.Government of Punjab* (1972) P.L.D. S. Ct. 139, 246-47.

[145] This explains cases such as *The State v. Dosso*, [1958] P.L.D. S. Ct 533 (Pakistan), *Uganda v. Commr of Prisons, ex p. Matovu* [1966] E.Afr. L.R. 514 (Uganda) and *Madzimbamuto v. Lardner-Burke* [1968] 2 S.Afr. L.R. 284 (Southern Rhodesia). See T.O. Elias, 'The Nigerian Crisis in International Law' (1971) 5 Nigerian Law Journal 1.

[146] Here there is no judicial duress because the new order has become permanent.

[147] Recall that a successful coup is the destruction of one order (in this case a democratic system of government) and the creation of a new order (permanent military rule). Where the State reverts to democratic government, then it follows that the new order of the usurpers (military rule) was not efficacious.

[148] '[S]uch military power is usurped power from the elected representatives to whom the people of Nigeria entrusted power democratically'. *Per* Uwaifo J.S.C. in *A.G., Federation v. Guardian Newspapers Ltd* [1999] 9 N.W.L.R. 187, 211. It also usurps the constitutional right of the people to choose their leaders and to be governed in accordance with the constitution.

[149] Doing just that in respect of the immunity clause contained in the Constitution of 1979, Fatayi-Williams CJN stated in *Uwaifo v. A.G, Bendel State & Ors* (1982) F.S.C. 124 at 145 : 'At the end of their rule, they (the Military) handed down a constitution wherein they made certain that future

himself had said: 'Never, not even in the earliest formulations of the Pure Theory of Law did I express the foolish opinion that the propositions of the Pure Theory of Law 'bind' the Judge in the way in which legal norms bind him'.[150]

By examining the concept of suspension closely, we see that it is merely a shorthand but inapt way of describing the impairment of the expression and enforcement of the people's will to be governed in accordance with their constitution. Now that the impediment to the expression and enforcement of the will has disappeared, all that remains is for a judge to discover the will of the Nigerian people, as expressed in the Constitution of 1979.[151] It is for the courts to discover and interpret the laws of Nigeria. If the Constitution of 1979 has, in truth, never been abrogated, it then means that the courts have the duty under that constitution to pronounce as a nullity any document that pretends to be a constitution. It makes no difference that the courts purport to adjudicate under the Constitution of 1999. As that constitution is void, the courts will, in fact, be adjudicating under the Constitution of 1979, which never disappeared. To refuse to do this is not legitimate judicial restraint; it will be an abdication of the judiciary's constitutional duty.[152] To be sure, this is not a task for the legislature, since it is a legal nonsense to amend a void constitution.

The virtues of the argument for the constitution's annulment are many. First, it is eminently sensible. Rather than accord an enduring validity to the acts of usurpers, this argument recognises that whilst they are in power, the expression and enforcement of the will of the Nigerian people is invariably impaired; however, when the military depart, willingly or through superior force, the will reasserts itself. Second, it enables the post-1966 Nigerian constitutional cases to be viewed in proper perspective. These cases which upheld the laws of the military were simply decisions given under duress. The courts were not enforcing the will of the Nigerian people, since its expression was impaired by superior force. Now that the military have departed, those decisions have no precedent value. Third, it establishes beyond all doubt that military rule is an aberration and, therefore, when the military depart their laws must be de-legitimised completely. Presently, a

---

administrations would not be given a free hand to dig up skeletons of any legislation with which they were involved for scrutiny. This is the purport of section 6(6)(d) of the 1979 Constitution.'

[150] Hans Kelsen, 'Professor Stone and the Pure Theory of Law' (1965) 17 Stan. L. Rev. 1128, 1134.

[151] If the courts were to rule otherwise, this would be tantamount to accepting that the soldiers have somehow abrogated the will of the Nigerian people (as opposed to merely impairing the will), as manifested in the 1979 Constitution. This would be the equivalent of accepting that a decree can legislate that the sex of the author of this chapter has changed from male to female. To use a simple analogy, when an armed robber invades and subsequently leaves one's house, the will of the master of the house reasserts itself. All the instructions of the armed robber, such as forbidding the calling of the police, become a nullity; the armed robber's constitution (which was based on his impairment of the householder's constitution) ceases to apply as soon as he leaves. This is implicit because the householder exercises legislative, executive and judicial powers at once. In the case of a country where there is a separation of powers, there is a need for a judicial pronouncement annulling the instructions of the usurper of constitutional authority. Therefore, it is the duty of Nigeria's courts to annul the instructions of the military.

[152] See *Marbury v. Madison*, 5 U.S. 137 (1803).

military decree is automatically recognised as an 'existing law'[153] and can only lose its validity if (a) it conflicts with the constitution which the military itself have imposed on Nigeria or (b) it is repealed by the legislature and its repeal does not violate the terms of the constitution given to Nigeria by the military. This explains why the decree on the Remuneration of Heads of State is automatically recognised. It also explains why successful coup plotters against Nigeria's democracy have never been prosecuted. Finally, by establishing the illegality of even the successful execution of a usurpation, it encourages respect for the constitution. As Fieldsend J. has stated in the *Madzimbamuto* case:[154] 'Nothing can encourage instability more than for any revolutionary movement to know that, if it succeeds in snatching power, it will be entitled ipso facto to the complete support of the pre-existing judiciary in their judicial capacity'. It is worse if the adventurers know that their actions will be validated even when they have relinquished power. There is, therefore, a need to substitute the present rule of perpetual validity with a rule of temporal validity. As Yaqub Ali J. said in the *Jilani* case:[155]

May be, that on account of his holding the coercive apparatus of the State, the people and the Courts are silenced temporarily, but let it be laid down firmly that the order which the usurper imposes will remain illegal and the Courts will not recognize its rule and act upon them as de jure. As soon as the first opportunity arises, when the coercive apparatus falls from the hands of the usurper, he should be tried for high treason and suitably punished. This alone will serve as a deterrent to would be adventurers.

Having debunked the first objection against the annulment of the Constitution of 1999, the three remaining objections shall now be examined with a view to determining whether they are valid objections.

A. Will there be legal chaos?

Recall that the second conceivable objection to the annulment of the constitution is that the same vice that taints this constitution also taints every other decree promulgated by the military, and if every such decree is to be denied recognition, there will be a legal vacuum and resultant legal chaos. According to this view, it is better to simply recognise all the decrees of the military (and, therefore, accept the 1999 Constitutionas valid), since if we pronounce one military decree invalid on account of the fact that it was promulgated in defiance of the supremacy clause of the Constitution of 1979, then we must do likewise in respect of every other decree. The flaw of this argument is that it seeks to validate an unlawful act on account of the fact that its unlawful progeny are numerous. In a situation where the consequences of an unconstitutional act are widespread, one should strive to formulate a rule or rules that would allow the courts to cherry-pick between necessary and undesirable outcomes. It cannot be a sensible proposition that all

---

[153] S. 315 of the Constitution of 1999.
[154] *Madzimbamuto v. Lardner-Burke* [1968] 2 S.Afr. L.R. 284, 430.
[155] (1972) P.L.D. S.Ct 139, 243.

unconstitutional acts and their consequences must be recognised. To do this will make nonsense of the law. The law must attach the badge of illegality to all constitutional violations. However, a refusal to recognise laws that are intended to legalise the usurpation (such as the immunity clause) does not mean that the laws passed by the usurping government which are necessary to the maintenance of organised society should not be recognised.[156] Two rules can be devised to aid the cherry-picking process. They are termed the *presumption of non-recognition* and the *rule of displacement*.

According to the first rule, all military decrees will be subject to the presumption of non-recognition because they were promulgated in defiance of the supremacy clause of the Constitution of 1979. This is necessary to de-legitimise all decrees.[157] However, since it will lead to legal chaos if the presumption were to be applied with ruthless logic, its application needs to be mitigated. The mitigation exercise is not, however, an exercise in palm tree justice. It must be based on the solid ground of principle. Such a principle is the rule of law. As was pointed out in the *Re Manitoba* case,[158] the rule of law not only means the supremacy of the law and, therefore, the absence of arbitrary power, it also 'requires the creation and maintenance of an actual order of positive laws which preserves and embodies the more general principle of normative order'. Clearly, if the presumption of non-recognition were to be applied in an unmitigated fashion, it will offend this aspect of the rule of law principle. It will mean that the legal order which has purportedly regulated the affairs of those subject to Nigerian law since 31 December 1983 will be destroyed and the rights and obligations arising under all military decrees will be invalidated. Since the rule of law is a principle of Nigerian constitutional law, it is necessary to devise a principle which at once recognises the unconstitutionality of military decrees, while at the same time avoiding a legal vacuum and ensuring respect for the rule of law. This is the function of the second rule, the rule of displacement.

Pursuant to this rule, where it will be unjust and inconvenient not to recognise a particular decree, the presumption of non-recognition should be displaced. The two prongs of this rule are cumulative. The presumption will not be displaced in respect of decrees which infringe the fundamental norms of the legal order, such as the decree repealing the Constitution of 1979 and the decree promulgating the Constitution of 1999. These two decrees seek to supplant the fundamental law of

---

[156] A similar distinction had to be made by Oputa J. (as he then was) in *John Oduah II and anor. v. Akubueze and ors* (1970 and 1971) ECSLR 185, in regard to the validity of a writ of summons that had been issued by the High Court of Biafra (a secessionist State which was subsequently defeated). The question that arose after the civil war was whether the writ was a nullity because it was issued by an illegal regime. This was what Oputa J said at 188-189:

'During the civil war and in spite of the civil war it was necessary to maintain law and order even in areas controlled by the illegal regime... A distinction ought to be drawn between acts, even of an illegal regime, necessary for the preservation of peace and good order among citizens and acts which aid and foster the rebellion.'

[157] If such decrees were not de-legitimised, it would logically follow that the military can write a constitution for Nigeria and Nigerians would have to apply it. This would be akin to the householder obeying the words of an armed robber even after the armed robber has departed!

[158] [1985] 1 R.C.S. 721, 749 (Canada).

the land. The case of decrees promulgated for the maintenance of organised society is, however, different. Such decrees – and it is expected that the vast majority of decrees promulgated by the military government would fall under this category – should easily satisfy the first and second prongs of the displacement rule.[159]

The workability of these rules can be tested by examining how they would operate in relation to two decrees, to wit, the Remuneration of Former Presidents and Heads of State (and other ancillary matters) Decree[160] and the Companies and Allied Matters Decree.[161] Both decrees will be subject to the presumption of non-recognition since they were promulgated by the military; however, because it will be unjust not to recognise the Companies Decree (it does not infringe a fundamental norm of the legal order) and it would also be inconvenient not to recognise it (it would be impossible to unscramble the egg as companies have been formed under the decree) the presumption should be displaced. On the other hand, the presumption should not be displaced in respect of the decree which rewards coup plotters, since it would not be unjust to refuse to recognise it (a decree that allows the usurper to reward himself for infringing the supremacy clause of the Constitution of 1979 is one that infringes a fundamental norm of the legal order) and it would not be inconvenient to refuse to recognise it.

These two rules should enable the courts to cherry-pick in a consistent fashion between necessary and undesirable outcomes with no consequent legal chaos. This is preferable to the present rule where all decrees are accorded automatic recognition pursuant to the *existing law* clause of the Constitution of 1999.[162] Once the court accepts these rules, it will be open to anyone with *locus standi* to invoke them. It would, however, make much sense for the Federal Attorney-General to compile a list of all decrees promulgated between 31 December 1983 and 29 May 1999 and seek a declaratory judgment invalidating those decrees in respect of which the presumption of non-recognition ought not to be displaced.[163] This is better than

---

[159] It may, however, be argued that if all military decrees are to be subject to the presumption of non-recognition, this will then mean that the electoral decree – under which elections were held in 1999 – will be affected and, therefore, the legality of the elections can be challenged on this ground. The response to this argument is that the electoral decree will be saved by the rule of displacement, since it paved the way for the restoration of the will of the people. Put differently, it would be unjust and inconvenient not to recognise the electoral decree.

[160] Decree No. 32 of 1999.

[161] Cap. 59, Laws of the Federation of Nigeria 1990.

[162] S. 315. A military decree, as an 'existing law', will be invalidated only if it can be demonstrated that it conflicts with the constitution given to Nigeria *by the military*.

[163] One who strives for theoretical purity may argue that when the Attorney General seeks a declaratory order, the electoral decree under which the President was appointed is at that point subject to the presumption of non-recognition and that accordingly, until the presumption is displaced, the position of the President and the Attorney General are invalid; and if this is so, the person purporting to be the Attorney General can hardly come to the court to ask for the presumption to be displaced. The argument can be countered by arguing that all governmental positions can be validated under the doctrine of necessity. This would mean that the Attorney General's position will be automatically validated and he should then be able to apply for declaratory relief invalidating those decrees in respect of which the presumption ought not to be displaced. Since the doctrine of necessity only validates that which is necessary, it would operate to prevent a legal vacuum but will not operate to validate or further the usurpation.

leaving it to the courts and litigants to invoke the presumption on an *ad hoc* basis, as this would only lead to uncertainty.

B. Is the Constitution of 1979 also tainted?

The second objection is that if the Constitution of 1999 is annulled on the ground that it is founded on an illegality, then this should apply to the Constitution of 1979, since it was also promulgated by the military. This argument sees the fact of promulgation as a vitiating ground. But this is wrong. The true position is that where a constitution has legitimacy, its promulgation by a usurper is not a vitiating ground. Professor Nwabueze puts it this way:[164]

If the substantive content of a constitution is freely agreed and adopted by the people either in a referendum or through a constituent assembly popularly elected for the purpose,[165] then it is their act, although promulgation may, in the interest of formalism and regularity, have been done by an existing State authority. Promulgation in this context is a purely formal act which should not detract from the popular will.

The promulgation by a usurper of a constitution is not a vitiating ground where the constitution is itself legitimate, since it means that the people have re-expressed their will in the new constitution. Critics may, however, argue that the Constitution of 1979 is not legitimate; and if that is the case, its promulgation by the military authorities is a vitiating ground. Indeed, it could be contended by such critics that the suspension and abrogation of the Constitution of 1979 was not a crime against the Nigerian people, because this constitution did not represent the will of the people, and that the relevant starting point should be the republican constitution. Such critics will then assert that since the republican constitution itself cannot really be described as an act of the people, its violation in 1966 had no legal consequence. If this argument were to be accepted it will become impossible to argue that the future violation of the supremacy clause of the Constitution of 1999 will have any legal consequence either, since that constitution is undoubtedly illegitimate. There would, therefore, be an endless cycle of validated coups.

At the beginning of this chapter, it was, however, shown that unlike the independence Constitution of 1960 and the republican Constitution of 1963, which both had a problem of legitimacy on account of the fact that they were not adopted by the Nigerian people, the Constitution of 1979 does not suffer from this vice. A study of the legislative history of the Constitution of 1979 will demonstrate that it was *largely* the product of an elected constituent assembly of citizens. True, some members were appointed by the military government of the day. But this

---

[164] See B.O. Nwabueze, *The Presidential Constitution of Nigeria* (1982) 1.

[165] It could be argued that the members of the constituent assembly were not elected for the purpose, since they were merely elected by the local councils acting as electoral colleges. This argument is, however, not valid, since one of the purposes behind the local government reforms of 1976 was that the local governments would serve as electoral colleges to constitute the constituent assembly. See *Guidelines for Local Government Reform* (1976). See also, T. Mamman, *The Law and Politics of Constitution-Making in Nigeria, 1862-1989: Issues, Interests and Compromises* (1998) 173.

imperfection is not a great one, since the appointees were a tiny minority. As stated earlier, such a minority could in no way have overridden the views of the elected members. More importantly, whilst it is true that some provisions of the constitution were imposed by the military, this impurity is not sufficient to erase the fact that the supremacy clause of that constitution was the product of the Nigerian people and it expresses their will to govern themselves democratically. It is this clause that was violated by the military in 1983. It is this breach that renders the illegitimate Constitution of 1999 invalid. As for the provisions inserted into the Constitution of 1979 by the then military government,[166] they too should be subjected to the two tests developed earlier, that is, the presumption of non-recognition and the rule of displacement. The court should be able to use its power of severance to cut off the offending provisions from this constitution.[167] The principle explaining this power of severance is that those offending provisions are not a part of the collective will. Therefore, they have no constitutional status within the Constitution of 1979.

C. Will there be a Constitutional Vacuum?

The final argument against the annulment of the constitution is that it will lead to a constitutional vacuum. It has been argued that the will of the Nigerian people to be governed democratically, as reflected in the supremacy clause of the Constitution of 1979, could never have been abrogated by fiat. All that the suspension decree did was to impair its expression and enforcement. Accordingly, now that the source of the impairment has disappeared, the constitution – which could never have been abrogated on the fiat of one man – should reassert itself. There will, therefore, be no vacuum. However, the question may be asked, how can the constitution be applied when certain fundamental changes have occurred in the polity, such as the creation of States? The simple answer is that decrees introducing such changes will be saved from the presumption of non-recognition through the application of the rule of displacement. Under that rule, it will be unjust and inconvenient not to recognise the decrees on State creation, since it will be impossible to unscramble the egg.

---

[166] Such as s.6(6)(d) of the Constitution of 1979.
[167] One such provision is found in ss. 274(5) and (6) of the Constitution of 1979, which entrenches certain decrees in the Constitution, such as the Land Use Decree. Severing this provision from the Constitution will not have the effect of putting in jeopardy the existing system of land tenure, since severance does not mean that the statute will disappear. It has been held in *Enugwu v. Okefi* [2000] 3 N.W.L.R. 620, that such statutes are not part of the Constitution – they have only been rendered extraordinary by virtue of s 274(5).

## VIII. CONCLUSION

The four conceivable objections against the judicial annulment of the Constitution of 1999 have not withstood scrutiny. The way is, therefore, clear for the courts to discover the Constitution of 1979. By unearthing this constitution, the courts would be establishing that a constitution, which is a statement of the collective will, cannot be abrogated by the fiat of one person – which was what literally occurred. The effect of such a ruling will be momentous. This would be the most significant development in Nigerian constitutional law since independence. It would mean that the Federal Attorney General would have *a duty* to institute criminal proceedings against General Buhari and his accomplices for treasonable felony. Indeed, nothing will preclude a private citizen from bringing a private prosecution. The obstacle to a successful prosecution – the immunity clause in section 6 of the Constitution of 1999 – would no longer exist. This would send a clear signal to the military that even the successful execution of a coup still has its risks. This may very well mark the end of military coups in Nigeria. However, just as criminal penalties do not guarantee the end of the phenomenon of bank robbery, a rule of deterrence cannot guarantee the end of coups in Nigeria. That it cannot offer such a guarantee is, however, no reason to discount it altogether. After all, we do not do away with penalties for robbery simply because such penalties do not guarantee the end of robbery. To reduce significantly the possibility of a coup what is needed, in addition to a rule of deterrence, are measures designed to prevent a failure of democracy, such as electoral reform to increase access, eliminate rigging and ensure fairness, the removal of obstacles that prevent the governed from holding those who govern accountable, such as the enactment of a Freedom of Information Act, the firm rejection of the current rule of *locus standi* and the upholding of the rule of law.[168] A failure of democracy leads to considerable resentment amongst those who have been excluded from centres of power. It also leads to a failure of government. These two consequences combine to create considerable public disaffection with the incumbents. It is at this stage that a coup becomes propitious.[169]

Although one could be forgiven for thinking that after the destructive era of military rule in Nigeria, there would be unanimity about the wisdom of prosecuting the coup plotters, it is, however, one of the many contradictions of Nigerian society that here sentiment may trump principle. The reason for this is that the seizure of power in Nigeria has the magical effect of conferring a considerable degree of respectability on the felons who have seized power; and after relinquishing power, they ensure that they remain viewed as statesmen. It explains why they promulgate mundane decrees which provide that former military leaders (with their spouses) are to take third position in the order of precedence after the serving President and Vice President at public functions and are entitled to a diplomatic passport for life

---

[168] For a wide-ranging discussion of other measures, N.A. Omoigui, 'On the Question of Preventing Coups in Nigeria' (Debate section in http://NigerianScholars.AfricanQueen.com/mainpage.htm.

[169] This appears to account for the recent coups in Pakistan and Côte d'Ivoire.

and to protocol within and outside Nigeria![170] From this sort of decree, we get an insight into the thinking of those who have ruled Nigeria for the past 16 years. The resultant culture explains the paradox that even those in the vanguard of civil society, who laboured greatly and suffered enormously for democracy, have never quite seen these retired coup plotters as the criminals that they are.[171] Consequently, seven arguments against such a prosecution may be advanced. First, it may be argued that since the military have renounced all interest in governance they are unlikely to stage a coup in the future, and, therefore, there is no need for a prosecution;[172] secondly, that a rule of deterrence is unnecessary once there is good government, as good governance is the panacea to coups;[173] thirdly, that such a

---

[170] S. 4, Part 1 of the Schedule to Decree No.32 1999.

[171] When this author wrote an article in the Nigerian newspaper, *The Guardian*, titled, 'Why General Buhari should be prosecuted', the editors of that paper (a paper that had been repeatedly persecuted by successive military administrations) changed the title to the less provocative 'Back to the 1979 Constitution'. See *The Guardian*, 23 December 1999. Rather surprisingly in its editorial of 17 March 2000, titled 'Pinochet's Nemesis' the paper announced that the Pinochet case has set an important precedent and that the 'former dictator must be made an example in the interest of the Chilean people who suffered under his rule in order to enhance the moral health of the world as a whole.' It is hoped that *The Guardian* will now champion the crusade to ensure the prosecution of those who violated the Nigerian Constitution on 31 December 1983.

[172] This is the argument of those who simply wish to bury their heads in the sand. Such persons put too much weight on the assurances of ex-generals and ignore the competition for power by those in the military class who were not 'lucky' enough to have had political appointments during military rule. Such soldiers, once in control of strategic positions in the military, have every incentive to stage a coup at a propitious time. This author's article in *The Guardian* (23 December 1999), opened thus:

'Is it outside the bounds of possibility that our democracy may at some point in the future be imperilled by a military coup? The recent Pakistani coup – after over 10 years of civilian rule – serves to remind us that once the military have tasted political power, it is a formidable task to make them relinquish permanently the thought of re-tasting power'.

A day after its publication, the armed forces of Côte d'Ivoire staged a successful coup against the civilian government in power. The military are likely to assume power when they sense that civilian resistance to their putsch is unlikely, such as when a civilian democracy misgoverns or subverts democracy. It is a certainty that once a civilian government misgoverns and time dims the people's memories of the cruelty and incompetence of military rule, the soldiers will be back. Already, a senator was reported in the Nigerian Press as calling on the military to return. See 'Atiku, military condemn call for coup' *The Guardian*, 8 February 2000.

[173] This is a vacuous view. Elections bring bad governments and it is elections – not soldiers – which ought to be used to get rid of bad governments. If the slogan 'Never Again' (which is now common in Nigeria) means anything, it must mean that even when Nigeria has the worst civilian government – when democracy is most vulnerable – soldiers must never usurp political power. See, T. Ogowewo, 'Never Again: An end to Coups in Africa' *African Topics*, Issue No. 30 (November-December 1999) 21. Others have said that civilians can stop coups by mass civil unrest. But it is difficult to envisage the Nigerian people (at their present level of socio-political development) rising up against coup plotters, *especially at a time when civilians misgovern*. There are a number of reasons for this. First, Nigeria's military have shown a considerable disrespect for human life. In the minds of the citizenry, there is a real possibility that those who resist will be mowed down. Second, the generality of Nigerians – who certainly cannot be described as highly sophisticated political creatures – have too much at stake in any existing *status quo* to want to sacrifice everything for democracy. Finally, many of those who were recently elected do not seem to be the likely guardians of Nigeria's new democracy. It will be unrealistic to expect them – many were on the side of the last dictatorship – to act as sentries to ward off constitutional transgressors. Others have said that all that is necessary is that an anti-coup clause should be inserted into the constitution, which would provide that the constitution cannot be suspended. There is a grave fallacy

prosecution will threaten Nigeria's nascent democracy;[174] fourthly, that a prosecution would send a signal to future successful coup plotters never to relinquish power;[175] fifthly, that the real culprits who should be prosecuted are not the coup plotters, but those that subsequently looted Nigeria's treasury;[176] sixthly, that the prosecution would turn into a witch-hunt;[177] and finally that the coup was popular and this validates it.[178]

---

in this argument. Once it is accepted that the military can suspend the supremacy clause of the Constitution, it then follows that they can suspend any such clause.

[174] This argument is without merit. The risk is non-existent where the constitutional transgressors no longer have a following in the military – which will be the case when they have retired from the military. In fact, such prosecutions will only strengthen democracy by protecting it from future attack. This is a certain gain. It makes sense to discount a non-existent or tenuous risk when considering this certain gain. Therefore, the prosecution of those who overthrew the government (and those that aided and abetted this offence with their endless transition programmes) carries no risk to Nigeria's democracy, but it certainly has the clear benefit of protecting the present and future civilian governments from the menace of military adventurists. The current trial of General Ishaya Rizi Bamaiyi (Rtd) (the former Chief of Army Staff) for the attempted murder of a newspaper publisher proves this.

[175] To appreciate the weakness of this argument it is important to bear in mind that very few military governments in Nigeria (even under the present rule of non-deterrence) have relinquished power to a civilian democracy voluntarily (two out of eight to be precise). The argument assumes that there will always be coups (which we must learn to live with) and the prosecution of coup plotters will simply mean that they will not leave office. So the argument implicitly subscribes to the view that it is preferable to have a continuous cycle of coups and a very low hand-over rate, rather than a rule of deterrence, which has a chance of bringing this cycle to an end. This must be a gloomy prospect. A rule of deterrence makes future coups unlikely.

[176] True, it will be a travesty if those who have looted Nigeria go unpunished. But those who made such unaccountable looting possible must first be punished.

[177] The argument here is that the prosecution would not stop with the actual coup plotters and those who aided and abetted it; it would extend to those persons who served in the military government down to the last military government which handed power to the civilians. The trick with this argument is that it attempts to stretch the application of the rule of deterrence to such an extreme extent that it begins to lose touch with the sensibilities of the people. When this happens, the entire project loses credibility. It is, therefore, necessary to confront this argument. The people who should be prosecuted for treasonable felony are not those who served in a military government, but those who actively planned a coup to subvert democracy. Others who should be prosecuted will include those who aided and abetted this offence through endless transition programmes. This would not include those who instituted a return to civilian rule. Another variant of the argument is that if General Buhari is prosecuted, then General Gowon (Nigeria's surviving military leader who assumed power after the first democracy was overthrown on 15 January 1966) should also be prosecuted. The answer to this is as follows. First, since those to be prosecuted should be those who instigated a coup against a civilian democracy and those that aided and abetted this offence, such a prosecution is not possible, since Gowon was not party to the first coup – this was by Major Nzeogwu and his fellow majors who are now beyond the reach of earthly justice. It is, however, possible to make a case against Gowon for aiding and abetting the offence by instituting a long transition programme which he even extended. This will have a salutary effect, in that if there is a coup against a democracy and this is followed by a counter-coup, those behind the counter-coup should have a duty to immediately hand over power to the surviving arm of the civilian government (such as the judiciary which never ceases to function even in a military regime). This surviving arm will then have the constitutional duty to restore a full democratic government. There is no reason why the military should institute their own transition programme under such circumstances. I wish to thank John Ofutu for drawing my attention to this very important point.

[178] To accept this argument is to accept that the military can intervene whenever there is a bad civilian government. There is no part of the 1979 Constitution which gives the military this function. This is the function of the electorate. Therefore, any alleged public acclamation in 1983 does not validate the

To all of these arguments, which have been respectively debunked, there can be one response, in the form of the words that fell from the lips of another Buhari, the disgraced former Speaker of the House of Representatives, who had to step down when he admitted to forgery and perjury. He said that his humiliation had shown him that 'in our new democracy, nobody, no matter how highly placed, will be above the law'.[179] He was subsequently convicted.[180]

The Nigerian legal establishment instinctively advance spurious and simplistic arguments to validate past military rule and decrees *in a democracy*, without an eye to the cost of military rule in terms of lost lives, distorted values, and the deterioration of the nation's infrastructure. It is most irresponsible of Nigerian scholars to fail to focus on the totality of costs inflicted on Nigeria by military rule in a discourse such as this. Surely, it is high time that the right to constitutional government is seen as the most important of all fundamental rights. After all, where this right disappears, all other fundamental rights are in jeopardy.

---

offence committed by the soldiers. What the vanguards of civil society ought to do is to make it easy to kick out bad civilian governments and not support an unfounded rule that allows the soldiers to come back when there is a bad civilian government. Nigeria's experience of military rule suggests that the soldiers inflict more damage on the country than the elected politicians. Of course, if a civilian government turns out to be undemocratic by thwarting the constitution, then a coup against such a government, if carried out for the express purpose of restoring constitutional government, will not be treason if power is handed over immediately to the legitimate civilian government. Here, it is the civilian government which subverted the constitution, not the group that restored democracy.

[179] 'Forgive Me, Says Buhari', *PostExpress*, 24 July 1999.
[180] In a brazen disregard for the rule of law the President recently misused the prerogative of mercy to grant a presidential pardon to Buhari, the convict. See 'Govt pardons ex-speaker, Buhari, and 14 others', *The Guardian*, 2 June 2000.

Chapter Fourteen

# ETHNICITY, CONFLICT AND CONSTITUTIONAL CHANGE IN RWANDA AND BURUNDI

Guglielmo Verdirame[*]

In most African countries the introduction of a constitution after independence was a process guided by the former colonial powers. In some cases the constitution was literally handed over by the colonial power without any local constitutional debate effectively having taken place. The predominant constitutional models in this initial phase were the Westminster model, which formed the basis of many constitutions in the former British colonies, and the French Constitution of 1958, from which many Francophone countries in Africa drew inspiration. Besides adopting the British system of parliamentary democracy, the Westminster model was also characterised by the presence of a Bill of Rights based on the European Convention of Human Rights.[1] The French Constitution of 1958, on the other hand, was essentially an attempt to reconcile the parliamentary system with a directly elected and powerful president.[2]

---

[*] Junior Research Fellow, Merton College, Oxford.

[1] Nwabueze, *Constitutionalism in Emergent States*, 1973. De Smith, *The New Commonwealth and Its Constitutions*, 1964. Read, 'Bills of Rights in the World: Some Commonwealth Experiences', in *Verfassung und Recht im Übersee*, Vol. 6, 1973. Nwabueze, *Presidentialism in Commonwealth Africa*, 1974.

[2] Bidegaray, Emery, Seurin, *Droit constitutionnel et institutions politiques*, 1983. Lavroff, *Les systemes constitutionelles en Afrique noire. Les Etats francophones*, 1976. Conac (ed.) *Les institutions constitutionnelles des états d'Afrique francophone*, 1979. The 1958 Constitution is still in force in France today.

When France adopted its new constitution in 1958, French colonies had to choose between independence and membership of the Communaute Francaise created under that consitution. Under the Communaute Francaise, colonies were granted autonomy but all matters relating to defence and foreign policy were left to France. Article 88 (Title XIII) of the 1958 Constitution exemplifies the colonial vision that permeated the 'new' constitutional arrangement that France was seeking with its former colonies in order to contrast the calls for independence: it states that 'the Republic or the Community may make agreements with States that wish to associate themselves with the Community in order to develop their civilisations'. Indeed, 'France aimed to promote the advancement of the Africans within a framework that for the time being would be dominated by Frenchmen but within which the Africans would undergo preparation to play progressively larger parts. This policy would lead to the integration of the African territories into the Republic and the gradual emancipation of their inhabitants as individuals rather than to the severing of ties with France. As a result of this essentially assimilationist policy, Africans acquired French citizenship and representation in territorial assemblies, federation

The constitutional experience of Rwanda and Burundi differs from that of most other African countries. Indeed, their first constitutions derived from neither the French nor the Westminster models. This is mainly due to the fact that the constitutional arrangement did not form part of the negotiations between the independence movements and Belgium, which had administered Rwanda and Burundi under a mandate of the League of Nations since 1919. The pre-colonial history of both countries is important in that they were both characterised by a strong centralised monarchic power and by profound social cleavages. At the end of the first constitutional cycle,[3] subsequent processes of constitutional amendment followed ethnic tension, violent clashes and, in some cases, mass killings.[4] Such amendments were seldom introduced through the application of the procedure for constitutional amendment and normally resulted from the tacit replacement of an existing constitutional order, from *coups d'état* and, more recently in the case of Rwanda, from negotiations among warring factions. This led to the dismantling of the post-independence constitutional order within only a few years after independence. The new constitutional system was introduced surreptitiously and was essentially authoritarian. In the late 1980s and early 1990s the process of democratisation led to the creation of new constitutions which were, however, short lived.

The frequent resort to violent means as a way of amending the constitution illustrates the extent to which the rule of law has not affirmed itself in Rwanda and Burundi. Without the creation of stable constitutions that protect fundamental rights and the resort to legal procedures for amending existing constitutional norms, the rule of law will only remain a shallow legal motto and the ethnic question will be solved outside a rational-legal framework.

The following chapter analyses the constitutional experience of Rwanda and Burundi since independence. The adoption of the first constitutions will be considered and the processes that led to the establishment of an altogether different constitutional order within such a short time will be analysed. The theoretical framework which distinguishes between 'formal constitution' and 'living constitution' can provide a useful model. The 'formal constitution' is, in brief, the written constitution, the norms contained in the actual constitutional text. The 'living constitution' is, on the other hand, the complex of written and unwritten

---

councils, and such metropolitan bodies as the National Assembly in Paris' (Gardinier, 'The Historical Origins of Francophone Africa', in Clark, Gardinier (eds.) *Political Reform in Francophone Africa*, 1997, p.12). Of all the French colonies, only Guinea rejected the arrangement and gained independence in 1958.

[3] The expression 'first constitutional cycle' to indicate the post-independence constitutional phase is used by De Vergottini (*Diritto Costituzionale Comparato, Parte IV*: 'Lo Stato di recente indipendenza', 1993).

[4] Chrétien, *Le défi de l'ethnisme. Rwanda et Burundi: 1990-1996*, 1997, especially Première Partie, 1: 'L'immatriculation ethnique, vocation de l' africanisme interlacustre?'. Reyntjens, *L'Afrique des Grands Lacs en crise. Rwanda et Burundi: 1988-1994*, 1994, pp. 17-53.

norms that provide 'the fundamental organisation of society'.[5] The degree of discrepancy between the formal constitution and the living constitution can vary: in some cases, constitutional norms formally still in force may cease to apply as a result of the creation of a customary rule by consent. In other cases, a whole constitutional order may be repealed following a *coup d'état*. Furthermore, many authoritarian regimes disregard written constitutional norms in particular those relating to the protection of fundamental rights. The actual 'strength' of a written constitutional norm, as opposed to its avowed formal rank, will depend on different factors. The theoretical framework of living vs. formal constitution facilitates the investigation into constitutional systems in which the written text of a constitution often ceases to provide fundamental norms and procedures, and norms of constitutional rank are introduced without applying the legal procedure for amending the constitution.

## I. BACKGROUND

The population of Rwanda and Burundi is made up of three main groups: the Hutus account for about 80-85 per cent of the total, and the Tutsis and a small Twa minority comprise the rest of the population (Tutsis around 14-15 per cent and Twas 1-1.5 per cent). Whether Tutsis and Hutus are ethnic groups is debated among historians and anthropologists.[6] However, in this chapter, the terms 'ethnic' and 'racial' will be used with respect to Tutsi and Hutu identities. It is important to stress that such terms cannot bear the same significance they have in the context of European history. The term 'super-clan' could be more appropriate in some respects, although it conceals the process of racialisation of Rwandan and Burundi society set in motion during colonial times.

In examining the pre-colonial past, there is often the tendency to idealise that period as one of stability and peaceful and harmonious co-existence: the creation of the 'myth of merry Africa' has proven quite attractive to many.[7] The history of Rwanda and Burundi before colonisation is, on the contrary, one of complex and unequal social relations.

---

[5] De Vergottini, *Diritto Costituzionale Comparato*, 1993, 130. Mortati, *La costituzione in senso materiale*, 1940. Romano, *L'ordinamento giuridico*, 1918.

[6] In *Prosecutor v Akayem*, ICTR-96-4-T, in part reported at 37 *ILM* (1998) 1.3.99, the International Criminal Tribunal for Rwanda has dwelled on the nature of Hutu and Tutsi identities.

[7] Rhoda Howard, 'Group versus Individual Identity in the African Debate on Human Rights', in An-Naim, Deng (eds.), *Human Rights in Africa*, 1990, p. 164. See for instance Basil Davidson, *The Black Man's Burden*, Nairobi, 1992, p. 251 when he writes with reference to Burundi: 'In those pre-colonial times, we are told, the king and his princely henchmen, the mwami and his ganwa, had been able to hold a structural balance of interest and obligation between Tutsi and Hutu. This was the balance which colonial overlordship had destroyed'. The main historical responsibility of the colonial authorities in Rwanda and Belgium is not so much the fact that they undermined an unfair and unequal social system based upon castes; their main responsibility is having exacerbated the existing conflict, using it for their own political convenience. For a different account on the pre-colonial era: Rwanda Prunier, *The Rwanda Crisis: History of a Genocide*, 1995, 21-23.

The origin of Hutus and Tutsis is an area of great controversy that exemplifies the ways in which the past can be used in order to justify the ideologies behind the conflicts of the present. Furthermore, the construction of genealogical myths serves the purpose of justifying current identities and is a crucial step in the identity-building process of the group. According to the most commonly believed account, the Tutsis are a cattle-raising Nilotic population which invaded the area inhabited by the Hutus and imposed their rule around the seventeenth century. Tutsis and Hutus speak the same language and there are no significant differences in religious affiliation or customary practices. In the pre-colonial period, the Hutu and Tutsi identities were closer to social groups and castes rather than ethnic groups. Transitions from one group to the other occurred and, in some areas, were indeed quite common. Such transitions still take place nowadays, but to a more limited extent. The most notorious case is that of Paul Kajuga who headed the interahamwe[8] responsible for the genocide of 1994: he was a Tutsi himself by birth who became Hutu and embraced Hutu extremism. In Rwanda such transitions occurred within the system of the 'ubuhake', the contract between a Tutsi patron and a Hutu client that gave the latter the right to own cattle normally reserved exclusively to the Tutsis. The client and the patron shared the calves born from the original cattle. With time and subject to the approval of his patron, the Hutu client could become Tutsi.

Rwanda and Burundi were characterised by some differences in the political and institutional structures in the pre-colonial period. In Burundi the royal clan, Ganwa, constituted a group which claimed to be separate from Hutus or Tutsis. Although members of the Ganwa married only Tutsi women of the Abyangaruru clan, they did not identify themselves as either Hutus or Tutsis. The perception that the king (mwami) had no racial affiliation served the purpose of 'avoiding the juxtaposition between the rulers and the ruled'.[9] In spite of the pre-colonial experience, the short-lived monarchy after independence failed to establish itself as a *super partes* institution. The Rwandan monarchy was, on the other hand, 'a stratified and highly centralised kingdom much more impervious to any kind of mobility than Burundi'.[10] The mwami was more closely associated with the Tutsi aristocracy and worshipped as a semi-divine figure. The last small Huth kingdoms that had maintained some independence were incorporated into the Rwandan monarchy at the beginning of this century with the help of the colonial power.

During the colonial period Hutu and Tutsi identities underwent a process of radical transformation as a result of different factors. Firstly, the Belgian colonial authorities maintained the system of indirect rule initiated by the Germans. In doing so, they relied on the Tutsi elite and Hutu chiefs were dismissed and replaced with

---

[8] Interahamwe ('those who work together') was the most important extremist militia during the genocide, and was responsible for planning and carrying out a lot of the killings.
[9] Darbon, Hoiry, *Pouvoir et integration politique: les cas du Burundi et du Malawi*, 1982, 10.
[10] Bayart, *The State in Africa: The Politics of the Belly*, 1993, 122.

Tutsis.[11] Secondly, the approach of the Belgian colonialists, and in particular of the missionaries, to the question of identities was essentially racist. They saw Tutsis as descendants of a superior race and born leaders, whilst the Hutus were thought inferior. On the basis of this belief Tutsis were given exclusive access to the educational institutions which were entirely controlled by the Catholic Church.[12] The Belgian colonial authorities and the Catholic missionaries failed to comprehend the social caste nature of the Hutu-Tutsi cleavage and interpreted those identities as racial identities.[13] Power can shape identities very rapidly, and within two generations Hutu and Tutsi identities acquired the ethnic and racial significance that the colonialists had originally read into them.[14]

The colonial policy of favouring Tutsis changed after the second world war

---

[11] Timothy Longman, 'Rwanda: Democratisation and Disorder: Political Transformation and Social Deterioration', in Clark, Gardiner (eds.), *Political Reform in Francophone Africa*, 1997, p. 288: 'German and Belgian colonial policies, however, eliminated the pre-colonial system of flexibility and complexity and solidified social categories into distinct ethnic identities'. See also Prunier, *op. cit.*, 23-40.

During the first world war the Belgians occupied Rwanda and Burundi defeating the German forces. After the end of the war, the end of German colonial domination over the two countries, and indeed over any African country, was sealed by the terms of the peace treaty imposed on Germany. The two former German colonies came to be nder the Mandate of the League of Nations.

[12] Prunier, *op. cit.*, 31 ff.

[13] 'Ces catégories correspondaient à d'anciens clivages sociaux, les Hutu étant plutôt agriculteurs et les Tutsis plutôt éleveurs sans que l'on puisse parler non plus de classes sociales. Ces groupes fonctionnaient un peu comme des superclans, dotés de vocations différenciées et en rivalité autour des fonctions et des prébendes redistribuées par les cours royales ou princières' (Chrétien, *op. cit.*, 1997, p. 13).

In Burundi there is also a considerable Protestant presence. The Catholic missions operated mainly in the north and in the centre of the country, while the Protestant missions began to evangelise the southern regions in the years preceding the second world war. Although such religious differences should not be overplayed, they constitute another important variable in Burundi history (See: Weinstein, *Conflict and Confrontation in Central Africa: The Revolt in Burundi*, 1972, p. 19).

[14] On the shaping of identities see: Anderson, *Imagined Communities*, and Vidal, *Sociologie des passions*, 1991. On the effects of colonial policies on the social fabric in Burundi, see: Darbon, Hoiry, *Pouvoir et integration politique: les cas du Burundi et du Malawi*, 1982, Chapter II, Part II.

The process of transformation of social castes into ethnic and racial identities during the colonial era can hardly be underestimated. Rwandese and Burundi refugees, interviewed in Kenya in the course of a socio-legal study on refugee rights carried out by the writer for the Refugee Studies Programme at University of Oxford, used such expressions as Hutu or Tutsi 'blood' and 'intimate nature'. A large number of the interviewees were of mixed parentage. When the author/interviewer observed that talk of Hutu or Tutsi blood was so much more meaningless given the incidence of mixed marriage, his remarks were usually dismissed (interviews with Rwandese and Burundi refugees, conducted in Nairobi from April to June 1997). The attitude of host countries towards Rwandese refugees varies a great deal. In Tanzania, efforts were made to integrate the refugees in the local population. In Uganda Rwandese refugees settled down mainly in Buganda which already hosted the descendants of Rwandese who had arrived there from earlier migrations. The Banyarwanda, as they were referred to, faced persecution in Uganda particularly in the early 1980s under Milton Obote. Many of them decided to join the Yoweri Museveni's National Resistance Army which entered Kampala in January 1986. However, even under Museveni the Ugandan authorities failed to integrate the Rwandese refugees. Such failure resulted in the strengthening of Rwandese identity amongst those refugees who began to prepare their return to Rwanda by force allegedly with the help of the Ugandan government.

mainly as a result of the need to isolate the Tutsi elite - by then associated with the anti-colonial struggle. However, the nefarious racialisation of the Hutu-Tutsi cleavage was there to stay. The social dynamics changed also as a result of the impact of such a powerful idea as equality on a profoundly unequal social order like that of pre-colonial Rwanda and Burundi, based on the acquiescence of the Hutu majority to rule by the Tutsi minority.

The years that preceded independence were characterised by ethnic turmoil in both countries. In Rwanda ethnic clashes resulted in mass killings and in the displacement of hundreds of thousands of refugees, mainly Tutsis, in neighbouring countries. Following independence, Rwanda and Burundi had opposite experiences in many respects: in Rwanda the Hutu majority obtained political power whereas in Burundi the Tutsis maintained control of the military apparatus as well as the political machinery.[15] What both countries have in common is the continued role played by the Hutu-Tutsi cleavage in the social and political arena, as well as a history of violence and displacement resulting from that conflict. Even before independence thousands of Tutsis had been forced to leave Rwanda following a massacre that killed hundreds. Under Kayibanda's rule, which lasted for twelve years, Rwanda was subject to an authoritarian and highly personalised regime: although the Hutu-Tutsi conflict was apparently dormant for a number of years, the violent enforcement of the quota policy in 1972 resulted in the dismissal of many Tutsi employees and in the expulsion of Tutsi students from schools and universities. In the same year, the Tutsi-led regime in Burundi organised the killing of hundreds of thousands of educated Hutus in one of the bloodiest massacres in modern times. Those educated Hutus who managed to escape death left Burundi. Further outbreaks of violence took place in Burundi in 1988 and in Rwanda in 1990. In April 1994 after the killing of President Habyarimana the extremist militias of the Rwandese Government (interahamwe) tried to eliminate the entire Tutsi population of Rwanda. About 800,000 Rwandans, including also many Hutu opponents of the extremists, lost their lives in the 1994 genocide.[16]

From the point of view of constitutional development, both countries had in common constitutions which were unable to lay the foundations for the rule of law and to provide the rational-legal framework necessary for the solution of conflicts

---

[15] The reality is obviously more complex. In Burundi, a section of the Tutsi group, the Bururi clan, is the one which is effectively in control. Opposition to the authoritarian rule of the regime comes from the Hutus but also from Tutsis from different clans. In Rwanda, on the other hand, another important cleavage is that existing between Hutus living in the northern provinces of Ruhengeri and Gisenyi and Hutus living in the southern and central provinces. President Habyarimana came from Gisenyi as did many of the key people in his regime. 'From a comparison between Burundi and Rwanda it emerges that the Rwandese revolution has played an important role in the evolution of power in Burundi. The Burundi power feared that the ethnic majority would transform itself into a political majority, like in Rwanda', (Reyntjens, 'L'Afrique des Grands Lacs en Crise: Rwanda-Burundi: 1988-1994', Paper published on internet, 22 May 1997, p. 2).

[16] The most detailed and researched account of the Rwandese genocide is *African Rights, Death, Despair and Defiance*, 1995, 2nd edition.

and for social and political developments. The written constitution was often disregarded and changes in the constitutional structure occurred more often as a result of coups d'état or violent confrontations.

## II. THE CONSTITUTIONS ADOPTED AFTER INDEPENDENCE

When Rwanda and Burundi became independent on 1 July 1962 no constitution was 'handed over' to them. However, there were some important differences in the constitutional situation of the two countries. In Burundi a provisional constitution had been in force before independence. The National Assembly had approved it, but it had been abrogated just before independence. Within a few months a new constitution was prepared and was promulgated on 16 October 1962. In Rwanda, on the other hand, no constitutional structure was in place at the moment of independence and the constitution was only thereafter drafted and adopted.

The procedure that was followed in the adoption of the first constitutions in Rwanda and Burundi is also quite exceptional if compared with the constitutional experience of most African countries that had become independent at the same time. Both Rwanda and Burundi witnessed a lively constitutional debate. In Rwanda, the Constitutional Assembly debated the constitutional project for about a year, from October 1961 to October of the following year.[17] Furthermore, the Rwandan people abolished the monarchy in a referendum which was held on the same day as the elections for the National Assembly. The final text of the Constitution was approved after four different readings. Although the main model of inspiration was the Senegalese Constitution of 1959, some of its provisions were based on the French Constitution, and, in some cases, on the Belgian Constitution.[18] The constitutional amendment procedure contained in that Constitution was particularly burdensome. It required a very high majority both for proposing an amendment bill - which had to be signed by two-thirds of the members of the Assembly - and for passing the proposed amendment for which the vote of four-fifths of the members was necessary. An amendment bill threatening the republican form of the state, the integrity of national territory and democratic principles could not be submitted to the Assembly.[19]

In Burundi, the Constitution, which had come into force on 16 October 1962 with retroactive effect, was also largely the result of internal factors and local debate. That Constitution, which replaced the provisional one, was essentially monarchic and conferred significant powers on the king.[20] The amendment of the

---

[17] 'Unlike the constitutions in the majority of African countries, the Rwandese Constitution is not a 'constitution of jurists. Its text was debated by the Assembly for a long time' (Reyntjens, *Pouvoir et Droit au Rwanda: Droit publique et evolution politique 1916-1973*, 1985, p. 358).
[18] Reyntjens, *op. cit.*, p. 359 ff.
[19] Art. 107.
[20] Although the 1962 Burundi Constitution concentrated power in the king, the creation of a Parliament had a significant impact on the Burundi political society. Indeed, Parliament became a symbol of concurrent power different from the mwami (Darbon, Hoiry, *Pouvoir et integration*

constitution was made particularly difficult: Article 119 established that once the National Assembly had declared that a particular constitutional provision would be amended, the two legislative Chambers were dissolved. After the elections the new Chambers, together with the king and the Crown Council, would identify the provisions to be subject to constitutional reform. No special majority was required either for the initial declaration of the legislative body nor for the amendment to be passed.

The Constitutions which were adopted by both countries were, thus, autochthonous. Although earlier constitutions obviously offered a model for the constitutional law-makers in Rwanda and Burundi, what distinguishes the constitutional experience of these two countries from other African countries in the decolonisation period is the predominance of a national constitutional debate as the decisive factor in the constitutional process. It is in a way ironic that countries in which the impact of the colonial period was particularly pervasive and produced long-lasting consequences received little interference from the former colonial power in the critical phase of the transition to independence.

## III. THE AUTHORITARIAN PERIOD

The constitutional structure put in place after independence did not last for very long in either country. Within a few years both Rwanda and Burundi were left with an altogether different constitution. The changes to the formal constitution were normally introduced without resorting to the procedure that had been originally envisaged for amending the constitution. The surreptitious introduction of authoritarian institutions unveiled the defeat of the rule of law in Rwanda and Burundi.

In Burundi, the progressive erosion of the 1962 Constitution began in early 1963. The Government led by André Muhirwa arrested the President of the National Assembly and the Minister of Public Works despite the existence of a constitutional provision that explicitly prohibited the arrest and detention of any member of Parliament.[21] Following the elections in May 1965 which gave a vast majority of the seats in the National Assembly to Hutu candidates, the country plunged into a state of civil war. A Hutu uprising in the central and northern regions of the country was repressed violently. As would become practice in Burundi constitutional history, the Constitution was amended after the ethnic clashes and in disregard of the procedure for amending the Constitution.

The most significant change was the overthrow of the monarchy in 1966. In November 1966 the self-appointed President of the Republic, Michel Micombero,

---

*politique: les cas du Burundi et Malawi*, 1982, p. 45 ff.). In the view of Darbon, the 1962 Constitution was the first step in a process of challenge against the monarchic institution which was an historical inevitability (*op. cit.*, p. 63).

[21] Art. 42.

declared the end of the monarchy and the introduction of republican institutions. The overthrow of the monarchy has been explained by modernisation theorists as a historical inevitability resulting from the conflict between the traditional authority represented by the king (mwami) and based on theocratic legitimacy, and the emerging bureaucratic and political elite whose legitimacy was essentially rational-legal in nature.[22] It would be a mistake, however, to interpret that event as the work of a modern bourgeoisie eager to break with the past and establish a new political and constitutional system based solely on rational-legal legitimacy. On the contrary, the new elite established an oligarchy and based its power on ethnic allegiances and clan loyalties.

Following the change in the form of the state, other important tenets of the constitutional order were modified. The Décret-L1966 vested legislative power in the President of the Republic and confined the National Assembly to a strictly consultative function. Within five years the formal Constitution had been virtually repealed. Some of its provisions were still formally in force, but they did not retain any normative strength, let alone constitutional authority. The constitutional order that was in place at the end of that process was authoritarian. It conferred both legislative and executive powers on the President and did not safeguard individual and collective freedoms. The Decret-Loi 1/144 of 20 October 1971 consolidated that order by creating the Supreme Council of the Republic which took over the depleted powers of the National Assembly. The Supreme Council of the Republic was entirely composed of officers from the Tutsi-dominated army.[23]

A new Hutu uprising took place in 1972. The repression was even more violent than in the past. The systematic massacre of the Hutu elite was organised and carried out amid international indifference. About 300,000 people were killed and many more became refugees in Eastern Zaire.[24] The events of 1972 consolidated the power of the ruling elite and literally wiped out the opposition. The Constitution adopted in the aftermath of those events entered into force on 1 August 1974. It consecrated the one-party system and gave the President wide legislative and executive powers thus consolidating the despotic power of the small elite responsible for the horrific massacres which had taken places two years earlier.[25]

The 1974 Constitution was adopted following an authoritarian procedure. Not only was the procedure still formally in force for amending the previous Constitution completely ignored, but there was also no public pronouncement on the new Constitution. The Supreme Council of the Republic approved it and the

---

[22] Darbon, Hoiry, *op. cit.* On modernisation: Huntington, *Political Order in Changing Societies*, 1968.
[23] 'By including most ranking officers, Micombero may have hoped to achieve a broad-based support among his officer corps. It also provided a forceful counterweight to civilian ministers who continued to pressure Micombero on a number of issues' (Weinstein, *Conflict and Confrontation in Central Africa: The Revolt in Burundi*, 1972, p. 24).
[24] Deo Hakizimana, *Burundi: le non dit*, 1990. Weinstein, *op. cit.*
[25] Arts. 18 and 48. The President at the time was still Michel Micombero.

President of the Republic promulgated it. The provisions on the amendment of the Constitution also reflected the authoritarian nature of the new Constitution. Indeed, Article 63 accorded to the President the power to initiate the procedure for amending the Constitution. No specific provision is made with respect to the approval of the Constitution by any elected body.

The coup which took place in 1976 did not bring any significant change in terms of constitutional order. It brought to power a different group of army officers, whose constitutional agenda - at least in the beginning - hardly differed from that of their predecessors. The unwritten constitutional order of Burundi was one based on the authoritarian rule of a small elite, which imposed its will through violent means and repression. Part of that order was also the segregation of the largest ethnic group and its exclusion from the exercise of political power as well as from equal access to education. The 1976 coup did not alter this order, as it was simply the result of the struggle for power taking place between opposing factions within the ruling elite.

However, the new regime headed by Colonel Bagaza undertook an effort of constitutional creation a few years after gaining power. This led to the adoption of a new Constitution, the third formal text in less than twenty years of independence. The Constitution was approved in a referendum in November 1981. That Constitution did not constitute a significant break in the authoritarian trend upon which the country had embarked. Indeed, it preserved the one-party system,[26] stated that the leader of the single party was the only candidate in the presidential elections,[27] and conferred wide powers on the President.[28] Chapter IX dealt with the procedure for the amendment of the Constitution. The power to initiate the procedure was a concurrent attribution of the President and the National Assembly. In the case of a proposal of amendment put forward by the President the consultation with the Central Committee of the Party was required. In order to be approved the proposal needed to receive two-thirds of the votes of the National Assembly. Article 78 stated that the republican nature of the state, national unity and territorial integrity could not be subject to any amendment.

The Bagaza regime was overthrown by the same means it had used to overthrow its own predecessor. In 1987, Major Buyoya led a military plot against Bagaza, which, in practice, did not change much in the country. The Buyoya coup was yet another example of the struggle for power within the ruling elite,[29] this time

---

[26] Art. 22.
[27] Art. 29, II.
[28] One substantive difference with the 1974 Constitution lay in the legislature. Arts. 42-51 regulated the creation of a National Assembly which was the main legislative organ.
[29] Indeed, Micombero, Bagaza and Buyoya shared a common 'agreement to exclude' ('*ad excludendum*') against the Hutu majority. Presidental changes occurred only as a result of palace plots and the perception that the President may not be able to preserve the Tutsi-Burundi oligarchy in power despite all the opposition. The statistics confirm the constant exclusion of the Hutus from power: in 1985 only four ministers out of 20 were Hutu, 17 members of the National Assembly out of 65, one

originating from the fear that Buyoya was losing control of the situation: the threats to suspend bilateral aid from some European countries bore testimony to that. From a constitutional point of view, the coup confirmed - if any confirmation was still necessary - that constitutional legality had come to mean very little and that changes of government were the result of a violent coup rather than any constitutional procedure.

The Buyoya regime faced considerable internal opposition from its onset. It reacted to the formation of a clandestine Hutu party, Palipehutu, with the usual systematic repression. The progressive deterioration of the situation in the north of the country led to an uprising in August 1988. Thousands of civilians were killed in a massacre that, although on a smaller scale, was conducted with a systematic brutality similar to that of 1972.[30] After those events, the Buyoya regime made some efforts towards national reconciliation. The larger presence of Hutu ministers in his government and the appointment of a Hutu Prime Minister did not significantly alter the balance of power in that the opposition movements were not yet allowed to participate in the process and key institutions like the army were left unaffected by the changes. It was not until 1992 that multy-partyism was introduced and a new Constitution enacted.

The authoritarian transformation of the political and constitutional system was more gradual in Rwanda after independence. The 1962 Constitution gave the Rwandan Parliament wider powers than the ones conferred on the Burundi parliament in the post-independence constitutional arrangement. It was not only the main legislative body but it could also control the President and his government and even dismiss individual ministers or the entire government with a vote of no-confidence. Its real powers were progressively eroded through the intervention of the President and the concentration of power in the executive.[31] During the first two legislatures following independence, the parliament was still a force to be reckoned with. It amended the bills presented by the government and tried to oppose the authoritarian devolution of the country. The control of the government on the electoral process and the restrictions on freedom of expression and assembly ensured the 'taming' of the Parliament to the will of the executive. As a result of this, during the third legislature 'there was no criticism of the Government, no rejection or amendment of bill'.

The erosion of the constitutional role of the parliament occurred initially without any formal constitutional amendment. A series of constitutional amendments were introduced in 1973 strengthening the power of the President and eliminating the constitutional limit of three consecutive presidential mandates.[32] This would have allowed President Kayibanda to stand for re-election in the fourth

---

ambassador out of 22 (see Reyntjens, *L'Afrique du des Grands Lacs en Crise*, 1994, p.41).

[30] See, for instance, Amnesty International's Report on those events: Burundi: Killings of Children by Government Troops, October 1988.

[31] Reyntjens, *op. cit.*, 1985, p. 365-402.

[32] Reyntjens, *op. cit.*, 505.

mandate. However, a few months after those amendments were approved a coup led by General Habyarimana overthrew the Kayibanda regime. The new regime adopted an altogether new Constitution in 1978 which incorporated the authoritarian form of the state into a written text. Like the Burundi Constitution of 1974, the 1978 Constitution explicitly accepted the single-party system by decreeing that Mouvement Révolutionnaire National pour le Développement was the only political group (formation politique unique).[33] Unlike the 1981 Burundi Constitution, however, the Rwandan Constitution does not contain such a detailed regulation of the single party and gives more limited powers to the party organs. With respect to the procedure for amending the constitution, for instance, the party does not play any constitutional role. The procedure is vested concurrently with the President and the National Council for Development. A majority of two-thirds of the members of the National Council is required for an amendment bill to be considered by the Council which will need a majority of three-quarters to pass it. Subject matters left outside the sphere of possible constitutional amendment include also the democratic principles of the republic besides the republican form of the state and territorial integrity.

## IV. THE RECENT YEARS: SHORT-LIVED CONSTITUTIONS, VIOLENCE AND UNCERTAINTY

The winds of change that have blown over the African continent since the late 1980s did not leave Rwanda and Burundi unaffected. The core of the constitutional reforms of the late 1980s and early 1990s regarded the introduction of multipartyism and free elections. In many countries such process was accompanied by momentous constitutional changes and, in some cases, by the adoption of an entirely new constitution.

Rwanda preceded Burundi in the adoption of constitutional reforms and the introduction of multipartyism. In 1991, the new Rwandese Constitution entered into force. The regime that had ruled the country for nearly twenty years was compelled to pursue a policy of political and legislative reform by a series of factors of which the process of democratisation taking place in many other African countries at the time was only one.[34] An important factor was the military operation carried out by the Raggroupement Patriotique Rwandaise (RPF), a rebel movement based in Uganda.[35] The escalation in the RPF's military activities weakened President Habyarimana's regime which could not contrast the demands

---

[33] Art. 7.
[34] See Reyntjens, *op. cit.*, 1994, pp. 103-125.
[35] On 1 October 1990, the Rwandan Patriotic Army launched an attack on the north-eastern region of Rwanda. Its troops came from Uganda, where a large number of Rwandan refugees had lived for nearly three decades. At the time of the attack, the RPA declared its primary objectives to be the acceleration of the process of democratisation and the quest for a long-lasting solution to the problem of the return of the refugees from Uganda.

of the internal opposition for political reform.[36]

The 1991 Constitution was drafted by a commission (Commission Nationale de Synthèse) entirely appointed by the President. The final text was not subject to referendum for approval but simply passed by the National Development Council on which only members of the ruling party sat. Although it formally introduced multipartyism,[37] the Constitution, enacted without any process of popular consultation and approval, was doomed to fail 'to provide the entire body politic the fixed and lasting foundation that is a condition for the continual development of the State free from disturbance'.[38] Within a few months the Government was obliged to come to terms with the reality of the military strength of the RPF and, shortly after the entry into force of the Constitution, began negotiations with the leadership of the rebel movement. The legal consequence of these negotiations was a change in the constitutional structure of the country. Indeed, between September 1991 and August 1993 a series of agreements were signed between the RPF and the Rwandan Government. Such agreements formed the basis for the Arusha Accord which created a 'negotiated constitutional order'.[39] The Accord was superior in rank to the Constitution and, in case of conflict between the two, the former would prevail over the latter. Furthermore, a large number of constitutional provisions were explicitly amended by the Accord. The adoption of such a procedure for the amendment of existing constitutional norms demonstrated the inadequacy of the 1991 Constitution and, in particular, the fragility of the machinery for the amendment of the Constitution set out in Article 96 which simply stated that the President of the Republic and the National Assembly had the power to initiate the procedure of constitutional revision. It also added that 'any project or proposal of constitutional amendment which modifies the republican nature of the State, the territorial integrity and the democratic principles on which the Republic rests cannot be taken into consideration'. This procedure was not followed in the introduction of substantial changes to the constitutional structure which took place only two years later. With hindsight, we can say that the 1991 Constitution contained norms devoid of the strength typical of constitutional norms.

The Arusha Accord did not, however, provide the stability that it aimed to created. On 6 April 1994 the plane carrying President Habyarimana and his

---

[36] 'In Rwanda, the 'War of October' simultaneously pushed the government to accept substantial political reforms and made a democratic transition more difficult by augmenting the coercive capabilities of the government and increasing the level of insecurity in the country' (Longman, *op. cit.*, 294).
[37] Article 7 of the Constitution said: 'All political parties fulfilling the legal requirements participate in the elections. Their establishment and the exercise of their activities is free provided that they respect democratic principles and do not aim at changing the republican nature of the state, territorial integrity and security'.
[38] Hermann von Mangoldt, *The Concept of the Rule of Law and Governmental Forms in the United States*, 1938.
[39] Reyntjens, 'Constitution-making in Situations of Extreme Crisis: The Case of Rwanda and Burundi', *Journal of African Law*, 1996, II, p. 235.

Burundi counterpart was shot down. This incident triggered off one of the greatest tragedies of modern times. A provisional government made entirely of extremists was formed. Hutu militias (interahmwe) with the help of the armed forces killed hundreds of thousands of Tutsis and moderate Hutus in a deliberate and long-planned attempt to eliminate all Tutsis. In about three months, the genocide in Rwanda caused the death of around 800,000 people.[40]

The Government that was installed after the end of the civil war and of the genocide in July 1994 was dominated by the RPF. Constitutional changes were once again introduced. The Fundamental Law of 5 May 1995 indicated that the constitutional order was made of four different texts, with that Law at the top of the hierarchy. A Protocol of Agreement signed by the RPF and other political parties was also given constitutional rank second only to the Fundamental Law. The Arusha Accord was the third set of norms having constitutional rank and the 1991 Constitution was to be deemed in force only insofar as its provisions were not inconsistent with the provisions contained in the other text.

The new constitutional order has been defined as 'a piece of subtle and smart constitutional engineering which attempts to hide the monolithic character of the exercise of power. Under the labels of 'power-sharing' and 'national unity', which are necessary for international consumption, one discovers a constitutional order allowing the victorious political-military party to pull the strings. The restructuring of power in favour of the (vice-)presidential institution through the extension of its competencies and its predominance over the governmental branch of the Executive, as well as through its control over the Legislature, in which the military tilt the balance in its favour, allows the RPF to exercise a political monopoly, while avoiding creating an image of concentrated power. Of course, the analysis presented here shows only the constitutional side of the hegemonic project. Military force and secret service activity, intimidation and the use of sheer violence are much more compelling for the other political actors, but the study of these physical means is beyond the scope of this contribution'.[41] Such an analysis fails to understand the context in which the change in the constitutional order took place. A genocide is no common event in the history of a country. Expecting a government installed just after such a tragic and unique event to respect the legality that had been agreed before the genocide is, to say the least, not reasonable. On the contrary, the constitutional history of many countries seems to suggest the contrary: after tragic events like those which occurred in Rwanda in 1994, a quiet return to a pre-existing legal order is the exception rather than the rule.

As correctly remarked by Reyntjens,[42] however, a weakness in the newly created constitutional order is the lack of specific provisions establishing a clear procedure for future amendments of constitutional norms. The procedure contained

---

[40] African Rights, *op. cit.* Prunier, *op. cit.* Chrétien, *op. cit.*, 201-375.
[41] Reyntjens, *op. cit.*, 1996, 238.
[42] Ibid.

in the 1991 Constitution is, theoretically, still in force, but constitutional norms of higher rank were created after the Constitution without resorting to that procedure. That procedure can be applied only to amend the provisions of the 1991 Constitution itself, but it would be rather paradoxical if it was followed to amend the higher constitutional norms contained in the subsequent acts, like the Arusha Accord, the Protocol of Agreement and the Fundamental Law. How these acts can be amended remains unclear and certainly contributes to a situation of legal uncertainty that can only be acceptable as part of a transitional arrangement.[43]

The experience of Burundi is in some ways similar, at least as far as the legal issues underlying the constitution-making process are concerned. In that country the democratisation process began later than in Rwanda. Multipartyism was introduced only in 1992. The free elections held in June 1993 led to the victory of the Melchior Ndadaye candidate of the main opposition party (FRODEBU). The Burundi Constitution that had ensured the transition to democracy was approved by referendum in March 1992. The norms on the amendment of the Constitution were more detailed than the ones in the Rwandan Constitution. Articles 180-182 gave power to initiate the procedure to the President, after consultations with the Government National Assembly after a resolution adopted by the absolute majority of its members. For the approval of an actual amendment, proposed by either the executive or the legislative, the vote of four-fifths of the Assembly is required, a particularly high quorum. The limits to constitutional amendment include the republican nature of the state, national unity and territorial integrity, like the Rwandan Constitution. However, in addition to these matters, Article 182 identifies the secular character of the state as a fundamental principle which cannot be subject to constitutional amendment. Furthermore, the procedure for amending the Constitution cannot be initiated in times of serious internal disorder. A referendum on the proposed amendment could take place subject to the decision of the President of the Republic.[44] His presidency came to a violent end a few months

---

[43] A recent constitutional amendment of great importance was adopted in February 2000. It concerns the establishment of community-based tribunals which would have jurisdiction over genocide cases, except for the so-called first tier of cases (i.e. individuals accused of greater involvement or planning).
[44] Article 89 of the French Constitution of 1958 constituted the model for the norms on constitutional amendment in many Francophone African countries. Both the Rwandan and Burundi Constitution, however, departed from that model as far as the limits to constitutional amendment were concerned. The French Constitution indicates only the republican nature of the Government as a constitutional principle which cannot be amended. On the procedures for constitutional amendment in Francophone African countries, Reyntjens remarks: 'Unlike the English-speaking countries, where the procedures for constitution-drafting and constitutional amendment are generally 'open' and participatory (often involving constitutional commissions hearing the views of the public and of experts, and constituent assemblies debating in public sessions), in francophone Africa they are marked by vagueness and lack of organised public debate. In most of these countries, it is extremely difficult to know, even approximately, how a constitution is made or amended. The major part of the preparation of a draft is conducted in private, popular reaction and participation is not invited, and in fact discouraged. The first contact of the public with the new constitution is generally on Referendum Day, if a referendum is held at all', (Reyntjens, 'Recent Developments in the Public Law of Francophone African States', *Journal of African Law*, 1986, II, p. 88).

after he had been elected: he was assassinated during a coup d'état orchestrated by the Tutsi-led armed forces.

The 1992 Constitution which had paved the way to the democratisation process did not survive for too long. Although formally still in force, the dubious interventions of the main constitutional organs, including the Parliament and the ethnically divided Constitutional Court, undermined the actual normative strength of the Constitution. By 1994 under the pressure of the armed forces most political parties had signed a document 'Government Convention' which is hierarchically superior to the Constitution. Article 6 states that the 'Constitution remains valid only insofar as it is not contrary to the Convention'. The Government Convention also contains a series of rules on the share of power between opposition and majority. All the posts in the government and in the diplomatic missions were to be divided between the party that had won the elections (FRODEBU) and the opposition, led by the Tutsi-dominated UPRONA. Quite significantly, the army and judicial posts were left out of the agreement.[45] Moreover, the 1992 Constitution stated that following the death of the President, elections should take place within three months.[46] Once again a document which introduces substantial modifications to the constitutional structure was adopted without following the procedure for constitutional amendment set out in the Constitution. In July 1996, a *coup d'état* brought Major Buyoya back to power, establishing yet another authoritarian system to replace the constitutional order. Negotiations between the Government and the Opposition have been taking place since 1996, convened first by Julius Nyerere and, after his death, by Nelson Mandela.

## CONCLUSION

The constitutional process in Rwanda and Burundi has been marked by failures. All significant constitutional changes in both countries resulted from coups d'états, 'hidden' amendments and, in the case of Rwanda in 1992, from negotiations between two opposing factions. The procedures designed in the written constitutions for amending the constitution were seldom followed. This is at the

---

[45] The army has been historically dominated by Tutsis from the Bururi province. Its accountability as well as its commitment to the democratic process are very questionable. The army together with militias of Tutsi extremists carried out massacres of Hutu activists since after the assassination of President Ndadaye in October 1993 and even before the army-led coup which re-installed Major Buyoya into power in July 1996. The district of Kamenge in Bujumbura, inhabited mainly by Hutus, was entirely wiped out in a few months, despite the presence of FRODEBU in the civilian authorities. The civil war in Burundi has caused the death of hundreds of thousands of civilians since October 1993 and has led to the displacement of many more in neighbouring countries.

[46] Art. 85, VI: 'The election of the new President of the Republic takes place within a period which cannot be shorter than one month and longer than three months (since the Constitutional Court has affirmed that there is a vacuum), with the exception of force majeure stated by the Constitutional Court'.

same time cause and consequence of the erosion of the rule of law in both countries.

Ethnic conflict has played a crucial role in the history of the two countries. It is certainly no coincidence that major institutional and constitutional changes occurred during or in the aftermath of major explosions of ethnic violence. The Constitutions normally ignore the ethnic problem, concealing it behind the slogans of 'national unity' and 'reconciliation'. However, the failure of the law-makers to devise a legal system which can satisfactorily deal with the ethnic cleavage instead of ignoring it has exacerbated the conflict, contributed to instability and to the recourse to violent means for resolving social conflicts.

Chapter Fifteen

# CONSTITUTIONAL CHANGE IN THE UNITED KINGDOM

Peter Oliver and Adam Tomkins[*]

## I. INTRODUCTION: THE STRANGE NATURE OF THE BRITISH CONSTITUTION

The constitution of the United Kingdom is a strange creature, especially when it is compared with other modern national constitutions, but it is not quite as odd as it first appears. Despite the fact that every other constitution discussed in this book is (said to be) of the 'written' variety, whereas the UK constitution is not, it is the similarities rather than the differences between the UK and other constitutions which are most notable. Despite the unusual form which the UK constitution takes, it shares with written constitutions all the problems of continuity and change with which public law has to grapple, however it is structured. This is no doubt a slightly unfashionable thing to say: most students and commentators already familiar with a written constitution who later come to study the UK constitution find it to be (at best) only very distantly related to the system they have already encountered. Similarly, increasing numbers of British constitutional observers are calling for radical constitutional reform which in many cases is designed to lead to a new written constitution. Against both of these positions we seek in this chapter to defend the old British constitution, not in the sense that we deem it to be perfect and in need of no renewal - far from it - but in the more limited sense that we seek to argue that despite its peculiar form, the UK constitution is one which is worthy of the name, and is one which merits comparative study in a collection such as this.

The 'UK constitution' is not a phrase which constitutional commentators frequently use. The proper name of the State is the United Kingdom of Great Britain and Northern Ireland. More usually we talk of the 'British constitution', a

---

[*] Both of the School of Law, King's College, London. Our thanks to Brian Bix and Stephen Tierney for their helpful comments on an earlier draft of this essay.

This essay was completed in August 1997. It has only been possible to comment on the new Labour Government's fast-moving constitutional reform agenda as of that date.

term which conveniently excludes Northern Ireland.[1] Britain is an amalgam of three nations: England, Wales and Scotland. These three nations enjoy two legal systems: England and Wales are ruled by English law and in Scotland Scots law applies. Constitutional lawyers in England tend to focus on the position in England, and even though there are important and often illuminating differences between English and Scots constitutional law,[2] the term 'British constitution' is usually employed as an expedient cover for these differences, as is so often the case when people in England talk of Britain.[3] That said, and because (as we shall see) conventions are important to our topic, we shall adopt these conventions and refer to the 'British constitution', on the understanding that we claim only to describe the English view of it.

The editors of this collection very sensibly sent to each of the contributors a questionnaire listing the issues which the editors wished to be included for consideration in each chapter. The first question asks, 'When did the present constitution come into force?'. This is the fascination of the British constitution. Even a simple and straightforward question such as this, which could be answered in one line in the USA, Ireland, France, Germany or pretty much anywhere else, could be the subject of several tomes in Britain. In Britain the constitution has always been in force, but then again, it never specifically came into force. Let us try to explain the apparent meaninglessness of this statement.

Perhaps what the editors mean by their question is, 'When was the document which you call 'the Constitution' written?' Well, there is no such document in Britain. This is why the British constitution is often referred to as an unwritten constitution. The frequency with which the latter term is used does not reduce the extent to which it is unhelpful and misleading. Much of the British constitution *is* written. In fact, almost all of it is written down somewhere. Similarly, there is much unwritten constitutional law (and even more unwritten constitutional practice) in States where there is a document called 'The Constitution'. The text of the US

---

[1] As we will. The changing constitutional relationship between Britain and Northern Ireland is a subject as provocative and complex as to merit a chapter to itself. We found that we could not do justice to it here. Rather than squeezing it into a too small number of pages, we have left this topic entirely for another day.

[2] There are many examples. The position of the crown and its relationship with the law is different in Scots law and in English law: see A. Tomkins, 'Crown Privileges', in M. Sunkin and S. Payne (eds), *The Nature of the Crown* (Oxford: Clarendon Press, 1999). Most strikingly, perhaps, judicial review has developed in Scotland in significantly different ways from England, especially as to the scope of judicial review: see W.J. Wolffe, 'The Scope of Judicial Review in Scots Law' [1992] *Public Law* 625. The Scottish view of parliamentary sovereignty is also different: see, e.g., C. Munro, *Studies in Constitutional Law* (London: Butterworths, 1987), ch. 4.

[3] A point made brilliantly by Tom Nairn in 'Sovereignty after the Election: Scotland and the Union', paper delivered to the Charter 88 Sovereignty Seminar, Birkbeck College, University of London, June 1997. Again, we will focus in this paper on English law, or on what might be called the English legal interpretation of the British constitution. The point is not to ignore Scotland, but to leave the Scottish view for the Scots, who would no doubt explain it better than us.

constitution, for example, makes no mention either of the cabinet or of congressional committees, both of which play powerful and important roles in contemporary American constitutional governance. What the term 'unwritten constitution' means is that there is no single document entitled 'The Constitution' which takes precedence over other, non-constitutional, laws. But the absence of such a piece of paper does not mean that Britain has no constitution. It simply means that Britain does not pretend, unlike almost all other States, that its constitution is written down in a single document.

Where then is Britain's constitution? There are many answers to this question, answers which will depend on what we mean by the word constitution. Rather than engage in a lengthy (and almost certainly unsuccessful) process of trying to come up with some sort of universal definition of 'constitution', we take as the British constitution that which talks of the State and its institutions; of relations between those institutions; and of relations between individual citizens and the State, or between State and society. For example, laws dealing with the composition of Parliament we would describe as constitutional, as they relate to an institution of the State. Similarly, laws or practices relating to the government, its powers and composition, to the judiciary and to the head of State would be constitutional. Doctrines such as the rule of law, the separation of powers, the responsibility of Ministers, and the sovereignty of Parliament would also be constitutional for us as they all concern the relations between the various institutions of State. Similarly, the regulation of civil liberties and other human rights, of voting, of nationality and citizenship: all of these would be constitutional matters, as they relate to relations between the individual and the State.

This is a deliberately broad understanding of what it is to talk of constitutions. One of the most obvious things about this understanding is that it does not seek to reduce the constitutional domain entirely to one of law. A number of the matters identified in the preceding paragraph as 'constitutional' would not in Britain be properly regarded as strictly legal. The doctrine of individual ministerial responsibility provides a good example. This is undoubtedly a constitutional doctrine in that it concerns limitations on the powers of government Ministers, and the relations between Ministers and Parliament,[4] but it could hardly be described as legal, in any usual sense. The doctrine is not enshrined in law. If it is breached no-one can go to court to have it enforced or to have sanctions imposed on those who have (allegedly) breached it. Rather, it has developed over time into an expectation which may, if disappointed, lead to certain political consequences. If, for example, a Minister lies to Parliament, then Parliament (and for that matter the public) will expect that Minister to resign. This has become such a strong expectation that we want to reinforce it with the language of constitutionalism. We know that we cannot actually enforce it through any judicial mechanism, but we

---

[4] The details of the doctrine of ministerial responsibility are examined below in the section of this chapter on constitutional conventions.

nonetheless want to have recourse to compelling and powerful rhetoric if we think that our strong expectations that Ministers must act responsibly and must not lie to us (or to our elected representatives) have been ignored. We therefore say that not only is the idea of ministerial responsibility one which is in fact recognised in British political practice, but that in addition, it ought to continue to be recognised in the future. This normative feeling which we want to keep hold of is commonly expressed through the language of constitutional convention. So we are able to say not only that 'as a matter of fact Ministers resign if they lie to Parliament, and that they resign in these circumstances is a good thing' but also that 'the constitution decrees that Ministers should resign if they lie to Parliament'. We are able to say this even though it is written nowhere and despite the fact that we could not go to court to have it enforced.

The importance of this for our purposes is that if we are to talk of constitutional amendment in the context of the British constitution, then we are talking not of a subject which is exclusively legal or juridical. It is not simply that there is a strong political element in constitutional change, but that it is through political processes that the British constitution can be changed, as much as it is through legal processes.

## II. CONSTITUTIONAL SOURCES: SOME HISTORICAL BACKGROUND

Why is there this diversity in the British constitution? Why has Britain persistently bucked the trend towards the written constitutional document? The answer is historical. Nation States acquire new written constitutional settlements for a variety of reasons. They gain independence from an imperial force (as in the USA in 1776). Or they lose a war and suffer the imposition of a new constitution (as in West Germany in 1945-48). Or they undergo civil war and internal political revolution (as in France in 1789). In other words, written constitutional settlements tend to follow on from political earthquakes of a magnitude Britain simply has not experienced in the past three hundred years. Britain has been successfully invaded (twice, in 55BC by Julius Caesar and in 1066 by William the Conqueror), and Britain has suffered a civil war (1642-49) which led, briefly, to political revolution (Oliver Cromwell's commonwealth between 1649 and 1660, when the monarchy was restored). But all of this really happened too early. The idea of the written constitutional settlement was born out of the political philosophy of the European enlightenment in the eighteenth century - the work of John Locke, Jean-Jacques Rousseau, Montesquieu and Tom Paine, whose (often English) ideas were of course nowhere less well received than in England. If English politics had been as restive during the eighteenth century as it had been in the seventeenth then the contemporary British constitution might well look very different indeed. It is an accident of history that Britain does not have a written constitution: the seismic political events have taken place, but not at the right times.

Consequently, the story of the development of the modern British constitution is less bloody and a lot longer than it might have been. There is no one starting date, but three from the seventeenth century offer themselves as obvious candidates: 1603, 1660 and 1688. In 1603 Queen Elizabeth died. Her demise marked the gradual death of the Tudor, or Ancient, Constitutional Order. Her successors were unable to hold the country together. Regional antagonisms, religious intolerance and parliamentary power all grew during the first four decades of the seventeenth century, culminating in the civil war of the 1640s during which all these tensions (geographic, religious and political) combined to begin the process of transforming England from the royal polity which it had been until 1603 into the parliamentary monarchy which it had become by 1688. For a while, it seemed that the civil war might lead to the complete eradication of the monarchy as a force in English government: King Charles I was beheaded in January 1649 and Parliament ruled alone for eleven years. But in 1660 the monarchy was restored, and Charles II became king. If only one thing was clear in 1660 it was that the monarchy would not be the same as it had been before the civil war. But quite what it would be was another question, which was not to be resolved until 1688 when an Act was passed with the misleading title of the Bill of Rights.

This title is likely to mislead for two reasons. First, it is not a bill but an Act - it is not a proposal for Parliament to debate but a binding Act of Parliament. Secondly, it is not a Bill of Rights in the sense in which we commonly understand that term today. The modern understanding of a Bill of Rights is of a list of rights and freedoms (such as the right to life, freedom of speech and freedom of conscience) which the individual enjoys as against the State. But the 1688 Bill of Rights is a list of rights which Parliament has as against the crown. Under the Bill of Rights, the crown lost its powers to tax: only Parliament may now do this (Article 4). Similarly, no army or militia may be kept by the State during peace-time without Parliament's specific authority (Article 6). Further, parliamentarians may not be prosecuted or sued in the crown's courts in respect of things which they say or do during parliamentary business (Article 9). The Bill of Rights remains one of the written corner-stones of the unwritten British constitution. It marks an important point along the path which the British constitution has taken since 1603: namely, the gradual move of the centre of power from the crown to Parliament.

Even though Montesquieu, the author of the modern version of the doctrine of the separation of powers, was reportedly influenced in his formulation of the doctrine by what he perceived to be the constitutional position in England (during a period, we should not forget, of the *ancien regime*, before the French revolution), the British constitutional order has only ever recognised two powers - crown and Parliament - and not the three which Montesquieu identified. The story of the development of the modern British constitution is in large part the story of the struggle of power between these two great constitutional forces: crown and Parliament. The importance of the short seventeenth century (1603-88) is that this period marked the shift in the balance of power from the crown to Parliament. But this period did not mark the end of the battle: merely a decisive moment in its course. As we shall see as this chapter unfolds, the struggle continues.

The story of constitutional amendment in Britain which this chapter seeks to tell is structured around this basic theme: the ongoing struggle between the forces of the crown and those of Parliament for constitutional ascendancy. We look in turn at each of the main sources of constitutional authority in Britain, starting with the crown and its prerogatives and then at its common law; then moving on to Parliament and its legislation. In looking at each of these formal sources of constitutional law, we examine how they may be amended by each of the main actors on the constitutional stage: that is to say, by the executive, by the judiciary, and by Parliament. Finally, we examine in some detail the troublesome 'conventions' by which the crown's government has sought to recapture at least some of the constitutional high ground. In the conclusion we discuss the issue of where external influences might fit in to this domestic structure - especially as regards the law and jurisprudence of the European Union. We end with a brief overview of the extensive programme of constitutional reform on which Tony Blair's Labour government was elected in May 1997.

## III. THE CROWN PREROGATIVE

The crown prerogative may now be defined[5] as 'the remaining portion of the crown's original authority ... whether such power be in fact exercised by the Queen herself or by her Ministers'.[6] Nine hundred years ago the prerogative powers[7] covered virtually the whole range of possible governmental jurisdiction - the sovereign's sway was virtually unlimited. But gradually, in a process of what we characterise as constitutional amendment, these powers were reduced to a status which, at least in its most important elements, resembles the status of the executive in other constitutional systems. So just as the President of the United States of America can conclude treaties, declare war and emergencies, sign bills and pardon offenders, so can the Queen or (by convention) her Ministers. We can see,

---

[5] There is an academic dispute over the definition of the prerogative which is not pursued in any detail here. Briefly, a first view, put forward by Blackstone, *Commentaries*, I, p. 239 in 1765 and supported by Professor H.W.R. Wade in this century (see H.W.R. Wade, *Constitutional Fundamentals* (London: Stevens, 1980), pp. 46 *et seq.*), interprets the prerogative as referring to acts which *only* the sovereign can do - powers to enter into contracts, employ people, set up compensation schemes, etc. are all therefore excluded. Professor Dicey, the courts (see, e.g., *AG v. De Keyser's Royal Hotel Ltd.* [1920] AC 508, p. 526 per Lord Dunedin, *R v. Criminal Injuries Compensation Board, ex parte Lain* [1967] QB 864 (Div. Ct.)) and most commentators adopt a less restrictive view, essentially to the effect that anything 'the executive government can lawfully do without the authority of an Act of Parliament is done in virtue of the prerogative'. (A.V. Dicey, *An Introduction to the Study of the Law of the Constitution*, 10th ed. (London: Macmillan, 1959) (first published edition 1885), p. 425). The second of these approaches is adopted here.
[6] A.V. Dicey, *An Introduction to the Study of the Law of the Constitution*, 10th ed., pp. 424-5. The prerogative is also 'a term which has caused more perplexity to students than any other expression referring to the constitution'. *Ibid.*, p. 424.
[7] The focus in this section is on prerogative powers. But full consideration of the crown prerogative would take in rights, such as treasure trove, and immunities, such as immunity from suit, and even duties, such as the crown's duty to protect subjects within the realm. See A. Tomkins, *op. cit.*, note 2.

therefore, that there is both an historical and a functional explanation for the attribution and continued existence of prerogative powers in the present-day British constitution.[8]

What would a list of prerogative powers under the present-day British constitution look like? Textbook writers regularly attempt this task, and the standard approach is to divide prerogative powers into those which are still exercised by the sovereign personally, and those which are exercised on her behalf by her Ministers. Without any pretence of exhaustiveness, competence under the prerogative can be summarised briefly as follows.[9]

First, there are the prerogative powers which are exercised with some degree of personal input by the sovereign. These include appointment of the Prime Minister, summoning Parliament, dissolving Parliament, and assenting to parliamentary bills. Secondly, there are a good number of prerogative powers which are exercised by the Prime Minister or other Ministers: foreign affairs (signing, ratifying or rejecting international treaties); defence of the realm (declaring war, ordering British forces into armed combat,[10] internment of enemy aliens; organising the armed forces,[11] keeping the peace within the realm); administration of justice (grant of pardons, appointment of judges); appointments to the civil service and other public offices; etc.

The prerogative may be exercised with widely varying degrees of formality. For example, in the conduct of the day-to-day foreign policy discussions the power may be used without any special documentary form. At the other extreme, the prerogative may justify detailed legislation such as the Civil Service Order in Council 1982 which grants power to Ministers to exercise further discretionary powers.[12] As we shall see, primary competence under the prerogative relates closely to (secondary) exercise of such power.

In the *Case of Proclamations* (1611), Coke CJ stated that 'the King hath no prerogative but that which the law of the land allows him'. Over 150 years later, Lord Camden CJ declared in relation to all executive powers, including the prerogative, that justification for a claim of power could only lie in 'our books' and

---

[8] For elaboration on these approaches see A. Le Sueur & M. Sunkin, *Public Law* (London: Longman, 1997), pp. 267-9.

[9] See 8(2) *Halsbury's Laws*, 4th ed. 1996, para 801 *et seq*.

[10] There was no prior parliamentary approval before troops were sent to recent conflicts: the Falkland Islands, Kuwait and Bosnia.

[11] It is this head of jurisdiction which gives the Ministry of Defence the power, for the time being, to prohibit homosexuals from serving in the armed forces. See *R v. Ministry of Defence, ex parte Smith* [1996] 1 All ER 257 (CA). This situation could well change with incorporation of the European Convention on Human Rights.

[12] Margaret Thatcher used powers granted under the Civil Service Order in Council 1982 to ban trade unions from GCHQ, thereby provoking the legal tussle which culminated in *Council of Civil Service Unions v. Minister for Civil Service* [1985] AC 374. Day-to-day matters of management and employment are now governed by the Civil Service Order in Council 1995 (as amended by the Civil Service (Amendment) Order 1995 and the Civil Service (Amendment) Order 1996).

'[i]f it is not to be found there, it is not the law'.[13] Today, despite the existence of well-known books on the prerogative such as Chitty[14] and Halsbury,[15] the ground occupied by the prerogative in our constitution has not been mapped in detail. This century, for example, the government has claimed authority under the prerogative to intercept private communications.[16] Although this area has now been covered by legislation,[17] there have always been doubts as to whether the earlier power had been properly claimed.[18]

Prior to the seventeenth century, it may have been true to say that the prerogatives of the crown were those which the sovereign claimed.[19] In other words, the sovereign's exercise of the prerogative gradually poured content into this constitutional sphere until the courts and Parliament summoned up the will to oppose such claims. It seems that after 1688 the sovereign's behaviour would no longer determine the legal delimitation of the prerogative. As Lord Camden CJ stated in *Entick*, '[w]ith respect to the practice [of the prerogative], if it goes no higher [than 1688], every lawyer will tell you, it is much too modern to be evidence'.[20] In other words, no matter how often the sovereign repeated an unconstitutional act, such precedents could not carve out new jurisdiction under the prerogative.

Does this mean that the executive no longer has the ability to amend the prerogative of its own accord? It is possible to imagine in the abstract that, given the vast range of historical powers exercised by the crown, some less important ones may have fallen into disuse unnoticed even by dedicated historians and legal scholars. Others, such as the power to press subjects into the service of Her Majesty's Navy, may have been followed more closely and eventually consigned to the bin of desuetude. To this extent, we can say that the action or inaction of the executive affects jurisdiction under the prerogative.

However, it is the tendency of the executive to *expand* its powers which naturally attracts the greatest interest from constitutional observers. Strictly speaking, the executive cannot of its own accord expand its powers under the prerogative, but it is easy to imagine how the executive tests the outer edges of its authority by occasionally 'trying it on'. The example of wire-tapping has already been mentioned.[21] Another example is provided by *R v. Secretary of State for the Home Office, ex parte Northumbria Police Authority*[22] in which the Court of

---

[13] (1611) 12 Co. Rep. 74; *Entick v. Carrington* (1765) 19 St. Tr. 1030.
[14] *Prerogatives of the Crown* (London: Butterworths, 1820).
[15] *Op.cit.*
[16] See *Malone v. Metropolitan Police Commissioner* [1979] Ch. 344.
[17] Interception of Communications Act 1985.
[18] See, e.g., R. Brazier, *Constitutional Reform*, (Oxford: Oxford University Press, 1991) p. 89.
[19] According to Professor Dicey, 'during the earlier periods of our history ... the King was the source of law'. *Op. cit.* p. 183.
[20] *Entick v. Carrington* (1765) 19 St Tr. 1030.
[21] See notes 16 and 17 and accompanying text.
[22] [1988] 1 All ER 556.

Appeal declared that it was within the crown's prerogative powers (to maintain the peace) to make available plastic bullets and CS gas canisters to police. Although amendment to the extent of the prerogative was confirmed by the judiciary, the decision by the executive to exercise controversial powers in conditions propitious to any potential litigation clearly has an important role in the development of the prerogative. Furthermore, the attitude of the Court of Appeal clearly did nothing to dissuade future governments from trying the same strategy. According to Nourse LJ, 'the scarcity of reference in the books to the prerogative of keeping the peace within the realm does not disprove that it exists. Rather it may point to an unspoken assumption that it does.'[23]

The same process of executive-initiated power grabbing can be seen in an even more topical and controversial case. The entry of the United Kingdom into the European Community was brokered by intensive executive action and the agreements were eventually signed under prerogative powers. The brief text of the European Communities Act 1972 disguised the extent to which powers resembling prerogative powers were given to the executive. Tony Benn MP and Andrew Hood have argued that by virtue of participation in European law-making decisions of the Council of Ministers, the UK executive has gained a new sphere of powers which it can exercise independently of Parliament.[24] Furthermore, EC law so made now has the potential to prevail over an Act of Parliament, by virtue of *Factortame*[25] and other key constitutional decisions of the European Court of Justice.[26]

If we shift the focus away from attempts by the executive to carve out new pockets of constitutional jurisdiction under the prerogative and look instead at particular exercises of such powers, matters appear more straightforward. One of the themes identified above is that occasionally executive practice pours content into a previously unexplored area of potential executive jurisdiction. But if we look for a moment at acknowledged prerogative powers, such as the power to regulate the armed forces, the specific exercise of such powers is not without constitutional significance. The decision of the executive to prohibit homosexuals from serving

---

[23] *Ibid.*
[24] A. Benn & A. Hood, *Common Sense: A New Constitution for Britain* (London: Hutchinson, 1993), pp. 64-73. The standard reply is that Parliament can repeal the 1972 Act and thereby reassert its authority. Whatever the strength of this argument as a matter of UK law, it is doubtful as a proposition of EC law and highly unlikely as a matter of politics and economics. A stronger reply to Benn and Hood is that EC law, especially treaty amendment, involves a degree of parliamentary participation. In the case of EC directives, there is some opportunity for parliamentary scrutiny in advance of approval by the Council of Ministers and ultimately directives are brought into UK law by Act or statutory instrument. But even these points must be moderated by noting, first, that the timing of parliamentary scrutiny of EC law may be such as to make it virtually irrelevant (see A. Cygan, 'The Scrutiny of EU Legislation by the House of Commons after Maastricht' [1995-6] 6 *KCLJ* 38) and, secondly, that the doctrine of direct effect devalues the importance of national incorporation.
[25] *R v. Secretary of State for Transport, ex parte Factortame (No. 2)* [1990] 1 AC 603.
[26] See cases cited at notes 67-9, 72 and 73.

in the armed forces may be amended at any moment by further executive action.[27] The same is true of the institution by prerogative of a criminal compensation scheme and the subsequent amendment of it by prerogative.[28]

What of amendment of the prerogative by the judiciary? It became clear in the seventeenth century that the courts rather than the sovereign would declare the existence and define the extent of the prerogative.[29] While having its source in custom, the prerogative would from then on be embraced by the common law.[30] As part of the seventeenth century settlement, the courts would limit the sovereign's ability to expand power by prerogative, Parliament would abolish the prerogative courts (the notorious Court of the Star Chamber), and the vacuum created by limited monarchy would be filled by a sovereign parliament. No part of the arrangement provided the judiciary with any specific power to expand or contract the prerogative. The ability to develop new 'custom' relevant to the prerogative being frozen as of 1688,[31] it was simply up to the courts to declare existence and define extent. As Diplock LJ confirmed as late as 1965 '[i]t is 350 years and a civil war too late for the Queen's courts to broaden the prerogative'.[32]

But the development of the common law is a creative business. Some judges, such as the Court of Appeal in the *Northumbria* case, are inclined to use the common law-making power vested in them to expand the prerogative at the behest of the executive. Other judges, such as Lord Camden CJ in *Entick*, stoutly refuse to manipulate the prerogative to suit the government of the day. In the residual sphere that is the enduring prerogative, it is clearly the courts which declare, confirm, define and re-define this constitutional jurisdiction.

In the discussion of the common law constitution below it will be apparent that the courts also amend prerogative powers by virtue of the ever-strengthening jurisdiction of judicial review.[33] To illustrate this point, let us take the prerogative

---

[27]   *R v. Ministry of Defence, ex parte Smith* [1996] 1 All ER 257 (CA). It may also be *required* as a result of incorporation of the European Convention on Human Rights.

[28]   As has recently been made clear, this statement has to be modified to take into account the rare case where Parliament has legislated to replace a prerogative scheme with a legislative one but where the latter has not yet been brought into force. The member of the executive empowered to bring the statutory scheme into force may not simply abandon this scheme and resort to a new prerogative version. The fact that Parliament has given the Minister the power to bring the statutory scheme into force means that he or she is not obliged to do so but the Minister must at least keep the option open until Parliament directs otherwise. See *R v. Secretary of State for the Home Office, ex parte Fire Brigades Union* [1995] 2 WLR 464.

[29]   *Prohibitions del Roy* (1607) 12 Co. Rep. 63 and *Case of Proclamations* (1611) 12 Co. Rep. 74.

[30]   As Monro notes, '[s]trictly speaking, the prerogatives are recognised, rather than created, by the common law, for their source is in custom'. C. Munro, *Studies in Constitutional Law* (London: Butterworths, 1987), p. 159.

[31]   See *Entick v. Carrington* (1765) 19 St Tr. 1030.

[32]   *BBC v. Johns (Inspector of Taxes)* [1965] Ch. 32.

[33]   The House of Lords has confirmed the ability of courts to review the exercise of a limited range of prerogative powers. See *Council of Civil Service Unions v. Minister for Civil Service* [1985] AC 374 and *R v. Secretary of State for the Home Department, ex parte Fire Brigades Union* [1995] 2 WLR 464.

power to issue passports. Since *R v. Secretary of State for Foreign and Commonwealth Affairs, ex parte Everett*,[34] it has been clear that this power must be exercised in conformity with the judicially-developed requirements of natural justice or fairness. Until *Everett*, political sanctions might have followed abuse of this power, but if the government was willing to ride out such pressure, the power was otherwise uncontrolled. Looked at in this light, the judicial amendment to the prerogative represented by *Everett* and similar cases is of a radical nature.

The orthodox answer to the question 'how is the prerogative amended?' is that the job is left to Parliament. Prerogative powers are created by pre-1688 custom, declared and defined by the courts, and gradually reduced by a sovereign parliament. This process has recently been summarised by Lord Browne-Wilkinson:[35]

The constitutional history of this country is the history of the prerogative powers of the Crown being made subject to the overriding powers of the democratically elected legislature as the sovereign body. The prerogative powers of the Crown remain in existence to the extent that Parliament has not expressly or by implication extinguished them.

Essentially four separate types of interaction between legislation and prerogative can be identified, and each of these will be discussed briefly below.

First, Parliament may enact legislation which is clearly incompatible with a pre-existing prerogative power. Where, for example, in the *De Keyser* case[36] legislation imposed a duty to pay compensation to an owner whose premises were requisitioned for military purposes, the government could not rely on an independent prerogative power to avoid paying compensation. Where the statute blows hot and the prerogative blows cold, then hot it is. The standard analysis of *De Keyser* is that the prerogative remains 'in abeyance'[37] for so long as the legislation is in place.

A second type of interaction occurs where the prerogative and legislation are

---

[34] [1989] QB 811.
[35] *R v. Secretary of State for the Home Department, ex parte Fire Brigades Union* [1995] 2 WLR 464, p. 474. In this quotation, Lord Browne-Wilkinson appears to underestimate the extent to which the prerogative powers have been transferred, not to the democratically elected legislature but to the executive which directs it.
[36] *Attorney General v. De Keyser's Royal Hotel Ltd.* [1920] AC 508. In May 1916 the crown took possession of the respondent's hotel in order to provide accommodation in London for the Royal Flying Corps. The crown denied that the owners had any legal right to compensation, claiming instead that any moneys paid would be on an ex gratia basis. The owners yielded up possession under protest and without prejudice to their rights, and subsequently asked for a declaration that they were entitled to compensation under the Defence of the Realm Act 1842. The House of Lords held that where the 'whole ground of something which could be done by the prerogative is covered by the statute, it is the statute which rules' (Lord Dunedin, pp. 524-5). Lord Parmoor (pp. 567-8) spoke in similar terms, stating that where the power of the executive has been placed under parliamentary control and 'directly regulated by statute', the executive no longer derives its powers from the prerogative but from Parliament.
[37] Lord Atkinson, *ibid.*, pp. 539-40.

potentially compatible.[38] In such cases the executive may continue to exercise power under both heads of jurisdiction and the courts may ultimately approve of such action. This occurred in the *Northumbria* case where the Court of Appeal accepted that the Home Secretary had acted under powers set out in the Police Act 1964, but that the government's prerogative power 'to maintain peace in the realm' was also available, undisturbed by Parliament's statutory intervention.

A third situation arises where the prerogative and legislation are potentially compatible but Parliament has opted to clarify whether it wishes the prerogative to be abolished or maintained. An example of the latter can be found in s.33(5) of the Immigration Act 1971 in which it is provided that 'this Act shall not be taken to supersede or impair any power exercisable by Her Majesty in relation to aliens in virtue of Her Prerogative'.[39] It is in this instance that the power of Parliament is clearest and where the judiciary's competing power to interpret most restricted. It should also be remembered that simple provisions such as s.33(5) serve the executive and would be included at its behest.

A final scenario is rarer but also illustrates the competing forces involved in amendment. It may be that legislative provisions clearly incompatible with the prerogative are not to be brought into force until such a time as a designated Minister determines. Parliament can be said to have expressed its will from that moment on, but given that the provisions are not in force there is no application for the *De Keyser* rule whereby the prerogative would be left in abeyance. This situation arose recently when the government decided to replace a criminal compensation scheme set up in the 1960s with a statutory scheme set out in the Criminal Justice Act 1988.[40] The scheme was to come into effect on 'such day as the Secretary of State may ... appoint'.[41] Subsequent Home Secretaries failed to

---

[38] There are numerous uncontroversial examples of such compatibilities. For example, regarding the sovereign's personal prerogatives, only a certain number of Ministers can be appointed by her at any one time (House of Commons Disqualification Act 1975, s.2). The Bill of Rights 1689 prohibits the 'raising or keeping of a standing army within the kingdom in time of peace unless it be with consent of Parliament' (the authorisation is given by the Army Act 1955 which is renewed annually). The power to keep the peace within the realm is clearly alive, as seen in the *Northumbria* case, but it would be surprising if such a power were governed entirely by prerogative (in fact, there have been important legislative amendments to this power, notably, the Civil Defence Act 1948, the Public Order Acts 1936, 1986, the Criminal Justice and Public Order Act 1994 and the Prevention of Terrorism (Temporary Provisions) Act 1989). Whereas there are important prerogative powers relating to pardons, there has also been important statutory intervention to deal with miscarriages of justice and compensation: (e.g. Criminal Justice Act 1988, s.133(1)). Prerogative governs the appointment of the judiciary (by the crown but with the Lord Chancellor and PM's advice), but statute governs matters such as the number of judges and the payment of pensions. Parliament intervened early on to amend the prerogative regarding dismissal of judges: that which had formerly been 'at the pleasure of the crown' became 'during good behaviour' under the Act of Settlement 1700.

[39] This example is suggested by Le Sueur & Sunkin, op cit, p. 282.

[40] See *R v. Secretary of State for the Home Department, ex parte Fire Brigades Union* [1995] 2 WLR 464. The Criminal Injuries Compensation Act 1995 repeals sections 108-17 of the Criminal Justice Act 1988 and makes provision for a scheme of payments of a standard amount of compensation calculated in accordance with a tariff prepared by the Secretary of State.

[41] Criminal Justice Act 1988, s.171(1).

implement the statutory scheme and in 1994 the Home Secretary announced that the 1988 provisions would be repealed and the enduring prerogative scheme modified in favour of less generous payouts. Thus an attempt by the executive to amend its exercise of the prerogative in the face of a clear (if not yet in force) expression of parliamentary will came before the courts by way of judicial review. The House of Lords decided that even though the statutory scheme was not yet in effect, a provision empowering the Home Secretary to bring it into force was law, and such a power had to be exercised properly, in this case by taking into account the existing expression of Parliament's will. The House of Lords could have reasserted the executive's power to determine freely the content of its decisions under the prerogative; instead it preferred Parliament's desire that the Home Secretary bring the statutory scheme into force, adding a judicially created requirement that the Home Secretary keep the option to do so open rather than abandoning it and implementing a new prerogative scheme.

One might expect that by now the remaining prerogative jurisdiction would have been claimed by Parliament. However, Parliament's agenda is largely determined by the government and there is little incentive for the latter to limit its own powers. Whereas the seventeenth-century settlement purported to give sovereign powers to Parliament, significant prerogative powers were held back and have now been appropriated by Her Majesty's government. Academic writers,[42] and policy institutes,[43] have suggested that key prerogative powers should be codified, but the issue, if considered at all, inevitably slips well down each new government's legislative agenda.

## IV. THE COMMON LAW

The common law constitution needs to be mentioned almost in the same breath as the prerogative. As we have seen, the prerogative finds its origin in custom but it is now recognised as a part of the common law whose (shifting) boundaries are determined by the courts. In fact, the idea of judicial supervision of the sovereign's powers was asserted before the key seventeenth-century decisions of Chief Justice Coke.[44] Bracton stated in the thirteenth century that the King was not subject to men, but to God and to the law.[45] God's law might be the preserve of the Church or possibly the Chancellor, but 'the law' came to mean the common law when, in

---

[42]  E.g., R. Brazier, *Constitutional Reform op. cit.* p. 89, recommends, for example, that each prerogative power should be expressly abolished and replaced in statutory form by an equivalent power together with adequate safeguards.

[43]  E.g., Institute for Public Policy Research, *A Written Constitution for the United Kingdom* (London: Mansell, 1993) p. 1.

[44]  E.g. *Case of Proclamations* (1611) 12 Co. Rep. 74 and *Prohibitions del Roy* (1607) 12 Co. Rep. 63.

[45]  'Ipse autem rex non debet esse sub homine sed sub Deo et sub lege, quia lex facit regem', *De Legibus et Consuetudinibus Angliae*, f. 5 b, cited by Coke CJ in *Prohibitions del Roy* (1607) 12 Co. Rep. 63.

the early seventeenth century, the courts needed support for their challenge to the Stuart kings.

The common law includes the full range of judge-made law, from contract's offer and acceptance to medical negligence in tort, but it is possible to pick out a selection of key court decisions which are clearly of constitutional significance. Professor Dicey even asserted that the British constitution was 'a judge-made constitution'[46] and noted that in the absence of a codified bill of rights, British subjects were protected by the courts and the common law.[47]

What might be included in the common law part of the constitution? Classic decisions such as the *Case of Proclamations*, *Prohibitions del Roy* and, especially, *Entick v. Carrington* have already been mentioned. Over a century ago, the courts sought to control the broad discretionary powers of public bodies by insisting, for example, that the rules of natural justice be followed,[48] and more recently such judge-made rules have increased dramatically.[49] These cases should no doubt be included in the common law constitution. In the sphere of civil liberties, in addition to *Entick v. Carrington*, one could cite *Beatty v. Gillbanks*[50] (freedom of assembly), *Derbyshire County Council v. Times Newspapers*[51] (freedom of expression) and *R v. Secretary of State for the Home Department, ex parte McQuillan*[52] (freedom of movement), to name but a few. How then is the common law part of the constitution amended?

The executive has a relatively minor role to play in amending the common law constitution. Governments constantly test the limits of their power,[53] and argue their cases strenuously when brought before the courts, but the law-creating and amending decisions belong to the judiciary and, beyond the judiciary, Parliament. The way in which the judiciary amends the common law constitution can be

---

[46]   A.V. Dicey, *An Introduction to the Study of the Law of the Constitution*, 10th ed. (London: Macmillan, 1959), p. 196.
[47]   *Ibid.*, p. 195.
[48]   *Cooper v. Wandsworth Board of Works* (1863) 14 CB (NS) 180 (the right to a fair hearing), *Dimes v. Grand Junction Canal Proprietors* (1852) 3 HLC 759 (the rule against bias).
[49]   The phenomenal rise of judicial review dates from the 1960s and takes in such key decisions as: *Ridge v. Baldwin* [1964] AC 40 (application of rules of natural justice not dependent on the nature of the decision-making body); *Padfield v. Minister of Agriculture* [1968] AC 997 (wide executive discretion provided for in legislation subject to judicial standards); *Anisminic Ltd v. Foreign Compensation Commission* [1969] 2 AC 147 (legislative exclusion of judicial review no bar in case where an authority or tribunal has exceeded its jurisdiction); *Council for Civil Service Unions v. Minister for the Civil Service* [1985] AC 374 (judicial review available on three grounds: illegality, irrationality and procedural impropriety - also available in relation to certain prerogative powers); *R v. Secretary of State for the Home Department, ex parte Doody* [1994] 1 AC 531 (duty to provide reasons). See generally, P. Craig, *Administrative Law*, 3rd ed. (London: Sweet & Maxwell, 1994); P. Cane, *An Introduction to Administrative Law*, 3rd ed. (Oxford: Clarendon, 1996); H.W.R. Wade & C.F. Forsyth, *Administrative Law*, 7th ed. (Oxford: Clarendon, 1994).
[50]   (1882) 9 QBD 308.
[51]   [1993] AC 534.
[52]   'Freedom of movement, subject only to the general law, is a fundamental value of the common law.' [1995] 4 All ER 400, p. 421.
[53]   See for example the discussion of the *Northumbria* case in the section on the prerogative.

illustrated by the fate of two important cases: *Entick v. Carrington* and *Beatty v. Gillbanks*. Examples of legislative amendments to the common law are legion. We begin with the judiciary.[54]

In *Entick*, Lord Camden CJ in the Court of Common Pleas preserved a sphere of individual liberty: namely, freedom from illegal search and seizure. Messengers authorised by one of the King's principal Secretaries of State had broken into Entick's house and taken papers belonging to him. Sued for trespass, the messengers argued that the Secretary of State's warrant authorising the action was legally justified given the need of any government to quieten 'clamours and sedition'. Lord Camden CJ denied that such an *explanation* could be an adequate legal *justification*: 'If it is the law it will be found in our books. If it is not to be found there it is not the law'.[55] This statement is striking in the context of a constitutional system which is said always to have had an unwritten constitution. Presumably, Lord Camden was referring to the books which recorded the custom of the sovereign (and therefore described the nature of the prerogative), the common law and statute. But the insistence on identifying a source of constitutional power was important for another reason. The case also appeared to stand for a central principle of constitutionalism, the rule of law: that whereas citizens are free to do anything except that which the law prohibits, the State and its officials can do nothing except that which the law permits. As such, *Entick* is rightly seen as a central piece in the common law constitution, and, from our perspective, a spectacular example of law-creating and constitution-amending.

But that which the common law creates it can also change or deny. Just over two hundred years after *Entick*, the courts were presented with another opportunity to affirm the citizen's freedom from illegal search. In many Western constitutions illegal search embraces illegal telephone tapping.[56] However, in *Malone v. Metropolitan Police Commissioner*,[57] Malone found himself unable to persuade Sir Robert Megarry VC that a citizen deserves protection when he discovers that the police have been intercepting his telephone calls without any obvious statutory authority and with no justification under the prerogative. Neither the constitutional freedom from illegal search nor the constitutional principle of the rule of law, apparently affirmed in *Entick*, were of any consequence. The *Malone* case appeared to indicate that the State, like the citizen, was entitled to do anything except that which the law prohibited it from doing - the rule of law turned on its head - and that freedom from illegal search was illusory in situations where the search had no

---

[54] On the related issue of how rules and practices of precedent may affect constitutional amendment by way of common law, see generally J. Farrar & H. Dugdale, *Introduction to Legal Method*, 3rd ed. (London: Sweet & Maxwell, 1990); W. Twining & David Miers, *How To Do Things With Rules*, 3rd ed. (London: Weidenfeld & Nicolson, 1991) and Smith & Bailey, *The Modern Legal System*, 2nd ed. by S.H. Bailey & M.J. Gunn (London: Sweet & Maxwell, 1991).
[55] (1765) 19 St. Tr. 1030.
[56] See e.g., in the United States, fourth amendment and *Katz v. United States* (1967) 389 US 347; and, in Canada, s.8 of the Charter of Rights and Freedoms and *R v. Duarte* [1990] 1 SCR 30.
[57] [1979] Ch 344.

effect on any other right which the common law recognised.[58] It is not hard to see that another judge could have taken a very different, and constitutionally more robust, view. For the time it prevailed, *Malone* clearly amended the common law constitution. And though the specific situation is now governed by the Interception of Communications Act 1985, the judicial attitude which the case reflects may not have disappeared, with the result that other constitutional protection under the common law may be in jeopardy.

Another example of the ebb and flow of common law protection of constitutionally significant rights can be seen in a century of development since *Beatty v. Gillbanks*.[59] Despite the existence of less liberal decisions at the time,[60] *Beatty* appeared to inject some force into the individual's claim to freedom of assembly in the United Kingdom. The case affirmed that the Salvation Army's freedom to assemble was not to be limited simply because another group (the Skeleton Army) threatened to act illegally in relation to that assembly. However, in another time and in other contexts, the courts have been less eager to protect this constitutionally significant freedom. In the 1930s, in the case of *Duncan v. Jones*,[61] the King's Bench Division decided that the police had a duty to break up an assembly and prevent an activist from speaking where others present might be induced to breach the peace. By the 1980s, this principle had been extended so as to allow police to prevent would-be protesters from attending a picket site if a breach of the peace was feared, notwithstanding that the police intervention occurred more than a mile away from the assembly.[62] The variable judicial protection of a free assembly has recently been amended in detailed fashion by Parliament, a phenomenon to which we shall turn below.

Before leaving this discussion of amendment of the common law part of the constitution by the judiciary, it is important to point out that European courts - the European Court of Human Rights and, especially, the European Court of Justice - have effect on the development of the common law, either directly or indirectly, via the British courts. The *Malone* case was an example of a British court refusing to fill a gap in the common law with the assistance of the European Convention on Human Rights and its associated jurisprudence. But since then the House of Lords has shown some willingness to take heed of the Convention in developing, for example, the court-made rules on remedies.[63] More recently, in the *Derbyshire*

---

[58] In *Entick*, the plaintiff could rely on the fact that the search amounted to civil trespass, whereas in *Malone* the interception of telephone communication did not amount to a violation of any law, civil or criminal.

[59] (1882) 9 QBD 308.

[60] See *Humphries v. Connor* (1864) 17 ICLR 1 and *O'Kelley v. Harvey* (1883) 10 LR Ir 105.

[61] [1936] 1 KB 218.

[62] See *Moss and others v. McLachlan* [1985] IRLR 77 (QBD).

[63] *Attorney General v. Guardian Newspapers (No. 2)* [1990] 1 AC 109, p. 283, where Lord Goff referred to the ECHR in developing the equitable doctrine of breach of confidence. For our purposes, it is of no significance that the remedy was equitable in origin; it is only important that it was judge-made and judge-developed.

case, the House of Lords has denied that it was controlled by the Convention in developing the law of libel,[64] but it is impossible to believe that what we stubbornly refer to as the development of the common law in that area is not markedly influenced by the Convention.[65] The Court of Appeal in *Derbyshire* was more open in this regard.[66]

However, it is the European Court of Justice (ECJ) which has amended the common law constitution in the most profound manner. Prior to the entry of the United Kingdom into the European Community in 1973, the ECJ had established a series of principles which went beyond the Community treaties, but which in the Court's view were essential to the development of the Community. Foremost amongst the cases were *Van Gend en Loos* (1963)[67] which established the principle of direct effect, *Costa v. ENEL* (1964)[68] which set out the doctrine of the supremacy of European law and the *Internationale Handelsgesellschaft*[69] litigation of the early 1970s which established that such supremacy applied to constitutional as well as ordinary domestic law. By section 3(1) of the European Communities Act 1972, Parliament directed the courts of the UK to treat decisions of the ECJ as binding precedent.[70] The central principle of the common law British constitution is that Parliament can make any law whatever and that no institution may challenge such parliamentary enactment.[71] Before 1972 it would have been inconceivable for a British court to order that an Act of Parliament be disapplied pending final judgment. And yet this is what happened in the *Factortame* litigation. The House of Lords had initially ruled that, as a matter of English law, it had no jurisdiction to grant such interim relief in terms that would involve overturning an Act of the United Kingdom Parliament.[72] It was not surprising, given the growing

---

[64] *Derbyshire County Council v. Times Newspapers* [1993] AC 534. Lord Keith stated that the decision was based on 'the common law of England' without finding any need to rely upon the European Convention.

[65] Of course, if the present government fulfils its election promise of incorporating the Convention, the judges may be specifically instructed to amend the common law so as to conform. Lord Hoffman was recently quoted as saying that if the Convention is incorporated '[t]here is not going to be a queue of statutes to be 'struck down', but what is going to be affected ... is the common law.' ('Rights: how the law lords line up', *Independent*, 25 July 1997, p. 18). (See now Human Rights Act 1998, s.6).

[66] *Derbyshire CC v. Times Newspapers* [1992] 3 WLR 28 (CA). For a discussion of the Court of Appeal and House of Lords decisions in *Derbyshire*, see Bix and Tomkins (1992) 55 *MLR* 721 and Bix and Tomkins (1993) 56 *MLR* 738.

[67] [1963] ECR 1.

[68] [1964] ECR 585.

[69] [1970] ECR 1125.

[70] Section 3(1): 'For the purposes of all legal proceedings any question as to the meaning or effect of any of the Treaties ... shall be treated as a question of law (and, if not referred to the European Court, be for determination as such in accordance with the principles laid down by and any relevant decisions of the European Court).'

[71] See A.V. Dicey, *An Introduction to the Study of the Law of the Constitution*, 10th ed., *op. cit.* p. 40; *Pickin v. British Railways Board* [1974] AC 765, pp. 787-8; *Manuel v. Attorney General* [1983] Ch. 77, p. 86.

[72] *R v. Secretary of State for Transport, ex parte Factortame Ltd.* [1990] 2 AC 85.

constitutional jurisprudence of the ECJ,[73] that the ECJ informed the House of Lords that the latter did have the jurisdiction to grant such interim relief. The European Court of Justice clearly contributed to an amendment of the common law rules of the UK constitution at least to this extent. The larger issues relating to UK sovereignty and EC law will be discussed in greater detail in the section of this essay dealing with Acts of Parliament.

Putting the European issue aside for the moment, in orthodox terms, as we have already noted in relation to the crown prerogative, Acts of Parliament are the master key to the constitution. In theory, any amendment is possible, just as any Act of Parliament must be heeded by the courts. Therefore, Parliament may at any time amend the common law constitution and has done so regularly. Following on from the examples selected above, we can note that the common law relating to illegal searches and seizures has been amended principally by the Police and Criminal Evidence Act 1984, the Interception of Communications Act 1985, the Security Service Act 1989, the Intelligence Services Act 1994 and the Police Act 1997; the common law regarding freedom of assembly has been radically altered by the Public Order Acts 1936 and 1986 and the Criminal Justice and Public Order Act 1994; and the common law rules regarding the sovereignty of Parliament have been altered, with the assistance of the ECJ, by the European Communities Act 1972.

Acts of Parliament prevail and can apparently therefore amend all there is to amend in the British constitution. A number of comments must be made here, however. First, prominent members of the judiciary, Lord Woolf[74] and Sir John Laws[75] for example, have recently made radical suggestions, admittedly in extra-judicial contexts, to the effect that some parts of the common law constitution - for example, the position of the judiciary and rights such as freedom of expression - are beyond Parliament's reach. President Cooke of the New Zealand Court of Appeal (now Lord Cooke) has already committed such unorthodoxies to judicial

---

[73] Especially *Amministrazione delle Finanze dello Stato v. Simmenthal SpA* [1978] ECR 629 in which the ECJ held that directly applicable rules of Community law 'must be fully and uniformly applied in all the member States from the date of their entry into force and for so long as they continue in force' and that 'in accordance with the principle of the precedence of Community law, the relationship between provisions of [EC law] and that national law of member-States ... is such that [EC] provisions and measures ... by their entry into force render automatically inapplicable and conflicting provision of ... national law ...' (p. 643).

[74] Rt. Hon. Lord Woolf of Barnes, 'Droit Public - English Style' [1995] *Public Law* 57, p. 67 where Lord Woolf presents a scenario in which 'a party with a large majority in Parliament uses that majority to abolish the courts' and asks whether 'the courts then accept that the legislation means what it says'. '[M]y own personal view is that they do not'. On p. 69, he goes on to say that 'I myself would consider there were advantages in making it clear that ultimately there are even limits on the supremacy of Parliament which it is the courts' inalienable responsibility to identify and uphold'.

[75] Sir John Laws, 'Law and Democracy' [1995] *Public Law* 72, pp. 84, 87. (See also the reply by the present Lord Chancellor, Lord Irvine, 'Judges and Decision-Makers: The Theory and Practice of Judicial Review' [1996] *Public Law* 556.)

decisions.[76] In comparative constitutional terms, this amounts to the same sort of arrangement as occurs in countries where some parts of the constitution are said to be unamendable, at least by ordinary amendment procedure.

A second comment is that despite the formal ability of Acts of Parliament to amend any part of the British constitution that is amendable, the formal position disguises the reality that, under the Blair government and for most of the Thatcher reign, a large majority in the House of Commons translates into domination of the legislature by the executive. The Act of Parliament may be the master key to the constitution but, when the government enjoys a majority of the size elected in 1983, 1987 and 1997, the key remains in the possession of the Prime Minister and the cabinet.

## V. ACTS OF PARLIAMENT

This component of the constitution is easier to define, though more difficult to delimit. It is simply that part of the United Kingdom constitution which is made up of Acts of Parliament having constitutional significance.[77] The definition is frustratingly circular but there is no avoiding the fact that what is included is a matter of judgment rather than legality. Whereas the amendments to the United States, Australian and Malaysian constitutions can be identified by the fact that a special procedure has been fulfilled and the text of the constitution changed as a result, this is not true of the UK constitution where the procedure for the enactment of the Sex Discrimination Act 1975, for example, is identical to the enactment of the Dangerous Wild Animals Act 1976: in each case approval by the House of Commons, the House of Lords and the sovereign must be obtained. The recent tendency to use referendums in relation to key constitutional changes (membership of the European Community in 1975 and devolution in 1979 and 1997) is of great constitutional significance but as yet such procedures are not legally binding on Parliament whatever their potentially overwhelming political or conventional significance.

What might be included in the statutory part of the United Kingdom constitution? Textbook writers typically list uncontroversial candidates for

---

[76] E.g., *Taylor v. New Zealand Poultry Board* [1984] 1 NZLR 394, p. 398.

[77] It should not be forgotten that subordinate legislative instruments, especially those relating to the European Communities Act 1972, can also have constitutional significance. The discussion here will not deal with such provisions. Generally speaking the amendment of statutory instruments is an executive act, subject to any fundamental amendment which Parliament might wish to make to the parent or primary statute.

With regard to subordinate legislative instruments, it should be noted that some such provisions, known as Henry VIII clauses, allow Ministers to repeal or amend Acts of Parliament and are, as such, relevant to the discussion in the present chapter.

membership: the Bill of Rights 1689,[78] the Act of Settlement 1700,[79] the Act of Union with Scotland 1707, the Representation of the People Acts, the Parliament Acts 1911 and 1949, the Public Order Acts of 1936, 1986 and 1994,[80] for example. Statute books for students of constitutional law helpfully provide collections of relevant primary and secondary legislation ranging from the Children and Young Persons (Harmful Publications) Act 1955 to Order 53 of the Rules of the Supreme Court.[81] For our purposes, the precise delimitation of the list is not so important as the way in which any Act of Parliament is amended.

With the exception of a very small number of private members' bills which might be of constitutional significance,[82] new constitutional legislation and amendments to new and old legislation are initiated by the government of the day. Whereas constitutional amendments in other jurisdictions may be initiated by the people,[83] or by the regions,[84] the co-ordination of constitutional change in the United Kingdom is monopolised by the executive. This is not to deny that momentum for change may often come from the public or the regions, or from vocal sections thereof; however, there is no formalised constitutional role for them.[85] Therefore, in very concrete fashion, it is the executive which sets the agenda for constitutional amendment.

Is there any role for the judiciary in the process of amending Acts of Parliament? The judiciary has always had an important task to perform in the interpretation of statutes. It is a well-known principle of interpretation that, for example, statutes which limit the rights of the subject are restrictively interpreted.[86] Once constitutionally significant legislation has been passed, powers are often delegated to members of the government to ensure its proper implementation. It is here that the rapidly expanding field of judicial review gives to the judiciary a

---

[78] The Bill of Rights 1689 was amended recently by the Defamation Act 1996.

[79] The Act of Settlement 1700 which regulated the succession to the throne on the failure of Queen Anne's issue was amended by His Majesty's Declaration of Abdication Act 1936.

[80] The full short title of the 1994 statute is Criminal Justice and Public Order Act 1994.

[81] See e.g. *Blackstone's Statutes on Public Law*, 7th ed. by P. Wallington & R. Lee (London: Blackstone Press Ltd, 1997).

[82] E.g. the Abortion Act 1967 proposed by David Steel MP.

[83] The present amending procedure of the Swiss Federal Constitution provides separate methods for dealing with a total revision and with a partial revision of the Constitution. A partial revision may be proposed by a popular initiative, requiring signatures of 100,000 voters. See Articles 118, 121 of the Swiss Constitution.

[84] In Canada, provincial legislatures may initiate constitutional amendments which, in most cases, must then be ratified by at least seven provinces representing 50 per cent of the population of Canada and by the two federal houses, the House of Commons and the Senate, before proclamation by the Governor General. See the Constitution Act 1982, ss. 38-49.

[85] As noted above, this may be changing at the political or conventional level with the introduction of referendums as an implement of constitutional change. But as the current devolution process illustrates, even the involvement of the public and the regions is carefully orchestrated by the national government.

[86] See Sir Rupert Cross, *Statutory Interpretation*, 3rd ed. by J. Bell & G. Engle (London: Butterworths, 1995) pp. 175-80.

highly significant constitutional role. The courts ensure that the decision-maker keeps within the four corners of the enabling legislation, acts reasonably and conforms with the basic principles of natural justice or fairness. Occasionally, the government has requested that legislation be drafted so as to exclude or restrict the possibility of judicial review. The courts have stubbornly resisted such attempts to marginalise them and in so doing have effectively reasserted a constitutional role.[87]

A recent trend to expand the range of litigants who can be granted standing to seek judicial review has slightly but significantly handed some of the initiative for constitutional change back to the public.[88] If, for example, the Commissioner of Police for London with the consent of the Home Secretary abused his powers in making an order (under section 14A(4) of the Public Order Act 1986) prohibiting all trespassory assemblies for a specified period, willing litigants of various shapes and sizes would surely emerge to challenge the encroachment on free assembly. Both the substantive and the procedural rules relating to judicial review guarantee that this constitutionally important role is fulfilled.

It goes without saying that Parliament can amend its own laws. The courts may interpret them, as we have already seen, but if Parliament's will is clearly expressed then the Act of Parliament should be heeded, subject to what was said earlier about court-imposed limits to Parliament's sovereignty. But this only really answers the question whether a particular exercise of Parliament's power can be amended.

A more difficult question is whether Parliament can itself amend the ambit or the nature of its own power. Can it eliminate certain matters from its supposedly all-encompassing legislative jurisdiction, or can it make it more difficult for it to legislate on certain matters?

Dicey's famous answer is 'no' - that it is a logical requirement of Parliament's sovereignty that no Parliament can bind a future Parliament.[89] Professor Hart has given this the convenient label of 'continuing sovereignty'[90] and Professor Wade has provided the most persuasive explanation for it, that is, that the continuing nature of Parliament's sovereignty is a historical, pre-legal or political fact (i.e., the seventeenth-century settlement) which it is beyond the power of Parliament to change, or the judiciary to ratify.[91] This state of affairs has the virtue of allowing each generation, or more accurately, each generation's rulers, to make its own laws, constitutional or other.

Hart thought that continuing sovereignty was still the rule in the United

---

[87] See *Anisminic v. Foreign Compensation Commission* [1969] 2 A.C. 147.
[88] *R v. Inspectorate of Pollution, ex parte Greenpeace Ltd* (No. 2) [1994] 4 All ER 329; *R v. Secretary of State for the Environment, ex parte Friends of the Earth* [1994] 2 CMLR 760; *R v. Secretary of State for Foreign Affairs, ex parte World Development Movement* [1995] 1 All ER 611.
[89] Dicey, *op. cit.*, p. 68.
[90] H.L.A. Hart, *The Concept of Law*, 2nd ed. (Oxford: Clarendon, 1994), p. 149.
[91] H.W.R. Wade, 'The Basis of Legal Sovereignty' [1955] *Cambridge LJ* 172, p. 188.

Kingdom in the 1960s.[92] But Hart was also clear in stating that continuing sovereignty is not the only plausible version of sovereignty. He gave the name 'self-embracing' sovereignty to the view that Parliament can, as part of its sovereignty, limit its own powers.[93] The best way of explaining this view is to say, contrary to Professor Wade, that parliamentary sovereignty is itself a rule of the common law and that like other rules of the common law it can be changed by Parliament. According to this analysis, the fact that the ambit of Parliament's powers remained unlimited for so long was not because this was a logical requirement, as Dicey suggested, but because Parliament had not yet chosen clearly to limit its legislative competence, or that even if it had, the courts had not yet ruled definitively on the matter. Has this situation changed?

One might have thought that the process of granting independence to Commonwealth jurisdictions would have confirmed the view that Parliament could limit its own powers. Had it not, in relation to so many former colonies, required that no future Act of Parliament apply to the newly independent country in question?[94] Whatever the view in the latter country (i.e., categorical rejection of any power inhering in the Westminster Parliament), the British courts appeared to be at best agnostic on such questions, and tended toward the attitude that a court's duty was to heed Acts of Parliament whatever their subject matter.[95]

However, the European Communities Act 1972 and *Factortame* indicate that times have changed. Together they show that the courts now implicitly accept Parliament's ability to alter the nature of its own sovereignty. The pre-1972 rule regarding Parliament's sovereignty was that Parliament could pass any law whatever and that no institution would challenge its ability to do so.[96] The 1972 Act said not only that the courts must construe even a post-1972 Act of Parliament

---

[92] Hart, *op. cit.*, p. 149. The passage in which this view is expressed is unchanged from the first edition of the *Concept of Law* which was published in 1961. However, continuing sovereignty was clearly not the rule in the many Commonwealth countries which had accepted that the UK Parliament had terminated its powers in granting to them independence: e.g., the Mauritius Independence Act 1968 (UK) or the Canada Act 1982 (UK).

[93] George Winterton agrees that continuing and self-embracing sovereignty are the only two logically coherent possibilities, but he noted (G. Winterton, 'The British Grundnorm: Parliamentary Supremacy Re-examined' (1976) 92 *LQR* 591) that much of the debate exists in a middle region inhabited by manner and form restrictions on parliamentary sovereignty, such as the European Communities Act 1972 and, incidentally, most proposals for a United Kingdom Bill of Rights.

[94] E.g., Mauritius Independence Act 1968 (UK), s.1(2): 'No Act of the Parliament of the United Kingdom passed on or after [independence day] shall extend, or be deemed to extend, to Mauritius as part of its law; ...'; and the Canada Act 1982 (UK), s.2: 'No Act of the Parliament of the United Kingdom ... shall extend to Canada as part of its law.'

[95] See *Manuel v. Attorney General* [1983] Ch. 77. For an analysis of constitutional independence from Canadian and New Zealand perspectives, see P. Oliver, 'The 1982 Patriation of the Canadian Constitution: Reflections on Continuity and Change', (1994) 28 *Revue Juridique Thémis* 875-914, reprinted in J.-L. Baudouin *et al*, eds., *Mélanges Jean Beetz* (Montreal: Thémis, 1995) 799-838; and P. Oliver, 'Cutting the Imperial Link: Canada and New Zealand', in P.A. Joseph, ed., *Essays on the Constitution* (Wellington: Brooker's/Sydney: Law Book Co., 1995) 368-403.

[96] See A.V. Dicey, *An Introduction to the Study of the Law of the Constitution*, 10th ed., *op cit.*, p. 40; *Pickin v. British Railways Board* [1974] AC 765, pp. 787-8.

consistently with European law, but that in the case of clear conflict, the courts should 'give effect' to EC law (and therefore the 1972 Act). As a result of the 1972 Act, *Factortame* and *R v. Secretary of State for Employment, ex parte Equal Opportunities Commission*,[97] British courts must prefer European law to an Act of Parliament where there is conflict between the two. In areas of EC jurisdiction, Parliament's competence is limited and courts are obliged to challenge acts which go beyond this newly constrained competence. It would seem that the pre-1972 (common law) rule regarding Parliament's sovereignty has been altered at the initiative of Parliament itself.

The point is *not* that Parliament has already conceded sovereignty to Europe - our claim is much smaller. The point is that *Factortame* indicates that the courts will accept Parliament's own attempts to alter what had previously been the common law rules regarding the nature of its sovereignty. Once that is acknowledged, then it would seem that all things are possible. Parliament could exclude matters from its sovereignty or, more plausibly, it could make it more difficult for future Parliaments to legislate in certain areas, and the courts could be instructed to ensure that this happens. Parliament's re-discovered constituent powers could be used to create an entirely new written constitution.

If it is accepted that Parliament has constituent as well as legislative powers, then it would be possible, contrary to popular assumptions, to enact a written constitution immediately and to instruct the British courts to take on the role of constitutional review. However, it seems to us that, once a few overdue changes have been made, it would be more desirable to build up a constitution gradually. This would be typically British but also preferable in many ways. Other countries have, out of necessity, created entirely new constitutions at one moment in their history, but this is not the only way of proceeding, of course.

One of the best justifications for the doctrine of continuing parliamentary sovereignty is that it assumes that no one generation - or its elected representatives - has a monopoly of wisdom. The problem with the 'continuing sovereignty' version is that one generation's supposed preference for continuing sovereignty prevents subsequent generations from accomplishing constitutional change.[98] If we accept self-embracing change, or viewed otherwise, the possibility of Parliament legislating to change the common law relating to the nature of its own sovereignty, then all things really may be possible.

---

[97] [1995] 1 AC 1.
[98] See J. Finnis, 'Scepticism, Self-Refutation and the Good of Truth' in P. Hacker & J. Raz, ed., *Law, Morality and Society: Essays in Honour of H.L.A. Hart* (Oxford: Clarendon, 1977) 247, pp. 254-6, for a more elaborate version of this argument.

## VI. FROM POLITICAL PRACTICE TO CONSTITUTIONAL CONVENTION: THE CROWN'S GOVERNMENT STRIKES BACK?

In the preceding sections we have seen how amendment of the constitution is formally a matter for the courts and for Parliament, although we have also seen how the government is additionally involved in various attempts to shape or manipulate change. In this section, the focus moves more clearly onto the government as the prime mover in constitutional reform, and in the extensive role played by the executive in the creation and amendment of constitutional conventions.

Constitutional conventions are a problem. Unlike our previous three constitutional sources, it is unclear even whether constitutional conventions exist. Certainly they exist as an important source of the constitution for many commentators: from Dicey to Jennings to the authors of the leading textbooks of the moment,[99] but even among these scholars there is some debate as to whether conventions can sensibly be described as sources of constitutional *law*. What is clear is that there is a series of political practices which are deemed to be of such significance that they attract a normative character, and the phrase 'constitutional convention' is then used to convey this sense of obligation. While the ignoring of an established political practice would carry no constitutional sanction, to say that a convention of the constitution has been breached raises the stakes considerably.[100]

Before we can discuss how they might be changed, and how their amendment affects the development of the constitution as a whole, we need first to address the issue of how constitutional conventions are to be recognised. It is clear that constitutional conventions are different from the types of constitutional laws discussed in the previous sections. Constitutional conventions are created neither by courts of law nor by the legislation of Parliament. Neither are they part of the crown prerogative. Nor are the effects of breaching a convention the same as the consequences of breaking a law. While repeated breach of a constitutional convention will place the convention in doubt, no legal sanction can ensue. No court can enforce a convention, although courts may have reference to a convention in order to determine the scope of a law, as in the famous case, *Attorney General*

---

[99] See A.V. Dicey, *Introduction to the Study of the Law of the Constitution* (London: Macmillan, 1885), Chapters 1 and 14; Sir Ivor Jennings, *The Law and the Constitution* (London: University of London Press, 5th ed., 1959) Chapter 3; A.W. Bradley and K.D. Ewing, *Constitutional and Administrative Law* (London, Longmans, 12th ed., 1997) Chapter 2; S.A. de Smith and R. Brazier, *Constitutional and Administrative Law* (Harmondsworth: Penguin, 7th ed., 1994) pp. 27-48; and G. Marshall, *Constitutional Conventions: The Rules and Forms of Political Accountability* (Oxford: Clarendon Press, 1984), Chapters 1 and 13.

[100] Perhaps it is better not to view constitutional conventions and political practices as discrete entities, but as different points along a single continuum: for a brief exposition of this view, see C. Munro, *Studies in Constitutional Law* (London: Butterworths, 1987) pp. 59-60.

*v. Jonathan Cape* in which the Lord Chief Justice (Lord Widgery) referred to the constitutional convention of collective ministerial responsibility in order to determine whether the publication of a former cabinet Minister's diaries would be in breach of confidence.[101]

Distinguishing laws from conventions is the easy part of the equation. The more difficult part is how we are to differentiate between constitutional conventions (which are of some normative value) and mere political practices (which are merely descriptive and prescribe nothing). This problem is neatly illustrated by the traditions of budget day. Every year the chancellor of the exchequer delivers to Parliament a budget speech in which the government's fiscal and monetary policy for the ensuing financial year is set out. Great secrecy surrounds the preparations for the budget. Very few people outside the Treasury will know in advance of budget day what the chancellor will say. On the morning of budget day, the chancellor will present his proposals to his cabinet colleagues - and this will be the first most of them know of what the chancellor's plans are. Later in the morning the chancellor habitually takes a walk in St James's Park to feed the ducks. During the afternoon he will deliver his speech to the House of Commons and there will follow several days of debate. That evening the chancellor will appear on national TV to explain and defend his proposals. Opposition spokesmen will make official TV appearances over the course of the following evenings attacking the chancellor's policies. Which of these are mere habits, traditions, or political practices, and which are constitutional conventions, and how can we tell?

Writing in the 1930s, Sir Ivor Jennings suggested a three-stage approach to the question of how to distinguish constitutional convention from mere political practice.[102] In brief, he argued that, first, for a mere tradition to be elevated to the status of constitutional convention, there had to be some lengthy precedence of the convention/tradition having been observed;[103] secondly that the actors on the constitutional stage (here, the chancellor and his cabinet colleagues) had to feel bound to continue to observe the convention/tradition; and thirdly, that there had

---

[101] [1976] QB 752. Breach of confidence is a legal doctrine which is enforceable in courts of law. Lord Widgery was unsure as to whether the doctrine would apply in the case of a former cabinet Minister's diaries. After hearing argument on the issue and on the supposed constitutional importance of collective cabinet responsibility (a constitutional convention), he ruled that the doctrine of breach of confidence could in principle apply, but would not prevent the publication of the diaries in the case before him, on the ground that by the time they were to be published, the materials would no longer be confidential, as they related to cabinet proceedings from over a decade previously.

[102] Sir Ivor Jennings, *The Law and the Constitution* (first published 1933) (London: University of London Press, 5th ed., 1959) p. 136.

[103] Other commentators have suggested that in some limited circumstances, such as where all parties agree that a certain course of action is appropriate, a constitutional convention can be established more quickly. See G. Marshall, *Constitutional Conventions, op. cit.*, pp. 8-9. One example of this might perhaps be the convention (if that is the right word) of holding a referendum before Parliament devolves power to a region of the UK. This was the course adopted in the devolution campaigns for Scotland and Wales in 1978-79, and again in 1997-98.

to be some good constitutionally-related reason justifying or explaining the convention/tradition. Let us apply these tests to aspects of the budget day story, as recounted above.

To take first the requirement for an annual budget: is this a convention or a mere practice? It appears that all three of Jennings' tests are met here. As for length of precedence, there has been an annual budget day for a considerable time:[104] as long ago as 1853 the future Prime Minister Gladstone was busy making his parliamentary reputation as chancellor of the exchequer by making memorable (and very lengthy) budget speeches.[105] There is a very good constitutional reason for an annual budget speech. Under the 1688 Bill of Rights only Parliament may tax the people. Under the Finance Acts (the legislation which the budget speech in effect introduces) Parliament authorises the government to collect certain taxes at certain rates, but this is not a permanent authorisation: it must be renewed every year. Tax in Britain is permanently temporary. Without an annual Finance Act the government would be powerless to tax. It used to be that the budget would be delivered on a Tuesday in March. This was changed in the early 1990s when the annual spring budget (concerning taxation) and autumn financial statement (concerning government spending) were merged and the combined budget is now set out in November. This change could not be said to be a breach of constitutional convention. The important thing is that there is a budget every year, not that there is a budget every March.

What of the secrecy which surrounds the contents of the budget in the run-up to budget day? Again, this aspect of budget day would appear to meet Jennings' criteria. The economy could lose significantly if a privileged few in the City were to learn of the budget's details in advance of budget day. Keeping the majority of the cabinet in the dark until the morning of budget day reduces the risk of leaks. When Hugh Dalton (Attlee's chancellor during the post-war Labour government in the late 1940s) informed journalists of some of the details of the 1948 budget shortly before going into the House to deliver his budget speech, he was forced to resign from the government. The walk in the park, on the other hand, could not be said to share any such grave consequences. No chancellor would have to resign simply for refusing to take a stroll!

Finally, what of the evening TV broadcasts? This is more difficult. Would it be unconstitutional for the television networks to prevent the chancellor and his

---

[104] Peter Hennessy's authoritative account of the civil service suggests that the annual budget was established by a civil servant named William Lowndes, whose treasury career lasted from 1675-1724: see *Whitehall* (London: Fontana, 1990) p. 26.

[105] Gladstone's budget speech of 1853 was described by Lord Morley as 'one of the great parliamentary performances of the century'. See E. Taylor, *The House of Commons at Work* (London: Macmillan, 9th ed., 1979) p. 149. Gladstone's two periods as Chancellor (1852-55 and 1859-66) were extremely important to the future development of Parliament's role in overseeing the finances of the government. It was Gladstone who in 1861 established the office, which continues to this day, of Comptroller and Auditor General. See generally, I. Harden, 'Money and the Constitution' (1993) 13 *Legal Studies* 16.

political opponents from appearing on TV to defend or attack the budget proposals? It may be in breach of their licence agreements, but that is another matter. It could be argued that there is a good constitutional reason for this practice: namely, the explanation and critique of the government's plans to the electorate. A badly informed electorate is a negation of democracy, which is clearly a constitutional matter (in that it concerns relations between the State and its citizens). It is certainly arguable that for the chancellor to refuse to make such a broadcast would be to diminish his political accountability to the electorate, but whether this is properly classified as a constitutional matter must be doubtful. The constitution provides (as we shall see) that Ministers are accountable to Parliament, not to TV audiences. For this reason, despite its democratic importance, the post-budget TV broadcasts are probably not constitutional matters and would not therefore fall within Jennings' test.

What can be clearly appreciated from this analysis is that distinguishing a binding constitutional convention from a mere habit or tradition is not always easy. All constitutions suffer from this problem to some extent: under the US constitution, for example, we might argue that it was an unwritten constitutional convention that no president would serve more than two terms, and then Franklin Roosevelt did, only to see the constitution formally amended to prevent future recurrences.[106] Similarly, while the text of the constitution provides that the president shall 'from time to time give to the Congress information on the state of the union' it has now become an established practice - a constitutional convention perhaps -that the president shall make an annual state of the union address to Congress each January.[107] But the problem is no doubt exacerbated in the unwritten British constitution, which relies more than most on the unwritten practices of accepted political behaviour. Among the most important of these, which are most commonly ascribed the status of constitutional convention, are the following.

Before a Bill may become an Act of Parliament, it has to be passed by both Houses of Parliament (Commons and Lords) and also receive the royal assent: this is a matter of law.[108] It is said to be a constitutional convention, however, that the monarch will not refuse her royal assent to a Bill which has been duly passed by both Houses. The last time the royal assent was refused in relation to such a Bill

---

[106] The twenty-second amendment, ratified in 1951, provides that 'no person shall be elected to the office of the president more than twice'.

[107] See US constitution, article 2, section 3. It has to be admitted that this might merely be a peculiarly English way of looking at the US constitution. American constitutional commentators generally prefer to focus exclusively on the text of the constitution, as interpreted of course by the supreme court. Even those more imaginative scholars who have sought to read unwritten restraints into the constitution have done so primarily by reference to the structure of the text, rather than by referring to observable political practice. See, e.g. L.H. Tribe, *American Constitutional Law* (New York: Foundation Press, 2nd edn, 1988) and P. Bobbitt, *Constitutional Interpretation* (Oxford: Blackwell Press, 1991).

[108] See *Pickin v. British Railways Board* [1974] AC 765.

was in 1708 when Queen Anne refused to grant her assent to the Scottish Militia Bill.

There has to be a general election at least every five years.[109] Before there is a general election, Parliament must be dissolved. The dissolution of Parliament is a matter for the monarch (it is a crown prerogative exercised by the monarch herself, and not on her behalf by her Ministers). All of this is a matter of law. As a matter of convention, however, it is for the Prime Minister of the day to decide when the dissolution should take place (within the legal five year limit), and the monarch may not refuse to dissolve Parliament once the Prime Minister has requested it.[110] Similarly, the monarch may not usually insist that Parliament is dissolved where the Prime Minister does not want this to happen.[111]

The very existence of the Prime Minister and of the cabinet are matters of convention. No law provides for their existence, although the Prime Minister's salary (and the salaries of his colleagues) is a matter which is recognised in law.[112]

Among the most important of all conventions are those which concern the responsibility of government. It is said that there are two conventions which regulate this: the convention of individual ministerial responsibility and the convention of collective ministerial responsibility. The former provides that Ministers are individually responsible to Parliament for the actions, policies and decisions of their departments; and the latter states that all the government's Ministers are jointly responsible for the government's policies - individual Ministers may not evade responsibility for a particular part of the government's policy simply because they disagree with it. Ministers in this position will either have to keep their disagreements quiet or resign.

---

[109] Septennial Act 1715, as amended by the Parliament Act 1911, s.7.

[110] This is the basic position. It is possible, however, that a royal refusal to grant a Prime Minister's request might be constitutional in certain exceptional circumstances. Suppose that at a general election one party is returned with a good working majority of MPs (let us say a majority of 50). Twelve months later the leader of the opposition dies, leaving the opposition parties in turmoil with no obvious successor. The Prime Minister notes that the government is doing very well in the opinion polls and decides to seek a dissolution in order to exploit the weakness of the opposition in an attempt to increase his party's majority in the Commons. It is difficult to see why it would be unconstitutional for the monarch to refuse to dissolve Parliament in such circumstances. See further R. Brazier, *Constitutional Practice* (Oxford: Clarendon Press, 2nd ed., 1994) Chapter 9.

[111] Again, there may be exceptions. During the constitutional crisis of 1909-11 the Liberal government (which had been elected in 1906 with a landslide majority in the Commons) could not get its budget proposals through a very Conservative House of Lords. Eventually, the Prime Minister, Asquith, asked the King if he would create 400 new Liberal peers to prevent the government from going bust. The King was uncomfortable with the idea, and insisted that a general election should be held whereby the views of the country could be tested. If the Liberals won the election and still could not get the House of Lords to vote for their budget proposals, then the King would oblige Asquith's request. In the event, the Liberals did win the election (but only very narrowly - losing their landslide majority in the Commons) and the Lords, fearing that they would be swamped by unwelcome new Liberal peers, reluctantly passed the budget as the lesser of two evils. This débâcle led to the Parliament Act 1911, which limited the powers of the House of Lords, especially as regards money bills. See R. Brazier, *ibid.*

[112] Ministerial and other Salaries Act 1975.

This is not an exhaustive list, but it gives a flavour of the extent and importance of unwritten political rules to the British constitutional order. In order to consider how they might be changed and what broader implications the processes of changing constitutional conventions have for British constitutional law, let us consider recent developments concerning the supposed convention of individual ministerial responsibility. Unusually for a constitutional convention, the doctrine of individual ministerial responsibility is written down. Each Prime Minister since Attlee (1945-51) has issued to all government Ministers a rule book, known as *Questions of Procedure for Ministers* (or *QPM*). This rule book used to be secret until John Major published his version of it in 1992. Paragraph 27 of that version explained the doctrine of individual ministerial responsibility in the following terms:

Ministers are accountable to Parliament, in the sense that they have a duty to explain in Parliament the exercise of their powers and duties and to give an account to Parliament of what is done by them in their capacity as Ministers or by their departments. This includes the duty to give Parliament, including its select committees, and the public, as full information as possible about the policies, decisions and actions of the government, and not to deceive or mislead Parliament and the public.

Ministerial responsibility is always a contentious issue, because there will always be acrimonious demands by a gleeful opposition that a government Minister should resign if the obligations of ministerial responsibility are breached, demands which will usually be resisted by an embarrassed government anxious to save face. The sanctions for breaching the obligations of paragraph 27 are political. It is the Prime Minister (with the assistance of the head of the civil service, the cabinet secretary) who polices and is responsible for the operation of *QPM*. But the Prime Minister is unlikely to feel inclined to call for the resignation of one of his Ministers unless that Minister's future position in the government is politically embarrassing or untenable. The practices of ministerial responsibility were particularly controversial during John Major's years in office (1990-97). Mr Major's government suffered from more ministerial resignations than most, many of which were not only politically damaging to the Conservative government, but were also personally embarrassing for the Prime Minister. To illustrate the ways in which changing conventions can contribute to changing the constitution, and the power which this gives to the government, we will examine the experiences of the Major government as regards individual ministerial responsibility in some detail. Towards the beginning of John Major's tenure in No. 10, the most prominent ministerial casualties were David Mellor and Norman Lamont. Mellor and Lamont were not only good friends of the Prime Minister, they were also close and trusted political allies. Mellor was Secretary of State at the Department of National Heritage. He was married. He had an affair with an unemployed Spanish actress who sold her story to a tabloid newspaper. Mellor was in deep trouble and the Prime Minister found himself under intense pressure to call for his resignation. However, despite the unwelcome bad publicity, John Major demonstrated a trait which was to become a fatal hallmark of his (i.e. loyalty) and he stood by his disgraced Minister. Some weeks later, in September 1992, it was disclosed that Mr Mellor had gone on holiday at the expense of some Palestinian contacts. When his judgment was once again being publicly questioned, Mr Mellor found that as an already damaged figure, he could not survive this storm, and he resigned.[113]

Meanwhile, Norman Lamont was busy as chancellor of the exchequer spending billions and billions of pounds on unsuccessfully trying to keep sterling afloat in the European Exchange Rate Mechanism (ERM). The Conservatives had taken the UK into the ERM at an exchange rate which turned out to be economically unsustainable. Inevitably, the markets piled in to put pressure on a weak but chronically over-valued pound, resulting in huge losses to the exchequer. No Conservative Minister apologised. Nobody resigned. Despite this Mr Lamont found that he had the loyal support of his friend, the Prime Minister. However, as time went by and it became clear that Mr Lamont was not likely to recover in the public's eye,[114] the Prime Minister came to understand that the chancellor's position at the Treasury could no longer be sustained, and in May 1993 he offered him a less senior post in the cabinet, which in a huff of hubris Mr Lamont refused to accept, so ending his ministerial career.

These events rocked the Major administration, and in the autumn of 1993 the Prime Minister decided to relaunch his government with a new 'back to basics' campaign, with an emphasis on individual moral duty and family values. This turned out to be somewhat unwise on the Prime Minister's part, as rather too many of his colleagues in Parliament (and in the government) appeared not to practise these virtues in their private lives. A number of Conservatives were exposed by the media as having had extra-marital affairs, including the environment Minister Tim Yeo, who was forced to resign.[115] More disturbingly, two broadsheet newspapers, the *Guardian* and the *Sunday Times*, began to sniff at a bigger scandal: one related not to dishonest sex but to dishonest money. A number of Conservatives were accused of having accepted cash to ask parliamentary questions on behalf of lobbyists - contacts which the MPs had failed to disclose, contrary to the rules of the House of Commons. In July 1994 two junior government aides, Graham Riddick and David Tredinnick, were exposed by the *Sunday Times* and were forced

---

[113] For a more detailed account of Mr. Mellor's resignation, see D. Woodhouse, *Ministers and Parliament* (Oxford: Clarendon Press, 1994) pp. 77-86.

[114] Mr. Lamont's difficulties were compounded by stories in the tabloids to the effect that he had been caught buying cheap champagne and cigarettes at an off licence near Paddington station resulting in prurient speculation as to with whom these treats were to be shared. It was also alleged that a female tenant of Mr Lamont's London flat was offering various sexual services from his premises. Mr. Lamont was reported to have used departmental assistance (and money) to secure the woman's eviction.

[115] Also embroiled in sex or personal scandals of one degree or another were Tory MPs Steven Norris, David Ashby, Gary Waller, Hartley Booth, Richard Spring, Stephen Milligan, and Michael Brown. See D. Leigh and E. Vulliamy, *Sleaze: The Corruption of Parliament* (London: 4th Estate, 1997) p. 150. See also R. Brazier, 'It *is* a Constitutional Issue: Fitness for Ministerial Office in the 1990s' [1994] *Public Law* 431.

to quit their posts as parliamentary private secretaries (the first step on the ministerial career path).[116] Later that year, the *Guardian* exposed three Ministers, Tim Smith, Neil Hamilton and Jonathan Aitken (the last of whom was a member of the cabinet) as having substantial financial interests which they had failed to disclose on the *Register of Members' Interests*.[117]

During all of this time, the Major government knew that it was sitting on a steadily ticking time bomb. In November 1992 a court of appeal judge, Sir Richard Scott, had been appointed by the government to chair a public inquiry into the government's covert policy on trade with Iraq between 1984-90. It appeared that the government had authorised the export to Iraq of defence equipment and so-called dual-use goods which could be used by Iraq in the manufacture of weapons, despite the fact that the government had publicly stated that no such goods were to be sold to Iraq. Moreover, Customs and Excise, one of the government's prosecuting authorities, had brought criminal proceedings against a number of companies which had been engaged in this process. The most famous of these companies (Matrix Churchill) argued in their defence at trial that the government had known all about the nature of their trade with Iraq and had approved of it. When this argument proved to be successful and the Matrix Churchill trial collapsed amid the (alleged) perjury of a former government Minister (Alan Clark), the Prime Minister appointed Scott to look into the entire story. Scott conducted high profile public hearings throughout 1993 and 1994, and would eventually issue a report which the government feared would have to lead to further resignations. Foremost in the firing line was William Waldegrave, who had been one of the Ministers responsible for government policy on Iraqi trade at the critical time.[118] The Scott inquiry's report was eventually published in February 1996. Despite

---

[116] See Leigh and Vulliamy, *ibid.*, pp. 170-72. It was due to these various sex and financial scandals that John Major established the Nolan committee to examine (and to reassure the public about) standards in public life. The first report of the committee was published in May 1995 as Cm 2850. See generally, D. Oliver [1995] *Public Law* 497.

[117] Established in 1974-75, the register provides an official listing of MPs' interests. See Erskine May, *Parliamentary Practice* (London: Butterworths, 21st ed., 1989) pp. 384-90. All three resigned from the government, and all found that by the summer of 1997 their disgraced political careers were in tatters. Tim Smith stood down at the 1997 general election when it became clear a matter of weeks before polling day that if he did not, the opposition candidates would withdraw, allowing an independent anti-sleaze candidate to stand, behind whom all opposition supporters could unite. Mr. Hamilton refused to stand down when he found himself in the same position, but lost his (previously safe) constituency, Tatton, to the independent anti-sleaze candidate, Martin Bell, after the Labour and Liberal Democrat candidates withdrew from the ballot. Mr. Aitken lost his Thanet seat in the Labour landslide of May 1997, and shortly afterwards lost his libel case against the *Guardian*, costing him £1.8 million. See, generally, Leigh and Vulliamy, *ibid.*, especially on the Hamilton case.

[118] Mr. Waldegrave was not solely responsible for this, but by the time the Scott report was published, he was the only Minister to remain in the government who had been involved in formulating the policy over Iraq. Of the other two, Lord Trefgarne had left the government in 1992, and Alan Clark did not contest the 1992 election, although he was returned to Parliament in 1997.

being heavily criticised in the report, Mr Waldegrave did not resign. Why not?[119]

By 1996 the government had changed the rules. The meaning of the constitutional convention of individual ministerial responsibility had been changed by the government in three critical ways so that, by 1996, despite the scathing criticisms of the Scott report, the government could ensure that its Ministers would remain fully protected. What were these changes, and how did the government manage to secure them? The first of them, which directly helped Mr Waldegrave, related to the requirement that Ministers should not mislead Parliament. This principle was altered by the government by the inclusion of the adverb 'knowingly', so that Ministers would now only be constitutionally responsible if they knowingly misled Parliament. Inadvertently misleading Parliament, even if the Minister should have known that what he was saying to Parliament could not have been true, would now attract no constitutional sanction, according to the government. How did the government do this?

The key was paragraph 27 of *Questions of Procedure for Ministers* (which we quoted from above). *QPM* might be the most authoritative text on the doctrine of ministerial responsibility, but it is unusual as a constitutional source in that it is a governmental text (issued by the cabinet office under the Prime Minister's name) and can therefore be changed by the government without prior parliamentary or judicial approval, authority or even consultation. This is what the government did here. The first sign that the government was intending to change the wording of paragraph 27 came in 1994 when John Major himself wrote a letter to the Treasury and Civil Service Committee (a select committee of the House of Commons) which was at that time conducting an investigation into the role of the civil service. In his letter, Mr Major stated that 'it is clearly of paramount importance that Ministers give accurate and truthful information to the House. If they *knowingly* fail to do this, then they should relinquish their positions except in the quite exceptional circumstances of which a devaluation or time of war or other danger to national security have been quoted as examples'.[120] Following on from this, in the government's response to the Nolan committee's report on *Standards in Public Life* in May 1995, the principle contained in *QPM* was redrafted. The government stated that 'Ministers are accountable to Parliament for the policies, decisions and actions of their departments and agencies' and that 'Ministers must not *knowingly* mislead Parliament and the public and should correct any inadvertent errors at the earliest possible opportunity. They must be as open as possible with Parliament and the public, *withholding information only when disclosure would not be in the public*

---

[119] For a full analysis of the Scott report and of its constitutional implications, see A. Tomkins, *The Constitution After Scott: Government Unwrapped* (Oxford: Clarendon Press, 1998), especially Chapter 1.

[120] Letter dated 5 April 1994, emphasis added. Cited in the government's response to the Treasury and Civil Service Committee's report on *The Role of the Civil Service* (HC (1993-94) 27). See *The Civil Service: Taking Forward Continuity and Change* (Cm 2748, January 1995).

*interest*.[121]

Does this matter? For our purposes, yes it does, as it represents an example of the power which conventions give to the government. This was a change in the constitutional regulation of the government which was inspired by and executed by the government. Moreover, it was a change which has resulted in the lessening of that regulation. Ministerial responsibility has been reduced as a result of the government's changes. As Vernon Bogdanor has argued, 'the formula 'knowingly mislead' ... does not provide for a situation in which a Minister has been negligent or incompetent, in which he failed to apprise himself of things that he ought to have known'[122] and in failing to account for such a situation, the newly drafted convention leaves the government less responsible than it was before. This is, then, an example of the government changing the constitution deliberately to suit its own needs - an illustration, perhaps, of Thomas Paine's famous criticism of the British constitution: that in Britain it is the constitution which is accountable to the government, rather than the government which is accountable to the constitution.[123]

But the Major government's tinkerings with ministerial responsibility did not stop there. In September 1994 six armed IRA prisoners attempted to escape from Whitemoor maximum-security prison in Cambridgeshire. The prisoners had obtained guns and semtex explosive and had tried to shoot their way out of jail. On 3 January 1995 three very high-risk prisoners escaped from Parkhurst high-security prison on the Isle of Wight. Michael Howard, the Home Secretary, appointed Sir John Learmont, a retired army general, to inquire into prison security in England and Wales. Learmont's report was published in October 1995.[124] The report was highly critical of the prison service and of the entire system of prison management, from the level of prison governors and more junior staff all the way up to the chief executive of the prisons agency and to the Home Office and its ministerial team. When the Learmont report was published, a huge political storm broke out, and the opposition called for the Home Secretary's resignation. Mr Howard refused to resign, however, and instead called for the resignation of Derek Lewis, the chief executive of the prison service, a civil servant for whom the Secretary of State is constitutionally responsible.[125] When Mr Lewis refused to resign, Mr Howard dismissed him.[126] This was quite unprecedented. Never before had a civil servant

---

[121] The Government's Response to the First Report from the Committee on Standards in Public Life, Cm 2931, July 1995, annex A. Emphasis added. This report is considered in A. Tomkins, 'A Right to Mislead Parliament?' (1996) 16 *Legal Studies* 63.
[122] Vernon Bogdanor, 'Ministerial Accountability', (1997) 50 *Parliamentary Affairs* 71, at p. 74.
[123] See Thomas Paine, *Rights of Man* (part one, 1791) (ed G. Claeys, Indianapolis: Hackett, 1992) p. 42.
[124] *Review of Prison Service Security in England and Wales and the Escape from Parkhurst Prison*, Cm 3020, October 1995.
[125] Civil servants are not themselves directly responsible to Parliament, although they may be called upon to give evidence to select committees.
[126] Mr. Lewis issued a writ for wrongful dismissal, but the action was settled before it came to court. For newspaper coverage of the story, see the *Guardian*, 18-20 October 1995. See also Derek Lewis, *Hidden Agendas: Politics, Law and Order* (London: Hamish Hamilton, 1997).

been forced in this way to accept responsibility (and its consequences) in place of a Minister.[127]

Why was it Mr Lewis who was held to be responsible in this way, and not the Minister? Michael Howard claimed in Parliament that he as Secretary of State was responsible only for policy matters, and the problems which had been identified in the Learmont report were operational concerns, not matters of policy. The person responsible for operational matters was the chief executive, not the Secretary of State, and therefore Derek Lewis was responsible, not Michael Howard. The Secretary of State would naturally have to come to the House of Commons and explain - or give an account of - what had happened (he was in that limited sense accountable to Parliament) but he was neither personally nor constitutionally responsible for what had gone wrong. Thus, here we have the second example of the Major government's rewriting of ministerial responsibility: namely the notion that Ministers are responsible to Parliament only for matters of policy, and not for operational concerns. The purported distinction between policy and operations is not only novel, it is also very difficult.[128] There are two levels of criticism: the first relates specifically to Michael Howard and his relationship with Derek Lewis (i.e., that Mr Howard was in fact deeply involved in both operational and policy matters as regards the prison service), and the second is more general. It is extremely difficult to know how to classify something as either policy or operational. For example, is a decision to reduce prisoners' visiting time a policy or an operational decision? What about over-crowding, or the re-introduction of slopping out, or staff shortages, or deciding to keep a set of prisoners confined in their cells for twenty-three hours per day - are these policy matters or operational matters, and how can we tell? In trying to get both Messrs Waldegrave and Howard off the hook, the Major government rewrote the rules, paying scant regard to constitutional precedents, and despite the fact that the implication of their actions was to leave future governments less constitutionally responsible than the constitution had once provided for.

In effect, the Major administration succeeded in drawing a distinction between ministerial accountability and ministerial responsibility. Ministerial *accountability* to Parliament, it argued, consisted of a Minister's ultimate duty to account to Parliament for the work of his department. This would mean that in the last resort Ministers could be challenged about any action of the civil service, since civil servants act on behalf of and are accountable to government Ministers, and

---

[127] Although for earlier developments concerning Ministers seeking to rely on legal advice of their civil servants in order to duck accusations of irresponsibility, see D. Woodhouse [1993] *Public Law* 412.

[128] There is some argument as to how novel this position is. Other Ministers had sought to rely on the distinction earlier in the Thatcher/Major years: see the exchange between James Prior (Secretary of State for Northern Ireland) and Enoch Powell over responsibility for escapes from the Maze prison in Northern Ireland: HC Deb, Vol 53, cols 1042-61 (9 February 1984), reproduced in M. Allen and B. Thompson, *Cases and Materials on Constitutional and Administrative Law* (London: Blackstone Press, 4th edn, 1996) pp. 277-79.

Ministers alone are accountable to Parliament. Ministerial *responsibility* arises only where a Minister is directly and personally involved in an action or decision and implies that the Minister carries personal credit or blame for that action or decision. These attempts at constitutional amendment did not go unnoticed. The public service committee of the House of Commons (a departmental select committee monitoring the department of public service) drew up a report into these matters which was extremely critical of the government's position.[129] The committee argued that the constitutional accountability of the government should not be a matter left entirely for the government to determine, and that Parliament should involve itself more deeply in what the government was trying to do. As a result of the committee's work, shortly before Parliament was prorogued in March 1997, both Houses of Parliament passed resolutions on ministerial responsibility, which for the first time lay down in a parliamentary text (rather than in the government's own *QPM*) what the requirements of ministerial responsibility are.[130] The resolutions state that:

Ministers have a duty to Parliament to account, and to be held to account, for the policies, decisions and actions of their departments ... It is of paramount importance that Ministers should give accurate and truthful information to Parliament, correcting any inadvertent error at the earliest opportunity. Ministers who knowingly mislead Parliament will be expected to offer their resignation to the Prime Minister ...

This is the first time that a constitutional convention has been codified in this way by Parliament. Its importance for our purposes is that it prevents future governments from changing further the convention of individual ministerial responsibility without first going through Parliament. No longer is this convention, at least, the exclusive preserve of the government of the day. In the unwritten constitution, that is an important constitutional breakthrough.

By way of summary, then, the executive creates constitutional conventions through its actions (hence the position of the Prime Minister and of the cabinet, for example). Occasionally the executive will codify conventional rules, as in *QPM*, but we have seen that this does not prevent the government making sometimes significant amendments, as illustrated by the stories we have recounted here from the period of John Major's government. The courts play a passive role in this, commenting on constitutional conventions only where necessary as a part of legal reasoning (as in the *Jonathan Cape* case, mentioned above).[131] As for Parliament,

---

[129] See Public Service Committee, *Ministerial Accountability and Responsibility*, HC (1995-96) 313.

[130] See HL Deb, Vol 597, col 1055 (20 March 1997) and HC Deb, Vol 292, cols 1046-47 (19 March 1997).

[131] Cases such as the Supreme Court of Canada's rewriting of the Canadian constitutional amendment formula in 1981 are exceptional: see *Reference re Amendment of the Constitution of Canada* (1982) 125 DLR (3d) 1 (on which see C. Turpin, *British Government and the Constitution* (London: Butterworths, 3rd ed., 1995) pp. 93-102). Decisions such as this one are to some extent

while it can hardly be said to stand on the sidelines with the courts, it does not often play a leading role. Again, this is well illustrated by the resolutions on ministerial responsibility. The resolutions were initially the suggestion of the public service committee, a back-bench all-party select committee of the House of Commons,[132] but although the committee provided the starting point, the resolutions as passed were the result of extensive redrafting by the government and then negotiation between the three main parties in both Houses of Parliament. Parliament, in the form of the public service committee, had a role, but always one which was effectively subordinate to the government party machine and its whipped MPs.

## VII. CONCLUSION

We have come full circle. We started by outlining the historic tension between the crown and Parliament and by looking at the role of each of them in creating and amending the constitution. We considered the core legal components of the UK constitution - prerogative, common law and statute - and analysed the various ways in which each is amended. We have seen that whereas Parliament was in Dicey's time placed at the apex of the constitution it is the executive which has over the course of the twentieth century regained the ascendancy - as illustrated most clearly in the area of constitutional convention. Whatever we might think of the appropriateness of describing conventions as constitutional, they certainly give great flexibility (and power) to the government of the day to change the constitution in a way which few written constitutions have emulated. Perhaps that is the lesson of this chapter: namely, that it is not its unwritten form which marks the British constitution out as unusual, but rather it is the way in which its constitutional rules are so weakly entrenched. The most obvious conclusion to draw from this chapter, perhaps, is that it is so easy to change the British constitution, whatever source of constitutional law is at stake.

There are two ways in which current arrangements are being mobilised to make constitutional change more difficult - to begin the process of entrenching the British constitution. On the one hand, in this essay we have talked mainly of the internal, domestic constitution. While we have occasionally referred to Europe - to the EC and to the ECJ as well as to the Council of Europe and the ECHR - we have not considered at any length the ways in which these institutions have contributed to constitutional amendment from the outside, from the perspective of the external constitution. Over the past twenty years or more, both the EC and the ECHR have

---

explained by the existence in Canada of a reference procedure, whereby constitutional questions may be referred to the court for an advisory opinion - no such jurisdiction exists in English law (although compare Art. 177 of the Treaty of Rome and the jurisdiction of the European Court of Justice).
[132] See the committee's report, *Ministerial Accountability and Responsibility*, HC (1995-96) 313, para 60.

made significant reforming contributions to British constitutional law,[133] but for our purposes their influence is more interesting in terms of the ways in which they are now beginning to be used both within the UK and on the continent of Europe as devices for entrenching European norms of public law into the British constitution. In the field of judicial review, for example, a number of judges have begun to argue that the jurisdiction of judicial review ought to be expanded so that acts of public administration can be struck down by the courts not only if they violate the existing principles of judicial review (that is to say, illegality, irrationality and procedural impropriety) but also if they infringe basic rights, such as the right to life or freedom of speech.[134] Thus far we should be careful not to overplay the importance of such arguments - we are talking of only a small handful of controversial judges in a still small number of cases[135] - but it is clear that serious judicial consideration is being given to the role which European standards such as those of the ECHR can play in the British constitution as a way of enhancing the judicial hand in its struggle to keep the executive under control and within the rule of law.

The second way in which a greater degree of entrenchment can be detected comes, ironically, from the government. After eighteen years in opposition, in May 1997 the Labour party was elected to form a government. Tony Blair's new Labour party won the general election with an overwhelming majority of 179 MPs. It was elected on a manifesto which included a significant commitment to wide-ranging constitutional reform. The first item on the government's agenda was devolution

---

[133]   On the contribution of the EC, see for example the changes which the UK's membership of the EC has brought about to the understanding of parliamentary sovereignty, especially as regards issues such as sex discrimination: see for example, *R v. Secretary of State for Transport, ex parte Factortame* [1990] 2 AC 85; *R v. Secretary of State for Employment, ex parte Equal Opportunities Commission* [1994] 2 WLR 409; and *Webb v. EMO* [1995] 1 WLR 1454. The ECHR and its enforcement bodies in Strasbourg have made significant contributions in areas such as prisoners' rights, and due process - especially as regards Northern Ireland. See, among many other examples, *Golder v. UK*, Series A, No. 18, (1975) 1 EHRR 524; *Silver v. UK*, Series A, No. 61, (1983) 5 EHRR 347; *Ireland v. UK*, Series A, No. 25, (1978) 2 EHRR 25; and *Brogan v. UK*, Series A, No. 145-B, (1988) 11 EHRR 117. See generally, C.A. Gearty, 'The United Kingdom' in C.A. Gearty (ed.) *European Civil Liberties and the European Convention on Human Rights: A Comparative Study* (Deventer: Kluwer, 1997) Chapter 2.

[134]   For cases, see *R v. Home Secretary, ex parte Leech* [1993] 4 All ER 539; *R v. Cambridge Health Authority, ex parte B* [1995] 2 All ER 129; and *R v. Ministry of Defence, ex parte Smith* [1996] 1 All ER 257. For articles and lectures by judges, see Sir John Laws, 'Is the High Court the Guardian of Constitutional Rights?' [1993] *Public Law* 59, 'Law and Democracy' [1995] *Public Law* 72, and 'The Constitution: Morals and Rights' [1996] *Public Law* 622; Sir Stephen Sedley, 'The Sound of Silence' (1994) 110 *Law Quarterly Review* 270 and 'Human Rights: A 21st Century Agenda' [1995] *Public Law* 386; and Lord Woolf, 'Droit Public - English Style' [1995] *Public Law* 57. See also the troika of essays by Sedley J published in the *London Review of Books*, volume 19, numbers 9-11 (May and June 1997). In this drive towards greater recognition of civil liberties in English law, these judges have been supported by a small but vocal and influential group of academic constitutional lawyers, representing a further factor in constitutional amendment which we have not discussed in this essay: namely, scholarship. See T.R.S. Allan, *Law Liberty and Justice: The Legal Foundations of British Constitutionalism* (Oxford: Clarendon Press, 1993) and de Smith, Woolf and Jowell, *Judicial Review of Administrative Action* (London: Sweet and Maxwell, 1995) especially Chapter 13.

[135]   See F. Klug and K. Starmer, [1997] *Public Law* 223.

to Scotland and to Wales. Within weeks of having been elected, the government introduced a Scotland and Wales (Referendums) Bill which provided for referendums to be held in Scotland and in Wales asking whether the people of those nations wanted power to be devolved from Westminster to Edinburgh and Cardiff.[136] White papers on devolution were published in July, along with a green paper on the future of regional government in London.[137] Even if all the various proposals for devolution and regional government come into effect, they could of course be repealed by a subsequent Parliament. But it is interesting that the government has decided that a part of the process towards devolution - in Scotland, Wales and London - is to hold a referendum. There is no legal requirement to hold a referendum in these (or in any other circumstances) and the government and Parliament are legally at liberty to ignore the results of the referendums, but they are nonetheless of some significance to the issue of constitutional amendment. There is a strong political argument - but we stress it is no more than this - that an amendment introduced on the back of a referendum should be reversed only on the back of a further referendum. This is plainly an attempt by the Blair government to entrench (politically, at least) the constitutional changes which it has introduced, making it harder for a future Parliament or a future government to reverse them.[138]

In addition to devolution the Labour government also plans to incorporate the European Convention on Human Rights into domestic law, to enact a Freedom of Information Act, and to abolish the voting rights of (most) hereditary peers in the House of Lords.[139] Further, a number of potential changes to the House of Commons were also highlighted. The manifesto stated that 'the House of Commons is in need of modernisation' and that a special select committee of the House should be set up to look into its procedures. Further, 'Prime Ministers questions will be made more effective [and] ministerial accountability will be reviewed so as to remove recent abuses'.[140] Indications were also given that the Nolan committee would be invited to conduct an inquiry into the funding of political parties, and that a referendum would be held on the voting system for the

---

[136] The Scottish referendum also asked whether voters wished the Scottish Parliament to have limited tax varying powers, so that it might raise (or lower) income tax rates by as much as 3% measured against the rate set by the Chancellor in his budget.

[137] See *A Voice for Wales*, Cm 3718; *Scotland's Parliament*, Cm 3658; *New Leadership for London*, Cm 3724. White and green papers are documents published by the government. White papers set out the policy which the government wishes to put into effect in a later Act. Green papers set out a variety of proposals for discussion and consultation.

[138] For the avoidance of doubt, the white paper on Scottish devolution stated that 'the UK Parliament is and will remain sovereign in all matters: but as part of the government's resolve to modernise the British constitution Westminster will be choosing to exercise that sovereignty by devolving legislative responsibilities to a Scottish Parliament without in any way diminishing its own powers. The government recognises that no UK Parliament can bind its successors'. See *Scotland's Parliament*, Cm 3658, para 4.2.

[139] *Because Britain Deserves Better* (London: Labour Party, 1997) pp. 32-35.

[140] *Ibid*, p. 33.

House of Commons.[141]

These plans may come to nothing, following the pattern of attempts by previous Labour governments to introduce constitutional change,[142] but they certainly indicate that the substance, as well as the procedure of constitutional reform is likely to dominate public lawyers' concerns for the foreseeable future. If only one thing is clear from this essay, it is that everything can change. But it may be that even this rule is changing, and that in the future, constitutional amendment will become a more controlled process, with greater constraints on the government being exercised not only by Parliament and the courts, but also by the people. That really would be a constitutional amendment worth celebrating.

---

[141] *Ibid.*
[142] Labour governments during the 1960s and 1970s tried but failed to reform the House of Lords, to introduce devolution to Scotland and to Wales, and to introduce a greater degree of open government and freedom of information.

Chapter Sixteen

# THE CHANGING CONSTITUTION: AMERICAN CONSTITUTIONAL AMENDMENT AND THE LIMITS OF ARTICLE V

Stephen Tierney[*]

*Malum est consilium quod mutari non potest*
(*Publilius Syrus*)

## I. INTRODUCTION

In the relatively short history of modern liberal democracy and of the written constitutional instruments by which popular government is secured in most countries, the endurance of the US Constitution for over two hundred years is particularly noteworthy. Although this longevity is especially significant given that on only twenty six occasions has successful recourse been had to the amendment procedures within the Constitution,[1] it might not be entirely churlish to suggest that the Constitution's survival may better be viewed as an achievement in spite of, rather than on account of this statistic. That a constitution which was designed in 1787 to accommodate the interests of a small settler population has endured, with so few enumerated revisions, to fit the needs, at least in political terms, of the world's leading economic and military superpower, is indeed remarkable. However, radical changes have taken place in the social, economic, demographic, geographic and political fabric of the United States, changes so fundamental to the nation's self-understanding that they have demanded accommodation in constitutional terms whether or not that accommodation has formally manifested itself by means of Article V.

This chapter will examine how flexible the American amendment article has been in providing for the challenges of changing times. In doing so it will address in section II the mechanics of formal constitutional amendment enshrined in Article V. This will involve consideration of the constitution's formation and of the historical process from which the constitution as a whole and Article V in particular emerged, before leading on to an analysis of some of the ambiguities and complexities inherent within Article

---

[*] The University of Edinburgh.
[1] The amendment provision is to be found in Article V of the Constitution.

V, which continue to bedevil its interpretation. Section III will extend beyond the issue of formal constitutional amendment to address contemporary controversies over structural changes to the constitution, changes which have apparently been effected outwith the processes of Article V. This will comprise analysis, first of these extra-Article V modifications and re-evaluations in generally accepted renditions of constitutional meaning, and secondly, of the role assumed by the Supreme Court both in its interpretation of Article V, and in effecting, through its own jurisprudence, incremental constitutional change perhaps in tacit recognition of the rigidity of the Article V process.

## II. THE FORMAL PROCESS OF CONSTITUTIONAL AMENDMENT

A. Formation of the Constitution

The American Constitution which came into being in 1787 was very much the child of the War of Independence, and in particular of the War's defining moment, the signing of the Declaration of Independence.[2] The close connection between Revolution and constitution is clear as far back as 1776 when, with transformative zeal, the Continental Congress not only appointed a committee to draft the Declaration, but also assigned to another body the task of formulating an instrument on which might be based some kind of union of the states.

The first attempt at constitution building resulted in the Articles of Confederation which were first presented in draft form to the Continental Congress in 1777 and accepted by the states in 1781. Although these remained in force until 1788 they proved to be largely unsatisfactory, lacking as they did provision for strong central authority. The amount of autonomy remaining to each individual state meant that with their varying interests there was no prospect of central planning nor of the policies needed to stabilise the post-bellum economy. Therefore, to most delegates at the Philadelphia Convention, meeting in 1787 with a remit under the Articles to draft amendment of them, it was evident that a radical revision was required if a viable nation was to be forged from the existing loose confederation of ex-colonies.

The backdrop to Philadelphia with the revolutionary war not long ended was one of upheaval. Delegates came together from the several states representing a range of competing interests and the constitution which resulted was ultimately a consensus or series of compromises built upon the accommodation of these differing concerns and upon the defusing of tensions resulting from them.[3] It is useful to identify three particular tensions which put a strain on the task of constitution building and which

---

[2] An event which famously took place on 4 July 1776. As one commentator describes it: 'The creation of one republic out of thirteen colonies forms the last great drama of the Revolution'. Edward Countryman, *The American Revolution* (1985) p.175.

[3] Max Farrand, the great historian of the Philadelphia Convention, describes the Constitution as 'a bundle of compromises'. Quoted by Esmond Wright *Fabric of Freedom 1763-1800* (1965) at p.168. See also Gordon Wood *Creation of the American Republic 1776-1787* (1969).

required resolution at Philadelphia.

One particular dilemma following the Revolution was the diversity in outlook and the strong sense of independence felt to varying degrees by each of the thirteen colonies. The Articles of Confederation which had attempted to bind the new, independent states together had been forced to accommodate their strong sense of sovereignty and had done so by a lowest common denominator of acceptable central authority.[4] The nature of the Revolution and the eventual triumph of the colonies had made it clear that any new government arrangement involving these emerging states could not be unitary in nature. An important debate at Philadelphia, therefore, involved the need to build a central government apparatus which would be sufficiently strong to avoid the ills of the Articles of Confederation without at the same time destroying the autonomy of the states which still felt themselves to have ultimate control over their own affairs. The move then to federalism at Philadelphia was an attempt both to alleviate the inherent weakness of a confederacy composed of thirteen states all retaining individual sovereignty, and to avert the threat that if the thirteen could not agree on a stronger union of all, sectional interests would drive certain states into unions with one another on sectional or regional grounds.[5] The issue of federalism was thus the first great tension of Philadelphia and it required a sensitive and complex approach in order to enshrine within the constitution an acceptable division of powers both among the states themselves, and between the states and the emerging institutions of federal government.

A second and very specific set of problems facing the Philadelphia delegates were the economic and ensuing political difficulties which beset the colonies in the aftermath of the War of Independence. The revolutionary struggle had drained resources, and the need for rapid economic expansion was great. Again, however, the weakness of the Articles was an impediment to progress. Without strong central control it was extremely difficult to put in place planned economic restructuring of the country as a whole. Furthermore, the existing Continental Congress was denied the power to raise taxes which it needed not only to repay war debts but also to finance the army.[6] These pressures had a number of negative side effects. For example, certain states resorted to printing currency, as the war had exhausted reserves, a practice which led to conflicts between states and intensified economic disputes within states themselves among sectional or class interests. The need then for a constitution which would facilitate a unified and co-ordinated economic policy also added to the urgency of the Philadelphia deliberations.

A third strain on the Philadelphia process was slavery. An enormous dichotomy

---

[4] The various weaknesses of the Articles are outlined by Countryman, *op. cit. supra* n.2 at pp.179-180.
[5] This could have resulted in what one commentator calls the 'balkanization of the Union.' Thornton Anderson *Creating the Constitution: The Convention of 1787 and the First Congress* (1993) at p.13.
[6] It was important to maintain an army as further British attacks were still widely feared, but the difficulty of doing so with no central taxing powers was considerable. For example, seaboard states in the 1780s refused to allow the Continental Congress to collect duties on goods arriving at American ports. See Countryman, *op. cit. supra* n.2 at pp.183-5.

existed (even if not articulated as such by the delegates at Philadelphia[7]) between, on the one hand, the progressive political thought which lay behind the revolutionary struggle and which helped nurture emergent concepts such as personal autonomy, participatory democracy, and the moral equality of man, itself made manifest in civic citizenship, and on the other hand, the primeval state of human bondage embodying as it did the antithesis of these values.[8]

B. Ideology, constitution building and early amendment

The foregoing pressures demanded of the framers a deft touch in laying down a constitution which would prove acceptable to the competing interests of the day and yet would endure in changing times. Issues such as developing a federal system, increased centralisation of the economy, and the entrenchment of slavery were very much current concerns and as such they suggested that the constitution as established in 1787 would not be final and definitive.[9] An amendment process was therefore needed to facilitate change in light of prevailing circumstances.

Another variable in drafting a constitution which could endure was the dramatic

---

[7] It has been suggested by one writer that slavery was not in fact a source of much dispute at Philadelphia - Esmond Wright *Fabric of Freedom 1763-1800 op. cit. supra* n.3 at pp.169-170. If nothing else, however, it was central to the vital discussions over representation which was certainly a problematic subject. At issue was the question of how slaves were to be counted for the purposes of both representation and taxation. A number of northern states believed that slaves should not be counted for the former purpose, as they enjoyed almost none of the attributes of citizenship, but included for the latter purpose as property. Southern states where slave ownership was greatest sought the inclusion of slaves on citizenship grounds, in order to guarantee these states more representation, but excluded for taxation purposes. In the end a compromise was reached whereby a slave would count for three-fifths of a person with regard to representation in the lower House of Congress - US Const. Art. I, s. 2. Further evidence that slavery was a crucial issue is reflected in Article V itself which included, as one of only two unamendable provisions, a twenty year period during which Congress was forbidden from interfering with the slave trade. (See US Const. Art. V cited in full below).

[8] Gouveneur Morris of Pennsylvania described this difficulty as 'the dilemma of doing injustice to the Southern States or to human nature'. Quoted by Countryman *op. cit. supra* n.2 at p.190. The result was the three-fifths compromise (see n.7 *supra*). Note also William M. Wiecek, 'The Witch at the Christening: Slavery and the Constitution's Origins', in Leonard W. Levy and Dennis J. Mahoney ed. *The Framing and Ratification of the Constitution* (1987) at p.167. The compromise arrived at between the slave states and the free states was to prove so untenable that the remaining tensions would result in the bloodiest war in American history (as well as in a series of amendments in the wake of this war). This disaster and the continuing acrimony between North and South would remain an open wound at the heart of American society with continuing constitutional implications as the southern states persisted in using their remaining constitutional powers for a century after the end of the Civil War to deny the civil rights of African Americans until a combination of further constitutional amendment, federal legislation and Supreme Court activism attempted to enforce at least basic civil rights in the South.

[9] This was accepted by delegates at Philadelphia. For example, George Mason of Virginia stated: 'Amendments ... will be necessary, and it will be better to provide for them, in an easy, regular and Constitutional way than to trust to chance and violence.' M. Farrand ed. *I The Records of the Federal Convention of 1787* (Yale University Press, New Haven, 1937) at pp.202-3, quoted by Walter Dellinger 'The Legitimacy of Constitutional Change: Rethinking the Amendment Process' (1983) 97 *Harvard Law Review*, 386 at p.431. See also Sanford Levinson ''Veneration' and Constitutional Change: James Madison Confronts the Possibility of Constitutional Amendment' (1990) 21 *Texas Tech Law Review* 2443 at p.2445.

ideological transformations of the seventeenth and eighteenth centuries. These ensured that the constitution would have the firm handprint of the new ideology of liberalism.[10] The effect of liberal ideology and, in particular, the theories of Hobbes, Locke and Paine on the framers, is well documented.[11] What was particularly novel about post-Revolutionary ideology in America was the idea that individual rights might be entrenched within a constitution. This notion was not adopted at Philadelphia, however, and the omission of explicit entrenchment of fundamental individual rights provoked widespread discontent and even threatened ratification of the constitution itself.[12] Reactions against the failure to entrench individual rights within the new constitution provoked the first use of the amendment process in order to correct this anomaly and secure the so-called Bill of Rights, an initiative led by James Madison.[13]

C. 'Higher law' and Article V

The desire to entrench individual rights as 'higher law' was part of the larger design to protect the constitution as a whole from frequent change at the behest of differing interests. The American Constitution was one of the first modern codifications of democratic governance and as such was instrumental in the development of many concepts now commonplace in constitutional theory. Doctrines such as separation of powers, federalism, and constitutional supremacy over ordinary law, have acquired their contemporary meaning largely by virtue of their location within the American Constitution and by their subsequent refinement through the workings and development of the constitutional machine itself.

Of particular importance for a study of the amendment process is the notion of constitutional supremacy. The US Constitution was conceptualised as a higher body of law forming the supreme norms of the emerging American state, a concept which led the framers to conclude that the protection of these norms from the passing whims of

---

[10] For a discussion of the emergence of democracy both ideologically and in practice prior to the Revolution see Jackson Turner Main *The Sovereign States 1775-1783* (1973) chapter 4. For the development of popular government in the provincial congresses and conventions see especially pp.127-8. Note, Main concludes that in the pre-Revolutionary period: 'the colonies were becoming democracies characterized by local sovereignty.' p.141.

[11] See generally Bernard Bailyn *The Ideological Origins of the American Revolution* (1967) and Gordon S. Wood *The Radicalism of the American Revolution* (1993).

[12] See Countryman, *op. cit. supra* n.2 at p.197-198 and Anderson *op. cit. supra* n.5 at p.176-8. It has been suggested that the objection to the omission of a Bill of Rights may have been a debating tactic by those delegates opposed to ratification, see Robert Bork *The Tempting of America: The Political Seduction of the Law* (1990) at p.93. The tension between majority rule and individual rights became widely known as the 'Madisonian dilemma'. This was and is the dilemma (named after the man who identified it as such, James Madison) between popular rule, usually manifesting itself through governance by the majority, and retained individual rights which may not be infringed even by the majority.

[13] The Bill of Rights is in fact the first ten amendments to the Constitution adopted in 1791 which guarantee fundamental rights such as freedom of speech, religion, criminal due process, etc.

majoritarianism would require to be effected through constitutional entrenchment.[14] The internal shield by which the constitution would preserve its own supremacy was to be an elaborate procedure for constitutional amendment crucially involving super-majorities at each stage of the process.[15] Thus the idea of supremacy of the constitution is integrally related to the process of constitutional amendment. The most important way in which the consensus reached at Philadelphia would be accepted as a founding, authoritative text and system of entrenched ultimate rules for a new nation was its capacity for change if required and yet its relative security from frequent transformation, whether total or partial. If the constitution was to be legitimated as higher law it would have to guarantee government security but at the same time not tie a governmental system based on popular consent to the will of its founding generation. As will be seen, Article V and its requirement for the consent of super-majorities in both the proposal and ratification of amendments, more than any other provision, sets the constitution apart as 'higher law' and as a founding text.[16]

D. Constitution building and the problem of rigidity

Philadelphia was a process of compromise particularly on the issue of federalism. The emergence of the constitution as entrenched 'higher law' and the central role of the amendment provision in establishing this, requires an analysis of how the drafting of the amendment provision was itself the product of compromise and how this process was tied up with the general settlement between central power and residual state power.

The clear impetus for many in forming the constitution was the desire to build a nation and, of the founders holding this view, none was more influential than James

---

[14] The experience of the English common law, which in the late 18th century was at the mercy of the developing doctrine of the legislative supremacy of Parliament, could well have served to limit the imaginations of those searching for a model of higher law by which to form a more effective union of the sovereign states in 1787. Madison's goal was to lay the foundation of the Constitution in the will of the people, not merely in the consent of legislatures. This was to be achieved by appealing directly to the people for the Constitution's ratification. Assent to the Constitution, therefore, had to be 'the *unanimous* assent of the several States that are parties to it, differing no otherwise from their ordinary assent than in its being expressed, not by the legislative authority, but by that of the people themselves.' *The Federalist* No. 39 *in The Federalist Papers*, Penguin, 1987. The question of ratification of the Constitution itself will be addressed below.

For an indication of how revolutionary the concept of a written constitution was, it is instructive to recall the words of John Marshall in one of the most important cases in the history of the Constitution, where he offered the view that its written nature was the 'greatest improvement on political institutions' which the American Constitution had brought about. *Marbury v. Madison* 5 US (1 Cranch) 137, 178 (1803).

[15] It has also been suggested that the very idea 'of incorporating within a constitution a provision for its own amendment was largely an invention of the Constitutional Convention in Philadelphia.' Douglas Linder 'What in the Constitution cannot be amended?' (1981) 23 *Arizona Law Review* 717 at p.719 referring to C. Friedrich *Constitutional Government and Democracy* 4th ed. (1968) p.138.

[16] It has thereby earned the accolade of 'arguably the single most important procedural provision in the Constitution' David R. Dow 'The Plain Meaning of Article V' in Sanford Levinson ed. *Responding to Imperfection: The Theory and Practice of Constitutional Amendment* (1995) at p.117.

Madison.[17] As discussed, political and economic divisions among the states had already made this task difficult. There was also, however, a legal problem since the amendment provision in the Articles of Confederation, if adhered to literally, would prevent any constitutional change without the unanimous consent of all the states. This might have been beneficial in protecting the Articles as a constitution but had the side effect of gridlock as each state had in effect a veto over proposals for amendment.[18] The Philadelphia Convention, it will be recalled, was given a remit to amend the Articles by the Articles themselves and so any reworking of them would in turn require the consent of all thirteen states. This level of difficulty helped focus the minds of the delegates as they attempted to draft a less restrictive amendment process for a new constitution. What was needed was a provision which would deny the federal government *carte blanche* to change the constitution to suit its own ends as and when it saw fit, but which would at the same time be more flexible than the unanimity requirement contained in the Articles.

It was generally accepted that the Articles of Confederation were wholly inadequate and in particular that the amendment veto they contained would have to be modified.[19] There were, however, two dilemmas. First, a process which would allow amendments by bare majority could lead to constitutional instability, jeopardising the other agreements at Philadelphia which were to be entrenched in the new constitution as higher law; and, secondly, a deal had to be struck which would appease those who were concerned that either the states or the federal government would be given too great a role in the amending procedure.

The compromise reached was Article V and in order to properly understand its meaning the development of this compromise requires exploration. The amendment process which was eventually enshrined in Article V can be divided into two parts - proposal and ratification. It seems that of the two, the issue of ratification was less

---

[17] Attempts to demythologise the motivations of the 'founding fathers' have led to much disagreement among historians. On one side of the debate are those who see the founders as crusaders for liberty. Just as they had fought a war for freedom so now were they creating a document that would enshrine it. Edward Countryman expresses this viewpoint thus: 'The Revolution had been a struggle to secure American liberty, and the Constitution was liberty's greatest protection.' Countryman *op. cit. supra* n.2 at p.176. On the other hand, perhaps beginning with the revisionist work of Charles A. Beard (*An Economic Interpretation of the Constitution of the United States*, (1913)) the Constitution has been seen as a means of enshrining not ideals but the self interest of its founders. 'For Beard, the Constitution marked not much more than a triumph for men who were on their way to wealth at other men's expense.' Countryman at p.176. Whatever their motivations, men like Madison clearly saw a firmly grounded Constitution as a *sine qua non* to survival of the Union.

[18] For Madison '(t)he first step ... was to end the possibility that one state's veto could prevent any change at all, no matter how much the other states might want it.' Countryman *op. cit. supra* n.2 at p.186. As Madison himself stated: 'Could anything in theory be more perniciously improvident and injudicious than this submission of the will of the majority to the most trifling minority?' Quoted in Sanford Levinson, *Texas Tech Law Review op. cit. supra* n.9 2443 at p.2448.

[19] Madison saw the Articles as a whole to be completely unworkable and, accordingly, he arrived at Philadelphia with a worked out agenda designed to replace them entirely. 'He had worked out 'amendments' to the Articles which, in effect, eliminated the Articles themselves and started once again from the beginning.' Countryman *op. cit. supra* n.2 p.186.

controversial to the constitution's framers.[20] There was general agreement that ratification should lie in the hands of the several states, rather than, for example, the federal legislature. As a compromise between differing proposals that an amendment should require ratification either by all of the states unanimously (which would be no improvement on the Articles' amendment provision) or that it should simply demand ratification by two-thirds of the states, the Convention decided that ratification should be by three-quarters of the states.[21]

The important issue remaining to be resolved was where the power to propose amendments should lie.[22] The issue of balance there came to a head. That there should be a balance between the federal Congress and the states, giving either an opportunity to propose amendments was advocated by Madison in this formulation: 'The Legislature of the United States whenever two thirds of both Houses shall deem it necessary, or on the application of two thirds of the Legislatures of the several States, shall propose amendments to this Constitution...',[23] they would be valid subject, as mentioned above, to ratification by three-quarters of the states. This was opposed by those delegates such as George Mason of Virginia, who, anxious to preserve the powers of the states, sought to deny Congress any role in the amendment process.[24] Mason and others were concerned that this provision would replace an earlier proposal which read '[o]n the application of the Legislatures of two thirds of the States in the Union, for an amendment of this Constitution, the Legislature of the United States shall call a Convention for that purpose.'[25] Madison's alternative not only introduced a role for Congress, it excluded the state-led convention method and left the final say on all

---

[20] As Dellinger writes: 'The Philadelphia Convention readily agreed upon a method for ratifying proposed amendments to the new Constitution.' Walter Dellinger, 'The recurring Question of the 'Limited' Constitutional Convention' (1979) 88 *Yale Law Journal* 1623 at p.1625.

[21] M. Farrand ed. *II The Records of the Federal Convention of 1787, op. cit. supra* n.9 at 555 as cited by Dellinger, *Yale Law Journal op. cit. supra* n.20 at p.1625.

[22] Dellinger cites this as 'a critical question.' *Yale Law Journal op. cit. supra* n.20 at p.1625. See Dellinger generally (pp.1624-1630) for an excellent discussion on how Article V took shape. See also Thornton Anderson *op. cit. supra* n.5 at p.156-8, and Gerald Gunther 'The Convention Method of Amending the United States Constitution' (1979) 14 *Georgia Law Review* 1 at p.13-17.

[23] M. Farrand ed. *II The Records of the Federal Convention of 1787, op. cit. supra* n.9 at 559 as cited by Dellinger, *Yale Law Journal op. cit. supra* n.20 at p.1628. See the opening section of Article V below where a similar phrase to this is incorporated.

[24] See Levinson, *Texas Tech Law Review op. cit. supra* n.9 at pp.2445-6. The Thirteenth Virginia Resolve, May 29, 1787, also sought to exclude any Congressional role, M. Farrand ed. *I The Documentary History of the Ratification of the Constitution* 245 (M. Jensen ed. 1976). See also Gerald Gunther, *Georgia Law Review op. cit. supra* n.22 at p.14.

[25] M. Farrand ed. *I The Documentary History of the Ratification of the Constitution* 269 cited by Levinson, *Texas Tech Law Review op. cit. supra* n.9 at p.2445 and Dellinger, *Yale Law Journal op. cit. supra* n.20 at p.1627. Had this alone been the process of proposal the opposite danger of excessive state control would emerge. As Gunther writes: '[the] amendment process would have been initiated solely by the states; the role of Congress would have been minimal; and the convention would have been the sole source of amendments and apparently could have made changes in the Constitution on its own, without any further requirement of ratification'. *Georgia Law Review op. cit. supra* n.22 at p.14.

proposals with the Congress.[26] In order to balance Madison's proposal, two supporters of Mason, Eldbridge Gerry from Massachusetts and Gouverneur Morris of Pennsylvania, were successful in arguing that a convention method of proposal be reinstated to supplement Madison's draft clause.[27] The final form of Article V which embraced this compromise and accordingly established a balance both between state and federal power, and between rigidity and ease, establishing as Levinson puts it, 'two quite separate paths to constitutional amendment',[28] can be seen below.

A remaining task in launching the new constitution was the need to circumvent the Articles' demand for unanimity since strictly speaking the new constitution was an amendment of the Articles. Unanimity among the thirteen states would have been a virtual impossibility (Rhode Island had not even sent delegates to Philadelphia and both it and North Carolina initially refused to ratify) and so the Articles were overridden and state legislatures, which had the power to ratify under Article XIII of the Articles,[29] were bypassed in the process of ratifying the new constitution. This was done first by way of a resolution passed at Philadelphia declaring that the constitution be submitted not to state legislatures but 'to an assembly or assemblies of Representatives, recommended by the state legislatures to be expressly chosen by the people, to consider & decide thereon',[30] and, secondly, by the application of Article VII of the new constitution which, by the time the final draft was prepared, required the approval of only nine of the thirteen states to ratify these 'amendments' to the Articles.[31]

---

[26] As Gunther continues: 'An all-powerful convention had been the sole proposing mechanism at the outset; Madison's compromise eliminated the device altogether.' *Georgia Law Review op. cit. supra* n.22 at p.14.
[27] M. Farrand ed. *II The Records of the Federal Convention of 1787, op. cit. supra* n.9 at 629 as cited by Gunther, *Georgia Law Review op. cit. supra* n.22 at p.15.
[28] Levinson, *Texas Tech Law Review op. cit. supra* n.9 at p.2446. That the final form was a balance is expressed by Madison. Article V, he wrote, 'guards equally against that extreme facility, which would render the Constitution too mutable; and that extreme difficulty, which might perpetuate its discovered faults.' Federalist 43, *The Federalist Papers op. cit. supra* n.14 at p.284.
[29] Article XIII of the Articles of Confederation provided: '[no] alteration [shall] at any time hereafter be made in [these Articles...,] unless such alteration be agreed to in a Congress of the United States, and be afterwards confirmed by the Legislatures of every State'. U.S.C. xxxv, xxxviii (1976) cited by Walter Dellinger, *Yale Law Journal op. cit. supra* n.20 at p.1625 n.6.
[30] Quoted by Countryman *op. cit. supra* n.2 at p.187. This was part of Madison's plan to appeal directly to the people (see n.14 above): 'in such a ratification by the people themselves of the several States as will render it clearly paramount to their Legislative authorities'. Quoted by Russell L. Caplan *Constitutional Brinksmanship: Amending the Constitution by National Convention* (1985) at p.5.
[31] Some have even considered that this process made ratification of the Constitution illegal. See for example, Bruce Ackerman 'The Storrs Lectures: Discovering the Constitution', (1984) 93 *Yale Law Journal* 1013 at p.1058, and Edward Countryman who writes: 'What the Convention had done was illegal by any standard that held when it first assembled. Its first illegality was the decision to bypass the whole procedure that the Articles themselves specified for their own amendment. Its second was the delegates' decision to abandon their assignment of proposing amendments and draft a whole new document'. Countryman, *op. cit. supra* n.2 at p.192. In the end a role for the existing Congress was found, but Countryman describes this as 'window dressing , for nothing could hide the fact that the Convention had far exceeded its mandate.' p.193. For the opposite view see Akhil Reed Amar 'Popular Sovereignty and Constitutional Amendment' in Sanford Levinson ed. *op. cit. supra* n.16 89 at pp.92-95.

## E. Article V

The Congress, whenever two thirds of both Houses shall deem it necessary, shall propose amendments to the Constitution, or, on the application of the legislatures of two thirds of the several States, shall call a convention for proposing amendments, which, in either case, shall be valid to all intents and purposes, as part of this Constitution, when ratified by the legislatures of three fourths of the several States, or by convention in three fourths thereof, as the one or the other mode of ratification may be proposed by the Congress; provided that no amendment which may be made prior to the year one thousand eight hundred and eight shall in any manner affect the first and fourth clauses in the Ninth Section of the First Article; and that no State, without its consent, shall be deprived of its equal suffrage in the Senate.[32]

The brevity and seeming simplicity of Article V belies both the level and the extent of the controversy and contention which it has provoked.[33] In section III two questions in particular which have been raised in a number of guises by various commentators with regard to Article V will be addressed both in relation to wider notions of non-formal constitutional change and in terms of the Supreme Court's approach to constitutional amendment. These are: is it the exclusive mechanism by which the American Constitution can be amended?; and, to what extent is it meaningful to consider American constitutional change taking into account only the numbered amendments to the Constitution and without reference to the alterations which have taken place in the historical and political structure which underpins it?

For now the apparent, literal meaning of Article V together with the two methods of proposing amendments which it countenances will be considered. One initial observation which ought to be made is that the balance reached at Philadelphia, requiring as it does a super-majority at both proposal and ratification stage, fell on the side of rigidity. Constitutional amendment in the US is accordingly difficult to achieve, and this difficulty has increased since 1787 with the growth in the number of states.[34] An immediate complication is that Article V contains two methods for both the proposal and the ratification of amendments, both of which require varying forms of super-majority consent at each stage of the process, as follows:

---

[32] US Const. Art. V. The last two clauses introduce non-amendable provisions - i.e. preventing interference with the slave trade for twenty years referred to above and guaranteeing to each state equal suffrage in the Senate. For an overview of how these two provisions found their way into Article V see Douglas Linder, *Arizona Law Review op. cit. supra* n.15 at pp.721-722.

[33] It has been argued that the amendment process in the US is in fact not clear at all. In the words of one American commentator: 'a satisfactory amendment process demands, at a minimum, that the rules for the adoption of an amendment be clearly understood. Judged by such a standard, our amendment process is seriously flawed.' Dellinger, *Harvard Law Review op. cit. supra* n.9 at p.387.

[34] It is worth noting that at the time the Constitution was drafted ratification only required acceptance by ten of the thirteen states and also that legislative workloads were far lighter than they are today where the consent of busy legislatures (or state conventions) in thirty-eight states is needed. It has been suggested that the rigidity of the American amendment process strongly influenced the framers of the Canadian constitution in the decade leading up to 1867 and explains in part why they were prepared to leave amendment of the British North America Act 1867 with the British Parliament which could amend it simply by way of ordinary legislation. (The author is grateful to Peter Oliver for this observation).

*Proposal*

1. 'The Congress, whenever two thirds of both Houses shall deem it necessary, shall propose amendments to the Constitution'.[35]
2. 'The Congress, ... on the application of the legislatures of two thirds of the several States, shall call a convention for proposing amendments by way of convention'.[36]

*Ratification*

1. By the legislatures of three quarters of the states; or
2. By convention in three quarters of the state.
In either case as Congress proposes.[37]

F. Proposal of amendments by convention

In any analysis of the textual meaning of Article V most confusion and controversy is provoked by the possibility of amendments to the Constitution being proposed by conventions, particularly as this method has never been used. Given that the other method of proposal, i.e. by Congress, and both methods of ratification, are relatively uncontroversial, discussion of the mechanics of amendment will be restricted here to the convention method of proposal. The first difficulty is the lack of guidance provided by Article V which is silent as to: the purpose of such conventions, how they should be composed, and what powers they have. Secondly, it is unclear whether or not, if a convention is called with a limited remit, Congress or any other body could prevent it from going beyond this remit and proposing what amounts to a reworking of the entire Constitution. A third point which leads from the second is, if it is the case that a convention can be called with a limited remit and is so called, could amendments which do not adhere to this remit become part of the Constitution if ratified by three fourths of the states?

The fact that these issues are crucial and yet remarkably unresolved contains obvious dangers. A convention although ostensibly called for a specific purpose could, if not held to that purpose alone by the Constitution, become a runaway train in effect proposing a new constitution for ratification. Furthermore, the text of Article V offers little if any interpretative guidelines on whether a convention can or should be limited and if so by whom. One powerful argument to the effect that a convention cannot be limited is that if it could be, the state legislatures in calling it could set its agenda, a state of affairs which would entrust them with excessive power. Walter Dellinger in

---

[35] This provision is relatively uncontroversial and hitherto has been the only one used.
[36] This has never been used but has nonetheless provoked considerable controversy, as will be discussed below.
[37] Of the two methods of ratification possible only once has there been ratification by convention. The other twenty-five amendments have been ratified by state legislatures. For a step-by-step summary of the amendment process see Russell L. Caplan *op. cit. supra* n.30 at p.viii -ix.

support of this argument analyses the intentions of the framers. He refers to Article V's nature as a compromise provision designed to withhold exclusive power from Congress to propose amendments and from the state legislatures both to propose and ratify them. Therefore, in the case of proposal by the states, suggested amendments come not from the state legislatures directly but through a convention called by two-thirds of these legislatures. This indicates for Dellinger that the framers wanted the involvement of a 'national forum'. The purpose behind this, i.e. allowing proposals to come from a 'national' convention, would be defeated if the state legislatures could limit the subject matter which such a convention could consider: '[i]f the state legislatures could not only control the text of the proposed amendment, but also limit the convention to that subject, effective proposal power would have been shifted to the state legislatures'.[38] This view is not conclusive and there is a strong body of opinion which argues that conventions, or at least applications for them, can be limited in their remit.[39]

G. The limited convention issue - what role Congress?

In practical terms Congress may have a crucial role to play in determining the scope of constitutional conventions. If the state legislatures request a limited or indeed unlimited convention, what may prove decisive is Congress' preparedness to comply with this request. Dellinger, as has been observed, suggests that Congress cannot require a convention to adhere to a limited agenda even should the states request it.[40] Albeit that a request for a single issue convention was received, and a convention with a limited remit called, there may be no way thereafter to prevent it from discussing and voting on other issues. If delegates, as is most likely, are popularly elected in their respective states, it is possible that they would assume a commission to alter the Constitution in other areas in a similar way, and drawing upon a similar populist mandate to that assumed by the delegates to the Philadelphia convention, Congress in such an event would perhaps simply refuse to submit *'ultra vires'* proposals for ratification. This tactic would, however, be as constitutionally questionable as attempting to impose limits on the convention in the first place. Congress could also face intense political opposition if public opinion considered the convention to have put forward a legitimate and popular set of proposed amendments, which the country at large was anxious to consider for ratification. The last resort, if Congress was unclear as to the constitutional

---

[38] Dellinger, *Yale Law Journal op. cit. supra* n.20 at p.1630. See Gunther, *Georgia Law Review op. cit. supra* n.22 at p.13 who also argues that the remit of a convention once called cannot be controlled by either Congress or the applying states.
[39] For a discussion of the alternative view that limited applications for a convention are valid see Gunther, *Georgia Law Review op. cit. supra* n.22 at p.6 n.14 and at p.12. That such limitation is possible is implied in a number of initiatives in recent years, which call for single issue conventions to propose amendments. A prominent example is the application to Congress by Delaware in 1975 for an amendment to ensure a balanced federal budget each year. Del. H. Con. Res. No. 36 (1975), and 125 Cong. Rec. S1307 (daily ed. 8 Feb. 1979). This makes clear that the convention is intended to have power only to propose this specified amendment. Such an application is invalid according to Dellinger, *Yale Law Journal op. cit. supra* n.20 at p.1634.
[40] Dellinger, *Yale Law Journal op. cit. supra* n.20 at p.1624.

position, would be to take the question to the federal courts, but as will be observed below the courts, and in particular the Supreme Court, have been extremely restrained in addressing Article V, leaving its interpretation largely to the Congress.

## III. CONSTITUTIONAL AMENDMENT AND CONSTITUTIONAL CHANGE

In a technical dissection of the mechanics of Article V it is important not to lose sight of the fact that constitutions develop by way of alterations in received understandings of meaning as well as through formal processes of textual amendment. In this context, changes in the perceptions of constitutional actors as to the US Constitution's substance have served to constitute developments in the Constitution's structure even in the absence of reference to the formal amendment mechanism contained in Article V. To evaluate constitutional change in this broader sense it is important to address both the limitations of Article V and the otherwise flexible nature of the Constitution - a Constitution which has had to adapt to altering circumstances even when it has not always been possible to activate the laborious process contained in the Constitution's amendment provision.

The remainder of this chapter will address two fundamental issues which relate to the wider issue of American constitutional development. First, is the broad inquiry into constitutional change outwith the confines of Article V, within which two questions will be posited:

1. Is Article V the exclusive mechanism by which the Constitution can *formally* be amended?
2. Even if Article V is the exclusive mechanism for formal amendment, is bare analysis of its process and the twenty-six amendments which that process has produced, sufficient to explain the extent of American constitutional change since 1787?

The second issue is the role played by the Supreme Court in American constitutional development. Again two questions will be asked which mirror the first two questions set out above:

3. Correlating to the question of whether or not Article V is the exclusive mechanism by which the Constitution can formally be amended is the query: what role has the Supreme Court played in developing the meaning and delineating the scope of Article V?
4. The question of whether or not simple reference to the twenty-six numbered amendments to the Constitution is sufficient to explain the extent of American constitutional change again begs an associated inquiry in respect of the role of the judiciary, namely: to what extent has the Supreme Court played a role in developing the substantive meaning of the Constitution through its own creative/activist jurisprudence?

A. Constitutional development and the limits of Article V

*1. Is Article V the exclusive mechanism by which the Constitution can formally be amended?*

The problems in elucidating the meaning of Article V which have been discussed in Section II are compounded by a school of thought which contends that, in any event, Article V is not the exclusive means by which the Constitution might be amended. This is a very radical approach put forward in its most strident form by Akhil Reed Amar.[41] He asserts that Article V sets out the exclusive way in which *ordinary* government, namely Congress and the state legislatures, can amend the Constitution. This does not detract, however, from the sovereignty retained by the people, a sovereignty which may manifest itself through popular constitutional revision, and, if need be, reconstitution of the organs of government. Amar states plainly: 'Article V nowhere prevents the *People* themselves, acting apart from ordinary government, from exercising their legal right to alter or abolish government, via the proper legal procedures.'[42] Amar argues that the federal division of power between national and state government, which Madison took to be at the heart of the Constitution, was an attempt to divide sovereignty. Divided sovereignty was, however, widely seen as illogical by other delegates at Philadelphia, such as James Wilson. Instead men like Wilson put their trust in, and in turn entrusted the Constitution to, popular sovereignty, which could ultimately manifest itself in majoritarianism.[43]

The implications of this approach for Amar are, bearing in mind his reference to 'proper legal procedures', first, that a bare majority of those voting in a national election might *ratify* amendments provided they were proposed in conformity with Article V, and secondly, that a majority of voters can even *initiate* the amendment process: 'I believe that Congress would be obliged to call a convention to propose amendments if a majority of American voters so petition; and that an amendment could be lawfully ratified by a simple majority of the American electorate.'[44] In justifying this contention Amar traces the origins and legitimacy of the Constitution back to simple

---

[41] Akhil Reed Amar in Sanford Levinson ed. *op. cit. supra* n.31. See also Amar 'Philadelphia Revisited: Amending the Constitution Outside Article V' (1988) 55 *University of Chicago Law Review* 1043.

[42] Amar in Sanford Levinson ed. *op. cit. supra* n.31 89 at p.90.

[43] 'A fundamental principle for republican government was that the majority should rule, and divided sovereignty betrayed that fundamental principle'. Amar in Sanford Levinson ed. *op. cit. supra* n.31 89 at p.115.

[44] Amar in Sanford Levinson ed. *op. cit. supra* n.31 89 at p.89 n.1. See also Amar, Philadelphia Revisited etc. *op. cit. supra* n.41 1043 at p.1065. This approach must rely for its legitimacy either upon evidence that the Constitution itself provides for this retained popular sovereignty, or that there is some right to popular sovereignty, perhaps emanating from natural law, which vests the ultimate power to alter the Constitution in a majority of the people, despite attempts in Article V to impose a super-majoritarian requirement upon the amendment process. Amar hints that it might be both: 'first principles and various other parts of the federal Constitution require us to abandon the seeming exclusivity of Article V itself'. Amar in Sanford Levinson ed. *op. cit. supra* n.31 89 at p.108. A critic of Amar, David Dow, rejects either of these as possible justifications for Amar's theory. David R. Dow 'The Plain Meaning of Article V' in Sanford Levinson ed. *op. cit. supra* n.16 117 at pp.124-125 and 137-138.

majoritarian will and asks: 'Why does not a simple majority of the national People - for the Constitution forms one national People from the formerly distinct thirteen state peoples - retain an analogous legal right to alter or abolish its Constitution outside Article V?'[45]

It can be argued that Amar's thesis is flawed for a number of reasons. First, his approach seems to contradict Article V and the careful compromise worked out at Philadelphia. The balance between establishing a stable Constitution, requiring a supermajority at each step in the amendment process, and at the same time dividing this amendment power between the federal government and the states, was precisely struck. The history of the Constitution and its commitment to protecting different interests through the separation of powers, the establishment of federalism and the entrenchment of individual liberties in the first ten amendments, appears to bear out this analysis. The rationale of the Constitution was compromise among competing interests, a compromise which could only be maintained by preventing a bare majority from wresting absolute control of the process of government.[46] Secondly, Article V contains the only mechanism for amendment referred to in the Constitution. If the established doctrine, *expressio unius est exclusio alterius,* meaning that the expression of one thing is the exclusion of another, is applied, this suggests that Article V is indeed the exclusive vehicle for formal constitutional change.[47] Thirdly, to argue that Article V does not restrain amendment by simple popular majority would seem to undermine Article V itself. As Schauer argues: '[a]lthough Article V does not specify in so many words that the procedures specified therein shall be the sole method of amending the Constitution, nor does it contain the words 'inter alia,' any fair literal reading of the text of Article V produces the conclusion that nothing *in* the Constitution textually authorises methods of amendment other than the two alternative procedures established in Article V itself.'[48] And lastly, retained majoritarian control over the amendment process begs the ultimate question, why embark at all on a constitutional enterprise in order to balance power between central government and the country's constituent states if provisions cannot be entrenched and protected from majority rule? The American Constitution is a federal project which reserves powers to the states, but that very

---

[45] Amar in Sanford Levinson ed. *op. cit. supra* n.31 89 at p.104.

[46] A similar sentiment is expressed by David R. Dow in his critique of Amar's approach: 'When we look at the structure of the Constitution, and in particular at Article V, what we see is that our political essence reflects an individualist commitment to majoritarianism coupled, concomitantly, with a radical individualist commitment to the sanctity of certain principles. We believe in majority will, *and* we believe in the idea that certain ideals transcend the vicissitudes of majority will'. Dow in Sanford Levinson ed. *op. cit. supra* n.16 117 at pp.143-4. See also John R. Vile 'Legally Amending the United States Constitution: The Exclusivity of Article V's Mechanisms' (1991) 21 *Cumberland Law Review* 271.

[47] See Frederick Schauer 'Amending the Presuppositions of a Constitution' in Sanford Levinson ed. *op. cit. supra* n.16 145 at pp.146-7. See also Dow in Sanford Levinson ed. *op. cit. supra* n.16 117 at p.127.

[48] Schauer in Sanford Levinson ed. *op. cit. supra* n.47 145 at pp.146-7. Again Dow is of this view, claiming that any other interpretation 'renders Article V supererogatory'. Dow in Sanford Levinson ed. *op. cit. supra* n.16 117 at p.127. This seems to be not only logical simply by reference to constitutional interpretation, it is also in line with any meaningful review of the origins and purpose of the Constitution. See for example James Madison, The Federalist no.43, *The Federalist Papers op. cit. supra* n.14.

federalism is at risk if power lies in the hands of a simple national majority.[49]

It seems difficult to accept that Article V does not constitute the exclusive formal means by which the Constitution may be amended. One thing which can be taken from Amar's theory, however, is the light he casts on the limits of formalism.

## 2. Is analysis of the text of Article V and the twenty six amendments which it has produced sufficient to explain the extent of American constitutional change?

There is no question that the meaning of the Constitution has changed in many ways over the past two hundred years and that not all of these changes can be explained by, or have been brought about by way of, the sparse text of the twenty-six amendments.[50] It is necessary to consider the impact of social and political developments on constitutional meaning if a more accurate interpretation of that meaning is to be gained. Indeed, so fundamental have been the constitutional developments (i.e. changes in the accepted understanding of the Constitution as a narrative of superior norms) wrought without reference to Article V, that it is arguably misleading to assert that the Constitution has only been 'amended' by means of Article V procedure, and therefore that the simple statement that the Constitution has been amended only twenty six times is at best meaningless and at worst plain wrong.[51]

Bruce Ackerman, who has addressed this issue at length in his book *We the People: Foundations*[52] identifies two periods in American history as seminal epochs of constitutional change or transformation. The first is the Reconstruction period following the Civil War of 1861-65 which radically altered the balance of power between the states and the federal government, and the second is the growth in government which took place during the New Deal era as the Democratic Party led by President Roosevelt sought to promote intervention in the economy to cope with post-Depression problems. In a detailed argument Ackerman sets out his view that significant constitutional changes, what he terms constitutional transformations or 'unconventional

---

[49] As Dow writes: 'The suggestion that Article V is not the exclusive mode of amendment contradicts that bedrock principle of federalism and leads inexorably to the disappearance of states.' Dow in Sanford Levinson ed. *op. cit. supra* n.16 117 at p.142. He also takes issue with Amar's apparent contention that popular sovereignty and majoritarianism are synonymous. 'By *popular* sovereignty ... we mean that the people, in contradistinction to God or the king, hold this power.' p.119. It may be rule by the majority but 'can also be understood as a plurality, a super-majority, or even the will of an appointed oligarchy of lawmakers.' p.120. See also John Vile, *Cumberland Law Review op. cit. supra* n. 46 at pp.292-294.

[50] The difficulty of the process must go some way to explain why there have only been twenty-six formal amendments when by 1977 over five thousand bills proposing amendments had been introduced in Congress. See S. Rep. No. 724, 95th Cong., 2d Sess. (1977) cited by Walter Dellinger, *Harvard Law Review op. cit. supra* n.9 386 at p.427.

[51] Exponents of this approach are Sanford Levinson, Stephen M. Griffin and Bruce Ackerman. Levinson, for example, says that to suggest there have been exactly twenty-six amendments is 'simpleminded and atheoretical'. Sanford Levinson 'Introduction: Imperfection and Amendability' in Sanford Levinson ed. *op. cit. supra* n.16 3 at p.7. See also Stephen M. Griffin 'Constitutionalism in the United States: From Theory to Politics' in Sanford Levinson ed. *op. cit. supra* n.16 37, and Bruce Ackerman 'Higher Lawmaking' in Sanford Levinson ed. *op. cit. supra* n.16 63. See also Bruce Ackerman *We the People: Foundations* (1991).

[52] *Op. cit. supra* n.51.

adaptation[s]'⁵³ took place without the application of Article V during these dramatic periods in America's development.⁵⁴

What is more, Ackerman sees such 'transformations' as legally legitimate. In a thesis which has similarities to that put forward by Amar, he considers that while Article V provides *one* way in which the Constitution may be amended, it does not necessarily restrict constitutional amendment to this process. 'None of its [Article V's] 143 words says anything like 'this Constitution may only be amended through the following procedures, and in no other way'. The Article makes its procedures sufficient, but not necessary, for the enactment of a valid Constitutional amendment'.⁵⁵

Ackerman's argument that the Constitution was transformed during Reconstruction and the New Deal is perhaps not as radical or challenging to accepted understandings of the amendment process as it may at first appear. All constitutions develop over time without the need for a textual explanation or legitimisation of every change in interpretative nuance. The same applies to ordinary law. Courts imperceptibly change, and are indeed often entrusted explicitly or implicitly with the power to change, the meaning of statutes and accepted common law through the process of interpretation, a process which must be guided to some extent by the background of developing times. Just as ordinary courts develop the ordinary law, so a constitutional court may play the same role in developing a living constitution to adapt to changing circumstances. This observation does not, however, detract from the importance of Ackerman's observation that there have been periods in American constitutional history where the meaning of the Constitution has changed fundamentally without textual support, i.e. where transformations have occurred which go beyond modifications in interpretation to alterations in the accepted meaning of the Constitution which is being interpreted. The two periods on which Ackerman focuses are good examples but it is also possible to identify other, if less dramatic constitutional changes, such as the growth of presidential power, the changing reality of where the war power lies etc.,⁵⁶ which have occurred

---

[53] Ackerman in Sanford Levinson ed. *op. cit. supra* n.51 63 at p.69.

[54] 'After these two transformations, American government was very different from anything the Founders had experienced. No longer had We the People established a decentralized federal system that allowed white men to pursue their self-interest within a market economy. Americans had constituted a powerful national government with unquestioned constitutional authority to secure the legal equality and economic welfare of all its citizens regardless of the state in which they happen to live.' Ackerman in Sanford Levinson ed. *op. cit. supra* n.51 63 at pp.67-68.

[55] Ackerman in Sanford Levinson ed. *op. cit. supra* n.51 63 at p.72. The similarity to Amar is reflected in the similar criticisms levelled at Ackerman. For example, in a review of his book *We the People: Foundations* (1991) *op. cit. supra* n.51, Cass Sunstein emphasises that the American Constitution is a written text, therefore '[u]nwritten amendments simply are not amendments.' Cass Sunstein 'New Deals', New Republic, 20 Jan. 1992 32 at p.34. Ackerman's approach, however, differs from Amar's in that it does not depend upon the 'originalism' of Amar's eighteenth century interpretation of constitutional formation as a process predicated upon popular sovereignty. Ackerman relies upon more modern, and in his terms more complex, observations. Ackerman in Sanford Levinson ed. *op. cit. supra* n.51 63 at p.72 n.4.

[56] The war power is perhaps one of the most striking examples of how the President's power has grown. In terms of the text of the Constitution the power to declare war rests with Congress (US Const. Art.1 s.8) whilst the President's role is restricted to that of Commander in Chief of the Army and Navy (Art.2 s.2). Levinson, however, argues that if the Ackerman/Griffin line is taken it may be possible to say that based upon accepted understandings, the following may be considered to be an amendment of the Constitution:

without reference to Article V but which have arguably altered the parameters within which constitutional interpretation operates.[57]

It seems necessary to distinguish between constitutionality in a formal, technical sense and the political reality of transformation in generally accepted constitutional norms. Complete transformations of constitutions can take place outwith the permitted remit of the existing Constitution - perhaps an obvious example as cited by Ackerman is the American Constitution itself which was founded by a process which arguably usurped the existing Articles of Confederation but which nevertheless became the founding text for the country.[58] By extrapolation, the same process can apply to less extensive constitutional changes where alterations in received understandings of the meaning of constitutional provisions can effect what are tantamount to informal 'amendments' to the Constitution, albeit that these 'amendments' lack formal articulation by reference to Article V procedure.[59]

It is possible to argue that constitutions do change not only by adherence to the mechanisms provided for in the Constitution itself, but whenever there is a change in the political and social assumptions which underpin it.[60] Schauer argues that what allows a democratic constitution to endure and continue to enjoy legitimacy is not its strict adherence to formalism but, ultimately, popular acceptance. The reason the American Constitution has authority as far as American people, judges and officials are concerned is not that it is a document purporting to exercise this authority - any document could do this - but that it is seen to be authoritative. Therefore, abstract legal arguments about the 'legality' of constitutional change are of limited utility or relevance. What matters is that the Constitution was at the time and continues to be accepted as the legal rule of recognition for the US. The fact that it became so by revolution is of little import and indeed shows the limitations applying when one attempts to understand the legitimacy of constitutional change merely by analysing

---

'The President may declare war on relatively insignificant foreign countries without formally consulting Congress'. Levinson in Sanford Levinson ed. *op. cit. supra* n.16 3 at p.8.

[57] For the view that the Constitution has also been changed by way of constitutional conventions (i.e. conventions in the sense of accepted norms which regulate constitutional practice, as opposed to conventions provided for under Article V), see Dellinger, Harvard Law Review *op. cit. supra* n.9 at p.431 n.236.

[58] Ackerman compares the developments after the Civil War and in the 1930s to the 'unconstitutional' activities of the delegates to the Philadelphia convention which went beyond the amendment powers vested in them by the Articles of Confederation: 'Both Reconstruction Republicans and New Deal Democrats refuse[d] to follow the path for constitutional revision set out by their predecessors; like the Federalists before them, they transformed existing systems of higher lawmaking - what is more, they were perfectly aware of the unconventional bootstrapping operation in which they were engaged.' in Sanford Levinson ed. *op. cit. supra* n.51 63 at p.71.

[59] Frederick Schauer takes this process of external constitutional transformation and asks if it might not extend to smaller scale revision also: 'If displacing a constitution takes place outside of that constitution, then is it possible that displacing part of it may take place outside the constitution as well, and, if so, that amending it may also occur outside of the constitution?' in Sanford Levinson ed. *op. cit. supra* n.47 145 at p.145, see also pp.156-157.

[60] Frederick Schauer writes: '[C]onstitutions are thus necessarily always subject to amendment as their supporting presuppositions are amended, even though it cannot be the case that the amendment of those supporting presuppositions can be thought of in anything other than factual or other prelegal terms.' in Sanford Levinson ed. *op. cit. supra* n.47 145 at p.148.

constitutional text.[61] The legitimacy of the American Constitution cannot be derived from either the text of the Articles or from its own text, yet legitimate it is.[62]

The Constitution is able to adapt to changing circumstances by the application of norms not found in the text of the Constitution and indeed by leaving to desuetude some which are found there. Schauer cites an example of this and suggests that if the three branches of government together with the American people came to consider as no longer acceptable the Second Amendment which protects the right to keep and bear arms and thereafter treated it as though it had been annulled, then it could be said that the Constitution no longer contained the provision. Amendment can therefore take place on two levels:

On the constitutional level, it can take place within the contours of the constitution itself, either according to a literal reading of an amending clause, or according to an interpretative understanding of what the constitution encompasses. But because constitutions owe their 'constitutionality' to logically and politically antecedent conditions, the process of constitutional amendment may also take place at another level, when these logically and politically antecedent conditions are themselves amended. Because these *a priori* conditions are not themselves legal or constitutional in any important sense of those terms, however, it remains necessarily the case that constitutions are always subject to amendment by changes - amendments - in the practices of a citizenry, in the practices of its officials, and in the practices of its judges.[63]

To conclude on the issue of formalism it seems accurate that, in a formal sense, Article V is the exclusive means by which the Constitution might be amended. However, many uncertainties still attach themselves to Article V, the most important of which would appear to be whether the use of the convention method to propose amendments can or cannot be restricted. Important though these issues are, it is impossible to look at American constitutional change as an exclusively rigid, textual affair. The alteration, for example, in the balance of power between state and federal government over the past two hundred years cannot be explained away by a simple analysis of the twenty six numbered amendments. It is clearly the case that historical processes of centralisation and the need for increased federal authority at various stages of American history have led to a realignment in the federal/state relationship to an extent that the present day authority of the central government would be unrecognisable to the framers of the Constitution. That this process of centralisation has taken place often without reference to Article V speaks generally of the fluidity of constitutional development. It also speaks at least in part to the stringent demands of an amendment mechanism which so often prevents its own use in cases where a swift and adaptable

---

[61] Schauer in Sanford Levinson ed. *op. cit. supra* n.47 145 at pp.152-4.
[62] Schauer focuses on the 'heroic efforts' (p.147) of people like Ackerman and Amar to expand the meaning of Article V or to argue for its non-exclusivity. Similarly he takes issue with their opponents such as Dow for falling into the same trap: 'All suppose that the internal resources of the Constitution, however those internal resources are defined, provide the only or most appropriate way of thinking about the process of constitutional change.' p.147.
[63] Schauer in Sanford Levinson ed. *op. cit. supra* n.47 145 at pp.160-1.

constitutional response is required to meet the changing moods of the day.[64]

B. The Supreme Court, Article V and the limits of formalism

*3. What role has the Supreme Court played in developing the meaning and delineating the scope of Article V?*

The completion of any discussion on the amendment process requires consideration of the role played by the Supreme Court in American constitutional life. Since the revolutionary judgment of *Marbury v. Madison,* where the Court asserted its power to review Congressional legislation for its constitutionality,[65] the Supreme Court has become the final word on constitutional interpretation, thereby creating for itself a pivotal role at the heart of the political system. At the same time as the Court affirmed its ultimate authority in constitutional interpretation it was also conscious of the limits placed upon this authority. Its interpretative role sprang from the intention of the founders not to entrust any one branch of the federal government with excessive power. Therefore, just as the President and Congress have limited spheres of activity, so too does the Supreme Court, a point which was accepted by the Court itself in *Marbury* when it recognised that there exist some constitutional questions which remain issues of political discretion, vested in the other branches of government.[66]

The doctrine which has developed whereby the Court has delimited its own area of activity is known as the 'political questions' doctrine.[67] This has been applied by the

---

[64] This difficulty perhaps explains in part why 'transformations' in Ackerman's terms have occurred without reference to Article V. The difficulty of using Article V is recognised by Ackerman himself: 'The formalist's obstacle course may stifle the expression of constitutional movements that, after years of mobilized debate that has penetrated deeply into the consciousness of ordinary citizens, won the support of a decisive and sustained majority.' He calls this obstacle course 'institutional resistance' and considers that it has held great dangers: 'At two of the greatest crises in their constitutional history, Americans were face to face with a very grave risk of a false negative. If they chose to play punctiliously by the rules of Article V, Reconstruction Republicans and New Deal Democrats confronted the clear and present danger that their long and successful struggle to mobilize the People for fundamental change would be stifled by legalistic nitpicking.' *Op. cit. supra* n.51 pp.85 and 86. For a discussion of how the rigidity of the amendment process was one reason why it was not resorted to by President Roosevelt in order to overcome the resistance of the Supreme Court to his New Deal policy see Stephen Griffin *op. cit. supra* n.51 pp.51-53.
[65] 'A law repugnant to the Constitution is void'. *Marbury v. Madison* 5 US (1 Cranch) 137, 179 (1803).
[66] 'The province of the Court is, solely, to decide on the rights of individuals, not to enquire how the executive, or executive officers, perform duties in which they have a discretion. Questions in their nature political, or which are, by the constitution and laws, submitted to the executive, can never be made in this court.' 5 US (1 Cranch) 137, 170 (1803), see also pp.165-6 and p.177.
[67] The political questions doctrine has been set out most authoritatively in the case of *Baker v. Carr* where certain matters were declared to be non-justiciable where there is a 'textually demonstrable constitutional commitment of the issue to a co-ordinate political department.' *Baker v. Carr* 369 US 186, 217 (1962). Despite this, and the subsequent elaboration in *Baker* at p.217 of the factors which can make issues political questions, the political questions doctrine and how far it restrains the courts is unclear. Laurence Tribe is of the view that it does not mean that there are areas of the Constitution which due to their political nature the Court will not interpret but that there are powers vested in the other organs of government which do not produce any rights which the Court can enforce. The Court can interpret the relevant constitutional provisions and at that stage declare, if necessary, that there is not relative thereto a judicial power to enforce

Court in its approach to Article V and has resulted in the Court declaring that a number of important questions involving the proper meaning of the amendment provision be left to Congress to resolve. For example, the Court has held that: Congress can choose the method of ratification of an amendment;[68] similarly it can set a time limit within which the ratification process must be completed;[69] the determination of whether or not an amendment not ratified within a reasonable period of time lapses is again a matter for Congressional discretion;[70] and by the same token Congress can decide whether or not a state may ratify a proposed amendment which it has previously rejected.[71]

Other important issues of interpretation have arisen concerning Article V and it is unclear if they fall within the political questions doctrine. For example, it is not certain whether Congress can extend a time limit which it has set for ratification. This point was put to the test with regard to the so-called (and ultimately unsuccessful) 'Equal Rights Amendment' which was proposed in 1972. In 1978 Congress extended the period for ratification to 30 June 1982 (the original deadline for ratification had been 22 March 1979).[72] Another point which arose in this context was whether or not a state

---

rights. See Laurence Tribe *American Constitutional Law* 2nd ed. (1988) pp.96-102 (esp. p.97).

[68] In terms of US Const. Art. V, either by 'three fourths of the several States, or by convention in three fourths thereof'. *United States v. Sprague* 282 US 716, 730 (1931).

[69] The Court has declared that 'ratification must be within some reasonable time after the proposal. Of the power of Congress, keeping within reasonable limits, to fix a definite period for the ratification we entertain no doubt.' *Dillon v. Gloss* 256 US 368, 376 (1921). In this context a seven-year limit set by Congress was not open to question.

[70] The requirement set out in *Dillon v. Gloss op. cit. supra* n.69 that any time limit be reasonable may not apply any more since *Coleman v. Miller* 307 US 433 (1939). Here it was stated: '[the] petitioners contend that, in the absence of a limitation by the Congress, the Court can and should decide what is a reasonable period within which ratification may be had. We are unable to agree with that contention.' p.452. To adjudicate on the reasonableness of the time limit would involve the Court in issues of political, social and economic background, 'which can hardly be said to be within the appropriate range of evidence receivable in a court of justice.' pp.453-4.

[71] This was held in *Coleman v. Miller op. cit. supra* n.70 to be a political question 'pertaining to the political departments, with the ultimate authority in the Congress in the exercise of its control over the promulgation of the adoption of the amendment.' Chief Justice Hughes at p.450 with the concurrence of Stone and Reed JJ. The Supreme Court therefore would not consider the issue as there was 'no basis in either Constitution or statute for ... judicial action.' Dellinger is critical of the Court's deference here: 'I am at a loss to understand why this issue - a question of the proper interpretation of article V - should not be answered by a court in a case brought at a proper time by a litigant with a genuine stake in the outcome'. Walter Dellinger, *Harvard Law Review op. cit. supra* n.9 at p.420.

The Court's general approach begs the question of whether or not Congress can be said to have general control of the entire amendment process. Four justices in *Coleman* were prepared to accept that Congress had absolute control: 'Undivided control of that process [amendment] has been given by the Article [V] exclusively and completely to Congress', a power which is 'subject to no judicial review.' *op. cit. supra* n.70 at p.459. Laurence Tribe is of the view however that this absolutist position is now doubtful: *op. cit. supra* n.67 at p.101. This issue, which has provoked much controversy, is at the heart of a learned and lively debate between Tribe and Walter Dellinger. See two articles by Dellinger and one by Tribe in (1983) 97 *Harvard Law Review* 386-450. Dellinger describes the present situation of Court deference to Congress as 'disastrous' p.387. Tribe on the other hand considers this picture to be a 'caricature' and a 'straw man' p.433. He contends that Congress cannot usurp Article V. See also John R. Vile 'Judicial Review of the Amending Process: The Dellinger-Tribe Debate' (1986) 3 *Journal of Law and Politics* 21.

[72] For further details see Tribe *op. cit. supra* n.67 at p.1586.

can later reject an amendment after ratification. Although by 1978 thirty-five of the required thirty-eight states had ratified the amendment, further to Congress extending the time limit for ratification, three states voted to rescind. Both the extension and the question of later rescission were tested before a federal district court. The court held, first, that the extension of the time limit by Congress was unconstitutional and, secondly, that ratifications could be rescinded and could not then be treated as ratifications by Congress.[73] In the end however this decision on both counts was stayed by the Supreme Court[74] and finally it was declared moot.[75] The second time limit had expired without sufficient ratifications, even counting the three states which later rescinded. This meant that the Supreme Court did not have to decide on the power of the states to rescind earlier ratifications or on the proper limit of the judicial role here, leaving vague another important issue in the application of Article V.[76]

Crucial to the Supreme Court's deference to Congress over the amendment issue is the idea of 'promulgation' of amendments. The Supreme Court in *Coleman v. Miller* referred to a Congressional power to promulgate amendments following ratification.[77] The idea of promulgation appears to give the Congress wide discretion on how to interpret the application of Article V and, in particular, power over the uncertainties surrounding ratification which the Court prefers to leave to the federal legislator. It has

---

[73] *Idaho v. NOW* 529 F.Supp. 1107 (D.Idaho 1981).
[74] 455 US 918 (1982).
[75] 459 US 809 (1982).
[76] It seems to be at least arguable that the power to extend deadlines is a logical implication of Congress' power to set a time limit in the first place, especially if Tribe *American Constitutional Law op. cit. supra* n.67 is correct and that since *Coleman v. Miller op. cit. supra* n.70 that time limit need not be 'reasonable'. This leaves the question uncertain. According to Tribe 'it would probably have been up to Congress to decide, if 38 states had ratified by the dead-line, whether to count the three rescinding states toward the required 38, notwithstanding their legislative change of mind.' Tribe at p.1586 n.7. Dellinger *Harvard Law Review op. cit. supra* n.71 also admits that the rescission question remains uncertain: 'Any candid discussion of the question of rescission should begin by acknowledging the absence of any clear answer to the question whether article V permits states to withdraw ratifications.' p.421. See also p.423.

Importantly this confusion does not bode well when one recalls the confusion over the convention method of amendment proposal contained in Article V and the debate as to whether or not a convention can be limited in its remit and who is to decide as to its composition and rules of operation. It is possible, if not likely, that judicial deference would extend to the operation of any convention. Given the potential power of a convention the lack of clarity over its scope under Article V is made worse by the uncertainty over who can determine that scope, Congress or the courts. Even Tribe says: 'To call such a convention in this state of uncertainty may well be a prescription for constitutional chaos, suggesting that a second convention ... should be avoided unless compelling circumstances warrant taking the drastic step of calling one, or unless article V is itself first amended to clarify the process of amendment by convention.' Tribe advocates a more activist judicial role here given that the purpose of a convention is to give the states power to propose amendments where Congress is reluctant: 'substantial judicial inquiry into procedural determinations by Congress on whether a convention has been properly called seems justified.' p.102 n.41. See also Gerald Gunther, *Georgia Law Review op. cit. supra* n.22 at p.11.

[77] *Coleman v. Miller op. cit. supra* n.70. The concept of promulgation also arose in *Goldwater v. Carter* 444 US 428 (1979). Justice Rehnquist with the concurrence of three other justices cited Chief Justice Hughes' judgment in *Coleman* with approval where Hughes stated 'Congress in controlling the promulgation of the adoption of a constitutional amendment has the final determination of the question whether by lapse of time its proposal of the amendment had lost its vitality prior to the required ratifications.' *Coleman v. Miller* p.456. See *Goldwater v. Carter* pp.430-1.

been criticised as an additional step in the amendment process which is not provided for in Article V.[78]

One justification advanced for the Supreme Court's obeisance to Congress over Article V is the fear that if the Court played too activist a role it could interfere with amendments which were designed to over-turn in whole or in part Supreme Court decisions.[79] The threat of the Supreme Court blocking numerous revisions of its own decisions does not appear to be very likely, however, even were the Court to play an activist role in interpreting Article V and in setting out procedural guidelines for its application. In the first place, very few amendments have been inspired by Supreme Court decisions,[80] and those that are related to decisions of the Court need not be seen as criticisms of them as having been wrongly decided. It is possible for the Congress or the states to seek an amendment to the Constitution pursuant to a decision by the Supreme Court which they accept was correctly reached on the law as it stood, and vice versa it is possible for the Supreme Court to reach a decision which the Constitution demands but which by personal inclination the judges concerned might have preferred not to have reached had the Constitution permitted an alternative outcome. In the latter case the judges may tacitly support moves to amend the constitutional provision which forced this decision upon them.

Secondly, an active role for the courts on the mechanics or procedure of Article V in no way implies that the Supreme Court would develop this to interfere with the substance of amendments themselves. The idea that adjudication on issues such as Congressional time limits for ratification or the status of rescissions would enable the Court to interfere, or that for whatever reason the Court would attempt to interfere, with the content of amendments, seems highly unlikely as such a manifest usurpation of power by the Court would almost certainly provoke a constitutional crisis. The Court, even if asserting an activist role in the process of amendment, would seem to have little, if any, scope for meddling with the substance or merits of a particular amendment, even in the unlikely event that it sought so to do.[81]

---

[78] 'This conception of the amending process is, in my view, a disastrous rendering of Article V.' Dellinger, *Harvard Law Review op. cit. supra* n.71 386 at p.387. Note Dellinger says promulgation has 'no foundation in the text of the Constitution' p.398. He also argues it contradicts the convention method of amendment proposal (p.399) and is contrary to other Supreme Court decisions such as *Dillon v. Gloss* which suggested that 'proper' ratification was a justiciable matter (Dellinger at p.402 and pp.412-413).

[79] This concern was expressed by Justice Powell in *Goldwater v. Carter* 444 US 428, 430 n.2 (1979).

[80] Dellinger at p.414 quotes J. Choper *Judicial Review and the National Political Process* (1980) who is of the view that only four amendments were intended 'to overcome the court's view.' Choper p.49. One example is that of the eleventh amendment which, in denying the Court jurisdiction to hear any case brought against a state by citizens of another state or a foreign country, repudiated an earlier Court decision. The amendment was later challenged on the grounds that it had been invalidly adopted. Its validity was, however, upheld unanimously by the Court, with the unequivocal statement 'that the amendment being constitutionally adopted, there could not be exercised any jurisdiction, in any case, past or future, in which a state was sued by the citizens of another state, or by citizens, or subjects, of any foreign state.' *Hollingsworth v. Virginia* 3 US (3 Dall.) 378, 382 (1798).

[81] Laurence Tribe is less convinced of this. He considers that the proposal of amendments 'almost inevitably reflects a deep national dissatisfaction with the way constitutional law - elaborated in our system principally by the courts - has theretofore resolved the matter.' *Harvard Law Review op cit. supra* n. 71 at

*4. To what extent has the Supreme Court played a role in developing the substantive meaning of the Constitution through its own creative/activist jurisprudence?*

The Supreme Court's deference to Congress in terms of the formal process of amendment belies the prominent role it has played, through certain seminal decisions, in shaping and developing the meaning of the Constitution. That a constitutional court should play an important role in constitutional development is perhaps inevitable. Those who draft a written constitution can never envisage, and thereby account for in its provisions, the various social changes it will require to accommodate in the trajectory of its future elaboration. Even modern, detailed constitutions require to be modified through later explication by courts of their terms. Therefore the US Constitution, which is both long in age and short on detail, in particular leaves a great deal of scope for debate as to the correct application of its terms to matters not foreseen by the Constitution's framers. It is perhaps inevitable then, given the structure of the US Constitution and the role the Supreme Court has carved out for itself since *Marbury v. Madison*,[82] that it is the Court which is so often turned to for definitive interpretation of constitutional terms.

This active role which the Court has assumed since *Marbury* is, unsurprisingly, not without controversy. Critics of the Court's approach point to what they consider to be excessive 'activism' in its interpretation of constitutional provisions, activism, they contend, which offends against the intricate network of divided and shared powers enshrined in the Constitution. This concern is often coupled with a suspicion that the Supreme Court in, for example, setting aside acts of Congress as unconstitutional or in restricting the authority of the states, is often doing so not simply through a *bona fide* belief that these branches of government have exceeded their constitutional authority, but in order to pursue its own policy preferences. These critiques are met with equally stalwart defences of an assertive judicial role provoking a very lively debate as to the correct mode of interpretation which should be applied by the Supreme Court.[83] In his attack on the Supreme Court's 'activist' approach to constitutional interpretation, Robert Bork argues that judges ought to be 'politically neutral'[84] and that they should inform their decisions by reference to the original intentions of the Constitution's framers. It is for judges to *apply* law, including the Constitution, not to *make* law or, effectively, amend the Constitution, as they see fit.[85] The main focus for Bork's

---

p.436. There is therefore a danger in excessive judicial involvement both on issues of amendment process and substance, the two of which are not always easy to distinguish, p.444. Dellinger taking issue with Tribe does not share his 'highly implausible assertion' that the disputes over Article V procedure and disputes over the merits or substance of particular amendments are difficult to separate, p.447.

[82] *Op. cit. supra* n.14.

[83] An illuminating insight into this debate can be gained from, on the one hand, the polemical critique of judicial activism launched by Robert Bork in *The Tempting of America op. cit. supra* n.12, and in turn the criticism of Bork and his analysis made by Ronald Dworkin and originally appearing in a series of articles, now conveniently collected in *Freedom's Law: The Moral Reading of the American Constitution* (1996) (see especially, the Introduction and chapters 12-14).

[84] Robert Bork *The Tempting of America op. cit. supra* n.12 at p.2.

[85] Bork *op. cit. supra* n.12 at pp.4-5.

criticism is the Warren Court (the Court presided over by Chief Justice Earl Warren from 1953-1969) which assumed a very active role in advancing a liberal political agenda through progressive decisions in areas such as racial desegregation, the rights of the criminal suspect, and general individual rights such as freedom of religion and privacy.[86] For critics such as Bork, many of these decisions were reached in an arbitrary and value-laden way on matters reserved by the Constitution to the other branches of government or to the states, and as such they upset the compromises on separation of powers and federalism[87] which were so carefully constructed at Philadelphia.[88]

Within this debate between Bork and his critics surface countless claims and counterclaims. Nonetheless, it is perhaps possible to identify three particularly important allegations of the dangers inherent in judicial activism advanced by 'conservative' critics of the Court such as Bork, and responses to these fears put forward by his 'liberal' opponents, most notably Ronald Dworkin. First of all at risk, it is claimed, is the democratic principle that the judiciary should not be entering the realm left by the Constitution to the 'political' organs of government which have electoral mandates to make policy decisions.[89] This is given short shrift by Dworkin. For him, Supreme Court judges are an integral part of the political process and can bring to complex issues of political morality a principled position removed from the various influences which colour decision-making in the workings of ordinary politics.[90]

---

[86] The Warren Court greatly influenced American public life in a number of diverse ways but one undercurrent which seems to have been central to a number of important decisions was the quest for greater social equality. This view is supported at least in part by Bernard Schwartz, who writes: 'If one great theme recurred in the jurisprudence of the Warren Court, it was that of equality before the law - equality of races, of citizens, of rich and poor, of prosecutor and defendant.' *A History of the Supreme Court* (1993) p.279.
[87] For an argument that the Court's activism has in particular been aimed at the states see Stephen Griffin in Sanford Levinson ed. *op. cit. supra* n.51 pp.57-8.
[88] Bork *op. cit. supra* n.12 p.4. From Bork's critique it may be concluded that if the Supreme Court is usurping the proper role accorded by the Constitution to the Congress and the state legislatures and through its decisions it goes so far as to alter the meaning of constitutional provisions, it can be said that the Court is undermining Article V and the amendment process itself through what Ackerman might call 'transformative opinions'. (See Ackerman in Sanford Levinson ed. *op. cit. supra* n.51 63 at p.82).
[89] When the Court acts in an activist way and develops constitutional meaning it is often forced to go beyond a declaration of general principle into assuming a detailed quasi-legislative role. For example in *Miranda v. Arizona* 384 US 436 (1966) the Court extended procedural protections for the criminal suspect to the states and in doing so laid down detailed rules on police examination of suspects. Bork writes: '*Miranda* reads more like the work of a legislative drafting committee than a judicial opinion.' p.94. Similarly in *Roe v. Wade* (see below) the Court, having declared a right of abortion to be protected by the Constitution, went on to set out three stages, trimesters, of pregnancy and detailed when and in what regard a state could regulate abortion in each of these stages. In his dissent Justice Rehnquist suggested that this approach 'partakes more of judicial legislation than it does of a determination of the intent of the drafters of the Fourteenth Amendment.' p.174. During deliberation in the *Roe* case a letter was sent by Justice Stewart voicing his concern that the draft decision of Justice Blackmun was 'inflexibly 'legislative''. Quoted by Bernard Schwartz *op. cit. supra* n.86 at p.354.
[90] He goes so far as to suggest, albeit as a tentative possibility, that 'judicial review may provide a superior kind of republican deliberation' to the ordinary political process, *op. cit. supra* n.83 at p.31. The central role which Dworkin sees for judges in the political process is legitimated by his development of a different account of democracy from that of the established 'majoritarian premise'. Dworkin uses a model which he calls the 'constitutional conception of democracy'. This 'denies that it is a defining goal of democracy that collective decisions always or normally be those that a majority or plurality of citizens would favour if fully

Furthermore, Dworkin is not advocating that the judges should invade the realms of authority left by the Constitution to the other branches of government, but simply that it is the proper role of the courts to interpret the Constitution and to decide whether or not the Constitution does intend to leave certain matters to, for example, the Congress.[91]

The second conservative criticism is that overtly political decisions made by the Court undermine the legitimacy of the Court as a 'neutral' arbiter which derives its credibility from attempting to reach decisions in an objective way above the fray of partisan politics. The notion of the neutral judge however, is for Dworkin nonsensical. 'Constitutional politics', he writes 'has been confused and corrupted by a pretense that judges ... [can] use politically neutral strategies of constitutional interpretation'.[92] What is needed is a candid admission by judges that their judgments are not and cannot be value neutral, coupled with a conscious application by them of moral principles in the process of adjudication: 'fidelity to the Constitution and to law *demands* that judges make contemporary judgments of political morality, and it therefore encourages an open display of the true grounds of judgment, in the hope that judges will construct franker arguments of principle that allow the public to join in the argument'.[93]

Thirdly, the conservative would contend, a court which brings a creative or activist approach to constitutional interpretation in order to advance a particular social or political agenda leaves as its legacy a dangerously malleable precedent. Activist methods can be adapted by a later court with a different outlook in enabling it to pursue an alternative programme which may result in the reversal of many of the decisions of the earlier court.[94] This is indubitably a legitimate concern. In following Dworkin's line of reasoning it is possible to suggest that a court, searching transparently for principles of political morality will reach decisions which are relatively consistent with one another, or at least decisions following a more consistent pattern of justification than adherence to spurious notions of original intent would be likely to produce. Nonetheless there is no guarantee, and in fairness Dworkin does not seek to provide any such

---

informed and rational. It takes the defining aim of democracy to be a different one: that collective decisions be made by political institutions whose structure, composition, and practices treat all members of the community, as individuals, with equal concern and respect.' *op. cit. supra* n.83 at p.17. The political institutions which he has in mind include the courts, 'the majoritarian process encourages compromises that may subordinate important issues of principle. Constitutional legal cases, by contrast, can and do provoke a widespread public discussion that focuses on political morality.' *Op. cit. supra* n.83 at pp.30-31.

[91] Bork, writes Dworkin 'appeals to the truism that elected legislators, not judges, ought to make law when the Constitution is silent. No one disputes that, of course; people disagree only about when the Constitution *is* silent' *op. cit. supra* n.83 at p.273.

[92] *Op. cit. supra* n.83 at p.37.

[93] *Op. cit. supra* n.83 at p.37. This allows Dworkin a swipe at another of Bork's fundamental reference points, namely 'original intent' which will be considered in more detail below. Dworkin suggests that this doctrine 'serves only to allow judges to treat their personal political convictions as neutral constitutional law', thereby creating the very danger it is supposed to preclude. *Op. cit. supra* n.83 at p.304.

[94] This by implication politicises the appointment process. It was widely considered that the opportunities to appoint justices to the Supreme Court, which fell to Presidents Nixon, Ford, Reagan and Bush, were used to appoint 'conservative' judges who would to some extent 'turn back the tide' of Warren's egalitarian agenda. The importance of 'transformative judicial appointments' 'as a central tool for constitutional change' is highlighted by Ackerman in his discussion of the New Deal. Bruce Ackerman in Sanford Levinson ed. *op. cit. supra* n.51 63 at p.81.

guarantee, that the search for principles in the Constitution by different judges will not result in very different conclusions. This is perhaps inevitable when judges approach adjudication in a highly politicised environment. The development of a principled, coherent and consistent jurisprudence would remain a perennial difficulty, and the risk would be that a court unsure of its role would attempt either to shadow what it perceives to be the political mood of the day, or, more specifically, to mirror the political hue of the government.

As mentioned, Bork's prescription for a proper approach to adjudication by the Court is two-fold. First, the Court should not pursue any political agenda, and secondly it ought to be guided by the original intent of the Constitution's framers. These two principles should be distinguished.[95] The latter directive, that judges should adhere to original intent, requires that a judge should identify what effect the framers of a constitutional provision intended it to have, a very difficult if not impossible task. It also makes no allowance for the changes in the meaning of words over time or developing notions of what the words or phrases used in the Constitution's text might mean. In short, any serious attempt to apply this principle would sacrifice flexibility in the development of constitutional meaning for the sake of a largely spurious, historical search for the precise intentions formulated by draftsmen over two hundred years ago.[96] A further criticism of original intent as a recommended judicial approach to adjudication is that it can be used as justification both for those judges who seek to exercise a minimalist role in constitutional interpretation, and for those who take an activist approach and who read into original intent a green light for this. It is possible for different observers who claim to favour the 'originalist' method to reach very different conclusions on the correctness of many seminal Supreme Court decisions.[97]

Bork's second prescription, that the Court ought not to adopt a particular political agenda, is more convincing, at least where such an approach by the Court manifests itself as 'result-oriented' jurisprudence, whereby in its extreme form the Court allegedly

---

[95] Dworkin uses similar notions when he refers to 'constraints of integrity and history', respectively. *Op. cit. supra* n.83 at p11.

[96] Dworkin on the other hand does not dismiss the importance of reference to the framers of constitutional provisions, but his approach is both more subtle and more responsive to the need for flexibility than a crude attempt to elicit a definitive 'original intent' from historical constitutional provisions. For Dworkin it is the *words* of the framers which count, not the ascription of specific intent behind those words: 'We turn to history to answer the question of what they intended to *say*, not the different question of what *other* intentions they had. We have no need to decide what they expected to happen or hoped would happen, in consequence of their having said what they did'. *Op. cit. supra* n.83 at p.10.

[97] For example, Michael Perry is a critic of Bork's interpretation of the Constitution whilst also claiming to advocate an 'originalist' approach: Michael Perry *The Constitution in the Courts: Law or Politics?* (1994) pp.8-9. Importantly Perry distinguishes between 'originalism' which for him is simply an approach to interpretation of the constitutional text, and a second element to interpretation which is the role that the Court should play 'in bringing the *interpreted* constitutional text to bear in resolving constitutional conflicts.' p.9. Crucially originalism does not imply judicial minimalism. They can go hand in hand, but need not. In other words one can be both an originalist and in favour of judicial activism. The main concern in this chapter is with the latter which when applied excessively can lack legitimacy. As one commentator writes of Warren, he 'was the paradigm of the 'result-oriented' judge, who used his power to secure the result he deemed right in the cases that came before his Court.' Schwartz *op. cit. supra* n.86 at p.284.

reaches a decision in a case fitting in with a political agenda which it has constructed and then attempts to develop legal arguments to justify this decision.[98] The criticisms levelled at 'result-oriented' jurisprudence are generally familiar - for example: that it is disingenuous for a court to arrive at a policy decision and then to pretend that it is the product of careful legal argument; that it is inappropriate for judges to become involved in policy choices to which they are by training unsuited and for which they are in political terms unaccountable; and that *in extremis* result-oriented jurisprudence can constitute an illegitimate usurpation of powers vested by the Constitution in other organs of government. The difficult issue is again where to draw the line between creative interpretation of constitutional terms and fundamental alterations in accepted understandings of supreme legal norms which result in changes to the fabric of constitutional meaning.[99]

Dworkin's critique of Bork does not, however, involve acceptance that judges may approach cases with a view to giving effect to their own political or moral perspectives. The principles which they must seek in applying those parts of the Constitution which require the application of political morality demand that they fit their decisions within a consistent constitutional theme.[100] Dworkin rejects the idea that judges have no democratic imperative or are unable to undertake this role.[101]

In the context of this ongoing debate it is instructive to consider one or two examples of judicial activism as exercised by the Supreme Court which have come in for particular criticism from Bork and others. The focus of much of Bork's critique are two constitutional amendments themselves - namely the Fifth and Fourteenth. These are the two so-called 'due process' amendments.

The Fifth, which applies to the federal government, states *inter alia*,

No person shall ... be deprived of life, liberty, or property, without due process of law ....

The Fourteenth, which sought to protect the civil rights of freed slaves in the aftermath of the American Civil War, extended the due process clause to the states as well as introducing other protections including an 'equal protection' provision, thus:

---

[98] The selective use of an activist approach when it suits the Court's agenda would certainly seem to be a matter of concern. Schwartz suggests that Chief Justice Warren took this approach: 'Warren followed the canon of judicial restraint in the economic area, but he felt that the Bill of Rights provisions protecting personal liberties imposed more active enforcement obligations on judges.' *op. cit. supra* n.86 at p.275. Defences of judicial prioritisation of individual rights do of course exist. Dworkin's famous 'rights as trumps' argument is a prominent example.

[99] This dilemma echoes the discussion above of the theses put forward by Amar and Ackerman.

[100] 'Judges may not read their own convictions into the Constitution. They may not read the abstract moral clauses as expressing any particular moral judgment, no matter how much that judgment appeals to them, unless they find it consistent in principle with the structural design of the Constitution as a whole, and also with the dominant lines of past constitutional interpretation by other judges.' *Op. cit. supra* n.83 at p.10.

[101] The suggestion that judicial review can provide 'a superior kind of republican deliberation' was noted above, *op. cit. supra* n.90.

...No State shall make or enforce any law which shall abridge the privileges or immunities of citizens of the United States; nor shall any State deprive any person of life, liberty, or property, without due process of law; nor deny to any person within its jurisdiction the equal protection of the laws ....

For many commentators including Bork these provisions are largely if not exclusively procedural protections which should apply in the exercise of the law. They have, however, been interpreted by the Supreme Court to have substantive content resulting in the doctrines of 'substantive due process' and 'substantive equal protection'. Under the doctrine of substantive due process (whether articulated as such or not) the Court has at various stages of its history declared certain substantive rights to be protected by the due process provisions of the Constitution. For example, in 1857 the Supreme Court read into the due process clause of the fifth amendment a constitutional right to own slaves.[102] The same clause in the fourteenth amendment was applied in 1905 to protect the right of contract in relation to business.[103] A more recent controversial application was the 1973 decision of *Roe v. Wade* which found within the Constitution a right of abortion.[104] This right was itself based upon the right of privacy which the Court had earlier found also to be protected by the Constitution.[105]

Substantive equal protection is a more modern development[106] and was used by the Court particularly under Chief Justice Warren to develop rights to substantive equality. This has also been criticised by Bork for going beyond what he calls the primary purpose of the ratifiers who intended the provision to deal only with racial discrimination. This interpretation seems dubious given that there is no reference

---

[102] *Dred Scott v. Sandford* 60 US (19 How.) 393 (1857). The decision by Chief Justice Taney states: 'The rights of property [under the Constitution] are united with the rights of person, and placed on the same ground by the fifth amendment to the Constitution, which provides that no person shall be deprived of life, liberty and property without due process of law.' p.450. The property rights he had in mind included slavery. This judgment is savaged by Bork: 'His transformation of the due process clause from a procedural to a substantive requirement was an obvious sham, it was a momentous sham, for this was the first appearance in American constitutional law of the concept of 'substantive due process''. *Op. cit. supra* n.12 at p.31. Bernard Schwartz agrees: 'Taney was, for the first time in Supreme Court jurisprudence, holding that the Due Process clause has a substantive as well as a procedural aspect.' *A History of the Supreme Court op. cit. supra* n.86 at p.117.

[103] Mr J. Peckham: 'The general Right to make a contract in relation to his business is part of the liberty of the individual protected by the 14th amendment of the Federal Constitution.' *Lochner v. New York* 198 US 45, 53 (1905). Perry criticises *Lochner* as a misuse of the due process clause. Michael Perry *op. cit. supra* n.97 at p.163. He goes on to state 'the approach of the majority in *Lochner* ... collapses the distinction between the legislative function and the judicial function.' p.168.

[104] *Roe v. Wade* 410 US 113 (1973).

[105] *Griswold v. Connecticut* 381 US 479 (1965). In *Roe* the Court said: '[the] right to privacy, whether it be founded in the Fourteenth Amendment's concept of personal liberty and restrictions upon state action, as we feel it is, or, as the District Court determined, in the Ninth Amendment's reservation of rights to the people, was broad enough to encompass a woman's decision whether or not to terminate her pregnancy.' This decision has also been bitterly attacked by Bork as 'the greatest example and symbol of the judicial usurpation of democratic prerogatives in this century.' p.116. See also John Ely *Democracy and Distrust: a Theory of Judicial Review* (1980).

[106] Its first use is generally accepted to be the case: *Skinner v. Oklahoma* 316 US 535 (1942).

specifically to race in the fourteenth amendment. If a narrow construction is to be taken of original intent it is clear that the framers did not intend the amendment to make racially segregated schools unconstitutional. Yet it was held to do this in the case of *Brown v. Board of Education*[107] (a decision incidentally supported by Bork).[108]

Although it seems that the use of original intent arguments to attack substantive decisions on both due process and equal protection is largely spurious given the difficulty in identifying such intent, and the constitutional gridlock this approach would produce if adhered to comprehensively, expansionist Court decisions in this area may still be open to more convincing criticism as examples of result-oriented jurisprudence.[109] The changing, and at times contrasting, content of the substantive protections which have been secured by the Court at different times in its history emphasise how policy choices vary according to the political balance of the Court at the time. A 'conservative' court may choose to protect slavery or freedom of contract (*Dred Scott* and *Lochner*) while a 'liberal' court may find a right to abortion (*Roe*) or a right of racial minorities to affirmative action[110] to be immanent within these provisions.[111]

Dworkin's appeal for the judicial application of principles founded on political morality carries much conviction as well as considerable credibility.[112] There must,

---

[107] 349 US 294 (1955).
[108] See Bork's evidence to the Congress at the time of his proposed nomination to the Supreme Court. US Congress, Senate Committee on the Judiciary, *Nomination of Robert H. Bork to be Associate Justice of the Supreme Court of the United States: Hearings before the Senate Judiciary Committee*, pt. 1, 100th Cong., 1st sess., 1987, p.286. See Dworkin pp.13-14 and p.5 for particularly biting criticism of what he sees to be Bork's inconsistent approach on this issue.
[109] Bork seems at times to concentrate on this line of attack: 'Once the Court begins to employ its own notions of reasonableness in order to decide which classifications should be treated like race, it *cannot* avoid legislating the Justices' personal views.' p.64.
[110] *Regents of the University of California v. Bakke* 438 US 265 (1978).
[111] The Court has arguably even written into the Constitution additional provisions. Allegations of this arise with the case of *Bolling v. Sharpe* 347 US 497 (1954) where the Court seemed to extend the equal protection provision of the fourteenth amendment to the fifth amendment. In this case, dealing with racial discrimination in the District of Columbia which was governed by the fifth and not the fourteenth amendment, Chief Justice Warren acknowledged that the equal protection clause of the fourteenth amendment prohibited the states from maintaining racially segregated schools. He also accepted that the fifth amendment did not contain such a clause. However, 'the concepts of equal protection and due process, both stemming from our American ideal of fairness, are not mutually exclusive ... discrimination may be so unjustifiable as to be violative of due process.' p.499. He continued, 'In view of our decision [*Brown v. Board of Education*] that the Constitution prohibits the states from maintaining racially segregated public schools, it would be unthinkable that the same Constitution would impose a lesser duty on the Federal government. We hold that racial segregation in the public schools of the District of Columbia is a denial of the due process of law guaranteed by the Fifth Amendment to the Constitution.' p.500. Bork criticises this decision: '*Bolling* ... was a clear rewriting of the Constitution by the Warren Court' p.83. Ely is equally strident, stating that the idea 'that the Due Process Clause of the Fifth Amendment incorporates the Equal Protection Clause of the Fourteenth ... is gibberish both syntactically and historically.' *op. cit. supra* n.105 at p.32, quoted by Bork endnote 28 p.384.
[112] For example, the emasculation of the equal protection clause which would result from an original intent interpretation is clear. It has already been noted that this reading would not permit it to be used to justify school desegregation. The language of such a vague clause necessarily engages judges in moral choices. On

however, remain lingering doubt that this approach would really reduce the incidence of radical shifts in Supreme Court jurisprudence which result from changes in the political hue of the Court. What seems clear is that judicial activism and the debate it has fuelled is in some sense directly related to the difficulty in applying Article V. The arguments of Ackerman and Schauer and their observations of non-formal or non-literal constitutional development should also be recalled. Given the rigidity of the formal amendment mechanism and the difficulty in gaining super-majority support at both the proposal and ratification stages, it is possible that the Court in some of its most openly activist decisions, which nonetheless do often reflect a strong popular dissatisfaction with present constitutional arrangements,[113] acts as a safety valve releasing tensions in the body politic with a level of speed and flexibility which Article V is unable to match.[114]

## IV. CONCLUSION

It is now an almost universally accepted assumption among constitutional draftsmen that any constitution must be open to revision in order to accommodate fundamental shifts in popular understanding of how the political system is operating or ought to operate. It is also generally understood that constitutional change should be restricted to such important moments and should not become a vehicle for establishing as constitutional text the transitory political opinions of the day. The purpose of entrenching an amendment mechanism in a constitution, therefore, is both to legitimate the constitution for those generations who were not party to its drafting by allowing for change when required through a process of democratic deliberation, while at the same time restricting its operation to vital issues where some clearly definable national consensus for change exists.

The amendment process which found its way into the United States' Constitution was carefully constructed so as to deny either the federal government or the states the unilateral power to alter the Constitution by way of a simple majority. The resulting procedure, however, requiring super-majorities at each of two stages in the process, and which today in a country of fifty states depends upon the ultimate ratification of thirty-eight of these states, is extremely difficult to complete successfully. This difficulty is evident when it is considered that only twenty-six numbered amendments have been made to the Constitution since 1787. Given that the first ten amendments creating the Bill of Rights were added in 1791 and that the eighteenth and twenty-first cancelled one another out, this means that in effect only fourteen amendments have

---

this basis the hands-on approach of Dworkin, whereby judges seek for moral principles in a spirit of openness would seem be the better road forward in the absence of political will to amend the Constitution formally, for example by way of an Equal Rights Amendment on gender equality.

[113] It is remarkable that, in the absence of an appropriate constitutional amendment or federal legislation, it was left to the Supreme Court to declare racial segregation in schools to be unconstitutional. See *Brown v. Board of Education op. cit. supra* n.107.

[114] For a critique of the rigidity of Article V see Anderson *op. cit. supra* n.5 at pp.155-6.

been added to the Constitution in over two hundred years. There can be little doubt that the rapid and extensive changes to American government which have taken place over this period cannot be explained simply by reference to these numbered additions to the text of the Constitution.

Bruce Ackerman in particular has identified in detail fundamental transformations in the American polity at various stages of the country's history, transformations which have affected how the Constitution is to be understood and applied and which have not been accorded formal legitimacy by way of Article V. In helping to bring about some of these alterations in constitutional understanding the Supreme Court has played a full role. It seems that on occasion the activism of the Court has, rightly or wrongly, supplied the omission of the excessively cumbersome Article V process. The benefits of a strict amendment device such as Article V, balancing as it does state and federal interests, are considerable in promoting constitutional stability. The advantages in introducing constitutional change through the 'back door' by way of Supreme Court activism are significantly less apparent. The price to be paid for a rigid amendment mechanism is a straining of both the capacity of non-formal processes to accommodate constitutionally the changing realities of American public life, and of the Supreme Court to legitimate these changing realities through seminal, and often controversial, constitutional decisions while still attempting to retain the framework of a consistent and principled jurisprudence.

Chapter Seventeen

# THE CREATION AND AMENDMENT OF CONSTITUTIONAL NORMS: A COMPARISON

Andrew Harding[*]

The chapters in this volume, in the main, are based on the proceedings of a three-day conference held at Cumberland Lodge, Windsor Great Park, by the British Institute of International and Comparative Law. The participants were students in law from many Commonwealth countries.

In my remarks at the end of the conference, I informed a slightly incredulous audience that, according to the current authorised version of comparative law, the entire proceedings of the conference were invalid.

After due reflection I think my remark was quite true. Comparative lawyers have in general either completely neglected public law or actually denied that public laws could be compared. This prompted me to think further about the nature of our discussions about the creation and amendment of constitutional norms. After all, this was no mere discourse about constitutional law in general. All the participants recognised that the process whereby constitutional norms come into existence and are changed is absolutely critical to the success of a constitution. In a real sense the rules governing the creation of constitutional norms are the most fundamental known to a legal system. It is quite likely that those who are charged with advising on constitutional drafting will in future consider these processes much more carefully than they have done in the past, when too many constitutions have emerged fully armed (but, alas, rather too scantily clad) from the head of Zeus without any broad discussion or any legitimacy in the eyes of the people whom they sought to subject to their provisions. If so, then those who seek to pronounce on these processes should consider their own processes, by which I mean those whereby they reach their generalisations and the evidence they examine. An essential part of the task is to consider how public law and comparative law relate to each other in the present era of globalisation, in which ideological distinctions

---

[*] Professor of Law in the University of London, Law Department, School of Oriental and African Studies.

have become far less pronounced, and are capable of being expressed or accommodated within a constitutional framework. This is a task for another day, and I do not pretend that this chapter lives up to the standards I presume to set out. But it is worth making a few points to begin with about the relevance of the kind of comparison undertaken.

One type of meaning of 'comparative law' sees the subject as an interesting and theoretical, but not essentially very useful, discourse about different kinds of laws and legal systems; in this sense comparative law is seen as serving purely intellectual ends in rather the same way as legal history, with which it has much else in common. The second kind of meaning sees comparative law as a practical method by which we can decide inter-jurisdictional questions to do with legislation, legal transplantation and legal development or reform, with the possible higher aim of unification or standardisation of principles of justice in pursuit of humanistic goals.

Comparative law in both of these senses was undertaken at Cumberland Lodge. We can call them 'theoretical comparative law' and 'applied comparative law'.[1] We were presumably principally concerned with applied comparative law, which might be seen as the business end of the subject, although personally I see the first type of comparison as being both important and useful, in that it creates an indispensable foundation or framework for the second. It is important to note here that the detractors of comparative law or its uses aim their fire at the second rather than the first meaning. Even Kahn-Freund, whose theory of comparative law I reject, wrote about the value of theoretical comparative law, and was indeed a masterful exponent of it.[2] His objection was, of course, not to comparative law as such, but rather to the uses or misuses to which it is put, one of which is its application in public law contexts.

Applied comparative public law has in fact been an important aspect of political history. At crucial points of constitutional settlement or legal reform, comparison has been increasingly influential. Revolutions and the establishment of new States and constitutions have raised comparison most forcibly: the making of the United States Constitution of 1787 embraced extensive comparison and changed forever the very meaning of 'constitution' everywhere else.[3] The makers

---

[1] Kahn-Freund refers to comparative law as either 'a tool of research or education' and as a 'tool of reform': 'On Uses and Misuses of Comparative Law' (1974) 37 *MLR* 1; see also his 'Comparative Law as an Academic Subject' (1966) 82 *LQR* 40. These are reproduced as Chapters 12 and 11 of Kahn-Freund, O., '*Selected Writings*' (1978).

[2] See n. 2 above.

[3] One could elaborate hundreds of examples. The influence of the British, French, Swiss and Dutch Constitutions on the United States, and of the latter on South America, India and Europe; the influence of the Prussian and the American on the Japanese; of the British in Belgium and Ireland; of the British, American and the Indian on those of the modern Commonwealth; of the French and Belgian on francophone Africa; of the Soviet Union on China and communist States, and so on. The most recent versions, the 1996 Constitution of South Africa and the 1997 Constitution of Thailand, both show numerous influences.

of each new constitution which is drafted cannot avoid having regard to all the precedents, commenting on them, adding to them, and thereby creating a new set of precedents. South Africa and Thailand afford fascinating current examples. These historical facts alone seem to me sufficient to scotch the idea that public laws cannot be validly compared: comparison is rife and always has been, and is on the increase. We have now, surely, enough evidence of the successes and failures of comparative public law to be able to establish some kind of a *modus operandi*, some body of experience, and some useful proverbs at least, to guide the lawgivers of the 21st century.

I cannot emphasise too much how serious a matter this is. If we are unable to make very good sense of it, then people may die, as they have done in large numbers, in the civil wars and other conflicts to which constitutional lawyers have made a rather too sizeable contribution. I would not go so far as to say that the Weimar Constitution caused Hitler's ascendancy and World War II, but it certainly greatly facilitated these events and its errors have imposed a kind of healthy scepticism on our view of constitutional law: Weimar was the Chernobyl of our subject. Is it fanciful to suggest that the appalling implosion of Rwanda was in part due to the failure to provide it with an appropriate constitution? Guglielmo Verdirame's chapter says it is not. Cambodia's inability to find a constitution was surely also a factor in the Khmer Rouge genocide. To adapt Marx, those who do not learn from history are condemned to repeat it, the first time as tragedy, the second time as even worse tragedy. The present fashion for constitutionalism in various parts of the world raises the pressing question,[4] *what happens if these new constitutions fail?* The answer to this might indeed be: Rwanda.

Hence one's attention is focused both on the technology of public law, that is the finding of effective mechanisms, as well as on the broader political context in which public law operates. Of all public laws, those relating to the creation and amendment of constitutional norms probably have the broadest possible context, because of their importance and their very close relationship to, or complexity with, the political process and political culture. This would make the comparison of the processes of constitutional change a classic instance of what orthodox comparative law would see as inappropriate comparison; in fact, due to the role of mechanisms of constitutional change in undermining constitutions, our subject matter requires particularly urgent comparison, and some forward-looking theory, not narrow scepticism.

Theoretical comparative public law has been slow to develop and is still unclear in its outlines. As far as method is concerned it has no canons, nor even proverbs, though it is quite well organised in the sense of having a fairly well-developed taxonomy.[5] The comparison of forms of government was known in the ancient world of Greece and Rome, particularly to Aristotle, who organised his

---

[4] For which I am indebted to John Hatchard.
[5] See, e.g., Wolf-Phillips, L., '*Constitutions of Modern States*' (1968).

research students to mount a huge research project on 158 constitutions.[6] Comparison of public law regimes was not, however, subjected to rigorous analysis until the 20th century, and not to analysis at all until the 18th century, when the diversity of States which existed in the ancient world finally reappeared.

Scholars of government in most cultural traditions, finding actual examples generally too dangerous, have contented themselves with images of Utopia, following the Platonic rather that the Aristotelian example. The long night of comparative public law between the ancient world and the enlightenment was thus illuminated by philosophers who ruminated on the nature of kingship and statecraft, rather than actual constitutions. I would suggest that the true origins of modern European constitutionalism lie in the evolution of city governments in the middle ages in the low countries, Germany, Switzerland and Italy, which seem like oases of modern legal thought in deserts of absolutist government. Many of the scholars who contemplated law and government actually participated in democratic government, though few followed the examples of Bartolus and Fortescue to actually write about it.

The European enlightenment produced thinkers who saw that the variegation of forms of government required some kind of comparative assessment: Montesquieu and de Tocqueville spring to mind; and Thomas Paine and Edmund Burke in a more polemical vein. The role of comparative public law scholars has also been prominent in the political process of constitution-making.[7] In the present century there have been many great comparative public lawyers: in Britain Lord Bryce, Sir Kenneth Wheare, Stanley de Smith, Sir Ivor Jennings, Geoffrey Marshal and Vernon Bogdanor (both of whom joined us at Cumberland Lodge), and many others; and, of course, many important works of comparative public law have been written.

By the time the First International Congress of Comparative Law assembled in Paris in 1900 it could not be said that comparative public law was on the crest of a wave, and a preview of the next half century or so would have reinforced the participants' scepticism about public law as a fit subject for comparison. Given the state of the world even in the year 2000 it is hardly surprising - it is even forgivable - that the participants in the Congress took for their subject matter private law in

---

[6] Unfortunately only the Constitution of Athens has come down to us (though the Politics discusses briefly the Spartan, Cretan and some other constitutions), but it shows an acute appreciation of the economic and political context of constitutional change. Strangely enough, there is little discussion in Aristotle of the process whereby constitutions came into existence or were amended. The usual method was the appointment of a wise lawgiver, such as Solon or Lycurgus. Solon committed his memoirs to poetry and went into voluntary exile for 10 years after reforming the Athenian Constitution, an interesting precedent for modern Constitutional Drafting Committees! The Greeks left behind little advancement in terms of insight into the mechanisms of constitutional change, as opposed to the general principles governing their evolution. It seems that in general constitutions changed simply by the passing of a law, or where that proved impossible, by revolution; a notion of a higher order of legal rules seems not to have existed.

[7] The American federalists (Madison, Hamilton and Jay), Rau in India, Jennings in Malaya, etc.

Europe. It was this field which offered some hope of progress and a manageable empirical base. Although this Congress and its progeny have stood in the way of the inclusion of comparative public law within the discipline of comparative law, its participants, had they survived until today, might well have congratulated themselves that their vision - the unification of European private law - had been largely achieved, and that their neglect of public law as being, unlike private law,[8] too much related to politics and political structure, was entirely justified. The very success, however, of European legal unification (they would be compelled to note) has made the next stage, political union, an issue for comparative public law. The Treaty on European Union requires the development of the institutions of the EU to take into account the different traditions of European States.[9]

However, the way in which the great tradition of comparative law has proceeded gives cause for dismay at its self-defining narrowness. In the first place it adopts a very narrow definition of law, and an extremely conservative view of its field of activity, ignoring in its theory its practical successes. Secondly, it is highly Eurocentric in that it is concerned only with the civilian and common law systems of Europe and North America; non-European laws do not figure at all, or else are unintelligently or inaccurately described. And thirdly, it totally precludes or ignores even the consideration of public law.[10] At Cumberland Lodge the discussions constantly broke all three of these restrictions, and so they ought. We dared not just to compare public laws, but to compare those very public laws which, being closest to the political process, are most open to the charge of lack of comparability.

The main point about Kahn-Freund's scepticism about public law (to take the best articulation of the orthodox view: most comparatists have not troubled themselves with public law) is that it is based on a world view which is now grossly outdated. He even used the Berlin Wall to symbolise the developments which led him to his point of view:

I referred to a wall: the wall which separates East from West Berlin is a symbol of the development [i.e. the diversity of political structures]. The geographical and demographic factors and even the social and economic structures would not stand in the way of a transplantation of legal ideas and institutions between the Federal Republic of Germany and the German Democratic Republic. It is still the same German nation. If the thought of such transplantation appears today to be ludicrous end even frivolous, the reasons are purely political - they are environmental factors of which Montesquieu could have no conception.

The proliferation of new public-law regimes since 1989 has not simply unified Germany. Central and Eastern Europe, followed by Russia and the Caucasus,

---

[8] The assumption that private law did not relate to these structures would not be accepted by most academics today.
[9] Treaty on European Union, 1992, Art F(1).
[10] I have, however, noticed that the prospectus for the Bristol International Congress of Comparative Law 1998 devotes as many as 9 of its 54 hours to comparative public law topics.

Southern and Eastern Africa and Latin America, and parts of Central, Eastern and South East Asia, have contributed to the process. Even in the West European heartland of constitutional government, even in the United Kingdom, where the constitution changes without being observed by the naked eye, public-law reform is gathering pace. The forces which, incredibly, led to the illegality of the communist party in Russia at the moment it was legalised in South Africa, may yet bring North Korea or Cuba under a constitution which looks more like that of, say, South Korea or Brazil than that of the Soviet Union;[11] and may yet provide constitutional stability in Africa and peace and democracy in the Middle East.

What would Kahn-Freund make, I wonder, of the constitutional debates in Thailand during 1997, or the success of Nepal in using legal transplantation to move smoothly from medieval monarchy to modern democracy in only seven years.[12] In the coffee-shops of Bangkok, apart from the stock market, they talked of little in 1997 but the comparing of constitutions. The 1997 Constitution is riddled with implied references to other constitutions. Discussions have revolved around which of these would suit Thai conditions and should be inserted in the new Constitution.[13] Few would, I think, be forced to describe this discourse as totally illegitimate. However, to confine constitutional debate in the way Kahn-Freund would demand would be to deny an opportunity to achieve the kind of legality and accountability Thailand desperately needs to escape from its economic malaise. If the attempt fails, it will be due not to too much comparison, but too little or the wrong kind of comparison. Who, after all, are comparative lawyers to say that Thailand's attempt to cope with globalisation must not be served by an independent Election Commission, or South Africa's by its Constitutional Court, or Nepal's by its multi-party democracy, because such things are neologisms in terms of what went before? Who are we to deny these countries the benefit of the kind of legal analysis which will ensure that these experiments work? If the goddess of justice changes her clothes from system to system, who are we to deny her the right to deck herself in her chosen colours?

Kahn-Freund would I think be forced to concede that applied comparative public law is rife, but he might well retort that this merely proves his point that it is *differences between* political structures which stand in the way: it is just that the

---

[11] For myself, the period of the velvet revolution was best characterised by the banner in Wenceslas Square in Prague which read: "Poland - 10 years; Germany - 10 months; Hungary - 10 weeks; Czechoslovakia - 10 days!". The author clearly had a few scruples about comparative public law, but he or she was clearly right in pointing out how quickly ideas spread and how easy it sometimes is to overthrow a public-law regime.

[12] The Constitution of Nepal (1990) imports many ideas from abroad, and also adds some interesting home-grown features such as opposition participation in the appointment of major officials. Transfers of power and other indications lead to the conclusion that this Constitution works.

[13] The Thais are keen comparative lawyers, which is due perhaps to their uncolonial history and their having a free selection of the world's laws. During the reign of King Chulalongkorn, prior to the legal reforms of 1908, jurists from the United States, Britain, France, Belgium, Japan, and Ceylon extensively advised the King on legal reform. The new Constitution continues this tradition, and adds a number of interesting home-grown features.

differences have been suddenly removed. This would be somewhat disingenuous, because he points to differences between the democracies of the 1970s, such as France, Britain and Germany, to justify his thesis, and the differences between the democracies of the 1990s are actually even greater. He might also still question whether the transplanting of public laws will be successful if it is not carefully executed. At this point we might have to agree with him. It would be tragic, and an indictment of comparative public law, if the present period of experimentation were to result in legal chaos due to the lack of wisdom of the reformers. The indications, however, are that the lessons of failed experiments in the 1950s and 1960s, which are, of course, seized upon by Kahn-Freund as crucial evidence, have been learned. Even those countries which, like Egypt, Taiwan, Nepal, Hungary, Thailand, South Africa, Brazil, Uganda and South Korea, have not had much in the way of democratic institutions and constitutional government previously, seem to be establishing a firm foundation for the new public laws, and developments in Asia, Africa and Latin America give rise for some cautious optimism about the chances of improvement.

## COMPARING THE PROCESSES OF CONSTITUTIONAL CHANGE

I hope that the foregoing establishes some kind of credibility for what follows. In the next section I seek to do what the comparatists say I cannot, namely to set out in a comparative mode the main conclusions reached by the country chapters so as to obtain a conspectus of the subject-matter, and then proceed to comment on them and draw some general conclusions. I do not, of course, go so far as to indulge in applied comparative public law, but that is only a matter of space and opportunity. In principle the lessons of Cumberland Lodge can, I think, be applied in new constitutional situations. The reader will make a judgment on this, but for myself the accumulated experience of the countries is highly illuminating.

(a) Australia

The influence of both the British and American, and in relation to the amendment process itself, the Swiss, precedents can be seen in the creation of the Constitution of Australia (1900), a country which has provided much innovation in public law, including constitutional law. Yet, as Professor Leslie Zines' chapter indicates, constitutional amendments have played little or no part in this process. Despite the fact that the amendment process was not seen originally as onerous, the practical result has been a remarkable, century-long, story of stability, the electorate having displayed a singular reluctance to assent to any marked constitutional changes at all. The requirement that a Bill to amend the Constitution be supported by a majority of all electors voting and a majority of electors in a majority of the states[14]

---

[14] Constitution of Australia, s. 128

(i.e. four out of six) seems to have provided a rigid rather than a flexible Constitution, with approval being obtained for only eight out of 43 proposals to date. In general only politically neutral amendments supported by all the states have been approved. Whether the amendment process has any implied limitations remains a matter of dispute.

However, this picture should be qualified by some other considerations. First, the Constitution of Australia is, like the Constitution of the United States, a rather short document burdened with little detail, rendering amendment less necessary than in other constitutional systems. Secondly, constitutional change has in fact taken place despite the lack of use of the amendment process, conventions and judicial decisions having assumed the role of agents of change.

The Australian experience indicates that careful attention to precedent (elements of both the British and American Constitutions being rejected as inapplicable), and to the process of ratification (this took nine years and involved approval by the state electorates rather than legislatures) can produce remarkable results. If one counts 1975 as an unfortunate aberration due to a defect of vagueness, the Constitution has worked well for Australia and its comparative rigidity seems to have been an important factor in its success.

(b) Brazil

The Constitution of Brazil (1988), which displays American, French and Portuguese influences, was also the outcome of a Constituent Assembly, which comprised members of both houses of the legislature and sat during 1987; this process was both subject to public approval and open to public input: several articles were the result of public initiative.

Under Article 60, proposals for constitutional amendment may be made by one third of the members of the Chamber of Deputies of the Federal Senate, by the President, or by more than one half of the Legislative Assemblies of the Units of the Federation, and must be passed by both Houses at two readings and by at least a three-fifths majority of the members;[15] however, a constitutional amendment may not (under 'petrous' clauses) be aimed at abolition of the federal structure; direct, secret, universal and periodic elections; the separation of powers; or individual rights. Under a concept known as 'circumstantial entrenchment' constitutional amendments may not be undertaken during a period of emergency, when certain individual rights may, however, be restricted.

It is interesting to note that, while previous Brazilian Constitutions have been fairly stable in that they have required infrequent amendment, the present Constitution has been amended 22 times in nine years. The discussion by Luciano Maia shows that this is *not*, however, an index of political instability; rather, in the

---

[15] Internal rules of both Houses require a delay of 5 sessions between the first and second readings before the amendment bill goes to the other House.

Brazilian context, it indicates the increased seriousness attached to the Constitution, the complexity and extensiveness of the document, and the need for liberalisation of the economy.[16] Thus the process of constitutional amendment may be frequently resorted to in the interests of progressive reform, rather than destruction, of the constitutional order. For developing constitutional systems this is an important point.

(c) Canada

Canada presents special and tortuous problems which act as a reminder that the amendment process has to be tailored very specifically to the political circumstances of each country. The process and analysis of Canadian constitutional politics undertaken by Chris Ram cannot be fairly or readily summarised here, but the Canadian experience indicates forcefully not only the difficulties and the importance of achieving an amendment process which carries legitimacy and maintains a supportable balance between stability and flexibility, but also the need to ensure that the amendment process provides for participation of groups who are specially affected. It is the nature of this participation which has bedevilled the search for a solution which is sufficiently flexible but also sufficiently stable to keep Canada together.

For the time being the amendment process contained in the Constitution Act 1982, ss. 38-49, provides five different methods of amendment depending on what is sought to be amended. The general provision requires a simple majority in each House of Parliament, the Senate being presently appointed and not elected, but representing provincial interests, plus resolutions of the legislatures of at least seven of the ten provinces representing at least 50 per cent of the national population. Some amendments require the assent of all ten provincial legislatures. An Act of 1996 requires a federal minister introducing an amending bill to secure first the consent of each of five defined regions of Canada.[17] There is no referendum requirement in the amendment process; this reflects a Canadian belief that referenda obstruct consensus-building by polarising opinion and alarming the minority (Quebecker and aboriginal) populations. The amendment process as presently defined (even after ten attempts to define it over half a century) does not carry assent, particularly of these populations, who wish to have a defined form of participation in the process. The result of the process of defining the Canadian constitution has probably created more 'constitution-fatigue' than the process of defining the constitution of the Holy Roman Empire.

---

[16] Most of the amendments since 1988 have concerned economic rather than purely political reforms, and the latter have also been liberal.
[17] i.e., of the governments of five groups of provinces.

(d) Commonwealth Africa

Commonwealth Africa (consisting of 18 countries) is now the world's most experienced region in terms of modern constitution-making, having produced no less than 13 new constitutions since 1990 (Cameroon, Ghana, Lesotho, Malawi, Mozambique, Namibia, Seychelles, Sierra Leone, two in South Africa, Uganda, and two in Zambia), only two of the 18 (Botswana and Zimbabwe) having retained their independence constitutions. Earlier efforts at the time of independence foundered because the resulting constitutions were not related to African needs and had not been subject to public discussion before adoption (for example, Ghana, Kenya, Malawi, Tanzania, Uganda, and Zambia).

The process of constitutional change has featured military coups, dictatorships and one-party States rather than the amendment processes described extensively here. Where amendment processes have been used, special majorities have not prevented the undermining of the constitutional order: where the constitution can be consigned to oblivion, its amendment is not likely to present difficulty. It is too early to say how many of the new constitutions will survive, but from John Hatchard's survey it seems likely that in those cases in which the creation of constitutional norms is dominated by a small group of actors, the result will be the same as previously. In those cases in which there has been extensive public participation and no executive tinkering with the resulting recommendations, or those in which the constitution has been drafted by a broadly representative assembly, the chances of success are increased. South Africa has introduced two innovations in the creation of constitutional norms by including the Constitutional Court in the process of approval, and a 'cooling-off period' of 30 days following the introduction of an amendment bill in the Assembly.

Much the same considerations apply to the amendment process. A variety of practice is revealed, encompassing the need for a special parliamentary majority (65 per cent, two thirds, 75 per cent, and even 100 per cent in Zimbabwe up to 1990), and/or a referendum (Zambia, Malawi, Sierra Leone), which also may require a special majority (for example, 60 per cent in Seychelles), and even total unamendability (as in Namibia). The African experience indicates that the special parliamentary majority is inadequate to protect the constitution from destruction (as, for example, in Zimbabwe post-1990), due to domination of one party (compare also Tanzania, Zambia, Seychelles, Namibia, Mauritius and Ghana). The key element in the creation and amendment of constitutional norms is public participation, and there is also a case for treating some provisions such as fundamental rights provisions, as a special case (Namibia), assuming that provisions given special protection have first been given public approval.

(e) France

It is a commonplace that some countries, when they wish to amend their constitution, create a new one, while others, when they wish to create a new constitution, amend the existing one. Sophie Boyron places France firmly in the former category: France has adopted 15 written instruments since 1789, thus blurring the distinction between constitutional creation and amendment. Even the comparatively abiding 1958 Constitution displays a tendency to oscillate between emphasis on presidential and parliamentary power according to the political make-up of the *Assemblé Nationale* and the possibility of 'cohabitation'. The phenomenon of constitutional sclerosis due to revolving-door governments (104 between 1870 and 1940; 21 between 1946 and 1958) seems, under the Fifth Republic, to have been overcome, and the 1958 Constitution underwent careful scrutiny, being promulgated after receiving overwhelming support at a referendum.

The amendment process has, however, given rise to difficulty, due to lack of clarity about which method is to be applied. Article 89 allows either the President (on a proposal of the Prime Minister) or parliamentarians to present a proposal for revision. The President may choose whether to submit it to the Congress (i.e. *Assemblé Nationale* and *Senat*) or to referendum. No revision may take place while the integrity of French territory is in jeopardy (compare Brazil here), and the republican nature of the constitution is beyond abolition. Article 11, which contains a presidential power to hold a referendum, has been used (once successfully, once unsuccessfully) to by-pass Article 89. Article 89 has been used eight times; two amendments are minor, two consequential on European integration, and four have substantially altered the nature of the separation of powers, giving more power to the legislature and the judiciary. Apart from formal amendment, as with other historic constitutional systems such as Britain and the United States, constitutional practice and judicial decisions have also played a large part in France's constitutional evolution.

(f) Germany

The German Basic Law (BL) is unusual in providing (by what is known as the 'eternity clause': Article 79(3) BL) for the unamendability by any means of certain of its provisions, namely those relating to the federal structure and the participation of the *Länder* in the legislative process, fundamental rights, democracy and the rule of law. This means that there are in essence three rather than two levels of rules in the German legal system, and raises the possibility (which has not so far occurred) of a constitutional amendment being struck down by the Constitutional Court. The general rule, however, under Article 79 BL, is that the Constitution can only be amended by a statute providing expressly for an alteration to its wording; such a statute does not require any different procedure compared with an ordinary statute, but must be supported by two thirds of the members of the *Bundestag* and the *Bundesrat*. The requirement of expressness was imposed by a decision of the Constitutional Court. The possibility of an additional referendum requirement was rejected in order to protect the people from manipulation by demagogues.

The result of the apparent rigidity of the BL is, however, that no less than 43 amendments have been enacted since 1949. As with India and Malaysia, the length and complexity of the BL is clearly a factor in explaining the large number of amendments: many of them have dealt with matters one would normally expect to be dealt with by ordinary legislation.

The fundamental problem of stability versus flexibility is complicated by Article 146 BL which envisages the BL ceasing to have effect on the day on which a constitution adopted by a free decision of the German people enters into force. As Sven Reckewerth indicates, this would appear to mean that, in spite of the eternity clause, the entire BL could be replaced as a result of a referendum. This possibility appears to undermine the notion that reserving the power of constitutional amendment to the legislature is a guarantee of stability.

(g) Hungary

Hungary, as presented by Gyorgy Szoboszlai, is a fascinating problem of stability versus flexibility, the process of transition to a liberal democracy requiring flexibility in order to achieve stability. In 1989 an effectively new Constitution was enacted by amendment of the old (1949) Constitution, which required a two-thirds majority in the unicameral Parliament. Given the ease with which the Constitution has been amended, the flexibility allowing for transition becomes a problem when the fundamental rules of the new order require entrenchment. While the two-thirds requirement is now seen as too flexible, there is no agreement on what the requirement should be.

(h) India

The Constitution of India, influenced by those of the United Kingdom, the United States, Canada and Australia, is one of those longer documents which requires frequent amendment of detail as well as broad principle, and 76 amendments have been passed since 1950, the amendment process itself not being exempt from amendment. Article 368 provides for a two-thirds majority in both houses of Parliament; however, the ratification of at least half of the state legislatures is required for the amendment of certain provisions affecting the states.

The almost universal problem among developing countries of one-party dominance of the amendment process has led to an original solution, which receives extensive treatment by Mathew Abraham: the Supreme Court's controversial doctrine of implied limitations on the amending power. This doctrine postulates a distinction between amendments which destroy the basic structure of the Constitution and those that do not, and under it the judiciary defines and is the guardian of the basic structure. This structure is defined as the supremacy of the constitution; the democratic form of government; the separation of powers, and the secular character of the constitution. The scope of the doctrine thus extends to attempts to abolish the doctrine itself by constitutional amendment.

Acknowledging the creativity of the Indian judiciary in this development, and the felt need to counterbalance the flexibility of the Indian Constitution, it is hard to see how it could be recommended as a universal restriction on amendment powers, enticing as it is, unless the doctrine derives support from the actual text of the constitution (compare Italy, Namibia, Germany and Brazil). Even express absolute limitations on the amending power might be dangerous: a constitution which cannot bend could well snap. The power of judicial review itself in the United States was invented as a matter of constitutional interpretation, and so the absence of text is not an absolute bar. It is surely, however, preferable that an intention to define the scope of the legal system's most fundamental law in a particular way should be clear rather than imputed.

(i)  Ireland

Ireland provides further support for the referendum formula. The 1922 Constitution provided that, following an eight-year period of flexibility in which only an ordinary Act was required, a Bill to amend the Constitution would only succeed if passed by both Houses of the *Oireachtas* and a majority of registered voters (or two thirds of those actually voting) at a referendum. The 1937 Constitution, which expunged all references to the Crown, and constituted Ireland as a Republic, was adopted after a plebiscite. This Constitution departed from the British precedent by adhering to constitutional supremacy and allowing constitutional review of legislation by the High Court and Supreme Court. It continued the method of amendment set out in the 1922 Constitution, except that a majority of votes at a referendum being cast in favour of an amendment satisfies the referendum requirement. The subsequent Irish experience is rather similar to that of Australia. While several important amendments were passed by ordinary legislation during a three-year transition period (1938-41) in which only an ordinary Act of the *Oireachtas* was required, only 15 amendments have been passed in the subsequent 57 years, and only very few of these have been controversial or fundamental (and these have mainly concerned Europe and issues of personal morality rather than the system of government). Padraic Taylor's review of case law shows the importance of the role of the courts in reviewing legislation against fundamental rights, and also in controlling the constitutionality of the amendment process itself. The increased tendency towards activism in the Irish judiciary has reduced the need to fill out the fundamental rights provisions with amendments in order to give citizens the full measure of these rights; the theme running through their decisions is identified by Padraic Taylor as the recognition of the paramount role of the people in the making, operation and amendment of the Constitution.

(j)  Italy

Following the end of World War II the Constitution of Italy of 1948 was drafted by a tripartite Commission under the authority of an elected Constituent Assembly, the people of Italy having already decided in a referendum to adopt a Republic in preference to monarchy. Like other constitutional systems, the Italian has been deeply influenced by its historical experience, and leans on the side of rigidity, providing for extensive checks on the executive, which is parliamentary in form. These include decentralisation of power to regional entities and a Constitutional Court having power to check the constitutionality of legislation.

Under Article 138 a law for constitutional revision, and laws for implementation of the Constitution, may be proposed by the government, a Member of Parliament, a Regional Assembly, or 50,000 electors, and must be approved on two occasions within a three-month period by each house of the bicameral Parliament. As with Brazil, such a law may not provide for alteration of the Republican form of the Constitution; and, as with India, the Constitutional Court has power to prohibit a constitutional revision which conflicts with the general and fundamental provisions of the Constitution. The referendum principle and the special majority principle are interestingly combined: if the law is not passed or is passed but does not obtain a two-thirds majority of both houses, then one fifth of the members of each chamber, or 500,000 voters, or five Regional Assemblies may, within three months, call for a referendum. This procedure has been invoked only for minor revisions.

One result of this constitutional rigidity has been a long-standing inability (contrast France post-1958) to solve the problem of revolving-door governments. As indicated by Paolo Galizzi, this problem has exercised constitutional reformers continually since 1983 and remains unresolved.

(k) Malaysia

The Constitution of Malaysia, influenced principally by India and the United Kingdom, presents a classic case for the opponents of "special majority" entrenchment. Despite the provision of a requirement that a Bill for amending the Constitution should be passed by a two-thirds majority in both upper and lower houses of Parliament, the Constitution has been subjected to persistent tinkering over the 43 years since independence. Most of the 23 amending Acts, effecting almost 300 separate amendments, have been destructive of fundamental rights, parliamentary democracy, federalism, judicial independence, or some other feature of the original Constitution; only a few, such as those bringing the traditional monarchy within the rule of law and creating Malaysia in 1963, have been ameliorative, although many have been inconsequential and due to the length and complexity of the document.

The continued enjoyment by the Government of a two-thirds majority in Parliament (the upper house being largely appointed by the executive) for 43 years does not in my opinion reflect a consensus about constitutional change: in fact, each successive amendment has been the subject of bitter controversy. The Indian doctrine of implied limitations on the amending power, which might have provided a check, has been argued unsuccessfully in the courts. Paradoxically, although the original Constitution was the product of a colonial Constitutional Commission, and did not, as a result, acquire an aura of permanence, its survival has made it (in its unamended form) a touchstone of democracy. Although constitutional change has reflected an overwhelming desire for social stability in a pluralistic society, its present function seems to be to increase executive power without limit.

Much the same may be said of Singapore, which also suffers the ill effects of 'two-thirds syndrome'.

(l) Rwanda and Burundi

As Guglielmo Verdirame shows, these countries provide harrowing, indeed pathological, examples of the failure of constitutionalism and the rule of law, reflected in the failure of the constitutional amendment process, in which constitutional and governmental change have been brought about by *coup d'etat*, violence and genocide rather than through prescribed procedure. An uneasy and unequal balance of caste-relations in pre-colonial times was disturbed by colonialism, which failed to substitute a better method of achieving social stability, and exacerbated social cleavage. The independence constitutions, although autochthonous and not dictated by the colonial powers, clearly did not reflect the underlying social realities, and in the case of Rwanda spiralled into one of the worst genocidal episodes in human history.

The rigidity of the constitutions may be a factor. In Rwanda a special legislative majority of four-fifths was required for a constitutional amendment, and in Burundi the dissolution of the National Assembly was required. In both countries highly authoritarian regimes emerged shortly after the espousal of constitutional government, and constitutional changes ignored the democratic processes by which the original constitutions had been adopted. Even the recent, ostensibly more democratic, multi-party constitutions carry no real conviction, and the failure to specify a clear amendment process indicates that violence may return as the principal method of amendment unless more permanent institutions can take root.

(m) United Kingdom

The British example, discussed by Adam Tomkins and Stephen Oliver, shows how, in an unwritten, flexible and evolutionary constitution based on parliamentary supremacy, it is not just Parliament which can amend the Constitution, but also the courts and the executive, and that constitutional amendments can embrace a wide variety of laws and conventions. The comparable cases of New Zealand and Israel probably support this hypothesis. The fact that the UK Constitution is in theory (and in practice with regard to its detail) dangerously (or conveniently) flexible has to be considered along with the entrenchment in practice of its major premises. For example, it is doubted whether the courts would submit to abolition of their powers, even though parliamentary supremacy would seem to indicate that they have no alternative. This latter doctrine, as Tomkins and Oliver indicate, is already restricted in practice, if not also in law, by, for example, the operation of the law of the European Union, and by the increased resort to the referendum as a prerequisite of constitutional amendment. The use of the referendum creates an expectation that a reversal or amendment of a reform adopted or tested by this means would itself require a referendum. The big test of the UK constitution's unique method of combining flexibility with settled criteria of legitimacy will no doubt come with the settlement of several important constitutional issues over the next few years, notably Scottish and Welsh devolution, the abolition of voting rights of hereditary peers, the bill of rights, and the issue of the European single currency.

(n) United States of America

The provision by Article V of the Constitution of the United States of America of an amendment process requiring special majorities both of Congress (two thirds of the membership of each House) and the states (three fourths) has had a profound influence on the entrenchment of later constitutions. The comparative rigidity which this process creates has been rendered more extreme by a four-fold increase in the number of states in the union (indicating that 38 of the 50 states must ratify to complete an amendment), so that only 26 amendments (and substantively actually only 14 since the constitution-making process was completed) have been effected in 211 years. This rigidity is, however, balanced out by two other related factors, which are discussed by Stephen Tierney. The Constitution is short and deals in generalities. Its words are open to varying interpretations by the organs of State, notably by the Supreme Court, which assumed an extensive power to interpret the Constitution, this very power being its first major act of constitutional interpretation. Judicial review has been subject to careful self-limitation, however, when it comes to the interpretation of the amendment provision itself. And decisive events in American history have resulted in constitutional amendments occuring gradually and without formal process - for example, the enlargement of federal powers and the right of equality following the Civil War and the abolition of slavery, and the New Deal of the 1930s.

The whole represents a balance of forces which has provided remarkable stability, yet has allowed for evolution and sometimes sharp changes of direction. Perhaps the only mistake has been for constitutional lawyers to imagine that what works for the United States will work in other polities.

## SOME CONCLUSIONS[18]

It is, of course, extremely difficult to draw up rules about constitutional amendments which guarantee satisfaction of the two fundamentally conflicting

---

[18] This section is based on notes I took at Cumberland Lodge. It is, of course, tendentious to present the proceedings of an entire conference in a few short paragraphs, and I cannot affirm that they represent a consensus or a majority opinion. However, they are my own version of and reaction to what was said, and they are at least contemporaneous.

purposes of having such rules, namely to prevent unwise alteration of long-established constitutional rules for reasons of political or other expediency, but to allow for measured and reasonable constitutional development according to changing circumstances. In other words, amending a constitution should be neither too hard nor too easy. What exactly is meant by the word 'too' in the last sentence can only be judged precisely in relation to actual political facts and values in a given society at a given time. I would summarise my own view of the experiences set out at Cumberland Lodge with this general prescription: *constitutional amendments should be made difficult, once the constitution has settled into its foundations.*

Britain, Australia, Germany and the United States (one could also add Japan) have made it hard in practice to amend the Constitution but have experienced a high degree of stability without inhibiting constitutional change unduly.[19] It could, of course, be argued that, on the other hand, rigidity may well lead to inability to solve deep flaws in the document which may become apparent, such as the governmental instability experienced in France and Italy. Constitutional stability and the stability of constitutional development are, of course, often due to factors other than the amendment process itself, as Ireland, the United Kingdom and the United States show.

It seems to be a necessary consequence of having a highly controlled or rigid constitution that a greater role is thereby in practice given to the judiciary to interpret or develop the constitution, and explore areas not traditionally regarded as within judicial competence. This seems to me to be desirable, because I have come to trust judges more than politicians in these matters, the latter tending to wish to tinker with constitutional rules for often short-term political advantage. This approach is reasonable, and not in my view undemocratic: judges are concerned to take a discrete and long-term view of the polity, whereas most politicians are concerned with securing votes at the next election. Safeguarding the constitution is not a political task, but, as it were, a meta-political task; judges determine the extent and framework within which political debate occurs, rather than taking sides in such debate. This view is unfashionable in some quarters, and, of course, judges do in a sense take sides; however, it is often overlooked that for judges to take a narrow view of their role is also a form, and often a more pernicious one, of taking sides. Judicial involvement can also extend to scrutiny of constitutional amendment proposals, which is also, it seems, desirable. To extend this as far as judicial pronouncement on the formal validity of constitutional amendments (as distinct from judicial control over the actual process of amendment) is controversial in terms of its effect on the separation of powers, and should be clearly mandated by the constitution itself.

The power of amending a constitution cannot be vested either in principle or

---

[19] In Britain's case this is due to institutional and ideological sclerosis rather than any rule of law, as in theory the British is the easiest Constitution to amend.

in practice exclusively in the executive or in the legislative branch. To amend a constitution is simply not the same as making an ordinary law, and demands a wider form of agreement. This proposition received unanimous support at Cumberland Lodge. That wider form of agreement may involve one or more of the elements of general election,[20] referendum,[21] renewal of a federal bargain,[22] legislation (including perhaps State and federal legislation with or without special majorities),[23] convening of a constituent body, or adjudication.[24] We have noted also the difficulty of distinguishing between amending the constitution and creating a new one.[25]

A constitution is a profound expression of political culture, and should be securely based on the concept of autochthony. This means that a constitution must be tailor-made, not off-the-peg, and the constitution-making process must be carefully designed to reflect the wishes of the people. I would add that this is a particular difficulty for the developing countries of the Commonwealth, where constitutions on the Westminster model have tended to be imposed regardless of the need for supportive and gradually absorbed mechanisms such as political parties, a competent judiciary, and a free but responsible press. It should be noted that even autochthony and public participation are not guarantees of success, but they appear to increase its chances. I would add that even these considerations ignore the dynamic nature of constitutional law in the developing countries, and that the constitution should *develop* autochthonously, not just *be created* autochthonously. To that extent constitutional change can be for the better, not just for the worse, and therefore in the developing (and post-communist) countries the constitution should not, in practice, be too difficult to amend, provided the amendment process involves a broad measure of political consensus before the change is made. This position contradicts the proposition that the rigid constitution is best: I resolve this in my prescription above by saying that developing countries should be allowed flexibility in constitutional development up to the point at which the constitution can be said to have settled into its foundations. As Simon Bolivar says (of South America compared with Europe) in Marquez's *The General in his Labyrinth*, 'do not expect us to do in twenty years what you have imperfectly done in two thousand'.

Another interesting point was raised at Cumberland Lodge by a number of female participants: where do women fit into the process of constitutional change? Women do seem to be largely absent from the discussion of constitutional changes to a greater extent than in other legal changes. This very volume contains only one

---

[20] Britain, Belgium, Denmark.
[21] Switzerland, Ireland, Australia, Philippines.
[22] Canada.
[23] Everywhere.
[24] India, France.
[25] France, Germany, Italy. Thailand has accomplished amendment by creating new Constitutions, each successive document being virtually a comment on its forerunners.

chapter by a female author. Has the ancient replacement of the Goddess of the Earth by the God of Heaven resulted in our constitutions reflecting a deep-seated paternalism? The point is a fascinating one, but no real answer was provided other than to say that female participation is a function of the general process of political representation and public participation: recent constitutional processes, for example in South Africa and Thailand, have, however, involved more specific forms of female participation through the involvement of the civil society in the constitution-drafting process.

## A CONUNDRUM FOR THE FATHERS AND MOTHERS OF THE MARTIAN CONSTITUTION

In a novel by Ray Bradbury there is a pleasing episode in which a father, a new resident of Mars, goes for a walk with his two children, promising them a sight of some real Martians. He asks the children to look over the edge of a cliff into a still pool of water, and they are surprised to see their own reflections. 'You are the Martians', says the father.

This expresses a psychology which must have been experienced by many who migrated to North and South America in the 17th to 19th centuries, and suddenly realised that they were Americans. The emergence of a distinctly American way of life was expressed pre-eminently by the development of American constitutions. Indeed, those constitutions (both of North and South America) profoundly affected the whole notion of a constitution, and its relation to freedom and responsible government as expressed in the nation State, all over the world.

Imagine that in a few decades' time we decide to colonise Mars.[26] This is not such an unlikely event. A Japanese company is already investing millions of dollars in the design of a Martian environment which will support life; and *Time* magazine recently predicted the colonisation of Mars by 2044. The pressure of population and environmental degradation will probably compel the colonisation of the solar system. To provide for stability and development for the new Martian colony, we will need a constitution. In drafting it, we will face the age-old conundrum: what rules will best secure stability of the constitutional scheme without precluding orderly constitutional development?

Rather than dictate from early 21st century England the future of a Mars I will probably never visit, and basing my answer on the conclusions drawn from the above discussion, I would answer the conundrum by placing it within a frame of reference rather than giving a direct answer.

First, the answer will be dictated by the political circumstances of the colony, which I hope will include an appropriately colonial idealism embracing justice, freedom, equality, fraternity and sorority, internationalism, and a general

---

[26] The choice of Mars enables me to focus on the ideal while neatly avoiding discussion of any awkward actualities. Colonies have always been law-givers' paradises, from the 6th century BC Greek and Italian colonies of Sicily to 18th century America.

determination to avoid of all of the constitutional horrors which have occurred on Earth.

Secondly, the process for deciding what the Constitution of Mars will look like will be crucial, and so will the process whereby we construct this process. Hopefully, they will be informed by precedent, critically examined and representative of the actual Martians, including, of course (with an eye to recent Australasian case law) any indigenous and linguistic Martians we may find there, who may have their own idea of the good constitution and their role in its amendment.[27] The results of their labours should be put to a free vote of all Martians.

Beyond that, the delegates and the Martian electorate should have regard to earthly experience with the main object of avoiding its repetition. In particular they should note the unfortunate consequences of special legislative majorities, which entrench the first thoughts of dead legislators with the arrogance of living ones. If there is one thing we learned at Cumberland Lodge, it was that the process of creation and amendment of constitutional norms is too important to be left to members of the legislature, even an unusually large proportion of them; the legislature is after all but a creature of the constitution. But I think we also learned that it is not necessary to have *one process* for amending every provision of the constitution: different provisions may properly be entrenched to different degrees and in different ways, depending on the precise nature and purposes of the constitution itself. The people must play the largest part in the process, which should allow them (for better or for worse) *their* will rather than that of their representatives or their ancestors, but it should be a will expressed through an extended process allowing for full and informed consideration and second thoughts. After all, it is only through being treated as Martians that they will become Martians.

And one other thing. All Martian schools should teach the Martian Constitution, and the first law school on Mars should have a course in Martian and comparative constitutional law, for which I hope BIICL (perhaps renamed the British Institute of Interplanetary and Comparative Law) will make copies of this book freely available. The course instructor would do well to begin her course by quoting these careful words of Aristotle, who founded our subject, and her students would be wise to give them the closest attention.

Just as he will not be a good builder who does not use the rule or the other instruments of this kind, but takes his measure from other buildings; so he will not be a good lawmaker or a serious Statesman who gives his laws or administers the affairs of the State with a view to, or in imitation of, the actions of others or of the constitutions of actual human communities as, for instance, those of the Lakedaimonians or of the Cretans. For a copy of that which is not beautiful cannot itself be beautiful... We shall attempt, on the basis of our collection of Constitutions, to find out what things contribute to the preservation or the

---

[27] I am indebted to Piers Gardner for this perceptive observation.

destruction of States in general and what things help to preserve or to destroy particular types of constitutions, and finally also for what reasons some States are well governed and others the opposite. For once we have considered these problems, we shall, perhaps, be better able to discern what the best State must be like, and also how each given type of State must be ordered, and what laws and customs it must have in order to function as well as possible.